WHO'S WHO IN THE COSMIC ZOO?

A GUIDE TO ETs, ALIENS, GODS & ANGELS

BOOK THREE:

Who Are The Angels?

Ella LeBain

Who Are The Angels?
Book Three: A Guide to ETs, Aliens, Gods & Angels

Copyright © 2016 by Ella LeBain.

All rights reserved.
ISBN-13: 9780692806296
ISBN-10: 0692806296

---

no part of this publication may be reproduced, stored in a retrieval system or transmitted in any way by any means, electronic, mechanical, photocopy, recording or otherwise without the prior permission of the author except as provided by USA copyright law.

Published by Skypath Books, LLC
3051 W. 105th Ave., #351961 | Westminster, Colorado 80031
USA 1.720.977.9110 | www.skypathbooks.com
Where the Sky Is the Limit!
"The Heavens declare the glory of God." (Psalm 19:1)

Book design copyright © 2016 by Skypath Books, LLC. All rights reserved.
Cover Art Illustration by Lori Garcia, www.TLCUnlimited.com
Editing contributions by Colleen Vaughn Henderson

Published in the United States of America ISBN:
1. Religion / Theology / eschatology
2. Religion / Ancient Mysteries

CONTENTS

INTRODUCTION... xiii
   I Love God!... xviii
CHAPTER ONE 1
The Clash Of Two Kingdoms 1
   The War in Heaven 3
   Angel Linguistics 4
   Legions of Angels vs. Legions of Demons 5
   Welcome to the Grand Experiment 8
   Angels and Sex..8
   Angelic Warfare 20
CHAPTER TWO..27
The Angelic Government...27
   Who Are The Twenty-Four Elders? 30
   Who Are The Four Living Creatures 34
   The Sons of God 37
   Extraterrestrial Sons of God? 40
   Life On Other Planets?..41
   The Truth is Stranger Than Fiction!....................................46
CHAPTER THREE 48
The Celestial Hierarchy of Angels 48
   The Elohim 49
   BeneElohim 50
   Angels As Dimensions 51
   Seraphim 51
   Cherubim...54
   Ophanim or "Thrones" 55
   Dominions..57
   Principalities..58
   Rulers..58
   Powers 58
   Authorities 59
   Archangels 59
   Angels 60

- Angels are Teachers 61
- Kabalistic View 62
- Angels Intercede Between God and Humans 63
- Angels of the Nether World 63
- Angelology in the Quran 65
- Guardian Angels of the Nations 66
- Who Is Michael? 67

CHAPTER FOUR 71
Angel Protocol 71
- Invoking the Names of Angels 73
- God Confounds The Names of Angels 74
- Angel Worship 76
- Spiritual Fraud 81
- The Son Superior to Angels 82
- Angels are Inferior to Humans 84
- Judging Angels 87
- Why Angels Will Be Judged by Man 91
- Angels Evolve Through Human Evolution 93
- Philo on Angels 93
- Ranking: Archangels or Angels? 96
- The Angel of the Lord 98
- Christophany or Wrestling Angels? 104
- Are You Pulling My Leg? 105
- The Jealousy of Angels 106
- What's in a Name? 107

CHAPTER FIVE 114
Celestial Warriors: Extraterrestrials With Extraordinary Powers 114
- Who are the Hosts of Heaven? 114
- Lost in Translation? 115
- The Presence of Cosmic Evil 117
- Do Not Worship the Hosts 117
- The Lord of Hosts 122
- Heaven's Army 123
- The Creation of Angels 125

CHAPTER SIX 127
The Fallen Angels 127
- Angels and Sex 127
- Names and Sins of the Watchers - the Origin of Evil on Planet Earth 127
- The Destiny of the Fallen Angels & Watchers 131

CHAPTER SEVEN 133
The Watchers, the Nephilim and "Satan's Ministers." 133
    The Watchers in the Bible. 134
    The Watchers in Jewish Midrash 135
    The Watchers in 1 Enoch. 136
    The Origin of War. 139
    The Watchers in Jubilees 142
    The Watchers in 2 Enoch. 143
CHAPTER EIGHT 146
Stars Who Fell From Heaven 146
CHAPTER NINE. 151
Fallen Angels or Evil Spirits? 151
    The Demons (Aliens) Tremble at the Name of Jesus Christ 153
    Time Always Tells The Truth. 154
    The Horns 156
    The Forbidden Bible. 160
    Vampires 165
    Alien War on The Human Race. 166
    Fallen Angels and The Jezebel Spirit. 168
    So, Who Was Jehu? 169
    True and False Prophets 175
    What is the Church of Thyatira? 176
    Thyatira and New Agers. 180
CHAPTER TEN. 185
Purgatory 185
    Earth School. 190
    Investing in Our Spirit 194
    To Be Healed, You Must Be Broken 197
    Beyond Forgiveness 198
    Second Chances and Rebirth 200
    Heaven is For Real 207
    On Karma 209
    Generational Sins and Curses 210
    The End of the Cycle of Rebirth. 212
    Can a Deceased Spirit Return to Earth? 214
CHAPTER ELEVEN 219
Is Hell For Real?. 219
    Define Hell 221
    Dante's Inferno. 224

    Duel Dimensions 225
    Jesus Preached to the Dead Spirits 228
    The First and Second Deaths 230
    The Transfiguration 233
    Hell is Not Forever 236
    Hell was Created for Satan and His Angels 236
    The Abyss of Tartarus 238
    Saved From Hell 239
    Visions of Hell 240
    Hell is Separation From God 241
    What does it mean to have the fear of God? 244
    Spiritual Blindness 246
    Spiritual Deafness and Spiritual Muteness 246
    The Unbelief of the Jews 249
    The Reward for the Faithful 249
CHAPTER TWELVE 251
The World of the Wondrous – The Kingdom of God 251
    Discernment Is The Way 253
    The Supernatural Battle 254
    Satan's Doom 256
CHAPTER THIRTEEN 259
The Coming Kingdom 259
    What is the Kingdom of God? 260
    Kingdom History 262
    The Keys of the Kingdom 265
    Who is Called to the Kingdom? 268
    The Heavenly King Lives Through His People On Earth 275
    Why People Reject His Kingdom 276
    Who Gets Rejected From The Coming Kingdom 279
    Who Are the Citizens of the Kingdom? .282
    War Against the Kingdom 285
CHAPTER FOURTEEN 289
The Harvest of Angels 289
    The Final End of Satan: 292
    The Angels Separate The Good Earth Humans from the
    Evil Earth Humans: 292
    The Reapers 297
    The Great Judgment 298

    Spiritual Weapons 299
    Evangelical Angels? 300
CHAPTER FIFTEEN 303
Ascension Or Rapture? 303
    The Day and Hour Unknown 307
    Raptured! 316
    Who is the Restrainer? 327
    The Technology of the Rapture 330
CHAPTER SIXTEEN 338
The Second Coming and Nibiru 338
    The Death Star, Nibiru, Hercobulus, Wormwood 340
    The Pole Shift and Bible Prophesy 343
    Blue Kachina vs. Red Kachina 347
    Earth Changes From A Binary Brown Dwarf? 353
    New Heavens And New Earth 356
    Signs of the End of the Age 357
    What is The Day of The Lord? 360
CHAPTER SEVENTEEN 364
The Cosmic Christ 364
    The Power And Authority Of Jesus Christ 366
    The Word Became Flesh 367
    The Cosmic Christ Defeats The God Of This World 369
    Old Testament Prophecies Fulfilled in Jesus Christ 371
    The Book of Enoch Prophesies Jesus Christ 391
    Did Jesus quote the Book of Enoch? 399
    Jesus calls Enoch Scripture: 405
    The Destruction of Satan 406
    Is Jesus The Cosmic Christ? 407
    Lord Of The Cosmos 410
    Religious Spirits 411
    Destiny For Believers Of Christ 414
CONCLUDING WORDS 417
    Angels, UFOs and Mars 418
    Mars Exopolitics 419
    The Chief Cornerstone and the New Jerusalem 420
    End Time Apostasy 427
    The Seven Churches of Revelation 432
    Disclosure of ETs, Aliens and Angels 436

Who Are The Human Angels?..................................441
NOTES AND BIBLIOGRAPHY.................................447
ABOUT THE AUTHOR..459
Who Is Ella LeBain?..461

DEDICATION

This book is dedicated to the Lord of the Cosmos, The Lord of Heaven and Earth, without whose loving support, guidance and protection, this manuscript would not have been possible, for which I am forever grateful.

In addition to, I am dedicating this book to all those wounded by religion, all atheists, agnostics, and especially to those who consider themselves religious. May you all find something useful within the pages of this book to heal your soul.

ACKNOWLEDGEMENTS

My deepest gratitude goes to my loving and devoted husband and daughter, without whose love and support, this manuscript would not have been possible. They have stuck with me through all the spiritual battles and never stopped believing in my vision and goal. They are my true loves and soul mates whom I am blessed to be journeying with through this earth experience.

INTRODUCTION

> "The harvest is at the end of the world,
> and *the harvesters are the angels*."
> (MATTHEW 13:39)

> "Then another angel came out of the temple,
> calling in a loud voice to
> the One seated on *the cloud*, "Swing Your sickle and reap,
> because *the time has come to harvest; for the crop of the earth is ripe.*"
> (REVELATION 14:15)

Who Are the Angels? What or whom are they harvesting? Are you part of their end time harvest? Are there good angels and evil angels? How can you tell them apart? Let's explore and discern.

In Book Three of *Who's Who in The Cosmic Zoo?* I am going to not only prove to you the reality of angels, but demonstrate how to discern between the fallen angels and the faithful angels of heaven. We will view their protocols, examine their hierarchy and discover the pivotal role they play at the end of this age. We will see how this understanding can create a paradigm shift in your present thinking and give you hope.

Another recurring theme in this book series is that not all aliens are extraterrestrials, not all extraterrestrials are alien. This is an important difference which I am exposing and expanding on through knowledge and understanding of both scriptures, history, linguistics and archeology. This was my thesis statement as was laid out and proven in Book One.

In Book Two, I continued to prove that many extraterrestrials were mistakenly called gods by the ancients and that some of them actually did have 'god' complexes. History tells us some of them demanded worship from earth humans, through the erection of temples.

Here in Book Three, I'm going to continue to prove that there are good angels and evil angels (fallen angels, demons), and that *not all* extraterrestrials are alien demons as the Christian fringe insists! This is evidenced in Scripture. Likewise, not all extraterrestrials who ride in spaceships are of the dark side. I will point out to you, in continuation from Book Two, that the ancient alien 'gods' of our past are all mentioned in the Bible, some as aliens and some as 'gods.' I cited as proof that even the Lord of the Old Testament decreed that He will punish 'the gods'; if there weren't any other gods, then just to whom was He referring? (See, 1 Samuel 28:13; Zephaniah 2:11; Jeremiah 46:25; Isaiah 24:21-22; Exodus 15:11; 20:3; 22:28; 23:13; Deuteronomy 5:7; Job 1:6; 2:1; Psalm 96:5)

I see myself as a Kingdom missionary to all of Christendom. I believe I am called to liberate Christendom from its bondage to pagan Rome, which lies at the root of Protestant and Catholic cultural norms today. In this way, I can identify with the angels, as they too work to spread accurate knowledge of the Word of God. My important message to announce to Christendom is that of liberation from Rome and from the Draconians who have sabotaged religion.

As a Messianic Jew, I believe I was called to expose the lies of the Church of Rome to help liberate the body of Christ from the Draconian implants which have manipulated and controlled Christianity for millennia. This spiritual tyranny has caused many to reject Christ! This is because many Christians have been so abusive, judgmental and cultish. As I've said in previous books, "you can't throw the baby out with the bathwater", meaning just because Christians are flawed, doesn't mean Christ is less than perfect. He's the only One who can save humanity. I have got good news for you; your salvation is not solely dependent on you, but upon Him.

> "For it is by grace you have been saved, through faith—and this is not from yourselves, it is the gift of God—not by works, so that no one can boast."
>
> (Ephesians 2:8,9)

All who are Christian need accurate knowledge of how deliverance works. Key to this knowledge is *spiritual legal ground*. As I lay out *spiritual legal ground* in the angelic realms then you'd be wise to take heed of the information within the pages of these books.

I will prove that *not all* ETs or aliens are demonic, which seems to be the mainstream angelology of the modern Christian church. In view of the fact that few churches touch on the subject or teach it at all, it nevertheless appears to be an adopted belief system by those on the fringe. It is my hope that more Christian churches will begin to examine and teach this topic through Scripture as I have, benefitting from my research. We are in the Last Days, the End Times, the culmination of history, and the message of this research is that of being able to recognize good angels, who are assigned to help save and harvest humanity for God's Coming Kingdom, from evil ones who seek to deceive. This message just may save many souls from the mass alien deception!

This half-baked angelology which teaches that all aliens are demonic seems to be rooted in the Bible stories of the giants and Nephilim. The Book of Enoch, frequently quoted by Christ Himself, makes it very clear that the evil spirits of the earth are the spirits of the dead Nephilim Giants of the past. These evil dead are stuck in earth's astral plane until Christ returns. This is demonstrably true. However, the rest of the basis of this angelology, that *all ETs and Aliens are demons,* is rooted in fear and ignorance of what the Bible Scriptures actually do state, which I illuminate to you within the pages of this book, and my entire five book series, *Who's Who in the Cosmic Zoo?*

Christians seem to have a problem accepting the fact that aliens and extraterrestrials are real, and do in fact exist, yet when they do accept it, they believe them to be all fallen angels and demons. That is a half-truth, and you know what they say about half truths? Be careful that you do not get hold of the wrong half. As I prove throughout this series, that discernment is the spiritual muscle that Heaven wants humans to exercise during these end times of this present Age.

New Agers, on the other hand, tend to believe that ETs and aliens are real, only their viewpoints are skewed by their half-truth that they're here to help us evolve, advance and even save us from ourselves. Again, another half-truth, that totally lacks discernment. I am here to bridge the two hemispheres into truth for you. Christians resent and demonize New Agers for their viewpoints on aliens, because Christians are in fear that it's all part of a Mass Deception to enslave humankind. That is part of the story, which I laid in Book One of *Who's Who in the Cosmic Zoo?* However, in Book Three, we're going to get into the weeds about just 'who' the angels really are, both fallen and faithful, so both New Agers and Christians can come away with more understanding and discernment of what's really going on in the spirit and supernatural realms between the two kingdoms of angels.

Most New Agers come out of Christian Churches, and either have started their own New Age churches, or have broken away from the religious side of Christianity and identify themselves as *spiritual*. However, because the New Age is so broad, and encompasses not just spirituality, but health, wellness, self-improvement, and ancient history, Christians demonize New Agers for breaking away from the church to follow occult spirits, who channel falsehoods and deceptions masquerading as light from fallen angel demons and aliens. I exposed the alien agenda of the Grays, Reptilians, Draconians, Insectoids, Annunaki, Nephilim, etc., in Book One, which is an A-Z Compendium of ETs, Aliens and Inter-dimensionals reported by contactees, abductees, experiencers and government whistleblowers. Being an experiencer myself, this work took me literally decades to compile and research, which was not without battles for my very soul.

Christians just can't get their head or faith around the fact that God actually created extraterrestrials who live on other planets and are somehow connected to earth's ancient history. But, the Truth is Stranger Than Fiction, and yes, Christians are correct about the clash between the two kingdoms, but seem to fail in their knowledge or understanding of the very fact, that the Lord they worship as the King of Universe and Creator of Heaven and Earth, would allow earth humans to just hang out here with just a bunch of fallen angels, Nephilim, alien demons. This is where I come in, because scripture is glaringly clear that the Lord of Hosts of the Celestial Armies, actually rules over millions, if not billions of extraterrestrials, which I'm going to prove to you throughout this book.

But first allow me to connect one dot for the skeptical, the term 'New Ager' actually comes from the Bible, which points to the New Age to come, which is the Golden Age, aka the Millennial Reign of Christ on earth, or Heaven on Earth. Another typical New Age term would also be the Earth being raised into the Fifth Dimension. Remember the song in the 1960s, *The Age of Aquarius*, by the group, 'The Fifth Dimension'? It's all connected.

> "But those who are considered worthy of taking part *in the age to come* and in the resurrection from the dead will neither marry nor be given in marriage, and they can no longer die, <u>for they are like the angels</u>. They are God's children of the resurrection."
>
> (Luke 20:35-36)

It's important to distinguish that both groups hold half of the truth, and I'm going to present both sides herein, in order to connect the dots, with the hopes that both sides reading this book series, will be made whole. I'm going to revisit this schism in the Churches towards the end of this book by reconciling both sides with suggestions for both to meet through the Messiah/Christ. But in the meantime, let's begin with the following passage from the Exobiblical Book of Enoch:

> "But now the giants who are born from the (union of) the spirits and the flesh shall be called evil spirits upon the earth, because their dwelling shall be upon the earth and inside the earth. Evil spirits have come out of their bodies. Because from the day that they were created from the holy ones they became the Watchers; their first origin is the spiritual foundation. *They will become evil upon the earth and shall be called evil spirits.* The dwelling of the spiritual beings of heaven is heaven; but the dwelling of the spirits of the earth, which are born upon the earth, is in the earth. The spirits of the giants oppress each other, they will corrupt, fall, be excited, and fall upon the earth, and cause sorrow. They eat no food, nor become thirsty, nor find obstacles. And these spirits shall rise up against the children of the people and against the women, because they have proceeded forth from them."
>
> (1 Enoch 15)

Introduction

We are living in an age of knowledge, where that which has been concealed is now being revealed on many levels. It's truly apocalyptic! Most people don't know that the original translation of the word 'apocalypse' in ancient Greek actually means 'Revelation', or the "Lifting of the Veil". It most certainly does not mean disaster. An apocalypse (ancient Greek:ἀ ἀποκάλυψις apokálypsis, from ἀπό and καλύπτω meaning "uncovering"), translated literally from Greek, is a disclosure of knowledge, or revelation. Apocalypse is a disclosure of something hidden from the majority of humankind from an era dominated by falsehoods, misconceptions and deceptions.

> "...for there is nothing concealed that will not be disclosed, or hidden that will not be made known." (Matthew 10:26)

> "The time is coming when everything that is covered up will be revealed, and all that is secret will be made known to all." (Luke 12:2)

> "For there is nothing hid, which shall not be manifested; neither was anything kept secret, but that it should come abroad." (Mark 4:22)

Yes, many aliens are demonic, and do not have the best interests of the human race at heart, but I will prove through Scripture that the Lord of Hosts commands His own very powerful celestial army of extraterrestrial angels, who have been and will continue to, kick the living daylights out of the bad ETs, and aliens. Yes, the *Truth is Stranger Than Fiction*, and holding to the motto of this book series, we, the human race, are living in the crosshairs of this very real ancient *Star Wars* battle taking place on, inside and above planet earth as well as in our neighboring solar system.

In this book, I will prove to you the authenticity and authority of the Words in the Book of Enoch that matches Bible Scripture in both the Old and New Testaments. In fact, as I have been saying throughout this book series, all the Great Rejected Jewish Texts are relevant and were written for such a time as this.

We can gain great insight when we compare the rejected Jewish texts to the modern testament scriptures, such as discerning the difference between demons, fallen angels and evil spirits. Indeed, they are all under the auspices of the Kingdom of Darkness but they are not all the same. They do operate as a kind of compartmentalized hierarchy and network together but there are differing levels of powers and influence over human behavior and spirit.

The Book of Enoch details the origin of demons. It states that demons were already in existence during the time of the fall of the sons of heaven. According to 1 Enoch 19, demons are the spirits which go forth from these angels.

> "Here shall stand in many different appearances the *spirits of the angels* which have united themselves with women (fallen angels). They have defiled the people and will lead them into error so that they will offer sacrifices to the demons as unto gods, until the great day of judgment in which they shall be judged till they are finished."
>
> (Enoch 19:1)

Before I get started, I want to give acknowledgement to G. Cope Schellhorn, who inspired me more than any author. A friend gifted me with his book, *Extraterrestrials in Biblical Prophecy,* which was life changing to me, back in 1992. He proved, without a shadow of a doubt, that the Bible is the best proof and evidence for the ET/Alien presence on earth, both in the ancient past and through future End Time scenarios detailed in prophecies. While most of the world sits waiting with baited breath for some type of *official* form of disclosure from an authority in government, the Bible, along with its rejected Jewish texts (Exobiblical- Pseudepigrapha-Apocrypha), have been telling us for millennia that we are not alone on planet earth, and never have been.

I Love God!

For those who didn't get to read *Who Is God?* Book Two of *Who's Who in The Cosmic Zoo?* here's a brief synopsis to get you going into this book, *Who Are the Angels?* Book Three.

How can one love God if they don't know **who** he is? Some have been told there is only one god, however, Scripture tells us otherwise. The god of this world is called satan, which in Hebrew literally translates as 'adversary'. There are many adversaries to the God of Love. Many people blame the Creator God for what satan does because they can't tell the difference between their source of supernatural origins, so much so that many now identify themselves as atheists. As I've proved in previous books, there is more than one satan or adversary, which is why I generally do not capitalize the word 'satan'.

This is why discernment, is the most important *spiritual muscle* to develop in these times. Things are going to get even weirder, supernaturally speaking. In the last days of the end of this present age, we're going to be seeing aliens and demons one minute, and mighty godly extraterrestrial interdimensional angels the next.

As we read in Isaiah 5:20, there is a curse on those who confuse the discernment of good and evil, by calling good evil and evil good, synonymous as when you blame the Lord God for the works of Satan.

Introduction

> "Woe unto them that call evil good, and good evil; that put darkness for light, and light for darkness; that put bitter for sweet, and sweet for bitter!"
>
> (Isaiah 5:20 - KJV)

Likewise, the same goes for those who think all ETs are fallen angels or all aliens are demons. I am not even sure where or from whom many Christians get this angelology, although the Christian fringe is now packed with various authors touting it as a religious teaching in spite of the fact that the Bible, and all of the rejected Jewish texts, say otherwise. This is why I wrote *Who Is God?* to prove *who* the God of gods is in relation to the other gods. We see who are His angels, the extraterrestrial messengers, guardians and warriors of His heavenly hosts, in comparison to the fallen 'alien' angels who live inside and around the space of earth and this solar system.

This is all in the Scriptures, concealed to most Christians due to a plethora of mistranslations from Hebrew to English, along with deliberate cover ups of sacred text by the Church of Rome. That's history.

Knowing the identity of God is the most important and valuable relationship you will ever have in your life. Are you listening to the voice of His Spirit or the voice of the Counterfeiter? Can you tell them apart?

If you're confused between the two voices, you're not alone. Some big Bible characters couldn't tell them apart either. This surprising fact too was covered up and lost in translation, when it could have served as a serious edifying Bible Study for all those who struggle with their faith today. I reveal their names, stories and literal translations of *who* and which of the cast of Biblical characters are actually speaking, in Book Two: *Who Is God?*

English Bibles use two words when God speaks; 'God' and 'LORD.' The word 'LORD' covers up the sacred name of the Lord Yahuah, but the English word 'God' is a mistranslation. Nine times out of ten, when the English Bible uses the word 'God,' the original Hebrew actually says Elohim. In Hebrew, El means God, however, Elohim is in its masculine plural form, which literally translates as 'gods' or 'God's sons'. Big difference in meaning, when reading Bible stories from the original Hebrew.

I point out when it is the Lord Yahuah *who* shows up versus when it is the Elohim instead. English Bibles do not do these stories justice in translation, and this creates misunderstanding as to *who* is exactly intervening in human affairs. This leads to false theologies.

The Elohim were created beings, translated 'sons of God' or, as 'God's sons,' which can also be translated as 'Els', or gods. The Bible tells us that they serve as a council in the Courts of Heaven. This is important foundational knowledge because in order to discern *who* the Twenty-Four Elders of Revelation are, you must first have the correct understanding of *who* the Elohim are, which I will reveal to you in relation to the Elders.

The Scriptures tell us that the Elohim had sons, who later became known as fallen angels. The Book of Enoch tells us that there were two hundred Bene HaElohim who fell from their first estate and mated with earth women and produced giant offspring known as Nephilim, which in Hebrew means, fallen ones, or rejects. (See, Jude 1:6, Genesis 6:4)

> "And the angels who did not keep their positions of authority but abandoned their proper dwelling (left their first estate) —these he has kept in darkness, bound with everlasting chains for judgment on the great Day."
>
> (Jude 1:6)

This mistranslation of the very words *God*, *gods*, and *angels* in the Scriptures is the reason why Christians can't see that the Bible really is an historical account of extraterrestrials who actually serve the Lord and His Kingdom of Heaven on earth. These good angels battle the fallen angels and the counterfeit gods over the minds, bodies and souls of the human race.

Who Is God? Book Two of *Who's Who in the Cosmic Zoo?* is 570 pages of Scriptural translations corrected from Hebrew to English. This book reveals the extraterrestrials in Biblical history and Biblical prophecy, pinpoints and exposes their enormous fleet of spaceships, all under the command of the Lord of the Heavenly Hosts, *Adonai Tzebayot*. This title literally translates as 'commander of celestial armies' and is another name for the God of the Old Testament. All of this important information was concealed in the translations from the original Hebrew.

Ephesians 6:12 tells us, "We war not against flesh and blood, but against powers, principalities, rulers of the darkness of this present world and spiritual wickedness in the heavens."

I spent the entire length of Book One of *Who's Who in the Cosmic Zoo?* analyzing and proving *who* these powers, principalities, rulers of this present world are, and *who* and what is the spiritual wickedness in the heavens. For a Christian to suggest that all alien or extraterrestrial life is demonic is a half-truth. And you know what they say about half truths, be careful that you don't get hold of the wrong half.

In Book One, I exposed the true meanings of the words *alien, extraterrestrial,* and *interdimensional.* To recap, not all aliens are extraterrestrials, as many actually live *inside* the earth. Not all extraterrestrials are alien, as many are human, made in the image and likeness of God, the Elohim, as described in the Bible Scriptures. Yet both can be interdimensional. This is why discernment is the major theme in this book series, as it is so sorely needed in identifying *who* is *who*, for the sake of communications.

Introduction

Many people use the term *alien* to describe anything that they do not understand, or anything that is different than us. For instance, a Christian would never say that Jesus was an alien, even though many New Agers and Ufologists might use this incorrect term to describe Him. Jesus Himself claimed to be extraterrestrial, when He said, He *was not of this world*, and His Kingdom *is not of this world*. By very definition, that qualifies Him as *extraterrestrial*. This is an indisputable scripture which most Christians believe yet do not understand that Jesus is *'out of this world'*. Even though many call Him alien, He is in fact far from it by its very definition because He is human, the Son of Man, and according to Scripture, we are made in His image and likeness. Aliens are **not** human, for example, non-human intelligences. For a Christian to suggest that all aliens are demonic is inaccurate. This error is due to miscommunication and misunderstanding of the language used to describe celestial beings, as well as those alien life forms that exist on and *inside* the earth. There are alien lifeforms that are extraterrestrial as well. Jesus is not an alien life-form, He is human and the very image of God in the flesh. This is an important distinction when discerning between ETs, aliens, gods and angels.

> "Jesus said, "My kingdom is not of this world. If it were, my servants would fight to prevent my arrest by the Jewish leaders. But now my kingdom is from another place."
>
> (John 18:36)

> "They are not of the world, even as I am not of the world."
>
> (John 17:16)

> "Then Jesus told them, "You are from below; I am from above. You are of this world; I am not of this world."
>
> (John 8:23)

> "I have given them Your word and the world has hated them; for they are not of the world, just as I am not of the world."
>
> (John 17:14)

> "They are of the world. That is why they speak from the world's perspective, and the world listens to them."
>
> (1 John 4:5)

Does any true believer in God and Jesus really think that God doesn't have a plan to deal with these aliens? He most certainly does! His plans are laid out all over

Scriptures which have been concealed through mistranslations, transliterations of key words and the names of God, and the suppression of the Great Rejected Jewish Texts. I prove through Hebrew linguistics, history, a little archeology and corroborating Scriptures that these rejected Jewish texts did indeed contain the Word of God.

Too many Christians think that Disclosure, or the exposure of the alien presence on earth, is going to instigate some alien gospel. Again, this is only half the story. When experiencers talk about ETs or aliens without knowledge of God's mighty extraterrestrial army, they speak of an incomplete picture, which can be a deception in and of itself. They are also missing the true gospel, written all over the Jewish Scriptures and written into the very stars themselves. Book Five – *The Heavens* reveals how the Gospel of Salvation was first written into the stars, before it was even given to the scribes on earth. This is God's own astrology, which the fallen sons of heaven, those two hundred Bene HaElohim, then distorted by teaching men a corrupted version of the names and true meanings of the stars which the Creator has spread out in the heavens.

> "And I saw another *angel fly in the midst of heaven*, having *the everlasting gospel* to preach unto them that dwell on the earth, and to every nation, and kindred, and tongue, and people. Saying with a loud voice, 'Fear God, and give glory to him; for the hour of his judgment is come: and worship him that made heaven, and earth, and the sea, and the fountains of waters.'"
>
> (Revelation 14:6,7)

This is a clear indication that extraterrestrial messengers will be preaching the eternal gospel of salvation through Yeshua/Jesus to the entire world at the very end of days, which will be the last bastion of Grace, and very last window of opportunity to repent, right before the wrath of God engulfs the planet. Christians must take note of this, as it clearly describes an ET (angel) flying in a space vehicle through the atmosphere, coming into the air space of the earth or *into the midst of heaven*, in *midair* above the earth, as other translations interpret the KJV words. Obviously, this has to be the skies above earth, as how else could they be preaching the gospel from midair to all the peoples of the earth? As they are speaking in a loud voice to all the various peoples so that everyone in all the nations can hear them simultaneously, they may be using some type of public announcement system within their spacecraft. Their job and their role in the very last days is announcement.

Essentially, almost every spiritual system incorporates a belief in angels. But just *who* are they? Jewish Angelology describes a hierarchy of angels, adopted by Christianity, which further believes that angels played a role in Bible history and prophesy. Just how much of an individual role these angels play varies, depending on the type of Christian teaching. New Agers not only believe in angels, but tend to worship them, and invoke them. We're going to explore and discern throughout this book the ways and means of how to tell if you are dealing with Heaven's angels who serve the Lord and His Kingdom of Heaven, or if you are working with the god of this world and his fallen angels, the counterfeits who masquerade as Heaven's angels.

New Agers tend to believe that the angels will save them, whereas Christians believe only Jesus can save them. New Agers believe that extraterrestrials are space brothers coming to save the planet and to help humans ascend. Christians typically do not believe in extraterrestrials but believe all aliens are demons and fallen angels, and that one can only be raptured through faithfulness to Jesus Christ. So, who is right, and who is wrong, and how can we discern the truth?

Most Christians are not aware of the fact that about ninety percent of so-called *New Agers* actually once identified as *Christian*, but left the churches for a variety of reasons. One of the most common of these reasons is their wounding from the false Religious Spirit, expressed through the cult mentality which often exists in many denominations, leading to the hypocrisy that emanates from many so called Christians. Besides, these New Age people tend to be truth seekers, and when they discovered that there are other books in the Bible which were omitted, they began to search elsewhere, and to create their own churches. However, just for clarities sake, the term *New Ager* didn't actually come about till the 1990s. It actually comes from the Bible, the *Book of Revelation*, which speaks of the Age to Come, the Millennial Reign of Christ on Earth, which I have identified as the Astronomical Processional Age of Aquarius.

So, perhaps Christians are the real New Agers! If they are following the Scriptures and the Bible Prophesies closely, they are supposed to represent the Kingdom of Heaven on earth, which will manifest on earth in the Age to come, the New Age of Aquarius. I'm very much a *word* person. Words matter. When words are twisted and become misconstrued out of ignorance, bigotry or a complete lack of understanding of linguistics and history, then people get subjugated and marginalized due to misunderstanding.

It is true that many New Agers succumb to the New World Order Agenda and are being used, unbeknownst by them, through their naiveté and enthusiasm for contact with ETs and Aliens. Most are unaware that they are being deceived by the channelings from so-called space brothers, angels and spirit guides. I have exposed much of this in Book One and Book Two, and will continue down this path to teach discernment of spirits here.

There is a strong *occult* influence in the New Age movement, which Christians find false and objectionable, and they are correct for doing so. There is an *alien agenda* at work to deceive the masses, which I have exposed in Book One. Unfortunately, according to my research, there aren't many Christians who teach the Divine remedy for this, which is what you will learn within the pages of this book. The Bible Scriptures are full of extraterrestrials who serve the heavenly armies, which are on specific assignments on earth now. These are without a doubt, the good ETs and yes, many may be classified as aliens, because of their giant stature, their interdimensional abilities and their advanced intelligence, but suffice it to say, they appear human nevertheless. Most people call them 'angels'.

Many living today don't realize, unless you're as old as me, that book stores from the 1950s that used to sell books on the occult, spirit communications, etc., were originally called *Occult Book Stores*. Then in the late 1970s, that moniker changed to *Metaphysical Book Stores*, as many scientifically inclined subjects were added, such as the study of quantum physics, chemistry, healing, energy awareness, etc. It was only towards the late 1990s that that label changed again to *New Age*, which encompasses self-help, health, psychology, healing modalities, the body-mind-spirit connection, on top of the usual metaphysical information of the past.

Jesus made it very clear in Matthew 24 and 25 that He would return at the *end* of this age. He was referring to the Processional Age of Pisces. The ancients were well-aware of Astronomical cycles, which is why at the end of this book, I'm going to reveal to you that Revelation Chapter 12 was written in the language of Astrology and Astronomy.

The fact that you're reading this book now means that Jesus hasn't returned yet, and the Age of Pisces isn't complete. However, there is a great deal of information He relates to us in His Prophesies which refer to this very time in which we live. Information can be found regarding how to discern the times, how to discern the 'signs in the heavens' and the very important role His angel armies will play at the end of this age.

I am going to present a body of knowledge here on how our ancient history fits into the End Times Prophecies, then you can decide for yourself.

Remember, the only thing that travels faster than the speed of light is thought. Are we there yet?

The Truth is Stranger Than Fiction!
www.whoswhointhecosmiczoo.com

CHAPTER ONE
THE CLASH OF TWO KINGDOMS

> "For we wrestle not against flesh and blood, but against principalities, against powers, against the rulers of the darkness of this world, against spiritual wickedness in heavenly places."
> (EPHESIANS 6:12)

How does one find freedom amidst the clash of two kingdoms?
Do Angels play a bigger role in human affairs on earth, than we may realize?
Angels wage war against other angels, so how do we tell them apart?
Is there such a thing as Human Angels born on earth?

Book Three, *Who Are the Angels?* is the continuation of Book One and Book Two of *Who's Who in The Cosmic Zoo?* Here we will focus on the discernment of angels. We know that there is war in heaven between groups of angels. We have already established that the two hundred sons of the Elohim fell from heaven, came to earth, mated with earth woman, and created a race of Nephilim, Giants. That's what Enoch and Genesis 6 tell us. There is more detailed history to that story.

Angels who serve and belong to the Kingdom of Heaven operate under God's laws and protocols. The fallen angels, however, follow a different set of marching orders. If humanity is to succeed on earth, we must get to the point, where we can discern them apart, and not allow ourselves to be misled by the counterfeits, who use earth humans as pawns in their space war.

There is a battle going on in the heavens, above and inside the earth, over all the nations of the earth between the kingdom of darkness and the Kingdom of Heaven, the Kingdom of God. For those of you who have read Book One of *Who's Who in The Cosmic Zoo?* you'll remember that I spent Book One identifying just *who* are the powers, principalities, rulers of the darkness of this present world and spiritual wickedness in the heavens mentioned in Ephesians 6:12.

According to the Scriptures, the end of days is a real life scenario right out of *Star Wars*. All the apocalyptic prophesies point to a time on earth when angels will fly through the air with the last and final call for salvation through repentance. Warships are literally released from inside the earth in order to torment humankind, but are ordered not to harm the grass.

> "And the fifth angel sounded, and I saw a *star fall from heaven unto the earth: and to him was given the key of the bottomless pit.* [This was no ordinary star, but an extraterrestrial angelic being, because the scripture refers to the star as a 'him' and 'he'.] And he opened the bottomless pit; and there arose a smoke out of the pit, as the smoke of a great furnace; and the sun and the air were darkened by reason of the smoke of the pit. And there came out of the smoke locusts upon the earth: and unto them was given power, as the scorpions of the earth have power. [The vision of locusts are of spacecraft, locusts have been compared to helicopters, or some type of flying armored vehicle, with weapons attached to them, like the stingers of scorpions]. And it was commanded them that they should not hurt the grass of the earth, neither any green thing, neither any tree; *but only those men which have not the seal of God in their foreheads.* And to them it was given that they should not kill them, but that *they should be tormented five months*: and their torment was as the torment of a scorpion, when he strikes a man. *And in those days shall men seek death, and shall not find it; and shall desire to die, and death shall flee from them."*
>
> (Revelation 9:1-6-emphasis mine)

> "And I saw another *angel fly in mid heaven*, [clearly the description of an extraterrestrial flying in a spacecraft in the skies above earth, also known as mid-heaven] having the everlasting gospel to preach unto them that dwell on the earth, and to every nation, and tribe, and tongue, and people, saying with a loud voice [through a PA system], "Fear God, and give glory to him; for the hour of his judgment has come: and worship him that made heaven, and earth, and the sea, and the fountains of waters."
>
> (Revelation 14:6, 7-emphasis mine)

We are in a clash between two kingdoms on earth. Humans are the prize. These two armies will launch all kinds of attacks on the human mind, body and soul, to try to break us. This is why, especially in these last days, life without knowing God is ultimate death. The promises of God are to those who believe in Him, who shall not perish, but have everlasting life. (John 3:16)

Chapter One: The Clash Of Two Kingdoms

The War in Heaven

"And there was war in heaven: Michael and his angels fought against the dragon; and the dragon fought and his angels, and prevailed not; neither was their place found any more in heaven. And the great dragon was cast out, that old serpent, called the Devil, and Satan, which deceives the whole world: he was cast out into the earth, and his angels were cast out with him.

And I heard a loud voice saying in heaven, "Now, is come salvation, and strength, and the kingdom of our God, and the power of his Christ: for the accuser of our brethren is cast down, which accused them before our God day and night."

And they overcame him by the blood of the Lamb, and by the word of their testimony; and they loved not their lives unto the death. Therefore, rejoice, ye heavens, and ye that dwell in them. Woe to the inhabiters of the earth and of the sea! for the devil is come down unto you, having great wrath, because he knows that he has but a short time."

(Revelation 12:7-12)

We need to understand our role in this warfare, how, with our faith and prayers, we actually have been given the power and authority, collectively, to win battles in the heavens. Human prayers are answered by God through the agency of angels. Yet, due to ignorance, and a lack of discernment, there are many on earth who have their prayers answered by fallen angels, all due to different types of bondages, confusion and wickedness.

When a human being prays without discernment, without faith in the Lord and Messiah, a prayer like: "help me, somebody help me;" or when someone enters into a Faustian-type contract with darkness, deception occurs. Recently there has been a growing desire to have contact with aliens. People aren't fussy, they just want to see or hear from ET, as there is little to no discernment in their request, many have reported that they couldn't care less who answers their call when questioned about it. These people are visited by someone, frequently someone in a masquerade of false light and techno-wizardry as 2 Corinthians 4:4 affirms:

"Satan, who is the god of this world, has blinded the minds of those who don't believe. They are unable to see the glorious light of the Good News. They don't understand this message about the glory of Christ, *who is the exact likeness of God.*"

And no wonder, for Satan himself masquerades as an angel of light."

(2 Corinthians 11:14)

Who Are The Angels? — Ella LeBain

This is what this five-book series, *Who's Who In The Cosmic Zoo?* teaches and exposes, that not all aliens or extraterrestrials are benevolent and not all angels are serving the Kingdom of Heaven (Light). We need to understand this spiritual warfare between the angelic realms, which began in ancient times, at the start of the last galactic war. Yes, the Truth Is Stranger Than Fiction, and our world, both the seen and the unseen, are a lot like *Star Wars*, or *Star Trek*. I kid you not!

I'm sure you must be thinking, why are humans such a prize? There are so many humans who are demonstrating outright evil and wickedness in the way they treat their own kind, as well as the horrific abuses they are capable of visiting upon animals. When I see and hear of the stories of the tactics of ISIS, how these human beings viciously rape, torture and abuse women, children and animals, and then see actual videos of the cruel, barbaric ways they kill both humans and animals, I can only have one conclusion: this is most definitely *not* human!

Crimes against humanity is evidence of an alien force amongst us. While possessing the human mind, soul and body, these fallen angels and their draconian hierarchy manifest their intense hatred for us humankind. They are behind all the wars on this planet, all the abuses, all the perversions, all the torture, persecution and torment of the human race, in all its races and genders. But let's face it, they particularly have it in for the female side of humanity, which we witness from the ancient past. We are going to explore and understand the underlying roots of sexism, which I began in Book Two: *Who Is God?*

One thing we have learned about our history is that it not only repeats itself, it also comes around full circle as a revolution, seeking closure. In this ancient extraterrestrial-alien-gods-angels-timeline, a great deal of unfinished business is seeking resolution, and will find it, for good or bad, depending on which side of this battle you find yourself.

So much of our history is lost in the buried past. Humanity is essentially a species with amnesia[1], and we can't really expect to move forward if we are disconnected with our past. Our genetic memories, with which we are all born, link us to the past through our ancestors, but where does this all stop? Just how far and deep into the past do we need to go in order to understand the challenges facing today's generation?

Angel Linguistics

In Hebrew, the word for angel (Malachim) primarily means 'messenger' or more literally 'messenger of/from the kingdom.' It comes from the Hebrew root word, 'Melechk' which means king, combined with the Hebrew root word which means 'to send,' thus combined, translates to "sent from the King, or Kingdom." Malachim also are seen as the shadows of God, as it is the shadows which define the light. All Malachim are

Chapter One: The Clash Of Two Kingdoms

both extraterrestrial and interdimensional messengers. However, the English word 'angel' was derived from the Greek the word 'angelos' which meant intermediary. Angels are intermediaries and messengers between God and humans. Since they reside primarily in the upper heavens, they are considered as 'extraterrestrials.'

When the Lord Yahuah in the Old Testament was referenced in Psalm 91:11, 'He will give His angels charge over us', He was referring to His multitude of extraterrestrial servants, the messengers and warriors which are under His command. Angels are powerful extraterrestrial, interdimensional beings who serve God's Kingdom of Heaven and humankind on multiple levels.

As with all challenges to identity, you have to be able to first know and identify the original before you can rightly discern the counterfeit. Fallen angels have been classified in the demonic realms as arch-demons, which fall within a further hierarchy. Fallen angels masquerade as light beings, and can both pretend and project themselves as heavenly beings, ascended beings and space brothers. As I proved in Book One, fallen angels lost their first estate, and were downgraded into the alien bodies of Grays, Reptilians and Hybrids, the result of the Lord's curse. Their history is that of creating monstrosities on earth, reaping mixed genetic seeds. The Grays are essentially clones which do not have progeny, and depend on genetic engineering and cloning. These have manipulated themselves into many differing types which I detailed in Book One. These Grays are behind most abductions, which is the method they use to obtain genetic material from humans to create an alien-human hybrid race.

The reason the Bible refers to satan as the Dragon and the Beast is literal, not metaphorical. The fallen son, also called the fallen cherub of heaven, was thrown down to earth to inhabit the bodies of the Reptilians, who are genetic mutations from the dinosaurs, which I also revealed in great detail in Book One. The race of these Reptilian beings are called Draconians, shortened as Dracs, as they are Beasts. They are a militarized hierarchy broken up into a type of caste system, similar to that of the Hindu Brahman. They follow the head of the Beast who is Lucifer/Satan. They believe they are the true owners of planet earth, and will fight to retain it and its resources.

LEGIONS OF ANGELS VS. LEGIONS OF DEMONS

Legion is a word that can describe armies. The Hebrew word for armies is *Tzeveyot*. *Adonai Tzeveyot* is the Lord of Hosts, which specifically translates to Lord of Celestial Armies.

Many people believe in angels, but have no idea where they come from or whom they serve. Some angels, as extraterrestrial messengers, serve the Creator God, while others serve the adversary of the Creator God, Satan in Hebrew, also called Lucifer, also Sammael, also Baal, ad infinitum. You can see the catalogue of his many names in Book Two: *Who is God?* my Chapter on *The Office of Satan*.

Throughout human history, angels as extraterrestrial messengers have appeared before men and women, often being mistaken as gods as they have intervened quite often in the affairs on earth. Angels as extraterrestrial messengers are essentially agents on assignment, sent on a mission from a higher authority, a divine source which cares for humankind, as well as to effectuate God's Divine Will on earth.

The Bible is by far the largest compilation of evidence of extraterrestrial contact with Earth inhabitants. As you will see in the following pages, a great deal of the original meaning was lost in watered down translations. Many Scriptures obviously reveal extraterrestrials in all their technological glory, yet modern man has had his spiritual eyes blinded from seeing these truths. As the saying goes, the truth is stranger than fiction. Science fiction, much of which has been proven to be more prophetic than fictional, has indeed become science fact in this age of knowledge.

It is proverbial that man believes what he wants to believe, but for all of us who take the Scriptures seriously must therefore read through these passages with a new perspective. According to Born Again believers, it is only the Holy Spirit Who gives the power of Rhema, or the true Revelation of the Logos, The Word Who is Jesus Christ, by bringing true meanings to light. I am certainly not the first to see these truths revealed in the Bible, nor will I be the last. We live in an age of knowledge, in a time where secrets and mysteries are now being revealed to humankind. The revelation of the true identities of these celestial beings is now being exposed in these End Times, also known as the 'Apocalypse,' which is the Great Unveiling of Truth. I pray every eye reading these words will be touched by the Rhema of the Holy Spirit to witness Truth to your inner man, so you can *see* what I *see*.

In the Scriptures, angels are never described as having wings. They are *always* described as looking human. Many of the angels are considered ultraterrestrial, meaning having interdimensional capabilities, or the ability to move through the different dimensions. Some of them would simply appear, come through a window or wall, and then disappear. Others would descend on a ladder, as in the classic Biblical UFO story of 'Jacobs Ladder' in Genesis 28. Here Jacob witnessed ETs coming and going down a ladder from heaven. He then physically struggled with one of these angels, or extraterrestrials, and refused to let him go until the angel blessed him. Clearly the ladder was an extension from a spaceship which these extraterrestrial angels were utilizing. This is why angels were later depicted in artwork with wings, because it was ancient man's way of communicating that they had the ability to fly.

As a matter of fact, some angels, do have winged appendages, also known as bird men. The Halo and the wings in artwork, depicted their auric field, which was made

Chapter One: The Clash Of Two Kingdoms

of light. But for the most part, all the angels who show up in the Bible stories, are men, and their wings are either hidden or non-existent.

The ancient astronaut theory has implied that the wings drawn on these ETs were to depict a device that was used to transport them to and from their space ship, similar to our modern day jet pack. When observed by humans, it looked like an extension on the back, allowing them to fly through the air. As our ancestors knew only birds to fly through air, these ancient astronaut angels were drawn with bird wings to illustrate that they had the ability of flight.

The Kabbalah Book of Formation received through Abraham, in approximately 3700 BC, consists of a revelation of astrology, cosmology and the laws of reincarnation, and also describes the heavenly hierarchy of angels. Angels as extraterrestrial messengers are made up of wisdom, intelligence, mercy, strength, beauty, victory, dominions and splendor which is light energy. Angels, or extraterrestrial messengers, are put in charge of the celestial music, the frequency, vibration, color and sound of which keeps the universe in motion.

Human knowledge is given by God through the mediation of angels. In fact, every visible thing in this world is placed in charge of an angel. The Talmud states that not even a blade of grass can grow on the earth without an angel whispering to it to encourage it to grow.

Angels don't always have to bear wings of flight. The ancient astronauts of the past whose star ships and orbital stations landed on earth were often depicted as having wings. The tall, glowing beings who appeared and were later illustrated through the art of the Renaissance as human beings with wings and halos or auras were angels. Oftentimes their auras were so wide and colorful, artists depicted them as feathered wings, reproducing the layers of light and shadows seen in their aura. In Hebrew, the word for wings, *kanafim,* is exactly the same word used to describe the extenders or wings of an airplane. The fact that angels, extraterrestrial messengers, were illustrated with wings simply showed that they flew in vehicles with winged extenders. A lot of the artwork shows them in bubbles, with circles around them, which could be interpreted as being housed in a space ship as well as depicting their glowing auras. The ancient astronaut theorists believe them to be extraterrestrial messengers, and if you want to get literal, that's exactly what they are.

By definition, extra-terrestrial means anything outside the earth's atmosphere. Extra-terrestrial beings are often of advanced intelligence that surpasses our own. Many originate from outside of this star system. ET's have been known to work as angels on their missions to Earth, serving the family of light or office of Christ.

The term 'alien', however, has a completely different meaning. Alien means foreign life form. A foreign life form is comprised of completely different genetic codes. Many extra-terrestrial life forms share the same genetic coding as we do, perhaps because we are a strain of their seed, planted here many thousands of years ago. However, not all extra-terrestrials are aliens or angels and not all angels are extra-terrestrials or aliens.

So why the distinction? Many types of advanced life forms have been visiting us, some of which are working with and within the angelic orders, and are helping us to transform, transcend, and transmute the darkness and negativity of this world. They are equipping us with abilities to switch from one universe to another. We are being made aware of this parallel universe and given a choice to transfer over without coercion. This respect of our free will often serve as an indicator as to the level of advancement and intelligence of the extra-terrestrial being or angel.

Genetic manipulation to upgrade or downgrade species is as old as time itself. Our present abduction dilemma is nothing new. However, we must remember that, no mystery is ever closed to those with an open mind.

Welcome to the Grand Experiment

> "More and more we are finding that mythology in general though greatly contorted very often has some historic base. And the interesting thing is that one myth which occurs over and over again in many parts of the world is that somewhere a long time ago supernatural beings had sexual intercourse with natural women and produced a special breed of people."
>
> (Francis A. Schaeffer)

Earth is a social experiment, ordained and authorized by the Lord to allow ET and Alien races to seed the planet with various genetic mutations of the human race. This is why every culture is so different yet still human nonetheless. The experiment is to see if all these roots races which originated in the cosmos can get along together on earth. Not all races are of human origin, but all have blended with the human form and genetic code, opening up their chances of salvation through the Lord of Salvation.

> "The LORD will give strength to His people; the LORD will bless His people with peace."
>
> (Psalm 29:11)

Angels and Sex

Much of the sexual connection, from the extreme ends of the spectrum, the one end being the violations, the rape, abuse, mutilation and sexual immorality of all kinds,

Chapter One: The Clash Of Two Kingdoms

to the other extreme of loneliness and pain of the lack of a partner, are all the work of the same principality of the influence of fallen angels on humankind. It's all a form of bondage. This is one of the downsides that comes from sharing the planet with these fallen beings all being under the influence of an ancient curse.

The fallen angels also called fallen sons of heaven, fell into lust for the human woman. Their results, the fruit of their unions, are the miscreants called the Nephilim. These Giants later died and became the evil spirits of the earth who torment humans until the return of the Lord. They are responsible for orchestrating the abductions of millions, if not billions of human beings, harvesting their genetic seeds through the extraction of sperm and ovum.

Even fallen angels have tried to get in on this Grand Experiment by attempting to hybridize themselves into human form through Nephilim seed.

> "The Nephilim were on the earth in those days, and also afterward, when [because] the sons of God came in to the daughters of men, and they bore children to them. Those were the mighty men who were of old, men of renown."
> (Genesis 6:4 - NASB)

The Scriptures tell us that these beings sinned not only against humankind but also against the animals and all the creatures of the earth. They mixed the animal seeds with their own, creating hybrids and monsters. The practice of bestiality originates from the influence of fallen angels and their demons who seek to hold humanity in bondage to the very sins that angered the Creator. Both floods were unleashed upon the earth as punishment. The Lord promised with His Covenant Rainbow that He would never destroy the world by water again, but He never said anything about fire and brimstone. This is exactly what the Bible Prophesies say will happen when the Wrath of God is unleashed on earth to punish the wicked and all those who reject God's gifts of grace and salvation.

The horrible cruelty and abuse that takes place today against women, children and animals by Daesh, another name for ISIS, are directly influenced by fallen angel demons. This is exactly the kind of horrors that were rampant upon the earth in the days prior to the Noachian Flood and the Luciferian Flood, which destroyed the ancient civilization of Atlantis. The fallen angels were punished for their miscreations, for going against the Laws of Creation, established by the Creator.

> "And they began to sin against the birds, wild beasts, reptiles and fish."
> (Enoch 7:5)

"And their judges and rulers went to the daughters of men and took their wives by force (rape) from their husbands according to their choice, and the sons of men in those days took from the cattle of the earth, the beasts of the field and the fowls of the air, and taught the mixture of animals of one species with the other, in order therewith to provoke the Lord; and God saw the whole earth and it was corrupt, for all flesh had corrupted its ways upon earth, all men and all animals."

(Jasher 4:18)

The Books of Enoch, Jasher and Jubilees are considered Exobiblical texts, or Pseudepigrapha, but as I proved in Book Two: *Who Is God?* that these scrolls of Enoch were considered to be the Word of God by Jews, the early disciples and Jesus Himself, who all quoted from Enoch's scriptures. Enoch was the first scribe and prophet to coin the phrase, *Son Of Man,* which is exactly what Jesus Christ called Himself. Besides Enoch's scriptures, which this author considers to be the Word of God, there are multiple books that were rejected out of the Bible Canon, which are all considered to be *rejected texts,* mainly because they contained knowledge that was contrary to the political agenda of the Church of Rome who later became the Roman Catholic Church, and the sovereign Vatican City, which rules it.

All of the great rejected texts, including Enoch's Scrolls, were foundational scripture in Jewish beliefs, many of them were *too Jewish* for pagan Rome, others contradicted Church Agenda, which is what I proved in Book Two, *Who Is God?* Many modern-day Christians ignore.

Most of the rejected texts contain knowledge and End Times Prophesies that were written especially for times such as this. Enoch's scrolls described the story that is but a brief synopsis in Genesis 6 about the Nephilim aliens on the earth in ancient times, and how they got there, in the most detailed account of describing two hundred rebellious *sons of the Elohim* (Bene HaElohim), who mated with earth women and essentially created giants who behaved like monsters and sinned against both humans and animals.

Suffice it to say, this could be categorized as another example of the Grand Experiment on the earth. In Enoch 1:10 we learn that two hundred sons of the Elohim (also known as *Fallen Angels*), landed, yes landed in spacecraft on Mount Hermon during the days of Jared. Jared was born 460 years after Adam died (Genesis 5:15, 20). The story of Jared is found in greater detail in the rejected *Book of Jubilees,* another Jewish scroll which expounds on the Genesis account, and reveals the very date these extraterrestrial rebellious sons of heaven, also called, *Watchers,* descended to Earth which was 461 Annus Mundi, a date which Bishop Usher would later interpret as 3543 B.C. The *Book of Jubilees,* also describes these Watchers were specifically associated with Jared, who was fifth in line of Adam's descendants.[2]

Chapter One: The Clash Of Two Kingdoms

The *Book of Jubilees* tells us:

> "And in the second week of the tenth jubilee of Mahalelel took unto him a wife Dinah, the daughter of Barakel, the daughter of his brother's brother and she bore him a son in the sixth year and he called his name Jared for in his days the angels of the Lord descended on the earth, those so named the Watchers."

> "The Sons of God were sent down to teach mankind truth and justice; and for three hundred years did indeed teach Cain's son Enoch all the secrets of heaven and earth. Later, however, they lusted after mortal women and defiled themselves by sexual intercourse. Enoch has recorded not only divine instructions, but also their subsequent fall from grace; before the end they were indiscriminately enjoying virgins, matrons, men, and beasts."
>
> (Jubilees 4:15, 22)

> "And it came to pass when the children of men had multiplied that in those days were born unto them beautiful and comely daughters. And the angels, the children of the heaven, saw and lusted after them, and said to one another: 'Come, let us choose us wives from among the children of men and beget us children."
>
> (Enoch 6:1-3)

> "And it came to pass when the children of men began to multiply on the face of the earth and daughters were born unto them, that the angels of God saw them on a certain year of this jubilee, that they were beautiful to look upon; and they took themselves wives of all whom they chose, and they bare unto them sons and they were giants."
>
> (Jubilees 5:1-2)

> "And I Enoch was blessing the Lord of majesty and the King of the ages, and lo! The Watchers called me – Enoch the scribe – and said to me: Enoch, thou scribe of righteousness, go, declare the Watchers of the heaven who have left the high heaven, the holy eternal place, and have defiled themselves with women, and have done as the children of earth do, and have taken unto themselves wives: Ye have wrought great destruction on the earth: And ye shall have no peace nor forgiveness of sin: and inasmuch as they delight themselves in their children [Nephilim], The murder of their beloved ones shall they see, and over the destruction of their children shall they lament, and shall make supplication unto eternity, but mercy and peace shall ye not attain."
>
> (1 Enoch 10:3-8)

W. F. Albright wrote, "The Israelites who heard this section recited unquestionably thought of intercourse between angels and women." [3] Essentially, this is how the myth began, which brings us to today's fantasies of sex with aliens. Lilith was Adam's first wife, who rebelled against him and the Lord. Per the *Book of Giants* and the *First and Second Books of Adam and Eve*, she chose evil, so was transformed into a demon, to steal the lives of babies and torment men through lust. Lilith became the succubus that oppresses men in their wet dreams, and is aligned with today's Gray aliens, who perform all kinds of sexual experiments on humans. They also program humans towards different types of sexual lusts and perversion. This is why many abductees report different types of sexual abuse and molestation, and are forced into having all kinds of sex that is perverted and contrary to their normal sexual orientations.

I think it's important to include as many different viewpoints as possible, which are exobiblical, because so much of the great rejected texts, were concealed and covered up for political reasons, from the true history most theologians were taught, not to mention that they contain God's prophecies for the end of this timeline for humankind as we know it now, which I referred to in Book One, as the *Evadamic Race*. Jesus promises upon His return, to transform humanity back into the glory bodies, which was lost with Adam, when the Annunaki genetically manipulated human DNA after Adam's fall and the dispensation of the curses by the Lord.

God has always raised up his resistance on earth to the god of this world. Those who kept the faith back in ancient times, were front line and center witnesses to the presence of these fallen corrupted supernatural extraterrestrials on earth, that created the Grand Experiment on earth, by choosing to mingle their genetic seed with earth women thereby producing human-hybrid-giants called Nephilim, which in Hebrew specifically translates to *fallen ones or rejects*, who have been dubbed by researchers as *fallen angels*.

We have historicity in Bible scriptures of their record. The Book of Jasher, another rejected Jewish text, tells that the first generation of Nephilim offspring lived longer than five hundred years and ended up killing each other off. Their fathers were judged harshly and sentenced to everlasting chains of darkness, and were buried under the earth for *seventy generations*.

> "And all the sons of men departed from the ways of the Lord in those days as they multiplied upon the face of the earth with sons and daughters, and they taught one another their evil practices and they continued sinning against the Lord. And every man made unto himself a god, and they robbed and plundered every man his neighbor as well as his relative, and they corrupted the earth, and the earth was filled with violence. And their judges and rulers went to the daughters of men and took their wives by force from their husbands according to

Chapter One: The Clash Of Two Kingdoms

their choice, and the sons of men in those days took from the cattle of the earth, the beasts of the field and the fowls of the air, and taught the mixture of animals of one species with the other, in order therewith to provoke the Lord; and God saw the whole earth and it was corrupt, for all flesh had corrupted its ways upon earth, all men and all animals. And the Lord said, I will blot out man that I created from the face of the earth, yea from man to the birds of the air, together with cattle and beasts that are in the field for I repent that I made them. And all men who walked in the ways of the Lord, died in those days, before the Lord brought the evil upon man which he had declared, for this was from the Lord, that they should not see the evil which the Lord spoke of concerning the sons of men."

(Jasher 4:16-20)

"And He said "Thy spirit will not always abide on man; for they also are flesh and their days shall be one hundred and twenty years. And He sent His sword into their midst that each should slay his neighbor, and they began to slay each other till they all fell by the sword and were destroyed from the earth. And their fathers were witnesses of their destruction), and after this they were bound in the depths of the earth forever, until the day of the great condemnation when judgment is executed on all those who have corrupted their ways and their works before the Lord. And He destroyed all from their places, and there was not left one of them whom He judged not according to all their wickedness."

(Jubilees 5:8-11)

The Book of Jasher also mentions Enoch quite a bit. Enoch was reported to have taken trips back and forth to heaven and earth. He was revered and feared, because He must have been one of the powerful humans that was not corrupted by the genetic downgrading of humankind, but managed to keep all twelve of his strands of DNA, which today many would call a superhuman, or extraterrestrial. Enoch was taken up to heaven and never died.

"The sons of men were greatly afraid of Enoch, and they feared to approach him on account of the Godlike awe that was seated on his countenance; therefore, no man could look at him, fearing he might be punished and die."

(Jasher 3:20)

The Book of Enoch discerns the imprisonment of the Watchers and their final judgment at the end of seventy generations.

"And the Lord said unto Michael (the Prince/ArchAngel): 'Go, bind Semyaza and his associates who have united themselves with women so as to have defiled themselves with them in all their uncleanness. And when their sons have slain one another, (the Nephilim) and they have seen the destruction of their beloved ones, bind them [the two hundred Bene HaElohim aka Watchers] fast for *seventy generations* in the valleys of the earth, till the day of their judgement and of their consummation, till the judgement that is forever and ever is consummated. In those days, they shall be led off to the abyss of fire: and to the torment and the prison in which they shall be confined forever. And whosoever shall be condemned and destroyed will from thenceforth be bound together with them to the end of all generations."

(1 Enoch 10:11-15)

For *seventy generations* they are bound inside the earth. I discussed in Book One, as to what constitutes a biblical generation, which is key in understanding the timing of End Times Prophesies. Some bible scholars say a biblical generation is seventy years, others say its eighty years, while others believe it is one hundred years. Let's do the math. Seventy generations at one hundred years equals seven thousand years from the time these rebellious sons of the Elohim, were punished and bound inside the earth. Before the times of Moses, a generation was one hundred years, because humans lived to be up to nine hundred years old. However, after the flood, the genetic strain was weakened, and a generation became seventy years.

"As the sun was setting, Abram fell into a deep sleep, and a thick and dreadful darkness came over him. Then the Lord said to him, "Know for certain that for four hundred years your descendants will be strangers in a country not their own and that they will be enslaved and mistreated there... In the fourth *generation* your descendants will come back here."

(Genesis 15:16)

God said to Abraham that after four hundred years He would deliver Israel, "in the fourth generation". Here a generation is one hundred years (4 x 100 = 400 years). This is understood by the fact that Abraham had his promised child Isaac when he was exactly one hundred years of age. (Genesis 21:5) This makes it obvious, that the age of a man when his first child is born is the raw definition of a generation.

Nevertheless, notice that the full number (400 years) is exactly ten-times that of a regular generation of 40 years. Both 100 years and 40 years are considered generations in the Bible, depending on whether it was before Noah's flood or after the flood. However, the average of these two would be seventy years, which is also found

Chapter One: The Clash Of Two Kingdoms

in the bible, (Psalm 90:10). Seventy years is a generation consistent with the average age of a man at his death, rather than when his first child is born as with the example of Abraham.

40 + 100 = 140 years. 140 ÷ 2 = 70-years as a generation. It's also important to note that King David died at the age of 70 yet reigned 40 years. The bible then rounds the exact span of years in a "generation" to be 40 and 100 years as the primary usage, but on occasion, seventy years is used. The number 70 just happens to be the average of 40 and 100, which allows three different timeframes to work in numeric harmony to produce the numeric symmetry found throughout the bible. The usage of the 100-year generation predominates in the bible prior to the time of Moses when men lived longer, but was downgraded to 40 years after Moses. A generation of 70 years is also inferred in the books of Enoch and Jubilees, and is highly compatible with the jubilee system of the bible itself, (Daniel 9)[5]. The Shemitah cycles, seven years times seven years becomes the year of Jubilee, which is the beginning of the next super Shemitah cycle that began in 2015.

So, for what it's worth, the fallen angels who were bound in the earth for *seventy generations,* could be there for 7,000 years, or 4,900 years respectively depending on what number you assign for a *generation.* I'm going with a hundred years, because this was written down by Enoch who lived before the flood, when men lived to be nine hundred years old. I'm also going with the fact that these fallen angels were bound inside the earth prior to Noah's flood (approximately 3,000BC), which may have even happened after the first floods known as the floods of Lucifer, or the sinking of Atlantis, which scholars put at around 9,600BC or sometime in between. Remember the covenant that the Lord gave Noah after the last great deluge was His promise to never destroy the earth by floods again, which implied that He did it before. (Genesis 9:15)

It is my belief that the beginning of the book of Genesis 1 begins with the Spirit hovering over the waters, because that was the result of the Luciferian Floods aka the sinking of the Atlantean Civilizations in approximately 9,600BC. Enoch says, they will be bound until the Day of Judgment, which according to Revelation, comes at the end of this Age, the end of the processional Age of Pisces.

Scriptures tell us there were two hundred *Watchers* who went down to Tartarus, which is another level of hell inside the earth, where they were buried under the *valleys* of the earth. Tartarus contains underground rivers. I don't think it's any coincidence that the *Book of Revelation* prophesies the release of four angels that are bound in the Euphrates River.

> "The sixth angel sounded his trumpet, and I heard a voice coming from the four horns of the golden altar that is before God. It said to the sixth angel who had the trumpet, *"Release the four angels who are bound at the great river Euphrates."* And

the four angels who had been kept ready for this very hour and day and month and year were released to kill a third of mankind. The number of the mounted troops was twice ten thousand times ten thousand (200 million). I heard their number."
(Revelation 9:13-16 – NIV)

The *Book of Jubilees* states that demons were severely persecuting humans after the flood and Noah was asked to appeal to God to remove or subjugate them.

"And Thou knowest how Thy Watchers, the fathers of these spirits, acted in my day: and as for these spirits which are living, imprison them and hold them fast in the place of condemnation, and let them not bring destruction on the sons of thy servant, my God;

And the chief of the spirits, Mastêmâ, [who is Satan] came and said: "Lord, Creator, let some of them remain before me, and let them hearken to my voice, and do all that I shall say unto them;

And He said: "Let *the tenth part of them* remain before him, and let nine parts descend into the place of condemnation."
(Jubilees 10:1-9)

"And after this they sinned against the beasts and birds, and all that moveth and walketh on the earth: and much blood was shed on the earth, and every imagination and desire of men imagined vanity and evil continually. And the Lord destroyed everything from off the face of the earth; because of the wickedness of their deeds, and because of the blood which they had shed in the midst of the earth He destroyed everything."
(Jubilees 7:24,25)

Essentially this prophetic Jewish scripture claims that ninety percent of the Nephilim spirits who are demons are imprisoned in the abyss awaiting the final judgment. The remainder will be imprisoned in the bottomless pit at the beginning of the Millennium and then will be placed into the lake of fire. The ten percent allowed to roam the earth (today's gray aliens) are aware of this future punishment, which is why they asked Jesus, whom they recognized as the Son of God, not to place them in the abyss before the appointed time. This would explain and answer the age-old question, as to 'why' God allows suffering on the earth.

"And, behold, they (the demon spirits) cried out, saying, "What have we to do with you, Jesus, you Son of God? are you come here to torment us before the time?"
(Matthew 8:29 AKV)

Chapter One: The Clash Of Two Kingdoms

This scripture is extraordinarily revealing, proving that even the demons, the Gray aliens, and the Nephilim spirits, know that Jesus is the Son of God, and has power over them. They fear the Lord, because they know they are on borrowed time, and they are well aware of what happened to the other ninety percent of them.

"And the number of the army of the horsemen *were* two hundred thousand-thousand: (200 million) and I heard the number of them."
(Revelation 9:16 – KJV)

It's stated clearly in Bible prophecy that the End Time Space War will begin when two hundred million Nephilim soldiers, the Grays in similar formation to Storm Troopers or Clones in *Star Wars*, are going to emerge out of the Bottomless Pit in the Last Days.

"He unleashed against them his hot anger, his wrath, indignation and hostility – a band of *destroying angels*."
(Psalm 78:49)

The entire ninth chapter of Revelation refers to the aliens and their perverted space technology, all the weaponry that will emerge from *inside* the earth in the last days to torment the wicked of humankind. For those of you who never read it, here it is. Brackets and emphasis are mine.

The Fifth Trumpet
"And the fifth angel sounded, and I saw a star fall from heaven unto the earth: and to him was given the key of the bottomless pit. And he opened the bottomless pit; and there arose a smoke out of the pit, as the smoke of a great furnace; and the sun and the air were darkened by reason of the smoke of the pit. And there came out of the smoke locusts upon the earth: and unto them was given power, as the scorpions of the earth have power."

[St. John is describing his vision that they were like scorpions, but not scorpions. Many aliens, particularly gray aliens are insectoid like, have armored bodies. These are hybrids, with technology in their armor, like that of a scorpion, with the power to sting, or shoot people on earth. They are ordered not to harm any of the green plant life on the surface of the earth. Only those humans without the seal of God.]

"And it was commanded them that they should not hurt the grass of the earth, neither any green thing, neither any tree; but only those men which have not the seal of God in their foreheads. And to them it was given that they should not kill them, but that they should be tormented five months: and their torment *was* as the torment of a scorpion, when he strikes a man. And in those days shall men seek death, and shall not find it; and shall desire to die, and death shall flee from them."

[This is known as the Great Tribulation, or the Wrath of God, which is prophesied in Isaiah 66. They are ordered to torment the wicked of humankind, the unrepentant, the unsaved, and the unbelievers, these are the ones who rejected the Grace of God and His Salvation through Yeshua/Jesus. These people are not to be killed, but only to be tormented by these alien creatures.]

"And the shapes of the locusts *were* like unto horses prepared unto battle; and on their heads *were* as it were crowns like gold, and their faces *were* as the faces of men. And they had hair as the hair of women, and their teeth were as *the teeth* of lions. And they had breastplates, as it were breastplates of iron; and the sound of their wings *was* as the sound of chariots of many horses running to battle. And they had tails like unto scorpions, and there were stings in their tails: and their power *was* to hurt men five months. And they had a king over them, *which is* the *angel* of the bottomless pit, whose name in the Hebrew tongue *is* Abaddon, but in the Greek tongue hath *his* name Apollyon.

[The description is that of alien hybrid Nephilim Giants. This is what was done in the past, hybridizing animal, human and alien DNA, and taking the worst or most powerful from each, and creating monstrosities. Note that St. John said, they like horses, but they weren't real horses. They are probably some type of non-human intelligence which today we call aliens, and the sounds of their wings like chariots, are their spaceships, with weapons to hurt the wicked. The fact that this is a prophetic vision given to St. John by Jesus Christ, means that this is the plan God will use to punish the wicked on earth. This is the reason, the Lord did not destroy them all, and allowed satan to keep his ten percent out of the prison, for the end times. The King of the Abyss, Abaddon/Apollyon, is a despotic giant Nephilim Archon, from deep antiquity, held in the abyss to be unleashed at the end of the age, to lead the punishment of the wicked, who are doing the bidding of the Almighty.]

One woe is past; *and*, behold, there come two woes more hereafter."

The Sixth Trumpet
And the sixth angel sounded, and I heard a voice from the four horns of the golden altar which is before God, saying to the sixth angel which had the

Chapter One: The Clash Of Two Kingdoms

trumpet, "Loose the four angels which are bound in the great river Euphrates." And the four angels were loosed, which were prepared for an hour, and a day, and a month, and a year, for *to slay the third part of humankind.*

[The Third, is a repetitive theme throughout the Scriptures. I have connected this dot in Book Two, of how a third or a remnant were either saved or a third were punished. This is about the punishment of the wicked, those who are saved, will not be affected. This punishment will go on for 396 days.]

And the number of the army of the horsemen *were* two hundred-thousand thousand: (200 million) and I heard the number of them.

[For those of you who read Book One, you will remember the piece about satan amassing an army under the earth, fixing his spaceships that were broken from the last celestial war between the angels. He knows that the Armies of Heaven are returning with Christ, and he's been working day and night to rebuild his alien army of clones and ships, yes, just like in *Star Wars*. Yes, the Truth is Stranger Than Fiction!]

And thus I saw the horses in the vision, and them that sat on them, having breastplates of fire, and of jacinth, and brimstone: and the heads of the horses *were* as the heads of lions; and out of their mouths issued fire and smoke and brimstone. By these three was the third part of men killed, by the fire, and by the smoke, and by the brimstone, which issued out of their mouths. For their power is in their mouth, and in their tails: for their tails *were* like unto serpents, and had heads, and with them they do hurt.

[As I've proved in Book Two, that horses are the language of the prophets for spaceships, these were space chariots, which was what St. John could relate to and wrote down. Real horses do not spit fire, but space technology certainly does. These were not real horses, because he says they have the heads of lions, there are many types of spacecraft, that release fire, smoke and brimstone, which is Sulphur. Sulphur exists inside the earth. Abductees report the smell of Sulphur when they have been in ships or encountered Gray aliens. What St. John was seeing were alien hybrids and their spacecraft. The words mouth and tail refer to the front and back of the spacecraft.]

And the rest of the men which were not killed by these plagues yet repented not of the works of their hands, that they should not worship devils, and idols of gold, and silver, and brass, and stone, and of wood: which neither can see, nor hear, nor walk: Neither repented they of their murders, nor of their sorceries, nor of their fornication, nor of their thefts."

(Revelation 9:1-20, KJV)

Angelic Warfare

"And He is before all things, and by Him all things consist."

(Colossians 1:17)

We can get a glimpse into how angelic warfare operates in the Bible through the story of Daniel and his drama with Cyrus the King of Persia. In this story, it is rich with the interventions of two of the Bible's highest ranking angels, Michael and Gabriel, as well as the Lord of Hosts Himself, which is known as a 'Christophany' when the pre-incarnated Jesus Christ shows up to intervene. This story also deters any worship of the angels, just as centuries later, Paul warned against the worship of angels. This is relevant, because in the Middle Ages, people invoked many types of angels, both good and bad, who were assigned to do different things, which became a problem, so God intervened and changed the names of many of the Holy Angels, so humans couldn't abuse them through magical invocations anymore.

Then, the Book of the *Keys of Solomon* became *the* manual for magicians to create incantations to angels, which is an occult handbook for invoking demons. That book still exists, but all the angel names were claimed by the fallen angels, whose very job is to counterfeit Heaven's Angels. I'll go more into this in my chapter on *Angel Protocols,* however, in the Old Testament, we are introduced to the only two angels named in the Old Testament, Michael and Gabriel. In the book of Daniel, we are given insight into their difference in ranking, power and purpose. The Book of Tobit introduced the angel Raphael as well as several other demonic entities, it was believed to have been written in 800BC and was incorporated into the Catholic deuterocanonical books. The Book of Tobit and the other deuterocanonical books were not called Canonical but Ecclesiastical books.

God created these Principalities and Powers, both good and bad. In Ephesians 6:12, "For we wrestle not against blood and flesh, but against Principalities..." When we have disputes with people, we may think we are fighting an individual or corporation, but we are essentially wrestling against Principalities, Powers, and rulers of darkness that control the thoughts and minds of human beings that come against us. As above, so below, as the ancient hermetic law says. All things must first exist in the heavenly realms or spiritual realms before they can manifest on earth.

Chapter One: The Clash Of Two Kingdoms

Their chief agent in charge of that are the demons assigned to us under control of these Principalities and Powers sitting on the Thrones and Dominions. Likewise, angels are assigned to assist us to confront these evil forces, not just demons, but other fallen angels as well.

Daniel 10:5, 6 tells us:

"Then I lifted up mine eyes, and looked, and behold a certain man [In Hebrew, *one man*] clothed in linen, whose loins were girded with fine gold... His body also like the beryl, and his face as the appearance of lightning, and his eyes as lamps of fire, and his arms and his feet like in color to polished brass, and the voice of his words like the voice of a multitude."

What Daniel described in verse 5 and 6 is nothing more than an encounter with the Lord Jesus Christ in a pre-incarnated appearance, known as a *Christophany*. It is similar to descriptions of other appearances of angels in the Old Testament, but the Hebrew is specific, and this was no regular angel. *His Word* like the voice of a multitude? That's the Lord of Hosts, not one of His angels.

Here is the corresponding scripture from the New Testament, where similar if not the same type of descriptive words, just as a right and left leg walk together, which shows up in St. John's Revelation 1:12 where he saw the Lord Jesus Christ. He wrote:

"And I turned to see the voice that spoke with me. And being turned, I saw seven golden candlesticks; and in the midst of the seven candlesticks one like unto the Son of Man, clothed with a garment down to the foot, and girt about the paps with a golden girdle."

Now when you compare Revelation 1:12 to Daniel 10:5 we see the similarity reads, "Then I lifted up mine eyes, and looked, and behold a certain man clothed in linen whose loins girded with fine gold....", and continues to Revelation 1:14, "His head and his hairs were white like wool, as white as snow". Comparing that to Daniel 10:6, "His body also was like the beryl, and his face as the appearance of lightning...." and on to Revelation 1:14 describing His eyes, "and His eyes were as a flame of fire;" as does Daniel 10:6, "and His eyes as lamps of fire..." Revelation 1:15 tells us, "And His feet like unto fine brass, as if they were burned in a furnace." and Daniel 10:6 states, "and His feet like in color to polished brass....". Revelation 1:15, "and His voice as the sound of many waters," as in Daniel 10:6, "and the voice of His words like the voice of a multitude." You can see that two different Bible scribes were describing the same person, the Son of Man, who is the Lord Jesus Christ.

There are no coincidences. All the prophesies that have already been fulfilled throughout time were given prior to that fulfilment, which is evidence that God's Word is true. All these things that John saw were still things yet to happen. And in verse 12 through verse 15 John gives a description of what he was seeing and how he was perceiving Jesus.

This is none other than Jesus Christ that Daniel encountered. I am asserting that this was not a vision, but a real encounter with the Lord. As I've explained in Book Two; *Who Is God?* with respect to Ezekiel's so called 'visions', that they were in fact real events and encounters with both angels and the Lord Himself, but have been mistakenly interpreted as visions.

This was not the first time that Daniel saw the pre-incarnated Christ. He also saw Him, or at least heard Him, in chapter 8, which is the same person, Jesus Christ, who Daniel described in chapter 10:5 and 6 and who John described in the midst of those seven candlesticks.[6]

> "And it came to pass, when I, even I Daniel, had seen the vision, and sought for the meaning, then, behold, there stood before me as the appearance of a man. And I heard a man's voice between the banks of Ulai [literally the banks of the mighty leaders], which called, and said, Gabriel, make this man to understand the vision. So, he came near where I stood: and when he came, I was afraid, and fell upon my face: but he said unto me, Understand, O son of man: for at the time of the end shall be the vision."
>
> (Daniel 8:15)

We have no record that Daniel actually saw Christ here, but he heard His voice which said, "give him the understanding of the vision that he just saw"; was the command of the Lord of Hosts (Jesus Christ) commanding Gabriel to give him understanding of the vision.

However, another *Christophany* occurs in chapter 10, in verses 5 and 6, who is none other than the pre-incarnated Christ and the same description is given of the same Lord Jesus Christ in the Book of Revelation, chapter 1 that John saw in the midst of the candlesticks. Daniel 10:11, Gabriel begins speaking:

> "And he said unto me, O Daniel, a man greatly beloved, understand the words that I speak unto thee, and stand upright: for unto thee am I now sent. And when he had spoken this word unto me, I stood trembling. Then said he unto me, Fear not, Daniel: for from the first day that thou didst set thine heart to understand, and to chasten thyself before thy God, thy words were heard, and I am come for thy words. [Daniel's words were heard.] But

Chapter One: The Clash Of Two Kingdoms

the *prince of the kingdom of Persia* withstood me one and twenty days: but, lo, *Michael, one of the chief princes*, came to help me; and I remained there with the kings of Persia."

This 'prince of the kingdom of Persia' is not some earthly king. This is one of the princes of satan's kingdom holding its influence over the kingdom in Persia. No earthly king could keep any angel or fallen angel at bay. A human man would not have the strength or the power to keep these mighty beings at bay for three weeks, or twenty-one days. The Angel Gabriel was trying to get through with God's message of understanding of the visions for Daniel. But he could not break through because the king of Persia, one of these Principalities with a mighty Dominion, and probably with a mighty army behind him, was able to keep Gabriel from delivering the message to Daniel.

However, the Archangel Michael came, who is a more powerful and a higher ranking angel than Gabriel, and was able to put the prince of Persia in his place, thereby allowing Gabriel to go to Daniel and deliver the understanding of the vision, and complete his assignment for the Lord. Michael was powerful enough to restrain this evil prince of Persia, who was a fallen angel being that was clearly *not* on God's side, but working for Satan's Kingdom of Darkness.

The first words that Gabriel spoke to Daniel were an explanation of a delay in answering Daniel's prayer. He said that he had been detained for twenty-one days, the same length of time Daniel had been praying'. The 'Prince of Persia' had been standing in Gabriel's way and if Michael, the Archangel, had not come to his rescue, he would have been there still. What a powerful witness to the triumph of Heaven's Archangels.

Here the veil is lifted, and we are shown something of the workings of the *unseen realms,* and of the connection between the *Spirit World* and the affairs of nations on the earth. This 'Prince of Persia' was not Cyrus the King of Persia. Cyrus was human. No mere human being like Cyrus could withstand a supernatural being like Gabriel for twenty-one days in spite of the fact that Gabriel has less power than Michael, he is powerful nevertheless. The scriptures clearly teach that there is a Kingdom of Darkness that rules in an Archonic way over the nations, a kingdom which Satan reigns as the king, and that Kingdom is made up of *Principalities, Powers, Rulers of the darkness and spiritual wickedness in the heavens.* (Ephesians 6:12)

From this we see that Satan has his Kingdom organized as a militant hierarchy, compartmentalized and divided into Kingdoms and Principalities. These divisions correspond to the kingdom divisions of our earth. If Satan has the 'Prince of Persia' and a 'Prince of Grecia,' he probably has a Prince assigned over every nation. Satan has his limitations, as he is not an omnipresent or omnipotent being, so he is forced to depend upon his agents, the fallen angels. But just imagine how powerful are his 'Princes' that it takes a supernatural being, like Michael the Archangel, to overwhelm them, which Gabriel could not do alone.

Per the specificity of scripture, Michael did not necessarily *overcome* the evil prince of Persia, but he certainly was able to engage and occupy him long enough so that Gabriel could break free and get to Daniel with God's messages. We know what was going on during this power play through Job 1 and 2. These chapters describe the scene in the courts of heaven, where Satan and the *Bene HaElohim* go up and down from the earth. Satan and his rebels have continued access to the heavenly courts. During Daniel's drama, they were disputing the intervention of Gabriel while the Archangel (Prince) Michael, was already there to restrain the evil prince of Persia to clear the path for Gabriel's message to Daniel.

The fallen angels (i.e., Watchers) already knew the Angel Gabriel was trying to deliver the message the Lord wanted Daniel to hear, to explain things that were still yet to come. They were fighting against the knowledge being given to Daniel. Now just think about how many times in human history has information, truth and encounters with supernatural beings been covered up? Think about the burnings of the Library of Alexandria, which happened in two separate events, pretty much wiping out humanity's memory of deep antiquity, truly causing human education and science to enter into the *Dark Ages*, as a species with severe amnesia. Consider the fact that the spread of the Word of God has been intensely fought over by these angels all over earth. Is it any wonder that the Church of Rome, under the ruler of an Archonic Evil Prince, a fallen angel, that the Bible canon was edited, whole sections deleted and entire books rejected? Eighteen other Jewish scrolls, that were held as the sacred words of the Lord by the Jews and early church, were expunged and denied authenticity.

Think about this, only the kingdom of darkness wants humans in the dark, because that way, they can have power over us. Whereas the truth of our history, is held in the heavens, to be revealed during the Apocalypse, which is now. We are essentially getting our memories back of who we were, which can connect the dots to who we are. The fact that the very scriptures which were written for times such as this were covered up by the evil Prince of Rome between 325AD -360AD, is why we have so much confusion, dissension and discord in the Body of Christ today. As I've been saying all along, we may have unity in faith, but there is still no unity of knowledge or unity of spirit in the Body of Christ. And why is that? We can blame that on the kingdom of darkness winning a few battles along the way, to suppress knowledge and God's Word on earth.

So, while these angels were being held up, Christ came on the scene. He did not have any problem breaking though the obstructions. He went right through as the

Chapter One: The Clash Of Two Kingdoms

source of peace and calmness, and eventually a deep sleep came over Daniel, who was mourning and in agony. Daniel saw the pre-incarnated Christ, the same appearance of whom is described in the Book of Revelation chapter 1. Daniel 10:8 tells us what Jesus did for him:

> "Therefore I was left alone, and saw this great vision, and there remained no strength in me: for my comeliness was turned in me into corruption, and I retained no strength. Yet heard I the voice of his [Christ's] words, then was I in a deep sleep on my face, and my face toward the ground."

Jesus intervened, which reveals to us that no matter what angels obstruct or what we may entangle ourselves, Christ will always be there for us. We have a comforter and that is the Holy Spirit, *who* is promised to His faithful. The promises of God are that He will neither leave us or forsake us. Jesus brought Daniel comfort by putting him in a deep sleep until that angel broke through and was able to lift him up. So, the next time you experience a *hard heaven* for your prayers, pray for God's angels to prevail, pray for the Lord Himself to step in and intervene in your situation, and pray for warrior angels to take control of whatever spiritual blocks you're up against. Satan wants you to believe it's all your fault, that you're not *religious* enough, or good enough, or worthy enough, but these are all lies to keep you from being empowered with the ultimate truth, that the battle is the Lords. (2 Chronicles 20:15; 1 Samuel 17:47)

In conclusion, the story of Daniel proves that just as the angelic warfare was heating up in the unseen world, not a single thing could hold back the Lord Jesus from showing up and strengthening Daniel. With all the angels fighting, not a single one was a match for the Lord Jesus Christ in this pre-incarnated state. This is why those who are filled with His Spirit, *who* is the Holy Spirit, depend on Him for strength, comfort and protection, no matter what the angelic warfare weather may be, which still stands true today.

In Colossians 2, hundreds of years later, Christ has come and fulfilled everything that God said He would fulfil so we are complete and fully armed spiritually for warfare with these angelic beings.

> "Be careful not to allow anyone to captivate you through an empty, deceitful philosophy that is according to human traditions and the elemental spirits of the world, and not according to Christ. For in Him (Christ) all the fullness of deity lives in bodily form, (God in the flesh) and you have been filled in Him, *who is the head over every ruler and authority*. In him you also were circumcised – not, however, with a circumcision performed by human hands, but by the removal of the fleshly body, that is, through the circumcision

done by Christ. Having been buried with him in baptism, you also have been raised with him through your faith in the power of God who raised him from the dead. And even though you were dead in your transgressions and in the uncircumcision of your flesh, he nevertheless made you alive with him, having forgiven all your transgressions. He has destroyed what was against us, a certificate of indebtedness expressed in decrees opposed to us. He has taken it away by nailing it to the cross. Disarming the rulers and authorities, he has made a public disgrace of them, triumphing over them by the cross."

(Colossian 2:8-15 – NET Bible)

He made a public example of Principalities and Powers by disarming them, including Satan and his demons, after what He did for all of creation on the cross of Calvary. Those who put their faith in Him are complete in Him and made whole. Remember these words to those still in unbelief:

"But God chose the foolish things of the world to shame the wise; God chose the weak things of the world to shame the strong."

(1 Corinthians 1:27)

This was how He was able to shame the Archons, the rulers of the darkness of this present world, the principalities, the spiritual wickedness in the heavens, by one Godly act on the Cross of Calvary. In that moment, He took upon Him the punishment of all, being the blameless, unspotted lamb of God. They knew exactly *who* He was, and they trembled! As far as *spiritual legal ground* goes, this is an example of how evil is defeated with good.

Notes and References:

1. Robert Sepehr, *Species with Amnesia*, Createspace, 2015
2. Dr. R.H.C. Charles, *The Book of Jubilees* (London: A & C Black, 1902).
3. W.F. Albright, *Our Future is in Our Past*, W.F. Albright of Archeological Research, http://www.aiar.org/
4. Ella LeBain, *Who's Who in The Cosmic Zoo? Book One, A Spiritual Guide to ETs, Aliens, Gods & Angels, Third Edition,* Tate Publishing & Enterprises, 2013.
5. *What is Generation in the Bible?* http://www.bible-codes.org/old-prophecy_5c-Yeshua-codes.htm
6. http://www.teachingfaith.com/spiritual-warfare-ebook

CHAPTER TWO
THE ANGELIC GOVERNMENT

"I will give my angels charge over you."
~ PSALM 91:11

The stars are the windows of heaven, where the angels peek through.
~ OLD SAYING

This primordial drama between good and evil can be traced back to an angelic war in the heavens, involving those angels sent to earth as fallen, because of their nature and deeds. These secrets are now being revealed to humanity as part of the preparation for the end of days. We are being lifted out of the muck and mire, out of the bonds of darkness and negativity, the twisted shrouds of versions of the truth. We are learning the secrets of the heavens and of humanity's genesis.

What has and is now being revealed to us is that "missing link" in our evolution, which is extra-terrestrial intervention through genetic manipulation. It's quite a long story, paramount to which is our understanding the role of angels and extra-terrestrials in our planet's history and how this affects our present day.

The kink in our chain occurred when a group of renegade heavenly angels got hooked on the sexual kick they experienced through mating with the daughters of men. These angels were considered giants and so were their offspring. Further, they didn't stop with mating the ape-woman, they spread their seeds into the animals and beasts of the earth as well. When the Council of Elohim, the Celestial Governors, discovered the aberrations that these Nephilim had created, they destroyed most of the mutations through laser-like radiation and two major floods. As the Nephilim and fallen angels suffered as well, they were genetically damaged and bound to live inside the earth along with some leftover offspring, known as Sasquatch and Bigfoot.

Today, many refer to these genetically damaged beings as the Watchers. Some also call them the Grays. These aliens are ancient scientists, the ones responsible for the abduction of human beings. They do this in order to perform medical and sexual examinations, extracting genetic material from us, in an attempt to create a new race of beings, hybrids combining both genetic codes, which I will later expose as the

New Nephilim. Their intentions are nefarious to say the least, because they want to replace the present human model on earth with their new hybrid. These are nothing but clones, genetic mutations to house the *spirits* of the Nephilim, which the Books of Enoch told us, are bound to the astral realm of earth until the Final Judgment.

Many New Agers and Ufology enthusiasts are misled into thinking that these hybrids are some type of new and improved humanity, some go so far as to say that they are future bodies prepared for future incarnations for us. This is a deception, as it was the intention of the god of this world from the very beginning, to corrupt the image and likeness of God in humanity. This is the very reason and motivation behind all the perversions, and genetic downgrading of humankind, the dumbing down of the human genome, to use humans as a slave race to serve the fallen angels and their overlords on earth.

Let's be clear about discernment and distinction here, this is, nor has it ever been the Divine Will of the Lord, the Creator of Heaven and Earth to replace humanity with cloned hybrids or genetically modified human-alien robots. What is the Divine Will of the Lord when He returns is to transform humanity by restoring all twelve original strands of DNA into immortal humans, but that is promised only to those who are of the 'redeemed' of the Lord. Those who accept His Grace and Salvation in this life, are rewarded with the resurrected body and immortality in the Age to Come.

> "And Uriel said to me: 'Here shall stand the angels who have connected themselves with women, *and their spirits assuming many different forms* are defiling mankind and shall lead them astray into sacrificing to demons as gods, (here shall they stand,) till the day of the great judgement in which they shall be judged till they are made an end of. And the women also of the angels who went astray shall become sirens.' And I, Enoch, alone saw the vision, the ends of all things: and no man shall see as I have seen."
>
> (1 Enoch 19)

There are thirty-six tribes of giants mentioned in the Bible. There are twenty-two individual giants by name in the Bible. How many people actually asked the questions while listening to the famous Bible story of David and Goliath, "Why were there giants? Where did they come from?" Book One of *Who's Who in The Cosmic Zoo?* spends several chapters on the Giants, Nephilim, Fallen Angels and Annunaki discerning them from each other and connecting the dots to who they are today.[1]

Giant sons of the Elohim mated with earth women, producing Nephilim Giants, who later became the evil spirits of the earth. They were sentenced to torment humans till the Lord returns and puts them all in their place. I point out this fact because these beings were considered miscreants by the Creator God, who did

Chapter Two: The Angelic Government

not have a place for their deceased spirits, as He did not create them. *Nephilim* in Hebrew means fallen ones, or rejects. Instead they were bound to roam the earth's spirit realm, to torment and haunt humans, watching everything they do, which is why they are known as the Watchers. But *who* is watching the Watchers? The answer is the Lord Yahuah, His Elohim and His Malachim (extraterrestrial messengers aka angels).

> "And now, the giants, who are produced from the spirits and flesh, shall be called evil spirits upon the earth, and on the earth shall be their dwelling. Evil spirits have proceeded from their bodies; because they are born from men and from the holy Watchers is their beginning and primal origin; they shall be evil spirits on earth, and evil spirits shall they be called. [As for the spirits of heaven, heaven is their dwelling, but as for the spirits of the earth which were born upon the earth, the earth shall be their dwelling.] And the spirits of the giants afflict, oppress, destroy, attack, do battle, and work destruction on the earth, and cause trouble: they take no food, but nevertheless hunger and thirst, and cause offences. And these spirits shall rise up against the children of men and against the women, because they have proceeded from them."
>
> (1 Enoch 15:8-12)

If the *bene HaElohim* also known as the fallen angels, were giant beings, imagine what the Angels who didn't fall from heaven look like? They're huge, mighty, gigantic beings, about whom we are going to explore and learn their hierarchies and their protocol in Book Three, *Who Are the Angels?*

"And there were giants in those days..." (Genesis 6:4, 1 Enoch)

Angels govern every single aspect in the entire universe. Per the Talmud, nothing grows, dies, is repaired or healed, without the influence of Angels. The Cosmic process itself is made up of an enormous order of Angels, Devas, and Helpers of the Divine Plan. This Cosmogony involves the birth of stars, planets, galaxies and universes, as well as of course, the human race, both on the earth, as well as the extraterrestrial humans. The animal, plant and mineral kingdoms are all governed by their respecting Angels or Devas.

The word *DEVA* is a Sanskrit word, which means "to shine". Also, referred to in Sanskrit texts as the "shining ones', and the "resplendent" ones. The Sanskrit words for Archangel is *DHYAN CHOHAN*, who is considered to be one of seven high spiritual beings, or Lords, or Princes, who are "Intelligent conscious living Principles of the Logos". It's been said that the *Dhyan Chohans* are the same as the "Elohim" in the

Jewish Bible. Both Hebrew and Sanskrit are the two oldest languages on the planet. There are many parallels between Judaism and Hinduism. *Chohan* in Sanskrit, is equivalent to *Cohane* in Aramaic/Hebrew, which translates to mean 'Priest'. In fact, the 13th tribe, were the *Cohanes*.

Instead of 'gods' these beings may be regarded as the conscious, intelligent powers in Nature. In fact, they are divine intelligences charged with the supervision of Cosmos.[2] The term, *Chohan*, is not used in a specific sense, but rather in a generalizing manner; thus, it is applied to any celestial being.

All the world's literature down through the ages is abundant with myths, legends, fairy-tales and allegories regarding the presence, existence and intervention of Angels and/or Devas. The ages of belief in the Kingdom of Angels is strong evidence for the actuality of the seed of reality within those beliefs, a basis of fact upon which folklore is founded. Angels are real.

> "For we know that if our earthly house of this tabernacle were dissolved, we have a building of God, a house not made with hands, eternal in the heavens. For in this we groan, earnestly desiring to be clothed upon with our house which is from heaven:"
>
> (2 Corinthians 5:1-2 KJV)

WHO ARE THE TWENTY-FOUR ELDERS?

> "And around the throne were twenty-four thrones; and upon the thrones I saw twenty-four elders sitting, clothed in white garments, and golden crowns on their heads."
>
> (Revelation 4:4)

The book of Revelation speaks of twenty-four Elders, who are these beings? Are they Angels? Or Ascended Masters? Or are they the first of the Elohim, the council of gods, as analyzed and described in both Book One and Book Two. Yahuah, the Lord and Creator of Heaven and Earth, created the Elohim, who are the gods, or more specifically the sons of God. Could these twenty-four Elder beings be the first twenty-four the Elohim created?

The Book of Enoch tells us that two hundred Bene HaElohim were the sons of the Elohim (gods) who rebelled, came to earth to mate with earth women and created the Nephilim. These were the original fallen angels. That they left their first estate (Jude 6). However, the twenty-four Elders, may just be their fathers, and the beings who have remained faithful to the Creator and the Kingdom of Heaven. The

Chapter Two: The Angelic Government

Elohim are known as the council of gods. Could these twenty-four Elders be the inner circle of the Courts of Heaven?

Many theologians have misinterpreted the scriptures on Elders to be angels. But this is inconsistent with the rest of Scripture and here's why: Nowhere in Scripture do angels sit on thrones, nor are they pictured as ruling, reigning or wearing gold crowns. The twenty-four elders clearly are not angels which this verse reveals:

> "Then I looked and heard the voice of many angels, numbering thousands upon thousands, and ten thousand times ten thousand (ten million). They encircled the throne and the living creatures and the elders."
>
> (Revelation 5:11)

They are distinguished in their number from the angels. There are well over ten million angels, but only twenty-four elders. These beings are clearly human in nature, but divine as well. They are not deceased humans who made it to heaven and rule the inner courts of heaven with the Lord of lords, they were first sons, who are known as Elders. Remember Jesus is called the Lord of lords, because He rules over all the lords of other realms and lesser kingdoms. These crowned Elders are lords. But they give glory to the Lord of lords, King of kings, the One who the Book of Revelation says, wears *all* the crowns.

> "Then I saw heaven standing open, and there before me was a white horse. And its rider is called Faithful and True. With righteousness He judges and wages war. He has eyes like blazing fire, **and many royal crowns on His head**. He has a name written on Him that only He Himself knows. He is dressed in a robe dipped in blood, and His name is The Word of God...."
>
> (Revelation 19:11-13-NIV)

We know from scripture that these twenty-four Elders bow down and worship the Lord, the Lamb of God, who is worthy of praise, who is seated on the Throne of Heaven.

> "And He came and took the scroll from the right hand of the One seated on the throne. When He had taken the scroll, the four living creatures and ***the twenty-four elders fell down before the Lamb***. Each one had a harp, and they held the golden bowls full of incense, which are the prayers of the saints. And they sang a new song: "Worthy are You to take the scroll and open its seals, because You were slain, and by Your blood You purchased for God those from every tribe and tongue and people and nation...."
>
> (Revelation 5:7-9-NIV)

So, we know that the twenty-four elders listen to the prayers of the saints, because how else could they present the golden bowls full of their prayers, which the bible calls, incense? This is why these beings are gods, with a small 'g'. They serve the King of the Kingdom and His Divine Will for humanity.

Angels are ministering spirits, extraterrestrial messengers who come and go from heaven to earth. These beings are not Elder Angels, because Angels are ruled by princes, also known as Archangels. These beings are fully human, fully divine, created as sons of God, and have been serving and ruling probably since the beginning, which is why they are called Elders.

They can't be humans who have died, because they are presenting the golden bowls which are full of the prayers of the saints, who are the body of the Christ, the redeemed of humanity. They can't be dead saints, because then they would be carrying their own prayers, and scripture does not say that. This is why it is my conclusion that the twenty-four Elders, are the original council of gods that the Lord Yahuah created to serve His Universe. The fact that they are wearing golden crowns on their heads, proves they are human, but also Divine and appointed as lesser rulers in the Kingdom of Heaven under the Lord. These beings are His council.

Here is another scripture, that differentiates angels, the twenty-four elders and the Lord of Heaven. This section of scripture, when the Seventh Trumpet is sounded, reveals all three different characters, who each have different roles in the Kingdom of Heaven.

> "Then the seventh angel sounded his trumpet, and loud voices called out in heaven: "The kingdom of the world is now the kingdom of our Lord and of His Christ, and He will reign forever and ever." ***And the twenty-four elders who sit on their thrones before God fell on their faces and worshiped God***, saying: "We give thanks to You, Lord God Almighty, the One who is and who was; You have taken Your great power and begun to reign...."
>
> (Revelation 11:15-17)

Clearly the twenty-four Elders are god-like humans who have each been given thrones to rule over, perhaps different regencies of the universe, or earth, or both, we don't know for sure, but they are clearly Lords, Masters and Kings because they are given crowns and sit on thrones, yet they all submit to the Lord of lords, and worship Him. We also see, the role of the angel who acts as a messenger. Of course, these scriptures reveal the future, after the end of this age.

> "...And a second time they called out: "Hallelujah! Her smoke ascends forever and ever." And the twenty-four elders and the four living creatures fell down

Chapter Two: The Angelic Government

and worshiped God who sits on the throne, saying: "Amen, Hallelujah!" Then a voice came from the throne, saying: "Praise our God, all you who serve Him, and those who fear Him, small and great alike!"

(Revelation 19:4)

It is clear from this closing scripture in the book of Revelation, that the twenty-four Elders represent the church of heaven in the Kingdom of Heaven. The reason that the twenty-four elders could not represent the redeemed of humankind indicates it would have to include Israel, and because the redemption of Israel is not yet complete by Revelation chapter 4, when we first read of the twenty-four elders. The twenty-four elders also could not be the tribulation saints, because they too, have not been redeemed yet, until the second coming of Christ is complete, same as Israel.

Some have postulated that the twenty-four elders maybe the part of the 144,000? But scripture clearly differentiates between them, making the twenty-four elders distinct form the 144,000. Herein, we see that the 144,000 are singing to the elders and the four living creatures.

"Then I looked and saw the Lamb standing on Mount Zion, and with Him one hundred forty-four thousand who had His name and His Father's name written on their foreheads. And I heard a sound from heaven like the roar of rushing waters and the loud rumbling of thunder. And the sound I heard was like harpists strumming their harps.... ***And they sang a new song before the throne and before the four living creatures and the elders***. And no one could learn the song except the one hundred forty-four thousand who had been redeemed from the earth...."

(Revelation 14:1-3)

We can also eliminate that the twenty-four elders are not part of the great multitude either. In Revelation 7, also another scripture that defines the distinction between them and the praise from the great multitude:

"from the tribe of Zebulun twelve thousand, from the tribe of Joseph twelve thousand, and from the tribe of Benjamin twelve thousand. After this I looked and saw a multitude too large to count, from every nation and tribe and people and tongue, standing before the throne and before the Lamb. They were clothed in white robes, with palm branches in their hands. And they cried out in a loud voice: "Salvation to our God, who sits on the throne, and to the Lamb! And all the angels stood around the throne and around the elders and the four living creatures. And they fell facedown before the throne

and worshiped God,...Then one of the elders addressed me: "These in white robes," he asked, "who are they, and where have they come from?
(Revelation 7:8-11,13)

Let's face it, an elder wouldn't ask who are the multitude and where did they come from, if they were one of them. So clearly, this is eliminated, that the twenty-four elders do not come from the great multitudes, who are the redeemed of humanity by the way, that includes all those who were resurrected with Jesus and went to heaven, as he promised the thief on the cross with him, 'today you will be with me in paradise.' (Luke 23:43)

We know that the identity of the twenty-four elders when they are first described in Revelation 4 already had on their heads crowns of gold (Revelation 4:4) - they are already rulers. This contrasts with the group described in Revelation 5:9-10 who "shall reign on the earth" indicating a future reign. So, if the twenty-four elders are not the angels or the 144,000 or the great multitude or the redeemed that Jesus raises at the resurrection, then who are they? What is left? The sons of God, who are the Elohim (council of gods).

Who Are The Four Living Creatures

In Revelation 4:6–8; 5:11, four living beings are seen in John's vision. These appear as a lion, an ox, a man, and an eagle, much as in Ezekiel but in a different order. They have six wings, whereas Ezekiel's four living creatures are described as only having four. Are they the same four living creatures? Or are they a different set of living creatures? Let's discern.

> "In the midst of the Throne, and round about the Throne, were *four beasts* full of eyes before and behind. And the First Beast was like a *Lion*, and the Second Beast like a *Calf*, and the Third Beast had a face as a *Man*, and the Fourth Beast was like a *Flying Eagle*. And the four Beasts had each of them six wings about him; and they were full of eyes within; and they rest not day or night, saying, HOLY, HOLY, HOLY, LORD GOD ALMIGHTY, WHICH WAS, AND IS, AND IS TO COME."
> (Revelation 4:6-11)

The word translated *Beasts* should be translated as *Living Creatures*, reflected in the Revised Version. The word here translated *beast* (Zoon), is not the same as the one translated *beast* (Therion) in chapters eleven, thirteen, and seventeen. The word here used means a *living being* or *creature*, while the word used in chapters eleven, thirteen,

Chapter Two: The Angelic Government

and seventeen, means a *wild, untamed animal*. They are not angelic beings, for they are distinguished from the angels, who are mentioned as a class by themselves in Revelation 5:11. They are not representative of redeemed human beings, because they do not join in the Redemption Song. Revelation 5:8-10. The word *they* in this passage does not refer to the *Four Living Creatures*, but to the *Twenty-Four Elders*.

The *Four Living Creatures* are not in the same class with the Elders, for they have no thrones, crowns, harps or golden vials. They are the *Guardians* of the Throne of God, and accompany it wherever it goes, which implies that the Throne of God travels, because as I proved throughout Book Two: *Who Is God?* the Lord not only has a fleet of starships, but Motherships as well. And each time the Lord's spaceship lands in the Book of Ezekiel, these living creatures guard and accompany it. "He lays the beams of his upper chambers on their waters. He makes the clouds his chariot and rides on the wings of the wind." (Psalm 104:3)

In Ezekiel 1:24-28; there are four in number, which is the earth number, and therefore have something to do with the earth. That is, they are interested in the *re-genesis* of the earth to its former glory before the Fall. They have eyes before, behind and within, which reveals their intelligence and spiritual insight of things past, present, and what's to come. They are tireless in their service, for they rest not day nor night, saying, "Holy, Holy, Holy, Lord God Almighty, which was, and is, and is to come."

The first time these *Living Creatures* are mentioned in the Bible is in Genesis 3:24, where they are called *Cherubim*, but are not described. They were placed as guardians at the entrance to the Garden of Eden to prevent the re-entrance of Adam and Eve, and to keep the way of the Tree of Life. The place where they were stationed there was a Tabernacle, a place of worship to which Cain and Abel resorted to make their offerings, and that it was from there that Cain went out from the *Presence of the Lord*. (Genesis 4:16) This Tabernacle was most likely a spaceship, that the *Living Creatures* guarded.

When Moses was given the pattern of the Tabernacle on the Holy Mount, he was instructed to make the *Ark of the Covenant* with two Cherubim upon it. (Exodus 25:10-22) These Cherubim were guardians of the "Mercy Seat," or the place of God's *Presence* when He in His Shekinah Glory visited the Tabernacle. But it is not until Ezekiel had his vision of the Cherubim (Ezekiel 1:1-28; 10:1-22), that we have a description of what they are like.

Ezekiel describes them as having the likeness of a man, with four faces, and four wings, and feet like a calf's foot, and hands like a man's hand under their wings on their four sides. Their four faces were different. The front face was that of a *Man*, the right-side face was that of a *Lion*, the left side face was that of an *Ox*, and the rear face was that of an *Eagle*, and their whole body, back, hands, and wings, were full of eyes around about. (Ezekiel 10:12) In John's vision of the *Cherubim* or *Living Creatures* they are described like animals, the first was like a *Lion*, the second like a *Calf*, or a young *Ox*, the third had the face of a *Man*, and the fourth was like a *Flying Eagle*. John's *Living Creatures* had six wings, while Ezekiel's *Cherubim* had only four.

In Ezekiel's vision, the *Cherubim*, or *Living Creatures* were accompanied by the Holy Spirit (Ezekiel 1:12) and they traveled on wheels within wheels, which shows that they were on some tour or mission and a part of the Lord's spaceship technology, attended by the Lord, who sat on His Throne over their heads inside His starship (Ezekiel 1:25-28). However, the wheels are absent in St. John's vision, for the scene is in Heaven, the permanent home of the Throne of God. The *Living Creatures* in heaven are stationed there, they are not frequent travelers. They are not human, they are alien creatures.

In the camping and marching order of Israel in the Wilderness, there was a fixed relation of the Twelve Tribes to the Tabernacle. In camp the Tabernacle rested in the middle. The Camp of Judah, composed of three Tribes, rested on the East, with its Standard bearing the figure of a *Lion*. The Camp of Ephraim, composed of three Tribes, rested on the West, with its Standard bearing the figure of an *Ox*. The Camp of Reuben, composed of three Tribes, rested on the South, with its Standard bearing the figure of a *Man*. The Camp of Dan, composed of three Tribes, rested on the North, with its Standard bearing the figure of an *Eagle*. Consequently, the Tabernacle was in the center of the Camp, which was the place of God's *Presence*, and was surrounded and protected by figures of both Ezekiel's and John's *Living Creatures*.

The difference between Ezekiel's *Living Creatures* and John's *Living Creatures* can only be explained on the conclusion that there are different orders for *Living Creatures* and for *Cherubim*, while each adjust to the service they are created to perform. In Isaiah's vision in the Temple of the Lord seated on His Throne, he saw a heavenly order of beings that he called the *Seraphim*. They had six wings, like John's *Living Creatures*, who cried "Holy, Holy, Holy, is the Lord of Hosts: the whole earth is full of His Glory" (Isaiah 6:1-4), but they stood *above* the Throne, while Ezekiel's *Cherubim* supported the Throne, and John's *Living Creatures* were in the midst of and were placed around the Throne. In Book Two, *Who Is God?* I postulated that the difference between the *Seraphim* and *Cherubim* were the number of their wings, which in Hebrew is the same word used for the blades (wings) of an airplane. Both were aeronautic beings, with the ability to use their wings to fly and power the Lord's spaceship.

Whatever significant roles they both may have, there are different forms that the *Cherubim* or *Living Creatures* express and it is blatantly clear that neither of them represent the Church, the redeemed humanity or the *Twenty-Four Elders*, but are attendants or officials attached to the Throne of God nevertheless, because they summon the four Horsemen of the Apocalypse to appear (Revelation 6:1-8). They are intelligent creatures, because they speak and are devoted the Lord. One of them hands to the seven angels, the Seven Golden Vials filled with the Wrath of God. (Revelation

Chapter Two: The Angelic Government

15:7).³ And when they give glory and honor and thanks to Him that sits upon the Throne, who lives forever and ever, the *Twenty-Four Elders* fall down before Him that sits upon the Throne, and worship Him and cast their crowns before the Throne, saying, "Thou art worthy, O Lord, to receive glory and honor and power; for Thou hast created all things, and for Thy pleasure they are and were created." (Revelation 4:9-11)

The Sons of God

The "sons of God" are mentioned several times in scripture[4]. You can be a son of God three ways: 1) by Adoption; 2) by being begotten; or 3) by Creation. We can become sons and daughters of God by being adopted into His family when we accept Jesus' sacrifice on our behalf:

> "Having predestinated us unto *the adoption of children* by Jesus Christ to himself, according to the good pleasure of his will,"
>
> (Ephesians 1:5)

> "For as many as are led by the Spirit of God, *they are the sons of God*. For ye have not received the spirit of bondage again to fear; but ye have received the Spirit of adoption, whereby we cry, Abba, Father."
>
> (Roman 8:14-15)

> "And will be a Father unto you, and *ye shall be my sons and daughters*, saith the Lord Almighty."
>
> (2 Corinthians 6:18)

There is only one being who has become a son of God by being begotten, and that is Jesus:

> "For God so loved the world, that he gave his only begotten Son, that whosoever believeth in him should not perish, but have everlasting life."
>
> (John 3:16)

The genealogy of Luke 3 traces the generations from Jesus back to Adam and ends with this verse:

> "Which was the son of Enos, which was the son of Seth, which was the son of Adam, *which was the son of God.*"
>
> (Luke 3:38)

It is only Adam who was created directly by God (actually it was the Elohim that created Adam according to Genesis) that is called the son of God. As I've proved in Book One, Adam was created perfect. Perfect with all twelve strands of DNA. After the fall, Adam's offspring were genetically manipulated and downgraded to two strands of DNA, disabling the other ten strands, causing today's geneticists to see it, nevertheless having no idea why it's there, calling it 'junk DNA' because it's there but not switched on, like a disabled software program.

For those of you who read Book One of *Who's Who in The Cosmic Zoo?* will remember, that this piece dovetails into the Sumerian Cuneiform tablet's story of how a group of giant lizard men (Annunaki) from a planet called, Nibiru, genetically manipulated humans into a slave race to serve them, and use them to mine the planet for natural resources for gold and precious metals, to collect for them, to be used in their spaceships. But the promises of God through Jesus, are that his redeemed of humanity will be translated back into their glory bodies, which will be immortal, without blame or blemish upon Christ's return. The Elohim created Adam perfect. Yes, Adam was a son of God in this regard.[5]

Others in scriptures are all listed as the sons of earthly fathers. Not even Jesus is here listed as a son of God because He was not a son of God by being born on earth. Rather, He existed before the incarnation. Think of it - if God sent His Son to earth He had to have a Son to send. Just as He was about to leave Heaven and begin His mission to planet earth His Father did not say to Him something like: "I will see you back here in about 33 years, now go and become my Son." No; it would have been more like: "My Son, go now and you will rejoin me here in about 33 years."

So just who are the Sons of God? In Scripture, there are three types of uses of this term: Sons of God in the New Testament, Sons of God in Genesis, and Sons of God in the Book of Job.

> "Behold, what manner of love the Father hath bestowed upon us, that we should be called the sons of God: therefore, the world knoweth us not, because it knew him not."
>
> (1 John 3:1)

Two uses speak of the sons of God becoming involved with the daughters of men. This is a different use that will be spoken of on another page.

> "The Nephilim were on the earth in those days, and also afterward, when the sons of God came in to the daughters of man and they bore children to them. These were the mighty men who were of old, the men of renown."
>
> (Genesis 6:1-4)

Chapter Two: The Angelic Government

That leaves the book of Job where the sons of God are spoken of as coming "to present themselves before the LORD." (Job 1:6) This is a very interesting incident. It must be happening in heaven itself. In our look at the ways to become a son of God above, it seems these must fit in the option of becoming a son of God by creation. They were not begotten by God and they were not redeemed. Who were they? The next verse provides a clue:

> "And the LORD said unto Satan, Whence comest thou? Then Satan answered the LORD, and said, from going to and fro in the earth, and from walking up and down in it."
>
> (Job 1:7)

Satan came "among" the sons of God or as though he was part of this group. There is no verse ever calling any angel a son of God. Indeed, the Lord seems to challenge his being there. He asks "Whence comest thou?" or "where did you come from?" or "what is your position that gives you a right to be here?" God knows perfectly well where He came from - He doesn't need to ask to be informed; it is more of a challenge.

Satan's answer, justifying his presence, even gives a clue as to who the rest of the group is. He says:

> "... From going to and fro in the earth, and from walking up and down in it."
>
> (Job 1:7)

This is a way of stating his claim of ownership of the earth. It's what a person does when they acquire a new piece of property; they walk around in it to check it out - I have done it several times. It may also be a way of justifying his presence there - after all, that was the question. As prince or ruler of this world (John 14:30) he did indeed have some right to appear as its representative.

That God is challenging Satan's right to be there as the representative of Planet Earth is even more evidenced by His then drawing attention to Job, "a perfect and an upright man (verse 8)" - perhaps he could represent earth.

Adam lost his God-given dominion of this earth when he sinned and even Jesus referred to Satan as "the god of this world." (2 Corinthians 4:4) Satan could offer "all the kingdoms of the world" because it was given (or forfeited) to him by Adam:

> "And the devil said unto him, all this power will I give thee, and the glory of them: for that is delivered unto me; and to whomsoever I will I give it."
>
> (Luke 4:6)

Adam was crowned before his fall; he was the king with dominion (Genesis 1:26) of the earth:

> "For thou hast made him a little lower than the angels, and hast <u>crowned him</u> with glory and honor."
>
> (Psalm 8:5)

Obviously, the meeting recorded in Job 1 is not happening on the earth as that is where Satan came from to get there. In chapter 2, he again comes from the earth to another gathering with this same group before the Lord. As we saw above, in the genealogy of Luke, it is only Adam, the first man on the earth, who is called a son of God.

Extraterrestrial Sons of God?

Is it possible that the sons of God mentioned here are the equivalents of Adam - the first or representative men created on each of their respective worlds? Wouldn't that require that there are other populated planets with intelligent life; in fact, people who send representatives to heaven to take part in the government of the Universe?

Here is an interesting verse:

> "When the morning stars sang together, and all **the sons of God** shouted for joy?"
>
> (Job 38:7)

Some commentaries say that the two terms are equivalent. But how could that be? There are two groups mentioned and they are each doing different things. Scripture frequently refers to angels using the symbol of stars. The sons of God must be a different group. Angels are never referred to using this term. Consider this verse:

> "Now there was a day when **the sons of God** came to present themselves before the LORD, and Satan came also among them."
>
> (Job 1:6)

If the angels came. Satan, as an angel, would be among them and there would be no need to say "Satan came also." Here is another use of "sons of God:"

> "Beloved, now are we **the sons of God**, and it doth not yet appear what we shall be: but we know that, when he shall appear, we shall be like him; for we shall see him as he is."
>
> (1 John 3:2)

Chapter Two: The Angelic Government

This verse is not saying that we are angels. Let's look more closely at the context of that verse in Job 38:

> "Then the LORD answered Job out of the whirlwind, and said, who is this that darkeneth counsel by words without knowledge? Gird up now thy loins like a man; for I will demand of thee, and answer thou me. <u>Where wast thou when I laid the foundations of the earth</u>? declare, if thou hast understanding. Who hath laid the measures thereof, if thou knowest? or who hath stretched the line upon it? Whereupon are the foundations thereof fastened? or who laid the corner stone thereof; <u>When the morning stars sang together, and *all the sons of God* shouted for joy</u>?
>
> (Job 38:1-7)

The context is the creation of the world. The idea is that two separate groups - the morning stars (the angels) and the sons of God (the representatives of other worlds) - were both joyful at the creation of a new planet.

It has been said that, God's ultimate purpose is to make as many people as possible as happy as possible for as long as possible. Could God have made other inhabited worlds? Absolutely! Estimates are that there are 100 billion galaxies in the universe with 100-200 billion stars in each. This brings up the question, could there actually be other inhabited planets in the universe?

The meaning of the word, "universe" is derived from "one voice" which is in reference to the voice of God, by which all things were created. Genesis 1, And God said, "Let there be Light", He essentially "spoke" the world into existence, and He will end this world, with a breath and a Word as well.

Life On Other Planets?

Is there actually life on other planets? One might think, that's just science fiction with no place in the Bible? Well you might be surprised. The Bible not only hints at other inhabited planets, but there are scriptures that there are other worlds.

Let's look at some of the evidence suggesting that there might be other inhabited planets:

> "Hath in these last days spoken unto us by his Son, whom he hath appointed heir of all things, by whom also he made *the worlds*;"
>
> (Hebrews 1:2)

> "Through faith we understand that *the worlds* were framed by the word of God, so that things which are seen were not made of things which do appear."
>
> (Hebrews 11:3)

Some other versions will say "ages" instead of "worlds" and some say "universe" which of course, as we now know, includes other planets. After saying that "the worlds were formed by the word of God" the verse says that because of this, "things which are seen ..." Therefore, it cannot be referring to ages or time since time cannot be seen. "The worlds were formed (something that was made) so that things (with the result that) which are seen (we can see something).

When something was made, you could see it - you can't see ages or time. It was something physical that was made.

There is no doubt that there are other worlds, the question remains, are there inhabited planets? The Kepler telescope is identifying planets around stars within the habitable "Goldilocks Zones" of those star systems. Of course, it cannot tell if any of those planets actually harbors life yet, but if you read Book One of *Who's Who in The Cosmic Zoo?* I believe I made the case for the discovery of life on other inhabited planets and star systems, which has already been established by multiple contactees, witnesses and governments on earth. If you remember my thesis statement, *not all extraterrestrials are aliens, and not all aliens are extraterrestrials.*[6]

This is done by detecting small decreases in the amount of light emitted by a star as an orbiting planet crosses or transits (thus the name transit method) between the star and the Kepler telescope which measures variations in light very accurately. When multiple transits have occurred, it can be established that a planet is the cause. From various measurements, the size of the planet and its distance from the star it is orbiting can be determined as well as whether or not the planet is in the "habitable zone." This zone is where water could be present in liquid form, a prerequisite for inhabited planets; indeed for any life.

From the small portion of the sky that is being studied in this way, scientists can extrapolate the numbers found to larger portions of the sky. The latest estimate I heard is that there could be 64 billion such planets in our galaxy alone.

> "Wherefore seeing we also are compassed about with so *great a cloud of witnesses*, let us lay aside every weight, and the sin which doth so easily beset us, and let us run with patience the race that is set before us,"
>
> (Hebrews 12:1)

Chapter Two: The Angelic Government

"To the *general assembly* and church of the firstborn, which are written in heaven, and to God the Judge of all, and to the spirits of just men made perfect,"
(Hebrews 12:23)

Definitions for *general assembly* are:

- 1. a <u>festal</u> gathering of the whole people to celebrate public games or other solemnities;
- 2. a public <u>festal</u> assembly.

"General Assembly" is the term used by the United Nations for a meeting of the representatives of every member nation on earth. Could the firstborn be the first or representative people of each world?

"Unto me, who am less than the least of all saints, is this grace given, that I should preach among the Gentiles the unsearchable riches of Christ; And to make all men see what is the fellowship of the mystery, which from the beginning of the world hath been hid in God, who created all things by Jesus Christ: To the intent that now unto the *principalities and powers in heavenly places* might be known by the church the manifold wisdom of God,"
(Ephesians 3:8-10)

The word "men" is supplied just as it is in John 12:

"And I, if I be lifted up from the earth, I will draw all ***men*** unto me."
(John 12:32)

Notice that Paul is saying in Ephesians that his preaching will reveal something to people beyond this earth. Verse 15 also suggests a bigger family than we see on earth:

"For this cause, I bow my knees unto the Father of our Lord Jesus Christ, of whom the *whole family* in heaven and earth is named,"
(Ephesians 3:14-15)

"That in the dispensation of the fullness of times he might gather together in one all things in Christ, both which are in heaven, and which are on earth; even in him:"
(Ephesians 1:10)

God formed the earth to be lived on:

"For thus saith the LORD that created the heavens; God himself that formed the earth and made it; he hath established it, he created it not in vain, he formed it to be inhabited: I am the LORD; and there is none else."

(Isaiah 45:18)

Some might think this wording indicates that God created the earth to be inhabited and nothing else. However, the wording itself does not exclude the possibility that He created other inhabited planets. Heaven itself is inhabited:

"Take heed that ye despise not one of these little ones; for I say unto you, that in heaven their angels do always behold the face of my Father which is in heaven."

(Matthew 18:10)

God created the earth to be inhabited rather than creating it in vain. While this reasoning is not proof, we could ask: Did God who created the heavens (everything else beyond earth) create them in vain?

During creation week, God formed the previously "without form and void" (Genesis 1:2), earth, the sky and the sea into something habitable and then proceeded to fill them with life.

Consider this passage from the perspective of the universe:

"What man of you, having a hundred sheep, if he loose one of them, doth not leave the ninety and nine in the wilderness, and go after that which is lost, until he find it? And when he hath found it, he lays it on his shoulders, rejoicing. And when he cometh home, he calls together his friends and neighbors, saying unto them, rejoice with me; for I have found my sheep which was lost. I say unto you, that likewise joy shall be in heaven over one sinner that repents, more than over ninety and nine just persons, which need no repentance."

(Luke 15:4-7)

Could an application of this teaching be that the lost sheep represents this one lost world and the whole universe will rejoice when it is reunited with the (much) bigger family? There is no one on earth who needs "no repentance;" however, beings on the other (unfallen) worlds are correctly described this way.

Some people take the view that God and religion are only connected to this earth and the rest of the vast universe is totally in the realm of science or even science

Chapter Two: The Angelic Government

fiction and God has nothing to do with it or even with other inhabited planets if there are any. It's narcissistic and even arrogant to think we are alone, or the only inhabited world in the universe. Scripture says:

"And God made two great lights; the greater light to rule the day, and the lesser light to rule the night: *he made the stars also.*"

(Genesis 1:16)

Or they think that perhaps people have sinned on other planets. While I believe that God has granted free will to all His sentient creatures, the Bible says that sin started with Lucifer (Ezekiel 28:15) and he was cast to this earth (Revelation 12:9). Indeed, it seems that this earth has been quarantined from the rest of the universe and, I like to think that the vast universe (with, I am coming to believe, many inhabited planets) is eagerly awaiting to have this one lost sheep of a world reunited with them.

"And now, O Father, glorify thou me with thine own self with the glory which I had with thee before the world was."

(John 17:5)

"For I think that God hath set forth us the apostles last, as it were appointed to death: for we are made a spectacle unto the world, and to angels, and to men."

(1 Corinthians 4:9)

In the NIV the word for "world" is the "whole universe". The margin of the KJV for "spectacle" gives "theatre." Think of the Shakespearean line "all the world's a stage" with the rest of the universe watching. This is not a new concept, as in the Book of Ezekiel, we discover that when Ezekiel was taken up in the *wheels within wheels (spaceships) of Ezekiel,* he was shown what he described as a vision on the wall, but it was in real time, as he and the Lord watched the Israelites worship idols in His temple in Jerusalem, which provoked the Lord to jealousy. (See, Ezekiel 8-11) I proved in Book Two: *Who Is God?*, based on Hebrew Linguistics and mistranslations from Hebrew to English, that this was not just a dream/vision, but that Ezekiel's vision on the wall, was a television screen inside the spaceship, video-graphing this live event of the Israelites worshiping the Asherah pole, the image of jealousy for the Lord. This story proves that events on earth are and have been recorded, just as today we have cameras all over the place, this technology may be new to us, but there is nothing new under the sun! (Ecclesiastes 1:9). We're all be watched, and it's clear from Ezekiel's chapter that the Lord Himself is watching the watchers!

As I began this thesis in Book One[8] with the premise that the earth has been quarantined because of galactic sin, the prophecies tell us, that earth will be reunited with heaven and the entire universe/multiverse once it has been redeemed and cleansed from sin and wickedness after Christ's Second Coming.

THE TRUTH IS STRANGER THAN FICTION!
As the veil is now being removed from this ancient drama, we are beginning to understand not only our origin, but which of the gods, extra-terrestrial beings, angels or aliens have our best interest at heart, and which of them have their own evil agendas. The greatest tool we can hope and pray for in the times to come is *discernment*.[9]

"When pride comes, then comes disgrace, but with the humble is wisdom."
(Proverbs 11:2)

James Madison said, "If men were angels, no government would be necessary; If angels were to govern men, neither external nor internal controls on government would be necessary."

The question remains, which angels? Princes of nations are placed there by the king of the kingdom of darkness of this present world. This is why our world is in a constant state of turmoil. I do believe James Madison was referring to Heaven's Angels. Bible Prophecy tells us that during the age to come, the *Millennial Reign of Christ on Earth*, all the nations of the world will serve the Lord. The Kingdom of Heaven is coming to earth, governed by the Kingdom of God, which is made up of legions upon legions of faithful angels.

NOTES AND REFERENCES:

1. Ella LeBain, *Who's Who in The Cosmic Zoo? Book One, A Spiritual Guide to ETs, Aliens, Gods & Angels, Third Edition,* Chapter One. Tate Publishing & Enterprises, 2013.
2. Geoffrey Hodson, *The Kingdom of the Gods,* The Theosophical Publishing House, London, U.K., Adyar, India, 1952
3. http://www.sacred-texts.com/chr/tbr/tbr023.htm
4. *The Sons of God and the 24 Elders,* http://www.jesus-resurrection.info/sons-of-god.html
5. Ella LeBain, *Who's Who in The Cosmic Zoo? A Spiritual Guide to ETs, Aliens, Gods and Angels, First Edition,* 2012, Trafford, Indiana.

Chapter Two: The Angelic Government

6. Ella LeBain, *Who's Who in The Cosmic Zoo? Book One, A Spiritual Guide to ETs, Aliens, Gods & Angels, Third Edition,* Chapter One. Tate Publishing & Enterprises, 2013.
7. Ella LeBain, *Who Is God? Book Two, Who's Who In The Cosmic Zoo? A Guide to ETs, Aliens, Gods & Angels,* Chapter Three: Ancient Astronaut Theory, p.49, Skypath Books, 2015.
8. Ella LeBain, *Who's Who in The Cosmic Zoo? Book One, A Spiritual Guide to ETs, Aliens, Gods & Angels, Third Edition,* Chapter One. Tate Publishing & Enterprises, 2013.
9. Ibid.

CHAPTER THREE

THE CELESTIAL HIERARCHY OF ANGELS

> "For by Him all things were created that in heaven andthat are on earth, visible and invisible, whether *thrones* or *dominions* or *principalities* or *powers*. All things were created through Him and for Him."
> (COLOSSIANS 1:16)

"Knowledge is then gained through interpretation of the symbolic hierarchies. We must lift up the immaterial and steady our eyes of our minds to that outpouring of Light which is so primal indeed much more so, and which comes from that source of divinity, I mean the Father. This is the Light, which, by way of representative symbols, makes known to us the most blessed hierarchies among the angels. But we need to rise from this outpouring of illumination so as to come to the simple ray of Light itself."

(Pseudo-Dionysius)

In this chapter, we're going to explore the definition, purpose and hierarchical positions of angels or extraterrestrial messengers with respect to their assignments on earth and to earth humans.

In the Celestial Hierarchy, there are nine angelic orders. They are divided into Triads or Choirs, the First Triad consists of Seraphim, Cherubim and Ophanim (Thrones) who are considered angels (extraterrestrial guardians) of purity to govern all of God's Creation, the Second Triad consists of Dominations, Virtues, Powers, who are Angels of the Cosmos whose job it is to govern the Cosmic realms. The Third Triad consists of Principalities, Archangels, and Angels (extraterrestrial messengers) whose job is to be the Angels of our world, to govern the realms of Earth. The Ninth order are the Angels who are the closest to Humans. It is from this choir or category that we are given our own guardian and ministering angels. The Eighth

Chapter Three: The Celestial Hierarchy of Angels

order which consists of Archangels (Princes) are the Mighty Warrior Angels who conduct spiritual warfare and have been known to take down thousands of human armies at one time. These angels function as both heavenly messengers and soldiers.

The Lord of Hosts, as defined throughout this book series, in Hebrew, *Adonai Tzebayoth*, literally translates to the Lord of Celestial Armies. This is a military operation of the orders of Angels (extraterrestrial messengers and soldiers).

There have been many different Celestial Hierarchies throughout time based on different scriptural passages, ancient texts, visitations from the angels, and from other sources. The triads are sometimes spheres, ranging from three to five - with the choirs ranging from seven to eleven. The most comprehensive working theory that has stood the test of time was written by Pseudo-Dionysius.

Pseudo-Dionysius wrote Celestial Hierarchy, a highly influential outline that was later adopted by Thomas Aquinas [1225-1274] stating that the angels are arranged into nine choirs, which are grouped into three hierarchies, perhaps reflecting the Trinity.

THE ELOHIM

The word 'Elohim' is plural, meaning Gods, or a pantheon of Gods. In Hebrew, it is in the masculine plural participle. However, the words, 'Bene Elohim' or 'Bene HaElohim' literally translates as 'the sons of the sons of God'. This interests me greatly because the Bene Elohim, 'the Sons of God', comes up only twice in the Bible scriptures, whereas the word, 'Elohim' which is always plural, comes up more than 2,500 times in the Hebrew Old Testament. Due to the many translations, its literal meaning was lost in translation, as most English bibles translate Elohim as God, or the Lord. This is literally false, as 'Elyon' would be the Most High, also translated as the 'Almighty', or 'God on High', whereas Adonai means 'Lord'.

Many Christians believe that the Elohim is the Trinity of the Father, Son and Holy Spirit. As many Jews point out, there is no Trinity of God or Gods in the Bible.

Per Jewish tradition, there are ten orders of angels, with the Bene Elohim, the Sons of God being one of them. There are only a few times in the Bible where the two names are used to illustrate the difference between Elohim and Elyon:

> "And they remembered that God (Elohim) was their rock, and God Most High (El Elyon) their redeemer."
>
> (Psalm 78:35)

This implies that Elyon is Higher than the Elohim. The other instance where these names are distinguished is Genesis 14:18–19, "And Melchizedek King of Salem brought forth bread and wine: and he was the priest of the Most High God (El

Elyon). And he blessed him, and said, Blessed be Abram of the Most High God (El Elyon), possessor of heaven and earth: And blessed be the Most High God (El Elyon), which hath delivered thine enemies into thy hand."

The Elohim are *Governors,* a group of gods, or *Council of Gods* who govern, interact and act as God's intermediaries between the Almighty and human creation. Elohim literally translates to *gods*. The syllable 'El' literally means 'god', and is the root of Elohim which is plural. Elohim is a collective plural when the gods act in concert. Eloah is also another singular form both are used in the Old Testaments as proper names of God and are interchangeable with Elohim. These are the extra-terrestrials that have intervened with humanity from the beginning. The first section of Genesis, from 1:1 to 2:4 uses the plural 'Elohim' exclusively to describe the six days of creation; the sections following use the phrase *Yahuah Elohim* ("Lord of the gods") exclusively to describe the creation of the garden, Adam, and Eve. They infer that "the gods" created the Earth generally, and the "Lord God" created Adam and Eve.

BeneElohim

The Bene Elohim (sons of God) are in a completely different class and group than the angels. When they appeared and intervened to man in the past they were often mistaken as angels, i.e., messengers. The difference between Elohim (gods) and Bene Elohim (sons of God), are the Extra-Terrestrial races that God created (See, *Cosmic Drama Chart*)[1] to rule the Heavens. They all acknowledge and are in agreements with the Creator Father god and have not rebelled but uphold the laws of God throughout the Cosmos. These are the benevolent ETs of the Human Vine.

The Bene Elohim are listed as angels in the Celestial Hierarchy. They too are human extra-terrestrials. The *Book of Enoch* states that two hundred of the *Benei HaElohim* decided to marry human earth women. They were divided into groups of ten who then became known as the 'Watchers', also known as *fallen angels*. They produced offspring known as 'Nephilim'.

> The phrase *Benei HaElohim* appears only twice in the Old Testament in the Book of Job: "Now there was a day when the *Benei HaElohim* came to present themselves before *Yahuah,* and Satan came also among them."
>
> (Job 1:6)
>
> "Again there was a day when the *Benei HaElohim* came to present themselves before the Lord *Yahuah,* and Satan came also among them to present himself before the *Yahuah.*"
>
> (Job 2:1)

Chapter Three: The Celestial Hierarchy of Angels

In both cases, the *Benei HaElohim* are described as separate from *Yahuah*, and presenting themselves before Him, as in a conference or royal court. The *Book of Jubilees* and the *Book of Enoch*, which are factually consistent with Genesis and with each other, describe the 'Bene Elohim *as angelic beings lower in rank than* Yahuah Elohim.

Angels As Dimensions

Another way we can interpret the orders of Angels are as dimensions. Quantum physics has determined a total of eleven dimensions, including our familiar third dimension. This is interesting as, spiritually speaking, each of the orders of the Celestial Hierarchy resides and governs different dimensions. The scriptures say that the Lord has blanketed the heavens with a huge curtain. Could these be the curtains between the dimensions? Scripture says we see dimly as if through a glass, but one day we will see clearly. Our vision, even with our present technological wizardry, including the amazing Hubble Telescope which are our eyes into heaven, is still limited to what exists beyond the veils and curtains that separate the different dimensions of consciousness.

In Ephesians 6:12, it says, "We fight not against flesh and blood but against principalities, against powers, against the rulers of the darkness of this world, against spiritual hosts of wickedness in high places." It goes on to say, "For the weapons of our warfare are not carnal (worldly) but mighty through God to the pulling down of strongholds." (2 Corinthians 10:4) This is precisely how the order of angels comes into play. Just as God has His Celestial Orders and Hierarchy, there is a similar but counterfeit hierarchy of Cosmic Evil, which is kept in order by God's angels. I will elaborate more on this in the coming chapters.

Seraphim

Large light mother ships surrounded by orange, yellow, white fiery light. Seraphim is plural for 'Seraph'. Seraphim are sometimes called the fiery, flying serpents, mentioned in Isaiah 6:1-7, who serve as the caretakers of God's throne and continuously shout praises: "Holy, holy, holy is the Lord of Hosts. All the earth is filled with His Glory." The name Seraphim *means the burning ones*. The Seraphim have six wings; two covering their faces, two covering their bodies or feet, and two with which they fly. The archangel Seraphiel, is the chief prince or gatekeeper of the Seraphim.

Two of the Seraphim are named Seraphiel and Metatron, according to some accounts. Metatron is another name for Enoch. Seraphiel is said to have the head of an eagle. It is said that such a bright light emanates from them that nothing, not even other angelic beings, can look upon them. It is also said that there are four of them surrounding God's throne, where they burn eternally from love and zeal for God. They have been known to minister guidance for humanitarian and planetary causes.

The Seraphim rank as the highest order of God's Angelic Servants; they appear with six wings and four heads. They are known as *fiery serpents*, beings of pure light, angels of love, light and fire. The Seraphim keep negative energy from getting through to divinity. They shine so brilliantly with light that humans are unlikely to see them clearly and can mistake them as stars or glowing light ships.

The actual appearance of a Seraphim 'spirit-entity' is described in the *Book of Enoch*. The Greek translation used here is *drakones* which means *serpents*. Snakes and serpents have long been associated with demons. "Above it stood the seraphim: each one had six wings; with two he covered his face, and with two he covered his feet, and with two he did fly." (Isaiah 6:2) Seraphim are described as creatures with six wings and they can adjust their serpentine form. This indicates that we are dealing with serpents that can fly, and a dragon is very often described as a flying serpent.

The fiery, burning ones, the seraphim, are associated with the prophet Isaiah's vision of God in the Temple. The sixth chapter of Isaiah is the only place in the Bible that specifically mentions the seraphim. "In the year that king Uzziah died I saw also the Lord sitting upon a throne, high and lifted up, and his train filled the temple. Above it stood the seraphim: each on had six wings; with twain he covered his face, and with twain he covered his feet, and with twain he did fly. And the posts of the door moved at the voice of him that cried, and the house was filled with smoke. Then said I, Woe is me! for I am undone; because I am a man of unclean lips, and I dwell in the midst of a people with unclean lips: for mine eyes have seen the King, the Lord of hosts. Then flew one of the seraphim unto me, having a live coal in this hand, which he had taken with the tongs from off the altar: And he laid it upon my mouth, and said, Lo, this hath touched thy lips; and thine iniquity is taken away, and thy sin purged." (Isaiah 6:1-7)

Isaiah 6:2-4 records, "Above him were seraphs, each with six wings: With two wings they covered their faces, with two they covered their feet, and with two they were flying. And they were calling to one another: 'Holy, holy, holy is the Lord Almighty; the whole earth is full of his glory.' At the sound of their voices the doorposts and thresholds shook and the temple was filled with smoke." Seraphs are angels who worship God continually.

Each seraph had six wings. They used two to fly, two to cover their feet, and two to cover their faces (Isaiah 6:2). The seraphim flew about the throne on which God was seated, singing His praises as they called special attention to God's glory and majesty. These beings apparently also served as agents of purification for Isaiah as he began his prophetic ministry. One placed a hot coal against Isaiah's lips with the

Chapter Three: The Celestial Hierarchy of Angels

words, "See, this has touched your lips; your guilt is taken away and your sin atoned for" (Isaiah 6:7). Like the other types of holy angels, the seraphim are perfectly obedient to God. The seraphim are particularly focused on worshipping God.

Ann Madden Jones explains in her book *The Yahweh Encounters*, that the only mentioned difference between the Seraphim and Cherubim was the difference in their number of rotary blades or "wings".[2] The singular form of the word Seraph means not only *burning,* but also a symbolic creature named for its *copper color* and a poisonous serpent. Adding this together, we have a copper or amber colored poisonous serpent-like creature that was associated with the fire or burning, clearly an alien being. From Isaiah's experience, we know they had three pairs of wing-like appendages, flew in the air under pilot control, emitted smoke, and made such a noise and reverberations that the doors of the temple shook when one of them hovered overhead. This is the origin of the myths and traditions of flying dragons who were actually Seraphim.

During the Exodus, the people were discouraged and troubled by the long journey through wilderness and began to rebel against God and Moses leading them. "And the people spoke against God, and against Moses, saying, wherefore have ye brought us out of Egypt to die in the wilderness? for there is no bread, neither is there any water; and our soul loathes this light bread [manna]. And the Lord sent fiery serpents among the people, and they bit the people; and much people of Israel died." (Numbers 21:5-6)

Ann Madden Jones concludes that in the original Hebrew translation of *fiery serpents* was a reference to a "hissing" sound, and the definition of "fiery" was the same as the definition for Seraphim. It is the same Hebrew word, translated in one case as "fiery" in connection with a biting serpent (or something that hisses) and translated at a later date simply as "Seraphim." The strange serpents that were sent to "bite" the rebellious people were burning, hissing creatures, named for their copper (amber) colored bodies and their fiery appearance.

In the Book of Mormon, Nephi, the only prophet to call the Seraphim spaceships, also mentioned flying fiery serpents in 30:6. (Book of I Nephi 17:41) Between the time of Exodus till the later time of Isaiah, the name by which these crafts were identified had changed from "fiery serpents" to "Seraphim".

Ann Madden Jones postulates that the word 'bit' used in Numbers 21 meant *to strike with a sting,* as a snake would strike. Did the Seraphim use microwave or laser-type weapons against the people, the sting-like strike of which killed them outright, or caused deadly cancer or tumors to emerge later?

After the people confessed their sins and asked Moses to pray for God to stop the killing, the fiery serpents, the Seraphim, departed. God then instructed Moses to build a serpent of brass, put it on a pole, so that anyone who had been bitten by the fiery serpents could come to this brass serpent, and by beholding it, gazing upon at it, be cured. This procedure indicates that the bite of the fiery serpents was not a bullet-type wound which instantly killed, but was a sickening sting which was slow in its lethality and could be cured if treated in time.

> "And Moses made a serpent of brass, and put it upon a pole, and it came to pass, that if a serpent had bitten any man, when he beheld the serpent of brass, he lived."
>
> (Numbers 21:9)

Ann Madden Jones postulates that the serpent of brass was a complex type of radiation treatment device, similar to the radiation therapy used to treat cancer patients today.[3]

This was not the first time the Israelites were afflicted by radiation poisoning. The Ark of the Covenant killed thousands with boils and cancerous tumors, the result of intense radiation. The Cherubim and Seraphim may have used robotics, wielding fiery sword like weapons which had the power to 'sting' and 'bite' with radiation poisoning. We would describe these technological devices today as laser beams or laser wands.

Cherubim

Pronounced 'Kerubim' (plural) or 'Kerub' (singular), this angel is understood as a high-ranking Fire Being, those who guard the Garden of Eden, the Spaceships of Ezekiel, or the space ships of the Lord. They aare always seen wielding fire swords, or lasers. They are God's security guards, fierce, powerful and completely under the command of the Lord. They are the closest Guardians of the Creator. Lucifer was the highest the Cherubim, above all, but when he rebelled against the Lord and wanted to be god himself, he lost his high place in heaven. He was cursed with the body of a serpent, there to have dominion as the lord of darkness over the lower worlds, earth being of them. Cherubim are considered to be angels of harmony and wisdom, who guard the light and the stars. They channel positive energy from the divine, being angels of boundless love and of knowledge. As mentioned, they are known to function as the personal security guards of religious temples, as well as the space ships of the Lord.

The Angel Cherubiel is the chief or prince gatekeeper of the Cherubim. Cherubim or cherubs are angelic beings involved in the worship and praise of God. The cherubim are first mentioned in the Bible in Genesis 3:24, "After He drove the man out,

Chapter Three: The Celestial Hierarchy of Angels

He placed on the east side of the Garden of Eden cherubim and a flaming sword flashing back and forth to guard the way to the tree of life." We know that prior to his rebellion, Satan was a cherub from Ezekiel 28:12-15.

The Book of Ezekiel describes the "four living creatures" in chapter 1:5, as being the cherubim of chapter 10. Each had four faces—that of a man, a lion, an ox, and an eagle (Ezekiel 1:10; also 10:14)—and each had four wings. In their appearance, the cherubim "had the likeness of a man" (Ezekiel 1:5). These cherubim used two of their wings for flying and the other two for covering their bodies (Ezekiel 1:6, 11, 23). Under their wings the cherubim appeared to have the form, or likeness, of a man's hand (Ezekiel 1:8; 10:7-8, 21).

The tabernacle and temple, along with their articles, contained many representations of cherubim (Exodus 25:17-22; 26:1, 31; 36:8; 1 Kings 6:23-35; 7:29-36; 8:6-7; 1 Chronicles 28:18; 2 Chronicles 3:7-14; 2 Chronicles 3:10-13; 5:7-8; Hebrews 9:5). The imagery of Revelation 4:6-9 also describes cherubim. "Also before the throne there was what looked like a sea of glass, clear as crystal. In the center, around the throne, were four living creatures, and they were covered with eyes, in front and in back. The first *living creature* was like a lion, the second was like an ox, the third had a face like a man, the fourth was like a flying eagle. Each of the four *living creatures* had six wings and was covered with eyes all around, even under his wings. Day and night they never stop saying: "Holy, holy, holy is the Lord God Almighty, who was, and is, and is to come."

OPHANIM OR "THRONES"

The Greek *thronos* or Elders, also known as the *Erelim* or Ophanim, are classified as 'Virtues,' or 'Strongholds' which lie beyond the Ophanim, the Thrones or Wheels. Their primary duty is to supervise the movements of the heavenly bodies to ensure that the cosmos remains in order. They are a class of celestial beings mentioned by Paul of Tarsus in Colossians 1:16. They are living symbols of God's justice and authority. One of their symbols is the throne. These high celestial beings appear to be mentioned again in Revelation 11:16 - 'And the twenty-four elders, who were seated on their thrones before God, fell on their faces and worshiped God.'

Thrones are star ships. When the Lord was described as coming out of the heavens on his 'Throne', he was moving through the heavens on his space ship. The Ophanim Thrones are living mechanical devices, described in the bible as 'Wheels', or wheels within wheels, which is a description of a space ship. The Angel Ofaniel, is the chief or prince gatekeeper of the Ophanim.

> "The appearance of the wheels and their work was like unto the color of a beryl: and the four had one likeness: and their appearance and their work was as it were a *wheel within the middle of a wheel.*"
>
> (Ezekiel 1:16)

The *Ophanim* (Hebrew *ofanim*, translated as Wheels, also known as Thrones, from the vision of Daniel 7:9) are unusual-looking, even compared to the other celestial beings. They appear as a beryl-colored *wheel-within-a-wheel*, their rims covered with *hundreds of eyes*. They are closely connected with the Cherubim:

> "When they moved, the others moved; when they stopped, the others stopped; and when they rose from the earth, the wheels rose along with them; for the spirit of the living creatures [Cherubim] was in the wheels (Ophanim)."
>
> (Ezekiel 10:17)

These are clearly 'Living Light ships' under the command of the Creator God, Lord Yahuah.

> "And when the living creatures went, the wheels went by them, and when the living creatures were lifted up from the earth, the wheels were lifted up. And wheresoever the spirit was to go, they went, there was their spirit to go, and the wheels were lifted up over against them, for the spirit of the living creatures was in the wheels. When those went, these sent, and when those stood, these stood, and when those were lifted up from the earth, the wheels were lifted up over against them, for the spirit of the living creatures was in the wheels."
>
> (Ezekiel 1:19-21)

> "As for the Wheels, they were called in my hearing, the Wheelwork."
>
> (Ezekiel 10:13)

Many have pondered after reading the book of Ezekiel, was Ezekiel having a vision or was it a close encounter with ultra-terrestrials?

Wheels within wheels, being lifted up from the earth sounds to me like a space ship. But what's even more fascinating about Ezekiel's experience, is that he says the spirit of the living creatures he encounters were *in* the wheels. The Holy Merkabah, the Divine Chariot of God, as the word *Merkabah* directly translates from ancient Hebrew/Aramaic. The Wheels within Wheels were *alive* with the spirit of God. Ezekiel describes a *living* organism. He says that the creatures or cherubim as later referred to, were *one* with the wheels. That everywhere they went, the wheels moved with them.

Chapter Three: The Celestial Hierarchy of Angels

In recent UFO history, the Golden Merkabahs, as UFO Researcher Wes Batemen refers, is the bright fiery star ship that Carlos Diaz of Mexico City experienced as a living organism. According to Carlos Diaz, who actually took film footage of these Golden Merkabahs from 1991-1992 in Mexico City, said that these Golden Merkabahs, were the energy field of school teachers, and that when one of the school teachers went with him, he was able to manifest this glorious star ship. It looks like a golden amber fiery object, with wheels within wheels within the golden fiery glow. After viewing this film footage myself, I was amazed to see how the flower of life pattern and the sacred geometry of the Star of David particularly Metatron's Cube, was apparent within the wheels of golden and amber light.

The Golden Merkabah, is a living organism or living cell, a kind of plasma, which is quite different from the mechanical UFOs seen all over the world. These ships are made up of living energy, and as Carlos Diaz has observed, these Golden Merkabahs grow as beings enter it, as their bodies are immediately transformed into 'light-bodies' upon entering the energy field of these extraordinary star ships.

Dominions

The Dominions (Latin: dominatio, plural: dominationes), also known as the 'Hashmallim' in Hebrew. The Hashmallim hold the task of regulating the duties of lower angels. It is only with extreme rarity that these angelic Lords make themselves physically known to mortals. Instead, they quietly concern themselves with the details of existence. They are also the angels who preside over nations.

The Dominions are believed to look like divinely beautiful humans with a pair of feathered wings, much like the common representation of Angels. They are physically characterized as wielding orbs of light fastened to the heads of their scepters or on the pommel of their swords. The Dominions may possibly be equated with the Lords of Individuality, a hierarchy of Elohim. They inhabit the World of Life Spirit, which is the home of Christ, The Son in cosmology. The Dominions are also translated from the Greek term kuriotes or Lordships, related to the Lord Christ Jesus, and also as Leaders. They are presented as the hierarchy of celestial beings as Lordships.

> "For we wrestle not against flesh and blood, but against *principalities*, (Archdemons) against cosmic *powers*, (rebellious extraterrestrials) against the *rulers* of the darkness of this world (aliens, satans, fallen angels), against spiritual wickedness (evil spiritual hosts) in heavenly places. (the first dimension of heaven)"
>
> (Ephesians 6:12)

Principalities

The Principalities (Latin: principatus, plural: principatus) are shown wearing a crown and carrying a scepter. The Principalities are also translated, from the Greek term "arche", as Princedoms and Rulers (see Greek root in Ephesians 3:10). These are 'Princes' hence the word, 'Principalities.' On the light side, they are also known as 'Archangels', however, on the dark side, they are known as 'Archdemons.' On the light side, their duties are to carry out the orders given to them by the Dominions and bequeath blessings to the material world. Their task is to oversee groups of people. As beings related to the world of the germinal ideas, they are said to inspire living things to many things such as art or science. The Principalities may possibly be equated with the Lords of Form, a Hierarchy of Elohim astrologically associated to Scorpio, presented in The Rosicrucian Cosmo-Conception. They inhabit, in Rosicrucian cosmology, the World of Thought in the Region of Abstract Thought (higher region; the Christian Third Heaven), which is the home of Yahuah, The Holy Spirit.

Rulers

These celestial beings appear to collaborate, in power and authority (as implied in their etymology source), with the Powers (Authorities). Rulers develop ideologies whereas Authorities write the documents and doctrines. Both Rulers (Principalities) and Authorities (Powers) are involved in formulating ideologies. However, Rulers are more focused on specific lines of thought whereas Authorities are all-encompassing. This relates to both the good rulers and the rulers of darkness. Both have competing celestial hierarchies. Also known as Archons.

Powers

The Powers (Latin: potestas (f), plural: potestates) are the bearers of conscience and the keepers of history. The angels of birth and death are Powers. They are academically driven and are concerned with ideology, philosophy, theology, religion, and documents pertaining to those studies. Powers are the brain trusts: a group of experts who serve as advisers and policy planners. They are also the warrior angels created to be completely loyal to God, thus the only order created after the fall. Some believe that no Powers have ever fallen from Grace but others say that not only have some of them Fallen, the Devil was believed to have been the Chief of the Powers before he Fell (see Ephesians 6:12) Their duty is to oversee the distribution of power among mankind, hence their name.

Chapter Three: The Celestial Hierarchy of Angels

Paul used the term powers in Colossians 1:16 and Ephesians 1:21 but he may have used it to refer to the powers of nations, societies or individuals, instead of referring to angels.

AUTHORITIES

The Powers are also translated, from the Greek term "exousia", as Authorities (see Greek root in Ephesians 3:10).

These celestial beings appear to collaborate, in power and authority (as implied in their etymology source), with the Principalities (Rulers). Rulers develop ideologies whereas Authorities write the documents and doctrines. Both Authorities (Powers) and Rulers (Principalities) are involved in formulating ideologies. However, Authorities are all-encompassing whereas Rulers are more focused on specific lines of thought. Authorities specialize in putting those ideas into print and in producing actual documents.

Paul used the term rule and authority in Ephesians 1:21, and rulers and authorities in Ephesians 3:10. He may have been referring to the rulers and authorities of men or societies, instead of referring to angels.

ARCHANGELS

The word archangel comes from the Greek *archangelos*, meaning chief angel. It derives from the Greek *archo*, meaning to be first in political rank or power; and *angelos* which means messenger. This suggests that they are the highest-ranking angels. The word is only used twice in the Bible: 1 Thessalonians 4:16 and Jude 1:9. Only Michael and Gabriel are mentioned by name in the Bible. Michael is the only angel the Bible names expressly as an archangel. In Daniel, he is referred to as "one of the chief princes". The word "prince" here is the ancient Hebrew word 'sar,' which means: "a head person (of any rank or class), a chief, a general etc."

The name of the archangel Raphael appears only in the Deuterocanonical Book of Tobit (Tobias). Tobit is considered canonical by Catholics, Orthodox and some Protestants. Raphael said to Tobias that he was "one of the seven who stand before the Lord", and it is generally believed that Michael and Gabriel are two of the other seven. Another possible interpretation of the "seven" is that the seven are the seven spirits of God that stand before the throne.

They are said to be the guardian angels of nations and countries, and are concerned with the issues and events surrounding these, including politics, military matters, commerce and trade: For example, Archangel Michael is traditionally seen as the protector of Israel and of the Ecclesia (Gr. root 'ekklesia' from the New Testament passages), theologically equated as the Church, the forerunner of the spiritual New Israel.

Angels

The Angels, also known as the Malachim (messengers or angels), are the lowest order of the angels, and the most familiar to men. They are the ones most concerned with the affairs of living things. Within the category of angels, there are many different kinds, with different functions. The angels are sent as messengers to humans.

Jewish Angelic Hierarchy from the *Jewish Encyclopedia* gives a few different lists of the ten ranks of angels. Maimonides, in his Yad ha-Chazakah: Yesodei ha-Torah, counts ten ranks of angels in the Jewish angelic hierarchy, beginning from the highest:

1. Chayote Ha Kadesh
2. Ophanim
3. Erelim See Isaiah 33:7
4. Hashmallim See Ezekiel 1:4 explained in Ḥag. 13*b* as ḥayyot, who are sometimes silent [*hash*], and who sometimes speak [*mallel*]—they are silent when the word emanates from the Holy One, blessed be He! they speak when he has ceased speaking;
5. Seraphim
6. Malachim - Messengers, angels
7. Elohim – "Gods' Godly Governors"
8. Bene Elohim – "Sons of Godly beings"
9. Cherubim "like blooming youth," Ḳarabia (See, Talmud Hagigah 13b)
10. Ishim "manlike beings", see Daniel 10:5)

In "Maseket Azilut" the ten ranks of angels are given in the following order:

(1) Seraphim, with Shemuel [Ḳemuel] or Jehoel as chief; (2) ofanim, with Raphael and Ofaniel as chiefs; (3) cherubim, with Cherubiel as chief; (4) shinannim, with Ẓedeḳiel and Gabriel as chiefs; (5) tarshishim, with Tarshish and Sabriel as chiefs; (6) ishim, with Zephaniel as chief; (7) ḥashmallim, with Ḥashmal as chief; (8) malakim, with Uzziel as chief; (9) bene Elohim, with Hofniel as chief; (10) arelim, with Michael as chief.

These are the ten archangels that were created first; and over them is set Meṭaṭron-Enoch, transformed from flesh and blood into flaming fire.

Chapter Three: The Celestial Hierarchy of Angels

The *Book of Enoch* names the following archangels: Uriel, who rules the world and Tartarus; Raguel, who takes vengeance on the world of the luminaries; Michael, who is set over the most part of mankind and over chaos; Saraquael, who is set over the spirits; Gabriel, ruler of paradise, the serpents and the cherubim; Ramiel, whom God set over those who rise; and Raphael, who rules the spirits of men.

Angels are Teachers

Angels endowed with divine knowledge appear in the apocalyptic and rabbinic literature as the teachers of men. This is the so-called "whisper of the angels" Michael initiated Adam and Seth into the secrets of creation (Apocalypse of Moses 3:13) and taught Adam agriculture. The angels Michael, Uriel, and Raziel initiated Enoch into the mysteries of the world (*Book of Jubilees* 4:21; the *Ethiopian Enoch* 40:4, 5, 19:1, 72:1; and *Slavonic Enoch* 22:11, 33:6). Raphael imparted to Noah the secret of healing herbs (*Book of Jubilees* 10: 9-10). Michael initiated Abraham into the secret lore (Testament of Abraham 11-14).

The angel of the Face (Suriel) instructed Abraham in Hebrew, the language of creation and revelation thus enabling him to study the holy writings of the first fathers (Book of Jubilees 12:25). The angels understand only Hebrew (Ḥaggadah 16a; Soṭah, 33a), but the angel Gabriel knows seventy languages, all of which he taught to Joseph; "Beit Midrashot," 4:25, where Zagzagael ("Divine Splendor") is mentioned as the instructor in the seventy languages). Moses, who received all his knowledge from the angel of the face (Suriel) (Book of Jubilees 2, 3., etc.), was taught the art of healing by the angels when on Mount Sinai. Yefehfiah ("Divine Beauty"), the angel of the Law, and Meṭaṭron ("the Prince of the Face") taught him the mystery of the practical Kabala. The angel Zagzagael ("Divine Splendor") instructed Moses in the knowledge of the Ineffable Name (Deuteronomy 11). Uriel disclosed to Ezra the mysteries of life (2 Ezra 4:1). Suriel, the angel of the face, instructed Elisha in the laws of hygiene.

Occasionally the angels themselves gather amid joy and singing to listen to the initiated into the sacred lore of heaven. But at times they also betray jealousy and fear, begrudging man his knowledge of hidden things. Thus, they sought to dissuade the Most High from giving the Law to Moses (*Jewish Encyclopedia* 88b); but Moses pacified them by his arguments. In like manner they sought to drive Akiba out of the realm of paradise, as they did his colleagues Ben 'Azzai and Ben Zoma; but God Himself interceded, saying, "Leave this venerable sage unscathed; for he is worthy to make use of My glory" (Ḥaggai 15b).

Kabalistic View

For discernment sake, it is important to point out that there are three spellings of the Kabbalah, 1) Kabbalah; 2) Cabala; and 3) Qabala. The Cabala and Qabala which primarily runs two parallel currents that have both been used to invoke the fallen angels, in other words a Grimoire, a counterfeit of the Hebrew Kaballah. The Kabbalah which in Hebrew means *the receiving or the gift* is the revelation of secret knowledge from the Zohar. It has been kept off limits to the public for centuries, until the 1950s when Rabbi Phillip Berg was told by God it was time to share this knowledge to the world before the end of the age and the beginning of the Age of Messiah (the Age of Aquarius). The Kabbalah consists of Cosmology, Astronomy/Astrology and the Wheels of the Soul through Reincarnation through Tikune (the process of soul correction and evolution). The Hebrew Kabbalah does *not* condone magical ceremonies to invoke celestial beings. The Kabbalah is a vast study of knowledge which inspires its students to fill their human vessels with light and avoid the dark days which I will discuss further with respect to Cosmic Evil, Death Stars and the Dark Lords.

The practical Cabala or Qabala is bent on intervening, through magical incantations, the destinies of earthly lives by the higher powers through ceremonial magic, and is ever busy finding new names of angels able to control the lower forces. Such attempts are made by the Hermetic Order of the Golden Dawn, which used Hermetic Qabala, astrology, occult tarot, geomancy and alchemy and was practiced by various Masonic orders. At the turn of the 20th century Aleister Crowley took over the Order of the Golden Dawn, devolving it into the Argentium Astrum under the supposed auspices of a being he called Lam, whom he had conjured up while in Egypt. Crowley called up all kinds of demons while inside the Great Pyramid, and it is widely known that he later became possessed by the demon Choronzon when he opened the gates of Hell, where they both now reside.

The other books involved in the naming of angels or fallen angels for invocation, known as a Grimoire, are the *Sefer ha-Razim*. This is a list of angels for the months of the year. The *Sefer Raziel* is a collection of magical rituals, along with the *Greater Key of Solomon, The Lemegeton (The Book of Spirits)* and *Raphael's Ancient Manuscript of Talismanic Magic*. King Solomon was known for building his temple through invoking the aid of demons, or intelligences, which did all of his bidding. However, since God has changed the names of these angels, now when people try to use the magical seals in the *Greater Key of Solomon* they are in effect conjuring up from the Grimoire or fallen angels and demons.

On the other hand, we can consider the view of the Neoplatonic view of Emanation. The idea of the cosmic macrocosm, or the world in its totality as being the evolution of the image of God, has man as a microcosm. This has made man

Chapter Three: The Celestial Hierarchy of Angels

the object of Creation, so that in this view he ranks above the angels (Zohar, 3:68); while they, the angels, belong to the lower realm, to the world of formation (*Yezirah*), and not to that of Creation (*Beriah*), where belong the higher spirits. The angels are intellectual, spiritual beings, yet invested with a shining garb to make them visible to man. (Zohar, pp. 278-279)

ANGELS INTERCEDE BETWEEN GOD AND HUMANS

The angels mediate between God and man. They carry prayers up to the throne of God (Tobit 12, 15). Angels intercede for those who dwell on earth (Enoch 11:6; Job 33:23), which is to be translated: "If there be on his side one single messenger among a thousand pleading for him". They place the prayers and good deeds of the righteous before God, and in the same manner they also bring the sins of the evil-doers before Him (Enoch 99:3). They "write down and record all the deeds and lives before the face of the Lord" (Slavonic *Book of Enoch* 19:5). These records, in the Testament of Abraham, are called the "Books of the Cherubim" because they are kept by those angels.

Angels bring the souls of the righteous to heaven (Song of Solomon 4:12; Luke, 16:22).

Angels accompany the dead on their departure from this world. "Three bands of angels of the divine ministry [*mal'ake ha-sharet*], or peace [*hashalom*], accompany the righteous: the first singing, 'He shall enter in peace'; the second, 'They shall rest on their couches'; and the third, 'The one who walks in uprightness'" (Isaiah. 57:2).

But when a wicked man departs, three bands of angels of destruction (*mal'ake habbalah*) are described as accompanying him singing, "There is no peace, saith my God, to the wicked" (Isaiah 57:21).

The angels that execute God's judgment are called "the angels of punishment" (Enoch 56:1, 70:11, 63:1), *Satanim* (Enoch, 40:7), "angels of the dragon" = satan; Matthew 25:41. Their fierceness and their mode of punishment are described in the Testament of Abraham, A, 12, B, 11. They "sling the souls of the wicked from one end of the world to the other" These are under the leadership of six or seven archangels: Kezef, Af, Hemah (Deuteronomy 9:19), Mashhit, Meshabber, Mekalleh (Psalm 78:49: '*ebrah, za'am, zarah*); and above these is the angel of death (Testament of Abraham, 18.20).

ANGELS OF THE NETHER WORLD

In John's Apocalypse (Revelation 9:11), Abaddon (Hebrew) Apollyon (Greek) is the angel of the abyss.

In the Talmud, Dumah, the angel of silence (Psalm 95:17), is the prince of the nether world in whose charge are the spirits. He announces the arrival of newcomers in Sheol. According to the Midrash Konen, there are three princes placed at the three upper gates: (1) Ḳipod (the Persian *kapod* means "wolf"; see "Zendavesta," translated by Darmesteter, in "Sacred Books of the East," 13: 295); (2) Nagrasagiel, or Nasragiel, the prince of Gehinnom, who showed Moses the nether world and the sufferings of the wicked ("Bate Midrashot," 4:24); the angel messenger of Ahuramazda, Nairyo Sangha, to whose care the souls of the righteous are entrusted ("Vendidad," 19:34; Darmesteter, "Zendavesta,") In the Testament of Abraham, *A*, 13., two archangels are mentioned as assisting at the judgment of the souls: Doḳiel ("the weigher," Isaiah 40:15) and Puruel ("the fiery and pitiless angel," probably from *para'*, "paying"; *pur'anut*, "punishment"). In the Midrash Konen and Maseket Gan Eden and Gehinnom (Jellinek, "B. H." v. 44) the following angels of punishment are mentioned for the seven departments: (1) Kushiel ("the rigid one of God"); (2) Lahatiel ("the flaming one"); (3) Shofṭiel ("the judge of God"); (4) Makatiel ("the plague of God"); (5) Ḥuṭriel ("the rod of God"); (6) Pusiel (Puriel)— ("the fiery and pitiless angel") and (7) Rogziel ("wrath of God").

"Each angel has a tablet on his heart on which his name, combined with the name of God [*El*], is inscribed," says Simon B. Laḳish. This doctrine is based upon Psalm 68:18: "The Lord dwells in them," wherefore they are called Micha*el*, Gabri*el*, Rapha*el*, Uri*el*. They receive their name in accordance with their message, wherefore they cannot tell their names (Judges, 13:18).

"No single angel can carry out two messages, nor can two angels fulfill only one message. Of the three angels that came to Abraham, Michael, the guardian angel of Israel, brought the tidings of Isaac's birth; Gabriel, the angel of heavenly vengeance and of fire, had to overthrow Sodom; and Raphael rescued Lot" (Genesis 18:2). Michael to the right, Uriel to the left, Gabriel in front, and Raphael in the rear of the throne are stationed on the four sides of heaven (Midrash Konen).

Padael is the name given to the angel who appeared to Samson's parents in the apocryphal history of Philo ("Jewish Quarterly Review" 1898, p. 324). Zeroel ("Arm of God") was one of the angels who supported Kenaz in his battle against the Amorites; Nathaniel (Nuriel = "Fire of God"), the angel who saved the men cast into the fire by Jair, the judge, for refusing to worship his idols (*ibid.*). Over each force and element of life an angel is placed: one over the winds (Revelation 7:1); one over fire (*ibid.* 14:18); and one over water (*ibid.* 16:5).

In the Hebrew Enoch the following angel-princes are named: A few of these names recur in Enoch, 8 and 69. The angel of hail is introduced under the obscure name of Yurḳemo. The angel of night is called Lailah (Hebrew for night). The one set over the sea, Sarshel (like seashell). The angel set over the rain is Ridya, ("the Irrigator"); according to

Chapter Three: The Celestial Hierarchy of Angels

Kohut, "He resembles a calf, and is stationed between the upper and the lower abyss, saying to the one, 'Let your waters run down'; and to the other, 'Let your waters spring up.' Of the seven names of the earth seven angel names were formed: (1) Arẓiel, (2) Admael, (3) Ḥarabael, (4) Yabbashael, (5) 'Arẓiel ('Arḳas, *Slavonic Book of Enoch*, 24:2), (6) Ḥaldiel, and (7) Tebliel. They were stationed in the second heaven (see "Merkabah de-Rabbi Ishmael").

An angel set over the beasts is Thegri (Turiel means "bull-god,"). In Abraham of Granada's "Berit Menuḥah," are mentioned the angel Jehiel (Hayyel), set over the wild beasts; 'Anpiel, over the birds; Hariel (Behemiel), over the tame beasts; Shakẓiel, over the water-insects; Dagiel, over the fish; Ilaniel, over the fruit-bearing trees; Serakel, over the trees not bearing fruit.

"There is not a stalk on earth that has not its angelic star [*mazzal*] in heaven," a genuinely Persian notion. "Every single flower is appropriate to an angel" ("Bundahish," 27:24). The Talmud says: "Every blade of grass has its angel that bends over it and whispers, 'Grow, grow.'"

Angelology in the Quran

In the Quran, Jewish and Gnostic angelologies seem to be intermingled or counterfeited. In Mohammed's time the old Arabian goddesses, Al-Lat, Al-Uzza, and Manat, were spoken of as angels and daughters of God (Quran, 37, § 150, 53 § 20). The chief of all the archangels is Gabriel (Arabic=Jibreel); Mikaaiyl (Michael) comes next; whereas in the Jewish Bible, it's the other way around, Michael is the chief. This is evidence of counterfeiting scripture by fallen angels. As both the Judeo-Christian Bible came centuries, if not millennia before the Quran. The Gabriel of the Quran is not the same Gabriel in the Judeo-Christian Bible. Israfil (Sarafiel) who sounds the trumpet of the resurrection; and Azrael is the Archangel of Death in Islamic theology. Instead of four, there are eight Archangels that support the throne of God (Quran 49 § 17). Some angels have two, some three, others four wings. "They celebrate the praise of their Lord and ask forgiveness for those that are on earth". "Each man hath a succession of angels before and behind him" (Quran 13 § 12). The chief angel, who is in charge of hell, is Malik. According to the Quran, hell has seven doors (*sura* 15 § 44). Nineteen angels are set over the fire (Quran 74 § 30-31). Munkar and Nakir are the angels that interrogate the dead; and another angel, Ruman, makes each man write down his deeds. The Dictionary of Islam lists the names of other angels, used for invocations and exorcism, under "Da'wah" (incantation).

The angel Gabriel (Jibreel) is the most recognized angel, because in Islam this angel delivers the message of God (in the case of the Islamic prophet, Muhammad). Jibraaiyl/Jibril (Judeo-Christian Gabriel), the angel of revelation, who is said to be the greatest of the angels. Jibraaiyl is the archangel responsible for revealing the Quran to Muhammad, verse by verse. Jibrayil is known as the angel who communicates with all of the prophets.

Mikaaiyl (Judeo-Christian Michael), who provides nourishments for bodies and souls. Mikaaiyl is often depicted as the Archangel of mercy who is responsible for bringing rain and thunder to Earth. He is also responsible for the rewards doled out to good persons in this life.

Israfil/Israafiyl (Judeo-Christian Raphael), who will blow the trumpet twice at the end of time. According to the Hadith, Israafiyl is the angel responsible for signaling the coming of Qiyamah (Judgment Day) by blowing a horn and sending out a Blast of Truth. The blowing of the trumpet is described in many places in Quran. It is said that the first blow will destroy everything, while the second blow will bring all human beings back to life again to meet their Lord.

'Azrael/'Azraaiyl a.k.a Malak al-maut (Judeo-Christian Azrael), the angel of death. He is responsible for parting the soul from the body. He is only referred as malak al-maut, meaning angel of death, in the Quran.

Hamalat al-'Arsh, those who carry the 'Arsh (throne of God) (The Jewish Encyclopedia)

Guardian Angels of the Nations

In Daniel 10:20-21, the idea prevails that each nation has a heavenly guardian angel or prince. This would come under 'Principalities.' In Enoch 89:59, the seventy 'shepherds' are the 'guardian angels' of the seventy nations over whom Archangel Michael, who is Israel's angel-prince, is set as ruler. I am asserting that the Archangel Michael that New Agers claim to channel and invoke is *not* the real Archangel Michael! So many of these people are indifferent to or against Christ, and Israel, why would the real Archangel Michael listen to them? Archangels are not ordered about by humans, they exist to serve God and follow orders from on high via the Angelic Government/Hierarchy.

With these seventy-one angel-princes of the world sit in council, holding judgment over the world (Hebrew Enoch), each one pleads the cause of his nation before God (Genesis 11:7-8). At times, they accuse Israel; at other times they find especial merit in him. They are the "gods" whom the Lord crushes before He executes His punishment upon the nations in their charge (Exodus 12:12). These are the angel-princes of the nations, of Babel, Media, Greece, Syria, and Rome that Jacob saw in his dream ascending and descending the ladder (into a starship) (Genesis 28:12). The angel with whom Jacob wrestled was the angel-prince of Edom. God protects from the angel of death. By acts of benevolence the anger of the angel of death is overcome; when one fails to perform such acts the angel of death will make his appearance.

Samael (fallen angel), who is the head of all satans (enemies of God). The name of the angel of Egypt is Mizraim (Exodus) or Uzza; that of Persia's angel-prince is

Chapter Three: The Celestial Hierarchy of Angels

Dubbiel (means Beargod); (Daniel 7:5). But Michael, the angel-prince of Jerusalem, is set over all the seventy angels (Midrash; Genesis 132).

There is, however, a special angel-prince set over the world, Sar ha'olam (means 'Prince of the World'). The verses, Psalm 37:25; Isaiah 24:16, an angel of mankind is mentioned also (Apoc. Moses, 32). He has been identified, whether correctly or incorrectly, with Metatron. To fully resemble the court of the Persian King of Kings, the heavenly court is put in charge of a vice-regent, the *sar ha-Panim* ("Prince of the Divine Face"). Per the Testament of Job (52.), this vice-regent "sitteth upon the great chariot" (mothership); he is, according to Philo "On Dreams" (i. 25), "the driver of the chariot"; His "name is like the name of his Master" (Exodus 13:21), known under the name of "Metatron." This vice-regent is probably identical with the archangel Jehoel mentioned in Apoc. Abraham, as mediator of the ineffable name of God; also with Yehadriel; and perhaps also with Akathriel, the occupant of God's throne.

But alongside of Metatron is mentioned in "Maseket Azilut" (based on Job, 41:9), as "brother" and above him, Sandalfon, explained as Synadelphon ("twin-brother") and as "Sardonyx" (*Slavonic Book of Enoch*, 25.). The later Cabala places Akathriel above the twin-brothers Metatron = Enoch and Sandalfon = Elijah. Of well-nigh equal rank with Metatron and Sandalfon and Akathriel ("the crown of God"). (See, www.jewishencylopedia.com)

Beneath these are the seven heavens with Michael, Gabriel, Shateiel ("angel of silence"), Shahakiel, ("angel of Shahakim"), Baradiel, Barakiel, and Sadriel ("angel of order") as chiefs; and beneath them in the Velon, Galgaliel, and Ofaniel, Rehatiel, and Kokbiel as the angels of sun-wheel, moon-wheel, planets, and the other stars with all their hosts; the seventy-two angel-princes of the nations being stationed above these.

Who Is Michael?

Archangel Michael ranks as the highest and greatest of all of Heaven's angels, whether he shows up in Jewish, Christian or Islamic literature. His name in Hebrew literally translates to, *who is as God?* pronounced, *mee-chka-el*. He was worshipped as a god by the Chaldeans. He is Chief of the Order of not only Archangels, but Virtues, prince of the presence, angel of repentance, righteousness, mercy and sanctification; ruler of the 4th Heaven[5] (See, Book Five: *The Heavens*, Chapter on the Ten Heavens). He is known as the tutelary *sar* (angelic prince) of Israel, guardian of Jacob, and conqueror of Satan (bearing in mind, however, that satan is still very much around! While he appears to be unvanquished on earth, he has been defeated by Jesus Christ on the Cross of Calvary in the spiritual realms. The full manifestation will of satan's defeat will take place at the end of this present age in the final battle known as Armageddon, where the Lord Jesus Christ returns to end the battle of all battles over Jerusalem, with a breath and a Word.)

Michael is also called in satanic circles "The Alien Archangel Mik'ail Sabbathiel". Mik'ail was his Islamic name. Sabbathiel is his present satanic name.[6] Both systems believe Michael was the second born of all creation; the first born being Yeshua/Jesus, and the third born was Lucifer/Satan. All religions believe Michael is the leader of God's army, the Heavenly Order of Angelic Warriors. The general core opinion common to most belief systems is that when Lucifer/Satan first rebelled against the Creator God, Michael led the charge against his former brother and was ready to conquer and slay him. He was only prevented by his higher up, The Almighty God Himself, who instead chose to banish Lucifer/Satan and his rebellious fallen angel followers, from the Heavenly Realm. (See, Jude 1:6)

We know that Lucifer/Satan returned to Earth, and has been on a quest to destroy humanity ever since. He does this by corrupting the image and likeness of God within humankind. Witness the Cosmic Drama of the Garden of Eden! Ever since then he has been in constant battle with us humans and with the Lord's armies of extraterrestrial angels as well. Michael is ready to finally finish the war he could have ended many millions of years ago, by destroying Lucifer/Satan and his brother Abaddon. He will destroy them and all the demons that follow them, in the last and final battle over the earth called Armageddon. Michael is in charge of Israel and watches over the nation faithfully. He is the protector of Israel's armies, and his hand is behind all the supernatural victories of Israel since its rebirth in 1948.

There are stories told by the Egyptians that during the six-day war, they would encounter small groups of Israeli soldiers whom they outnumbered 3 to 1; and thinking the IDF was done, were stunned by the angelic intervention that took place. This was seen and revealed only to the Egyptians. They reported approaching the Israeli soldiers who were cornered in the foothills, and then a group of tall giant warrior angels appeared before them causing the entire Egyptian army to fall to their knees in fear and reverence. The Israeli soldiers did not 'see' what the Egyptians saw, but were saved from being overcome by them. This true story is but one of the miracles of the survival of Israel, attributed to angelic intervention. Michael rules over Israel, which is proof that New Agers are not invoking him, especially those who are anti-Semitic and hate Israel. Instead, they are getting the counterfeit Michael who works under Lucifer/Satan and serves the kingdom of darkness, which is sent to deceive undiscerning humans.

The Midrash Rabba (Exodus 18) credits Michael with being the author of the whole of Psalm 85. In addition, he has been identified with the angel who destroyed the hosts of Sennacherib, an achievement also ascribed to the prowess of Uriel, Gabriel, Ramiel. Michael is also known as well as the angel who stayed the hand of

Chapter Three: The Celestial Hierarchy of Angels

Abraham, on the point of sacrificing his son Isaac, having listened to the counterfeit god to sacrifice his son. (See Book Two: *Who Is God?* for the Hebrew Linguistics proving that the voice Abraham heard was not the Lord Yahuah, but the counterfeit god of this world who tested Abraham.) The Angel of the Lord who intervened was the Archangel Michael who, according to Jewish lore, sent his angel Tadhiel, Metatron and other angels to intervene and save Isaac, all part of the Genesis 22 story.

Per Ginzberg in *The Legends of the Jews*, "the fire that Moses saw in the burning bush had the appearance of Michael, who had descended from Heaven as the forerunner of the Shekinah."[8] This massive collection of the Haggadah, Jewish traditions surrounding the Biblical narrative, along with stories scattered throughout the Talmud and the Midrash, includes the oral traditions. The word *Midrash* is one of the many names for the Angel Metatron. Christians, however, believe that person to be a Christophany of Yeshua/Jesus Christ, who is the Great, "I Am". Both accounts may be true, as Michael is the protector of the Lord and Messiah of Israel, and they very well could have been working together to produce the fire, and the Lord's image.

Per Talmud Berakot 35, in the comment on Genesis 18:1-10, Michael is recognized by Sarah as one of three "men" whom Abraham entertained unawares. Legend speaks of Michael having assisted four other archangels, Gabriel, Uriel, Raphael and Metatron in the burial of Moses, as it was Michael arguing with satan for possession of the body of Moses.[10]

> "But Michael the archangel, when he disputed with the devil and argued about the body of Moses, did not dare pronounce against him a railing judgment, but said, "The Lord rebuke you!" (Jude 1:9).

To the Jews, Michael is the "Viceroy of Heaven" a title once applied to his adversary, HaSatan, before he fell. In *Baruch III,* Michael[11] "holds the keys of the kingdom of Heaven" which, traditionally, has been said of St. Peter, and per the Book of Revelation 1:18, it is Jesus who holds the keys of death and Hades. Along with Gabriel, Michael is the most pictured of the angels in the classic Renaissance work of the masters. He is depicted with wings and an unsheathed sword as the warrior of God and slayer of the Dragon. "Then war broke out in heaven. Michael and his angels fought against the dragon, and the dragon and his angels fought back." (Revelation 12:7)

Among the Dead Sea scrolls there is one entitled the *War of the Sons of Light Against the Sons of Darkness*. Here, Michael is called the "Prince of Light." He leads the angels of light in battle against the legions of the angels of darkness, who are under the command of the demon Belial, the spirit of lies. [12]

The Prince of Heaven, Archangel Michael, does not take orders from humans. This Commander of legions of angels within the Lord's Celestial armies cannot be invoked through witchcraft, tarot cards, or blue light, as many New Agers claim. This celestial being is second in command to the Lord of Hosts Himself, who is the Lord. The false Archangel Michael movement channeled by New Agers is nothing more than a masquerade of fallen angels, facilitated by the prince of darkness, through the agency of demonic intelligences who are none other than the Grays.[12]

NOTES AND REFERENCES:

1. Ella LeBain, *Who's Who in The Cosmic Zoo? Book One, A Spiritual Guide to ETs, Aliens, Gods & Angels, Third Edition,* Tate Publishing & Enterprises, 2013.
2. Ann Madden Jones, *The Yahweh Encounters: Bible Astronauts, Ark Radiations and Temple Electronics, A Controversial Interpretation of the Holy Bible,* The Sandbird Publishing Group, Chapel Hill, North Carolina, 1995.
3. Ibid.
4. Ibid.
5. Gustav Davidson, *A Dictionary of Angels: Including the Fallen Angels,* The Free Press, A Division of MacMillan, Inc., New York, 1967. p.193
6. Ibid.
7. Ibid., p. 194
8. Louis Ginzberg, *The Legends of the Jews,* 1909. Volume II. 303. http://www.pseudepigrapha.com/LegendsOfTheJews/index.htm
9. Ibid., Gustav Davidson, *A Dictionary of Angels: Including the Fallen Angels,* p.194
10. Ibid.
11. Ibid.
12. Ella LeBain, *Who's Who in The Cosmic Zoo? Book One, A Spiritual Guide to ETs, Aliens, Gods & Angels, Third Edition,* Tate Publishing & Enterprises, 2013, p.248-293

CHAPTER FOUR
Angel Protocol

"For He will command his angels concerning you to
guard you in all your ways."
(Psalms 91: 11)

"Praise the Lord, you his angels, you mighty ones who
do his bidding who obey His Word."
(Psalm 103:20)

The axiom, 'as above, so below' plays true. Just as we have all sorts of protocols on earth, so is it done in heaven. Angels follow protocols, as there is a definite Divine Chain of Command, as each and every one of them serve the Creator in a myriad of ways.

There are so many different facets of the study of angels. What I am mainly focusing on in this book is *discernment*. *Who* are the angels, really? We've already established that the word itself means messenger or intermediary, that they are not all fluffy winged beings, or chubby little cherubs; in fact, there is nothing little about the cherubim at all. God's extraterrestrial messengers, the angels, are the ones who are faithful to the Creator God, and are committed to doing His Will. These are the Angels of Light, or the benevolent ones. They are anything but fluffy! They are mighty, fearless warriors and ministers of God's Will, God's Truth and God's Healing.

"Funny thing, every time an angel appeared to someone in the Bible, the first thing he'd say was, "Fear not." ... I guess they were pretty spectacular."
- Gilbert Morris, *The Angels of Bastogne*

Music Is Said to Be the Language of Angels. Perhaps because the entire universe resonates to vibration, sound, frequency and light which are musical in nature. The Divine Order of the Cosmos is like a symphony inspiring the movement of the planetary spheres and solar systems, which are all kept in Divine Order by the Angels.

We know that every sound of the musical scale resonates to a color of the rainbow spectrum, and every color vibrates to a musical note. This is one of the languages of the Cosmos. There are angels who do nothing but sing praises to the Lord and make Divine music for the Creator.

> "Do not forget to entertain strangers, for by so doing some people have entertained angels without knowing it."
>
> (Hebrews 13:2)

Angels have been known to appear as human, in human form, yes, in the normal human size, well maybe just a little bit taller, just to show their stature; but they can be totally unobtrusive, humble and modest. They know that if they draw attention to themselves by showing up in their true form, that would distract from accomplishing their mission or assignment from the Creator, which is to serve humans while humans are unaware. The faithful messengers (angels) do not want humans to worship them, but to turn their gratitude and praise towards God alone. Then their mission is complete. These days, because there is a growing awareness of angels, there is a misunderstanding of their assignment and a misunderstanding of who they represent. In the past, many have strayed from the Creator by worshiping angels and invoking their names. It's understandable that these beings should inspire reverence and worship, especially when their true appearance can cause earth humans to tremble and fall down on the ground in fear. They are awesome beings! But let's look at what happens when earth humans get their angel protocols mixed up.

> "In the beginning, The Word was with God and the Word was God and the Word became flesh and dwelt among us."
>
> (John 1:1)

The Hosts of Heaven obey the Word of God. So, when it is spoken out loud and through the mouth of God's children empowered by Christ, the angels go into action in response to that Spoken Word of God. This is how prayers get answered, along with the help of the Holy Spirit who is also an immediate witness to the World.

The entire Bible is *not* the Word of God. The Bible *contains* the Word of God, yes God's actual Words. However, the Bible also contains the words of satan, fallen angels and sinful men and women. While the prophets spoke God's Word, they literally channeled it both orally and in written form. They also told the story which contains the words of God's enemies and other unrepentant characters throughout the Bible history. Funda-*mental* thinking says, the Bible is the Word of God, but you can't equate satan's words with those of God. They are part of the story and

Chapter Four: Angel Protocol

drama between satan and the Lord God in the Old and New Testaments, and satan and Jesus in the New Testament. The Bible also contains the words of fallen men and women, like King Saul, the evil Queen Jezebel, King Ahab, King Cyrus, King Herod, and Pontius Pilate. They are written in the Bible, which *contains* God's Word, but their words are most certainly NOT the Word of the Lord God. The exobiblical books of the Great Rejected Jewish Texts[1], also *contain* the Word of God, some of them more than others, like Enoch's scrolls.

Christians tend to forget that the Bible canon is also a *record* of historical events. Some scripture reflects the enemies of God speaking. The record of the despotic Kings, of the council of gods (Elohim) are recorded. We read what Satan speaks, what the Pharisees who challenge Yeshua/Jesus speak, and all their words are NOT God's Word, but records of history *within* the Bible, which *contains* the Word of God.

When people cherry pick scriptures that are NOT the actual Word of God, or which are the inserted words of the counterfeiter, they're not only taking words out of context, they are conflating one Bible character with another, which creates confusion. There's a whole cast of characters in the Bible. Not all of them serve the Kingdom of Heaven as their very words reflect!

Even in the Old Testament scriptures, which are quite specific in Hebrew, the actual names of God are lost with the insertions of the words, 'God' and 'Lord', when translated into English. Not all of them are actually representing the same character, as I proved extensively in Book Two: *Who Is God?*

However, I will prove to you herein Book Three: *Who Are The Angels?* that when you speak *out loud* God's Word through his prophets, angels go into action. This is how the Angels assigned to earth operate within the 'protocol' of the Kingdom of God on earth. When believers speak the Words of the Lord, in both the Old and New Testament, both Angels and the Holy Spirit go into action to answer those prayers, sometimes immediately. At other times, much prayer is necessary and it takes longer, because of God's Divine Timing and Will. Every prayer of repentance is answered with forgiveness, which leads to deliverance, which leads to healing, which in turn leads to peace, love and joy in the Holy Ghost. (Romans 14:17)

Invoking the Names of Angels

The names of angels formed a favorite study of the Essenes, Hasidim and Kabbalists in view of the magical cures effected by means of these names; for upon the accurate knowledge of the name and sphere of each angel, and of the power exerted by him on certain evil spirits, is dependent on the efficacy of the conjurers. In the Testament of Solomon, an apocryphal book belonging probably to the first century, King Solomon is introduced as giving his experiences on meeting the various demons, of each of whom he asks his name as well as the name of the angel that can overpower him. Asmodeus answers, that he is frustrated by Raphael, the archangel; another demon answers, Paltiel is his antagonist; a third, Uriel, etc. The magic book *The Sword of Moses*, published and translated by M. Gaster (London, 1896), is based upon the same principle, as are parts of the *Book of Raziel* ascribed to Eleazar of Worms. In Pseudo-Sirach the three angels, Sanuy, Sansanuy, and Samangaluf are said to have brought Lilith back to Adam, and when she turned child-murderess like Lamia, they were set in control over her.[2]

God Confounds The Names of Angels

In 2 Kings 24, we learn that in 589 BC Nebuchadnezzar II laid siege to Jerusalem, which culminated in the destruction of the city and the Holy Temple in 587BC. "At the siege of Jerusalem by Nebuchadnezzar, after the mighty hero Abika ben Gafteri had fallen, Hananeel, the uncle of Jeremiah, conjured up angels who struck terror into the hearts of the Chaldeans, thus setting them to flight. But God, having decreed the fall of the city, had changed the names of the angels when Hananeel summoned up the prince of the world by using the Ineffable Name, and he lifted Jerusalem into the air, but God cast it down again." The leading men of the city had conjured up the angels of water and of fire to surround the city with walls of fire and water; but God changed the names of the angels and punished the Israelites for their sins.

> "He sacrificed his own son in the fire, practiced sorcery and divination, and consulted mediums and spiritists. He did much evil in the eyes of the LORD, provoking him to anger."
>
> (2 Kings 21:6)

God changed the names so His angels couldn't be conjured up by magic. This is interesting, as many people today still believe they can use the *Seal of Solomon* or the mystical *Book of Raziel* or the *Cabbala/Golden Dawn* to invoke the names of angels to do their bidding. What they are really doing is conjuring up demons and fallen angels to come to their aid. Anybody who does this enters into a type of *Faustian Contract*, making a pact with the devil and with these fallen beings who are demons. Even though they may answer their invocations, and do as they are bid, the conjurer is literally entering into bondage through a *soul contract* with these *fallen angels*. There is so much of this going on these days, particularly in New Age circles, which are heavily saturated with demonic aliens and fallen angels. Masquerading as *light beings*, these demons are deceiving ignorant New Agers who invoke the names of angels and archangels for protection, guidance and all sorts of issues. It's a huge celestial con!

Chapter Four: Angel Protocol

One thing New Agers don't understand is that you cannot order God's angels. The Creator's heavenly hosts, His angels, extraterrestrial messengers and intermediaries, serve the Living God. They take direct orders from the Creator and His Lord of Hosts. They are not ordered around about by earth humans. They are only the *intermediaries,* recording and delivering prayers to the Creator. Those praying to or worshipping angels are mistakenly involved with the fallen angels, as God's heavenly hosts are not allowed to be worshipped and would deter any earth human from so doing. However, fallen angels do encourage worship of themselves, which is what fans the field of angel worship in New Age fields, along with using angel cards for divination and guidance. Regardless of whether one uses beautiful pictures of angels on the cards, or ancient tarot symbols, it is still divination.

> "Let no one be found among you who sacrifices his son or daughter in the fire, <u>who practices divination</u> or sorcery, interprets omens, engages in witchcraft, or casts spells, or who is a medium or spiritist or who consults the dead. Anyone who does these things is detestable to the Lord Yahuah, and because of these detestable practices the Lord Yahuah your God will drive out those nations before you. You must be blameless before the Lord your God."
>
> (Deuteronomy 18:9-13)

Being involved in the New Age circles for many years, I always thought the scripture in Deuteronomy was outdated, and only related to biblical times. However, after witnessing so much demonic oppression, outright deception and depression from the spirits who attach themselves to all those activities, I am now convinced the reason this was put into the scriptures was to warn us to stay away from such activities because they were and still are the <u>"legal territory" of demonic spirits, i.e., fallen angels</u>. The reason the Lord forbids it, is mainly for our own good so we can be free of the oppression of the deceptive spirits attached to them, in addition to the fact that the Lord considers it idolatry. I go into more details on *spiritual legal ground* in Book Four: *Covenants.*

> "But cowards, unbelievers, the corrupt, murderers, the immoral, those who practice witchcraft, idol worshipers, and all liars--their fate is in the fiery lake of burning sulfur. This is the second death."
>
> (Revelation 21:8)

This warning in the book of Revelation should make anyone in the New Age shudder, especially because there are so many who practice white witchcraft. Many think white witchcraft is all innocent but to the spiritual demonic realm, it is all the same. It's all about the *spirits* and the *demons* that are assigned to *all* witchcraft, black or white. For each sin, there are curses attached and demons put in charge of perpetuating those curses. There are areas of the heavens that are still under the curse because of cosmic evil and rebellion, just as there are aliens under that curse, many of whom even *look* cursed. They have lost their ability to procreate and rely solely on technology. They have lost all connection with the love energy and the spirit of God. There are many extraterrestrials in search of salvation and deliverance from these curses. Witchcraft is not limited to planet earth. Witchcraft is about rebellion, and it exists in the cosmos as well. This is the very reason it is prophesied in the book of Revelation that there will be a new heaven and a new earth. This will be witnessed when cosmic evil is obliterated.

The second death happens after you die physically, as your soul and spirit go back to the Creator to be judged. Those who fall into the categories mentioned in Revelation 21:8 are promised the second death, which is to cast to the lake of fire with all the satans and the fallen angels, the rebel extraterrestrials and cursed aliens.

> "Blessed are those who wash their robes. They will be permitted to enter through the gates of the city and eat the fruit from the tree of life. Outside are the dogs, those who practice magic arts, the sexually immoral, the murderers, the idolaters and everyone who loves and practices falsehood."
>
> (Revelation 22:14,15)

This is probably the worst fate for those who practice magic, as they will not be allowed into the Kingdom of Heaven, the new Jerusalem, The Heavenly City of Peace. They will not be allowed through the gates of heaven to eat of the tree of life. The New Jerusalem is literally out of this world. It exists in the upper heavens and will be brought down to the renewed earth, to become a beacon of light for all the cosmos, including all the faithful and the redeemed extraterrestrials as well.

> "The fear of the Lord is the beginning of Wisdom."
>
> (Proverbs 1:7, 9:10)

Angel Worship

The charge of angel-worship raised against the Jews, is decidedly unfounded. "Do not let anyone who delights in false humility and the worship of angels disqualify you. Such a person also goes into great detail about what they have seen; they are puffed up with idle notions by their unspiritual mind." (Colossians 2:18)

Chapter Four: Angel Protocol

Interestingly, we have come full circle, as the very same thing is happening today in New Age circles.

Angel worship was a characteristic of the Gnostics, not of the Jews. Christian Angelology may be described from the *Jewish Encyclopedia*: "The Coptic, the Abyssinian, the Greek, and the Roman churches adopted the invocation of angels in their liturgy; and since the tenth century the whole earth has been divided among the various tutelary angels and saints."[3]

Paul had probably the same Gnostic sect in mind to whom Celsus refers when he repeats the charge of Aristides. He tells of magical figures on which he found the seven angels inscribed: (1) Michael, with the figure of a lion; (2) Suriel, as a bull (*shor* or *tura* = Turiel; see Jerome on Hab. i. 14); (3) Raphael in a serpentine form; (4) Gabriel as an eagle; (5) Yalda Bahut with the countenance of a bear; (6) Erathaol as a dog; and (7) Onoel in the shape of an ass ("Apology," 14:4; see Origen, book 1, 26:6-34, 41). All of these are counterfeit angels. The rulers of the age, the fallen angels, essentially stole the names and perverted them into their image, creating a new form of angel worship, a form of magic to worship the fallen angels.

"And makes men as the fishes of the sea, as the creeping things, [that have] no ruler over them?" (Habakkuk 1:14) This is to say that all things on earth are ruled over by angels. The question remains, which angels? The Talmud says that not even a blade of grass can grow without an angel commanding it to grow. We know that God's angels play an integral role in maintaining creation. But there are fallen angels who oppose them and interfere with God's plans.

These fallen angels, called the seven archons, are also known as the rulers of this age and of the last age. It is to these fallen angels to whom Paul is referring, and of whom he speaks continually in his letters:

> "Yet among the mature we do impart wisdom, although it is not a wisdom of this age or of the rulers of this age, who are doomed to pass away. But we impart a secret and hidden wisdom of God, which God decreed before the ages for our glory. None of the rulers of this age understood this, for if they had, they would not have crucified the Lord of glory."
>
> (1 Corinthians 2:6-8)

But then the discernment is in who rules over them, and he goes on to say:

> "See to it that no one takes you captive through philosophy and empty deception, according to the tradition of men, according to the elementary principles of the world, rather than according to Christ. For in Him all the fullness of

Deity dwells in bodily form, and in Him you have been made complete, and <u>He is the head over all rule and authority</u>."

(Colossians 2: 8-10)

Being that Christ is the Head, He decides where His angels and extraterrestrials messengers go and what they do. As the Lord of Universe, He commands them and He orders their special assignments around the globe and around the universe. He is the CEO and they are His company. Here is the discernment: when a soul belongs to Christ, His angels are dispatched to you to fight your battles, guard your life, your family and possessions and perform all kinds of ministry. However, when a soul does not belong to Christ, but is open to the powers of the air, ruled by the god of this world, then it is his angels, the fallen angels and their mimicking demons, the spirit guides, who respond to your thoughts and answers prayers. They pretend to guard you, but in reality, they are holding you in bondage. The fallen angels and their demonic hierarchy are better than any Hollywood actor in creating the false image of pretending to be benevolent, light angels and spirit guides. These are probably the biggest deceptions of the New Age.

The worship of Angels is strictly forbidden, and considered idolatry, a sin that got the Israelites severely punished and ousted out of their land for over two thousand years.

The Jewish Encyclopedia comments on the prohibition of idolatry to the likeness of angels of the Ofanim and Cherubim. "He who slaughters an animal in the name of sun, moon, stars, and planets, or in the name of Michael, the great captain of the heavenly hosts, renders the same an offering to dead idols."[4] While today, New Agers aren't slaughtering animals, but they are making all kinds of offerings, prayers, affirmations and invocations to Michael. This is idolatry based on a false belief system. "Not as one who would first send his servant to a friend to ask for aid in his hour of need should man apply to Michael, or Gabriel, to intercede for him; *but he should turn immediately to God Himself*; for 'whosoever shall call on the name of the Lord shall be delivered.'"

Deliverance means freedom from bondage. Many New Agers are in bondage to fallen angels and they don't even realize it. They mistakenly call upon them, thinking they are the ones upstairs. "We war not against flesh and blood, but against powers, principalities, rulers of the darkness and spiritual wickedness in heavenly places." (Ephesians 6:12) The first and second heavens is where the fallen angels dwell.

I once spoke about going through deliverance to a New Age Healer, and she responded to me, 'what's that?' She is not alone, as there are many Christians who deny this power of God to liberate their minds, bodies and spirits while living in the flesh. Many Christians falsely believe that that can only happen in the afterlife. The Lord Jesus Christ is 'the' God of deliverance. The Holy Spirit is still delivering

Chapter Four: Angel Protocol

people today from all kinds of demonic strongholds, including the belief in counterfeit angels.

> "Then afterward I will pour out my spirit upon all mankind. Your sons and daughters shall prophesy, your old men shall dream dreams, your young men shall see visions; Even upon the servants and the handmaids, in those days, I will pour out my spirit. And I will work wonders in the heavens and on the earth, blood, fire, and columns of smoke; The sun will be turned to darkness, and the moon to blood, At the coming of the Day of the LORD, the great and terrible day. Then everyone shall be rescued <u>who calls on the name of the LORD Yahuah</u>;
>
> (Joel 3:1-5)

The following two verses reflects a pattern repetitive throughout the entire bible. When humans are visited by extraterrestrial angels of God, they prostrate themselves in awe and fear. They are immediately reprimanded and told not to do so. In the following verses, John is told twice that the angel or extraterrestrial messenger is equally a servant of God as is John, and that he must not worship the angel.

> "Then I fell down at his feet to worship him, but he said to me, "<u>*You must not do that*</u>! <u>I am a fellow servant with you and your brothers who hold to the testimony of Jesus</u>. Worship God." For the testimony of Jesus is the spirit of prophecy."
>
> (Revelation 19:10)

> "I, John, am the one who heard and saw these things. And when I had heard and seen them, I fell down to worship at the feet of the angel who had been showing them to me. But he said to me, "<u>*Do not do it*</u>! <u>I am a fellow servant with you and with your brothers' the prophets and of all who keep the words of this book. *Worship God*</u>!"
>
> (Revelation 22:8-9)

St. John is not alone; the Bible is full of angelic extraterrestrial contacts with human beings. From Jacob to Ezekiel to Joshua there are entirely too many to list here. In fact, Joshua was visited by one of the Lord's Commanders from His Celestial Army, known in the Bible as one of the hosts of the Lord. Joshua prostrated himself to the commander as well. However, because this was a commander, he was ordered to take off his shoes, because the Lord was declaring the place Gilgal, holy ground after delivering His people from the Egyptians. It is clear from the Hebrew words that this is no ordinary angel, but a high-ranking officer of the Lord's army. The words used are *sar, tzivah, Yahuah,* meaning: captain, commander or prince of the army of Yahuah. The commander did not tell Joshua to worship him, but declared that the place he stood was now holy ground because it was just delivered by the Lord and His army out of the hands of their enemies.

> "Once when Joshua was near Jericho, he looked up and saw a man standing before him with a drawn sword in his hand. Joshua went to him and said to him, 'Are you one of us, or one of our adversaries?' He replied, 'Neither; but as commander (captain) of the army of the Lord I have now come.' And Joshua fell on his face to the earth and worshiped, and he said to him, 'What do you command your servant, my lord?' The commander of the army of the Lord said to Joshua, 'Remove the sandals from your feet, for the place where you stand is holy.' And Joshua did so."
>
> (Joshua 5:13-15)

There is an important discernment here for those who have ears to hear in how to tell the Lord's holy angels from the counterfeit fallen angels. The counterfeit fallen angels thrive on the worship of ignorant humans. Historically they have encouraged worship, because they belong to the Office of Satan, whose agenda is to thwart humans from inheriting the Kingdom of Heaven. He thus perpetrates all kinds of idolatry on earth. An extraterrestrial angel who is faithful to the Kingdom of Heaven would never tolerate any human worship, and would immediately correct such ignorance, which they have done historically.

"Four keys are in the keeping of God exclusively and not in that of the angels: the keys of rain, of nourishment, of birth, and of resurrection" (Genesis 30:22; Deuteronomy 28:12) This is interpreted by rabbinical scholars as meant to *exclude* prayer to the angels. The invocations of angels occurring in the public worship were addressed to them as mediators, not as helpers. Many rabbinical authorities disapproved of such invocations based on the scriptures which forbids the worship of anything but God Himself.

We are told that after our translation into our immortal bodies, we will become like the angels, equal to them. Even now as in the past, they admit equality with us by saying they are <u>fellow</u> servants of God. Jesus said, "When the dead rise, (at the resurrection) people will neither marry nor be given in marriage; they will be like the angels in heaven." (Mark 12:25; Matthew 22:30) This means that we will be equal to the angels and extraterrestrials in heaven. We too will be immortal, consecrated interdimensional light beings serving God. This earthly life is a way for the Lord to separate the wheat from the chafe, to see who is worthy of the Kingdom of Heaven and who is not, which is why the mortal body is a temporary abode. Those who prove themselves worthy through faith in the Lord will receive their immortal bodies, just like the angels, and all will serve together.

Spiritual Fraud

Over the last two decades, there has been a rise in the popularity of angels. New Agers are constantly invoking them. Most people believe in the existence of angels, but so many distort who they really are, messengers who are on a mission from God. What has happened to many who have become despondent with religion and have lost, or never had a real live relationship with the Almighty, turn to New Age groups. Here angelology is a New Age lifestyle, they learn to worship the angels through invocation, prayer and divination through Angel Tarot Cards.

These angels who are being invoked are not God's Holy angels, but the counterfeit host of fallen angels and the demonic satans, the enemies of God. These demons will gladly answer any prayer to them, even those of the ignorant, as they *masquerade as angels*. While they can produce miracles and create seemingly benevolent outcomes, they are nevertheless keeping human kind from Christ. By deceiving mankind, the demons have won their souls in the end.

> "The coming of the lawless one(s) will be accompanied by the power(s) of Satan. He will use every kind of power, including miraculous signs, lying wonders, and every type of evil to deceive those who are dying, those who refused to love the truth that would save them."
>
> (2 Thessalonians 2:10)

They cleverly mix lies with some truth which hooks so many people into further deception. They tell humans what they want to hear, they beautify the language, and keep them ignorant. They *masquerade as ascended masters* as well as extraterrestrial commanders in chief. Again, archangels cannot be petitioned by humans, but only take orders directly from God. God's ministering angels act as intermediaries between humans and God, taking the prayers to God. The Lord of the Universe uses His angels to answer the prayers of humans. They work daily with the Holy Spirit on arranging circumstances and situations, by preparing the hearts and minds of humans to serve God through answering prayers. Can the counterfeit fallen angels answer prayers? You betcha! New Agers pray to a 'Divine Source', whom they do not address as the Lord Jesus Christ or the Heavenly Father, or even the Lord. In fact, many New Agers are goddess worshippers and speak of their god as *spirit*. This is not the Holy Spirit, but the spirit of the god of this world, who comes under the Office of Satan's principalities, princes and powers.

The only archangels that directly answer and channel to New Agers is Lucifer and his host of fallen angels. They masquerade as archangel Michael, archangel Gabriel, archangel Raphael, and so on. What New Agers are oblivious to is that Lucifer is a fallen archangel, and that he and his host of fallen angels all have the power and the intelligence to mimic and pose as archangels to those willing to invest in this delusion.

When humans worship angels, it is idolatry, and those prayers are answered by the fallen angels, who lay claim for that soul because they do not worship God. The fallen angels lull these misled humans into a false sense of security, causing them to think that benevolent beings are at their beck and call, but this is *spiritual fraud*.

There is a protocol for humans to worship and pray directly to God. Then they are assured the protection of God's holy angels, to the point of being at their side day and night, intervening without the human even having to pray for their support. There are numerous stories of unseen hands intervening in tragedies, protecting the innocent and the godly from danger. Sent by God the Creator, everyone has a guardian angel assigned to his soul. However, therein lies a battle, as many choose to ignore the promptings and leadings of their Holy Guardian Angel, and instead listen to the misguidance of their fallen angels and demons who are warring for their mind, body and soul.

The Creator God, or as Enoch puts it, *the Lord of the Spirits*, wants humans to worship and pray to Him and His Holy Spirit. Angels are then dispersed to humans to minister to them in all kinds of ways, and to answer these prayers to and for the glory of God. This is His promise: "For He will command His angels concerning you to guard you in all your ways; they will lift you up in their hands, so that you will not strike your foot against a stone." (Psalm 91:11,12) Many have experienced being 'lifted up' by an angel in the face of danger, or being pushed or pulled away from an oncoming car, or even a wild animal. Stories abound of the intervention of angels guarding humans from all kinds of harm.

The Son Superior to Angels

> "For to which of the angels did God ever say, "You are my Son; today I have become your Father"? Or again, "I will be his Father, and he will be my Son"? And again, when God brings his firstborn into the world, he says, "<u>Let all God's angels worship him</u>." "<u>Are not all Angels ministering spirits sent to serve those who will inherit salvation?</u>"
>
> (Hebrews 1:5,6, 14)

Chapter Four: Angel Protocol

All the angels are sent by the Lord to minister to humans. They all take orders from the Lord of Hosts. The angelic hierarchy is made up of the ministering angels, the ones working closest to humans, answering to the Archangels in charge of that group, who then in turn take orders from the Lord of Hosts. Prayers are answered through the ministry of angels. Prayers are spoken, recorded and brought up the hierarchy. When it takes a long time for prayers to be answered, it means there are battles in the heavens over that soul and over those issues. There is much legal ground that needs to be settled. For example, the state of the relationship of that particular soul with the Lord may give legal ground to Lucifer Satan and his fallen angels to keep that soul in bondage. This is the reason for many an unanswered prayer. Is the person living in sin? Are they giving their power away to idols? Are they in rebellion against God? Do they have a spirit of unbelief? Are they in bitterness? These are just a few of the issues that would cause the battle to go to Satan.

However, we are assured of the promise that if a person draws near to God, He will draw near to them. (James 4:8). He will then give His angels charge over you to keep you in all your ways. (Psalm 91) The promises of God are certain, if we put our trust in Him. If we put our trust in the seducing spirits of the New Age, those who exalt themselves and make all kinds of false claims of being ascended masters, ETs from a distant star, archangels and angels, we must think twice and discover that we have been taken, hook, line and sinker by the proverbial snake oil salesman. As I've said this before in this book series, and will reiterate it again, we can't go anywhere or complete any transaction in this world without showing our ID, so then why don't we demand the same kind of proof when we are approached by so called, ascended masters, ETs from a distant star, archangels and angels?

So, what is our litmus test? If a spirit cannot confess that Yeshua HaMashiach, (Jesus Christ) is Lord, then that pretty much identifies them as being part of the spiritual rebellion. Just because someone listens to the loudest voice in his head doesn't necessarily mean it is the right voice, or the voice of Truth and God. There must be more scrutiny, more discernment before humans give power away to seducing spirits, who are in an ongoing contest with the Creator and His Holy Angels over our bodies, minds and souls.

As we've already discussed in my chapter on the Celestial Hierarchy, there are several different orders or rankings of angels. The Bible references the following orders in the Old Testament: Elohim - "Godly Beings"; (Genesis 3:1, 38 occurrences) Cherubim with fiery swords (Genesis 3:24); Bene Elohim, "Sons of Godly Beings" (Genesis 6:2,4, 48:9; Job 1:6; 2:1;38:7); Erelim (Isaiah 33:7); Hashmallim (Ezekiel 1:4); Seraphim, the fiery ones (Isaiah 6:1-7); Ishim - "Manlike Beings", (Daniel 10:5); Malachim "Messengers" Angels (99 occurrences), all of which are different types of extra-terrestrial beings, all in service to the Kingdom of Heaven and thereby answering to its King, the Lord Jesus Christ.

Angels are Inferior to Humans

Believe it or not, angels, *malachim* were created to serve God and humans. However great the tendency to enlarge the number and the influence of the angels over our life there is, on the other hand, great stress laid upon the fact that the angels are in many respects inferior to man. Enoch, in 1 Enoch 15:2, intercedes on behalf of the angels, instead of having them intercede for him. None of the angels could see what he saw of God's glory, or learn the secrets of God as he knew them. Adam was to be worshiped by the angels as the image of God. Before his fall, Adam's place was within the precincts of God's own majesty, where the angels cannot stay. In the future, the righteous will again be placed nearer to God than the angels! Indeed, "they were inferior in intelligence to Adam, when names were given to all things" (Slavonic Book of Enoch, 24:3, Isaiah 9:27-38).

"The righteous rank above the angels" (Psalm 103:18; 1 Corinthians 6:3; Hebrews 2:5). "When Aaron in his vestments as high priest entered the Holy of Holies, the ministering angels fled in awe before him." "Israel is dearer to God than the angels; for Israel's praise is not confined to stated hours as that of the angels. Israel pronounces the name of God after two words: 'Hear, Israel'; the angels after three: 'Holy, Holy, Holy!' Israel begins the song of praise on earth and the angels in heaven chime in" (Psalm 104:1). The meaning of the word Israel, 'Yisra-el' in Hebrew, means to strive, struggle (Yisra) and to be ruled by God (El). "Angels minister to the saints" (Hebrews 1:13-14).

Redeemed human believers, the saints, will in the end *judge* the angels, not as humans but as transformed beings, immortal, as the Bible promises all those who inherit the Kingdom. The redeemed will be translated into incorporeal bodies, equal to the angels have now. Humans will be judging angels based on what they did or didn't do during their assignment as guardians, messengers and warriors on behalf of humanity, whom they have been assigned to 'harvest' for the Kingdom of Heaven. As Matthew 13:39 declared, that at the end of the age, the harvesters are the angels in the parables of the weeds.

> "...And He said, "The one who sows the good seed is the Son of Man, ...and the field is the world; and as for the good seed, these are the sons of the kingdom; and the tares are the sons of the evil one; and the enemy who sowed them is the devil, and the harvest is the end of the age; and *the reapers are angels*. So just as the tares are gathered up and burned with fire, so shall it be at the end of the age...."
> (Matthew 13:37-40)

Chapter Four: Angel Protocol

The redeemed, the ones the angels reap as a harvest at the end of this age, will be the group of humans that end up judging the angels. That's what the scripture implies:

"Do you not know that the saints will judge the world? And if you are to judge the world, are you not competent to judge trivial cases?" Do you not know that *we shall judge angels*?

(1 Corinthians 6:2)

"I declare to you, brothers and sisters, that flesh and blood cannot inherit the kingdom of God, nor does the perishable inherit the imperishable."

(1 Corinthians 15:50)

"Whoever sows to please their flesh, from the flesh will reap destruction; whoever sows to please the Spirit, from the Spirit will reap eternal life."

(Galatians 6:8)

The responsibilities of angels are to bring messages from one part of the universe to the other to God the Father and his Son Jesus the Christ and to execute their will. They are trained to watch humans who seek God and do this:

"He who dwells in the secret place of the Most High shall abide under the shadow of the Almighty."

(Psalm 91:1)

Dwelling in that secret place means praying and seeking the Lord, loving the Lord with all our heart, and all our soul. It means meditating on His word, His works, His creation. It means talking to Him. While there are many religions that do not practice direct communication with the Most High, because of belief in various saints, angels, priests as intermediaries, the Bible tells us that the only High Priest we need is the Lord Jesus Christ, who makes intercession for all believers, Who returns us back into communion with the Almighty Creator Father.

Some belief systems circumvent this direct communication by invoking angels and saints instead of bringing their prayers and petitions directly to God. While this variation may seem insignificant to believers, it is nonetheless an important detail when it comes to dealing with *legal ground* with respect to *who* and *what* is attaching to and guiding humans. This counterfeit is so subtle, and the laws of the scriptures are very clear in both the Old and the New Testaments, that we are to have no other gods before the Lord.

There are many different kinds of angels and extraterrestrials with all kinds of bodies, both physical, spiritual, inter-dimensional and elemental. All created beings have been given the ability to choose to obey the Law of God and His voice, or not to do so. When the angels sinned through disobedience, they were punished and bound into darkness. There have been many *stars who fell from heaven*, as fallen angels. (See, my chapter herein, *Stars Who Fell From Heaven*)

Ezekiel 28:11 is speaking of the leader of the fallen angels, Lucifer/Satan, the devil.

> "Moreover the word of the Lord came to me, saying, "Son of man, take up a lamentation for the king of Tyre, and say to him, 'Thus says the Lord GOD: You were the seal of perfection, full of wisdom and perfect in beauty. "'You were in Eden, the garden of God. Every precious stone was your covering: the sardius, topaz, and diamond, beryl, onyx, and jasper, sapphire, turquoise, and emerald with gold. The workmanship of your timbrels and pipes was prepared for you on the day you were created. "'<u>You were the anointed cherub who covers</u>. I established you. You were on the holy mountain of God. You walked back and forth in the midst of fiery stones. You were perfect in your ways from the day you were created, till iniquity was found in you.'"
>
> (Ezekiel 28:11-15)

Lucifer is being discussed in these verses because he was the one who walked in the midst of the stones of fire at the throne of God on his holy mountain. Verses 18 and 19 of the same chapter states that God will make Lucifer who became Satan into ashes and that he will be no more:

> "'. . . And I turned you to ashes upon the earth, in the sight of all who saw you. All who knew you among the peoples are astonished at you. You have become a horror, and shall be NO MORE forever.'"
>
> (Ezekiel 28:18-19)

This is the certainty that Lucifer, this leader of the fallen angels can be put to a final death (destroyed) even though he is made of spirit and created immortal.

Ezekiel 18:20 says that the soul that sins shall die. If this word *soul* can be translated as *life force*, then it relates to the angelic realm as well as the human realm. Only God can prevent humans from being resurrected into a new body containing that human's life force and only God can remove the life force from the bodies of angels.

Chapter Four: Angel Protocol

Lucifer convinced one-third of all the angelic beings to follow his rebellion (Revelation 12:3-4). Most of the rebel angels are now called the satans, or the adversaries, also known as demons or darker intelligences. Some inhabit alien bodies, while others have been incarcerated in a bottomless pit inside the inner earth until such time that the Creator Father will permit their release for their judgment:

> "But I want to remind you, though you once knew this, that the Lord, having saved the people out of the land of Egypt, afterward destroyed those who did not believe. <u>And the angels who did not keep their proper domain, but left their own abode</u>, He has reserved in everlasting chains under darkness for the judgment of the great day;"
>
> (Jude 1:5-6)

Judging Angels

> "Do you not know that we will judge angels? How much more the things of this life!"
>
> (1Corinthians 6:3)

Scripture teaches that the fallen angels will be judged by God (Isaiah 24:21-22; 2 Peter 2:4; Jude 1:6; Revelation 21:10). But Paul wrote that the saints will also judge angels? What does that mean? That we will judge angels? Clearly angels are above humans in their ability to go back and forth between heaven and earth. Their invisibility is superior to us in the flesh, they can manifest as human, look like any other person, blend right in and then disappear in a twinkling of the eye. They've been caught on camera coming to the aid of humans during accidents, and then disappear. There have been numerous testimonies of people being helped by the intervention of angels. I am one of them. They're interdimensional beings, humans, not so much. So why do we, the redeemed of the Lord, the harvest of God, are the ones who the angels gather up and present to the Lord of Hosts at the end of this present age, get to judge them? Let's discern.

> "This is how it will be at the end of the Age. <u>The Angels</u> will come to separate the wicked from the redeemed and throw the wicked into the Lake of Fire (burning furnace) where there is weeping and gnashing of teeth."
>
> (Matthew 13:49-50)

As I've shared previously, I've been saved multiple times through the intervention of my guardian angel and a band of angels. I even got a glimpse of an angel once putting me back in my bed, ever so gently, his arm was the size of a man's leg, he was a gentle giant. I've seen thirty-foot tall beings watching over the inter-coastal as the dawn was breaking, where I once lived in Indian Rocks Beach. I have heard the voice of my guardian angel multiple times. Once during a crisis, I wanted to give up and make the wrong choice, and my angel blocked me from that, which saved my marriage and family. So, I know first-hand how valuable my guardian angel is to me.

However, there were times when I would pray and hit a hard heaven, as I mentioned earlier. I learned this had to do with spiritual legal ground that I had to deal with before I could get my prayers answered. I think on these situations in my life, which I am grateful for God's salvation through the intervention expressed by my angels. But what about those angels who aren't doing enough for their assignments? What about those who perhaps didn't win the battles in the heavens over your life, who perhaps gave ground to the enemy and caused you pain and sorrow?

Unlike some of the fallen angels, Heaven's angels are not robots, you know, they are powerful celestial beings, but not all of them are equal in power, as we learned through the story of Daniel when he had to wait twenty-one days for the Angel Gabriel to interpret his dream to him, who was assigned by the Lord to do so, but was being blocked by the Prince of Persia, this was not the fleshly prince but the Fallen Angel-Archon. (See, Chapter One, *Clash of Two Kingdoms*, Section on *Angelic Warfare* herein). Even the Angel Gabriel was blocked from intervening in Daniel's life. So, the Lord ordered the Archangel Michael to engage in combat by holding back the Prince of Persia just long enough so the Angel Gabriel could get his message through. This is an important story giving us insight into how the angelic realm operates. Clearly, not all angels have the same abilities or power. So perhaps this could be one reason, we as the redeemed humans, would end up judging them, based on how they used their abilities especially when we cried out to the Lord for help, and specifically requested extra warrior angels to pull down strongholds.

> "For the weapons of our warfare are not of the flesh, <u>but mighty through God (through the agency of His Angels) to the pulling down of strongholds</u>."
> (2 Corinthians 10:4 – emphasis mine)

The angels are the ones dispatched to the pulling down of spiritual, Archonic, alien strongholds. They are the ones engaged in the battles over the issues, situation and conditions humans are faced with. This is the meaning of a 'clear heaven' versus a 'hard heaven.' The angels either gain victory by clearing the blocks i.e., strongholds, or lose battles based on the rules of engagement which is tied into spiritual legal ground, that allows Satan's realm to legally hold people in bondage. Of course, the more people pray, the more these prayers are lifted up to the courts of heavens, by our guardian angels and the Holy Spirit, the more angels are dispatched, because God is faithful to His own children on earth. More on this in Book Four: *Covenants*.

While we, in our present state cannot *order* the angels of Heaven, we can attract them through speaking God's Word, which they are obedient to and committed to serve. We can request them from the Lord of Hosts, to dispatch warrior angels to us, when we are in the midst of battles, we can also request ministering angels, when we are praying for the salvation of others. (See, Daniel 7:10; 1 Peter 1:12; Matthew 4:11; Hebrews 1:14) This is all within the Divine Will of God, and in accordance with His Living Word.

> "And of the angels He said, 'who makes his angels spirits, and his ministers a flame of fire.'"
>
> (Hebrews 1:7)

It's clear that what we can conclude from 1 Corinthians 6:3 passage is that God's redeemed children, will be given a higher position than the angels, if we will be collectively judging them. The Angels are sent to serve us. When the redeemed of the Lord are translated into their heavenly bodies, there will be a review of how the angels served us on earth.

> "Are not all angels ministering spirits sent to serve those who will inherit salvation?"
>
> (Hebrews 1:14)

> "The angel of the LORD encamps around those who fear him, and he delivers them."
>
> (Psalm 34:7)

> "For he will command his angels concerning you to guard you in all your ways;"
> (Psalm 91:11)

Coming next in this five-book series, in Book Four: *Covenants*, I detail how Psalm 91 is a covenant between the Lord and his faithful. It is a *conditional* agreement, which prefaces His covenant with the word, 'If', which leaves humans a choice. If we put our trust in the Most High God, then, and only then, will He put *His Angels* in charge of us, to keep us in all of our ways. This is an important discernment, because those who are in rebellion to the Lord, and who practice idolatry and worship other gods, will not get the Lord's Angels, but the god of this world, who is Satan's fallen angels to misguide them away from the Truth. We are created in God's image, and our redemption and salvation from the kingdom of darkness, is through Jesus Christ alone. Not the Christian religion, but through a personal relationship with the Messiah-King. (Galatians 3:13; 1 Peter 2:9; Luke 1:68; Ephesians 1:7).

> "For as much then as the children are partakers of flesh and blood, He (Jesus Christ) also Himself likewise took part of the same; that through death He might destroy Him that had the power of death, that is, the devil (Satan); And deliver them who through fear of death were all their lifetime subject to bondage. For truly He took not on him the nature of angels; but He took on Him the seed of Abraham."
> (Hebrews 2:14-16-AKV)

Herein lies the Spiritual Wisdom: Christ has been exalted above all the angels which seems reasonable that those who are in Him and made in His likeness (Romans 8:29; 1 Corinthians 15:49; Ephesians 4:24; 1 John 3:2) will share in His authority, including His authority over the angels:

> "...and the surpassing greatness of His power to us who believe. He displayed this power in the working of His mighty strength, which He exerted in Christ when He raised Him from the dead and seated Him (Jesus) at His right hand (Yahuah) in the heavenly realms, far above all rule and authority, power and dominion (the angelic realms), and every name that is named, not only in this age, but also in the one to come." And God (Yahuah) put everything under His feet (Jesus) and made Him head over everything for the church, which is His body, the fullness of Him who fills all in all.
> (Ephesians 1:19-23-Berean Study Bible, emphasis mine)

Additionally, we know that the Greek word for "judge," *krino*, also means "to rule or govern." This strongly indicates that we will have authority to rule over the angels. Most likely, the meaning of 1 Corinthians 6:3 is that believers in heaven will take part in the judgment of the extraterrestrials and how they interacted on earth during the times of man, and during the real *Star Wars* battle over the earth. For the promises of God, is that the redeemed will assist the Lord in judging the twelve tribes of Israel as well.

> "Jesus said to them, "Truly I tell you, at the renewal of all things, when the Son of Man sits on his glorious throne, you who have followed me will also sit on twelve thrones, judging the twelve tribes of Israel."
> (Matthew 19:28)

Chapter Four: Angel Protocol

"if we endure, we will also reign with him. If we disown him, he will also disown us;"

(2 Timothy 2:12)

"I saw thrones on which were seated those who had been given authority to judge. And I saw the souls of those who had been beheaded because of their testimony about Jesus and because of the word of God. They had not worshiped the beast or its image and had not received its mark on their foreheads or their hands. They came to life and reigned with Christ a thousand years."

(Revelation 20:4)

Let's not forget the beginning of His-Story, our history, which I laid out in Book One of *Who's Who in The Cosmic Zoo?* in my section, *From Adam's Failure to the Second Adam's Victory,* that it was God's intention all along for humans to rule the earth. When He returns and when our redemption is complete, we are promised to be restored into the kings and priests He intended us to be, and share in His Kingdom with Him, which includes judging the extraterrestrial angels along with him and how they behaved towards us on earth. Did they do everything they could in their supernatural powers for us, when we cried out to the Lord for help? Did they come to our aid when we were in trouble? Or were they negligent in their duties and service to God's creation? These are just a few issues we may face when we are called to reign with Christ in the New Age to come. How will we know what they did or didn't do? Everything is recorded by the Recording Angels, and every word is accounted for. (See, Matthew 12:36)

Another thing, we must keep in mind, is that when one third of heaven's angels rebelled and followed Lucifer in His rebellion to the Creator, two thirds of heaven's extraterrestrial angels remained faithful. Did they change over time? Was there mutiny within their ranks? Did they play both sides? Did they succeed in their responsibilities to save others? Remember the faithful angels witnessed first-hand the power of God, and saw what the Lord did to the fallen angels. This is why the scripture says, "the fear of the Lord is the beginning of Wisdom." (See, Proverbs 1:7: 9:10; Psalm 111:10) These angels knew full well, that if they were disobedient, they too would be punished for misleading God's children.

Why Angels Will Be Judged by Man

He said, 'Look! The Lord is coming with thousands and thousands of His holy ones, the angels. He will judge everyone. He will punish all wicked people (this includes the angels who have sinned) for all the wicked things that they have done. The Lord will punish these wicked people for all the hard words that they have ever spoken about him' (1 Enoch 15).

The angels are busy doing a lot, but they do not know everything. They look for the day when the elected saints will teach them the deep things of God. They are learning from humans through serving and ministering to us. 1 Peter 1:12 tells us that they want to understand these things, but they do not even understand why they are doing what they are doing. Many of them fear the Lord and obey Him because they do not want to be punished. When Proverbs 9:10 tells us, 'the fear of the Lord is the beginning of all Wisdom,' this applies to both humans and angels. The angels witnessed the punishment of many of their fallen comrades and know that if they disobey the Lord too, something similar will happen to them. Humans, however, aren't always that quick on the uptake, and are more inclined to explain away supernatural events in scientific terms, such as earth changes, mega storms and other 'acts of Nature'.

> "It was revealed to them that they were not serving themselves but you in regard to the things that have now been announced to you by those who brought you the good news through the Holy Spirit sent from heaven. <u>These are things that even the angels desire to look into</u>." The angels were not promised to rule in the Kingdom, the world to come or to be sons of God, "<u>And furthermore, it is not angels who will control the future world we are talking about</u>."
>
> (Hebrews 2:5).

There will be a day that even the angelic world will be examined to see if they have obeyed the laws of God. Why do angels need to be judged? Because at least one third of them have sinned and deserve death. Who will do this judging? Those who have entered into the Kingdom of God as spirit born children of God. Why will the saints end up judging the angels? Because all of their deeds and misdeeds will be exposed.

> "For now we see through a glass, darkly; but then we will see face to face: now I know in part; but then shall I know even as also I am known."
>
> (1 Corinthians 13:12)

In our present state, most of us do not see or understand the workings of the spirit realms and are therefore susceptible to all kinds of delusions, deceptions and confusions. When we see face to face, we will know the truth and we will be able to connect the dots of the spiritual behavior of the angels with the events of our lives and whether or not they handled matters correctly. Otherwise, why would the believers be called upon to judge them? Many angels are working towards receiving a higher reward, such as a heavenly promotion or even taking what they have learned from us and teaching it to others. There are other worlds and planets in the cosmos, over which the angels will be given governorship, if they prove themselves worthy through their earth ministries. Remember, many of these angels, or messengers, are extraterrestrials on assignment.

Angels Evolve Through Human Evolution

Each time a human is delivered from the darkness, an angel who works from the Office of Christ gets to keep his wings, or more appropriately is rewarded in heaven and gets to keep his job. There are literally hundreds of thousands of heavenly hosts and extraterrestrials whose love of God is expressed by serving and praising Him all day long. Remember that it is only the realm of angels in the spheres of the Celestial Hierarchy that work closely and directly with the world of us humans.

The upper dimensions of the Office of Christ includes, powers, principalities, dominions, archangels, cherubim, ophanim and seraphim, who do not get close to humans, as do the realm of angels. The angels job is to directly minister to us in all kinds of capacities. They are capable of taking on fleshly human form, of appearing in dangerous situations and helping us out of difficulty, only to disappear after we had been saved. The angels then report back up the ranks to the Office of Christ.

These angels carry the prayers of humans to God. The multiverse of the Celestial Hierarchy finds a way to answer even the toughest of prayers when the human prays directly to the Lord, and does not worship other gods or the angels. The Lord sends His ministering angels and authorizes miracles in the lives of humans. I will reiterate again, it is only through the authority of the Lord Jesus Christ and the Father in Heaven, that any kind of holy angel is dispatched to humans, whether that be healing angels, ministering angels, guardians, or warrior angels. He alone is the Lord of the Hosts of Heaven.

Likewise, the counterfeit angels are dispatched throughout the world through the Office of Satan and his principalities, powers and dominions. These dark angels or demonic influences war against the angels from the Office of Christ. It is through this cosmic warfare that evolution is taking place, both through earthly humans and angels or extraterrestrial humans. It is the darkness that defines the light, and the truth that exposes the deceptions.

Philo on Angels

Philo Judaeus of Alexandria, aka Yedidia, used allegory to fuse and harmonize Greek philosophy and Judaism. His method followed the practices of both Jewish exegesis and Stoic philosophy. His work was not widely accepted. "The sophists of literalness," as he calls them, "opened their eyes superciliously" when he explained to them the marvels of his exegesis. The goal of Biblical exegesis is to explore the meaning of the text which then leads to discovering its significance or relevance. Philo's works were enthusiastically received by the Early Christians.

Philo was inclined to accept the existence of angels as a fact far more than his allegorical system would lead one to suspect. He was prompted to do so through the example of the Stoics: "Beings whom other philosophers called demons, Moses usually called them angels"; they are "souls hovering in the air"; "some have descended into bodies; others have not thought fit to approach any part of the earth; and these, hallowed and surrounded by the ministrations of the Father, the Creator employs as assistants and ministers for the care of the mortals." "They report the injunctions of the Father to His children, and the necessities of the children to the Father. And, with reference to this, Holy Scripture represents them as 'ascending and descending.' . . . Not God, but we mortals are in need of a mediator and intercessor."[5]

"Souls, demons, and angels are things differing in name, but identical in reality. Yet, as men speak of God and of evil demons and of good and evil souls, so they speak of angels, calling them ambassadors of man to God and of God to man; and they are holy because of this blameless and honorable office. Others, on the contrary, are profane and unworthy, as is seen in Psalm 78:49 "He unleashed against them his hot anger, his wrath, indignation and hostility--a band of destroying angels."

It's important to note that the Greek word *daemon*, which is where we get the word *demon*, literally translates to *intelligences*. Perhaps Philo was onto something when he called out Moses apparent lack of discernment in calling them angels. If Moses was fooled by the vagaries between angels and demons, how much more can we humans, particularly New Agers, who seek after such supernatural and paranormal experiences, be deceived? We are told that the spirits of the Nephilim had no place to go when they died. Humans have a place in the afterlife.

There are dimensions inside the earth which we know as Hades (Hell), Paradise (Abraham's Bosom) and God's Holy fire (see my chapter in Book Two on *What Happens When You Die* for more details). We are also told that angels have their place, as Jude 5,6 tells us that some are being held in a prison before the judgment. Those who were not captured in the last Celestial War, however, are free to move through air. But the Nephilim, as the rejects, have no place, and are bound to the earth to hover in the air as evil spirits tormenting humans until the day of judgment.

> "But now the giants who are born from the [union of] the spirits and the flesh shall be called evil spirits upon the earth, because their dwelling shall be upon the earth and inside the earth. Evil spirits have come out of their bodies. Because from the day that they were created from the sons of God

they became Watchers: their first origin is the spiritual foundation. They will become evil upon the earth and shall be called evil spirits. The dwelling of the spiritual beings of heaven is heaven; but the dwelling of the spirits of the earth, which are born upon the earth, is in the earth."

(1 Enoch 15:8-10)

There is a subtle difference between the evil spirits, who are demonic, and the fallen angels, who are demonic in nature. Fallen angels are rebel extraterrestrials who have teamed up with the Office of Satan in the skies. Jesus gave all of His believers the authority to cast out demons and evils spirits, but He said nothing about fallen angels. The fallen angels are the principalities and powers that rule the darkness, who cause the spiritual wickedness in the atmosphere, spoken of in Ephesians 6:11-18. This is why we are told to put on the full armor of God against these dark forces. In doing so, we allow the Lord and His heavenly hosts of extraterrestrial angels to fight our battles for us in the other realms.

The Nephilim spirits and demons may masquerade as angels of light, as spirit guides and as the spirits of the deceased, but these are hardly angels. They are the ghosts that people often see hanging around and are described as being stuck between dimensions. While they have the ability to take on and mimic the looks and personality of deceased humans, this is nothing but a ruse and a deception, the purpose of which is to seduce humans into fascination with the paranormal, with mediums contacting the dead, and with haunted houses. These are the spirits that come through mediums in séances. These stuck Nephilim spirits have nothing better to do than to deceive humans and literally send them off on wild goose chases. Yes, the spirit realm is real and any spirit can masquerade as an angel, but not all are God's angels. You must have the light of the Holy Spirit in you in order to discern the truth.

Philo, however, calls angels (God's extraterrestrial messengers) *logoi*, "words," or "intellects".[7] "The LORD merely spoke, and the heavens were created. He breathed the word, and all the stars (heavenly hosts) were born." (Psalm 33:6) They are also called "God's own powers with whom the Father of the Universe consulted when saying: 'Let us make man in our image.' To them He gave the mortal part of our soul to form by imitating His art when He shaped the rational principle in us". Angels are the priests in the heavenly temple. And in the same manner as the rabbis speak of Michael/Metatron as the captain of the heavenly host, and the high priest Melchizedek, that offers sacrifice in the upper temple, and are the charioteers of God.

Philo says: "The Father, the Creator of the universe, gave to the archangel and most ancient *logos* ["word"] the privilege of standing on the confines, separating the creature from the Creator, and of interceding between the immortal God and the mortal, as ambassador sent by the ruler to the subject.[8] "I stood between the Lord and you,' being neither uncreated nor created, but between the two, pledge and security to the Creator and to the creature, a hope that the merciful God would not despise His work" (Deuteronomy 5:5)

Philo calls the archangels "the charioteer of the powers"; and Metatron with his seventy-two names, is called "the great archangel of many names".[9] There is a great archangel known as Angel Methraton or Metatron, who is the vice-gerent and representative of *El Shaddai*, (God Almighty) who is also called the Prince of Countenances (or the Prince of the Face), and the right hand masculine Cherub of the Ark, as Sandalphon is the left and feminine. Metatron has also been linked with Enoch. However, the high priest Melchizedek, is said to be the Lord Jesus Christ, who is the final sacrifice and intercessor between humans and the Almighty Father.

Ranking: Archangels or Angels?

Scripture is very specific when describing heavenly beings. Many have misinterpreted the phrase, 'an angel of the Lord', as a reference to God Himself. Hebrew is a very specific language however. We have passages that specifically say 'an angel of the Lord' visited, or 'one of the heavenly hosts', or even 'the commander of the Lord' as in Joshua. But only three scriptures in the entire Bible specifically make reference to an archangel. As I've mentioned earlier, archangels are princes. They are put in charge of nations and planetary spheres. They have armies amassed under them. They typically do not deal directly with individual humans.

There is no description of what Archangels look like in the Bible. The only Archangel mentioned specifically by name is Michael:

> "Yet Michael the archangel, when contending with the devil he disputed about the body of Moses, durst not bring against him a railing accusation, but said, The Lord Yahuah rebuke thee."
>
> (Jude 9)

Interesting that not even the great Archangel Michael rebuked Satan, but in some type of respectful 'archangel protocol' said, 'the Lord Yahuah rebuke thee'.

> "At that time Michael, the archangel (in Hebrew, the great prince, 'hasar hag-adol') who stands guard over your nation, will arise. There will be a time of distress such as has not happened from the beginning of nations until then. But at that time your people--everyone whose name is found written in the book--will be delivered."
>
> (Daniel 12:1)

Chapter Four: Angel Protocol

Here, we are told by the prophet Daniel that the great prince archangel Michael guards the nation of Israel. Come, let us reason together, and think about this, why would this great prince answer the prayers of New Agers who invoke him, when many of them are not only ignorant of who archangel Michael is to the Lord, but also harbor deep resentment towards Jews? I am certain the great prince Michael is chagrined at hearing their prayers and invocations, especially as they are being answered by counterfeit fallen angels.

> "For the Lord himself shall descend from heaven with a shout, <u>with the voice of the Archangel</u>, and with the trump of God: and the dead in Christ shall rise first:"
>
> (1 Thessalonians 4:16)

While this scripture doesn't specifically name which archangel's voice will give the shout to raise the dead in Christ, the scripture tells us that it is one of the Lord's princes, or archangels who will initiate the rapture.

Many misinterpret the passages of Luke 1: 26-36, that of an angel appearing to Mary to announce the birth of the child Jesus to her, as a reference to the archangel Gabriel. Nowhere does the scripture specify which angel or name this angel as an archangel, or *prince* in Hebrew. It specifically uses the word angel, which in Greek is 'angelos'. If the New Testament, written in Greek, meant to say archangel, it would have used the word, 'archistratege' meaning 'chief general', but it did not. My point is that an angel from the 'office of the Archangel Prince Chief Gabriel' was sent as a 'messenger', (the meaning of the Greek word, 'angelos') to deliver the good news to Mary. Notice that the name Gabriel is only mentioned once, to identify who the angel belonged to and or from whom he was dispatched. In the rest of the dialogue, the name of the angel is never repeated, but only referred to as 'the angel' or in Greek, 'the messenger' (angelos).

> "And in the sixth month <u>the angel Gabriel</u> was sent from God to a city of Galilee, named Nazareth, to a virgin espoused to a man whose name was Joseph, of the house of David; and the virgin's name was Mary. <u>And the angel came in to her</u>, and said, 'Hail, you that are highly favored, the Lord is with you: blessed are you among women.' And when she saw him, she was troubled at his saying, and cast in her mind what manner of salutation this should be. <u>And the angel said to her</u>, 'Fear not, Mary: for you have found favor with God. And, behold, you shall conceive in your womb, and bring forth a son, and shall call his name JESUS. He shall be great, and shall be called the Son of the Highest: and the Lord God shall give to him the throne of his father David: And he shall reign

over the house of Jacob forever; and of his kingdom there shall be no end.' Then said Mary <u>to the angel</u>, 'How shall this be, seeing I know not a man?' <u>And the angel answered</u> and said to her, 'The Holy Ghost shall come on you, and the power of the Highest shall overshadow you: therefore, also that holy thing which shall be born of you shall be called the Son of God. And, behold, your cousin Elisabeth, she has also conceived a son in her old age: and this is the sixth month with her, who was called barren. For with God nothing shall be impossible.' And Mary said, 'Behold the handmaid of the Lord; be it to me according to your word.' <u>And the angel departed from her</u>.

(Luke 1: 26-38, KJV)

As you can see, this was <u>not</u> the archangel Gabriel that visited Mary, but one of his messengers. As I've mentioned already, archangels are Princes and Chiefs, each with hundreds of thousands of hosts, or armies of lower ranking angles, warrior angels, ministering angels, and messenger angels working under them. As far as the celestial government goes, archangels each hold a special office. The angel of Gabriel that visited Mary was not the 'archangel' but one of his messengers. I realize that some may argue this, because Mary was carrying the Christ child, but if the scripture specifically said, 'the archangel Gabriel' as it did to describe the 'archangel Michael' twice, then that would be open to discussion, but this is not the case. Besides, everything about the birth of Jesus was humble, including his mother. She was chosen for her humility in the first place!! She was also a direct bloodline descendant of King David. Her genetics are a perfect match for Yeshua, who came with the Divine Blood of Yahuah, born for a divine purpose to be the final Lamb of God.

The Angel of the Lord

There are numerous scriptures in the Old Testament Bible which refer to Divine and supernatural intervention by visitations, describing 'an angel of the Lord' or 'the angel of Yahuah'. Many have misinterpreted these scriptures to name Jesus Christ. First, let me start off by saying that Jesus Christ is not and has never been an angel. Angels are created beings. Christ is a Creator, and while He does show up throughout the Old Testament, He is not described as an 'an angel of the Lord'. Secondly, Hebrew is a very specific language, as I've already mentioned throughout this book series. The language will specifically describe singular, plural, masculine or feminine in its lexicon. We know that the word for angel in Hebrew is *malach* or plural, *malachim*.

In the book, *Shocked by the Bible*, Joe Kovacs writes in his chapter, *"God The Father" is Not In The Old Testament"* that the man that wrestled with Jacob, was the Lord Jesus Christ.[10]

Chapter Four: Angel Protocol

I disagree with Kovacs on his point that the very words, 'God the Father' are not in the Old Testament. This is another classic case of knowledge being lost in mistranslations, or misunderstanding of Biblical Hebrew. In 2 Kings 18:2, the word, 'Abiyah' literally is translated to 'Yahuah the father,' or 'Yahuah is my father.' Every single translation from the Hebrew, translates Yahuah (YHVH) as LORD and God, which 'Abiyah' in Hebrew means, 'The LORD Yahuah God is my father'. Again, found in a parallel passage in 2 Chronicles 29:1. Abbah is Father in Hebrew. Abraham was originally Abram or Avram, who is known as the Father of the Nations, and the Father of Jews. Abiyah is Father God or God the Father.

It was a man with whom Jacob wrestled. Nothing in any of the verses implies this being who got down and dirty on the ground and physically wrestled with Jacob to the point of causing him to limp, was the Lord Jesus Christ, but an angel, a flesh and blood extraterrestrial messenger son of God. The Hebrew word used in this text is Elohim, which in every English translation is 'God'. However, Elohim is plural for the gods or sons of God, or more specifically, the 'Els', from the Father root, 'Elyon' or El Shaddai, which means the Almighty Creator. One of the Elohim, a 'son' of El Shaddai, visited Jacob, a strong man who had the power to bless him and change his name. It was the Elohim who first created Adam and Eve. The word Elohim first shows up in Genesis 1:26. Where the entire sentence uses the plural participles and plural pronouns. This was not Yahuah, but the 'Els', one of the gods or sons of God, also known as angels.

Some people believe that Jesus Christ shows up mysteriously multiple times as an angel in the Old Testament, known as a 'Christophany'. I will show you this is indeed the case in the book of Daniel. Remember, Jesus Christ is a Creator, not a created being, as are the angels and the ET messengers. In Jacob's case, I question why He would come out of heaven just to get down and dirty on the ground and wrestle it out with Jacob? This is where language matters. Many believe this because the scripture says Jacob's name was changed to Israel, meaning he wrestled with God and prevailed. But this doesn't necessarily mean it was *the* God, Jesus Christ.

The man described in Genesis 32 who wrestled with Jacob was no ordinary man, but an extraterrestrial. He clearly did not know Jacob's name, nor was he willing to tell Jacob his name when asked. He then gave him a new name, based on the encounter. The man still refused to tell Jacob his name, but the Hebrew records it as 'Elohim' meaning the man was one of the ELs. (See, my chapter, 'ELs' in Book One of *Who's Who in the Cosmic Zoo?*) One has to wonder, what was he hiding? The Bible tells us that the Lord knows every one of us by name. He even knows how many hairs we have on our head. The Lord would have known it was Jacob, because He created him. When the Lord appears in the Old and New Testament, He uses many names to describe the many sides of Him, but He never once evades the question about His name. (See my chapter, *Who Are the Biblical Gods,* in Book Two: *Who is God?*).[12]

"Then Jacob was left alone, and a man wrestled with him until daybreak. When he saw that he had not prevailed against him, he touched the socket of his thigh; so, the socket of Jacob's thigh was dislocated while he wrestled with him. Then he said, "Let me go, for the dawn is breaking." But he said, "I will not let you go unless you bless me." So, he said to him, "What is your name?" And he said, "Jacob." He said, "Your name shall no longer be Jacob, but Israel; for you have striven with God (Elohim) and with men and have prevailed." Then Jacob asked him and said, "Please tell me your name." But he said, "Why is it that you ask my name?" And he blessed him there. So, Jacob named the place Peniel, for *he said*, "I have seen God (Elohim) face to face, yet my life has been preserved." Now the sun rose upon him just as he crossed over Penuel, and he was limping on his thigh. Therefore, to this day the sons of Israel do not eat the sinew of the hip which is on the socket of the thigh, because he touched the socket of Jacob's thigh in the sinew of the hip."

(Genesis 32:24-32)

Angels work as intermediaries, messengers, like someone in our world who introduces the President before his speeches. This office is also part of angel protocol. In the case of Exodus 3, an angel of the Lord appears in a flame of fire to Moses, which leads him to check out this strange phenomenon, a burning bush that does not burn up. Moses approaches the bush and instead of speaking to the angel who was used to attract attention, he finds himself face to face with Yahuah. The angel of the Lord is not Jesus Christ, as Kovacs writes.

The scripture reveals the name of God as Yahuah. In fact, the Hebrew words, 'angel of the Lord' is 'malach Yahuah' which literally translates as Yahuah's messenger. However, when the Lord identifies Himself to Moses, He uses the word, 'Elohei' meaning 'god of', and then lists Abraham, Isaac and Jacob, and then concludes the sentence with the plural, Elohim. Yahuah is the Father of the Elohim, He is the 'El' in Elohim. While many may argue that Elohim is just another name for Yahuah, <u>it is plural</u>. In Hebrew, anything with the suffix 'im' indicates plurality, distinguishing the name Yahuah from the noun, Elohim, which translates as 'gods.'

Yahuah, is the Elyon, El Shaddai, the Almighty Creator of all the gods. But Moses is having an encounter with one God, not two, who is identifying Himself to Moses, and then when Moses asks Him who does He tell the Israelites He spoke to? The Lord answers him, with another name of God, which is 'Ehyeh, Asher, Ehyeh', I AM WHO (THAT) I AM. Then the Lord tells Moses, just tell them, 'Ehyeh' sent you. Meaning, 'I AM'. So much gets lost in translation.

Chapter Four: Angel Protocol

"There the *angel of the Lord* appeared to him in flames of fire from within a bush. Moses saw that though the bush was on fire it did not burn up. So, Moses thought, "I will go over and see this strange sight—why the bush does not burn up." When the Lord saw that he had gone over to look, God called to him from within the bush, "Moses! Moses!" And Moses said, "Here I am."

"Do not come any closer," God said. "Take off your sandals, for the place where you are standing is holy ground." Then he said, "I am the God of your father, the God of Abraham, the God of Isaac and the God of Jacob." At this, Moses hid his face, because he was afraid to look at God. (v. 2-6)

"And Moses said unto God Behold when I come unto the children of Israel and shall say unto them The God of your fathers hath sent me unto you and they shall say to me What is his name what shall I say unto them and God said unto Moses I AM THAT I AM and he said Thus shalt thou say unto the children of Israel I AM hath sent me unto you." (v.14,15)

Now, I can agree with Kovacs that when Moses was told to tell the children of Israel that I AM THAT I AM sent him, that this was a *Christophany* of Jesus Christ. In the Revelation of the New Testament, Jesus claims the name I AM. He also told the Jews in John 8 that 'before Abraham was, I AM,' for which they nearly stoned him. Yeshua HaMashiach was mentioned in Genesis 3:15 in the prophesy of the one who will crush the head of the serpent. In Genesis 1, He was the Word who became flesh. I agree that Jesus Christ was there before He was born as a flesh and blood man, died, was resurrected, and will always be. As Revelation 22:3 says, "I AM the Alpha and Omega, the beginning and the end, the first and the last." Be that as it may, He is not the angel of the Lord, but the very Lord of Hosts who commands the angels to do His bidding.

The Old Testament uses the Hebrew name Yahuah. Jesus said, "I and the Father are one, and no man comes to the Father except through me." This is an age-old mystery, for if they are one and the same, then how could Christ be the intercessor between God and man? There is clearly a higher deity, the Almighty Creator who has given His authority to Christ to be the Lord of lords and King of kings. To whom did Jesus pray? Who was He talking to when He said, Father? In my opinion, this is Yahuah. Yahuah is the Father of Yeshua, and they are one, in both spirit and in genetics, or bloodline. Jesus' blood had to be Yahuah's divine blood in Him, in order to accomplish His unique mission of being the final Lamb of God.

There are over 100 scriptures that include the words, 'the angel of the Lord', too many to list here. If we look at just one more, we can discover the protocol of the angel of the Lord as one preceding the voice of the Lord Himself, or to speak as a 'messenger' on behalf of the Lord. All of the scriptures are very specific, differentiating between the messenger and the originator of the message, the Lord Himself, by using different Hebrew words. Again, so much has been lost in translation. When people read the Bible, they are usually reading translations from the King James English version. The words for God, and the words for the angels, are obscured and their original specific meaning delineating exactly *who* is speaking, has been lost.

In the Genesis story of Abraham in chapter 22, Abraham hears a voice whom he *assumes* is the Lord, telling him to sacrifice his son Isaac. Remember the Lord is Yahuah. The Elohim is plural for gods or the sons of God. The voice Abraham first heard came from the Ha-Elohim, who tested Abraham. I have heard some people even say that this was Satan, which very well could have been, because Satan is the tempter, and the Lord does not tempt. Satan is also known as the counterfeit god. He pretends to be god, and it is possible that the biblical writer of Genesis did not know the difference between the two. As the scripture says nothing about Satan, it does use the words, *VeHa-Elohim Nisah* which literally translates to 'and the gods tested Abraham.'

After Abraham stacks up the wood on his donkey, he along with two men and his son Isaac head towards Mount Moriah to perform a sacrifice. All the while young Isaac is thinking they will be sacrificing an animal, as he has no idea he is the one to be offered into the fire. They arrive and Abraham begins to perform the deed, when an *angel of the Lord*, specifically, the words, *malach Yahuah* speaks to him, not once, but twice. The angel tells Abraham not to harm his son, and then delivers a message from Yahuah to Abraham.

Now doesn't it strike contradictory, as the Lord Yahuah Himself has decreed to Israel that sacrificing children in the fire is forbidden. So why would He, the Lord Yahuah, tempt or test Abraham in this matter?

> "For when you offer your gifts, when you make your sons to pass through the fire, you pollute yourselves with all your idols, even to this day: and shall I be inquired of by you, O house of Israel? As I live, said the Lord GOD, I will not be inquired of by you."
>
> (Ezekiel 20:31)

> "And you shall not let any of your children pass through the fire to Moloch, neither shall you profane the name of your God: I am the LORD."
>
> (Leviticus 18:21)

The answer is that it was <u>not</u> the Lord Yahuah who tested Abraham, but one of the gods of the Elohim. In the Hebrew, we have two distinct voices here, which are often confused as being the same voice, or the same god, and this is obviously not true. The voice of the Elohim is recorded as a plurality, while the voice of the angel of the Lord Yahuah is delivering a message from Yahuah. But Yahuah Himself does not speak at all during this entire episode. As the angel of Yahuah saves Isaac from being killed, a ram is discovered caught in the bush thistles, which is then sacrificed in Isaac's stead. Then Abraham declares the place, *Yahuah Yireh*, which means, Yahuah provides.

While God created a multitude of angels, there is one who stands out from all the rest of the *Malachim* angels as a King stands above his subjects. This is the '*King of Angels*', in Hebrew called, *Malakh Adonai*, or the '*Angel of the Lord*.' Unlike other angels who function as emissaries of God, *Malakh Adonai* is the representation, or very message of God Himself. His Word or Voice is *one* with the Person of the Godhead, just as the Spirit of God is *one* with Person of God.

The Hebrew words *Malakh Adonai*, is distinctly different than *malakh Yahuah*. It is unique in the sense that it means Lord of the Angels, or Angel of the Lord even though both words are used interchangeably throughout the Hebrew Bible. Remember the scriptures that King David wrote: "The LORD says to my lord: "Sit at my right hand until I make your enemies a footstool for your feet." (Psalm 110:1) The Hebrew words are *Yahuah Adonai*, which represents the second person of the Godhead, the firstborn son, Yeshua.

The words, *King of the Angels*, or *Angel of the Lord*, is named in approximately fifty scriptures in the Old Testament. He is first mentioned in Genesis 16:7-13, where He is called God. After He spoke with Hagar in the desert, she called him "The LORD" (Yahuah) and identified Him as El-Roi, the god who sees me in verse 13. He later appeared to Moses in the burning bush and identified himself as Yahuah, the God of Abraham, Isaac and Jacob. (Exodus 3:2); He led Elijah to Mt. Horeb (1 Kings 19); He commanded David to build the altar which later became the altar of the Holy Temple (1 Chronicles 21:18), and He mentioned in Psalm 34 and 35 as the Angel of Lord.

"The *angel of the Lord* (Yahuah) encamps around those who fear him, and he delivers them."

(Psalm 34:7)

In light of all this, we can be sure that when the words *Malakh Adonai* show up in scripture, it is the distinct manifestation of the LORD Himself. Isaiah the prophet called Him, the 'Angel of His Face.' (Isaiah 63:9) Being that Yeshua is the 'radiance of the glory of God and the exact imprint of His nature, who upholds the universe by the Word of His Power' (Hebrews 1:3), it's clear that the Angel of God's face is the "message of God" who was sent into the flesh of a human being (John 1:1, 14), none other than Yeshua, the King of the Angels, the Lord of Heavenly Hosts. Yeshua is *Melekh HaKavod*, the King of God's Glory (Psalm 24) and the *Adonai Tzebayot*, the Lord and Commander of Heavens Armies.[13]

CHRISTOPHANY OR WRESTLING ANGELS?

There are Christian interpreters like Henry M. Morris who state that the mystery man Jacob wrestled with was "God Himself and, therefore, Christ in His pre-incarnate state", citing Jacob's own evaluation and the name he assumed thereafter. The name Jacob means, "one who fights victoriously with God". Morris adds that God had appeared in the human form of the Angel of the LORD to eat a meal with Abraham in Genesis 18. These are known as Christophanies. But is this accurate, or could this mysterious man be an angel, an extraterrestrial messenger sent to thwart Jacob? Why would an angel get down and dirty with a human on the ground in a sweaty, gutsy old fashioned wrestling match? Why would a god lower himself into the dirt to do the same? Does this sound like the character of Jesus Christ? Let's discern.

It's important to remember that the wrestling match with the mysterious man or angel happened as Jacob was escaping from his father's home. He was on his way to the land of Canaan, being pursued by his twin brother Esau and an army of four hundred men. Jacob prepared for the worst. He prayed intensely to God, then tried to appease his brother by sending him a tribute of flocks and herds which he said was 'a present to my lord Esau from thy servant Jacob'.

Jacob then tried to save his family and flocks by sending them across the river Jabbok by night, re-crossing it again to send over his possessions. He was thus left alone in communion with God in the dark of the night. It was then and there that he had this mysterious encounter with this being who, according to Genesis 32:24-28, appeared as a man, who then later was referred to as a "God," in Genesis 32:28, 30 and Hosea 12:3, 5; and then again referred to as an angel in Hosea 12:4. The mystery man and Jacob wrestled until daybreak. When the being realized that he could not overpower Jacob, the man touched him on the sinew of his thigh (*hanasheh gid*) which caused Jacob to develop a limp (Genesis 32:31). It may be that Jacob's injury happened through the wrestling, and not from a simple touch, but 'to this day the people of Israel do not eat the sinew of the thigh that is on the hip socket' (Genesis 32:32).[14]

This is when Jacob demanded a blessing from this 'godly being', and the godly being declared that from that point on, Jacob would be called Israel (*Yisra'el,*) which in Hebrew means "one who struggled with the divine angel (or with a god)" (Josephus)[16], "one who has prevailed with God" (Rashi), "a man who sees God" (Whiston), "he

Chapter Four: Angel Protocol

will rule as God" (Strong), or "a prince with God" (Morris), from Hebrew: Sarah, "prevail", "have power as a prince").[17] (See, Strong's Concordance)

Because the language is unclear ("el" in *Yisra'el*) and inconsistent, and because this being refused to reveal his name, there are varying views as to whether he was a man, an angel, or God. Josephus uses only the terms "angel", "divine angel", and "angel of God", describing the struggle as no small victory.[18] All angels have the suffix, "el" after their names, which in Hebrew, literally means, of God. In fact, the first mention of the word that is often translated as 'God' in the Bible, is the Hebrew word, "Elohim" which is plural for 'gods'. The angel came from God, (the "Elohim") so he had the authority as an extraterrestrial messenger of the Most High, based on his encounter and contest with Jacob, to bless Jacob by giving him a new name. It was the least he could do, after his original mission failed, which was to destroy Jacob. His new name has since carried the plight and character of the Israelites and the Jewish people to this very day.

When Jacob asked this mysterious being's name, he refused to answer, yet afterwards Jacob named the place *Penuel* (which in Hebrew means "face of God"), and said, "I have seen God face to face and lived." To be literal, Jacob's words here were all in the plural. The Hebrew words he used for God is Elohim, plural for 'gods', and the word used for face is *panim*, plural for 'faces'. In the vernacular, the correct translation is, "I have seen the god(s) face(s) to face and lived."

I find this omission of the correct plurality throughout each and every translation from Hebrew to English. This consistently puts forward the word *God* in the singular form and ignores the plurality of the word, *Elohim*. Yet each and every other Hebrew word that is in its plurality is written out as plural, such as Malachim, the word for 'angels', and the singular is used only in conjunction to 'an angel of the Lord'. Jacob didn't see God with a big 'g' face to face, he saw one of the little 'gods' face to face, which was more likely an extraterrestrial messenger from the Elohim, or more popularly known as an 'angel.'

Are You Pulling My Leg?

So, Jacob wrestles with a man who changes his name, and implies that he's a god, but refuses to tell him his own name. If this mysterious god being was Yeshua or Jesus Christ, why would he withhold his name, when each time throughout scripture, Yeshua always answered affirmatively? The name *Yaakov* in Hebrew means 'leg puller'. Rebecca gave him this name because he was born holding onto his twin brother's heel. If this was a bona fide Christophany, why would Jesus have to ask Jacob what his name was when He already knew his name? Christ knows each of us by name. And after Jacob told the man or angel his name was Yaakov (Jacob), why then would he withhold what his own name was upon Jacob asking him? Isn't it proper etiquette, if you tell me yours, then I'll tell you mine? Whenever the Lord appeared throughout the scriptures and was asked His name, He always replied, though with various names, such as I AM THAT I AM (Ehyeh Asher Ehyeh), or I AM YAHUAH, the Lord your God, YHVH Elohei Tzibayoth (the Lord of Hosts) or even El Shaddai, or El Elyon, which all indicate the Almighty, the Most High God. This was definitely *not* the Lord, or Jesus who wrestled with Jacob.

This god-like being deliberately withheld his name for a reason. One possible reason was to hide who he really was, his real identity. Two, as Trachtenberg[20] theorized, the being refused to identify itself for fear that, if its secret name was known, magicians would try to conjure it up through incantations, something the Lord forbade. This is a serious issue which has gotten humans into a lot of trouble more than once, not to mention the angels who fell, and were bound and punished for revealing their names. Of one thing we can be sure, this angel (extraterrestrial messenger) was serving the Elohim, and following protocol.

In the 1939 book, *Jewish Magic and Superstition,* Trachtenberg states that according to Rabbi Shlomo ItzhakRashi, otherwise known as Rashi, the being was the guardian angel of Esau himself, sent to destroy Jacob before he could return to the land of Canaan, trying to answer the prayers of Esau.[21] When I saw this, I had an 'ah hah' moment! Makes perfect sense to me. This was definitely no Christophany, but it was an encounter with an angel, (extraterrestrial messenger) as scripture later revealed in Hosea 12:4, which uses the singular vernacular in Hebrew for angel (malach).

THE JEALOUSY OF ANGELS

To think that our Cosmic Drama, in which every human finds itself, began with the jealousy of angels toward humans is a sobering thought. God created both angels and humans, but He created angels first. When Lucifer rebelled, and was cast down from the high heavens, sent to earth as the 'Satan' adversary, his first goal was to try to destroy the humans that the Elohim created on earth.

The apocryphal book, *The First Book of Adam and Eve,* outlines the details of the story of the first humans and their tests and conflict with Satan. This was much more than just temptation over a piece of forbidden fruit in the garden of Eden.[22] Satan tried several times to destroy Adam and Eve, but each time God sent His angels to save them. It became a contest between Satan and God's angels. Satan was insanely jealous that God had placed humans above the angels. Satan, after all, was created first, as God's chief fiery Cherub of Light, Lucifer, the Light Bearer. How could these mere mortals have special status, higher than his own, and over all the angels?

There are many myths about Lilith, called the first Eve, who refused to submit to Adam and rebelled against him and the Creator. The story relates she invoked the holy name of God, fled from Adam and mated with Samael, the Fallen Angel, and was then cursed by the Creator and became a demoness. Legends say she caused jealousy between women, as she herself became jealous when the Creator gave Eve to Adam, a partner which worked out for him. Her jealousy was so intense that it has been said that she comes to steal and destroy the offspring of women. This is why special prayers are said as Jewish women near childbirth, to ward off the evil Lilith. In terms of archetypes, Lilith is the jealous woman. This archetypal pattern is repeated throughout the Old Testament, from Sarah and Hagar to Rachel and Leah and continues to this day. While the Lilith myth has been watered down over the centuries, and is known today as the first feminist revolt, the ancient texts say that Lilith is a fallen angel or demon who was cursed by the Creator.

What's in a Name?

A great deal of Book Two: *Who is God?* focuses on the importance of the names of God and their correct pronunciations. This is a vital issue because it conforms to the laws of vibration and sound. It is so easy to change the vibrational frequency of a name by changing one letter or syllable or vowel. The Hebrew language is a very specific one, as the root of a word can create dozens of derivatives. The meaning of a word can be altered just by changing the vowels around, as witness in the Tetragrammaton. (YHVH - Yud, Hay, Vav, Hay). According to the Masoretic texts, the authoritative Hebrew text of the Old Testament regarded universally as the official version of the Tanach, YHVH is pronounced 'Yahuah' which in English has been translated as 'Yahuah' *not* Yahweh. There is no 'W' sound in the Hebrew language. Depending on where the dots are, which signify the vowels in written Hebrew, the Tetragrammaton may also be pronounced as 'Yah-veh', which is the source of the word 'Yahweh'. In Hebrew, the 'v' sound and the 'w' sound have nothing in common. This is the name of the God of Israel, who created the Hebrew language, as well as the Hebrews themselves, also known as the Israelites.

The Jews, specifically, are of a tribe of Judah, hence the name, 'Judes' and 'Jews'. The name YHVH is so sacred to Jews that they never pronounce it, instead substituting the word 'Adonai' or 'Lord', each and every time YHVH appears in the Old Testament. English translations typically capitalize the word LORD in every place the Hebrew word YHVH appears, for emphasis that this is the Father Lord, not just any 'lord', or 'sir'. In modern Hebrew, the word, 'adonai' is used to address a man as one would use the word 'sir' in English.

Why you may ask, don't the Jews pronounce the name of the Lord, Yahuah? Besides the fact that they consider it to be the 'holy ineffable name of God' they are afraid to mispronounce it for fear of judgment. There is another occult reason for this fear, and that is, for fear of invoking the counterfeit god, who is called, *Yahweh Demiurge*, who is a serpent-dragon god, invoked in magical rituals.[23] (For more details, please see my chapters in Book Two: *Who Is God? Gods or ETs?* on *Who Are The Biblical God(s)?*, sub-section: *Yahweh or Jehovah? Yahweh, the Counterfeit God*)

This god, *Yahweh Demiurge* was worshipped by a faction of Jews. My readers may wonder; how can this be? But we need to remember ancient Jewish history. During times of animal sacrifices, the priest would put a blood sacrifice on the altar for the atonement of the sins of the people, and then he would offer another sacrificial goat to wander into the desert for Beelzebub and Azazel. The people feared these beings and believed it would appease them and thereby earn protection for their tribe. Historically speaking, the Israelites were rebuked and punished many times for worshipping and sacrificing to false gods, in this case a destructive false dragon-god who is a manifestation of satan! A serpent-dragon god named *Yahweh Yaldabaoth*!

Remember satan has a god complex, he is the counterfeit god. The name Jehovah is used in Freemasonry as a secret password, as well as the names, I AM THAT I AM. Initiates do not find out until they reach the 33rd degree that the god they are worshipping is Lucifer as Satan. The name Yahuah has become bastardized and blasphemed by Lucifer/Satan. It is his agenda to distort and pervert the sacred names of the Lord. This is why it is important to either pronounce the Tetragrammaton correctly, or, as the Jews believe, not at all, in order to play it safe, and avoid invokimg the counterfeit god and his demonic strongholds.

The slight difference in the pronunciation of the name of a god, or angel, can change the type of entity one is hoping will call. The counterfeit god knows this very well, and as I've said before, the devil is certainly in these details. Just think of how many ignorant Christians continue to speak the name of Yahweh, and even pray and worship him, in the mistaken belief that they are referring to the God of Israel when doing so? Too many in my opinion, which is the reason many Christian churches are infested with demons. Unbeknownst to them, they are literally calling the enemy in to fellowship! This is a prime example of where knowledge empowers and ignorance endangers.

Even the name of Jesus has been counterfeited. In John 5:43, He predicts this Himself, "I have come in my Father's name, and you do not accept me. Yet if another man comes in his own name, you will accept him." Firstly, His real name is Yahushua, which means, *Yahuah Saves*. The Greeks called him Iesus, the Indians and Arabs called him 'Issa', all of which mean *Savior*. Jesus is also a Spanish name, pronounced, 'hey-zeus'. Satan knows all about these subtleties, which is why he has

Chapter Four: Angel Protocol

a special demon named 'Jesus'. This is why the Bible specifically says that the way to test the spirits is to ask them to say that Jesus Christ came in the flesh.

> "This is how you can recognize the Spirit of God: Every spirit that acknowledges that Jesus Christ has come in the flesh is from God, but every spirit that does not acknowledge Jesus is not from God. This is the spirit of the antichrist, which you have heard is coming and even now is already in the world."
>
> (1 John 4:2,3)

I know many Christians who make a point, when using the Lord's name for healing and deliverance, to say the *'Lord Jesus Christ,'* to distinguish Him from the counterfeit demon, Jesus. I once dared to question this in a healing seminar done by a church leader, and was told, 'when I say the name Jesus, the demons know who I'm talking about'. That was a spirit of arrogance talking, not the Holy Spirit. The point is that we are immersed in a spiritual battlefield, and there are all kinds of traps and counterfeits, and spiritual discernment is an important tool now, for both believers and non-believers.

So, it goes with all the proper names and invocation of angels. When God changed their names, he also altered their vibration. In the year 587 B.C. this change caused the destruction of Solomon's temple in Jerusalem. The same goes for all the fallen angels, who were named first as angels of God, which is why they all have the suffix 'el' at the end of their names. 'El' means, 'of God'. So, God changed a letter or a vowel, marking the difference between a fallen angel and one of God's Holy Angels or a Son of God.

Take the name *Samuel*, who is one of God's prophets in the Old Testament. Samuel became the great prophet and judge of Israel who restored law, order, and regular religious worship in the land (1 Samuel 4:15–18; 7:3–17). However, *Samael* is the leader of the satans, he is one of the fallen angels that lords over the abyss, all that for just changing one letter in the name.

In Jewish lore, Samael is said to be the angel of death, the chief ruler of the Fifth Heaven and one of the seven regents of the world served by two million angels; he resides in the Seventh Heaven is an important archangel in Talmudic and post-Talmudic lore, a figure who is an accuser, seducer and destroyer, and has been regarded as both good and evil. Also called Sammael and Samil, he is considered in legend both a member of the heavenly host (with often grim and destructive duties) and a fallen angel, equitable with Satan and the chief of the evil spirits. One of Samael's greatest roles in Jewish lore is that of the angel of death. In this capacity, he is a fallen angel but nevertheless remains one of the Lord's servants. As a good angel, Samael supposedly resides in the seventh heaven, this is the one that Moses saw, who was so awesome it caused him to bow and pray. However, Samael is declared to be the chief angel of the fifth heaven. This is probably the prince that Enoch is referring to who is *fastened to the fifth heaven*.

The same goes for all the fallen angels who became demons (dark intelligences), and all the angels who were once known and invoked by name through magical ceremony. When the Creator Father God *changed* their names so humans could not order the heavenly angels around to do their bidding. Instead God cursed the magical arts by confounding the angel's names, so humans would get what they deserve for their idolatry, and conjure up the fallen angels and demons.

This is why the group of fallen angels, the Nephilim, run the Ashtar Command[24] (see my chapter on the *Ashtar Command* in Book One) named after Ashtoreth (Astarte), the Phoenician fallen angel goddess in the Old Testament who comes in many different forms and names.

It is generally accepted that the Masoretic "vowel pointing" adopted in 135 AD, indicating the pronunciation *'Aštōreṯ* ("Ashtoreth," "Ashtoret") is a deliberate distortion of "Ashtart", and that this is probably because the two last syllables have been pointed with the vowels belonging to *bōšeṯ*, ("bosheth," meaning abomination), to indicate that that word should be substituted when reading, so the reader does not invoke this demon inadvertently, by pronouncing its proper name. The plural form is pointed *'Aštārōṯ* ("Ashtaroth"). "Istar", or "Esther" are also derivations of Astarte.

The annual holiday Easter was actually named after this goddess. The hunt for Easter eggs commemorates the fertility goddess Astarte, and the bunny rabbit theme also comes from this spring festival to honor this fallen angel goddess. This is a clear indication of the competition between the fallen angels and the Creator Father God, in that Easter OVERLAPS the day of the resurrection of Jesus Christ and the feast of the Lord, which is the eight days of Passover that always happens on the first full moon after the vernal equinox. Yet unsuspecting Christians continue to this day to celebrate Easter with all its ceremonies to honor this fallen angel goddess, combined with celebrating Christ's victory over death.

Another instance, the title *Queen of heaven* as mentioned in *Jeremiah* has been connected with Astarte/Ashterah. In later Jewish mythology, she became a female demon of lust. For what seems to be the use of the Hebrew plural form *'Aštārōṯ* in this sense, see Astaroth. Astarte was accepted by the Greeks under the name of Aphrodite, who was known as the goddess love or lust. She then became known as Venus to the Romans. Today she is worshipped as Gaia, the Earth Mother, and as Mother Mary, still venerated as the 'queen of heaven.'

Ashtoreth also caused King Solomon to stray from the Lord. This created karma, as the Lord was not happy with Solomon's idolatry and his temple was destroyed twice.

Chapter Four: Angel Protocol

"As Solomon grew old, his wives turned his heart after other gods, and his heart was not fully devoted to the Lord Yahuah his God, as the heart of David his father had been. He followed Ashtoreth the goddess of the Sidonians, and Molech the detestable god of the Ammonites. So, Solomon did evil in the eyes of the Lord Yahuah; he did not follow the Lord Yahuah completely, as David his father had done. On a hill, east of Jerusalem, Solomon built a high place for Chemosh the detestable god of Moab, and for Molech the detestable (Nephilim) god of the Ammonites. He did the same for all his foreign wives, who burned incense and offered sacrifices to their gods. The Lord Yahuah became angry with Solomon because his heart had turned away from the Lord Yahuah, the God of Israel, who had appeared to him twice. Although he had forbidden Solomon to follow other gods, Solomon did not keep the Lord Yahuah's command."

(1 Kings 11:4-10)

The Syrian goddess Atargatic (Semitic 'Atar'atah) was generally equated with Astarte because the first element of her name appears to be related to the name Astarte. Astarte first appears in ancient Egypt beginning in the eighteenth dynasty, along with other deities who were worshipped by northwest Semitic people. She was worshipped fervently in her aspect of a warrior, often paired with the goddess Anat. In the *Contest Between Horus and Set*, these two goddesses appear as daughters of Ra and are given in marriage to the god Set, here identified with the Semitic name Hadad. Astarte also was identified with the lioness warrior goddess Sekhmet but seemingly more often blended, at least in part, with Isis to judge from the many images found of Astarte suckling a small child.

This is why the Ashtar Command, named after Ashtoreth the fallen angel goddess, call their mother ships after the four Archangels, Michael, Gabriel, Raphael, and Uriel. When humans try to contact these archangels, they are instead being received by the Ashtar Command, who masquerade as angels and disguise themselves as ascended masters. Thus, continues the celestial battle with the Creator Father God. The New Age cover 'Ashtar Command' is really the principality of Ashtoreth (Astarte), who has always been under the hierarchy of the Office of Satan. When New Agers pray and invoke these archangels, they are misled into a false sense of security by the counterfeit fallen angels.

"For we wrestle not against flesh and blood (human), but against principalities (fallen angels), against powers (evil spirits), against the rulers of the darkness of this world (Archons), against spiritual wickedness (aliens) in heavenly places."

(Ephesians 6:12)

NOTES AND REFERENCES:

1. Joseph B. Lumpkin, *The Lost Books of the Bible: The Great Rejected Texts,* Fifth Estate Publishers, Blountsville, AL. 2009.
2. *Jewish Encyclopedia,* http://www.jewishencyclopedia.com, West Conshohocken, PA, originally published in 1906.
3. Ibid.
4. Ibid.
5. Philo Judaeus of Alexandria, *idem,* "On Dreams," i. 22
6. Ella LeBain, *Who Is God? Book Two of Who's Who in The Cosmic Zoo? A Guide to ETs, Aliens, Gods & Angels,* Skypath Books, 2015.
7. Philo, Ibid.
8. Philo, Ibid.
9. Ibid.
10. Joe Kovacs, *Shocked by the Bible, The Most Astonishing Facts You've Never Been Told,* Thomas Nelson, Nashville, Tennessee. 2009.
11. Ella LeBain, *Who's Who in The Cosmic Zoo? Book One, A Spiritual Guide to ETs, Aliens, Gods & Angels, Third Edition,* Tate Publishing & Enterprises, 2013.
12. Ella LeBain, *Who Is God? Book Two of Who's Who in The Cosmic Zoo? A Guide to ETs, Aliens, Gods & Angels,* Skypath Books, 2015.
13. John J. Parsons, *Parashat Vayera-The Angel of the LORD, Further Thoughts on Parashat Vayera,* www.hebrew4christians.com
14. Henry M. Morris, *The Genesis Record: A Scientific and Devotional Commentary on the Book of Beginnings.* Grand Rapids, Michigan: Baker Book House. (1976). pp. 337, 499–502.
15. Wikipedia. < http://en.wikipedia.org/wiki/Jacob>
16. Josephus. *The Antiquities of the Jews,* Book II, 2.4.18
17. Strong's Concordance 3478, 8280, 6439.
18. Josephus. *The Antiquities of the Jews,* Book II, 2.4.18
19. Judah David Eisenstein, "Porging". *Jewish Encyclopedia.* New York City. (1901–1906). LCCN:16014703. Retrieved 2008-11-19.
20. Joshua Trachtenberg, *Jewish Magic and Superstition: A Study in Folk Religion,* New York: Behrman's Jewish Book House. 1939.
21. Ibid. Trachtenberg 1939, p. 80
22. Joseph B. Lumpkin, *The Lost Books of the Bible: The Great Rejected Texts,* Fifth Estate Publishers, Blountsville, AL. 2009.
23. Ella LeBain, *Who Is God? Book Two of Who's Who in The Cosmic Zoo? A Guide to ETs, Aliens, Gods & Angels,* Skypath Books, 2015. Chapter: *Gods or ETs?*

Chapter Four: Angel Protocol

Who Are The Biblical God(s)?, sub-section: *Yahweh or Jehovah? Yahweh, the Counterfeit God*

24. Ella LeBain, *Who's Who in The Cosmic Zoo? Book One, A Spiritual Guide to ETs, Aliens, Gods & Angels, Third Edition*, Chapter: *Ashtar Command*, Tate Publishing & Enterprises, 2013.

CHAPTER FIVE

CELESTIAL WARRIORS: EXTRATERRESTRIALS WITH EXTRAORDINARY POWERS

> "Thus the heavens and the earth were finished, and all the **hosts** of them."
> (GENESIS 2:1)

> "By the word of the LORD were the heavens made; and all the **hosts** of heaven by the breath of his mouth."
> (PSALM 33:6)

> "He unleased against them his hot anger, his wrath, indignation and hostility – a band of *destroying angels*."
> (PSALM 78:49)

WHO ARE THE HOSTS OF HEAVEN?

The words, *Hosts of Heaven* or *Heavenly Hosts* is used approximately twenty-five times in the Bible. The first time the word 'host' is used is in Genesis 2:1, and is defined by Strong's Concordance (6635) as "a mass of persons or things especially organized for war, an army." Often it refers to human armies. Two other words are translated as 'host' and used similarly, but 6635 is usually used to refer to the heavenly host. In Hebrew, the word for 'host' is *tzebayoth*.

In the Old Testament scripture, heavenly host refers specifically to angelic beings just as in Luke 2:13; "heavenly host praising God" at Christ's birth. It does not generally refer to celestial bodies, or to the cosmos in general.

Per the ancient astronaut theory, angels were nothing more than extraterrestrials who took the sides of certain groups and people. We see this clearly when it comes to the celestial armies, known as the hosts of heaven.

Chapter Five: Extraterrestrials With Extraordinary Powers

We are told not to worship the heavenly host, and God is declared "The Lord of Hosts" over two hundred times in the Bible. Unfortunately, modern theology almost always interprets the phrase "heavenly host" or "host of heaven" to mean the stars, planets, etc. ("array" or "starry hosts," in NIV), unless the context makes it absolutely unavoidable to do so.

The Heavenly Host, according to Wikipedia, is an army of good angels mentioned in the Bible. (Luke 2:13; Revelation 19:19) It is led either by the Archangel Michael, or by God Himself. Most descriptions of angels in the Bible are reminiscent of military terms, such as encampment (Genesis 32:1-2), command structure (Psalms 91:11-12; Matthew 13:41; Revelation 7:2), and combat (Judges 5:20; Job 19:12; Revelation 12:7). The Heavenly Hosts specific hierarchy differs slightly from that of angels as it encompasses more military services, whereas the hierarchy of angels is a division of angels into non-military services to God. The heavenly hosts participate in the War in Heaven and, according to some interpretations, will defeat Satan and his own army of satans (fallen angels) at the End of Days and be victorious.

In Milton's *Paradise Lost*,[1] Archangel Michael commands the army of angelic hosts loyal to God against the rebel forces of Satan. Armed with a sword from God's armory, he defeats Satan in personal combat, wounding his side.

The heavenly host as the Lord's army of faithful extraterrestrials will participate in the Final War in Heaven, the Star Wars-type battle against Lucifer/Satan and his rebel fallen angel army at the End of this Age, known as Armageddon. The heavenly host will be victorious.

According to the Bible, during the Luciferian Rebellion, Lucifer/Satan's forces were defeated by the Heavenly Host led by Archangel Michael (Revelation12:7-9). Lucifer/Satan and his followers still have access to the throne of God, however, which privilege he uses to accuse the followers of God (Zechariah 3:1; Job 1 & 2; Revelation12:10). Battles are constantly taking place between Satan's army and the heavenly host, however, open warfare will not break out in heaven until the tribulation period (Revelation 19:11-21). The heavenly host will be commanded by Jesus Christ.

Lost in Translation?

It's so interesting when studying the scriptures to note all the many different ways it has been interpreted. I have been using a website called *biblehub.com* which pulls up all the Bible versions, so you can see the difference in the choice of words that are used to convey every scripture. When it comes to the interpretation of the 'Hosts of Heaven' or 'Heavenly Hosts' there are some really drastic differences in the translations. The King James version has the most accurate translations, but it is clear that when compared to the New International Versions, the 'Heavenly Hosts' are changed to the 'stars of heaven,' or the 'stars of the sky,' or 'all the starry hosts'.

The word 'hosts' indicate an army or array of beings, which are extraterrestrials. These are not 'stars' per se, but may be considered 'stars' in the heroic sense of the word, as we may call a movie star a 'star.' These are clearly 'beings' which are mighty extraterrestrial celestial warriors.

In Genesis 1:15-17, the Hebrew word 'kawkuv' means stars. The Hebrew word for stars is used over twenty-five times in the Old Testament, and even the Hebrew word for "constellations" used in Isaiah 13:10. Occasionally, even this word for stars (which simply means "shining") is also used to refer to angels (extraterrestrial celestial beings) "when the morning stars sang together, and all the sons of God (Elohim) shouted for joy" (Job 38:7) - but never vice-versa. Do stars sing? Or are the stars actually celestial beings with voices? Therefore, "heavenly host" should almost never be translated as "vast array" or "starry hosts" as it was translated by the New International Version. This mistranslation obscures its true meaning. Host specifically implies a military grouping.

New Agers lack a strong understanding of the Biblical mandate NOT to worship the heavenly hosts. This lack of understanding leads many into receiving false spiritual doctrines from wicked heavenly hosts, the bad ETs and Aliens, the source of all cosmic evil, who are masquerading as space brothers, ascended masters and angels of light. Remember, Ephesians 6:12:

> "For our wrestling is not against flesh and blood, but against the principalities, against the powers, against the world-rulers of this darkness, against the spiritual hosts of wickedness in the heavenly places."

Those spiritual hosts of wickedness in the heavenly places, ruled by the prince of the power of the air, is Lucifer/Satan. 'Wherein in time past you walked according to the course of this world, according to the prince of the power of the air, the spirit that now works in the children of disobedience' (Ephesians 2:2).

Many people think that Satan lives underground in the abyss, but that is just one of the satans. Remember the word 'Satan' is Hebrew for adversary. He controls a hierarchy of demons and archdemons. The scripture is clear about Lucifer/Satan's control over the lower heavens, which explains all the UFO activity and all the battles that have been seen from the space stations. NASA and the Russian space stations have gotten UFOs being shot at by other UFOs on video. Clearly there is more than one group of UFOs battling over the air space over the earth. There are videos of armadas of UFOs patrolling the earth. The videos are too numerous to list, all one needs to do is Google it or visit YouTube and you will find scores of them.

Chapter Five: Extraterrestrials With Extraordinary Powers

These UFO's also comprise the heavenly hosts. Lucifer/Satan's control over the lower heavens allows his wicked heavenly hosts to flourish, so the two 'hosts' are in constant battle with one another over earth, and earths human inhabitants. This is why the Lord promises to create a new heaven and a new earth after the final battle is won, and Lucifer/Satan and all of his fallen angel demons are cast down in the lake of fire forever. Lucifer/Satan comes down from heaven to embody the antichrist during the seven-year tribulation period which happens after the rapture of the believers. In fact, the rapture of the church is his signal to come down and wreak havoc, for his last hurrah.

The Presence of Cosmic Evil

We have read in previous chapters about the many times people in the Bible wanted to bow down and worship the angels (extraterrestrial messengers) because of their power, light and glory, which was an awesome sight to see, but were told repeatedly, do not worship me, worship the Lord (Yahuah) your God, they are merely a servant. So, we see similar issues arising with the ancients when it comes to the hosts of heavens. However, because of the distinction of the two types of heavenly hosts, the Lord's army and Lucifer/Satan's army, we know that there is the presence of cosmic evil in the heavens. This is the very reason for the hosts of heaven, which are armies that do battle with each other over heavenly territories and over the Earth. This is the reason for the prophetic promise in both Isaiah and Revelation, from the Lord to create a new heaven and a new Earth, which will be free of cosmic evil, and therefore free of the cosmic war.

Do Not Worship the Hosts

The Old Testament Prophet Zephaniah included a strong judgment on Judah (Israel and the Israelites) because of "those who bow down on the roofs to worship the starry host, those who bow down and swear by the LORD and who also swear by Molech" (Zephaniah 1:5).

To *worship the starry host* is a clear violation of God's law in Deuteronomy 4:19, "When you look up to the sky and see the sun, the moon and the stars – all the heavenly array – do not be enticed into bowing down to them." The *starry host* includes the sun, moon, planets, and stars. These celestial bodies were worshiped by the pagan cultures of the day, and continue to be worshiped by pagans today. However, The Lord commanded His people to worship Him only and not bow down to other gods. (Exodus 20:3-4)

The violation of the first of the Ten Commandments became a perpetual problem in Judah. Zephaniah prophesied against it during the reign of King Josiah. Later, during Manasseh's reign, we are told that the king, "worshiped all the hosts of heaven and served them." (2 Kings 21:3) The prophet Jeremiah condemned the same practice: "The houses of Jerusalem and the houses of the kings of Judah—all the houses on whose roofs offerings have been offered to all the host of heaven." (Jeremiah 19:13) God's people were frequently tempted to worship heavenly bodies, while they were being led astray by false gods and their rulers.

The apostle Paul speaks of those who worship created things rather than the Creator (Romans 1:25). "They exchanged the truth about God for a lie, and worshiped and served created things rather than the Creator--who is forever praised." These created things include the stars, planets, ETs, aliens, gods and angels. While the heavens point to the glory of their Creator (Psalm 19:1-6); the heavens are not to be the focus of worship.

> "And lest thou lift up thine eyes unto heaven, and when thou seest the sun, and the moon, and the stars, <u>even all the host of heaven</u>, shouldest be driven to worship them, and serve them..."
>
> (Deuteronomy 4:19)

> "And hath gone and served other gods, and worshipped them, either the sun or the moon, or any of the <u>host of heaven</u>, which I have <u>not</u> commanded."
>
> (Deuteronomy 17:3)

> <u>"I saw the LORD sitting on his throne, and all the host of heaven</u> standing by him on his right hand and on his left... And there came forth a spirit, and stood before the Lord."
>
> (1 Kings 22:19-22; 2 Chronicles 18:18)

In this passage, it is obvious that the exact same word for 'host' cannot be mistaken here as "starry arrays" or "heavenly bodies," considering they stand around the throne and one of them answers the Lord's question to them. (See, Job 1:6)

The following verses are where the idolatrous worship of the <u>host of heaven</u> comes in, along with the idolatry to Baal, which the Israelites were severely punished for:

> "And they left all the commandments of the Lord their God, and made them molten images, even two calves, and made a grove, and worshipped <u>all the host of heaven</u>, and served Baal."
>
> (2 Kings 17:16)

Chapter Five: Extraterrestrials With Extraordinary Powers

"For he built up again the high places which Hezekiah his father had destroyed... and worshipped all the <u>host of heaven</u>, and served them."
(2 Kings 21:3)

In the following verse, the word, 'planets' can also be translated as constellations. Either way, since "heavenly bodies" are categorized by this word, "all the host of heaven" implies that the angelic hosts (extraterrestrials) occupy the heavenly realms.

"And he put down the idolatrous priests... them also that burned incense unto Baal, to the sun, and to the moon, and to the <u>planets</u>, and to <u>all the host of heaven</u>."
(2 Kings 23:5)

"For he built up again the high places which Hezekiah his father had destroyed... and worshipped all the <u>host of heaven</u>, and served them."
(2 Kings 21:3)

The following verse is an instance where "stars" may be the best rendering given its similarity to God's promise to Abraham - Genesis 15:5. However, it also implies that the angels (extraterrestrials) are considered numberless as well.

"As the <u>host of heaven</u> cannot be numbered, neither the sand of the sea measured: so, will I multiply the seed of David, and the Levites that minister unto me."
(Jeremiah 33:22)

This verse refers to the falling of Lucifer/Satan's celestial army. "And all the <u>host of heaven</u> shall be dissolved, and the heavens shall be rolled together as a scroll: <u>and all their host shall fall down</u>..." (Isaiah 34:4)

These are the fallen hosts or fallen angels (extraterrestrials) that have been at war against the Creator God. Isaiah 34 refers to the Judgment Against the Nations all of which had individual "gods" and idols (or "territorial spirits"), who worshipped the wrong set of <u>host of heaven</u>, and have been on the wrong side of the Creator Lord all these years.

"Thou, even thou, art LORD alone; thou hast made heaven, <u>the heaven of heavens, with all their host</u>, the Earth, and all things that are therein, the seas, and all that is therein, and thou preservest them all; <u>and the host of heaven worshippeth thee</u>."
(Nehemiah 9:6)

"And it waxed great, even to the host of heaven; and it cast down some of the host and of the stars to the ground, and stamped upon them. Yea, he magnified himself even to the prince of the host..."

(Daniel 8:10-11)

There is something about those host of heaven which inspires awe and worship in people. They are mighty celestial warriors, and humans are totally awestruck by them, which is understandable. The following scripture, in which Joshua was contacted by the 'captain' of the host of heaven, and his initial reaction was to bow down and worship out of reverence, is a prime example. In this instance, the 'captain' of the host of heaven, gives Joshua a command and tells him what to do. Of course, this is one of the most quintessential battle scenes in the Old Testament, when Joshua is given victory over the King of Ai and his army, which he could not have done of his own strength or by himself. He was assisted by the host of heaven.

"... when Joshua was by Jericho, he lifted up his eyes and looked, and behold, there stood a man over against him with his sword drawn in his hand: and Joshua went unto him, and said unto him, Art thou for us, or for our adversaries? And he said, nay; but as captain of the host of the Lord am I now come. *And Joshua fell on his face to the earth in reverence,* "I am at your command," Joshua said. "What do you want your servant to do? And the captain of the Lord's Host said unto Joshua, loose thy shoe from off thy foot; for the place where thou standest is holy. And Joshua did so."

(Joshua 5:14-15)

In the New International Version, it reads "as commander of the army of the Lord," and "The commander of the Lord's army replied..." This use of host obviously does not refer to stars and planets.

Of course, the rest is history. Joshua fought the battle of Jericho and the walls came tumbling down. He was aided by the captain of the host of heaven, that when Joshua and his army blew their shofars, they were backed up by the celestial army (host of heaven) who emitted a vibrational frequency which pulverized the stone walls. This was clearly one of many 'Divine Interventions' by the host of heaven in the Old Testament, as the Lord promised him, 'The LORD Yahuah said to Joshua, "See, I have delivered Jericho into your hands, along with its king and its fighting men.' (Joshua 6:2)

The following are two more passages with multiple counts of the phrase "host." In Daniel 8:10, the New International Version obscures the true meaning by running the terms "host" and "stars" together. This is a good example of when stars probably

Chapter Five: Extraterrestrials With Extraordinary Powers

mean angels - certainly the "starry host" thrown to Earth are fallen angels; Revelation 12:1. Just reading it tells you it can't mean literal stars - it's much more comparable to Isaiah 14:12 & Luke 10:18 (Lucifer's expulsion) but with good guy/bad guy roles reversed.

> "And suddenly there was with the angel a multitude of the <u>heavenly host</u>, praising God, and saying, Glory to God in the highest and on earth peace, goodwill toward men."
> (Luke 2:13)

This verse implies that "<u>the heavenly host</u>" are in a different class and rank than the first angel (extraterrestrial). (See, Romans 1:20, 25)

> "Then God turned, and gave them up to worship the <u>host of heaven</u>."
> (Acts 7:42) (KJV)

> "But God turned away and gave them over to the <u>worship of heavenly bodies</u>."
> (Acts 7:42 - NIV translations)

This is clearly one of those passages where the true meaning was lost in translation and the meaning was changed entirely. Here the term, <u>host of heaven</u> implies that these were the wicked heavenly hosts, and God turned away and gave them up to their idolatry. But it does not mean they were worshiping the heavenly bodies, which is the term generally used for planets. However, planet worship was prevalent during the Greco/Roman empires. In this verse, <u>the host of heaven</u>, were extraterrestrials not planets or stars. Unfortunately, many of the references in the Bible to extraterrestrials has been stolen and obfuscated by modern translations. Due to the fact that most Christians don't pay attention to these nuances because they do not *see* the true meaning of these words, the New Agers and UFO cults have emerged to fill that void.

The point is that the wicked, rebellious host of heaven are engaging in increased UFO activity at this time, preparing themselves for the final battle with the faithful host of heaven. Unfortunately, modern theology has been locked in a tradition of whitewashing the scriptural reality of wicked angelic hosts which dates back 1500 years. This pattern is typified today by poor renditions of passages that would illuminate our understanding of the UFO presence, but instead robs the church of her responsibility to warn the world of their past, present and future activity. Whether you view this as merely a poor translation, a spiritual stronghold, or a full-scale conspiracy theory, is up to you.[2]

"And it shall come to pass in that day, that the Lord shall punish the <u>host of the high ones that are on high</u>, and the kings of the earth upon the earth."

(Isaiah 24:21)

In Ephesians 6:12, it talks about warring not against the flesh, but against principalities, powers, rulers of the darkness of this present world and spiritual wickedness in the high heavens. The hosts of the High One that will be punished, and fall from the heavens like withered leaves, are all the extraterrestrials who have rebelled against their Creator.

"All the stars of the heavens will be dissolved and the sky rolled up like a scroll; <u>all the starry host will fall like withered leaves from the vine</u>, like shriveled figs from the fig tree."

(Isaiah 34:4)

The prophesy continues and is cross referenced in the New Testament, with the words of Jesus Christ Himself:

"Immediately after the distress of those days "'the sun will be darkened, and the moon will not give its light; <u>the stars will fall from the sky</u>, and the heavenly bodies will be shaken.'"

(Matthew 24:29)

The Lord of Hosts

"Who is this King of Glory? <u>The Lord of Hosts</u>, He is the King of Glory. Selah."
(Psalm 24:10)

There are 273 instances of the phrase "Lord of Hosts" in the Old Testament. The following is probably the most definitive use of this word referring to "armies" - whether human or angelic.

In the Old Testament, the name YHWH (Yahuah) and the title Elohim frequently occur with the word *tzevaot* or *sabaoth* ("hosts" or "armies", Hebrew: צבאות) as YHWH(Yahuah) Elohe Tzevaot ("YHWH God of Hosts"), Elohe Tzevaot ("God of Hosts"), Adonai YHWH Tzevaot ("Lord YHWH of Hosts") or, most frequently, YHWH/Yahuah Tzevaot ("YHWH of Hosts"). This name is traditionally transliterated in Latin as Sabaoth, a form more familiar to most English readers, because it was used in the King James Version of the Bible. Yahushua was the real name Jesus

Chapter Five: Extraterrestrials With Extraordinary Powers

Christ went by when he walked the earth. The name of the father Yahuah is in the son, meaning Yahuah is Savior. It was later truncated to Yeshua, and then some 1700 years later, the English name Jesus emerged. (See, my chapter on Tetragrammaton in Book Two, *Who Is God?* for more information) Being that all power and authority has been given to the son, Yahushua, aka Jesus Christ is the King of Glory, the Lord of Hosts, the Captain of Heaven's army.

Heaven's Army

Of the vastness of the armies of heaven the following description is given by Rav. Simon B. Lakish:

> "There are twelve mazzalot ["signs of the zodiac"], each having thirty armies; each army, thirty camps [castra]; each camp, thirty legions [compare Matthew 26:53]; each legion, thirty cohorts; each cohort, thirty corps; and each corps has 365,000 myriads of stars entrusted to it."[3]

> "Do you think I cannot call on my Father, and he will at once put at my disposal more than twelve legions of angels?"
>
> (Matthew 26:53)

> "When Moses went up in *the cloud* to heaven, Kemuel, the janitor of the first gate, with 12,000 angels of destruction under him, went to strike him, but succumbed. As he arrived at the second gate, Hadraniel, who exceeded the former 600,000 parasangs in length, came with his darts of fire to smite him, but God interfered. Finally, he came to the precincts of Sandalfon, the angel who towers above the rest by the length of 500 years' journey, and who when standing on Earth reaches with his head up to the hayyot, (Living Creatures, Merkavah, ie, spaceships). Standing behind the heavenly chariot, he weaves crowns for the Most High, while all the hosts of heaven sing, 'Blessed be the glory of the Lord from His place.' Before his fire even Hadraniel trembled; but Moses passed him also, the Lord shielding him. Then Moses came to the stream of fire which consumes even the angels; and God caused him to pass through unscathed. Next came Galizur ["Revealer of the Rock"], also called Raziel ["The Secret of God"], or Akraziel [the herald of God"], the angel who spreads his wings over the hayyot (living creatures, i.e., spaceships), lest their fiery breath consume the ministering angels. Finally, the troop of the mighty angels standing around the throne of glory threatened to consume Moses by the breath of their mouth: but Moses seized the throne of glory; and the Lord spread *His cloud* over him [Job, 36:9], and he received the Law despite the protesting angels."[4]

As I've pointed out in Book Two: *Who Is God?* the repetitive words for the Lord's spaceships are the clouds of heaven. The prophetic promise of Christ's return, is with the clouds of heaven, these are His heavenly hosts, His celestial army, prepared to claim victory over the Earth in the final battle known as Armageddon.

> "Look! He comes <u>with the clouds of heaven</u>. And everyone will see him--even those who pierced him. And all the nations of the world will mourn for him. Yes! Amen!"
>
> (Revelation 1:7)

Who are the clouds of heaven? More specifically, what are the clouds of heaven? The following verse, tells us He is coming 'in' the clouds of heaven, with great power and glory. These clouds that He and His elect arrive in are large motherships, more glorious than any modern-day UFO, the world has ever seen.

> "Immediately after the tribulation of those days shall the sun be darkened, and the moon shall not give her light, and the stars shall fall from heaven, <u>and the powers of the heavens shall be shaken</u>:
>
> (Matthew 24:29

The 'powers of the heavens' are the celestial hosts, the armies of heaven, particularly those who side with the Office of the Satans, they will be shaken on the Day of the Lord. The verse, the 'stars shall fall from heaven' does not relate in my opinion, to actual stars, but to the starry hosts, relating to the armies, who will crash down like the fallen angels. Then the following verses go into more detail, as to who exactly will be accompanying Christ in his 'cloud ships' upon His return to the Earth:

> "And then shall appear the sign of the Son of man in heaven: and then <u>shall all the tribes of the earth mourn</u>, and they shall see the Son of man coming <u>in the clouds of heaven with power and great glory</u>. And he shall send his angels with a great sound of a trumpet, and <u>they shall gather together his elect from the four winds, from one end of heaven to the other</u>."
>
> (Matthew 24:30-31)

Interesting that it is the job of His angels (extraterrestrial messengers) to first give the call, then these ETs gather His elect from all over the heavens. It is important when reading that verse to see the distinction between His angels and His elect. The question is, who are His elect? The other verse referring to the elect is Matthew

Chapter Five: Extraterrestrials With Extraordinary Powers

24:24, when Jesus warns of false prophets coming that will deceive even the elect. In that verse, His elect are His believers on the earth. However, in verse 31, His elect come from outer space, from all four corners of the heavens. Are these His heavenly hosts? His celestial armies? or does this imply that He has other believers around the universe? He did say in John 10:16, "I have other sheep that are not of this sheep pen. I must bring them also. They too will listen to My voice, and there shall be one flock and one shepherd." Perhaps these are the elect from the four corner of the heavens of which He speaks? This proves that *Yahushua HaMashiach*, Jesus the Christ, was not just the Savior of planet earth, but that He is the Cosmic Christ, the King of the Kingdom of Heaven.

THE CREATION OF ANGELS

"The angels of the face and of glorification, the angels of the elements of fire, wind, and darkness, of hail and hoar frost, thunder and lightning, of cold and heat, of winter and spring, summer and fall, of the abyss and night, of light and morning, were created on the first day." (Book of Jubilees, 2:2) According to R. Johanan in the *Jewish Encyclopedia,* he places the creation of the angels on the second day, referring to Psalm 104:4.[6] "He maketh his angels of winds" ("who maketh winds his messengers, and flames of fire his servants.") Per the *Book of Enoch,* God created them on the second day out of fire. The bodies of angels are radiant, their faces like lightning, their eyes as flaming torches. The food of angels is manna, of which Adam and Eve ate before they sinned. The angels of the Lord fed manna to the Israelites on their Exodus out of Egypt to Israel.

There are 496,000 myriads of angels (the numerical value of the Hebrew word *Malakoth*, which means 'Angels') sovereignty, or 499,000, the equivalent of the Hebrew word *Tzebayoth* which means 'hosts') who glorify God from sunrise to sunrise. These of course, are the faithful angels and hosts to the Creator. However, the ones who sided with Lucifer's rebellion, are the fallen angels and no longer glorify the Lord, even though they once enjoyed intimacy with him. As I've said before, and this point is important to reiterate, that for every fallen angel in rebellion there are two angels who remained faithful to the Creator. Hence the final battle will not be equal, but a complete obliteration of cosmic evil.

> "He rained down manna upon them to eat and gave them food from heaven. Human beings ate *the bread of angels*; He sent them food in abundance. He caused the east wind to blow in the heavens and by His power He directed the south wind."
>
> (Psalm 78:24-26)

The Lord shared the food of angels (extraterrestrials) with humans. Per the scripture, this was a nutritious mixture made fresh daily that came out of the sky. "And the house of Israel called the name thereof Manna: and it was like coriander seed, white; and the taste of it was like wafers made with honey." (Exodus 16:13)

Notes and References:

1. John Milton, *Paradise Lost,* 1667. http://www.paradiselost.org/
2. Guy Malone, *Hosts of Heaven,* 2007. http://www.alienresistance.org/hostsofheaven.htm
3. Rav. Simon B. Lakish, *The Jewish Encyclopedia* http://www.jewishencyclopedia.com, West Conshohocken, PA, originally published in 1906
4. Ibid.
5. Ella LeBain, *Who Is God? Book Two of Who's Who in The Cosmic Zoo? A Guide to ETs, Aliens, Gods & Angels,* Skypath Books, 2015. Chapter Four: *Mother Ships of The Lord,* subsections, *The Cloud Ships, The Clouds of Heaven.* pp. 71,75,77
6. R. Johanan, *The Jewish Encyclopedia* http://www.jewishencyclopedia.com, West Conshohocken, PA, originally published in 1906

CHAPTER SIX
THE FALLEN ANGELS

Alea iacta est — "The die has been cast."
~CAESAR

ANGELS AND SEX
The proclivity for excesses in sexual sin, from the one extreme of rape, abuse and mutilation, to the other end of the spectrum of loneliness and the pain of the lack of a partner, all fall under the same principality of fallen angels.

The fallen angels started out as the two hundred fallen sons of heaven, who fell into lust for the human woman. The results are the fruit of miscreations, the Nephilim, giants which became the evil spirits of the Earth doomed to torment human kind until the return of the Lord. The Books of Enoch name them, and record that many of them were imprisoned in the fifth heaven, being held till Judgment Day. We also have record in the Bible that some of them were imprisoned inside the Earth, only to be released on the Earth to be used to punish the wicked during the Bowls of God's Wrath being poured out on the unbelieving and rebellious humanity, who rejected the invitation of His Grace.

NAMES AND SINS OF THE WATCHERS -
THE ORIGIN OF EVIL ON PLANET EARTH
Names and Misdeeds of the Fallen Angels (aka the *Five satans*) are listed in 1 Enoch 69:2-12. 1 Enoch gives other lists of the names of the fallen angels as well.

After this judgment, they shall frighten them and make them scream because they have shown this knowledge of secret things to those who dwell on the earth. (1 Enoch 69:1)

There are 20 leaders in the 1 Enoch the section that mentions them which reads:

Now behold, I am naming the names of those angels! These are their names: The first of them is Semyaz, the second Aristaqis, the third Armen, the fourth

Kokba'el, the fifth Tur'el, the sixth Rumyal, the seventh Danyul, the eighth Neqa'el, the ninth Baraqel, the tenth Azaz'el, the eleventh Armaros, the twelfth Betryal, the thirteenth Basas'el, the fourteenth Hanan'el, the fifteenth Tur'el, the sixteenth SipWese'el, the seventeenth Yeter'el, the eighteenth Tuma'el, the nineteenth Tur'el, the twentieth Rum'el, and the twenty-first Azaz'el. (1 Enoch 69:2)

These are the chiefs of their angels, their names, their centurions, their chiefs over fifties, and their chiefs over tens. (1 Enoch 69:3)

These are the leaders of 200 angels, Bene Elohim - sons of God, in 1 Enoch who are turned into fallen Angels due to their taking of wives, mating with human women, and teaching forbidden knowledge.

Yeqon - "one who misled all the children of the angels, brought them down upon the earth, and perverted them by the daughters of the people"
(1 Enoch 69:4)

Asb'el - "one who gave the children of the holy angels an evil counsel and misled them so that they would defile their bodies by the daughters of the people"
(1 Enoch 69:5)

Gader'el - "he who showed the children of the people all the blows of death, who misled Eve, who showed the children of the people how to make the instruments of death such as the shield, the breastplate, and the sword for warfare, and all the other instruments of death to the children of the people. Through their agency death proceeds against the people who dwell upon the earth, from that day forevermore."
(1 Enoch 69:6,7)

Pinem'e - "demonstrated to the children of the people the bitter and the sweet and revealed to them all the secrets of their wisdom. Furthermore, he caused the people to penetrate the secret of writing and the use of ink and paper on account of this matter, there are many who have erred from eternity to eternity, until this very day. For human beings are not created for such purposes to take up their beliefs with pen and ink."
(1 Enoch 69:8-10)

Kasadya - "he who revealed to the children of the people the various flagellations of all evil - (the flagellation) of the souls and the demons, the smashing

Chapter Six: The Fallen Angels

of the embryo in the womb so that it may be crushed, the flagellation of the soul, snake bites, sunstrokes, the son of the serpent, whose name is Taba'ta"

(1 Enoch 69:12)

'For indeed human beings were not created but to be like malakim (angels), permanently to maintain pure and righteous lives. Death, which destroys everything, would have not touched them, had it not been through their knowledge by which they shall perish; death is now eating us by means of this power. Through their agency death proceeds against the people who dwell upon the earth, from that day forevermore.'

(1 Enoch 69:11)

And this is the number of Kasb'el, chief executor of the oath which he revealed to the kodesh (holy) ones while he was still dwelling in the highest in splendor.

(1 Enoch 69:13)

His name was then Beqa; and he spoke to Michael to disclose to him his secret name so that he would memorize this secret name of his, so that he would call it up in an oath in order that they shall tremble before it and the oath. He then revealed these to the children of the people, and all the hidden things and this power of this oath, for it is power and strength itself. The Evil One placed this oath in Michael's hand. These are the secrets of this oath -and they are sustained by the oath: The heaven was suspended before the creation of the world, and forever!

(1 Enoch 69:14-16)

Araqiel (also Arakiel, Araqael, Araciel, Arqael, Sarquael, Arkiel, Arkas) taught humans the signs of the earth. However, in the *Sibylline Oracles*, Araqiel is referred to not as a fallen angel, or Watcher, but as one of the 5 angels who lead the souls of men to judgment, the other 4 being Ramiel, Uriel, Samiel, and Azazel.

Armaros (also Amaros) in Enoch I taught men the resolving of enchantments.

Azazel taught men to make knives, swords, shields, and how to devise ornaments and cosmetics.

Gadriel taught the art of cosmetics.

Baraqel (Baraqiel) taught men astrology

Bezaliel mentioned in Enoch I, left out of most translations due to damaged manuscripts and problematic transmission of the text. Some believe Bezaliel is a derivative of Beelzebul.

Beelzebul is another form of the name Baal-Zebul ("Prince Baal"), one of the names of the ancient pagan god Baal. Earlier, Jews had mocked Baal-Zebul by referring to him as Baal-Zebub "Baal Fly" or, more literally, "Lord that flies". Today he is called Beezelbub. Baal-Zebub is referenced to in the Old Testament as the God of the city of Ekron (2Kings 1:6, 16). Here he is presented as the prince of demons.

It was a common belief among Jews and Christians that pagan gods were actually demons masquerading as divinities. It was also common practice for Jews during the times of animal sacrifices to prepare a special separate offering to Beelzebulb in the desert, as they believed sacrificing to him protected them from his fearful torments. That practice ended after the death and resurrection of Yeshua HaMashiach who is Jesus the Christ, the ultimate final sacrifice. The Temple sacrifices stopped completely when the 2nd Temple was destroyed in 70 AD, and the Jews were driven out of the land of Israel into the Diaspora.

Chazaqiel (sometimes Ezeqeel) taught men the signs of the clouds (meteorology).

Kokabiel (also Kakabel, Kochbiel, Kokbiel, Kabaiel, and Kochab), is a high-ranking, holy angel but, in general apocryphal lore and also in Enoch I, he is a fallen Watcher, resident of nether realms, and commands 365,000 surrogate spirits to do his bidding. Among other duties, he instructs his fellows in astrology.

Sariel (also Suriel) taught mankind about the courses of the moon (at one time regarded as forbidden knowledge).

Samyaza (also Shemyazaz, Shamazya, Semiaza, Shemhazi, Semyaza and Amezyarak) is one of the leaders of the fall from heaven.

Shamsiel, once a guardian of Eden, served as one of the 2 chief aides to the archangel Uriel (the other aide being Hasdiel) when Uriel bore his standard into battle, and is the head of 365 legions of angels and also crowns prayers, accompanying them to the 5th heaven. He is referred to as one of the Watchers. He is a fallen angel who teaches the signs of the sun.

Many can argue that these fallen angels came to jumpstart humanity and its culture, by teaching men the secrets of heaven and the art of war. After all, our galactic neighborhood is also filled with warfare. We find the end result of the Cosmic Drama between the forces of Light and the forces Darkness catalogued in the Book of Revelation. Many also believe that these fallen angels are even more violent than earth humans. As above so below.

"Then I saw an angel coming down from heaven, holding in his hand the key to the bottomless pit and a great chain. He seized the dragon, that ancient serpent, who is the devil, or Satan, and bound him for a thousand years. He threw him into the Abyss, and locked and sealed it over him, to keep him

Chapter Six: The Fallen Angels

from deceiving the nations anymore until the thousand years were ended. After that, he must be set free for a short time."

(Revelation 20:1-3)

THE DESTINY OF THE FALLEN ANGELS & WATCHERS

According to the *Book of Enoch*,[1] the Fallen Angels also known as the Watchers will be bound, imprisoned and vanished from the face of the earth.

'Then there came to them a great joy. And they blessed, magnified, and extolled YHVH (Yahuah) on account of the fact that the Name of that Son of Man (Jesus Christ) was revealed to them. He shall never pass away or perish from before the face of the earth. <u>But those who have led the world astray shall be bound with chains; and their ruinous congregation shall be imprisoned; all their deeds shall vanish from before the face of the earth</u>. Thenceforth nothing that is corruptible shall be found; for that Son of Man (Jesus Christ) has appeared and has been seated upon the throne of His splendor; and all evil shall disappear from before His face; he shall go and tell to that Son of Man (Jesus Christ), and He shall be strong before YHVH (Yahuah) the Lord of Hosts. Here ends the third parable of Enoch.'

(1 Enoch 69:27-29)

"They are demonic spirits who work miracles and go out to all the rulers of the world to gather them for battle against the Lord on that great judgment day of God the Almighty. "Look, I will come as unexpectedly as a thief! Blessed are all who are watching for me, who keep their clothing ready so they will not have to walk around naked and ashamed. And the demonic spirits gathered all the rulers and their armies to a place in Hebrew called Armageddon. Then the seventh angel poured out his bowl upon the air, and a loud voice came out of the temple from the throne, saying, "It is done." Then there came flashes of lightning, rumblings, peals of thunder and a severe earthquake. No earthquake like it has ever occurred since man has been on earth, so tremendous was the quake. The great city of Babylon split into three sections, and the cities of many nations fell into heaps of rubble. So, God remembered all of Babylon's sins, and he made her drink the cup that was filled with the wine of his fierce wrath. Every island vanished, and the mountains could no longer be found. From the sky, huge hailstones of about a hundred pounds each fell upon men. And they cursed God on account of the plague of hail, because the plague was so terrible."

(Revelation 16:14-21)

The Bible says, "that at the name of Jesus every knee should bow, in heaven and on earth and under the earth."

(Philippians 2:10)

NOTES AND REFERENCES:

1. R. H. Charles, (trans.). *The Book of Enoch,* 1917. http://www.sacred-texts.com/bib/boe

CHAPTER SEVEN

THE WATCHERS, THE NEPHILIM AND "SATAN'S MINISTERS."

"I have come to set the captives free."
- JESUS CHRIST

There are spirits in the material world. In fact, every single thing that happens in our third dimensional reality is orchestrated by spirits from the spiritual realms. There are several different levels to the heavens. The heavens are separated between the lower heavens and the higher heavens. What is known as the first and second heaven is where Cosmic Evil resides. This is what Ephesians 6:12 means when it says, "For we wrestle not against flesh and blood, but against principalities, against cosmic powers, against the rulers of the darkness of this world, against spiritual wickedness in heavenly places."

The cosmic powers, and the spiritual wickedness in heavenly places resides in the first heaven. These beings have the capability of space travel. They can travel from planet to planet and from one-star system to another, with some restrictions. The multiverse organizes itself according to cosmic vibrations, and as the low vibrational frequency of spiritual darkness and rebellion against the Creator of these cosmic beings is incompatible with loving and benevolent energies, they are denied access to the higher heavens and dimensions.

Subsequently, everything in our world is ruled by spirits, principalities (princes, Archangels, or ArchDemons), and the oligarchy of cosmic powers. In New Age vocabulary, there is such an emphasis on 'spirit guides.' Most of the time, people have no idea *who* these spirit guides are, but because they seem to be the loudest voice in their heads, they listen to and *believe* in them, without question, without discernment. They really believe that they are being guided and protected by their *spirit guides*. Most of these so-called *spirit guides* are in fact the fallen, masquerading as angels, goddesses from the past, ancient people, and even deceased family members. These are actually *cosmic intelligences* known as 'demons.' The Watchers, the Nephilim and

Satan's ministers are the cosmic intelligences known to us as demons. Remember, the word 'demon' comes from the Greek word for *intelligences,* which is 'daemon'.

THE WATCHERS IN THE BIBLE

> "When men began to increase on earth and daughters were born to them, the divine beings saw how beautiful the daughters of men were and took wives from among those that pleased them. The Lord Yahuah said, 'My breath shall not abide in man forever, since he too is flesh; let the days allowed him be one hundred and twenty years.' It was then, and later too, that the *Nephilim* appeared on earth - when the divine beings cohabited with the daughters of men, who bore them offspring. They were the heroes of old, the men of renown."
>
> (Genesis 6:1-4)

> "*God* (Elohim) stands in the Congregation of *God* (El), In the midst of *gods* (Elohim) He judges all the foundations of the earth are moved. "The 'gods' know nothing, they understand nothing. They walk about in darkness; all the foundations of the earth are shaken. I said: You are g*ods*, (Elohim) and all of you sons of the Most High (Elyon), nevertheless you shall die like men, and fall like one of the princes (sarim)."
>
> (Psalm 82:1, 5-7)

Many scholars agree that this part of the Psalm refers to the *fallen angels*. While Genesis Chapter 6 tells us that angels married women, it doesn't immediately condemn these acts as sin. It is their offspring, which become Nephilim, are later condemned and destroyed by Yahuah. Psalm 82 tells that the *Elohim* sinned, but does not tell how, nor does it specifically mention that they married women. It may have been that the angels sinned by reproducing or by rebelling and doing their own thing on the earth, which brought them into darkness. Certain passages in the *Jewish Midrash* talk of how angels are immortal and do not need to reproduce. Because humans are mortal, they must reproduce in order to achieve immortality in their descendants. Yet Psalm 82 does not refer specifically to angels, but to *gods*, to the Elohim. The Hebrew word for angels is 'malachim', which was never mentioned in the Psalm at all. This was a judgment on the *gods.*

There are myriads of unexplained phenomenon throughout history which have led people to believe that mankind has been visited by extraterrestrials. One group of alleged alien visitors who appear in some ancient texts are known as the "watchers." The Watchers have been regarded as a type of 'angel' rather than an extraterrestrial

Chapter Seven: The Watchers, the Nephilim and "Satan's Ministers."

entity. However, a careful study of these texts shows the Watchers to be in fact representative of being earthly beings, which means that these beings are not 'extraterrestrial' at all, but live and reside within the earthly realms, perhaps in another dimension, yet bound to the earth nevertheless.

> "Therefore God has highly exalted Him and bestowed on Him the name that is above every name, so that at the name of Jesus every knee should bow, in heaven and on earth and *under the earth*, and every tongue confess that Jesus Christ is Lord, to the glory of God the Father."
>
> (Philippians 2:9-11)

Under the earth, even though this passage was written approximately 2,000 years ago, displays the awareness of beings living *under the earth* was known.

The term *watcher* has gained a mystical connotation. In the three times it is used in the Bible, all occur during the prophetic dream of the Babylonian King Nebuchadnezzar. In one instance the allusion to a heavenly being seems apparent, *"a watcher and a holy one came down from heaven."* (Daniel 4:13) A revelation of troubling events to come is made to the dreaming king by the watchers as if in warning. However, a few verses later new meaning is added *"The matter is by the decree of the watchers, and the sentence by the word of the holy ones."* (Daniel 4:17) Here it becomes clear that the watchers and the accompanying holy ones are arbiters of the fates rather than messengers.

> "For we do not wrestle against flesh and blood, but against the rulers, against the authorities, against *the cosmic powers over this present darkness*, against the spiritual forces of evil in the heavenly places."
>
> (Ephesians 6:12)

The 'cosmic powers over this present darkness', refers to the Watchers, Nephilim, Fallen Angels, the satans, all the Demonic realm that attempts to interfere with and rule over the affairs of humankind. This is the material fragment of what many people see as UFOs in our skies today. USOs, or Underwater Submerged Objects, come from under the oceans and water beds of the earth, from underground and underwater UFO bases. These are *inside* and *under the earth* where the fallen angels, watchers, nephilim and the satans presently reside.

THE WATCHERS IN JEWISH MIDRASH

This is a passage from Jewish Midrash in which Hannah is praying for a child at Shiloh:

"Lord of the Universe! The celestials never die, and they do not reproduce their kind. Terrestrial beings die, but they are fruitful and multiply. Therefore, I pray: Either make me immortal, or give me a son!"

The Watchers in 1 Enoch

Who is Enoch? In Hebrew, Chanoch or Hanoch, in the book of Genesis 5, Enoch, the son of Jared, a great-grandfather of Noah, and father of Methuselah (Genesis 5:1-18). Enoch is often confused with Enos (or Enosh). Enos is recorded as a grandson of Adam (Genesis 5:5-6), and great grandfather of Enoch (Genesis 5:18).

"And Enoch lived sixty and five years and begat Methuselah: and Enoch walked with God after he begat Methuselah three hundred years and begat sons and daughters: And Enoch walked with God: and he was not; for God took him."
(Genesis 5)

God took Enoch, who never died. He ascended into a space ship, and a few hundred years later returned with two scrolls which were buried in the Dead Sea, our Dead Sea Scrolls. These are known as I Enoch and 2 Enoch (the Book of Secrets), as old as the books of Genesis, yet Enoch's books were not canonized into the Bible by the Catholic Ecumenical church fathers. This decision was made between 325 A.D. at the Council of Nicea though the whole doctrine was not complete until 360 A.D. at the Council of Constantinople.

The *Apocrypha* are the biblical books included in the Vulgate and accepted by the Roman Catholic and Orthodox canon but considered non-canonical by Protestants. These are not part of the Hebrew Scriptures. The word is originally Greek means "those having been hidden away", which were also called 'heretical'. The general term is usually applied to the books that the Protestant Christian Church considered useful but not divinely inspired. Given that different denominations have different beliefs about what constitutes canonical scripture, there are several versions of the apocrypha.

The *Book of Enoch*[1] was written centuries before the birth of Christ and yet is considered by many to be more Christian in its theology than Jewish. It was considered scripture by many early Christians. The earliest literature of the so-called Church Fathers is filled with references to this mysterious book. The early second century *Epistle of Barnabus* makes many references to the *Book of Enoch*. Second and Third Century Church Fathers like Justin Martyr, Irenaeus, Origin and Clement of Alexandria all make a big deal out of the Book of Enoch. Tertullian (160-230 C.E) even called the *Book of Enoch* "Holy Scripture".

Chapter Seven: The Watchers, the Nephilim and "Satan's Ministers."

The Ethiopic Church even added the *Book of Enoch* to its official canon. It was widely known and read the first three centuries after Christ. This and many other books became discredited after the Council of Laodicea. The Council of Laodicea was a regional synod of approximately thirty clerics from Asia Minor, that assembled about 363-364 AD in Laodicea, Phrygia Pacatiana. Thereafter, being under ban of those church authorities, afterwards it gradually passed out of circulation.

There are some Catholic bibles that include the Books of Enoch. The Coptic Churches in Egypt have included the Books of Enoch for millennia. The *Book of Enoch* was originally part of the Holy Bible; and was wrongfully removed by powerful evil people, as by the church fathers being led astray by the satans and fallen angels, who do not want you to read it, because of what it says about them. The church has long been a stronghold for the fallen angels, as from this seat of power they can efficiently distort the truth and deceive honest believers in their faith.

The *Book of Enoch* was acknowledged as Holy Scripture and quoted by Jesus Christ Himself; by his half-brothers James and Jude; by all of His Apostles and the whole Christian Church for several centuries before Mohammed Mustafa was given the holy Koran. Even in this book Enoch is greatly praised by God, and we are told that God "raised him to a lofty station". This praise is also recorded in the section of The Apocrypha called "The Wisdom of Joshua the son of Sirach", also known as "Ecclesiasticus".

Enoch was the first man to *ascend* to heaven and never die, and for that he should be honored. The fact that modern day Christians argue that the *Book of Enoch* had to be written after the flood, because everything was destroyed during the great deluge, show their lack of understanding. God's Holy Angelic forces handled those scrolls that Enoch was given and placed them in the caves. Remember Enoch was taken by God at the age of 365 years, but was then returned to earth some 200 years later. His scrolls were written to reflect the times before and after the great deluge and his scrolls were preserved by angels.

The *Book of Enoch* is divided into five basic parts, but it is *The Book of Parables* (37-71) which gives scholars the most trouble, for it is primarily concerned with a figure called "the messiah"; "the righteous one"; "the chosen one" and "the son of man." (Enoch 46:1-2) It is said that Jesus Christ Himself used the term 'the son of man' which came directly out of the book of Enoch. "There I beheld the Ancient of days whose head was like white wool, and with him another, whose countenance resembled that of a man. His countenance was full of grace, like that of one of the holy angels. Then I inquired of one of the angels, who went with me, and who showed me every secret thing, concerning this Son of man; who he was; whence he was; and why he accompanied the Ancient of days. He answered and said to me, 'This is the Son of man, to whom righteousness belongs; with whom righteousness has dwelt; and who will reveal all the treasures of that which is concealed: for the Lord of spirits has chosen him; and his portion has surpassed all before the Lord of spirits in everlasting uprightness'".

The opening verses of the *Book of Enoch* affirm to us that the revelations in this book were not meant for Enoch's generation, but for a rather remote generation, and of course the book would make more sense to the generations after Christ. We know that the early Church made use of the Book of Enoch, but it was then all but lost, until recent times. Perhaps this book was meant for our generation, as it is widely available today after being concealed for over a millennium.

The words of the blessing of Enoch were meant for the elect and righteous, who will be living in the day of tribulation, when all the wicked and godless are to be removed. 'And he took up his parable and said -Enoch a righteous man, whose eyes were opened by God, saw the vision of the Holy One in the heavens, which the angels showed me, and from them I heard everything, and from them I understood as I saw, but not for this generation, but for a remote one which is for to come.' (Enoch 1:1-3)

The reason for Enoch's books being considered apocrypha is primarily because of its devotion to the planets, and the stars of heaven, describing such detailed astronomical and astrological data that opposed the agenda of the church fathers. The church of Rome at that time held fast to the belief that the earth was flat and the center of the universe. Both Galileo Galilei and Giordano Bruno suffered terribly for their astronomical discoveries, which 2 Enoch confirmed and the church fathers rejected. The main body in I Enoch details the plight and fall of the Nephilim, the Fallen Angels, and the *satans* as he calls the *adversaries of God*, and their destiny to be bound inside the earth. They are even now used to tempt humankind, and will until the end of all battles, when the Lord Jesus Christ, to whom Enoch refers, will bind the fallen angels into the lake of fire to burn forever. Enoch's account perfectly coincides with the book of Revelation, though it was written several thousand years before St. John the Divine channeled the book of Revelation. If only the church fathers would have allowed I Enoch into the bible, it would have altered the face of the Judeo-Christian religion, plus having increased one's understanding of the nature of the spiritual battle in which we find ourselves engulfed.

The main sin of the fallen angels was that of revolting against *Almighty God, their Creator*. Because of this, they were cast down.

1 Enoch gives an account of the fall of the Angels from heaven. Chapter 6 talks of how the angels saw and lusted after the daughters of men, which corroborates Genesis chapter 6.

"In those days, when the children of man had multiplied, it happened that there were born unto them handsome and beautiful daughters. And the

Chapter Seven: The Watchers, the Nephilim and "Satan's Ministers."

angels, the children of heaven, saw them and desired them; and they said to one another, 'Come, let us choose wives for ourselves from among the daughters of man and beget us children.' And *Semyaza*, being their leader, said unto them, 'I fear that perhaps you will not consent that this deed should be done, and I alone will become (responsible) for this great sin.' But they all responded to him, 'Let us all swear an oath and bind everyone among us by a curse not to abandon this suggestion but to do the deed.' Then they all swore together and bound one another by (the curse) And they were altogether two hundred;"

(1 Enoch 6:1-7)

The angels descended on Mount Hermon during the days of Jared. There were 19 leaders mentioned in 1 Enoch, who were also called *'the chiefs of ten'* once they reached the earth:

"they took wives unto themselves, and everyone (respectively) chose one woman for himself, and they began to go unto them. And they taught them magical medicine, incantations, the cutting of roots, and taught them about plants. And the women became pregnant and gave birth to great *giants* whose heights were three hundred cubits. These *giants* consumed the produce of all the people until the people detested feeding them. So the *giants* turned against the people in order to eat them."

(1 Enoch 7:1-5)

The Origin of War

These Fallen Angels then taught women charms, enchantments, the cutting of roots, and the knowledge of plants. They taught men how to make various weapons and armor, and also arts and sciences. These acts led to an increase in lawlessness and warfare which angered the Creator that these angels would teach men how to fight and be at war. The men of earth then cried out to heaven, and the archangels (Michael, Uriel, Raphael, and Gabriel) cried out to the Most High *God*. In response, *God* sent Uriel to warn Noah that there would soon be a flood that would destroy the wickedness on earth.

"And *Azâzêl* taught men to make swords, and knives, and shields, and breastplates, and made known to them the metals and the art of working them, and bracelets, and ornaments, and the use of antimony, and the beautifying of the eyelids, and all kinds of costly stones, and all coloring tinctures. And there arose much godlessness, and they committed fornication, and they were led astray, and became corrupt in all their ways. *Semjâzâ* taught enchantments, and root-cuttings, *Armârôs* the resolving of enchantments, *Barâqîjâl*, (taught) astrology, *Kôkabêl* the constellations, *Ezêqêêl* the knowledge of the clouds, and *Sariêl* the course of the moon. And as men perished, they cried, and their cry went up to heaven . . ."

(1 Enoch 8:1-3)

"And then Michael, Uriel, Raphael, and Gabriel looked down from heaven and saw much blood being shed upon the earth, and all lawlessness being wrought upon the earth. 2. And they said one to another: 'The earth made †without inhabitant cries the voice of their crying† up to the gates of heaven. 3 And now to you, the holy ones of heaven, the souls of men make their suit, saying, "Bring our cause before the Most High."

(1 Enoch 9:1-4)

"The Archangels said to the Creator, 'Thou seest all things, and nothing can hide itself from Thee. Thou seest what *Azâzêl* hath done, who hath taught all unrighteousness on earth and revealed the eternal secrets which were preserved in heaven, which men were striving to learn: And *Semjâzâ*, whom Thou has given authority to bear rule over his associates. And they have gone to the daughters of men upon the earth, and have slept with the women, and have defiled themselves, and revealed to them all kinds of sins. And the women have borne giants and the whole earth thereby had been filled with blood and unrighteousness."

(1 Enoch 9:6-10)

There yet remained faithful Watchers still in heaven. These Watchers, two of which are named in the Bible, were faithful in their obedience to the Creator God. The book of Enoch and the Bible seem to treat the role of angels exactly the same.

They remained in their abode, and looked down upon the earth from heaven, and saw the exact nature of the corruption and depravity which had gripped mankind. Consequently, they took man's case to the Creator God.

Based on the scenario laid forth by the book of Enoch, it is only when the angels of the heavens of this earth approach God that He takes action. These were His appointed watchmen, or guardians, of the earth.

As long as things remained as they should, the angels could handle what happened on earth by acting in accordance with the Creator God's will. This, of course, is a hypothetical analysis of the Heavenly protocol. It is interesting the same protocol is described in both the Bible and the book of Enoch

Chapter Seven: The Watchers, the Nephilim and "Satan's Ministers."

Raphael was commanded to bind *Azazel* hand and foot, and to cast him into a hole that the Lord had made in the desert *Dudâêl*. Raphael threw rugged and sharp rocks and covered *Azâzêl's* face so that he would not see light. Michael was commanded to bind *Semyaza* and his associates inside the valleys of the earth, which is where they reside today. They will remain there until the Day of Judgment when he will be cast into the fire.

> "And heal the earth which the angels have corrupted, and proclaim the healing of the earth, that they may heal the plague, and that all the children of men may not perish through all the secret things that the Watchers have disclosed and have taught their sons. And the whole earth has been corrupted through the works that were taught be *Azâzêl*."
>
> (1 Enoch 10:5-9)

The *race of giants* produced from this union gave way to a brood of *evil spirits*. The evil spirits are the departed spirits of the giants themselves, and are bound to the earth to torment humankind. These spirits are not material or corporeal beings, but they torment mankind because they have proceeded from them, in other words, the spirits at one time were material and half human. According to 1 Enoch, these spirits will not be punished until the Day of Judgment, in contrast to the Watchers, who are punished both before and on the day of judgment.

> "But now the giants who are born from the union of the spirits and the flesh shall be called evil spirits upon the earth, because their dwelling shall be upon the earth and inside the earth. Evil spirits have come out of their bodies. Because from the day that they were created from the holy ones they became the Watchers; their first origin is the spiritual foundation. They will become evil upon the earth and shall be called evil spirits. The dwelling of the spiritual beings of heaven is heaven; but the dwelling of the spirits of the earth, which are born upon the earth, is in the earth. The spirits of the *giants* oppress each other, they will corrupt, fall, be excited, and fall upon the earth, and cause sorrow. They eat no food, nor become thirsty, nor find obstacles. And these spirits shall rise up against the children of the people and against the women, because they have proceeded forth from them."
>
> (1 Enoch 15)

1 Enoch 19 also gives a variation to the origin of *demons*. It implies that *demons* were already in existence during the time of the fall of the angels. According to 1 Enoch 10-16, the demons are the spirits which go forth from these angels.

> "Here shall stand in many different appearances the spirits of the angels which have united themselves with women. They have defiled the people and will lead them into error so that they will offer sacrifices to the demons as unto *Gods*, until the great Day of Judgment in which they shall be judged till they are finished."
>
> (1 Enoch 19:1)

THE WATCHERS IN JUBILEES

The *Book of Jubilees*[2] is also part of the *apocrypha* written around the 2nd century B.C. This is an account of the biblical history of the world from the time of creation to the time of Moses. It is divided into periods or Jubilees of 49 years each. For the most part the narrative follows the story in the book of Genesis, with some additional details such as the names of the daughter of Adam and Eve, and details the active role of a demonic entity called 'Mastema' who today is known as 'Satan'. We've already established that the word 'satan' is Hebrew for adversary, but this entity is called 'Mastema' who the *Book of Jubilees* describes as the Chief of the Evil Spirits, which is just another one of the many names of Satan.

Remember Lucifer persuaded one third of heaven's angels and extraterrestrials to rebel against the Creator. Lucifer then became 'Satan,' then so became the fallen those angels (extraterrestrials) who also became known as the 'satans' and the rebels, and a hierarchy of 'satans' was formed. This is why we see so many different names for 'Satan', there are many 'satans', who all have their place in the demonic hierarchy.

As God commanded the angels to bind all the evil spirits, Mastema came and asked the Lord that some of the spirits might be allowed to remain with him to do his will. God granted his request and allowed one tenth of the spirits to remain with Mastema, while the other nine parts would be condemned.

> "When Mastema, the leader of the spirits, came, he said: 'Lord creator, leave some of them before me; let them listen to me and do everything that I tell them, because if none of them is left for me I shall not be able to exercise the authority of my will among mankind. For they are meant for the purposes of destroying and misleading before my punishment because the evil of mankind is great.' Then he said that a tenth of them should be left before him, while he would make nine parts descend to the place of judgment."
>
> (Jubilees 10:8-9)

In the *Book of Jubilees* Mastema is the name given for Satan. The book gives another account of how the Watchers fell that is similar to *1 Enoch*. It explains that

Chapter Seven: The Watchers, the Nephilim and "Satan's Ministers."

the Watchers originally descended to the earth to teach mankind to do what is just, but they 'sinned with the daughters of men because these had begun to mix with earthly women so that they became defiled.' (Jubilees 4:22)

> Malalael "named [his son] Jared because during his lifetime the angels of the *Lord* who were called *Watchers* descended to earth to teach mankind and to do what is just and upright upon the earth."
> (Jubilees 4:15)

Jubilees also says that they were sent by *God, Himself*:

> "Against his angels whom he had sent to the earth he was angry enough to uproot them from all their (positions of) authority"
> (Jubilees 5:6)

Jubilees relates the fall of the angels similar to that of *1 Enoch*. *God* was displeased with the angels because of their lust for the daughters of men. The union of the angels and women is said to result in the bastard offspring of the *Nephilim*. In the Hebrew Bible, the word Nephilim translates to *fallen angels*, or *those who fell from heaven*. *Naphal* is the root word in Hebrew which means *to fall*. Their offspring became the reprobate *giants* that wreaked havoc on the earth and were later destroyed through the great deluge of floods.

> "For it was on account of these three things [fornication, uncleanness, and injustice - see Jubilees 7:20] that the flood was on the earth, since it was due to fornication that the Watchers had illicit intercourse, apart from the mandate of their authority, with women. When they married of them whomever they chose they committed the first acts of uncleanness. They fathered as their sons the *Nephilim*.
> (Jubilees 7:21-22)

The Watchers in 2 Enoch

2 Enoch also mentions a group of angels called the *Grigori*, who are similar to the Watchers. Their prince is called '*Satanail*'. The difference in this account as compared with the two previous accounts is that only 3 angels came down to earth to take wives and beget giants.

> "These are the *Grigori*, who with their prince *Satanail* rejected the *Lord* of light, and after them are those who are held in great darkness on the second

heaven, and three of them went down on earth to the place *Ermon*, and broke through their vows on the shoulder of the hill Ermon and saw the daughters of men how good they are, and took to themselves wives, and befouled the earth with their deeds, who in all times of their age made lawlessness and mixing, and giants are born and marvelous big men and great enmity. And therefore, *God* judged them with great judgment, and they weep for their brethren and they will be punished on the Lord's great day."

(2 Enoch 18:3-4)

Recognize this phrase? This was the motto of Book One of *Who's Who in The Cosmic Zoo?*:

"Be kind for everyone you meet is fighting a hard battle." - Philo 10 BC

Philo of Alexandria[3] (10 B.C.E.-50 C.E.) wrote a commentary of Genesis 6 called *Concerning the Giants*. In it, he emphasized that the passage was not a myth.

"And when the angels of God saw the daughters of men that they were beautiful, they took unto themselves wives of all of them whom they Chose."

(Genesis 6:2)

Those beings, whom other philosophers call demons, Moses usually calls angels; and they are souls hovering in the air. And let no one suppose, that what is here stated is a fable, for it is necessarily true that the universe must be filled with living things in all its parts, since every one of its primary and elementary portions contains its appropriate animals and such as are consistent with its nature; the earth containing terrestrial animals, the sea and the rivers containing aquatic animals, and the fire such as are born in the fire (but it is said, that such as these last are found chiefly in Macedonia), and the heaven containing the stars: for these also are entire souls pervading the universe, being unadulterated and divine, inasmuch as they move in a circle, which is the kind of motion most akin to the mind, for every one of them is the parent mind. It is therefore necessary that the air also should be full of living beings. And these beings are invisible to us, just as the air itself is not visible to mortal sight. But it does not follow, because our sight is incapable of perceiving the forms of souls, that for that reason there are no souls in the air; but it follows of necessity that they must be comprehended by the mind, in order that like may be contemplated by like.[3]

Chapter Seven: The Watchers, the Nephilim and "Satan's Ministers."

NOTES AND REFERENCES:

1. R. H. Charles, (trans.). *The Book of Enoch,* 1917. http://www.sacred-texts.com/bib/boe
2. *The Jewish Encyclopedia* http://www.jewishencyclopedia.com, West Conshohocken, PA, originally published in 1906
3. Philo, *Concerning the Giants* II: 6-9

CHAPTER EIGHT
STARS WHO FELL FROM HEAVEN

Jesus said, *"The stars shall fall from heaven."*
(Matthew 24:29)

Whenever the ancient texts refer to 'a star falling from Heaven,' these passages are referring to fallen angels, or rebellious extraterrestrials. This indicates that the stars of the Heavens may in fact be billions of God's angel, made of light and fire. Didn't He make the Cherubim as fire beings? Scientifically speaking, the stars are made of natural gases, but who empowers them? The Creator made them, the ancients named them as planets and believed them to be gods, and the stars themselves as angels. However, the stars were all named by God. [See my chapter on the *Divine Plan of Salvation as Written in the Stars*, in Book Five: *The Heavens*.] When Jesus spoke of the *stars falling from heaven*, I believe He was referring to the fallen sons and fallen angels who once were 'stars', both in the shining light literal sense and the celebrity sense as well. We on earth attribute someone who is a 'star' as meaning they once stood out, and were outstanding amongst the rest.

Jesus replied, "I saw Satan fall like lightning from heaven."
(Luke 10:18)

"The third angel sounded his trumpet, and a *great star, blazing like a torch, fell from the sky* on a third of the rivers and on the springs of water."
(Revelation 8:10)

"The fifth angel sounded his trumpet, and I saw *a star that had fallen from the sky to the earth.* The star was given the key to the shaft of the Abyss."
(Revelation 9:1)

"I, Jesus, have sent my angel to give you this testimony for the churches. I am the Root and the Offspring of David, and the bright Morning Star."
(Revelation 22:16)

Chapter Eight: Stars Who Fell From Heaven

"All the stars of the heavens will be dissolved and the sky rolled up like a scroll; all *the starry host will fall* like withered leaves from the vine, like shriveled figs from the fig tree."

(Isaiah 34:4)

"Though you soar like the eagle and make your nest among the stars, from there I will bring you down," declares the LORD."

(Obadiah 1:4)

"And *the stars of heaven fell to the earth*, even as a fig tree casts her untimely green leaves, when she is shaken by a mighty wind."

(Revelation 6:13)

"The fifth angel sounded his trumpet, and I saw *a star fall from heaven* unto the earth. The star was given the key to the shaft of the Abyss."

(Revelation 9:1)

"The third angel blew his trumpet, and a *great star fell from heaven*, blazing like a torch, fell from the sky on a third of the rivers and on the springs of water."

(Revelation 8:10)

"*The stars of heaven and their constellations will not show their light.* The rising sun will be darkened and the moon will not give its light."

(Isaiah 13:10)

"*All the stars of the heavens will be dissolved* and the sky rolled up like a scroll; all the starry host will fall like withered leaves from the vine, like shriveled figs from the fig tree."

(Isaiah 34:4)

"His tail swept a *third of the stars out of the sky and flung them to the earth*. The dragon stood in front of the woman who was about to give birth, so that he might devour her child the moment it was born."

(Revelation 12:4)

1 Enoch 85-90[1] gives a similar account of the fall of the angels. In these passages, a star (either *Semjaza* or *Azazel*) fell from heaven and began to pasture among the oxen (mankind). Both the book of Enoch and the Bible in a number of passages use the phrase, *"a star fell from heaven, or stars that fell from heaven,"* are all making

reference to Heavens Angels or God's Extraterrestrial Messengers. 1 Enoch 85-90 goes on to report that a *number of stars then fell and were transformed into bulls*. They began to cover the cows (the angels married mortal women), who then gave birth to elephants, camels, and asses (the giants). The oxen then became restless and began to fight, but they became prey to the wild beasts.

The Archangels then appear in the disguise of men. One seizes the first of the fallen stars and casts it into the abyss. A second gives the elephants, camels, and asses a sword so that they will kill each other. A third Archangel stones the other fallen stars and casts them into the gulf. The story then goes on to describe *the Maccabean revolt*, which leads to a description of the final struggle between good and evil.

The *Maccabean Revolt* can be read in its entirety in the rejected Jewish texts, *The Book of Maccabees*, which is read annually by Jews at the celebration of Hanukkah, the Festival of the Miracle of Light.

However, in dire circumstances, the cry must be taken to God, the Supreme Commander. The book of Enoch describes these times in the same nature as Genesis. These were some of the direst times the earth had ever known.

Like faithful soldiers they report to God what has been happening at their post, and how some of their fellow angels have rebelled once again. The book of Enoch, in essence, is a play-by-play of the brief passage found in Genesis 6. The faithful angels report the specific sins of certain angels, making special mention of *Azazel* and *Semjaza*. Based on this, it would be logical to assume these were the two most powerful of the rebellious Watchers.

Thus, in the following passage, "the holy ones of heaven" take the cause of man before God. And the Lord said to Gabriel, 'Proceed against the bastards and reprobates, and against the children of fornication: and destroy the children of fornication and the children of the Watchers from amongst men and cause them to go forth: send them one against the other that they may destroy each other in battle. (1 Enoch 10:9)

Indeed, *Semjaza* had been given authority by God to "bear rule over his associates". We know of at least two Nephilim children, Og and Sihon, descended from *Semjaza*. He was no doubt powerful. Could Gog and Magog be the children of the Nephilim or of *Semjaza* himself as well, who continue to this day to have a stronghold over some of the nations of the earth? Some Bible scholars have interpreted Gog and Magog as the land of Russia, which is known in the texts as Rosh. Could Gog and Magog be the Principalities that rule over this nation, which is destined, according to the prophetic Biblical timeline, to be brought down in the end times?

It seems that there is a threefold aspect to the sin of the Watchers in these accounts. First, it was a defilement of the essence of the angels to marry and engage in sexual acts with human women. Second, these unions between the angels and mortal women were considered evil in and of themselves. Because of the Nephilim and the evil created

Chapter Eight: Stars Who Fell From Heaven

by these unions, the Creator God ordered the great Flood of Noah's time to wipe them out. Finally, the *angels* sinned because they taught humanity how to war and revealed the secrets of the natural universe which *God* did not intend for man to know.

Herein lies the *Great Experiment* in which we all find ourselves. Human culture and human evolution has been initiated by the sins of these fallen angels. After the Creator ordered the floods to wipe the planet clean of their presence and of their offspring, humankind was allowed to evolve. Yet after the flood the evil spirits bound by the earth were allowed to torment humankind until the end of days. The Creator allows this to go on to test the souls of humans, to sort out which ones are worthy of His Salvation and His Kingdom on Earth, and which ones will be destroyed at the judgment. This makes life on planet earth a 'spiritual battle' between good and evil for every single soul, with humans being forced to make the choice daily between serving God or serving the dark forces. In the final death, those who have been taken over by the realm of the satans, the demonic fallen angels and their evil spirits will be destroyed forever.

The *Jewish Encyclopedia* states[2] that in the apocalyptic literature, the concept of fallen angels is widespread. Indications of belief in fallen angels, behind which probably lies the symbolizing of shooting stars, an astronomical phenomenon, are found in Isaiah 14:12. Throughout antiquity, stars were commonly regarded as *living* celestial beings (Job 38:7), when the *morning stars sang together* and all the sons of God shouted for joy.

The expression "*the morning-stars*" is used to account for the beauty of the principal star which, at certain seasons of the year, leads on the morning. It is applied naturally to those angelic beings that are of distinguished glory and rank in heaven. That it refers to the angel, seems to be evident from the connection; and this interpretation is demanded in order to correspond with the phrase "sons of God" in the other member of the verse. And all the sons of God - Angels - called the sons of God from their resemblance to him, or their being created by him. [3]

> "How you are fallen from heaven, *O Day Star, son of the Morning*! How you are cut down to the ground, you who laid the nations low! You said in your heart, "I will ascend to heaven; I will raise my throne above the stars of God (El); I will sit on the mount of congregation on the heights of Zaphon (the mount of meeting); I will ascend to the tops of the clouds, I will make myself like the Most High (Elyon)." But you are brought down to Sheol (the netherworld), to the depths of the Pit. Those who see you will stare at you, and ponder over you: "Is this the man who made the earth tremble, who shook kingdoms, who made the world like a desert and overthrew its cities, who would not let his prisoners go home?"
>
> (Isaiah 14:12-17)

Notes and References:

1. R. H. Charles, (trans.). *The Book of Enoch*, 1917. http://www.sacred-texts.com/bib/boe
2. *The Jewish Encyclopedia* http://www.jewishencyclopedia.com, West Conshohocken, PA, originally published in 1906
3. Albert Barnes, *Barnes Notes on the Bible*, Baker Books; 19th edition (February 1, 1983).

CHAPTER NINE
FALLEN ANGELS OR EVIL SPIRITS?

"And no wonder for Satan himself masquerades as an Angel of Light."
(2 CORINTHIANS 11:14)

There is a difference between the fallen angels and the evil spirits that dwell on the earth. Evil spirits are not dead people haunting the earth. It is the fallen angels who create evil and can be classified as demonic. To be clear, the fallen angels bring with them demon spirits. Remember the word, 'demon' comes from 'daemon', the Greek word which translates as 'intelligence'. Those in the realm of the demonic are knowledgeable, clever manipulators, very intelligent, but their agenda is evil, which classifies them as 'evil spirits'. Those of the realm of the demonic can trick humans into believing that they are being contacted by deceased family members, or ascended masters, or extraterrestrials. These demons are seducers, who come as 'angels of light', as their master, Lucifer, was once the Light bearer, so were all the fallen angels once created to bear light. They know how to put it over on us, they know exactly what buttons to push to get inside the minds and bodies of earth humans.

How clever these demons are! They are under the category of 'Watchers', so they literally watch and study us humans on earth. They know everything about human habits, special relationships and favorite things. When a spirit medium attempts to contact the dead, these demons just 'step in' for the actual deceased person. Because they have been watching and studying us for our entire lives, they know exactly how to mimic our loved ones and they know what we want to hear. They know exactly what to tell the spirit medium to 'hook' both the medium and the seeker in, making them believe that they have been contacted by their deceased loved one.

This is the reason that Lord warns several times in the Bible to stay away from spirit mediums. God in His mercy knows the game they are playing in the spirit realm, and wants His people to be protected from demonic influence, demonic deception and demonic interference. Remember these are seducing spirits! They tell you just enough truth to hook you in, but mix in lies and misguidance. They can make things happen, just to startle you into suspension of disbelief. This may sound unpalatable to many who are convinced that they are in contact with their dearly departed, but the truth is, they are being masterfully played by demons.

There is a hierarchy, a division between the fallen angels, demons and evil spirits, just as there is a hierarchy to the Creators archangels, angels and spiritual powers.

The evil spirits bound to the earth came from the horrific monsters, giants and hybrids that were the Nephilim. These abominations of creation had broken so many laws of the Creator that He ordered the floods to wipe them off the face of the earth and start all over again. The spirits that were housed in these aberrations were then bound to the earth to dwell and harass humans ever since. These spirits must all bow to the authority given to the Lord Jesus Christ. They fear the Lord and only those believers who carries the authority to cast out devils and evil spirits will they obey. They also follow under the Draconian/Satanic hierarchy, but they are neither here nor there, bound to an area of the spirit realm.

The bible teaches us that the spirits of these hybrid giants will not be resurrected:

> "Let not the dead live, *let not the giants* [repha'im] *rise again*: therefore, hast Thou visited and destroyed them, and hast destroyed all their memory."
> (Isaiah 26:14)

At some point, God will destroy the demonic spirits of the Nephilim and put them out of their misery. They are not part of His creation, and they have no future in His plan. He allows them to test humans, so from that day to this, they are still roaming the earth to see who they can harass, deceive and destroy.

Until the Kingdom of Heaven is set up on Earth, the Earth will be under the influence of fallen angel demonic principalities, powers and spiritual darkness in high places. Spiritual conflict is unseen but ongoing, and always manifests as attack, sickness, loss, war, conflict, and destruction among humankind. The Creator's angels are often in a battle with the fallen angels to fulfill God's will. Demons and the evil spirits of the departed Nephilim roam the earth seeking to torment and afflict humankind.

The fallen angels and the demons will be fully unleashed on the earth during the end of this age, when God's wrath is vented on unbelieving and unrepentant humanity. In the end, however, Christ will return and subjugate all who won't submit to God's authority, including Satan and the fallen host. Their punishment will be the lake of fire. The disembodied spirits of the giants will eventually be destroyed forever.

Gray aliens are part of the fallen angel demon hierarchy. The fallen angel demons and Watchers are equipped with extremely advanced technology. Again, this is another deception to awe humans. Many humans are fascinated by UFOs and their technology. They mistakenly think that just because these beings are more advanced

Chapter Nine: Fallen Angels or Evil Spirits?

technologically, we must make agreements with them to acquire their science. Yet, here is the *discernment*, just because a being, (alien, ET, fallen angel, demon) is more advanced technologically, certainly does not mean that they are more evolved spiritually, or 'of the light.'

Remember the math, only one third of heaven's angels rebelled against the creator and were therefore cursed and fallen, the rest of the two thirds remained faithful. These are the extraterrestrials of light, and these are the ones that are on the side of victory and aligned with the Kingdom of Christ against the cosmic evil forces. Earth humans must learn to *discern* between the different types of spacecraft and aliens. It is the final test of humanity.

The Demons (Aliens) Tremble at the Name of Jesus Christ

> "and whenever those possessed by evil spirits caught sight of him, the spirits would throw them to the ground in front of him shrieking, "You are the Son of God!"
>
> (Mark 3:11)

> "You say you have faith, for you believe that there is one God. Good for you! Even the demons believe this, and they tremble in terror."
>
> (James 2: 19)

So why would God allow the demonic realm to taunt, torment and deceive humans? The Lord uses the demons to punish, correct and discipline His children. This is considered a free will zone, meaning each of us have the freedom to choose between Good and Evil. The punishment for violating God's laws are the attacks and harassment from a demon, who can be instrumental in humbling a human being back to God, along with the conviction of God's Holy Spirit. When that happens, many humans will repent of wrong doing. Not all people do, as there are many stubborn rebels, but more importantly, there are those who are so oppressed and controlled by the fallen angels and the demonic realm that they do not even realize they are owned by them, and are bewitched by them. These misled people have been given a false sense of security and reality and consequently believe their lies are the truth.

There is a law in the hypnosis of mind control techniques, that if you tell someone a lie often enough, they will believe it as truth. This is the mantra of the fallen angels. The fallen angels masquerade as aliens, extra-terrestrials and ascended masters, and while they do offer lots of information and knowledge, the ignorant and undiscerning humans have become so hypnotized that they no longer question what they are told. They are so under the evil spell that they unfortunately do not know what has hit them until it is too late.

We are living in a time of Grace, which means that we humans have an opportunity to repent for ignorantly believing and following the doctrines of the fallen angels. Those who recognize the true doctrines of the Kingdom of Heaven will be saved from the deceptive and destructive path of the fallen angels, hence defining the true meaning to the phrase, 'being saved.' 'People perish from lack of knowledge and understanding.' (Hosea 4:6) It is so important to understand the true spiritual nature of this cosmic drama and its warfare. Not one single human is immune from it. The Divine Plan of Salvation was created to save us from what the fallen angels and their demons are perpetrating on humanity.

Jesus Christ was born and died for the sins of humankind. He bought back our souls and set them free. He achieved deliverance from the gods of this world, Satan and the fallen angels, by becoming a living sacrifice for the atonement of all sins and curses. While many have hardened our hearts and closed our eyes to this historical gift of grace, the fallen angels and Satan know who Christ is, both at the time of His embodiment, death and rebirth as well as now.

"Every knee shall bow, *in heaven and on earth and under the earth*, every tongue shall confess that Jesus Christ is Lord."

(Philippians 2:10,11)

That means every demon spirit in Satan's realm and the entire fallen hierarchy all tremble at the name of the Lord Jesus Christ. They all fear Him, because they know He is Lord, He has the victory and the keys of death and Hades and He has the power to use them or destroy them according to His will. This is why when the Lord wants to punish His people, He will use the demons. They obey His word and His will. Even Satan answers to the Lord. Satan's power is limited according to the will of God.

Time Always Tells The Truth

In 1942 C.S. Lewis[1] wrote *The Screwtape Letters* in 1942, five years before the first wave of "flying saucer" sightings began to hit the U.S. in earnest. In one particular letter to "Wormwood", the imaginary character, Screwtape, writes that he has *"great hopes that we shall learn in due time how to emotionalize and mythologize their science to such an extent that what is, in effect, a belief in us (though not under that name) will creep in while the human mind remains closed to belief in the Enemy."* C.S. Lewis had remarkable insight into the enemy's strategy, as soon became evident. His *Narnia*

Chapter Nine: Fallen Angels or Evil Spirits?

series is a startling look through all the interdimensional doorways and paths of travel which this very real spiritual battle between Christ and the pervasive cosmic evil continues to rage.

Particularly in his book,[2] *The Last Battle,* Lewis illustrates the *counterfeit* Aslan, who represents Christ, as an archetype of the coming Antichrist. The Antichrist will masquerade as a superman savior, deceiving most humans with his supernatural abilities, just as the *counterfeit* Aslan did through Narnia. C.S. Lewis even writes about how the real Aslan destroys the old Narnia and points the way to the real Narnia, which is in 'Aslans country', a metaphor for the New Jerusalem. This sacred place is promised to come down to the earth after Christ returns and wins the final battle against Satan and his fallen angels.

> "I had shown in *Passport to Magonia* that contact with ufonauts was only a modern extension of the age-old tradition of contact with nonhuman consciousness in the form of angels, demons, elves, and sylphs."
>
> (Jacques Vallée, 159)

John Keel[3] connected the dots to aliens and demons in *Operation Trojan Horse*:

> "Demonology is not just another crackpot-ology. It is the ancient and scholarly study of the monsters and demons who have seemingly coexisted with man throughout history.... The manifestations and occurrences described in this imposing literature are similar, if not entirely identical, to the UFO phenomenon itself. Victims of demonomania (possession) suffer the very same medical and emotional symptoms as the UFO contactees.... The Devil and his demons can, according to the literature, manifest themselves in almost any form and can physically imitate anything from angels to horrifying monsters with glowing eyes. Strange objects and entities materialize and dematerialize in these stories, just as the UFOs and their splendid occupants appear and disappear, walk through walls, and perform other supernatural feats."

In *Operation Trojan Horse*, Keel spoke of the intangible nature of the aliens and their craft as "transmogrifications tailoring themselves to our ability to understand."[4]

Dr. John Mack[5] made the same conclusion, that the aliens illustrate behavior resembling historical demons, but that the intangible nature of such is illustrated in how ETs traverse dimensional gateways, portals, and stargates. In *Abduction,* Mack wrote:

> "Quite a few abductees have spoken to me of their sense that at least some of their experiences are not occurring within the physical space-time dimensions

of the universe as we comprehend it. They speak of aliens breaking through from another dimension, through a 'slit' or 'crack' in some sort of barrier [gateway, portal], entering our world from 'beyond the veil.' Abductees, some of whom have little education to prepare them to explain about such abstractions or odd dislocations, will speak of the collapse of space-time that occurs during their experiences. They experience the aliens, indeed their abductions themselves, as happening in another reality, although one that is as powerfully actual to them as—or more so than—the familiar physical world."

The Horns

"The Lord is my rock, my fortress and my deliverer; my God is my rock, in whom I take refuge. He is my shield and the *horn* of my salvation, my stronghold."

(Psalm 18:2)

Horns have long been symbols of strength in ancient cultures, which is why the ancient heroes were illustrated with horns as in the famous Michelangelo sculpture of Moses.

Michelangelo's marble sculpture depicts Moses with horns, or tongs of fire according to the Bible, on his head. This was the normal medieval western depiction of Moses, based on the description of his face as "cornuta" ("horned", though other meanings are possible) in the Latin Vulgate translation of Exodus 34:29-35. The Greek Septuagint and Hebrew Masoretic texts use words meaning "radiant", suggesting an effect like a halo, though it has been argued that the Hebrew text remains unclear as to the original sense intended. Horns were symbolic of authority in ancient Near Eastern culture, and the medieval depiction had the advantage of giving Moses a convenient attribute by which he could easily be recognized in pictures crowded with other Israelites.[6]

Exodus 34:29-35 tells that after meeting with God, the skin of Moses' face became radiant, frightening the Israelites and leading Moses to wear a veil. Jonathan Kirsch, in his book *Moses: A Life*, thought that, since he subsequently had to wear a veil to hide it, Moses' face was disfigured by a sort of "divine radiation burn". This passage has led to one longstanding tradition that Moses grew horns. The horn theory is derived from a misinterpretation of the Hebrew phrase karan 'ohr panav (פָּנָיו עוֹר קָרַן). The root קרן Q-R-N (qof, resh, nun) pronounced, *kaw-ran*, literally

Chapter Nine: Fallen Angels or Evil Spirits?

means, "shone" or may be read as either "horn" or "ray of light", depending on vocalization. 'Ohr panahv (פָּנָיו עוֹר) translates to "the light of the skin of his face" or "light countenance of face."

Strong's Concordance includes in its definition of a horn which is *keren* in Hebrew, as something which can also be a musical instrument. As cornet, trumpet horn, an elephant's tooth, or ivory, also a corner of the altar, a peak of a mountain, or a ray of light, a power, hill, horn.

Interpreted correctly, these two words form an expression meaning that Moses was enlightened, that "the skin of his face shone," as with a gloriole.

Horns, in Moses' time, were a symbol of authority and power. Many gods, including Yahuah have been portrayed as having them. Kings and holy men were shown sometimes with exaggerated crowns with horns, as with the Vikings horned helmets. Another point of interest: Moses came down from the mountain with horns at the beginning of the astrological age of the Ram (Aries) stating, *"I am the Ram of God!"* Coincidence? There are old paintings showing Moses with the shining light of horns coming out of the top of his head, as if to show he was imbued with a special spirit. There is no doubt he was, but the horns were spiritual, not physical, as in other paintings showing auras around angels.

Elohim, comes from Ellu, meaning "the Shining Ones." "Shining Ones" is an ambivalent term used for both the Elohim and the Nephilim and their first born. The "Shining Ones" are often depicted with horns on their heads. This was a symbol of wisdom, but also of rulership. This is why shamans, priests, and kings adopted the convention of wearing hats with horns also, especially in the form of the crown. Their belief at the time was to primarily indicate that they were descendants of either the Atlanteans or the Lemurians and were endowed with power.

Interestingly, in more recent history, horns have been depicted as 'evil' and associated with Satan. During the Holocaust, Nazi propaganda portrayed Jews with horns, demonizing them. It's interesting that something that was once considered to be a symbol of strength, radiance and power, was then demonized as evil. But that's the nature of our present world of darkness and its principalities and powers which seek to distort all that is good and market evil as good in order to disguise their true colors.

Daniel wrote about horns in a fascinating way. When referring to *the little horn* coming out of the ten horns, many bible scholars believe him to be referring to the person known as the antichrist. Yet, what if this person, who will be known as the antichrist, who is to come as a man of peace at first, showing all kinds of signs and wonders and performing miracles, is in fact an alien being empowered from inside the earth? We know that the fallen angels and the 'satans' were bound to the bowels of the earth. Yet since the last angelic battle took place, they have been rebuilding their broken spacecraft, creating new weapons in preparation for the final battle with the Lord and his Heavenly Hosts.

What Daniel saw in his visions in terms of horns, iron, bronze and iron teeth, may in fact have been an alien invasion, something so foreign and alien to Daniel that he had no frame of reference in describing it. We've already established that in the ancient days, horns were considered symbols of strength and power, so perhaps Daniel was referring to 'strongholds' of powerful aliens and their spacecraft, which he describes as iron, bronze with iron teeth and feet.

> "After this I saw in the night visions, and behold, a fourth beast, dreadful and terrible, exceedingly strong. It had huge iron teeth; it was devouring, breaking in pieces, and trampling the residue with its feet. It was different from all the beasts that were before it, and it had ten horns."
>
> (Daniel 7:7)

In the most recent version of *The War of the Worlds*,[7] the 2005 Stephen Spielberg movie depicted robotic alien beings made of iron and heavy metal trampling everything underfoot. The fact that Daniel had a vision of this futuristic technology, and called it a beast, is vividly understandable. Even though it was not a biological entity as we consider beasts to be, it is rather a cybernetic hybrid beast, that was exceedingly strong, dreadful, terrible nonetheless.

> "I was considering the horns, and there was another horn, a little one, coming up among them, before whom three of the first horns were plucked out by the roots. And there, in this horn, were eyes like the eyes of a man, and a mouth speaking pompous words."
>
> (Daniel 7:8)

In this passage that refers to the coming antichrist, Daniel refers to a powerful being that appeared to look like a man but was full of arrogance. This most likely refers to an alien stronghold, particularly as he states he saw this *little horn* coming out of other horns, possibly a hierarchy of alien craft and strongholds.

> "The broken horn and the four horns that arose in its place represent four kingdoms which will arise from his nation, although not with his power."
>
> (Daniel 8:22)

Chapter Nine: Fallen Angels or Evil Spirits?

"Then the male goat magnified himself exceedingly. But as soon as he was mighty, the large horn was broken; and in its place there came up four conspicuous horns toward the four winds of heaven."

(Daniel 8:8)

The horn was broken, his power and his stronghold was defeated.

"All the horns of the wicked I will also cut off, but the horns of the righteous shall be exalted." (Psalm 75:10) The ten horns referred to in Revelation Chapter 17 that give their power and authority to the Beast shall be overcome by the Lamb. "And those who are with Him shall be called chosen and faithful."

(Revelation 17:14)

"I watched till thrones were put in place, and the Ancient of Days was seated; His garment was white as snow, and the hair of His head was like pure wool. His throne was a fiery flame, its wheels a burning fire;"

(Daniel 7:9)

This passage relates to the Lord Jesus Christ who is coming with His fleet of spaceships, often described in the Old Testament as 'thrones with a fiery flame' along with 'wheels burning with fire' or wheels within wheels as described by the prophet Ezekiel 37.

"And out of one of them came forth a little horn, which waxed exceeding great, toward the south, and toward the east, and toward the pleasant land."

(Daniel 8:9)

"And four great beasts came up from the sea, each different from the other."

(Daniel 7:3)

Likewise, the "little horn" is a political power for the same reason that the "ten horns" in Daniel 7:7-8 represent political powers; "horns" in the Bible often symbolize political kingdoms. Yet what if these political powers and kingdoms do not come from the earth's surface, but instead from inside the earth? What if these horns are strongholds from the 'satans' and the fallen angels, to rule the planet, both inside and out? What if these "horns" represent mission controls which exist on mother ships, or on bases that are within the earth, seeking power on the surface? Revelation talks about the "ten horns" that give their power and authority to the Beast. The four Beasts that comes from *out of the sea*? The Beast that comes from *inside the earth*? So, who is really running the show on planet earth? And why would the nations of the world give their power to a Beast?

Obviously, this is not just any Beast, but a Draconian Hierarchy which rules the interior of our planet, who want to take control of the minds of every human, and stop the arrival of the Kingdom of the God on earth. This is the Beast of old, that old Serpent or Dragon, known as the Devil, who controls the aliens from within the planet, responsible for seducing, deceiving and putting the nations and the inhabitants under hypnotic spells. They are being given their "last chance" as their days are numbered and spiritually speaking, they are already defeated foes.

These beings, the Beast and his Draconian hierarch, will turn on 'the whole works' and give it all they've got to pull the wool over the eyes of us humans, making us think that earth is being invaded by aliens from space, deceiving us into believing that earth is having its "first contact" with Extraterrestrials. But these beings are not 'Extraterrestrial' at all, they come from inside the planet, with corresponding bases inside other planets, such as Mars and the Moon. These beings are not benevolent, but will first come as 'Angels of Light', masquerading as benevolent ETs, hooking us humans into their dream of coming to 'clean up the planet's environment'. This is where treaties are made, technologies are exchanged, and 'Faustian' contracts are signed.

The prophesied 'Antichrist' is empowered by the Beast, the Draconian Satanic hierarchy from inside the earth.

Another possible interpretation for the horns could be the shape of the craft. Cigar shaped craft may have been seen as horns in ancient days, as a horn was a shape of something that came off of an animal, similar to a ram's horn. Cigar shaped crafts can also be described as having the shape of a horn.

The Forbidden Bible

The books that were not canonized into the Bible by the Catholic Church fathers in 325 A.D. are called the *Apocrypha* or *Pseudepigrapha*. All of the books were found together in scrolls at the caves of Qumran in Israel, written around the same time. The Books of Enoch are considered one of the Pseudopigrapha. Enoch's books were rejected as they did not fit the church's political agenda in 360 A.D. Enoch's books were read by the early disciples, even quoted extensively in the gospels. Besides, Enoch was way above the church fathers' heads when it came to knowledge. Enoch was the first to coin the phrase, 'son of man' which Jesus Himself used.

Enoch was the grandfather of Noah, and the father of Methuselah, the longest living man in the Bible. In my opinion, Enoch was the reason God chose to save

Chapter Nine: Fallen Angels or Evil Spirits?

Noah and his family, because of Enoch's DNA. Enoch was an elder forefather of Abraham, and the first man to 'ascend' into heaven, who was taken off the earth and brought back with his scrolls. If only the Books of Enoch were part of the bible today, the church, and the entire Judeo-Christian religions would be viewed in a whole different light. He holds so many key mysteries as to why things are the way they are, and literally fills in the gaps to what is missing in the book of Genesis. In fact, if the Books of Enoch were part of the Bible, it would extend the word of God even further to help us understand the spirit realm, the demonic, and who and what were the fallen angels in a more comprehensive way.

The *Book of Enoch* speaks of much devastation, chaos and corruption on Earth, as well as among the angels. Like Genesis, Enoch mentions 'giants' and 'the Watchers.' There were 'the satans' - the 'Sons of Heaven' - the 'angels of punishment' who were the 'instruments of Satan' - and the same specific Genesis angels: Michael, Raphael, Gabriel, only according to Enoch, the fourth archangel is Phanuel, not Uriel. 'God' is never mentioned; only plural gods or angels, however, Enoch refers to *the Lord of Spirits* each time he is talking about the one who has the authority over the heavens and the earth. He even goes into a long dissertation on Jesus Christ, thousands of years before he was even born. Enoch was taken to the mountaintop residence of the gods. He observed things that no earthly mind could understand. The angels 'corrupted the sons of man.' It was various human genus, with advanced technology, who played God and decided the fate of the children on Earth.

One of the main reasons for Enoch's ejection from the Old Testament could have been the accurate astronomy. Page after page concerns the sun, moon, yearly cycles and heavenly statistics. 'Paths of the sun and moon,' 'their stately orbits,' 'courses of the luminaries' and 'revolve in their circular chariots' are only a few quotes of Enochian wisdom.

> 'And I saw in the heaven running in the world, above those portals in which revolve *the stars that never set.*'
>
> (1 Enoch 75:8)

Aside from the circumpolar stars, we can only see stars as never setting from space. The ancients were fully aware of the circumpolar stars and used them for navigation. Stars that never set are his description of space ships.

Remember, it was the Church of Rome, during the time of Ecumenical editing, which condemned accurate astronomy. Many can relate to Galileo and Giordano Bruno, who suffered greatly for their accurate astronomical configurations. The Church's 'religious' officials wanted the public to think that the Earth was flat, that it did not move, and was in the center of all things. They are circulating that same lie today, using it as a psychological experiment, to see how many dependent minds would believe this nonsense. The Earth is not flat. There are multiple astronauts from the U.S.A., Russia and China who have witnessed first-hand the sphere of the Earth and are still alive today. The only thing that is flat is the ecliptic plane. This is an invisible plane based on physics. The apparent path of the Sun's motion on the celestial sphere as seen from Earth is called the ecliptic. The ecliptic plane is tilted 23.5° with respect to the plane of the celestial equator since the Earth's spin axis is tilted 23.5° with respect to its orbit around the sun.

During ancient times, mad scientists and demonic fallen angels cloned anything which they might covet. The mythological animals were real genetic experiments. They rebelled against the Creator and waged the Cosmic Wars of the gods. Nuclear warfare was not beyond the capability of the fallen angels. The deserts of today are the result of ancient, atomic wars. There is radioactive evidence in Israel at the site of Sodom and Gomorrah. In Ireland are rocks like glass, indicative of intense fire and heat. The floods were ordered by the Creator because all the perverted creatures, aberrations and hybrids along with their power-crazed, genetic engineers needed to be eliminated on a global scale. The Earth was a mess and needed to be wiped clean.

The creation story in Genesis, read from the perspective of our current awareness of genetic engineering, the interaction between the Sons of God and the fair daughters of men assumes a rather different interpretation:

> "And it came to pass, when men began to multiply on the face of the earth and daughters were born to them, that the sons of God saw the daughters of men were fair; so they took them wives of all whom they chose....There were giants on the earth in those days; and also after that, for the sons of God came in unto the daughters of men, and they bore children to them, and they became giants who in the olden days were men of renown."
>
> (Genesis 6:1–4)

The Hebrew word to describe demigods, or men of great renown, those who were said to be the offspring of the Sons of God and the daughters of men, is *Nephilim*. Interestingly, the word used to denote true giants, as far as great stature was concerned, was *Rephaim*. The Israelites found such giants among the Canaanite inhabitants of Palestine. Among these were the *Anakim* of Philisa and the *Emim* of Moab. Goliath was a Gittite or a Geburim, a man of great stature and bulk, but he was not a Nephilim.[8] (*See* Book One, Chapter on *Giants*)

In the 1 Enoch 7:12, one learns more of the non-terrestrial entities who desired the daughters of men: "It happened after the sons of men had multiplied in those days, that elegant, beautiful daughters were born to them. And when the angels, the sons

Chapter Nine: Fallen Angels or Evil Spirits?

of heaven, beheld them, they became enamored of them, saying to each other: Come, let us select for ourselves wives from the progeny of men, and let us beget children."

Scripture refers to the Nephilim as giants, the descendants of the offspring between the fallen angels and the rebellious sons of god and human women. These giants were monsters, full of iniquity, superhuman in size and equally wicked in their character, who had to be destroyed.

> "And God looked upon the earth, and behold, it was corrupt; for all flesh had corrupted his way upon the earth."
>
> (Genesis 6:12)

Most people do not believe in the Biblical story of Noah because of a basic problem: How could a few people gather ALL the animals, feed and care for them on board a ship for months? The answer comes from...who controlled the Earth thousands of years ago? The angels, the humans with the technology, built the Arks, collected the animals and caused the rains. The chosen animals were probably the best examples of their species and worth being saved. It is scientifically possible to place the DNA of all life forms in suspended animation and stored indefinitely. This was the cargo within the Arks. The samples of DNA would be revived later, after the waters receded. Nowhere in the Bible does it mention that Noah went out and gathered each animal. It only says Noah brought them into the Ark. If the 'life canisters' were all assembled for Noah by the gods and the simple people merely carried them in and secured them in place, then this does lend credence to the Noah story.

The world began again. In Genesis, it says that after the Great Flood, Noah went to live with the Elohim 'sons of gods.'

> "And the angels who did not keep their positions of authority but abandoned their proper dwelling (left their first estate) —these he has kept in darkness, bound with everlasting chains for judgment on the great Day. In a similar way, Sodom and Gomorrah and the surrounding towns gave themselves up to sexual immorality and perversion. They serve as an example of those who suffer the punishment of eternal fire."
>
> (Jude 1:6)

Jude 1 tells us that these beings lost their positions of authority in heaven. They were cast out into darkness. These are the fallen sons, aka fallen extraterrestrial angels of heaven.

The *Book of Enoch*, talks about 200 of the sons of God that came down to earth to mate with earth women. Not all the Elohim were involved in this. Remember the larger picture, that only one third of the stars (heaven's angels) followed Lucifer's rebellion against the Creator.

"The Sons of God came to present themselves before the Lord and Satan was among them" (Job 1: 6 and Job 2:1). They saw that the daughters of men were beautiful and took them as wives for themselves (Genesis 6:2) and beget children, the Nephilim, who were *on the earth in those days and also afterward* (Genesis 6:10). Thus, not only were there Nephilim in the days of Noah but also later in the days when the Israelites went into the Promised Land (Numbers 13:33). The clash between David and the giant Goliath happened after the flood. Sodom and Gomorrah were destroyed because of the immorality that the Nephilim created, again after the flood. Not all the giants perished after all, as many escaped into underground caverns inside the earth. After the nuclear destruction of Sodom and Gomorrah, the Nephilim do disappear from Scriptural evidence. However, many of their offspring and their genetic lines did continue as there have been historical accounts of giants living on the earth.

> "For God did not spare Angels when they sinned, but sent them to hell, (Tartarus) putting them into gloomy dungeons (chains of darkness) to be held for judgment; if he did not spare the ancient world when he brought the flood on it ungodly people, but protected Noah, a preacher of righteousness, and seven others."
>
> (2 Peter 2:4)

No one can fully comprehend the extent of spiritual warfare with demons, or the true meaning of extraterrestrials, unless there is understanding that these fallen angels are now masquerading as ETs. In some cases of UFO abduction, experiments are conducted still attempting to intermingle ETs with human females. The Grays involved in the abductions and the extracting of human bodily fluids, semen and ovum, are under the direction of the fallen angels who live inside the earth.

The original plan of the fallen angels was to create hybrid monsters and giants who would destroy the human family. This plan failed, not once but twice. So now they are working on creating a new human/alien hybrid that will take over the surface of the planet from us humans. The aim of the abduction phenomena is to obtain sperm and ova and other bodily fluids to create these new hybrids. The fallen angels move through New Age channels, lying to them by telling them that these hybrids are good and will be the future humans of the planet. The fallen angels promise the New Agers themselves will get to incarnate into new glorious bodies, becoming a space faring race, one that can handle living on earth and in space. Sadly, there are

Chapter Nine: Fallen Angels or Evil Spirits?

many of us who want to believe this so badly, who see it as a positive trend, and swallow it hook, line and sinker. It couldn't be further from the truth.

> "They sacrificed to demons, which are not God, gods they had not known, <u>gods that recently appeared,</u> gods your fathers did not fear."
> (Deuteronomy 32:17)

This verse clearly indicates that these were extraterrestrials with god complexes, fallen angels who visited earth and masqueraded as gods, demanding worship and sacrifice from the children of Israel. This got them into big trouble with the Lord of Israel. The Old Testament tells us that Yahuah turned His back on His own people because they followed other gods and worshipped demons, which He rightly calls idolatry.

Vampires

There are three kinds of vampires; the draconian types who drink human blood; the emotional vampire who drains our energy; and the psychic vampire who drains our life force. All vampires have demonic entities attached to them. Alien demonic spirits use emotional and psychic vampires to continue to drain the human life force with their negative energies. All are narcissistic at the core, totally self-centered. They manipulate us into self-sabotage, into victim consciousness, start the blame game, rile up anger, as they themselves are all deeply wounded at a soul level.

Jesus Christ is the only One who can kick out these kinds of devils. There is no other effective remedy in any 'Age'. In fact, the New Age has engendered its own group of energy vampires, through hypnotherapists, energy workers and yes, even massage therapists, and psychics. These are all in the business of helping others for a living, some of them not only to take our money, but also our energy. They end up draining us instead of uplifting us. Most of them are unaware that they are being used by energy vampires. The vampirism is all done by entity attachment. Let's not forget how scores of gurus have taken advantage of their followers, raping and stealing their money and their personal power.

These are enemies of humanity, and others who see humans merely as food. Depending on the type of Draconian species, some of us end up as 'physical' food for the carnivores in the case of physical abduction. Sometime the vampires feed energetically. Either way, it is bondage for those carrying these entities, as well as bondage for those being drained by them. Not all massage therapists have these attachments, as those who are aware of energy exchange know how to manage their own energy and do not subconsciously steal energy from their clients. But those who are unaware or have inroads to various occult activities are used to siphon energy from their clients for their entity attachments.

Sexual power is transferred particularly at the point of orgasm. If you are not in love or married, the union is not sanctified. An unholy alliance forms to which these energy vampires, gray aliens, demon spirits, can attach to both parties as a 'soul tie.' Until the soul ties are broken, the spiritual legal authority to drain energy from the victim remains, with the soul being drained periodically. These people feel like they're constantly caught up in drama, a real battle for their soul.

The only way out is through Christ. Jesus said,

"I AM the Light of the World. Whoever follows me will never walk in darkness, but will have the light of life."

(John 8:12)

"All authority in heaven and on earth has been given to me."

(Matthew 28:18)

Jesus Christ is the only one who can free a soul from vampiric entities. I am witness to that! I was saved from real vampiric entities who drained me of all my life force to the point of death, which was when I saw Jesus. I was taken out of my room of misery, and brought into a bright green valley where Jesus took my hand, walked with me and told me to tell my stories, and promised that I was going to finish and publish my books for Him. He taught me so much about spiritual warfare, spiritual legal ground and the reality of both good and fallen angels!

I had a lot of trouble sleeping in those days, but when I did, my visions were surreal, and I remember vividly being attacked by entities waking me up, who wouldn't let me sleep, and then I would see Jesus hanging on the cross, and two droplets of blood fell onto me. He once sent an angel to take me up to Him, because I was the victim of trafficking, which was vampiric witchcraft, and I woke up just as the angel was putting me back into my bed, and his arm that was holding me, ever so gently, was nearly as large as my body and I'm 5'5". My life force was restored and I was delivered from what felt like the darkest night of my soul, which lasted three and half years.

Alien War on The Human Race

Ephesians 6:12 couldn't be any clearer, "we are not warring against flesh and blood, but against power, principalities, rulers of the darkness of this present world, and spiritual wickedness in the heavens."

Chapter Nine: Fallen Angels or Evil Spirits?

I spent all of Book One identifying *who* these beings are. Now, we're going to get into how both fallen angel demons and Heaven's Angelic Host of extraterrestrials are on the front lines of this battle over earth's skies, earth's real estate and earth's inhabitants.

Knowledge empowers, ignorance imperils (Hosea 4:6)

Many are stuck in a state of ignorance, impatience and disbelief. Their disbelief is easily used against them, because people who refuse to believe in God are also blind to this spiritual and galactic battle taking place all around us, over us and through us. Humans are used as vessels and pawns in a cosmic chess game between the warring angels and so called ET gods.

Our human race is made up of multiple subgenera, many races, multiple hybrids, and varied cultures. Racism is being perpetrated by alien influence through implantation, programmed to divide and conquer humanity. These alien forces prey on humans through clandestine abductions, and implant humans with a programming to that is set to activate at an appointed time to be used by these aliens to create wars, discord and confusion, making humanity vulnerable to control. There is also a belief amongst UFO researchers that abductees are being used to create an alien-hybrid race, which is being raised in laboratories underground and off planet on ships, and will replace humans at some point.

Ephesians 2:2, "that you once practiced as you lived according to the ways of this present world and according to the ruler of the power of the air, the spirit that is now active in those who are disobedient."

The "ruler of the power of the air" is the god of this world, Lucifer/Satan. He controls a host of fallen angel demon aliens. Yes, the truth is stranger than fiction. The ones who carry out the abductions are generally different types of gray aliens. They are of a hive mentality, and simply follow orders. I shared stories in Book One[9] of *Who's Who in the Cosmic Zoo?* that proved that when you override their authority in the name of Jesus Christ, it immediately scrambles their marching orders, and they abort their mission, dropping people like hot cakes. Why? Well, even demons tremble in the name of the Lord, because they know He rules over all of them.

These gray alien forces work through the 'spirits of the air' which are ruled by the Leviathan Spirit, an archdemon, who twists communication between people and groups. This babel of words and twisting their original meaning to something else is causing severe misunderstandings between people.

The Python Spirit uses traps and spiritual attacks to literally "squeeze" the life-force out of you through in fighting, strife, draining your spirit, causing dis-ease and despair.

The Jezebel Spirit perverts all truth, trying to get you to believe the lies. This rebellious spirit purports turning truth into lies, lies into truth, darkness into light, light into darkness.

Isaiah 5:20, "Woe to those who call evil good and good evil, who put darkness for light and light for darkness, who put bitter for sweet and sweet for bitter."

The way to fight evil is with good, darkness with light, bitterness with sweetness, impatience with patience, hate with love, meanness with kindness, greed with generosity.

The way the Jezebel spirit works is through revenge (see Kings 19:2), by trying to disgrace, discredit, intimidate, and murder your good reputation. This is the "False Spirit" behind all the real false prophets and the spirit behind most false accusations on God's anointed.

Fallen Angels and The Jezebel Spirit

In the ancient land of Israel, Jezebel and Ahab were literally getting away with murder. They believed themselves to be above God's power to bring retribution against their many offenses. But God saw their sin and His response against them was Jehu. Today in America we have a power couple who embody the Jezebel and Ahab Archetype and the spirit demons that are attached to it in Hillary & Bill Clinton.

Allow me to share a secret with you, the JEHU anointing defeats the Jezebel spirit. The Jehu anointing comes from the Lord, not Jehu.[10] Jehu was anointed by the Lord to take down the house of Ahab and Jezebel and he did just that. Even though later in King Jehu's career he succumbed to idolatry, prevalent in ancient Israel due to the popularity of pagan gods, the Jehu anointing came from the Lord, and not Jehu. Just want to make that clear.

Contrary to popular belief, the Jezebel spirit is not a woman, it is a demon. All demons are male by nature. The odd name of this demon originates with the evil Queen Jezebel of the Church at Thyatira, who worshipped Ashtarte, not Yahuah. This demon, who existed before Queen Jezebel, released the *Religious Spirit* demon to steal, counterfeit and distort all the prophetic gifts from Yahuah. The story goes that the Church of Thyatira had dozens of false prophets in competition with Yahuah's anointed prophet Elijah.

Elijah won the spiritual contest, as Yahuah proved Himself to all of them and destroyed Jezebel's church and all her false prophets. But Elijah did not destroy Jezebel. King Jehu did. If you are someone who hates the *Religious Spirit* with all its deceptive, manipulative and judgmental practices, and you have a real passion for God's Justice, you too may have the Jehu Anointing.

Chapter Nine: Fallen Angels or Evil Spirits?

It doesn't matter what type of anointing it is, as there are many. Those who carry the Elijah Mantle and/or the Jehu Anointing have power over this ancient fallen angel and demonic attachments. This ancient spirit demon uses its human vessels, who carry this jealous and murdering spirit, that of being 'hell-bent on destroying God's true prophets, messengers, teachers, pastors and elders.' This spirits pervades churches as exactly one of its favorite hangouts. God allows it to test and strengthen His faithful and true believers and teaches them how to overcome through Him. This very spirit is the one that causes the church to be split between what Jesus called, "the separation of the sheep and the goats."

Whenever anyone attempts to thwart God's true agenda through His messengers, this spirit kicks up dust to deflect attention to itself through intimidation, manipulation, direct personal attacks on the messengers and their message. The Jezebellion (sounds like rebellion) religious spirit is in an ancient rebellion against the Lord Yahuah/Yahushua, which is another spiritual trap. Churches which focus on spiritual warfare, who do preach, pray and prophesy about Jezebel, are few and far between, and unfortunately offer little to no preaching on the Love of Christ or the Grace of God. Instead their battle axe rests on the authority in Christ. These churches will battle Jezebel spirits more than those who live by and through the Love of Christ and the Grace of God. It is Love that covers a multitude of sins. The ways of Love are spiritual weapons used in battles against Jezebellion Religious Spirits most successfully. Those are the overcomers prophesied in Revelation 12:11, who understand how to conquer the Jezebellion religious spirits in themselves and in their church.

So, Who Was Jehu?

Jehu was chosen and anointed by the Lord to become the new King of Israel and the destroyer of the household of Ahab. This is the way the Lord settled Ahab and Jezebels rebellion. This nasty couple became corrupted with power and terrorizing God's people and the Lord's anointed. They tried to murder the prophets of God. The Lord responded. This is what the Lord told Jehu when he was anointed King of Israel:

> "You are to destroy the family of Ahab, your master. In this way, I will avenge the murder of My prophets and all the Lord's servants who were killed by Jezebel."
>
> (2 Kings 9:7 NLT)

The Lord said in Psalms 105:15 and 1Chronicles 16:22, "Do not touch my anointed ones; do my prophets no harm." We see from this classic *archetypal* story, that the Lord meant business, and when God says, "Vengeance is mine, says the Lord," -- He ain't kidding.

He sent Jehu to Jezebel's palace and she verbally abused him, calling him names, and throwing scornful accusations at his good character. Everyone called her the tyrant of Israel, who was intimidating and powerfully nasty and narcissistic. Then Jehu comes along and kills her, just like that. Here's how it went down:

Jezebel called her servant eunuchs to deal with Jehu. But then Jehu cried out:

"Who is on my side?" And two or three eunuchs looked out at him. "Throw her down!" Jehu yelled. So, they threw her out the window, and her blood spattered against the wall and on the horses. And Jehu trampled her body under his horses' hooves.

Then Jehu went into the palace and ate and drank. Afterward he said, "Someone go and bury this cursed woman, for she is the daughter of a king." But when they went out to bury her, they found only her skull, her feet, and her hands.

When they returned, and told Jehu, he stated, "This fulfills the message from the LORD, which he spoke through his servant Elijah from Tishbe: 'At the plot of land in Jezreel, dogs will eat Jezebel's body. Her remains will be scattered like dung on the plot of land in Jezreel, so that no one will be able to recognize her.'"

(1 Kings 9:32-36)

Aside from killing Jezebel and all the members of Ahab's family, who had encouraged the people to worship false idols, Jehu ordered his men to kill all the priests of the pagan god, Baal, in the temple. He then converted the pagan temple into a public toilet. Jehu reigned as King of Israel for twenty-eight years. When he died, he was buried in Samaria, and his son Jehoahaz became the new king. The full story of Jehu is found in 2 Kings, Chapters 9 and 10.

The story of the evil empire of King Ahab and Queen Jezebel is archetypal in so many ways. Firstly, it teaches the lesson that marrying the wrong person can bring down a Kingdom or an empire. Secondly, King Ahab represents all men who are cowardly. This was a man who had it all. He had royal blood, God's anointing, wealth and power, yet he succumbed to a pagan gentile witch, instead of keeping with one of his kind.

At first Ahab and Jezebel were unequally yoked, until Ahab allowed himself to be dominated and put under her spell, and controlled by foreign gods, which is what Jezebel brought to the marriage. These fallen angels that she worshipped, succeeded in getting Ahab to turn his back on his God, and there lies his downfall. If Ahab

Chapter Nine: Fallen Angels or Evil Spirits?

went to the Lord with repentance and cried out for the Lord's help, it would have been a whole different story, as the Lord would have helped Ahab, because the Lord is faithful to His faithful. But Ahab rebelled against the Lord and followed after other gods. The Lord took his hand off Ahab, and allowed him to die in his battle against the Syrians, but protected King Jehoshaphat.

The other archetypal character is of course Jezebel. She was narcissist and controlled by Baal, who is called Allah today. She belonged to a church full of eunuchs and false prophets. She was prideful and rebellious in the face of the Lord, as is the spirit that controlled her. The demon that inhabited Queen Jezebel was in existence long before Jezebel was ever born. This is important to remember when pointing fingers at women and assuming all women are Jezebels if they put on lipstick.

The demon involved with Jezebel was the Religious Spirit. She was heavily involved with her Church of Thyatira. They thought they were all that, the top of the top, you know in the kingdom, they were full of wealth, knowledge and also full of themselves. They worshipped the pagan gods, multiple gods, not one. They were programmed from day one, through the demons attached to these fallen angel gods, to use anyone who fell into their religious trap, to use to wage war against the Lord and Creator.

Humans have long been used as pawns in this ancient battle between the fallen angels and the Lord against whom they rebelled. That's why they piggy back on all those who are in rebellion against the Lord, His people, Jews and Christians, and all true believers. This is the ancient archetypal drama that all spiritual and religious people must overcome. We are encouraged to hope in the Lord for the strength, power and intelligence to overcome them.

The Jezebel spirit is the Religious Spirit. It is the spirit-demon that creates spiritual arrogance, spiritually snobbery, a judgmental attitude, and is also known as the 'Accuser'. It points fingers, and fingers blame on others, void of a forgiving heart It is jealous of the power of the true believer. It can't acknowledge God's gifts in another. Instead it wants to steal the gifts or murder the believer, or disparage people in positions of authority and power in the Church.

The Jezebel demon usually goes right after the pastor and his wife, because these are the heads of the church. If this demon can't establish an Ahab archetype in the pastor, they will attempt to establish a Jezebel archetype in the pastor's wife. Either way, the heads of churches all get tested by this demon, and when they prove themselves worthy by showing faithfulness to the Lord, He delivers them. They then get power over this demon spirit. If they don't show faithfulness to the Lord, they are used by the demon. It's not my style to embarrass or slander others, so I'll let you relate it to those whom you know. However, it is very much my purpose to expose the spirit behind evil attitudes that hurt people, and the Religious Spirit is most definitely one of them. The Jezebellion Religious Spirit is full of fear-mongering and intimidation. If you don't do things their way, you are excommunicated from the church.

So many people think that the Jezebel spirit affects only women who are seductive or manipulative with sex. This is only one of its ways, but the root of it is spiritual witchcraft. If sexual seduction can work their spell in to have power over others, then it's just another feather in its cap, but sex is only a fragment of this demon. Its root is to control through religion. It is the Religious Spirit, which is the accusing spirit, the spirit of fundamentalism, strife and persecution. This is the demon that causes apostasy due to spiritual and religious woundings of rejection, judgmentalism and hypocrisy.

Today we have what I call the Modern-Day Pharisee. The same spirit that was in control of the Pharisees and Sanhendrin during the Roman rule of Israel, at the time of Christ. These people basically strain a gnat but swallow a camel, because this demon blinds them spiritually. They follow the letter of the law instead of the spirit of the law. With all their knowledge, they were puffed up with pride and fear of losing power, which is why they missed their Messiah. This is also called the High Priest Curse, but I'm going to unpack that in Book Four: *Covenants,* and how that pervades todays religions.

When people hunger more for power than for the Lord in their lives, they open up the spiritual legal ground for this demonic stronghold to take up residence in the heart, mind and soul of a religious or political leader. So, what is the remedy? Elijah was faithful and listened to the Lord. That is why the Lord took him up, and saved him from death. Elijah was one of the Ascended Ones. He never died. This is the reason for the tradition amongst Jews to expect his return at any time. Jews show their faithfulness to Elijah every year at the Passover Seder by setting a place for him, and pouring out a glass of wine. They make a point of praying for his return during the Seder, opening up the front door of their house to symbolically invite him in. This is a good practice, because by doing so, you are inviting the spirit of Elijah, called the Elijah mantel.

Many of us believe that Elijah will be one of the two prophets to return during the last days, the end of this age, as prophesied in the Book of Revelation. The other one expected is Enoch, who was the only other prophet to ascend to the heavens without dying. Both were literally taken off the earth. Of course, this was done by the Lord's spaceships and His heavenly host.

Elijah didn't kill Jezebel, King Jehu did. And remember, this Jezebel spirit lives on in the world today, because of the demon behind her and the fact that Queen Jezebel never received a burial, as did all royalty. Instead she was trampled on by horses, ouch, and then left to be eaten by dogs. All that was left were her bones scattered all over Jezreel, completely unrecognizable.

Horses have been used in battle for millennia, sometimes as weapons. They typically weigh a ton, and have the power to hurt you badly if you're not careful. Horses follow orders, intuitively, spiritually, and they listen to their leaders. In this case, they

Chapter Nine: Fallen Angels or Evil Spirits?

listened to Jehu. To be torn apart by dogs is not a very nice way to die. Remind this demon spirit of that when you confront it, and instead of you being intimidated by it, it will fear you! Remember, greater is He that lives within you, than He who lives in the World. (1 John 4:4)

The Jehu anointing is 'chutzpah'! It is a spirit of bravery and fearlessness in the face of her insults, false accusations and manipulations. It is the spirit that refuses to be intimidated by bullying and intimidation. The Jehu anointing is the spiritual warrior spirit that carries God's Divine Justice with it.[1]

Chutzpah is what believers must seek in prayer when confronting the Ahab/Jezebel archetypes and Jezebellion demons. These are not limited to women, but attack both men and women equally. They play on weaknesses. Men who are people pleasers, afraid of what other people think of them, open the door to this demon, and with it comes its Jezebel match in one form or another. What King Ahab lacked, King Jehu made up for with a heart of steel. Jehu's name is within the name of the Lord, Yahuah. In fact, in Hebrew Jehu is Yehu. Yehu-Yahuah. (Just connecting the dots here folks.) Jehu in Hebrew means, Yahuah is He.

Believers today who are faced with similar battles must rise up with Yehu's spirit to take back the reigns from the controlling demons that have taken advantage of them. We must stop living in fear of what other people think of us. It is the mission of End Time spiritual warriors to rise up and bind these ancient evil spirits and their demonic strongholds. Principalities are the vast iron strongholds that can only be taken down by the matching Kingdom Prince and His angels.

By doing your part in your own world, clearing your own dramas, and aligning with others who are also fighting the same battles, we can draw the attention of Heaven's archangels and pull down this evil stronghold once and for all! You will know the freedom it brings if you try and take a step out in faith. In Heaven's Kingdom, attributes like faith, fearlessness, courage and bravery are all rewarded. All of us are citizens of heaven, (Philippians 3:20) are in partnership with the Lord and His Heavenly Hosts, who are the good angels.

Our relationship here is similar to that of the partnership between a horse and rider. The union is rooted in the rider's thoughts and feelings, to which the horse's acts are a response. It is the rider who must take leadership, then the horse follows. It is the same way when we engage heaven's angels to fight our battles for us. We signal our intention by demonstrating faith, courage and affirming the Word of God, to which heaven's angels are obedient and faithful. Let's face it, the only way to win battles that are rooted in ancient demonic strongholds established by fallen angels is to attract the help of heaven's Kingdom, and to have *that* connection, you must be saved by the King, the Mashiach-Nagid, the Messiah King Jesus.

Who Are The Angels?   *Ella LeBain*

"I will put my angels in charge of you, to keep you in all of your ways," (Psalm 91:11) is a covenant. However, if you read the entire Psalm, it's a *conditional contract agreement*. It's not a given to be protected by the Lord's angels, as you first must put your trust in the Lord, and dwell in the shadow of the Almighty, El Shaddai. Who is El Shaddai? All the English Bibles translate it as the Almighty or the Most High, but as I shared in Book Two: *Who is God?* Hebrew is a very specific language and all the letters, words and roots have meanings. El means God. The Hebrew word, *Shad* or *shaddaim* means breast or breasts. Being under the shadow of the Almighty, and under the feathers of His wings, is to be in a very safe and nurturing place indeed! Picture a bird as she extends her sheltering wing over her young. This is how the Lord watches over us and 'keeps us' in all of our ways. The name of God in the form of *El Shaddai* reveals the *Divine Feminine* side of the Kingdom of God. *El Shaddai,* is the nurturing, protective side, the *breast feeder*.

I reveal more deeply the true meaning of Psalm 91 which is a Covenant between the Lord and His people in Book Four: *Covenants*. This Covenant, is very much a conditional one, it reveals that not all people are being guided by The Kingdom of Heaven's Angels.

As I have urged you throughout this book, I want you to start thinking in terms of living inside a Kingdom. I want you to ask yourself, to which kingdom do I belong? Don't expect to be allowed into a kingdom if you are an enemy of the king! The difference between the two kingdoms is vast. Because the Kingdom of Darkness is inhabited by masters of deceit and counterfeit, the only way to tell them apart is by examining the state for traces of rebellion against the Lord.

The Kingdom of Heaven is the source of true Love, Light and Truth. These inhabitants are the redeemed of the Lord, the ones who are just grateful for being saved, the ones who feel they owe the Savior such a great debt of gratitude that they will serve Him till He takes them home, away from earth. This is what it means to be a citizen of heaven while residing on earth, "our citizenship is in heaven", as the Kingdom of Heaven is *governed* by the Kingdom of God. Jesus said, "The Kingdom of God is within you." Those who submit their hearts and lives to the Lord get heaven's angels. Those who are in rebellion have the fallen as companions. Oh, you better believe it, they can seduce and make you feel like they are helping you, but they are really diverting you away from heaven.

Grays are fallen angels and have been around since antiquity. There's nothing new under the sun. They are depicted in art and immortalized in stone. They use technology like holograms to show you visions. As I pointed out in my analysis of Ezekiel's alleged 'vision', it wasn't so much a vision as a real encounter with the living Lord aboard His divine starship and His angels. That is exactly what was recorded here, the details of Ezekiel's encounters of being taken up and down in the Lord's starships.

Chapter Nine: Fallen Angels or Evil Spirits?

The counterfeiter uses holographic technology to produce visions while the Lord will reveal Himself or parts of His Kingdom, like His Angels, to you. The Lord gives dreams and visions, but they usually are within the mind; the counterfeiter uses techno-wizardry to put up a veil and create an illusion. The Lord's presence in your life will *lift* that veil and reveal truth to you. The difference is that the kingdom of darkness blinds you with deception and confusion, whereas the Kingdom of Light is about waking up to the spiritual reality of God, His Redeemer-Kinsman and His holy angels.

True and False Prophets

"Watch out for false prophets. They come to you in sheep's clothing, but inwardly they are ferocious wolves. By their fruit you will recognize them. Do people pick grapes from thornbushes, or figs from thistles? Likewise, every good tree bears good fruit, but a bad tree bears bad fruit. A good tree cannot bear bad fruit, and a bad tree cannot bear good fruit. Every tree that does not bear good fruit is cut down and thrown into the fire. Thus, by their fruit you will recognize them."

(Matthew 7:15-20)

When confronting with Jezebel spirit, always confront by reminder it of Queen Jezebel's death on the grounds of Jezreel, where Jezebel was eaten by dogs, so no one could bury her. (See 2 Kings 9:6-10)

The Religious Spirit twists the Word of God to alter its meaning to justify its own agenda. The Pharisees did the same thing by interpreting the Word through the letter of the law rather than understanding the *'spirit'* of the Law.'

Jesus tried to explain to the Pharisees the spirit of the law whenever He prefaced His teaching as "it has been said, it has been written, but I say to you...."

The Legalistic Spirit holds you to the literal interpretation without revelation of the spirit behind it. Jehu did not fight Jezebel on this own, he recruited supporters when he said, "Who is on my side? Who?" (2 Kings 9:32)

To defeat Jezebel, you must have God. You also need reinforcements and you can't do it without God. Learn to discern and then you can ignore all her "tactics", like intimidation, false accusations, seduction, witchcraft, because, in the end, this is God's Holy Battle. Jezebel operates by a false spiritual authority, empowered by fallen angels and gray alien demons who do her bidding. Jezebel influenced and persuaded King Ahab to lead Israel into idolatry and sexual immorality, which led to the downfall of the ancient kingdom, Jewish persecution and exile.

> "Rebellion is as the sin of witchcraft."
>
> (1 Samuel 15:26)

The Lord always gives time and space to repent, but Jezebel (Ashtarte) never repents, therefore, she gets judged in Revelation 2:21 and is destroyed by Jesus in Revelation 2:20-23.

When we battle Jezebel, we need to understand this is an Archon-principality, something we cannot take down alone. We need to be sure to battle in the strength and wisdom of the Lord for His Glory. Although Jezebel failed in ending Elijah's life, Elijah didn't finish off Jezebel, Jehu did and Elijah anointed Jehu.

What is the Church of Thyatira?

The Church of Thyatira was the church of Jezebel's false prophets. Jesus gave Thyatira and Jezebel space to repent in the last days of this present age. (Revelation 2:21-23)

Thyatira was the name of an ancient Greek city in Asia Minor, now the modern Turkish city of Akhisar (White Castle). The name Thyatira means 'sacrifice.' See, book of Kings and Revelation 3, and learn about the Church of Thyatira which rules over ALL false religions. Jezebel spirit is religious witchcraft, which are false prophets. Let's not forget what the Lord did to her, as she was eaten alive by dogs. One thing many Christians misunderstand is that scripture doesn't portray Jezebel as licentious, as 2 Kings 9:22 refers to idolatry, not sexual immorality. Jezebel was the enemy of God, because of her idolatry and rebellion to the Lord.

> "Because they rejected the Truth, for this reason God sends them a powerful delusion so that they will believe the lie."
>
> (2 Thessalonians 2:11)

"To the Church in Thyatira - "And Unto *the angel of the church* in Thyatira write; These things saith the Son of God, who hath his eyes like unto a flame of fire, and his feet are like fine brass; I know thy works, and charity, and service, and faith, and thy patience, and thy works; and the last to be more than the first. Notwithstanding I have a few things against thee, because thou sufferest that woman Jezebel, which calleth herself a prophetess, to teach and to seduce my servants to commit fornication, and to eat things sacrificed unto idols. And I gave her space to repent of her fornication; and she repented not. Behold, I will cast her into a bed, and them that commit adultery with her into great tribulation, except they repent of their deeds.

Chapter Nine: Fallen Angels or Evil Spirits?

"And I will kill her children with death; and all the churches shall know that I am he which searcheth the reins and hearts: and I will give unto every one of you according to your works. But unto you I say, and unto the rest in Thyatira, as many as have not this doctrine, and which have not known the depths of Satan, as they speak; I will put upon you none other burden. But that which ye have already hold fast till I come. And he that overcometh, and keepeth my works unto the end, to him will I give power over the nations: And he shall rule them with a rod of iron; as the vessels of a potter shall they be broken to shivers: even as I received of my Father. And I will give him the morning star. He that hath an ear, let him hear what the Spirit saith unto the churches."

(Revelation 2:18-29)

The Thyatira period of the church is thought to be during the church "dark ages" when the Roman Catholic Church reigned from about 538 A.D. to the start of the Protestant reformation in the 16th Century. Jesus rebuked Thyatira for "suffering" Jezebel, which essentially means "putting up with" this antichrist spirit, and losing their battle against her false teachings. Jezebel was the wife of King Ahab, who led Israel into Baal worship and Sun worship (See 1 Kings 16:31, 1 Kings 21:25). Today's Baal worship has become Islam. Allah is a composite name of Baal, Ilyat and Enlil. Today that Sun worship has become Roman Catholicism. See, Book Two: *Who Is God?* Chapter: *Who Is Allah?*[11]

In 1 Kings 18:13 it says that Jezebel murdered the prophets of the Lord God. During the spiritual church age of Thyatira, the Church of Rome elevated Mary, Mother of Jesus, above Him through their worship of her. The Church of Rome transformed the already established Babylonian religion, which was the worship of the Sun god Mithras and his mother Semiramis, into the Roman Catholic Church. Their rule and influence lingers in the remnant of the Roman Empire, which has led God's people into sun worship and idolatry, causing the faithful to be killed. In the Bible prophecy, a woman is used as a symbol of a church. The woman in white in Revelation 12 represents God's true church and the harlot woman in Revelation 17 and 18 represents an apostate fallen church.

So, who is this woman Jezebel? We know it isn't the original Jezebel from the Old Testament, because she was killed. This is spiritual Jezebel who, from 538 A.D. through the sixteenth century, led God's people into idolatry and persecuted and killed God's true believers, the saints. This is none other than the Roman Catholic Church. Remember Jezebel worshipped Astarte in 1 Kings. As I've connected this dot previously, the Jezebel demon comes from Astarte (Ashtarte, Ashtar) who is an ancient fallen angel archon. The fact that it is nick-named 'the Jezebel spirit', is partly archetypal and partly the fact that its true history precedes the story of King Ahab and the evil queen Jezebel in the first and second book of Kings of the Old Testament.

> "Jezebel is a figurative name, alluding to Ahab's wife, who slew the prophets of the Lord, led her husband into idolatry, and fed the prophets of Baal at her own table. A more striking figure could not have been used to denote the Papal abominations."
>
> (Review and Herald, Vol 8, Oct 16, 1856)

When you learn how to discern the truth about the antichrist spirit, you will understand who the Roman Catholic Church represents, and why it committed the atrocities against Jews and true Christians throughout the centuries. Therefore, Jesus rebuked His people for putting up with the abominations that infiltrated His church. Many openly surrendered to Roman Catholic apostasy out of fear of public chastisement, inquisitions and persecution. The people were weakened by fear and ignorance, and therefore did not put up enough of a fight to rebuke and stop the infiltration of evil that flooded God's church. In the Thyatira church age, apostasy was openly and defiantly rampant, even more so than in the Pergamos church age. Just as Jezebel in the Old Testament killed the prophets of God, the Roman Catholic Church murdered the true Christians who would not go along with her false teachings.

What's interesting is that Jesus Christ says this woman Jezebel calls herself a "prophetess". How many people do you know who are self-proclaimed prophets? Therein lies the Jezebel spirit. True prophets do not call themselves prophets. While the church claims to be doing God's work, in truth it has become a fallen church, doing the work of Satan. Jezebel isn't a prophet of God; she is a false prophet of the god of this world, who is Satan. The Roman Catholic Church claims to be doing God's work, but as we can see from her false teachings and her history of killing God's people, she is doing the work of Satan. Pedophilia is at the center of satanic ritual abuse, which is at the core of Roman Catholic Priesthood. More people have left the Catholic Church to become atheists because of the psychic and religious wounds received from its demonic religious spirit, masquerading as God's priests and authority on earth, but they are nothing but the whore of Babylon. Jesus repeatedly says, 'come out of her, Babylon.' Repent! (Revelation 18:4)

> "In the same way, I tell you, there is rejoicing in the presence of the angels of God over one sinner who repents."
>
> (Luke 15:10)

Chapter Nine: Fallen Angels or Evil Spirits?

In His great mercy, Jesus gives Jezebel (this apostate church) time to repent. That time is coming to an end at the end of the Church Age, also known as the Age of Grace. However, she refuses to repent, and in open defiance continues to reject the truth of God's Word by leading many into apostasy. The Roman Catholic Church openly rejected the Word of God by exalting the popes in place of Jesus Christ, and misleading its followers down the path of great apostasy. I know many 'recovering Catholics' who have become New Agers, because in their heart of hearts, they are good and spiritual people, but could no longer participate in a church full of hypocrisies and outright rebellion to God. Many of these recovering Catholics are so wounded by religion (and religious spirits) they are wary of joining other churches. This is how satan divides and conquers, through the religious spirit, the Jezebel spirit. The Holy Spirit which is the Spirit of Christ must be sought after above all other spirits, that we may find the true peace, love and joy promised to all those who follow the Lord (Galatians 5:22).

The children who Jesus says He will kill are those who commit fornication with this apostate church in Revelation 2:23, the ones who are in open rebellion against the truth of God's Word. God is merciful and full of wisdom and understanding. He knows who His faithful are, (sheep) and who are Christians in name only (goats). There are and have been countless members of the Roman Catholic Church whose hearts are devoted to the Lord Jesus Christ. Jesus isn't saying that He is going to kill everyone who was and is a member of this apostate church.

Most of us are blithely ignorant of church history, including the offshoots of Catholicism, of other denominations and even of non-denominational churches who are still unconsciously and unknowingly following the Constantine and Nicaean Creeds. These creeds are anti-Jew, anti-the God of Israel and Antichrist. There are many who are living in complete ignorance, as the truth has not been shown to them by the pastors whose job it is to shepherd and feed the sheep. God will judge these people by how they lived up to the light and knowledge they did possess.

The children to whom Jesus is referring as coming under His judgement in Revelation 2:23 are those who, after the truth has been shown them, reject the truth in rebellion against God and continue to follow Jezebel in apostasy, because of spiritual pride and stubbornness. Then God's mercy will come to an end and they will be killed in the last days. God's mercy is conditional upon our repentance of our sins and turning to the truth and living by it, through the power that God gives us through Christ's righteousness (Ephesians 6:14; Isaiah 59:17). The Lord still has some of His people within the Roman Catholic Church, along with other fallen and apostate churches, which is why He tells His people to COME OUT OF BABYLON. There are many Born Again Catholics who are waking up to the truth. They are promised salvation, but that salvation isn't promised to those who pray to His obedient and humble mother, Mary, who was never given authority to forgive sins or deliver souls from the many bondages of satan. Only Jesus Christ aka Yeshua HaMashiach, has that power and authority.

When Jesus said "to the rest in Thyatira" in Revelation 2:24, who have not known the "depths of Satan", He is talking to the small groups of people who lived throughout the Middle Ages and till the end of this present Age who want to remain loyal to the true apostolic Christianity and Judaism, which was rejected by the Church of Rome. Upon them God put no further burden than to be faithful to the light which was theirs, which Jesus says "HOLD FAST" to that truth which you have! These people, who are faithful in heart and deed to the Lord, these are the souls to whom the Lord will be faithful on the day of judgement.

Thyatira and New Agers

The term "New Age" is inaccurate, inappropriate and deceiving. Most of the New Age practices are revivals of ancient occult rites and rituals, nothing new. It's all old age, an ancient theme recycled, rebirthing itself, nothing else, nothing new. Why are most New Agers followers of ancient Egypt or ancient Native Indians, or ancient Atlanteans? The list goes on, but you get the picture. It is important to remember history, because we need the wisdom of its lessons. To be *enchanted* by the past to the point where you're living in it is regressive to your growth and evolution.

The Church of Thyatira (1-2 Kings) is the presentation of today's New Age mindset. The real "New Age" is the Age to come, which is the Kingdom of Heaven manifest on earth. The New Age essentially *is* when Heaven comes to earth. Bible prophecy calls it, "The Millennial Reign of Christ on Earth," which coincides with the shift of the Processional Age of Pisces into the Processional Age of Aquarius. Are we there yet? Almost! Truth be told, the believers in Christ and His Coming Kingdom are the true *New Agers*. All those whose names are written in the Lamb's Book of Life will partake of the Kingdom to come on earth. Now, for those Christians reading this, I hope that shifts your perspective a bit.

Remember 95% of the *New Agers*, whom Christians despise, reject and fear, actually came out of the Christian churches for a variety of good reasons. Christians need to recognize that, and own it on some level. Jesus came to save all sinners. He never said that one sinner is more important than the other. This type of funda-*mental* judgmentalism which has caused so many people to leave Christian churches is the Jezebel spirit. If Christians of today are not going to be filled with the lovingkindness, compassion and understanding of Christ, then you tell me, what's the point of calling yourself a Christian?

Chapter Nine: Fallen Angels or Evil Spirits?

Did Jesus not die for new agers and pagans too?

The presence of the religious spirit in immature Christians, many of whom were saved out of New Age practices, is evidence of continued demonic oppression. These immature Christians frequently malign and persecute their brothers and sisters with whom they previously bonded. This is NOT the will of God. What God calls His redeemed to do, is to go back where you came from and share the good news of the gospel of Grace with them. Or, in my case, write books for them, so that they may have understanding. Knowing the Messiah Lord Jesus, and knowing the old camp, and being able to discern the differences, illustrates the truths in both camps that only the Messiah can bridge together. He is active between Jews and Christians. He is, after all, the Messiah of all peoples.

The coming apostasy will take place because we are in the time of the Apocalypse, the time of revelation. Many New Agers already see through the lies of the Apostate church, which is the reason so them end up in New Age churches, or some kind of blend of the two. The other reason for the apostasy is the veil being removed. This is particularly troubling to fundamentalists who have been taught an incomplete story, believing in replacement theology, and therefore, do not recognize the offenses done by the Church of Rome to the Lord's people, the Jews, in their blatant attempt to dilute the Jewishness of Jesus from their Bible canon.

Jews and New Agers tend to look outside the box of fundamental Christianity. For Jews, Christians were the enemies for millennia. The Jews are traditionally blamed for the death of Christ. This blame, together with the false teachings of replacement theology, gave reason for persecution beyond belief. The New Agers seek knowledge, enlightenment and ascension. Jesus died for both these groups of people. Christians need to remember that.

Sadly, there is more scorn and disdain for Jews and New Agers than there are Christian missionaries and outreaches. True, there are many Messianic Congregations, but as I've already pointed out in Book Two[12] *Who is God?* many of these are plagued with the religious spirit and are nothing but modern day Pharisees. These congregations teach the need to compete with Judaism, steal Jewish identity, and follow the Jewish religion to the 'T' in order to be considered worthy of the Kingdom.

I got good news for you. Jesus freed everyone, especially His own people, from the *curse of the law, the letter of the law, and the judgment of the law*. The Sabbath, for instance has been a great source of controversy within both Judaism and Christianity, as to when the Sabbath day properly begins. Jews will argue over the timing of it, being the first light of the moon, and so are in bondage to the old ways of the Levitical Law, also known as legalism. Christians got diverted by the Roman decree that changed the Sabbath day to Sunday, which was always the day for sun worship. But Jesus said,

> "During the high priesthood of Abiathar, he entered the house of God and ate the consecrated bread, which was lawful only for the priests. And he gave some to his companions as well." Then Jesus told them, "The Sabbath was made for man, not man for the Sabbath. Therefore, the Son of Man is Lord even of the Sabbath."
>
> (Mark 2:26-28)

One of the most refreshing gifts enjoyed through God's Grace is that we are invited to rest in Christ. He cares less about us keeping our OCD religious rituals than He cares about us trusting and depending on Him for our restoration.

This, along with all the other problems that exist in the churches, is why we need the Messiah to straighten us all out. As I concluded in Book Two, we may have unity of faith in Christ, but there is still no unity of knowledge and little to no unity of spirit within the churches, and this becomes the devil's foothold and the spiritual legal ground to attack, oppress and create division amongst the Body of Christ. It's a Jezebellion trap folks. Did you fall for it?

The 'Love' piece must be continually cultivated within all groups of believers. Finger pointing is the office of the Accuser of the Brethren, which is foundational of the church of Jezebel and the basis of the Jezebel spirit. Accusing others comes from self-righteousness. God hates self-righteousness and hypocrisy. Jesus said, 'take the log out of your own eye first before you start picking on your brother!' It is way more important to show kindness to other believers than to judge and reject them because they think differently from you, or hold different perspectives, revelations or knowledge.

There is a counterfeit spirit which operates fully on narcissistic psychological projection, rooted in jealousy and competition. It brands a leader as 'false' because of something they don't like, which essentially is the spirit on them being threatened with truth, which they identify as unpopular, in face of the fact that the Lord is using the minister and their ministry in a mighty way. Then they disparage one another on line! This a betrayal of the true gospel, as true prophets and people of God don't go in for nasty tactics of Jezebellion spirits rooted in spiritual pride. I'm sure many of you would agree with me, there's plenty of hate and woundedness to go around, but not enough love and understanding.

True believers do not broadcast how many times a day they pray online, or how much money they gave, which Jesus forbade. He wants worship to be unto Him, no matter the form. There are those who puff themselves up and imply they are more spiritual, more religious than any other; then in the next sentence they trash talk some brother or sister for this or that online, discrediting them and debunking them. This is as far from being Christ-like as it can get, and is the reason so many Christians leave Christian churches. The Religious Spirit has a great deal for which to answer for!

Chapter Nine: Fallen Angels or Evil Spirits?

Those less knowledgeable than we are not false, just as those more knowledgeable are not more true. If we have yet to achieve a level of understanding comparable to that of our fellow-believers, we have a lot to learn, and can be thankful for the opportunity and guidance of mentors and seniors in the faith. There is no room for jealousy in the Kingdom of God. Together we can learn to discern what is false in God's eyes, as how our heavenly Father sees us all is as children who need to grow.

People who claim to be Christians represent Christ, and in Him was no arrogance, rejection or judgment. Bearing the fruit of the Spirit, our lives are a witness to the transformational power and Grace of Jesus. When Christ accepts us with all our flaws, then we too must learn to accept others who may not think like us, but are far from false.

It is a sin for Christians to reject Jews who accept Jesus. The Christian community may feel threatened by Messianic Jews, when they should see them as an integral link in the cause to build bridges between Christians and Jews. If a Christian believes in Genesis 12:3, "And I will bless them that bless thee, and curse him that curseth thee: and in thee shall all families of the earth be blessed," then this applies to Jews who accept Jesus as well, though they may look askance at the many different cults of Christianity. Why should any Jew leave their religion because of accepting Jesus, who was a Jew? You're in a relationship with the Messiah, who accepts you as you are, where you are, as should other Christians. Tolerance goes both ways.

Christians must let go of false attitudes inspired by the Church of Rome, which became the Roman Catholic Church at the first millennia. Christians have no excuse for closing their eyes to the power plays of the Church of Rome over the Jews, the Jewishness of Jesus, and their bastardization of the God of Israel. When Gentiles get saved, they need to rely on Jesus to show them the Father. The Father is Yahuah, the God of Jeshurun (Israel). The beings behind ancient Rome are ancient enemies to the Lord. When you understand that, everything else makes sense. You immediately want to repent of swallowing lies and following idolatry, for which the Lord punished Israel severely. If the Religious Spirit-demon blinds us into continuing to practice the ancient religions of Rome, which are Babylonian in essence, then so will the suppression of Jews, the rejection of the God of the Jews, and its Hebrew Bible also continue.

No man can successfully put God in a box, in spite of the many who've tried and failed. That is the demon of spiritual narcissism, which says, 'He is my Jesus, you can't have Him'. This is utter foolishness! We do not have a monopoly on God. People need to come out of the Babylon of the past. The reason we study the past is to become aware of the lessons it is supposed to be teaching us. But if we fail to learn these lessons, we're doomed to repeat its negative patterns and attitudes. This is why we need an attitude adjustment in our spirits. When people walk with the living God and are filled with His Spirit, miracles happen. This is a true "mark" of God.

Notes and References:

1. C.S. Lewis, *The Screwtape Letters,* published by Geoffrey Bles, U.K., 1942
2. C.S. Lewis, *The Last Battle,* published by The Bodley Head, U.K., 1956
3. John Keel *Operation Trojan Horse,* ISBN 978-0962653469 G.P. Putnam and Sons, NY, NY, 1970. p. 192
4. Ibid., (Keel 266).
5. Dr. John Mack, *Abduction, Human Encounters with Aliens,* Scribner, (August 1, 2007), p.402
6. Michelangelo di Lodovico Buonarroti Simoni, *Moses,* Wikipedia-Moses/Michelangelo c. 1513 – 1515, San Pietro in Vincoli, Rome.
7. Stephen Spielberg, *War of the Worlds,* 2005.
8. Ella LeBain, *Who's Who in the Cosmic Zoo?* Book One, Third Edition, Chapter on *Giants,* p.208, Tate Publishing, 2013.
9. Ibid. p.280-289.
10. Jennifer LeClaire, *Satan's Trio: Defeating the Deception of Jezebel, Religion and Witchcraft,* Revelation Media Networks, Chosen Books, Minnesota. 2014.
11. Ella LeBain, Book Two: *Who Is God?* Chapter Twenty-Two: *Who Is Allah?* p.359, Skypath Books, 2015.
12. Ibid.

CHAPTER TEN

Purgatory

> "If any man's work shall be burned, he shall suffer loss:
> but he himself shall be saved; yet so as by fire."
> (1 Corinthians 3:15)

The concept of purgatory dates back before the time of Jesus, which includes the worldwide practice of praying for and caring for the dead, with the belief in their afterlife *purification*. These roots are found in Judaism, from Christianity sprang. The Church of Rome, which later became the Roman Catholic Church, made a fortune out of a strongly held belief in Purgatory. They adopted these beliefs from ancient Jewish texts such as the Book of Maccabees, the book that details the miracle of the burning lamp for eight days in the temple, which is celebrated annually as Hanukkah. 2 Maccabees 12:43-46 supports the doctrine of purgatory as an ancient Jewish belief, which is still read in Jewish Funeral Homes till this day, encouraging the living to pray for the dead, so their sins maybe forgiven. The Chinese Buddhists also practice similar traditions of making offerings on behalf of the dead who they believed suffered numerous trials when passing over. The word purgatory comes from the root word, *to purge* or *to purify*.

The ancients believed that purgatory was a place between heaven and hell where souls were purified by a *spiritual fire*, which comes from God, a place of repentance from their sins and ungodly attitudes, a place to achieve at-one-ment with God, and get back into His mercies. Of course, this concept goes against today's mainstream Christianity. There are many Christians today who adopt the false beliefs of the Church of Rome, yet are vehemently opposed to any chance of salvation after death, and typically do not believe in Reincarnation either. As I proved in Book Two, *Who Is God?*[1] that reincarnation is deeply rooted in Judaism. There are more scriptures that point to God's grace through reincarnation than the *one* rogue scripture in Hebrews 9:27, that Christians seems to think points in the other direction. Here in this chapter, we are going to explore if the belief in purgatory has any basis in Scripture, and why this belief is held in Judaism and Catholicism, but no longer accepted in today's mainstream Christianity. Let's discern.

Purgatory is a type of dimensional holding place for souls that died without the benefit of the Savior, who were not exactly wicked and evil, but were not entirely righteous either. Purgatory is a place of grace from the Creator that allows souls a chance to purify themselves in the 'Holy Fire' of God. This is the place where souls may receive another chance at life as they are not worthy of paradise, as it is the will of the Creator that no soul be sent to hell or the lake of fire for eternity.

The Lord mentions this holy purging fire when speaking through his prophet Zechariah:

> "In the whole land," declares the LORD, "two-thirds will be struck down and perish; yet one-third will be left in it. This third <u>I will bring into the fire; I will refine them like silver and test them like gold</u>. They will call on my name and I will answer them; I will say, 'They are my people,' and they will say, 'The LORD is our God.'"
>
> (Zechariah 13:8-9)

This passage relates to the end time Jews who will be saved during the time of Jacob's troubles, the seven-year tribulation under the final antichrist. The two thirds the Lord refers to are the ones who will perish, the one third left will be the remnant He will save. But first He will put them through the 'holy fire' to refine them, and purge them of all their ungodly attitudes and unbelief. He tells us they will call out to His name, and He will answer them, as this fire will bring them to the acceptance that Yeshua is their Lord.

St. Augustine distinguished between the purifying fire that saves and eternal consuming fire for the unrepentant. Both St. Clement of Alexandria (c. 150-215) and his student Origen of Alexandria (c. 185-254) developed a view of purification after death; they drew upon this notion that the holy fire is a divine instrument from the Old Testament, and juxtaposed this in context of the New Testament teaching of baptism by fire, from the Gospel and purification through trial after death from St. Paul. Origen argued against soul sleep, stating that the souls of the elect immediately entered paradise unless not yet purified, in which case they passed into a state of punishment, a penal fire, which is conceived as a place of purification, as purgatory, not hell. For both Clement and Origen, the fire was neither a material thing nor a metaphor, but a "spiritual fire".

St. Catherine of Genoa[2] wrote a treatise on Understanding Purgatory, which she titled, *Fire of Love* after the disastrous plague of 1493, when she watched four fifths of Genoa perish including her husband. Her insights continue to inspire many Christians. She understood that the reason souls of the faithful are placed in purgatory was to purge them of all the rust and stains of sin of which they did not have

Chapter Ten: Purgatory

the opportunity to rid themselves in life. She said that the souls who are in purgatory did not choose to be there, that this is done by the ordinance and the Grace of God. In purgatory, they cannot turn their thoughts back to themselves, or say, 'such sins I have committed for which I deserve to be here', or, 'I wish that I had not committed them for then I would now go to Paradise', or, 'that person will leave sooner than I', or, 'I will leave sooner than will he.'

In purgatory, they can have no memory either of themselves nor of others, whether good or evil. That they are there to be within God's ordinance, to merge back with the light of God which is all truth, all love and all light. In this light, they no longer think of themselves as one is conditioned to on earth, but are happy to be in the divine goodness. They are there to purge themselves of all ungodly attitudes and to make right with God.

St. Catherine wrote that there are all different types of degrees of purgatory, from Charity, to Happiness, to Repentance, to Spiritual Hunger, to Hell in Purgatory, to Mercy and Justice in Purgatory, to a type of 'Joyful Suffering', to Sins being Revealed in Purgatory, to Purification, to Contentment and to the Fire of Love.

The Grace of God allows for all of this. Yet there are many rebellious souls who have become instruments of evil who do end up in Hell. Purgatory is for all those in between, those who are ignorant of God's laws, those who tried to do good but made lots of mistakes, those who did not know God, and all those who were misled by the god of this world (Satan), in all his many forms and disguises, who subsequently believed in his lies all their life. Through God's Grace many are given this chance to purify their souls of all iniquity, unrighteousness and unrepentance. This is the place where a soul is given another chance through God's Mercy. It is from this place, known as purgatory, or God's holy fire, that souls are allowed to reincarnate on earth and try again. This was the belief of the ancients, before the Church of Rome usurped the Jewish Scriptures in 325AD.

Visions of purgatory abounded; Bede,[3] who wrote *Historia Ecclesiastica* mentions a vision of a beautiful Heaven and a lurid Hell with adjacent temporary abodes. In the 7th century, the Irish abbot St. Fursa described his foretaste of the afterlife, where, though protected by angels, he was pursued by demons who said, "It is not fitting that he should enjoy the blessed life unscathed..., for every transgression that is not purged on earth must be avenged in heaven." On his return, he was engulfed in a billowing fire that threatened to burn him, "for it stretches out each one according to their merits... For just as the body burns through unlawful desire, so the soul will burn, as the lawful, due penalty for every sin."

If the soul accepted Christ as Savior, there is grace over their sins and they are forgiven. If not, the souls, depending on their deeds, are sent through a purging process to atone for all ungodly attitudes and behavior in an in-between place, betwixt paradise and hell, which has been called 'Purgatory' by the Catholics or 'Bardo' by the Tibetans.[4]

The lake of fire was prepared for the Devil and his angels (Revelation 21:8), not for humans, so when people miss the mark (an old archery term which is where the word 'sin' comes from), then out of the Grace of God, He judges them based on what was missed and allows them another chance to purge from sin. In Hebrew, it's called *Tikune* which is the path of correction so out of God's Grace, another chance at life as a spirit having a human experience is granted. Circumstances are arranged through who the parents will be to serve the soul's purging of their errors, and allows them the opportunity, one more time, to realize God's Divine Plan of Salvation, within the boundaries of life on earth.

Until the world is changed, the earth is still under the curse, and to be reborn under the Prince of Darkness, principalities and powers, serves as a place of trying men's souls. However, there is an expiration date! On rebirth out of purgatory, which is the end of the world, all souls pass through the final Judgment and the second death (Revelation 20:14). This terrible fate will be determined by weighing all the chances souls are given to find the Kingdom of God and those who misuse them, or who are aligned with the rebel fallen angels, the satans, will enter into the second death.

This is why there is a dimensional doorway into a place in the lower heavens known as purgatory. The *Tibetan Book of the Dead* calls it 'Bardo.' Here the soul is put through a series of tests to discern truth from lie, illusion from reality and *purge* all ungodly attitudes. Hence the origin of the word, "Purgatory."

Most people who have Near Death Experiences report moving into the 'light', areas of purgatory where the Light of God itself bathes and purges all spirits and souls from ungodly, unloving attitudes and behaviors. Remember the ego which battles against the spirit of man and God in the human body is connected to the flesh, the physical experience, so when physical death happens, the ego dies with the body. One doesn't need to let go of the physical body in order to experience the death of the ego. There are many humiliating and disappointing experiences on earth that can provide the opportunity to accomplish ego death without having to let go of the body.

There have been a growing number of accounts by experiencers of NDEs who have reported feeling like they were being eaten, having their ears and body parts chewed and the feeling that they were being dragged down a dark spiral which they reported was like 'hell'. When they called out to the Lord Jesus Christ to save them, they all reported that immediately an angel of the Lord lifted them out of this downward dark spiral and brought them up to the Lord, who gave them another chance at life. Upon the soul's return to the bodies, they were miraculously brought back to life. This proves that there is a hell.

George Anderson[5] writes in his book, *Extra-Terrestrials: Friend of Foe?* that, "one of the allegations concerning the short Grays is that they have a way of deriving

Chapter Ten: Purgatory

nourishment from what leaves our bodies at the moment of death, that they are eaters of souls, who extract from our spirits a certain principle, through a process comparable to the extraction of hemoglobin from blood, which they use as food, burying the residue elsewhere in the universe, not on this planet."

Separation of the etheric body from the soul can also be brought about by malignant entities for predatory purposes, both during life and upon passing the frontier into death. Anderson goes on to explain that the etheric body is charged with energy that is neither as subtle as that of the soul, nor as coarse as that of the physical body, but is intermediate between them. This is a substance highly valued as nourishment by certain other life-forms, which include the Grays. This is what the Grays are after, which they are here to trap as we trap fur-bearing animals. We are now and have been for millennia, been used by the Grays as a food source, with almost zero awareness of the actual situation. Except mysteriously feeling drained, fatigued and depressed. [emphasis mine]. Anderson postulates that the continued survival of the Grays on Earth depends on our continued ignorance of this symbiotic relationship, in which the benefits are all strictly one-way.[6] (See, Book One of *Who's Who In The Cosmic Zoo?* chapter on Grays).

The Grays are essentially using us to keep them alive in a parasitic relationship. Fear is the emotion that they provoke and feed upon. Once you're afraid, they've got you. Fear puts your heart and mind out of sync and scrambles your energy patterns and throws your ability to think clearly out of focus, enabling them to take control of you.

When the church fathers eliminated almost but not quite all the references to reincarnation and extra-terrestrials in the Bible during the Council of Nicaea in 325-360 A.D., humanity's path to liberation was transformed into a 'soul-trap', making it almost impossible to escape.

According to the *Tibetan Book of the Dead*, 'during the process of dying one at first blacks out, then very briefly a colorless light shines. If one instantly without hesitation recognizes this colorless light and merges with it, with the inmost essence of one's being, one no longer needs to reincarnate. If this instantaneous recognition and union does not occur, the light starts to take on different colors. Each color becomes a path that leads to a different type of incarnation. The light takes on these colors, until a color appears that one is attracted to and goes toward, at which point it becomes a path. The colorless light in the Tibetan system would correspond to the supreme divinity of the Gnostics and the pathways of the colored lights to the deities and the demons of the lower realms of heaven.[7]

In modern terms, we call them extra-terrestrial and other dimensional entities. As already discussed in this book, under the section on Lucifer/Satan, interdimensionals can be both malevolent and benevolent. Satan and his fallen angels operate as interdimensionals, meaning they can appear and disappear at will in our dimension yet reside primarily in a dimension in the spirit realm. Interdimensionals and extra-terrestrials can be one and the same.

Earth School

Earth lives are a series of preparations and proving grounds to build character, to present opportunities to serve God and others, which can determine the kind of future life. Some get to come back here for a myriad of reasons, including contracts and agreements made with the dark forces. That soul must reconcile with God and itself through experience of all kinds of things only earth life can provide. Others get to go on to other worlds, live lives on other planets according to the resonance of their soul. Others get to live out their futures in space on ships.

Many jobs on earth are training ground for 'ship' life. Take the transportation business for example, on earth you may prove worthy by driving a cab, or a car service, or a bus driver or train or plane. If your inner life aligns with the Plan of the Creator, in the future life you may be given your own space craft to transport others. As you have proved yourself of good stewardship on earth, being responsible to others, you are rewarded with your own ship.

Jesus said, "In my Father's house there are <u>many mansions</u>." (John 14:2) The word *mansions*, in Hebrew means, abode or levels. As I've written in my chapters on *The Divine Law of Salvation*, and *The Word of God in the Stars*, that the word *mansions* is actually a celestial term, for celestial houses, i.e., star systems.

Everyone goes to their designated place after death. It all depends on who owns your soul. Satan and the fallen angels of his kingdom are not limited to this planet, they will take you to their underground Hades or Hell or use you as slaves on other planets, or Christ will set you free from them and their captivity of your soul. Jesus said, "I have come to set the captives free." (Isaiah 61;1; Luke 4:18)

"Hell was prepared for the Devil and his angels." (Matthew 25:41) Hell was not created for humans, however, when people follow Satan and his fallen angels and reject the salvation that Jesus Christ offers, that's where they end up. There have been a handful of NDE experiencers who have reported falling into the vortexes of hell, having their body parts chewed off and the life sucked out of them, only to have called out to the Lord to save them, which He did, and sent them back into their bodies and gave them another chance.

Purgatory is a place in between heaven and hell. It is a realm in another dimension through which many souls pass. The word 'purgatory' comes from the word to 'purge'. This is where the souls purge themselves from their ungodly attitudes to achieve at-one-ment with God. This is the place of the 'Light' that most NDE

Chapter Ten: Purgatory

experiencers speak, because it is bathed in the Light of God, but it is not paradise. It is a place where souls have the opportunity to make it right and await judgment before the Lord, if they would be worthy to receive another chance, or another incarnation, to find the path of the Lord and Salvation. Purgatory is a kind of Bardo as described in the *Tibetan Book of the Dead*.[8]

When the Bible says, "And as it is appointed to men once to die, but after this the judgment" in Hebrews 9:27 it doesn't necessarily mean that after judgment that man cannot be born again. After all Jesus Himself said, "I am the gate; whoever enters through Me will be saved. He will come in and go out, and find pasture." (John 10:9) The words, 'come in and go out' indicate that many get another chance at life through reincarnating. After each life, there is judgment for that life. After each lifetime, the soul returns back to the Lord to be judged for that particular incarnation. This is the first death. This is different from the Final Judgment which is talked about in the book of Revelation, which is the second death. The final Judgment happens at the end of time, which will be the end of the chances to reincarnate. All souls will be judged based on their 'cumulative' lives on earth. If they found salvation through Christ, and made themselves worthy, their souls will enter into eternal life. If not, then their souls will be destroyed. That is the second death.

"As above, so below." ~ Hermetic Law

The corporate world is also a mirror of ship life. Everyone has their role or mission to carry out. They are forced to work close to others, share space, alternate schedules, work together for a common cause. The Lord watches along with His many ET allies, His 'angels', to see who are worthy of future ship life in the Kingdom of Heaven. How humans behave towards one another in a close, often competitive environment, is the gauge of who is worthy and who is ready. The Kingdom of Heaven includes mansions, which are starships.

The same goes for healthcare, hospital workers, anyone who works within a hierarchy. Those in the military also have lots to learn and prove. So many warriors end up giving up their lives before their time for others. Again, this is why God's grace allows for reincarnation, as everyone is given another chance or as many chances as needed to become aware and conscious of our Creator's Divine Plan for the soul. There are probably a million and one reasons why souls are given the chance to reincarnate.

Finding the path of salvation, learning how to trust the Lord and live right for Him, learning lessons, completing love contracts, learning forgiveness as there is nothing to forgive in heaven, forgiveness can only be experienced in earth's duality, along with developing the fruits of tolerance, long-suffering, compassion, courage in the face of fears. You can't have courage without fear! The main reason why souls are allowed to reincarnate is to find the path of salvation on earth and reconcile the soul's earthly experiences with the Creator. How the Almighty determines who goes where and when is according to each individual soul's journey.

I am reminded of the powerful line from C.S. Lewis' *Chronicles of Narnia, The Voyage of the Dawn Treader*,[9] when Aslan sends Lucy back to earth, and she asks him if she will ever see him again, and he tells her, "In your world, I have another name, try to find to me." Of course, we know that name is Jesus Christ, because Aslan is the Christ character in *The Chronicles of Narnia*.

When Jesus said, "I Am the Gate; whoever enters through me will be saved, <u>he will come in and go out and find pasture</u>." (John 10:9) Coming in and going out is the biblical term for reincarnating. The soul comes back to God, and then goes out from the presence of God again reincarnating on earth or other planets as the case may be. Jesus also said, "In my Father's house there are many mansions, if it were not so, I would have told you; for I go to prepare a place for you." (John 14:2)

The very words, 'he will come in and go out, and find pasture' is indicative of the fact that many souls are allowed to reincarnate through God's Grace. There are so many soul reasons for reincarnation. Take unrequited love for example, how many people have waited faithfully for loved ones to come back from war and they never do. Even though they believed on the Lord, their experiences were of unrequited love, which left a hole in their souls. In God's grace and mercy, he allows them another chance in the earth life to fulfill their soul's experience and are given a new life to meet up with soul mates.

Other reasons for reincarnation are for soul correction, which in the Hebrew Torah is called, 'Tikune', which translates to 'correction', which many also interpret as karma. Let's say a soul was so deeply ingrained in some kind of sin but accepted Jesus at the end of their life. The Lord is faithful and just to forgive them, but as they never learned the soul lesson, they are allowed another chance at life, to live a godly life. There are so many reasons why souls are sent back to earth, too many to mention here. The point is, purgatory and reincarnation have always been a facet of the world's major religions, Judaism and Hinduism, up until the Church fathers deleted it in 325 A.D. It did not fit into their political agenda. Book Two, *Who Is God?*, has a more detailed chapter on the history of reincarnation, why it was deleted, and where are the several dozen scriptures left in today's Bible that points to its foundation in God's Grace and Divine Will.

1 Corinthians 3:11-15 is the most straightforward text in Scripture disclosing Purgatory:

"For no other foundation can anyone lay than that which is laid, which is Jesus Christ. Now if any one builds on the foundation with gold, silver, precious stones, wood, hay, stubble—each man's work will become manifest; for the Day will disclose it, because it will be revealed with fire, and the fire will test what

Chapter Ten: Purgatory

sort of work each one has done. If the work which any man has built on the foundation survives, he will receive a reward. If any man's work is burned up, he will suffer loss, though he himself will be saved, but only as through fire."

There is not a single Christian sect I know of that would deny this scripture speaks of the judgment of God where the works of the faithful will be tested after death. However, not that it says our works will go through "fire," literally and figuratively speaking. In Scripture, "fire" is used metaphorically in two ways: as a purifying agent (Malachi 3:2-3; Matthew 3:11; Mark 9:49); and as that which consumes (Matthew 3:12; 2 Thessalonians 1:7-8). Therefore, it is consistent as an appropriate symbol for God's judgment. Some of the "works" represented are being burned up and some are being purified. These works survive or burn according to their essential "quality."

What is being referred in 1 Corinthians 3:11-15, cannot be heaven because there are imperfections that need to be "burned up" (see, Revelation 21:27, Habakkuk 1:13). It cannot be hell because souls are being saved. So, what is it? The Protestant calls it "the Judgment" and Catholics agree. Catholics simply specify the part of the judgment of the saved where imperfections are purged as "Purgatory."

Remember Catholicism began after the first millennia AD. They took over from the Church of Rome. So many of their beliefs are rooted in what the Roman Emperors decreed, as is much of today's mainstream Christianity. But why do so many non-Catholic Christians deny this piece of history and traditional beliefs? Yet they hold onto other lies from the Church of Rome? As you can see, the Catholics adopted their beliefs from the Jewish scriptures, which God gave to the Jewish people to be the keepers of knowledge, wisdom and sacred revelations.

Suffering purges from sin and karmic debt is the meaning of Purgatory, the purging, cleansing, purification of the soul to return 'whole' back to God. It's all about God's grace, mercy, love and goodness. The purging of old stuff creates purity. Healing leads to wholeness, holiness, purity. God is patient with us. These different facets of the afterlife are in place, including the cycles of reincarnation, designed to achieve the same purpose, the return of the soul wholly back to God, free of karmic debt, purified through the suffering for sin. Once the soul finds salvation through Christ and submits to God's will, it is transformed into a new creation in Christ Jesus through faith. In grace, something miraculous happens, all are liberated and set free from all kinds of demonic influences hindering and blocking from the true greatness which is found in God.

The demons of earth life fight against the will of God. Once humans consciously choose to seek God through the deliverance offered through Christ and the Holy Spirit, divine intervention occurs, supernatural movement transforms the soul and its human vessel through miracle healings of mind, body and spirit, which could never have happened otherwise. That kind of profound transformation leads the soul heavenward, where we no longer need to reincarnate, but may choose to do so, as a Saint or Bodhisattva, only to do the will of God on earth to assist humanity, essentially as a human angel.

> "He who overcomes, I will make him a pillar in the temple of My God, <u>and he will not go out from it anymore</u>; and I will write on him the name of My God, and the name of the city of My God, the new Jerusalem, which comes down out of heaven from My God, and My new name."
>
> (Revelation 3:12)

Not go out from it anymore, means that there will be no more need for reincarnation and leaving heaven for an incarnation in the flesh. There will be no more need for being 'born again' in water. By overcoming the tests, trials and tribulations in the kingdom of darkness, (Lucifer/Satan's realm) He promises to make us 'pillars' in His temple. A pillar is a support, a mainstay, a tower of strength, that holds up its foundation. Another definition for a pillar is a leader or a rock. By being transformed out of the kingdom of darkness into the Kingdom of God, then there is no need to come back to earth and live another life in the flesh. The corporeal then becomes the incorporeal, the translation has taken place and the new light body of eternal life has been given instead of the body of flesh that dies.

> "The thief (Lucifer/Satan) comes only to steal and kill and destroy; I (Jesus) have come that they may have life, and have it to the full. "I AM the good shepherd. The good shepherd lays down his life for the sheep."
>
> (John 10:10,11)

Investing in Our Spirit

Investing in cleansing the spirit in life, in preparation for death, so you don't end up in the holy fires of purgatory is the wisest path to take, along with belief in God and what He's provided for us through His Divine Plan of Salvation. You can go straight to paradise and avoid both the fires of hell and of purgatory. Sin, error, mistakes, separates us from God. The purpose of the holy fires of purgatory is to bring our souls back into at-one-ment with God.

> "I have come into the world as light, so that whoever believes in me may not remain in darkness."
>
> (John 12:46)

Chapter Ten: Purgatory

> "Again Jesus spoke to them, saying, 'I AM the light of the world. Whoever follows me will not walk in darkness, but will have the light of life.'"
>
> (John 8:12)

There are so many sins that we don't even realize are separating us from God. We've believed the lie or we've allowed ourselves to be dumbed down in life. The more we invest in our spirit in this life, the greater our reward in the afterlife, the less we have to do later.

Spiritually speaking, most people wrestle with these issues at one time or another throughout their lives: judging others, blame, bitterness, resentment, lack of forgiveness, pride, hatred, self-hatred, jealousy, envy, rejection, fear, control issues, delving into the occult, practicing witchcraft, rebellion, unbelief, just to name a few. Just think of how many dis-eases are caused from the psycho-spiritual and emotional ills, which eventually manifest into the physical body, in the form of pain, cancer, heart disease, diabetes, stroke, autoimmune disorders, and a host of other related medical issues.

We know today that our spiritual health affects our physical condition, that if we deal with our spiritual essence, we can experience relief and healing in our physical bodies. So many people allow all of these spiritual ailments to grow inside them and over time it produces illness, both mental, physiological and physical. If we address these issues as sins that need to be confessed and repentance expressed to God, we can find healing we need as God promises us. We can avoid having to go through the 'purging' fires of purgatory and even hell in the afterlife.

> "The thing that has been, it is that which shall be; and that which is done is that which shall be done: and there is no new thing under the sun."
>
> (Ecclesiastes 1:9)

The spiritual condition that so many people find themselves in throughout their earth life, is one of unawareness that they are in error and sin, which causes them to feel separated from God. When their conscience is pricked, or convicted by God's Holy Spirit, they feel guilt and shame. They do not know how to handle these emotions, so they go deeper into denial, and suppress the issues, never really dealing with them. Eventually this leads them to the fires of purgatory in the afterlife. Purgatory's fire burns all sin away and allows the soul to face itself in the holy fire, the light of God. This is what the scripture means when it says, "For the wages of sin is death, but the gift of God is eternal life in Christ Jesus." (Romans 6:23)

> "If we confess our sins, he is faithful and just to forgive us our sins, and to cleanse us from all unrighteousness."
>
> (1 John 1:9)

However, if one follows the precepts of the Lord, which is to confess one's sins to God who is faithful and just to forgive you while still on earth, then you wouldn't have to experience the fires of purgatory, and could pass over directly to Paradise in the upper heavens. This is why it is wise to invest in one's spirit and soul while alive on earth, through confessing and repenting and asking the Holy Spirit to reveal all unconfessed sin while still alive. This is the work that allows the soul to pass the fires through belief in what Christ did for us on the cross by taking on the curses and the judgments upon Himself that was due us for all the errors and sins of humanity. Our belief in Him becomes the bridge to Heaven's Paradise.

> "Confess your faults one to another, and pray for one another, so that you may be healed."
>
> (James 5:16)

If we do not confess our faults, errors, mistakes, sins, then the guilt, shame, sadness, disappointment, anger, self-hatred, bitterness, is still in our memories and we are held captive and in bondage to those memories, with all the pain associated with them. In both psychological and New Age circles, this is known as the 'shadow self' now new and improved as a means to find hidden gifts, instead of confession and repentance to God. The Shadow is that which is lodged in the subconscious, where resides guilt, shame, blame, repressed anger, that part of us that needs clearing. This is the part of us that unconsciously controls many unforeseen negative events in our lives. New Age psychology says one needs to embrace it and find the gift in it, however, in the spiritual realm, this unresolved spiritual condition gives 'legal authority' to the fallen angels, the demonic realm and Satan's hierarchy to attack, torment and continue to hold a soul in bondage. Until that entire Shadow is brought before God for healing, through confession and repentance and applying the saving Grace which comes through Christ, we live in its darkness.

Many people mistakenly think that if they accept the Lord Jesus Christ, then all of their sins are automatically forgiven. If so, then why are so many believers still in pain? I have a friend whose father was a Christian minister most of his adult life, and died from a painful debilitating disease. After his death, he appeared to one of his daughters and told her he was in purgatory. Why? He had a lot of unconfessed sin in his life with which he never dealt. He was abusive to his children, which his pride would not allow him to deal with so he never addressed, and those mistakes created guilt and shame. Yes, he believed the Lord Jesus Christ was his Savior, but his spirit was burdened down with unconfessed sin and unrepentance. Both daughters are plagued by post traumatic stress from his abuse and do not have a real relationship with Christ. His life as a minister was waisted, because he couldn't even lead his own flesh and blood into right relationship with Christ, because he never knew that himself, instead he was misled all his life by the false Religious Spirit.

> "Draw near to God, and he will draw near to you. Cleanse your hands, you sinners; and purify your hearts, you double minded."
>
> (James 4:8)

In the Old Testament, the blood of lambs, goats, doves and bulls was sacrificed on the altar for the forgiveness of sins. Fortunately, that practice ended when Jesus Christ became the Lamb of God. His blood became the *final* sacrifice for *all* of man's sins, so we only need to apply it to our lives. While salvation is offered, it is not automatic. No one can take it for granted. One still needs to follow the precepts of the Lord and humble one's spirit before God, confess, repent and ask for forgiveness and accept the blood of Christ as their *covering* for at-one-ment with God. Then God is faithful and just to forgive, and *heal* us from all the affects and curses associated with those sins.

There are so many Christians that sadly do not make it to Paradise right away, for a number of reasons. This scripture is very revealing why: "Many will say to me on that day, 'Lord, Lord, did we not prophesy in your name, and in your name drive out demons and perform many miracles? Then I will tell them plainly, 'I never knew you. Away from me, you evildoers!' (Matthew 7:23,24)

Heavy stuff! Imagine believing on the Lord Jesus Christ and then getting rejected by Him? What did they do to deserve that? Well, think of all the many ministries there are that collect money in the name of Jesus, yet use it for selfish end. Think of all those who allow themselves to be corrupted by the powers of darkness yet cloak themselves as Christians, while their hearts are full of sin, pride and greed. There are many Christians, who are Christians in name only, who grieve the Holy Spirit. These are the people Christ will not allow into the Kingdom of Paradise and instead send them for punishment.

To Be Healed, You Must Be Broken

What does God want from us? "The Lord is close to the broken-hearted and saves those who are crushed in spirit." (Psalms 34:18) "The sacrifices of God are a broken spirit: a broken and a contrite heart, you, God, will not despise." (Psalms 51:17) A broken and contrite heart and spirit. It is the only acceptable sacrifice for God to honour our needs and request. Praises, prayers, good deeds, good behaviour, money, offerings, none of these are worth anything to God without a broken, contrite heart and spirit. No matter the different situations, the prayers project the same state of mind and heart we must have for God to be pleased and spiritually prosper us. "You do not delight in sacrifices, or I would bring it; you do not take pleasure in burnt offerings." (Psalms 51:16) Otherwise our "offerings" are a literal mockery.

Sometimes we may be ignorant of our lack of mercy, or unaware of an act displeasing to God. Are we willing to accept what God will reveal that to us? We must be broken and contrite for God to be able to show us our errors. So often pride stands in the way. When people feel convicted, they go into guilt, shame and blame and do not know how to deal with those emotions, so it gets stuffed down, lodged into the shadow self.

Oftentimes we may not be paying close attention to our emotions, which are often masked by natural armour, as a self defence mechanism, so we push things to the back of our mind, and excuse ourselves with the idea that 'it's not my problem'. We cannot be clear if we are unconcerned about an offending misperception which we have caused another, and are aware of it but without the compassion to remedy it. It *is* our problem! That is not a contrite spirit, but a selfish one. We need to search our heart, so God can reveal our need to be broken and contrite for His will. "Search me, O God, and know my heart: try me, and know my thoughts: And see if there be any wicked way in me, and lead me in the way everlasting." (Psalms 139:23-24) God will not despise a broken spirit, but He will not work through a *stubborn, prideful or rebellious* spirit.

BEYOND FORGIVENESS

Also, those who blaspheme against the Holy Spirit can never be forgiven. Blaspheming the Holy Spirit is a big deal. It is the only "unforgivable" sin that Jesus mentions. It is also described in three of the four gospels. The texts are Matthew 12:31-32, Mark 3:28-29 and Luke 12:10. Each passage says pretty much the same thing. Luke is the most concise,

> "And anyone who speaks a word against the Son of Man will be forgiven, but anyone who blasphemes against the Holy Spirit will not be forgiven."

The Holy Spirit is the last bastion of grace given on this cursed planet, is the one Being that brings people back to God, who creates miracles, converts hearts towards repentance, comforts and heals the brokenhearted, is the teacher of all truth and wisdom and is the giver of all spiritual gifts. (See Book Two, *Who Is God?* my Chapter on the Holy Spirit)

In Matthew and in Mark the warning against blaspheming the Holy Spirit comes directly after the Pharisees accuse Jesus of driving out demons through Satan's power,

Chapter Ten: Purgatory

using the name of Beelzebub in the text. Luke includes Jesus' words after the Pharisees are described as looking for a way to catch Jesus doing something wrong.

The conclusion is that blaspheming the Holy Spirit is accusing the work of the Holy Spirit as being the work of Satan, or, calling the Holy Spirit evil. It makes sense that this is really bad. The Holy Spirit is the Spirit of God and of Christ. It upholds the Divine Plan of Salvation through Christ. It is called Holy for a reason. We should revere the Holy Spirit and the fact that it dwells within us is truly an amazing blessing. To accuse the Holy Spirit as being anything but Holy is calling the Spirit of God the opposite, that of being evil.

The other way of defining the blaspheming of the Holy Spirit is of rejecting God, Christ and the Holy Spirit. There is a story in my next chapter of a man named Howard Storm who was an atheist all his life, who died while waiting for surgeons in a hospital and was taken down into the fires of hell. He called out to the Lord to save him, and was immediately rescued by an angel who brought him to Jesus Christ, where he then became a believer. The Lord sent him back into his body, he was saved from hell and was given another chance at life. He now serves the Lord as a minister. This story shows that rejecting God and Christ can send a person to hell, but because he did not blaspheme the Holy Spirit per se, but rejected only God in his ignorance and disbelief, he was forgiven and saved.

There are many New Agers who claim to be speaking with 'Spirit,' as they call it, thinking they are being given messages and insights from the Universal Spirit or the spirit of the Earth. This is *not* the Holy Spirit from whom they are hearing, it is a counterfeit spirit, and oftentimes the 'spirit' that is whispering thoughts into their heads is a demon spirit or a fallen angel spirit, which are all opponents of the Holy Spirit. Many psychics say, "'spirit' told me this or 'spirit' told me that," when their information is not coming from the Holy Spirit at all. These so called 'spirit guides' are gray aliens, watchers, demons and fallen angels, which all come from Satan's realm. Remember, Satan often masquerades as an angel of light.

The love and light motto so often bantered around in New Age circles was coined by Lucifer/Satan and the fallen angels. This often is a sign of frauds and fakes. The Holy Spirit leads people towards salvation through Christ, away from the counterfeit spirits, fallen angels, demons, grays, vampires, reptilians, and all of Satan's hierarchy on earth. No other spirit has the power to cast out demons, spirits of darkness, the fallen angels and all their falsehoods, to free people from the bondages of Satan, except the Holy Spirit.

I think the best way to guard against this unforgiveable sin is to get to know God. When you draw close to Christ and seek to know Him through His Word through prayer, fellowship and other spiritual disciplines, then you will come to know the Holy Spirit because the Holy Spirit guides us in our seeking and knowing Christ. If you know God, Jesus, and The Holy Spirit, then you probably won't wrongly accuse Him. However, to 'think' you are channeling the Holy Spirit when in reality you are channeling a fallen angel or demon spirit, may not be blasphemy, but it certainly is deception of the highest order.

SECOND CHANCES AND REBIRTH

In Ezekiel 37, which is the chapter on the Valley of the Dry Bones, the prophesy is to the dead of Israel in 585 B.C., into whom the Lord promises He will breathe, attach flesh and tendons, and bring them all back to life. Many people, both Jews and Christians, believe wholeheartedly that this prophesy was fulfilled in 1948 when the Jews were given back the land of Israel, which land suddenly was brought back to life after an 1800+ year drought. All of the descendants of the land, who were scattered for centuries during the Diaspora, returned also. All those who were called back to Israel were reincarnates lost in that Valley of Dry Bones, and were given another chance to cultivate the land under the laws of the Lord, as the Lord Yahuah promised in Ezekiel 37.

> "Then he said to me, "Prophesy to these bones and say to them, 'Dry bones, hear the word of the Lord! This is what the Sovereign Lord says to these bones: <u>I will make breath enter you, and you will come to life. I will attach tendons to you and make flesh come upon you and cover you with skin; I will put breath in you, and you will come to life</u>. Then you will know that I am the Lord.'"
>
> (Ezekiel 37:4-6)

On Reincarnation: "But the rest of the dead lived not again until the thousand years were finished. This is the first resurrection." (Revelation 20:5) This prophecy clearly indicates that the dead will live again (reincarnate) after a thousand years. 'Carne' means flesh in Latin, to reincarnate means for a soul to come back into the flesh. The Lord's promise in Ezekiel 37 couldn't be clearer, that He is the Lord of reincarnation.

Yes, reincarnation is in the Holy scriptures! It is not some New Age or demonic invention, as many Christians mistakenly believe. It is rooted in foundational Judaic beliefs, of which Yeshua Jesus spoke and the early church actually believed, until the Church of Rome deemed it heresy. Reincarnation does not fit into their political agenda, which is to fear the Church, submit now or go to hell. Christians need to *discern* between ancient Judaism and New Age beliefs. The replacement theology or supersessionism taught in Christian churches is clearly *not* scriptural or the word

Chapter Ten: Purgatory

of God. Resistance is rooted in ignorance of the roots of reincarnation, which is in Judaism. Their resistance may in fact reveal antisemitism and the desire to kill all things Jewish, which was the very motivation of the Emperors of the Church of Rome, who decreed anything Jewish to be anathema to Rome.[10] (See, Constantine's and Nicean Creeds).

After Book Two: *Who is God?* was published, I was attacked viciously by a group of Christians, who call themselves the *Wolf Pack* on the internet, over my chapter on reincarnation in the Bible. To suggest that it was *cognitive dissonance* is a gross understatement, as they went all out on an attack to discredit me as a Christian when in fact I am actually a Jew for Jesus, and sinned against God by slandering me to an entire group of 5,000 people. When made aware of their illegal actions, they immediately took their slanders down, but banned me from the group. They teach fear of anyone who doesn't think like them, or who displays a level above their limited knowledge, and brands everyone who doesn't think like them false. This is classic narcissistic projection, that when you point a finger at someone, there are actually three fingers pointing back on yourself. I think the fact that they call themselves the *Wolf Pack*, says it all:

"Watch out for false prophets. They come to you in sheep's clothing, but inwardly they *are ferocious wolves.*"

(Matthew 7:15)

These are people who are so blinded by funda-*mentalism*, and the *demonic religious spirit*, that they bear absolutely no fruits of the Holy Spirit, the spirit of Christ's love. They are modern-day Pharisees, crucifying Christ all over again, blaspheming those who actually do carry His Spirit. They are being controlled by the Jezebel spirit, which originates from the ancient church of Thyatira, who rebelled against the LORD of Israel. These are Christians who literally want to replace Jewish history with their own bastardized version of Christianity. This is a form of Replacement Theology, based on the belief that because the Jews rejected Jesus, that they, the Gentiles, are supposed to receive the inheritances from God, and anything Jewish is to be condemned. This is exactly what the Roman Emperors did, who oppressed Jews and ruled over Israel with an iron hand, over two thousand years ago, in spite of the fact that Jesus was Jewish, and stated He came to fulfill the law of the prophets. Matthew 5:17, "Do not think that I have come to abolish the Law or the Prophets; I have not come to abolish them but to fulfill them."

It was a group of Roman imperators which decreed anathema against the belief in reincarnation (from 325AD-360AD), who were not 'god' or 'gods', and Christians should discern the reasons for their decrees before following blindly. Christians who claim to be rooted in the Word should understand the Word, and its Jewish roots. It is clear that reincarnation was the LORD's plan from the beginning, to not allow satan to steal souls from Him. The Church of Rome decreed that anything Jewish was now heresy. So how is it that Christians who are supposed to stand for the Word of God, which includes both the Old and New Testaments, follow after Romans and not the actual Word of God? In my opinion, their rejection of the truth in this matter deems them the heretics, just as the thousands upon thousands of Jews and true Gentile Believers were persecuted, hanged, and burned at the stake by the Catholic Church by the Inquisition for being heretics of Rome. Remember this Woe (a woe is a curse):

"Woe unto them that call evil good, and good evil; that put darkness for light, and light for darkness; that put bitter for sweet, and sweet for bitter!"
(Isaiah 5:20)

The foundation of Christianity is rooted in the grace of God. "Moreover, where sin abounds, Grace abounds even more." (Romans 5:20) Sure there are people who may never be redeemed because they are children of the devil, as the scripture tells us. But for those who are the children of God, His grace is greater than any sin, and death doesn't separate us from the love of God in Christ Jesus.

"For I am convinced that neither death nor life, neither angels nor demons, neither the present nor the future, nor any powers, neither height nor depth, nor anything else in all creation, will be able to separate us from the love of God that is in Christ Jesus our Lord."
(Romans 8:38, 39)

After each life, each soul appears before the judgment seat of Christ, depending on their life and beliefs, some will get sent back (reincarnated) others will move on in the heavens, and others may be sent to hell. (See, my chapter herein, *Is Hell for Real?*)

Jesus said, "I AM the gate; whoever enters through me will be saved. <u>He will come in and go out</u>, and find pasture."
(John 10:9)

He will come in and go out, clearly indicates reincarnation. There is a myriad of reasons the Lord allows for rebirth. Think of how many people whose lives end abruptly, either through war, disaster or disease. Many who never get to complete their mission, or share their gifts, or those who end up with unrequited love. Souls who never heard or understood the Divine Plan of salvation, souls who were held in

Chapter Ten: Purgatory

bondage by Satan all their lives, and thousands of other reasons. Souls need to feel complete, souls need to experience all that God has to offer, including all the learning experiences that earth life provides, along with character building, as well as the balancing of karmic debts. What about those who have 'karmic contracts', many of which get carried over into their future lives. Jesus said, when you go in through Him, you can come in, go out and find pasture. 'Finding pasture' is finding a new life which only He can authorize. Whether or not you believe Jesus Christ is the Lord of the Spirits, as written in the ancient texts, everyone meets Him after they die, whether they believe in Him or not.

The Lord said, "Before I formed thee in the belly I knew thee; and before thou camest forth out of the womb I sanctified thee, and I ordained thee a prophet unto the nations." (Jeremiah 1:5) This verse clearly illustrates that before a person is conceived, the Lord knew them. Clearly reincarnation was written into God's Divine Plan of grace from the beginning of this human experiment we call earth life. There are many souls and spirits who are waiting on the Lord to allow them another chance at life. Only the Lord can authorize rebirth.

> "Lord you have been our dwelling throughout all generations...You turn man to destruction and then say, return, ye children of men; You carry them away as with a flood; they are as asleep, yet in the morning they are like grass which grows back up."
>
> (Psalm 90:1, 3, 5)

These scriptures clearly prove that rebirth is ordered by the Lord. The Lord is with us through all generations, yet man can only live one generation at a time, if that long. He can cause destruction to come on man, yet He will then return him back to life again to give him another chance. How many people die in floods or earthquakes, go to sleep, which is death, yet are returned back to life to have another shot at it on earth? The grace of God that allows and governs the laws of rebirth. "Do not be deceived, God cannot be mocked, for whatsoever a man sows, that shall he also reap." (Galatians 6:7)

> "My little children, of whom I travail in birth again until Christ be formed in you." (Galatians 4:19) clearly illustrates reincarnation for the purpose of becoming perfect sons of God.

> "And ye shall know the truth, and the truth shall make you free." (John 8:32) Free from rebirth on this planet of pain and suffering.

"For we must all appear before the judgment seat of Christ; that every one may receive the things done in his body, according to that he hath done, whether it be good or bad." (2 Corinthians 5:10) This relates to Karma.

"<u>Your dead will live; Their corpses (dead bodies) will rise</u>. You who lie in the dust, awake and shout for joy, for your dew is as the dew of the dawn, And <u>the earth will give birth to the departed spirits</u>." (Isaiah 26:19) This is the meaning of reincarnation, to be dead and then to live again.

After each life time, every soul and spirit appears before the Lord of all Spirits who is Jesus Christ for judgment. They then are processed in the afterlife for either spending time purging their spirits in purgatory, where they await another chance at life through rebirth and reincarnation, they are sent to hell as their deeds and heart may be that wicked. They may pass through to Paradise where they spend eternity with God, having completed their cycles of rebirth on earth.

The Lord of Justice who balances His judgments with mercy and justice will determine through righteousness who ends up where, and with what lot in life, to either pay off karmic debts or learn soul lessons, which are designed to bring us all back into at-one-ment with God, or those who come back to serve God with a mission. Think about this, if souls who are sent to the in-between holding place, which is known as purgatory, to be purged from ungodly attitudes, how much more can earth life provide the same kind of purging through trials, tribulations and adversities that we all face as human beings journeying through life on earth? The more we purge, repent, atone for our errors, karma, sins on earth, the less our souls need to do in the afterlife.

The Bible talks about being born again. The scripture actually poses the argument. How can a man be born again? While the Christian and Born Again Movement interpret this scripture to mean that we must be born again of spirit by being baptized in the Spirit and being baptized in water, the verse is so literal and so simple that many miss its double meaning. As Jesus often spoke in parables:

"There was a man of the Pharisees, named Nicodemus, a ruler of the Jews: The same came to Jesus by night, and said unto him, Rabbi, we know that thou art a teacher come from God: for no man can do these miracles that thou doest, except God be with him. Jesus answered and said unto him, Verily, verily, I say unto thee, except a man be born again, he cannot see the kingdom of God. Nicodemus said unto him, 'How can a man be born when he is old? Can he enter the second time into his mother's womb, and be born?' Jesus answered, 'Verily, verily, I say unto thee, except a man be born of water

Chapter Ten: Purgatory

and of the Spirit, he cannot enter into the kingdom of God. That which is born of the flesh is flesh; and that which is born of the Spirit is spirit. Marvel not that I said unto thee, Ye must be born again.'"

(John 3:1-7, KJV)

Ye must be born again, this part relates to rebirth, not just the rebirth of the spirit, but of water, in which substance all babies live inside the womb. There are so many people who may have a belief in God, but have so many other issues that only rebirth and reincarnation can resolve for the soul. Yes, this verse also means that we must be born again of Spirit while still living in the flesh, but how many people actually live it?

Reincarnation, which is allowed by the grace of God and authorized by Jesus Christ, has a beginning and an end. Because we are approaching the end of Time on earth, there will be an end of souls being allowed to reincarnate. This is why there are so many souls on earth now, because time is getting short and the opportunity to reincarnate will end soon. This is also why there are so many souls who have reincarnated with their 'karma stacked', meaning they are living and purging up to three to four lifetimes in one incarnation.

Some will be able to relate to what I'm talking about, who have had such intense suffering, and so many different chapters and stories with a number of different souls and soul mates that they've had to deal with, that those who are older may even think of their past as a past life, yet they are still in the same body. Also, this is why there are so many children today who are born 'old.' They are born with all kinds of gifts and wisdom clearly beyond their years, which they can only have acquired through prior lifetimes, their inborn skills, second nature to them now even at such a young age.

On the flip side, there are many born into so much suffering, we can see it is karma they are purging from past lives. The scriptures talk about generational sins and the curses attached to those sins being sent down to the descendants, until someone in that family line takes steps towards deliverance of family and generational curses that are attached to them and their ancestors. Only Jesus Christ has the power to break curses. "Christ redeemed us from the curse of the law by becoming a curse for us, for it is written: "Cursed is everyone who is hung on a tree." (Galatians 3:13) But what most Christians do not realize is that this is not automatic, but the individual believer must *appropriate* the work of the cross to themselves, their ancestors and the generational curses they inherit. Then the power of the cross may be fulfilled on them, and the power of the curses can be broken. (See, Book Four: *Covenants*, my chapter on *Cosmic Karma & Ancient Curses* for further elucidation).

After the final battle of Armageddon, when the Lord returns to defeat Satan and his fallen angels for the last time, they will be cast into the lake of fire for eternity and then the promise of a new heaven and a new earth can be fulfilled. That means the old earth passes away, nothing remains. The final judgment will determine which souls will end up in the Kingdom of Heaven for eternity and which souls who have consistently aligned themselves with Satan and his fallen angels and rebelled against God through all of their lifetimes accumulated will end up with them in the lake of fire.

> "And just as each person is destined to die once and after that comes judgment, so Christ was sacrificed once to take away the sins of many people; and he will appear a second time, not to bear sin, but to bring salvation to those who are waiting for him."
>
> (Hebrews 9:27)

There is judgement after each life and death; there are three types of judgments in the Bible, this is *not* the final judgment as so many Christians mistakenly believe because this scripture is so often taken out of context. Just as Jesus comes a second time, so will those who are reincarnated on earth at that time see him. The second coming says, that those who pierced him will see him coming and mourn. How is that possible, if those who crucified him are long dead and gone? The answer is they will be reincarnated to be on the earth at that appointed time, as it will be their last and final chance for repentance.

> "He said in a loud voice, "Fear God and give him glory, because the hour of his judgment has come. Worship him who made the heavens, the earth, the sea and the springs of water."
>
> (Revelation 14:7)

> "They are demonic spirits who work miracles and go out to all the rulers of the world to gather them for battle against the Lord on that great judgment day of God the Almighty."
>
> (Revelation 16:14)

> "Behold, I will create new heavens and a new earth. The former things will not be remembered, nor will they come to mind."
>
> (Isaiah 65:17)

> "As the new heavens and the new earth that I make will endure before me," declares the Lord, "so will your name and descendants endure."
>
> (Isaiah 66:22)

Chapter Ten: Purgatory

"Then I saw a new heaven and a new earth, for the first heaven and the first earth had passed away, and there was no longer any sea."

(Revelation 21:1)

Heaven is For Real

There are two recent stories of two very young boys who suffered severe trauma and left their bodies and both were taken up to heaven and met the Lord Jesus Christ. This proves that everyone who loses their life on earth goes first to the Lord before being sent back or sent anywhere. Many have been saying that God has chosen two new messengers to convey the same message He's been saying for centuries. Their full stories are in the books: *Heaven is for Real* by Todd Burpo[11] and *The Boy Who Came Back from Heaven* by Kevin and Alex Malarkey[12] whose book has now become a New York Times Bestseller.

In 2004, Kevin Malarkey and his six-year-old, Alex, were involved in a horrific car accident. The impact of the crash on Alex caused what is medically termed an "internal decapitation – his skull was detached from his spinal column. Alex was in a coma, the prognosis for survival was not good. When the accident occurred, the Internet spread the news of Alex's condition. He was the focal point of prayer from around the world. Two months later, Alex awoke with an incredible story to tell. He shared detailed recollections of the accident scene and the emergency room – neither of which he could have seen with earthly eyes. He talked about the music he heard in heaven – nothing like he had ever heard before. And he talked about his conversations with Jesus.

"The first thing I saw was the angels catch daddy," said Alex "The car hit us. I slammed into my seatbelt. Daddy flew out of the car and the angels caught him." When father Kevin first heard that story, he feared his son had brain damage from the collision. "I really did, because I thought he was imagining things," he said.

But it soon became clear Alex knew things she couldn't have known from the five senses. "He told me that he saw me go away in the ambulance, but I never told him I went away in an ambulance. Why would he think I was in an ambulance? Cause I didn't have any injuries." It was Alex that was taken away in the ambulance.

Alex's answer: "I was in heaven then."

Alex recounts talking to Jesus from above as he watched fireman take his body out of the car and put him on a flat board. He recalls his dad screaming, "Alex, Alex, Alex," making a phone call and talking to a man in a blue suit by the helicopter.

Alex remains paralyzed, but his experience has left him positive and upbeat – assuring anyone and everyone that he will one day walk again.

Alex was the first child ever to undergo a complex surgical procedure in which doctors replaced his ventilator with a breathing apparatus called a pacer. "He was the first child that we ever implanted with a ventilator," said Dr. Ray Onders. "Alex's injury is really like a decapitation. When I looked at his X-rays, it almost looked like his entire head was removed from his spinal cord."

The injury was not unlike the one suffered by actor Christopher Reeve. It was Dr. Onders who performed the surgery that got Reeve off the ventilator.

"The whole time I was there (heaven)," says Alex, "I was basically in God's palace." Here's his description of what he remembers: "When I arrived in heaven, I was inside the gate. The gate was really tall, and it was white. It was very shiny, and it looked like it had scales like a fish. I was in the inner heaven and everything was brighter and more intense on the inside of the gate. It was perfect. Perfect is my favorite word for describing heaven."

But Alex was also cautioned, he says, not to relate some of what he saw and was told in heaven – not even to his father. "We probably only know about 10 percent of what he knows," said Kevin. "I think he is very protective about it."

In the years since the 2004 accident, Alex has made remarkable progress. He can now stand for periods of time in a supportive frame and walk on a treadmill with assistance.

As for the other best-selling young author, Colton, his was the story of a wrongly diagnosed illness – a case of acute appendicitis and a badly ruptured appendix that went untreated for five days. Then the lifeless 4-year-old boy was rushed to the hospital for emergency surgery. When it was all over, Colton survived and recovered fully. But that was just the beginning of his amazing saga. Four months later, Colton began telling his parents things he could not or should not have known.

"Mom, I have two sisters," he said. "You had a baby die in your tummy, didn't you?" Sonja, his Mom, was shocked. When she asked him, who told him, he said, "She did Mommy, she said she died in your tummy." Todd and Sonja had never told their son about the miscarriage Sonja had before Colton was born. Colton went on to tell his mom that she was a girl and, "she looked familiar and she started giving me hugs and she was glad to have someone in her family up there."

Asked by his Dad about his hospital experience, Colton said: "You know, Dad, the angels sang to me while I was there." Colton said that while on the operating table he went to heaven and that he met his great-grandfather Pop. Colton says his grandfather didn't look like the man in the photo in his house, but instead looked like the man in the picture sent months later by his Grandmother, a young man without glasses.

Later he described Jesus, and he talked about Armageddon and how God told him his father would fight in the final battle. Although Todd was a pastor, he says he never talked details like this with his preschool-aged son. Now Colton's stories of Heaven are documented in his father's book titled *Heaven is for Real*.

Chapter Ten: Purgatory

ON KARMA

Karma is a Sanskrit word which relates to the law of cause and effect. Meaning your deeds, good or bad, will repay you in kind. This is exactly what the scripture in Galatians 6:7 says about the laws of sowing and reaping. "Whatsoever a man sows, that shall he also reap." This is a universal law. God set this system up, which we are all subject to. No matter what an individual's personal belief system is, the law is no respecter of person, or religion. Karma is created with every action, every thought, and every word.

"For every man shall bear his own burden." (Galatians 6:5) Clearly illustrates Karma, as each man must pay for what he has done, both good and bad whether it be in the present or future life. Think about this, where is justice, when someone repeatedly abuses, steals or murders in one life and no legal authority catches them or brings them to justice? All souls stand before God to be judged according to their deeds.

"His mischief shall return upon his own head, and his violent dealing shall come down upon his own pate." (Psalm 7:16); again, another reference to Karma and Judgment.

"Can a man take fire in his bosom and his clothes not be burned?" (Proverbs 6:27); clearly describes that nobody gets away with anything, even though it may *appear* that way in the physical life, every deed is judged in the afterlife at the Judgment seat of Christ.

"He who is pregnant with evil and conceives trouble gives birth to disillusionment. He who digs a hole and scoops it out falls into the pit he has made. The trouble he causes recoils on himself; his violence comes down on his own head." (Psalm 7: 14-16) Again, another reference to the fact that the laws of cause and effect (Karma) is at work in every life on Earth.

"God will render to every man according to his deeds." (Romans 2:6) Everybody is judged after each life according to what he has done.

"But I tell you that men will have to give account on the day of judgment for every careless word they have spoken." (Matthew 12:36) This means that after each life, everyone will be held accountable to the Lord for what they say.

"He that leads into captivity shall go into captivity: he that kills with the sword must be killed with the sword." (Revelation 13:10) This scripture clearly indicates that what goes around comes around. For example, take a man who has taken unfair advantage of women all his life, who has raped and abused them. When he dies, he will be judged and he will feel what it's like to be on the receiving end of his own abuse. He may be reincarnated as a woman who then is raped and abused. Some women come out of it, with an awareness and make something of their lives, others will live their lives as a victim without any awareness or consciousness that their souls may be reaping what they've sown in a past life. It seems like a vicious cycle, but the only end is awareness, confessing one's mistakes, and coming to God for healing and forgiveness to break the cycle of abuse in their lives, and in all their descendants.

> "And, behold, I come quickly; and my reward is with me, to give every man according as his work shall be."
>
> (Revelation 22:12)

"Ye judge after the flesh; I judge no man." (John 8:15) Without knowing what someone's karma is, how can one properly judge another?

"For life and death is in the power of the tongue." (Proverbs 18:21) Every word spoken becomes a living thing, either to minister life or death. "You have been trapped by what you said, ensnared by the words of your mouth." (Proverbs 6:2). This is where the principle comes from that you possess what you confess. This law confirms that we can create our reality with the words of our mouth.

> "Give, and it shall be given unto you; good measure, pressed down, and shaken together, and running over, shall men give into your bosom. For with the same measure that ye mete withal it shall be measured to you again." (definition of Karma, which is a Sanskrit word)
>
> (Luke 6:38)

Generational Sins and Curses

All of us are born into families and inherit a host of traits and characteristics from our ancestors. Spiritually speaking, we also inherit their sins, curses and the demons attached to all those errors and mistakes. How often have children been abused by the hand of their parents, and the anger that the parent felt at that time was then transferred to the child as an imprint. That child then grows up to carry their parents anger in their body and psyche. All the resentment and bitterness that goes with it causes that child to sin and carry on that pattern and repeat the cycle of abuse upon others. Generational sins and curses are a very real phenomenon that can only be broken through the saving grace of Christ.

> "The LORD is long-suffering, and of great mercy, forgiving iniquity and transgression, and by no means clearing the guilty, visiting the iniquity of the fathers upon the sons to the third and fourth generation."
>
> (Numbers 14)

Chapter Ten: Purgatory

"Ah, Lord Yahuah! You have made the heavens and the earth by Your great power and stretched out arm. Nothing is too great for You. You show lovingkindness to thousands, and repay the iniquity of the fathers into the bosom of their sons after them."

(Jeremiah 32)

"Then the Lord passed by in front of him and proclaimed, "The Lord, the Lord God, compassionate and gracious, slow to anger, and abounding in loving kindness and truth; who keeps loving kindness for thousands, who forgives iniquity, transgression and sin; yet He will by no means leave the guilty unpunished, visiting the iniquity of fathers on the children and on the grandchildren to the third and fourth generations."

(Exodus 34:6--7)

"You shall not bow yourself down to them, nor serve them. For I the LORD your God am a jealous God, visiting the iniquity of the fathers upon the sons to the third and fourth generation of those that hate me, and showing mercy to thousands of those that love Me and keep My commandments."

(Exodus 20:5,6; Deuteronomy 5:9,10)

Exodus 20:5 is among the ten commandments. According to covenants and legal authority, when a father misleads his family, the effects of that misleading are often felt for generations. This is because the father is being unfaithful to the covenant. God has stipulated that there are punishments to breaking the covenant with Him. This explains these verses that deal with the sins of the father being visited upon the children. If a father rejects the covenant of God and takes his family into sin and rejection, the children will suffer the consequences, often for several generations. Whether or not this is fair is not the issue.

It is important to remember that spiritually, every curse has assigned to it demons who then hold 'legal authority' over that person, to hold them in bondage until they confess, repent and apply Christ's blood of redemption. This is the only liberation from those ancestral curses. Sin is in the world, consequences of sin affected many generations. We can conclude that God will visit the iniquities of the fathers upon the descendants because the fathers have taught their children to fail also to keep their covenants with God. Yet, we see in the other verses a declaration of legality in dealing with people. There is no contradiction.

"For as in Adam all die, so also in Christ all shall be made alive."

(1 Corinthians 15:22)

The End of the Cycle of Rebirth

"Him who overcomes I will make a pillar in the temple of my God, and <u>he will not go out from it anymore.</u> (Never shall he leave it.) I will write on him the name of my God and the name of the city of my God, the new Jerusalem, which is coming down out of heaven from my God; and I will also write on him my new name." (Revelation 3:12) I think the key words here, is 'he will not go out from it anymore' which again clearly indicates that reincarnation and the law of rebirth may come to an end to those who overcome this earth and become a Master of the planet. This is the real meaning of 'Ascended Master'.

There will be no more need for being 'born again' in water. By overcoming the tests, trials and tribulations in the kingdom of darkness, Lucifer's Satanic realm, Christ promises to make us 'pillars' in His temple. A pillar is a support, a mainstay, a tower of strength, that holds up its foundation. Another definition for a pillar is a leader or a rock. By being transformed out of the kingdom of darkness into the Kingdom of God, then there is no need to come back to earth and live another life in the flesh. The corporeal then becomes the incorporeal, the translation has taken place and the new light body of eternal life has been given instead of the body of flesh that dies.

> "Giving thanks to the Father, which has made us meet to be partakers of the inheritance of the saints in light: <u>Who has delivered us from the power of darkness, and has translated us into the kingdom of the Son of His love,</u> in whom we have redemption."
>
> (Colossians 1:12-14)

The end of this timeline will be end of the reincarnation. Whatever level a person has achieved from their <u>cumulative lives</u> on earth, they will be faced with the judgment. There is what is called the first death and the second death. The first death is dying to the flesh, and the second death is having the soul thrown into eternal separation from God, because the soul never chose the path of redemption in its cumulative earth lives through the many cycles of reincarnation. Reincarnation is all about God's grace, about being given a second chance, and a third, and even up to 444 lifetimes for the reincarnated soul to prove its faithfulness to God. Each life is designed to bring us closer to God on earth. After each life, the soul is returned to the Lord, who is the Creator of the soul and is known as the Lord of Spirits. He is the judge of whether or not that soul deserves His mercy and grace for another chance at earth life.

So many Christians think reincarnation is not in the Bible, and they are wrong. As I've already proven there are multiple scriptures in the Bible that relate specifically to rebirth (reincarnation). After the cycle of rebirth is complete, all the souls will face

Chapter Ten: Purgatory

the final judgment. Yes, the Bible says, it is appointed to man once to die and then the judgment. (Hebrews 9:27), which is also true, as after each life, a soul goes back to the Lord for judgment, but that judgment can often result in being sent back to earth to find salvation, instead of being sent to hell.

This is highly controversial to most Christians, mainly because they have been told that there is no reincarnation, that there is just heaven and hell. They are obviously missing some important points, one from history, which was the fact that all Jews, including those Jews who began the early church, the disciples, all believed in rebirth. It is still to this day a Jewish tradition to name a baby with the first letter of the name of someone in the family who has passed on, due to the belief in rebirth, that the new life will take on the spirit of the deceased family member, which is in essence, what we call, 'reincarnation.'

Just as the people of John the Baptist's day thought he was the spirit of Elijah, and that Jesus was the reincarnation of Joshua, Jeremiah, or Elijah as well, this belief was in place all the way through 325 A.D., until the council of Nicaea deleted it from the canonized bible. This council chose which books and which doctrines would be upheld as gospel by the church, and which would be rejected as heresy. This is why reincarnation was taught in the church prior to 325A.D. Just because they decreed it as heresy didn't make it cease to exist. The council wanted all of Christendom to be on the same page, and they used the extreme of heaven or hell as a tool to manipulate people into submitting to the church and to the religion they taught, instead of allowing people to know the truth. The church founders thought that if people knew the truth, they would live as they pleased because they knew God would give them a second chance and allow rebirth. The earthly church fathers didn't want them to think this way.

The rejection of reincarnation is a form of mind control which exists to this day in the Christian churches, mainly because this is what they've been taught by the hierarch. This false teaching continues to permeate the leadership in the churches, and let's face it, most church goers do not do their own homework, and readily accept what the pastors tell them as 'gospel'.

Think about this, why would a God who is full of grace and mercy, slow to anger, and is just, allow people such as the six million Jews who were exterminated during the Holocaust to go to hell because they didn't believe in Jesus Christ? The truth is, He didn't. They had already been in Hell, and all the souls that suffered at the hands of the Nazis were reincarnated in the ensuing 'baby boom' which immediately followed WWII. Many actually reincarnated with memories of torture and past life trauma to work through. Many also reincarnated with shame for being Jewish, because of the humiliating persecution that they endured which was literally 'seared' into their souls. Yet, God in His infinite grace and mercy gave them a new life, and with that a new opportunity to find Him, and find healing and respite for their souls.

God is not as 'black and white' as many Christians make Him out to be. Yes, there is a hell, created for Satan and his fallen angels, and all those who follow him and reject God. But there is also a large gray area between heaven and hell. God understands that humans live in a kingdom of darkness that programs them to believe all kinds of lies about Him, angels, ETs, aliens, heaven and hell. God knows the truth because God is Truth. God has more love than we can imagine. There are all kinds of mitigating circumstances that cause a person to get sent back to earth. There are all kinds of live paths that have not been shown the salvation offered through Christ.

The Lord Himself prophesied that His own people would suffer at the hands of their enemies because they rejected Him. The Holocaust was the ultimate punishment. But was it? The Bible tells us that when the abomination of desolation happens (Daniel 9:27; 11:31; 12:11, Mark 13:14; Matthew 24:15) that the Israelites and Jews would suffer such persecution at the hands of the antichrist, far worse than the Holocaust. Why does this happen? They rejected their Messiah. During the Holocaust one out of every three Jews were exterminated. During the time of the antichrist, when he sets himself up in the resurrected third temple in Jerusalem and demands Israel to worship him, two out of every three Jews will die. The prophets tell us that the Lord will save only one third of His people. One third will be His remnant. One third will 'get it' and turn back to Him. Why does He allow these horrors to happen? He wanted Israel to acknowledge its sins towards Him, repent and turn back to their only Lord and Savior. This entire cosmic drama is all about Him.

CAN A DECEASED SPIRIT RETURN TO EARTH?

Mediums channeling the dead are actually being duped by the demons, the Watchers who watch everything a person does during his life and have the power to imitate in voice, and can even morph themselves into looking like that person. This explains why people see ghosts. Not all ghosts are disembodied spirits, but demons who are imitating those who have died to fool the living into thinking they are seeing ghosts. Many of them are actually being purged in the light and the holy fire of purgatory while the demons are masquerading as them to the living. This ruse has been going on for millennia.

> "I will set my face against the person who turns to mediums and spiritists to prostitute himself by following them, and I will cut him off from his people."
> (Leviticus 20:6)

> "Do not turn to mediums or seek out spiritists, for you will be defiled by them. I am the LORD your God."
> (Leviticus 17:10)

Chapter Ten: Purgatory

There is a reason these curses are in the Bible. The Lord knew how mediums and spiritists work, and how the realm of the fallen angels set it up to dupe the living. These commandments and advice was given to the people for their own good, so they would not open themselves up for deception and demon spirits.

The New Living Translation writes Leviticus 20:6 like this, which takes on a slightly different meaning: "I will also turn against those who commit spiritual prostitution by putting their trust in mediums or in those who consult the spirits of the dead. I will cut them off from the community." Committing spiritual prostitution is a heavily loaded indictment for someone who consults a medium or the spirits of the dead. Our culture is fascinated by those who can see ghosts, hear spirits and can talk to the dead.

There have been countless Hollywood movies made on the subject along with a rash of television shows where people are encouraged to participate in the audience while the medium allegedly talks to their dead loved ones. So many people are convinced that the medium is actually hearing from their dead loved one, especially when they tell them something personal that only they could know. But the demons, the watchers, who literally watch and record every single thing a person does in his entire life, know everything about a person's habits, personality and character, as well as all the circumstances in their lives leading to the death. These spirits can deceive mediums and do so all the time, making them think they are hearing from the dead person's spirit, when in fact they are communing with demons. This has been going on for millennia, one of Satan's oldest tricks in his book.

Every sin and curse has demons attached to it. This is their *legal right,* and sin is Satan's realm. There is an age-old parlor game, still going strong today, of "I'm hearing an initial, the letter 'M', does anyone in the audience have someone who died that begins with the letter 'M'?" How broad is that? If the medium was truly in communication with someone's deceased loved one's spirit, then they would hear their full name. The fact that they don't indicates fraud. Further, the deceased spirits do not have a 'soul tie' with the medium, which allows lines of communications to be open via telepathic links that were already established in their relationship on earth. In addition to the facts that deceased spirits and souls have laws to follow in communicating with the living. They are not allowed to just go around haunting and talking to anyone. There are protocols which are all kept in place through ministering angels, under the authority of the Lord, depending on the different levels and holding places where the spirit and souls reside in the afterlife.

There has always been fascination with the paranormal to prove that it is real. Yes, it is real, but it is *not* what people think it is. Demons, fallen angels, gray aliens are all real, and they orchestrate the things that go bump in the night, to lure and to entice the curiosity of humans.

This book is about discernment, and a huge area that requires discernment is that of putting our trust in mediums and consultations with our dead loved ones. What a deeply personal and sensitive issue this is, especially for the one who has lost someone, to have been preyed upon by the spirit world by being duped and deceived!

Perhaps this is why the scripture calls it spiritual prostitution or to prostitute oneself, because a prostitute is someone who stands in for the real thing, a fake, a phony who expects payment for the role that they play.

So why would the fallen angels, the demons go to all that trouble to trick people into thinking that they have been communicated by their deceased loved ones? Perhaps it's because they do not want humans to know the truth about what really happens after you die, that first the judgment and then a soul is sent to be cleansed and purged in purgatory, or punished in hell, or sent to paradise in the upper heavens. All that 'feel good, love and light' stuff is to keep one believing in a lie which to many is more comfortable than the truth.

Can a person receive communication from a deceased loved one? Yes, but not through a medium. If there is a 'soul tie' on earth, a telepathic bond has already been established and that soul can send a message to their loved ones, in the form of a dream or through telepathy. There are souls whose assignment in purgatory is to work with their loved ones to complete unfinished business of all sorts. They are ordered to do so and work side by side with guardian angels who guide them to work within the laws. Many souls, especially those in purgatory or awaiting their next incarnation, can have access to their loved ones on earth. The ones in hell, however, cannot and do not have access to their loved ones on earth. This is the area where the demon watchers masquerade as the deceased loved ones, getting the living to believe that the lost are doing well on the other side, and 'watching' over their loved ones on earth. This is a lie, as no one in the lower regions can watch anyone on earth or in the other dimensions in afterlife. Let's explore this further in the next chapter.

The Word of God teaches that every human spirit RETURNS to God when the body dies, "Then shall the dust return to the earth as it was: and the *spirit* shall return unto God who gave it" (Ecclesiastes 12:7). In God's hands, that *spirit* will either be carried to Heaven by angels, or sent to Hell to suffer torment (Luke 16:22-23).

Although hard to grasp, since God is often only viewed as a loving God, the Bible clearly teaches that God will take vengeance upon those who die in their sins, having not accepted the Salvation of Jesus Christ, "In flaming fire taking vengeance on them that know not God, and that obey not the gospel of our Lord Jesus Christ: Who shall be punished with everlasting destruction from the presence of the Lord..." (2 Thessalonians 1:8,9).

Chapter Ten: Purgatory

It is clear from the Bible that the spirits of the dead cannot return to speak with us, nor send messages through psychic mediums. Mediums are empowered by Satan, who become willing channels of Satan's power. There's is no doubt that some psychics are real, and do indeed possess Satanic power. Just because a supernatural phenomenon has been proved to be real doesn't mean it comes from the source of all light. The kingdom of darkness counterfeits all that the Kingdom of God has created. It has been documented in multiple cases that some psychics have helped criminal investigators in missing persons' cases. Demonic intelligences are at work here, masquerading as light. Just the fact that when it comes to crimes and sin, the devil's job is not just to get someone to sin, but to torment them for doing so. Satan dispatches special demons to expose other demonic activity. It's all in the name of spiritual legalism.

NOTES AND REFERENCES:

1. Ella LeBain, *Who Is God? Book Two of Who's Who in The Cosmic Zoo? A Guide to ETs, Aliens, Gods & Angels,* Skypath Books, 2015. Chapter Twenty-Eight: *What Happens When You Die?* p. 455-485
2. St. Catherine of Genoa, *Fire of Love! Understanding Purgatory,* Sophia Institute Press, Manchester, New Hampshire. 1996. (Originally published in France, 1493)
3. Venerable Bede, *Historia Ecclesiastica, Ecclesiastical History of the English People,* 731 AD. Bede's Ecclesiastical History of England, A.M. Sellar's 1907 Translation. From the Christian Classics Ethereal Library.
4. Karma Lingpa, *Tibetan Book of the Dead,* aka *The Bardo Thodol, Liberation Through Hearing During the Intermediate State, the Profound Dharma of Self-Liberation through the Intention of the Peaceful and Wrathful Ones.* (1326–1386)
5. George Anderson, *Extra-Terrestrials: Friend of Foe?* Illuminet Press; 1st Edition, (August 1993).
6. Ella LeBain, *Who's Who in The Cosmic Zoo? Book One, A Spiritual Guide to ETs, Aliens, Gods & Angels, Third Edition,* Chapter: Grays, p. 248-289. Tate Publishing & Enterprises, 2013.
7. Ibid, Karma Lingpa, *Tibetan Book of the Dead,* (1326-1386)
8. Ibid.
9. C.S. Lewis' *Chronicles of Narnia, The Voyage of the Dawn Treader,* Geoffrey Bles, U.K. 1952.
10. The Constantine and Nicean Creed, 365AD, Council of Laodicea, Stefano Assemani, Acta Sanctorium Martyrum Orientalium at Occidentalium, Vol. 1, Rome 1748, page 105 https://tjcoop3.wordpress.com/the-constantine-creed/

11. Todd Burpo, Lynn Vincent, *Heaven Is for Real: A Little Boy's Astounding Story of His Trip to Heaven,* Thomas Nelson, October 31, 2010.
12. Kevin and Alex Malarkey, *The Boy Who Came Back from Heaven: A Remarkable Account of Miracles, Angels, and Life beyond This World,* Tyndale House (June 30, 2010).

CHAPTER ELEVEN
Is Hell For Real?

"But rebels and sinners will both be broken,
and those who forsake the Lord will perish."
(Isaiah 1:28)

"The fearful and unbelieving shall have their part in the lake
which burns with fire and brimstone."
(Revelation 21:8)

The bible history tells us that when Jesus died on the cross, He went down into the pit of hell. There He fought the powers of darkness, rescued souls that were held in bondage, and took the keys of death and hell away from Satan. He was then physically resurrected and visited the earth before ascending to the highest position in Heaven. This act gave Him all authority over heaven, earth and *inside the earth.* So, where is the proof in the Bible that Jesus went down into hell after He was crucified?

Paul tells us in Ephesians 4:9 that Christ our Lord descended into Hell after He offered His life on the cross. "Now that He ascended, what is it, but because He also descended first into the lower parts of the earth?" Note here that Hell is described as having four parts.

Peter said in Acts 2:24 that "God hath raised up Christ, having loosed the sorrows of hell, as it was impossible that He should be holden by it." Christ released the faithful from Old Testament stories from hell. Peter also wrote in 1 Peter 3:19 that "Christ coming in spirit preached to those spirits that were in prison, which had some time been incredulous."

The prophet Hosea foretold the descent of Christ into Hell in Hosea 13:14 by placing these words into the mouth of the Messiah: "O death, I will be thy death; O hell, I will be thy bite."

The Prophet Zechariah foretold the redemption of those forefathers being held captive in the pit inside the earth: "Thou also by the blood of Thy Testament hast sent forth Thy prisoners out of the pit." (Zechariah 9:11) What could this mean except that the Messiah would free people from the underworld?

Colossians 2:15 refers to Christ's victory over the condemned angels who are the demons of Hell.

> "Despoiling the principalities and powers, He hath exposed them confidently."
> (Colossians 2:15)

> "Lift up your gates, O ye princes," which the medieval Gloss interprets: "that is–Ye princes of hell, take away your power, whereby hitherto you held men fast in hell".
> (Psalm 23:7)

In Ecclesiasticus 24:45, Siracides (author of Sirach) prophecies: "I will penetrate to all the lower parts of the earth."

> "I am the Living One; I was dead, and now look, I am alive for ever and ever! And I hold the keys of death and Hades."
> (Revelation 1:18)

It's quite clear from both the prophesies in the Old and the record of the New Testaments that part of the work of the cross of Calvary was to liberate the ancient saints who were being held as prisoners by satan and his demons in the pit of the earth, also known as hell. But just when you thought that the drama and fruits of Christ's crucifixion couldn't get any more sensational, here we are told another piece of the Victory won on the Cross of Calvary: that the bodies of dead people were being raised out of their graves. Well, this does make sense, because if He liberated them from the pit, they had to go somewhere. He had the power to give them their lives back, because as the Scripture tells us, He now holds the 'keys' of both Death and Hades.

> "Then Jesus shouted out again, and he released his spirit. At that moment, the curtain in the sanctuary of the Temple was torn in two, from top to bottom. The earth shook, rocks split apart, the tombs broke open and the bodies of many godly men and women (saints) who had died were raised to life. They came out of the tombs, and after Jesus' resurrection they went into the holy city and appeared to many people. The Roman officer and the other soldiers at the crucifixion were terrified by the earthquake and all that had happened. They said, "This man truly was the Son of God!"
> (Matthew 27:50-54)

Chapter Eleven: Is Hell For Real?

After Jesus died, many of the dead saints arose and walked the earth and appeared to other people. This seems to suggest that Jesus freed the dead saints from a sleep, so He probably went to the place of the dead and set them free. Remember that Jesus also rose from the dead and walked the earth before being taken up into Heaven. These saints of old who visited the earth probably were raised to heaven as well. There is no suggestion in the Bible that these saints continued to live amongst mankind. The fact that the dead rose at the same time as Jesus Christ's resurrection is a fulfillment of what Jesus said would happen in John 5:28-29: "Do not be amazed at this, for a time is coming when all who are in their graves will hear his voice and come out--those who have done good will rise to live, and those who have done evil will rise to be condemned."

So, where is hell in the Bible? The Hebrew word 'Sheol' appears 65 times. The King James version translates this Hebrew word 'Sheol', 31 times as "hell," 31 times as "grave," and 3 times as "pit." In the Old Testament, the King James version uses the word "hell" 31 times, but it's interesting to note that the same Hebrew word 'Sheol' was also translated into other words.

In the New Testament, the King James Version translates the Greek word *Hades* in all 10 places it occurs, as 'hell'. The King James Version also uses the words hell and hellfire when translating the Greek word *Gehenna* 12 times. Other Bibles translate the Hebrew word *Sheol* and Greek word *Hades* in different ways, some not using the English word 'hell' at all.

The Greek word *tartaroos* or *tartarus* from which Hell is translated in 2 Peter 2:4 describes the deep parts of the dark pit which is reserved for the fallen angels for punishment. This is the same place the demons who had possessed the swine did not want Jesus to send them, into the Abyss. Also, 2 Peter 2:9 places the deceased wicked in the same place as the fallen angels. In the KJV, the word 'hell', though not meaning the same thing in every verse, is used 54 times.

Define Hell
Let's define the language that talks about Hell:

HADES - hell, grave

1. Hades or Pluto, the god of the lower regions, the underworld;
2. Orcus, the nether world, the realm of the dead;
3. later use of this word: the grave, death, hell;

4. In Biblical Greek, it is associated with Orcus, the infernal regions, a dark and dismal place in the very depths of the earth, the common receptacle of disembodied spirits.
5. Usually Hades is just the abode of the wicked, Luke 16:23, Revelation 20:13,14; a very uncomfortable place.

GEHENNA - hell, hell fire

1. Hell, is the place of the future punishment call "Gehenna" or "Gehenna of fire". This was originally the valley of Hinnom, south of Jerusalem, where the filth and dead animals of the city were cast out and burned; a fit symbol of the wicked and their future destruction.

SHEOL pronounced, she-ole, underworld, grave, hell, pit

1. Sheol - the Old Testament designation for the abode of the dead;
2. place of no return;
3. without praise of God;
4. wicked sent there for punishment;
5. righteous not abandoned to it.

These scriptures tell us the location of Hell also called 'sheol', the underworld, the grave and the pit, are all *inside* the earth.

"then I will bring you down with those who go down to the pit, to the people of long ago. I will make you dwell *in the earth below*, as in ancient ruins, with those who go down to the pit, and you will not return or take your place in the land of the living."

(Ezekiel 26:20)

Notice that this scripture indicates that some people are dwelling *inside* the Earth below (the pit).

"I made the nations to shake at the sound of his fall, when I cast him *down to hell* with them that *descend into the pit*: and all the trees of Eden, the choice and best of Lebanon, all that drink water, shall be comforted in the *nether parts of the earth*."

(Ezekiel 31:16)

Chapter Eleven: Is Hell For Real?

Again and again, Hell (sheol, underworld, grave, hell, pit) is referred to as being *inside* the earth. It is not only another dimension, which exists side by side with heaven and the place known as purgatory, but it's a city, with a hierarchy.

"The LORD kills and makes alive; He brings down to Sheol and raises up."
(1 Samuel 2:6)

"Have the gates of death been revealed to you, or have you seen the gates of deep darkness?"
(Job 38:17)

"And you, Capernaum, will you be lifted up to heaven? No, you will descend to Hades! For if the miracles that were performed in you had happened in Sodom, it would have remained to this day."
(Matthew 11:23)

Saint Thomas Aquinas and doctors of divinity who followed his work, have divided hell (infernus) into four abodes[1]:

1. Purgatory (abode of those being purified)
2. Limbo of the Fathers (abode of the Old Testament faithful – now it's empty)
3. Limbo of the Children (abode for unbaptized children under the age of reason)
4. Gehenna (abode of the damned)

Gehenna is usually referred to as "the fires of hell". Saint Thomas Aquinas is clear that Christ did not descend into Gehenna. Christ's soul descended to the Limbo of the Fathers, also known as *Abraham's Bosom*:

"And it came to pass, that the beggar died, and was carried by the angels into Abraham's bosom: the rich man also died, and was buried in hell; And in Hades he lifted up his eyes, being in torment, and seeing Abraham far off, and Lazarus in his bosom."
(Luke 16:22,23)

In the Old Testament, the gates of Heaven were not open to human souls. Remember in Book One of *Who's Who in The Cosmic Zoo?* we discussed the comparison of the first Adam to the second Adam, who was Jesus.[2] The inheritance that the first Adam lost was restored by the second Adam who was Christ. Up until the death and resurrection of Jesus Christ, satan, who we know as the god of this world, held all soul's captive inside the earth after death. The faithful men and women in the Old Testament times remained in the Limbo of the Fathers until the death of Christ– that includes all those born from Adam right up to the thief on the other cross. Thomas Aquinas teaches that since the Old Testament faithful did not have the sacraments, Christ's descent into the inferno was for them as the sacraments are to us.

The Grace of God that comes from what Yeshua/Jesus did on the Cross Calvary spans the timeline of earth's history. Gods redemptive grace through Christ's sacrifice is not limited to present time, but was applied to the dead who were held captive in the different levels of hell, which fulfills the Old Testament prophecy which predicts the New Blood Covenant we are all under now until His return:

"He sent forth prisoners out of the pit, in *the blood of His testament*,"
(Zechariah 9:11)

Dante's Inferno

The 14th century poem, *Dante's Inferno*, gives insight into the nine levels or circles of hell. *Inferno* is only the first part of Dante Alighieri's epic poem *Divine Comedy*.³ It is followed by *Purgatorio* and *Paradiso*. *Inferno* tells the journey of Dante going through Hell, while he is guided by the ancient Roman poet Virgil. The fact that he related the levels to be circles, indicates the spherical shape of this vast city beneath the earth, which mirrors the sphere of the earth.

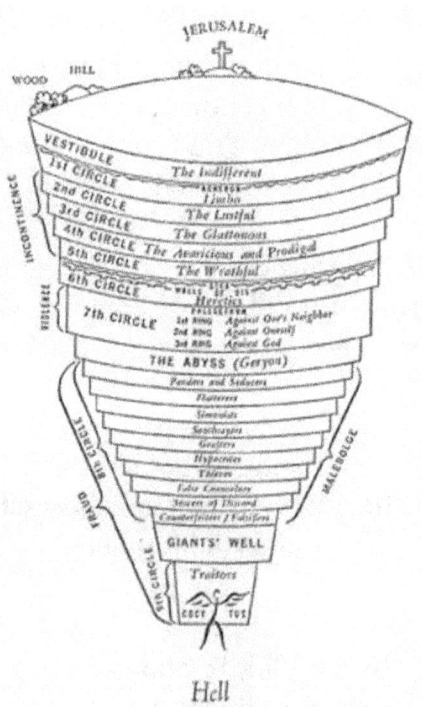

Hell

First Circle (Limbo)
Second Circle (Lust)
Third Circle (Gluttony)
Fourth Circle (Greed)
Fifth Circle (Anger)
Sixth Circle (Heresy)
Seventh Circle (Violence)
Eighth Circle (Fraud)
Ninth Circle (Treachery)

Chapter Eleven: Is Hell For Real?

The old expression, 'there's a special place in hell for what he did', may be associated with the fact that there are nine levels of hell. Each depends on the level of sins for the sinner. The fact that Jesus went into the pit to redeem and set the captives free, just as the prophesies promised He would, should encourage all people living now and reading these words to put their faith in the power of Christ's love and salvation for all sinners, no matter what amount of sin you may find yourself bound. If we repent, He alone has the power to set us free.

> "The Spirit of the Lord GOD is on me; because the LORD has anointed me to preach good tidings to the meek; he has sent me to bind up the brokenhearted, to proclaim liberty to the captives, and the opening of the prison to them that are bound;"
>
> (Isaiah 61:1)

> "The Spirit of the Lord is on Me, because He has anointed Me to preach good news to the poor. He has sent Me to proclaim deliverance to the captives and recovery of sight to the blind, to release the oppressed,"
>
> (Luke 4:18)

Duel Dimensions

The following story illustrates two places inside the earth reserved for the souls of the dead, one for the righteous and one for the wicked. They are separated by a chasm, so neither of the two can cross over to the another. The scripture speaks of these places as being *inside* the earth, as in the words of Jesus Christ Himself. The following account, told by the Lord Jesus Christ in Luke 16:19-31, gives us the actual words of a man in hell--notice how he is in torment, that he can see, that his tongue is hot and he is tormented in the flame. Notice how he wanted his brethren to be warned lest they too enter that place of torment. Notice how the only hope that his brethren had was to believe the holy scriptures as there would be no other proof:

> "Jesus said, there was a rich man who was dressed in purple and fine linen and lived in luxury every day. At his gate was laid a beggar named Lazarus, covered with sores and longing to eat what fell from the rich man's table. Even the dogs came and licked his sores. The time came when the beggar died and the angels carried him to Abraham's side. The rich man also died and was buried. In hell, where he was in torment, he looked up and saw Abraham far away, with Lazarus by his side. So, he called to him, 'Father Abraham, have pity on me and send Lazarus to dip the tip of his finger in water and cool my tongue,

because I am in agony in this fire. But Abraham replied, Son, remember that in your lifetime you received your good things, while Lazarus received bad things, but now he is comforted here and you are in agony. And besides all this, between us and you a great chasm has been fixed, so that those who want to go from here to you cannot, nor can anyone cross over from there to us. He answered, 'Then I beg you, father, send Lazarus to my father's house, for I have five brothers. Let him warn them, so that they will not also come to this place of torment. Abraham said to him, 'They have Moses and the prophets; let them hear them.' And he said, Nay, father Abraham: but if one went unto them from the dead, they will repent. And he said unto him, 'If they do not hear Moses and the prophets, neither will they be persuaded, though one rose from the dead."

(Luke 16:19-31)

Taken literally this means the world of the dead is divided into two regions, one for the wicked and the other for the righteous. The wicked are in torment in hell and the righteous are in peace with Abraham. There is a chasm between the two places that stopped either side from crossing to the other, yet they were able to see each other and even communicate.

This scripture proves that Jesus went to Hades/Hell after He was crucified on the Cross.

"For as Jonah was three days and three nights in the belly of a huge fish, so the Son of Man will be three days and three nights in the heart of the earth."

(Matthew 12:40)

This is literal and obvious of the fact that Jesus went *inside the earth,* to the heart of the earth, for three days and three nights. If this is the case, then how do the words of Jesus spoken to the thief on the cross, make sense.

"Then he said, "Jesus, remember me when you come into your kingdom." Jesus answered him, "I tell you the truth, today you will be with me in paradise."

(Luke 23:42-43)

The point is that Jesus was in the heart of the earth for approximately three days, after which time He walked the earth for a short time and then ascended up into heaven. If the reference to Paradise was heaven, then when Jesus said to the thief on the cross "that he would be in paradise with him today" would have to be a

Chapter Eleven: Is Hell For Real?

contradiction. Jesus was in the heart of the earth for three days and three nights. The only way that both scriptures can be explained without contradiction is to say that Paradise was also *inside* the heart of the earth, just separated by a chasm from Hell.

There are so many references to Paradise being *inside* the earth. The Hollow Earth Society believes that there are cities *inside* the earth, which is actually hollow, with the core being the central sun. This society bases its tenets on the hypotheses of astronomer Edmund Haley, of comet fame, who presented his theory in 1691 that the earth is hollow with several spheres within spheres. This would prove the different dimensions *inside* the earth.

In 1947 Admiral Richard Byrd flew his plane *inside* the opening at the North Pole and claimed to have witnessed cities and all kinds of beings and creatures, some of which had become extinct on the surface of the planet. I have discussed Admiral Byrd's trip in more detail in Book One, under the section of *Aghartians*,[4] but here we are talking about *spirits* and *souls* not physical beings as Admiral Byrd witnessed. It appears that the Inner Earth is a very busy place. The two places which are separated by a chasm are in another dimensional space of the inner earth. It is not physical but spiritual.

> "Heaven is under our feet as well as over our heads."
> ~Henry David Thoreau

Another story confirms the fact that there are two dimensions where souls and spirits go after they die, which are *inside* the earth.

We read earlier that when Lazarus died he went to Abraham's side and the rich man went to hell. In hell, the rich man looked up and could see Lazarus being comforted at Abraham's side. But neither could cross over to the other side because of a huge chasm. Luke 16:19-28 says the same thing. This holding place was where the righteous went after they died. It was a dimensional space *inside* the earth. This may even be purgatory, a place where souls go, which is not hell, but it is not heaven. It is the light, which many talk about who have had Near Death Experiences. This is why it says:

> "When he ascended on high, he led captives in his train and gave gifts to men. What does "he ascended" mean except that he also descended to the lower, earthly regions? He who descended is the very one who ascended higher than all the heavens, in order to fill the whole universe."
> (Ephesians 4:8-10)

The scripture is very clear that Jesus Christ descended to the lower earthly regions and then ascended to the highest heavens.

> "Since the children have flesh and blood, he too shared in their humanity so that by his death he might destroy him who holds the power of death--that is, the devil."
>
> (Hebrews 2:14)

> "When I saw him, I fell at his feet as though dead. Then he placed his right hand on me and said: "Do not be afraid. I am the First and the Last. I AM the Living One; I was dead, and behold I am alive forever and ever! And I hold the keys of death and Hades."
>
> (Revelation 1:17,18)

These scriptures indicate that Jesus was dead and is now alive, and now He also has the Keys of death and hell. We can see clearly that Jesus' mission to destroy the power that the devil had over death was a success! This is why He has the authority to share His power and authority with His believers.

Jesus Preached to the Dead Spirits

> "For Christ died for sins once for all, the righteous for the unrighteous, to bring you to God. He was put to death in the body but made alive by the Spirit, through whom also he went and preached to *the spirits in prison* who disobeyed long ago when God waited patiently in the days of Noah while the ark was being built. In it only a few people, eight in all, were saved from drowning through water."
>
> (1 Peter 3:18-20)

This scripture says that Jesus preached to disobedient spirits in prison who died before and during the flood of Noah. When Jesus defeated death, He proclaimed His victory to the wicked spirits in Hell, in other words He heralded their soon coming judgment, because He is the One they must pass through for the judgment. He also set the righteous spirits free to abide in Heaven. Those were the spirits that were in the holding place *inside* the earth, which may be purgatory.

> "But they will have to give account to him who is ready to judge the living and the dead. For this is the reason the gospel was preached even to those who are now dead, so that they might be judged according to men in regard to the body, but live according to God in regard to the spirit."
>
> (1 Peter 4:5-6)

Chapter Eleven: Is Hell For Real?

This scripture says that the Gospel, the Truth about the Kingdom of God, was preached to the dead and they were given another chance at life. Perhaps those who believed Jesus were then rescued from Hell and sent to Purgatory, where they had a chance to purge their spirits from all ungodliness and were later given another chance at life through reincarnation.

This verse relates to the resurrection of the righteous which happened as a result of Jesus Christ's victory over death and His journey to the world of the dead.

> "And the graves were opened; and many bodies of the saints which slept arose, and came out of the graves after his resurrection, and went into the holy city, and appeared unto many."
>
> (Matthew 27:52)

This verse suggests that Jesus Christ freed the dead saints from sleep, so He probably went to the place of the dead and set them free. These saints would have been in Paradise, see Luke 16:19-28 as quoted earlier, which was separated by a huge chasm from the spirits who were in hell.

After His journey into the underworld, Jesus rose from the dead and walked the earth for forty days before ascending and being taken up into Heaven in Yahuah's starship. These saints of old who walked the earth were probably taken to heaven as well because there is no suggestion in the Bible that these saints continued to live amongst humankind.

The fact that the dead rose at the same time as Jesus Christ's resurrection is a fulfillment of what Jesus said would happen:

> "Do not be amazed at this, for a time is coming when all who are in their graves will hear His voice and come out--those who have done good will rise to live, and those who have done evil will rise to be condemned."
>
> (John 5:28-29)

Also:

> "For the Lord himself will come down from heaven, with a loud command, with the voice of the archangel and with the trumpet call of God, <u>and the dead in Christ will rise first</u>. After that, we who are still alive and are left will be caught up together with them *in the clouds* to meet the Lord *in the air*. And so, we will be with the Lord forever. Therefore, encourage each other with these words."
>
> (1 Thessalonians 4:16-18)

Notice that the dead rise first, and at some stage all those believers who are still living will join them to meet the Lord in the air, which is known as the *Rapture*. Jesus Christ's victory over death has enabled the saints who have died to bypass Hades and go to Heaven as He did, the result of the victory over Satan who had previously the power of death. This power was stripped away from Satan at Christ's victory, when He took the keys of death and hell from him.

This scripture has always been used to support the *Rapture*. This is a hotly contested idea, as this could describe either the *Rapture*, or what happens at the second coming, which will occur at the end of the seven-year tribulation. My point in mentioning this scripture here is that it specifically says, 'the dead in Christ will rise first'. Where are these dead in Christ? This implies that they are not in the upper Heaven with the Lord, but 'sleeping' inside a dimension in the earth. As I've already established based on scripture, there is a paradise *inside* the earth. Heaven is *inside* the earth, as well as above us. This scripture clearly tells us that the Lord is coming *down* from heaven to the earth, to collect His own. The dead in Christ rise first, implying they come alive to the Lord. Perhaps they are sleeping? There are several scriptures that speak of the dead as sleeping. This means they are not in heaven with the Lord, but await their 'resurrection', or 'reincarnation' into the Kingdom of God or Heaven.

The following are more Bible scriptures on reincarnation, which also prove that the place of the dead is *inside* the earth.

> "But your dead will live; their bodies will rise. You who dwell in the dust, wake up and shout for joy. Your dew is like the dew of the morning; the earth will give birth to her dead."
>
> (Isaiah 26:19)

> "Multitudes who sleep in the dust of the earth will awake: some to everlasting life, others to shame and everlasting contempt."
>
> (Daniel 12:2)

> "for it is light that makes everything visible. This is why it is said: "Wake up, O sleeper, rise from the dead, and Christ will shine on you."
>
> (Ephesians 5:14)

The First and Second Deaths

Today when the righteous die, they go straight to heaven, but the wicked remain in the grave or in hell until the great day of judgment. This is why the book of Revelation talks about the first and second deaths.

Chapter Eleven: Is Hell For Real?

> "Blessed and holy are those who have part in the first resurrection. The second death has no power over them, but they will be priests of God and of Christ and will reign with him for a thousand years."
>
> (Revelation 20:6)

> "For the Lord himself will come down from heaven, with a loud command, with the voice of the archangel and with the trumpet call of God, and the dead in Christ will rise first. After that, we who are still alive and are left will be caught up together with them in the clouds to meet the Lord in the air. And so, we will be with the Lord forever. Therefore, encourage each other with these words."
>
> (1 Thessalonians 4:16-18)

Notice that the dead rise first, and at some unspecified point all those believers who are still living will join the dead to meet the Lord. Jesus Christ's victory over death has enabled the saints who have died to bypass Hades and go to Heaven as He did, as a result of the victory over Satan, who had the power of death. Jesus took the keys of death and hell from him, as we read earlier in Revelation 1:18. Today when the righteous die, they go straight to heaven, but the wicked remain in the grave/hell until the great day of judgment.

> "Then I saw a great white throne and him who was seated on it. Earth and sky fled from his presence, and there was no place for them. And I saw the dead, great and small, standing before the throne, and books were opened. Another book was opened, which is the book of life. The dead were judged according to what they had done as recorded in the books. The sea gave up the dead that were in it, and death and Hades gave up the dead that were in them, and each person was judged according to what he had done. *Then death and Hades were thrown into the lake of fire. The lake of fire is the second death.*"
>
> (Revelation 20:11-14)

The Bible tells us that the only ones who ascended to heaven before the death of Jesus Christ were Enoch, Elijah and Ezekiel. These three were all taken up in the Lord's spaceships. (See, Book Two: *Who Is God?* my chapter on *Ancient Technology and Biblical Astronauts*). However, there were some exceptions. We see that righteous men did ascend to heaven before Jesus Christ took back the power of death and Hades from Satan, for example on the Mount of Transfiguration where Elijah and Moses appeared with Jesus in heavenly glory. (See, Luke 9:29-31)

Enoch was taken up in one of the Lord's spaceships. Enoch came back after 300 years to deliver his scrolls which the Lord told him to write of his experiences on his spaceship and of the heavens. These experiences are in two books, 1 Enoch and 2 Enoch which I quote extensively in Book Two: *Who Is God?* Enoch was shown the secrets of the cosmos, and in 2 Enoch he writes in great detail of the star portals, the planets and God's astronomy. (See, Book Five: *The Heavens*) This is probably one of the reasons why the books of Enoch were rejected by the early church, as the consciousness of the time dictated that the earth was the center of the universe. This opinion prevailed throughout the dark ages, as seven hundred years later the Inquisition battled the works of Galileo Galilei and Giordano Bruno who thought otherwise. Who turned out to be right? Giordano Bruno and others like him knew something about astronomy and mathematics. If the church fathers canonized the book of Enoch, it would have proved them wrong and it certainly would have prevented the torture and persecution of Giordano Bruno and others like him.

Knowing what we know today as fact through science, we should realize that the minds of the Church fathers were tainted by fallen angels and religious spirits. These men had kept humanity in further darkness for so much longer when the truth was available, yet they rejected it because it didn't fit into their political agenda.

"Enoch walked with God; then he was no more, because God took him away."
(Genesis 5:24)

"By faith Enoch was taken from this life, so that he did not experience death; he could not be found, because God had taken him away. For before he was taken, he was commended as one who pleased God."
(Hebrews 11:5)

Elijah never saw death. He was taken up into Heaven while still alive, bypassing the holding place where Abraham dwelt, "As they were walking along and talking together, suddenly a *chariot of fire* and *horses of fire* appeared and separated the two of them, and Elijah went up to heaven in a whirlwind." (2 Kings 2:11)

As I've mentioned in Book Two in my chapter *Ancient Technology and Biblical Astronauts*,[6] the chariot of fire and the horses of fire, were biblical descriptions of the Lords spaceships. This is why it says, he went up to heaven in a whirlwind, which is what happens from the space ship.

Ezekiel was 50 years old when he began to have visions of a new *Temple*. He served as a prophet for at least 22 years, until Ezekiel's last supposed encounter with God occurred in April 570 BCE. (Ezekiel 29:17) His time of death and how he died

Chapter Eleven: Is Hell For Real?

has not been recorded which is why many believed he was taken up in one of the *Chariots of God* he described in such detail.

Moses was an exception to the fact that he was righteous and died but passed by the holding place *inside* the earth with Abraham, and ascended to heaven after his death:

> "But even the Archangel Michael, when he was disputing with the devil about the body of Moses, did not dare to bring a slanderous accusation against him, but said, "The Lord rebuke you!"
>
> (Jude 1:9)

Here we see that Michael the Archangel and the devil fought over Moses' body when he died, each one probably laying claim to why he should have Moses' soul. Satan most likely argued that it couldn't be taken because he had the power over death at that stage. It doesn't say who won, but the fact that Moses appeared in glory next to Jesus in the Mount of Transfiguration shows us the outcome of this dispute.

> "Jesus said, "Truly I tell you, some who are standing here will not taste death before they see the kingdom of God."
>
> (Matthew 16:28; Luke 9:27)

The Transfiguration

> "About eight days after Jesus said this, he took Peter, John and James with him and went up onto a mountain to pray. As he was praying, the appearance of his face changed, and his clothes became as bright as a flash of lightning. Two men, Moses and Elijah, appeared in glorious splendor, talking with Jesus. They spoke about his departure, which he was about to bring to fulfillment at Jerusalem."
>
> (Luke 9:27-31)

The fact that Jesus said to his disciples that some of them would not taste death before they saw the Kingdom of God, meant that some were destined to be lifted up into heaven.

Then the scripture tells us that they were all enveloped in a cloud, and a voice spoke to them out of that cloud. In Book Two, my chapter on *Ancient Technology and Biblical Astronauts*, I devote a whole section to the Clouds and the Cloud ships of the Lord, particularly the public-address system that was used over and over again when the voice of the Lord spoke, often described as a very loud voice out of the cloud. The Cloud was another word for the Lord's spacecraft, which were cloaked in the glory clouds.

> "While he was speaking, a cloud appeared and covered them, and they were afraid as they entered the cloud. A voice came from the cloud, saying, "This is my Son, whom I have chosen; listen to him." When the voice had spoken, they found that Jesus was alone."
>
> (Luke 9:34-36)

Both the Cloud, Elijah and Moses had disappeared. Spaceships come and go quickly. Many are interdimensional. In Book Two: *Who Is God?* I go into great detail on the use of the word *cloud* throughout the Scriptures, to describe the Lord's spaceships.[8]

> "and from Jesus Christ, who is the faithful witness, the firstborn from the dead, and the ruler of the kings of the earth. To him who loves us and has freed us from our sins by his blood,"
>
> (Revelation 1:5)

This scripture points out that Jesus is the first born from the dead. This suggest that there must be other people born from the dead to follow. Matthew 27:50-52 describes when the saints were resurrected after the crucifixion quoted above complements this point.

Only the power of God can raise the dead and this is what it means to be Born Again. The power that raised Jesus from the dead will also raise all those who belong to God when they die.

> "For as in Adam all die, so in Christ all will be made alive. But each in his own turn: Christ, the first fruits; then, when he comes, those who belong to him. Then the end will come, when he hands over the Kingdom to God the Father after he has destroyed all dominion, authority and power. For he must reign until he has put all his enemies under his feet. The last enemy to be destroyed is death. For he "has put everything under his feet." Now when it says that "everything" has been put under him, it is clear that this does not include God himself, who put everything under Christ. When he has done this, then the Son himself will be made subject to him who put everything under him, so that God may be all in all."
>
> (Corinthians 15:22-28)

Chapter Eleven: Is Hell For Real?

This scripture reveals a great mystery, being "all in Christ live". First Jesus, then the first fruits, then those that belong to Jesus Christ at His coming. The end will come when Jesus Christ destroys all dominion and authority. The last enemy is death. This will result in God the Father and His Holy Spirit being able to dwell in all. This fits in well with the teaching that Jesus Christ went to Hell, as to be victorious over it, and therefore destroying the One who had Power over death, namely the Devil.

It makes sense that when Jesus Christ died He went to Hell and defeated death and took the keys of death and of Hell from Satan. This victory means that Jesus Christ defeated death in a bid to make all things subject to Him. Death was the last enemy that needed to be conquered and now Jesus Christ has been exalted to the highest position in heaven by God. This victory has enabled all those who belong to God to be raised from the dead with the same power. Another reason the demons, aliens, fallen angels and Satan all tremble and submit to the name of Jesus Christ!

> Then Jesus came to them and said, "All authority in heaven and on earth has been given to me."
>
> (Matthew 28:18)

This victory has enabled all those who belong to God to be raised from the dead with the same power. Jesus is waiting for all his enemies to be made a footstool at his feet,

> "And God never said to any of the angels, "Sit in the place of honor at my right hand until I humble your enemies, making them a footstool under your feet."
>
> (Hebrews 1:13)

> "But when this priest had offered for all time one sacrifice for sins, he sat down at the right hand of God. Since that time, he waits for his enemies to be made his footstool, because by one sacrifice he has made perfect forever those who are being made holy."
>
> (Hebrews 10:12-14)

Then He will present His Kingdom to His Father so that the Father may dwell in all. Between now and then, the rest of the prophetic timeline needs to be revealed. The Truth as the Gospel of the Kingdom of God needs to be preached to the entire world. The Antichrist rises to power, and then the end shall come.

"And to make all men see what is the fellowship of the mystery, which from the beginning of the world hath been hid in God, *who created all things by Jesus Christ.*"

(Ephesians 3:9)

HELL IS NOT FOREVER

Hell is not forever, because God is going to destroy the heavens and the earth with fire after the millennium. If He destroys the earth and hell is inside the earth, then hell as a dwelling place will also be destroyed. However, there is a difference between hell and the Lake of Fire, which is spoken of in Revelation 20:14, when both hell and death are cast into the Lake of Fire.

"By the same word the present heavens and earth are reserved for fire, being kept for the day of judgment and destruction of ungodly men."

(2 Peter 3:7)

"Then I saw a new heaven and a new earth, for the first heaven and the first earth had passed away, and there was no longer any sea."

(Revelation 21:1)

"And death and hell were cast into the lake of fire. This is the second death."

(Revelation 20:14)

HELL WAS CREATED FOR SATAN AND HIS ANGELS

People say this all the time, "A loving God wouldn't put His creatures in hell." God is not willing that any should perish but that all should come to repentance (2 Peter 3:9). Hell was not created for man. Hell was created for the devil and his angels.

"Then shall he say also unto them on the left hand, depart from me, ye cursed, into everlasting fire, PREPARED FOR THE DEVIL AND HIS ANGELS."

(Matthew 25:41)

People go to hell because they choose the path of Satan and his fallen angels and reject the Lord Jesus Christ. God is holy and will not allow any sin in His kingdom. God is merciful and full of grace. People who die in their sins are forever banished from the presence of God to a fiery place called hell--a place of shame, contempt, and torment. Incidentally, Satan won't be ruling in the lake of fire. He'll be condemned

Chapter Eleven: Is Hell For Real?

and tormented just like everybody else; 'the devil...shall be tormented day and night forever and ever'. Hell was created as a place of judgment for Satan and those who followed him in their rebellion against God. This includes his fallen angel demons and the people they possessed. The Bible says that the devil and his angels will eventually be consigned to hell. Satan, the god of this world, WILL NOT always cause havoc. His doom is already foretold,

> "And the devil that deceived them was cast into the lake of fire and brimstone, where the beast and the false prophet are, and shall be tormented day and night forever and ever."
>
> (Revelation 20:10)

Human beings, who are created in God's image, are not meant to spend eternity away from the presence of God. The place God created for them is heaven and the Kingdom of God. Jesus spoke of this place that God has prepared for those who trust Him:

> "In My Father's house are many mansions: if it were not so, I would have told you. I go to prepare a place for you. And if I go and prepare a place for you, I will come again and receive you to Myself, that where I am, there you may be also."
>
> (John 14:2, 3)

If you do not belong to Jesus Christ, you belong to Satan. You don't have to be a card-carrying Satanist to serve Satan. You don't have to be a murderer, drunkard or drug addict, either. All you have to do is ignore and rebel against Jesus Christ. Remember the story of Lazarus in Abraham's bosom. The rich man was in hell, and Lazarus was in paradise with Abraham. This means that there are so many people of the world, who may appear to be successful, have riches, even fame, but if they reject the Lord Jesus Christ, they cannot enter into His Kingdom.

Think about it, why would a King allow someone into His Kingdom if he is against Him? Many ask, what about those who are righteous and holy but follow other gods, other religions? God has a place for them too, which may not be hell, but it is not paradise either. This is why there is reincarnation, as the grace of God allows souls the chance to find salvation while they are still alive. This is the purpose of the in-between place known as purgatory. One purges from their ungodly attitudes inside the light of god and awaits judgment. The Lord Jesus Christ in His mercy allows the soul another chance at life to find Him and find the path of repentance and salvation from the bondages of Lucifer and Satan. However, the wicked ones who die in their sins end up in hell.

> "Come now, and let us reason together, says the LORD: though your sins be as scarlet, they shall be as white as snow; though they be red like crimson, they shall be as wool."
>
> (Isaiah 1:18)

God does not want you in hell! Jesus Christ came to save you from that horrible place!

> "As I live, says the Lord GOD, I have no pleasure in the death of the wicked; but that the wicked turn from his way and live: turn ye, turn ye from your evil ways; for why will ye die..."
>
> (Ezekiel 33:11)

> "The Lord is not willing that any should perish, but that all should come to repentance."
>
> (2 Peter 3:9)

The Abyss of Tartarus

There is mention of a place called Tartarus in the Bible, which is for nonhuman spirits. This level of hell, or the abyss as it is called, is reserved for the rebellious angels and extraterrestrials who have sinned against the Creator both before and after the great deluge. Tartarus is not for human souls. "God spared not the angels that sinned, but cast them down to Tartarus (hell), and delivered them into chains of darkness, to be reserved unto judgment." (2 Peter 2:4). Tartarus means "dark abyss" or "place of restraint." This means that the fallen angels and Nephilim, the alien/human hybrids, are placed there to be released for judgment at a future date. They are not burning in the lake fire just yet.

According to Revelation 9:11, 'They had a king over them, who is the angel from the bottomless pit. His name whose name in the Hebrew tongue is Abaddon, but in the Greek tongue has his name Apollyon." This is an 'Archdemon,' who is in charge of them all at the bottomless pit. These evil spirits are being held, to be used in the final punishment upon the earth during the tribulation period. Revelation 9:1-10 describes these fallen spirits, as tormentors of men:

> "The fifth angel sounded his trumpet, and I saw a star that had fallen from the sky to the earth. The star was given the key to the shaft of the Abyss. When he opened the Abyss, smoke rose from it like the smoke from a gigantic furnace. The sun and sky were darkened by the smoke from the Abyss. And

out of the smoke locusts came down upon the earth and were given power like that of scorpions of the earth. They were told not to harm the grass of the earth or any plant or tree, but only those people who did not have the seal of God on their foreheads. They were not given power to kill them, but only to torture them for five months. And the agony they suffered was like that of the sting of a scorpion when it strikes a man. During those days, men will seek death, but will not find it; they will long to die, but death will elude them. The locusts looked like horses prepared for battle. On their heads, they wore something like crowns of gold, and their faces resembled human faces. Their hair was like women's hair, and their teeth were like lions' teeth. They had breastplates like breastplates of iron, and the sound of their wings was like the thundering of many horses and chariots rushing into battle. They had tails and stings like scorpions, and in their tails they had power to torment people for five months."

SAVED FROM HELL

Howard Storm[9] was a Professor of Art at Northern Kentucky University, and was not a very pleasant man. He was an avowed atheist and was hostile to every form of religion and those who practiced it. He often would use rage to control everyone around him and he didn't find joy in anything. Anything that wasn't seen, touched, or felt, he had no faith in. He knew with certainty that the material world was the full extent of everything that was. He considered all belief systems associated with religion to be fantasies for people to deceive themselves with. Beyond what science said, there was nothing else.

On June 1, 1985, at the age of 38, Howard Storm had a near-death experience due to a perforation of his stomach and his life was forever changed. His near-death experience is the most profound afterlife experiences ever documented. His life was immensely changed after his near-death experience that he resigned as a professor and devoted his time to attending the United Theological Seminary to become a United Church of Christ minister. His entire story can be read in his book, *My Descent into Death: A Second Chance at Life*.

Howard needed emergency surgery and was in Europe at the time and had to wait for the surgeons to arrive. This was very serious, and the surgeons did not get to him in time, so he died on the table. He said at first he didn't know he was dead, as he saw himself lying on the table, then he said beings began to chew at his ears and body, sucking the life force out of him and dragging him into a vortex of fire. He was so terrified, he called out to Jesus Christ to save him, and within an instant an Angel of the Lord was dispatched and rescued him out of the descending vortex of fire and brought him up to see the Lord. The Lord told him he was faithful to his call and that He was going to give Howard a second chance at life, so He put him back into his body, at which time, the surgeons had arrived and his heart beat resumed after being clinically dead, and they performed the life-saving surgery. Howard Storm survived and gave his life to the Lord Jesus Christ and became the Minister. Rev. Howard Storm of the United Church of Christ.

Howard Storm's story is one of the most remarkable conversion stories as you have an avowed atheist turned believer and minister of Christ. This is a man who understands the true meaning of the word 'Salvation.'

Visions of Hell

Another remarkable story, a Christian man named Bill Wiese[10] spent *23 minutes in Hell* in an out of body experience, which he writes about in his book called *23 minutes in Hell*. Bill has been a Christian for 37 years. He was not sent to Hell to be punished, but to experience what it was like so he could tell others that Hell was for real. Perhaps this was the proof that the rich man in the story of Lazarus wanted others to know, as these days, the unbelieving do not rely on scripture but will listen to the testimonies of those who have been there.

Bill Wiese was sleeping in his bed with his wife as he usually does and was woken up at 3:00 AM (known as the witching hour) and was given an 'out of body experience' from the Lord Jesus Christ. He was sent into a prison cell in hell with two grotesque demons who tormented him and tore his flesh. He said everyone was isolated and alone in cells. He saw the searing flames of hell, he felt total isolation, he was tormented by what he described to be *reptilian* creatures that appeared to be deformed, with sharp claws, bumps and scales all over their body and a huge jaw with long sharp teeth.[12] (See, my chapter on the Draconian/Reptilians in Book One of *Who's Who in The Cosmic Zoo?*)

Wiese said they were blaspheming and cursing God. He said they hated him and attacked him, they grabbed him and threw him into the wall, he said he felt their claws dig into his chest, they ripped his flesh right off his body that hung like ribbons. He said you have a body in hell, but most people were just skeletons with very little flesh left because they had all been tortured and tormented by these *reptilian* creatures. He said they hate humans with a hatred that is unimaginable. They have absolutely no mercy. They hate humans because they hate God, because God created humans in His image.

In the last days on earth, these demonic alien beings are being released to the surface. They influence people through the agency of spirits, thoughtforms and mind control. When people behave like these beings do, they are no longer behaving as human, but as alien. What ISIS is doing to men, women and children, is not human.

Chapter Eleven: Is Hell For Real?

Their hatred comes from these *reptilian* creatures, demons, who hate God for creating humans, and giving the earth to them.

This is a big part of the spiritual battle. The religious spirit comes from the *reptilians*, carried out through its Grays. It counterfeits, it denies, it mocks, it is full of unbelief. What this spirit has done to Islam is hellish, the killings, and particularly the way humans are being treated, is not human, it is demonic in its core and alien to the very nature of the human being.

There is hell on earth, and what Weise witnessed when taken to Hell, is now happening on the surface of the planet, through Islamists, Jihadists and the Caliphate. They are burning people alive, beating them while they are burning, chopping off body parts, often engaging in cannibalism (which is not a human trait but an alien behavior), raping women to death, raping babies and children, and beheading everyone who is not of similar belief. This is the *reptilian* spirit from hell inhabiting the lost souls of Islam.

HELL IS SEPARATION FROM GOD

He was then taken to a pit of fire, where he saw millions of people screaming on the top of their lungs while they were tormented by these demonic creatures who were all around the pit in all sizes and shapes, grotesque and deformed. He saw the people like skeletons with their flesh hanging off as he watched them burn alive in this pit of fire. Even though they had died and were sent to hell, they weren't really dead, they felt everything. Death in hell is really complete separation from God, which is what these people experienced. There was no good thing to comfort them. No hope. They were eternally lost. Bill said he wasn't sent into the pit, but he was shown it.

Bill says you have your full memory in hell but there is nothing good, he said you are exhausted all the time, there is no strength in your body, there is no air to breathe, yet you are conscious to experience all the torment which never stops, you are completely weak, void of any kind of strength. He experienced the putrid and rotting stench, deafening screams of agony, terrifying grotesque demons in the forms of snakes, maggots, worms and deformed spiders. He said nobody talks to each other. They are denied air to breathe, denied water to drink, denied food to eat and are also denied sleep. He said it is a completely hopeless state. There is no hope whatsoever.

He said he knew that he was down deep inside the earth, which is where hell is located right now. He said the Lord hid from his mind that he was a Christian, so that he could experience what people in hell feared and felt, that they were hopelessly lost forever. He said there is no conversation with anybody and the fear is beyond belief. Bill was once pulled down by a nine- foot shark during his life and survived, and the fear that he felt when the shark attacked him paled in comparison to the fear that he felt in hell. There was no comparison. Perhaps this was the reason the Lord chose him to experience this as a testimony to others, because he had survived a terrifying shark attack and lived. Bill said there is no mercy over you, due to the cruelty of *reptilian* demons who torment you over and over again. He said there are different levels of torment, different degrees of punishment. There is no relief.

Finally, the strong hand and Light of the Lord Jesus Christ appeared to him and lifted him out of the pit. When Bill saw the 'Light' he saw the Lord's feet and he said, 'Jesus', and the Lord answered him, "I AM." Then the Lord told him He wanted him to feel what these people felt, hopelessly lost, because it pains the Lord that any human should have to go to hell. He told Bill He didn't want to see one person go to hell, because He made hell for the devil and his angels, but man will go there if he doesn't listen and does not repent and come to the Lord. He said they need to repent of their sins and receive Him as their Lord and Savior. God wants people to know He doesn't want anyone to go there, He didn't make hell for man, but if man repents and recognizes that he is a sinner and that he needs a Savior, he will be saved from hell. He said that man thinks that if he is good enough with good works he can go to heaven, but this is not true, he needs to receive the Lord Jesus Christ, who is the Gateway to life eternal, and the Savior from hell and eternal damnation. Anybody who puts their trust in Him will not perish but have everlasting life. (John 3:16)

Then the Lord told him, "Tell them I am coming <u>very, very soon</u>!" Bill said He repeated Himself and said it twice. "Tell them I am coming <u>very, very soon</u>!" Bill says that he was given this vision, this out-of-body experience because the Lord wanted him to know what it felt like, so that he could tell others, so that they could avoid it. Remember the story of Lazarus and the rich man who wanted to tell others about hell but could not? This was done by the Lord's mercy. He chose Bill Wiese to be the witness, knowing that he could handle it. Bill said when he woke up and came back into his body he was screaming, traumatized. He shared that his wife prayed for him for over twenty minutes until he calmed down. He said that the Lord healed him of his trauma but did not take the memory from him so he could tell others. In his book *23 Minutes in Hell* he gives 150 different Bible verses that reference everything he experienced, though not as many as I am giving you here.

The Bible teaches that God loves us so much that the Creator of this universe, Jesus Christ, came to "taste death" for every man. Jesus Christ wasn't just some baby for a manger scene. He is God who came in the flesh to destroy the power of death and hell, He holds the keys! If you say yes to Jesus, hell won't be your final destination.

Regardless of whether you believe it or not, hell exists and the Bible says that it is never full.

These scriptures deal with hell and the lake of fire, where, at the final judgment, hell, death and those not written in the *book of life* will be cast to burn with fire and brimstone:

Chapter Eleven: Is Hell For Real?

"And the smoke of their torment ascends up forever and ever: and <u>they have no rest day nor night...</u>

(Revelation 14:11)

"And I saw the dead, small and great, stand before God; and the books were opened: and another book was opened, which is the book of life...And <u>whosoever was not found written in the book of life was cast into the lake of fire</u>."

(Revelation 20:12,15)

"And fear not them which kill the body, but are not able to kill the soul: but rather <u>fear him which is able to destroy both soul and body in hell</u>."

(Matthew 10:28)

"But I will forewarn you whom ye shall fear: <u>Fear him, which AFTER he hath killed hath power to cast into hell; yea, I say unto you, Fear him</u>."

(Luke 12:5)

"Wherefore if thy hand or thy foot offend thee, cut them off, and cast them from thee: it is better for thee to enter into life halt or maimed, rather than having two hands or feet to be <u>cast into everlasting fire</u>. And if thine eye offend thee, pluck it out, and cast it from thee: it is better for thee to enter into life with one eye, rather than having two eyes to be <u>cast into hell fire</u>."

(Matthew 18:8, 9)

"And <u>these shall go away into EVERLASTING punishment</u>: but the righteous into life eternal."

(Matthew 25:46)

"Who shall be <u>punished with EVERLASTING destruction</u> from the presence of the Lord, and from the glory of his power."

(II Thessalonians 1:9)

"And they shall go forth, and look upon the carcasses of the men that have transgressed against me: for <u>their worm shall not die, neither shall their fire be quenched; and they shall be abhorring unto all flesh</u>."

(Isaiah 66:24)

(speaking of hell), Where <u>their worm dies not, and the fire is not quenched</u>.

(Mark 9:44)

Sodom and Gomorrah...are set forth for an example, <u>suffering the vengeance of eternal fire</u>.

(Jude 7)

"Bind him hand and foot, and take him away, and cast him into outer darkness; <u>there shall be weeping and gnashing of teeth</u>."

(Matthew 22:13)

"The Son of man (Jesus) shall send forth his angels, and they shall gather out of his kingdom all things that offend, and them which do iniquity; and <u>shall cast them into a furnace of fire; there shall be wailing and gnashing of teeth</u>."

(Matthew 13:41-42)

"But the fearful, and unbelieving, and the abominable, and murderers, and whoremongers, and sorcerers, and idolaters, and all liars, <u>shall have their part in the lake which burns with fire and brimstone: which is the second death</u>."

(Revelation 21:8)

"<u>The wicked shall be turned into hell</u>, and all the nations that forget God."

(Psalm 9:17)

(referring to Lucifer), "Hell from beneath is moved for thee to meet thee at thy coming: it stirreth up the dead for thee...all they shall speak and say unto thee, Art thou also become weak as we? art thou become like unto us? <u>Thy pomp is brought down to the grave, and the noise of thy viols: the worm is spread under thee, and the worms cover thee...thou shalt be brought down to hell, to the sides of the pit</u>."

(Isaiah 14:99-11, 15)

"And many of them that sleep in the dust of the earth shall awake, some to everlasting life, and some to<u> shame and EVERLASTING contempt</u>."

(Daniel 12:2)

What does it mean to have the fear of God?

For the unbeliever, the fear of God is the fear of the judgment of God and eternal death, which is eternal separation from God (Luke 12:5; Hebrews 10:31). For the believer, the fear of God is something much different. For a believer, fear is reverence

Chapter Eleven: Is Hell For Real?

for God. Hebrews 12:28-29 is a good description of this: "Therefore, since we are receiving a kingdom that cannot be shaken, let us be thankful, and so worship God acceptably with reverence and awe, for our 'God is a consuming fire.'" This reverence and awe is exactly what the fear of God means for believers. This is the motivating factor for us to surrender to the Creator of the Universe.

Proverbs 1:7 declares, "The fear of the LORD is the beginning of knowledge." Until we understand who God is and develop a reverential fear of Him, we cannot have true wisdom. True wisdom comes only from understanding who God is and that He is holy, just, and righteous.

Deuteronomy 10:12, 20-21 records, "And now, O Israel, what does the LORD your God ask of you but to fear the LORD your God, to walk in all his ways, to love him, to serve the LORD your God with all your heart and with all your soul. Fear the LORD your God and serve him. Hold fast to him and take your oaths in his name. He is your praise; he is your God, who performed for you those great and awesome wonders you saw with your own eyes." The fear of God is the basis for our walking in His ways, serving Him, and, yes, loving Him.

Some redefine the fear of God for believers to "respecting" Him. While respect is definitely included in the concept of fearing God, there is more to it than that. A biblical fear of God includes understanding how much God hates sin, and the fear of His judgment on sin, even on the life of the believer.

Hebrews 12:5-11 describes God's discipline of the believer. While it is done in love (Hebrews 12:6), it is still a fearful thing. As children, the fear of discipline from our parents no doubt prevented some evil actions. The same should be true in our relationship with God. We should fear His discipline, and therefore seek to live our lives in such a way that pleases Him.

Believers are not to be afraid of God. We have no reason to be frightened of Him. We have His promise that nothing can separate us from His love (Romans 8:38-39). We have His promise that He will never leave us or forsake us (Hebrews 13:5). Fearing God means having such a reverence for Him that it has a great impact on the way we live our lives. The fear of God is respecting Him, obeying Him, submitting to His discipline, and worshipping Him in awe.

> "And he has given him authority to judge everyone because he is the Son of Man."
>
> (John 5:27)

Since no man is excluded from calling upon God the gate of salvation is open to all. There is nothing else to hinder us from entering, but our own unbelief.
~ John Calvin

Spiritual Blindness

'Jesus heard that they had thrown him out, and when He found him, He said, "Do you believe in the Son of Man?" "Who is He, sir?" the man asked. "Tell me so that I may believe in him." Jesus said, "You have now seen Him; in fact, He is the one speaking with you." Then the man said, "Lord, I believe," and he worshiped him. Jesus said, "For judgment I have come into this world, so that the blind will see and those who see will become blind." Some Pharisees who were with him heard him say this and asked, "What? Are we blind too?" Jesus said, "If you were blind, you would not be guilty of sin; but now that you claim you can see, your guilt remains."' (John 9:35-14)

Think about it, how many people are walking around this planet with visual eyesight, yet most are spiritually blind. When a person's eyes are truly open to the spiritual realm, we see the subtle warfare taking place hourly over every living soul. Those who 'hide' under the shadow of the Almighty are those who put their faith in God through Christ and experience a great deal of protection, but are not immune from the spiritual warfare, nonetheless. It is the Lord who fights their battles for them.

Likewise, there are many who put their faith in false gods, and those who listen to the loudest voice in their head, thinking they are being contacted by angels, ETs, aliens, ascended masters or their deceased loved ones, aka 'spirit guides'. These people also have a great degree of spiritual blindness, even those who are supposedly clairvoyant and can see auras and outlines of spirits. These people may have a certain degree of spiritual sight but many cannot tell one spirit from another, or which one is from the light of God, and which are the ones masquerading as light. This requires discernment as well. With that said, there are many who are gifted psychically, who can sense, see and hear the spirit realms, but are seduced by the fallen angels who masquerade as angels of light, deceased loved ones, ascended masters and angels.

Spiritual Deafness and Spiritual Muteness

There is a spirit called, 'the Spirit of Unbelief and the Deaf and Dumb Spirit.' Spiritually Satan blinds people's eyes, ears, and minds to the things of God. "He (Satan) has blinded their eyes and deadened their hearts, so they can neither see with their eyes, nor understand with their hearts, nor turn--and I would heal them." (John 12:40)

This spirit affects people in two ways, spiritually and physically. Satan uses this against us by making people blind and deaf and dumb spiritually. That means, that people do not have ears to hear, and become deaf in the spirit to the spirit of truth and discernment, which comes from the Holy Spirit. Instead, Satan gives you his spirit, which are demons to tell you lies in your ear, to make you feel good, and think you

Chapter Eleven: Is Hell For Real?

are hearing from spirit, when in fact you are being misled. You may want to hear, you may be hungry for the voice of God, but this spirit causes deafness to God's voice, and instead gives you another voice, a misleading voice to keep you temporarily happy.

The dumb spirit, or the spirit of muteness, interferes with our ability to understand, so that we cannot receive the spirit of wisdom and revelation. There are people who may read the Bible daily, yet there is a block over their mind, so no matter how much they read, they forget, and no matter how much they study, they still don't understand the true meaning. The deaf and dumb spirit makes you 'mute' spiritually. It renders one powerless. Inner conviction is replaced with tradition, theology, religion, and being taken over by *religious spirits*, as a form of godliness that denies the power of God. "Having a form of godliness, but denying the power thereof: from such turn away." (2 Timothy 3:5)

Physically speaking, the deaf and dumb spirit causes complete or partial deafness, ringing in the ears, (tinnitus), muteness, attention deficit disorder, dyslexia, mental illness, insanity, problems focusing, reading problems, and other learning disabilities. How many children today are misdiagnosed with attention deficit disorder, which comes from this spirit that is passed down through the family, due to the spirit of unbelief?

The spirit of unbelief is the root cause of the spirit of the deaf and dumb spirit. Jesus says three times in the scriptures when the disciples asked him why they couldn't cast out a demon from a boy. Matthew 17:17" "O unbelieving and perverse generation," Jesus replied, "how long shall I stay with you? How long shall I put up with you? Bring the boy here to me." Their unbelief was blocking them from kicking out the demon spirit in the boy. Not only their unbelief, but the unbelief of their generation, as it was a generational sin and generational curse of unbelief, on which the spirit of the deaf and dumb spirit piggy backs. If someone does not have faith, then Satan has the legal right to make them spiritually deaf, blind and mute.

The word 'generation' relates to the time, the age, the family, the city and the nation of that time.

Then, "Jesus rebuked the demon, and it came out of the boy, and he was healed from that moment. Then the disciples came to Jesus in private and asked, "Why couldn't we drive it out?" He replied, "Because you have so little faith. I tell you the truth, if you have faith as small as a mustard seed, you can say to this mountain, 'Move from here to there' and it will move. Nothing will be impossible for you." (Matthew 17:18-20)

In Mark 6, Jesus returns back to his hometown of Nazareth, he could not do any mighty works there because of their unbelief. The spirit of unbelief blocks miracles from happening. Jesus said to them, "Only in his hometown, among his relatives and in his own house is a prophet without honor." He could not do any miracles there, except lay his hands on a few sick people and heal them. And he was amazed at their lack of faith." (Mark 6:4-6)

In Mark 9:21, there was the desperate cry of a father to Jesus to "help his son, if you can." Then Jesus said to him, "It's not a matter of if I can, it's a matter if you can believe." But the father was so discouraged and beaten up by the spirit of unbelief, which had made his son deaf, dumb and mute, he wasn't able to believe in God. Out of desperation, the father cried out to Jesus and said, "Lord, I believe, help me overcome my unbelief!" Then Jesus cast out the deaf and dumb spirit from his son and the boy was healed.

It was the father's unbelief that prevented the disciples from casting the demon out, not the unbelief of the disciples. This is based on the scripture law, that the sins of the father are passed on to the third and fourth generation to those that do not believe. (Exodus 20:5) This was not just the father's sin of unbelief, but the 'generational' sin of unbelief that needed to be broken.

How many of us have parents or grandparents that scoff and mock our belief, and cause us to have blocks in the healing of our lives? How many of us are tempted into unbelief because we go for healings and the healing is not immediate? The generational sin and curse of unbelief must first be broken before we can experience complete liberation from this deaf and dumb spirit and have our spiritual ears, eye and mind opened to hear God's voice.

In my chapter on the Holy Spirit in Book Two, I mention the unforgiveable sin, which is blaspheming the Holy Spirit. "Blasphemy or sin against the Holy Ghost includes any willful, malicious, and slanderous word spoken against the person and work of the Holy Spirit, or ascribing the work of the Spirit to Satan." (Matthew 12:31-32). The reason it is the unforgiveable sin is because it is the willful rejection of Light and a deliberate insult to the last stronghold of God. He wants to bring about the cure and remission of sins and curses in this cursed world. When people do away with the only agent of God, there is no one to plead their case before God, and their souls are lost. However, one may blaspheme and insult the Spirit in ignorance and still be forgiven. "Even though I was once a blasphemer and a persecutor and a violent man, I was shown mercy because I acted in ignorance and unbelief." (1 Timothy 1:13) This means that even though this sin may be from ancestors, passed down through generations, doesn't mean we are a lost cause. Because of ignorance and unbelief, there is mercy. However, the generational sin and curse must first be broken in order for the deaf and dumb spirit to be released and healing to be restored. I focus on how to do this in Book Four: *Covenants*.

Remember, if demons are cast out, they can only be kicked out through Christ and his Holy Spirit. Satan cannot drive out demons, as a kingdom divided against itself cannot stand. Jesus said,

Chapter Eleven: Is Hell For Real?

"But if I drive out demons by the Spirit of God, then the kingdom of God has come upon you."

(Matthew 12:28)

The Unbelief of the Jews

"Then came the Feast of Dedication at Jerusalem. It was winter, and Jesus was in the temple area walking in Solomon's Colonnade. The Jews gathered around him, saying, "How long will you keep us in suspense? If you are the Christ, tell us plainly." Jesus answered, "I did tell you, but you do not believe. The miracles I do in my Father's name speak for me, but you do not believe because you are not my sheep. My sheep listen to my voice; I know them, and they follow me. I give them eternal life, and they shall never perish; no one can snatch them out of my hand. My Father, who has given them to me, is greater than all; no one can snatch them out of my Father's hand. I and the Father are one." Again, the Jews picked up stones to stone him, but Jesus said to them, "I have shown you many great miracles from the Father. For which of these do you stone me?" "We are not stoning you for any of these," replied the Jews, "but for blasphemy, because you, a mere man, claim to be God." Jesus answered them, "Is it not written in your Law, 'I have said you are gods'? If he called them 'gods,' to whom the word of God came—and the Scripture cannot be broken—what about the one whom the Father set apart as his very own and sent into the world? Why then do you accuse me of blasphemy because I said, 'I am God's Son'? Do not believe me unless I do what my Father does. But if I do it, even though you do not believe me, believe the miracles, that you may know and understand that the Father is in me, and I in the Father." Again, they tried to seize him, but he escaped their grasp."

(John 10:22-39)

The Reward for the Faithful

"My sheep listen to my voice; I know them, and they follow me. <u>I give them eternal life, and they shall never perish; no one can snatch them out of my hand</u>. My Father, who has given them to me, is greater than all; no one can snatch them out of my Father's hand. I and the Father are one."

(John 27:30)

Those who are faithful, who listen to the voice of God's Holy Spirit, through Christ will inherit the eternal life through the Kingdom of God. (see, Keys of the Kingdom)

"Life is a long lesson in humility." ~ James M. Barrie

NOTES AND REFERENCES:

1. Taylor Marshall, *Why Did Christ Descend Into Hell?* 2012. http://taylormarshall.com/2012/01/why-did-christ-descend-into-hell.html
2. Ella LeBain, *Who's Who in The Cosmic Zoo? Book One, A Spiritual Guide to ETs, Aliens, Gods & Angels, Third Edition,* Chapter Three: *The Clash of Two Kingdoms: The Cosmic Conflict,* subsection: *From Adam's Failure to the Second Adam's Victory,* p. 71-73.
3. Dante Aligheri. *Dante's Inferno,* Parts 1-3 epic 14th Century Poem *Divine Comedy, Purgatorio* and *Paradiso.* 1320.
4. Ella LeBain, *Who's Who in The Cosmic Zoo? Book One, A Spiritual Guide to ETs, Aliens, Gods & Angels, Third Edition,* Chapter Five: *Aghartians,* p. 98-104.
5. Ella LeBain, *Who Is God? Book Two of Who's Who in The Cosmic Zoo? A Guide to ETs, Aliens, Gods & Angels,* Skypath Books, 2015. Chapter Two: *Ancient Technology and Biblical Astronauts,* p. 21-46
6. Ibid.
7. Ibid.
8. Ibid.
9. Howard Storm, *My Descent into Death: A Second Chance At Life,* Harmony; First U.S. Edition (February 15, 2005).
10. Bill Wiese, *23 Minutes in Hell One Man's Story About What He Saw, Heard, and Felt in that Place of Torment,* Charisma House; 1st edition, January 30, 2006
11. Ella LeBain, *Who's Who in The Cosmic Zoo? Book One, A Spiritual Guide to ETs, Aliens, Gods & Angels, Third Edition,* Chapter Five: Draconian/Reptilians, p.154-177.

CHAPTER TWELVE

THE WORLD OF THE WONDROUS – THE KINGDOM OF GOD

> "And he said to them, to you it is given to know the mystery of the kingdom of God: but to them that are without, all these things are done in parables."
> (MARK 4:11)

P.D. Ouspensky[1], in his book, *Tertium Organum*, calls the 5th dimensional world, the "World of the Wondrous." He figured out mathematically, that there is a realm where all conditions are perfect. Jesus Christ called it the Kingdom of God. He said, "Seek ye first the Kingdom of God, and all things shall be added unto you." He also said, "The Kingdom of God is within you." This means it can only be reached through a state of consciousness. Jesus Christ said, to enter the Kingdom, we must become as a little child. Children are continually in a state of joy and wonder, and have faith.

New Agers believe in the 5th dimension, a place of harmony, understanding, brotherhood, sisterhood, good will towards all men, the Age of Aquarius. In the 1960s there was a music group called the '5th Dimension' and they wrote the song, 'The Age of Aquarius.' The 5th Dimension is the Kingdom of God, which happens during the Age of Aquarius. But how can anyone be allowed into the Kingdom of God if they rebel or hate the King? Jesus Christ, who has been given all *authority* over the heavens and the Earth and *inside* the Earth, is the Lord of the Kingdom of God. He will set up His Kingdom on Earth for one thousand years of peace. My sense is that if people really desire the Kingdom, the World of the Wondrous, the 5th Dimension, then they must accept Jesus Christ and not follow after the doctrine of demons.

> "Now the Holy Spirit expressly says that in the last days some will depart from the faith by giving heed to deceitful spirits and doctrines of demons, through the pretension of liars whose consciences are seared."
>
> (1 Timothy 4:1)

Many are already following the doctrines of demons, of fallen angels, and aliens, by believing in their lies, their manipulations of the truth of our history, of who and what they really are, and their deceptions. People are persuaded and hypnotised, put under a spell if you will, by falsely believing that because they are given channelled information which comes from a supposed angel, alien or ET, it must be true, real and relevant. Not so! How many people have been given information from channels which has turned out to be wrong? Too many!

The entities, fallen angels, demons, aliens, deliberately mislead people. Take the case of Sheldon Niddle[2], who channelled the book, *You are Becoming a Galactic Human*. He was given specific information which he channelled to his followers, to wait on the beaches of Hawaii in the early 1990s. He told them that they were going to be taken up by aliens in their spaceships and ascend to heaven! Many listened to him, hung out on the beach and waited and waited and waited and no one ever came. So, one needs to ask, who was he channelling? If these demons/aliens/fallen angels have no credibility, then why listen or believe anything else they have to say?

> "A large part of the available UFO literature is closely linked with mysticism and the metaphysical. It deals with subjects like mental telepathy, automatic writing and invisible entities as well as phenomena like poltergeist [ghost] manifestation and 'possession.' Many of the UFO reports now being published in the popular press recount alleged incidents that are strikingly similar to demonic possession and psychic phenomena."
> ~ Lynn E. Catoe, *UFOs and Related Subjects*:
> USGPO, 1969; prepared under AFOSR Project Order
> 67-0002 and 68-0003

I believe, based on past experience and research, that much of the information received through so-called "trance channels" should be discarded for several reasons:

1. Such information is often self-contradictory.
2. Channeled revelations often contradict "revelations" received through other "channels".
3. There are supernatural beings inhabiting the aerial realm whose very purpose and "assignment" is to counterfeit "divine" revelation in order to spread propaganda, confusion or mislead the seeker from the truth. This is often, accomplished by offering the seeker a substantial amount of "truth" in order to uphold one strategic lie.
4. Channeled information in most cases cannot be followed up by physical documentation or evidence.

Chapter Twelve: The World of the Wondrous

5. There are many indications that non-human beings, both supernatural and reptilian, are utilizing occult channels in order to carry out propaganda warfare against those who possess the truth. There is also much evidence that these alien beings have utilized witchcraft and occult movements (i.e. the serpent cults) since the earliest times in order to further their reptilian cause.

"But the UFO phenomenon simply does not behave like extraterrestrial visitors. It actually molds itself in order to fit a given culture."
- John Ankerberg, *The Facts on UFOs and Other Supernatural Phenomena*, p. 10

"We are part of a symbiotic relationship with something which disguises itself as an extra-terrestrial invasion so as not to alarm us." -Terrence McKenna [from a lecture]

"There seems to be no evidence yet that any of these craft or beings originate from outer space."
-Gordon Creighton, *Official 1992 Flying Saucer Review Policy Statement*

DISCERNMENT IS THE WAY

How can anyone have discernment if they are not investigating both sides? You have to have light to discern the darkness. And often it just takes a small crack of light to illuminate a dark room. Belief in Jesus Christ affords us His Holy Spirit to dwell within us. The Holy Spirit is known as the Mighty Counsellor, the Great Comforter. The Mind of Christ. His Spirit is our discernment or our 'litmus paper' to be able to tell *who is who* in the spirit world. Light and darkness cannot co-exist together.

Betrayal happens when one's desire to believe that something or someone is true is shattered by the truth that they were not who you thought they were. Most people living today can recall that experience. We've all at one time been bamboozled, have bought the 'line,' took the bait, and got hooked into buying into something that later turns out to be a false path. Too many times the desire to believe that someone or something really is what you want them to be, can totally obfuscate what is true and real.

"Do not let anyone who delights in false humility and *the worship of angels* disqualify you for the prize. Such a person goes into great detail about what he has seen and his unspiritual mind puffs him up with idle notions. He has lost connection with the Head, from whom the whole body, supported and held together by its ligaments and sinews, grows as God causes it to grow."
(Colossians 2:18-19)

The Supernatural Battle

As I've been saying throughout this book series, every human being that lives on the surface of planet Earth at this time is involved in an ancient battle over our minds, our bodies and our very souls. As Ephesians 6:12 says, we war not against flesh and blood, but against powers, principalities and world rulers of this present darkness, spiritual wickedness in heavenly places. These powers and principalities are the aliens. The spiritual wickedness in heavenly places comes from Lucifer or Satan's rebellion against the Creator Father God, along with the one third of heaven's angels and extraterrestrials that followed in his rebellion, have corrupted the heavens. However, they only have access to the first and second heavens, the upper heavens being off limits to them. See, Book Five: *The Heavens* for further elucidation. This is why the people of earth are seeing UFOs, which are for the most part the vehicles that belong to Lucifer's Satanic demonic army. This is also why it says in the book of Revelation that the Creator God plans to recreate the heavens and the earth.

> "Behold, I will create new heavens and a new earth. The former things will not be remembered, nor will they come to mind."
>
> (Isaiah 65:17)

> "Nevertheless we, according to his promise, look for new heavens and a new earth, wherein dwells righteousness."
>
> (2 Peter 3:13)

The heavens have been corrupted and put under a curse. There are other planets like ours that have been taken over by the cosmic rebellion. This is why I am asserting throughout this book that the Cosmic Christ, who is Yeshua, Jesus Christ, is the One that will end it. However, as all things in both the heavens and the earth follow divine order, everything happens in order as well. Before the Creator God recreates the heavens and the earth, and essentially wipes out the memory of all cosmic evil, there will first be a one-thousand-year reign of the Kingdom of God on earth. This is why Jesus instructed everyone to pray in the Lord's Prayer, 'Thy Kingdom Come, they will be done on earth as it is in heaven,' as eventually this will happen. God's Kingdom will be established and 'grounded' on the earth. It is what many call the Golden Age, the Age of Aquarius, a time of peace, brotherhood, sisterhood, harmony, and good will towards all humankind. And the King of that Kingdom is Jesus Christ, Yeshua, Emmanuel.

The end of this timeline is the battle of Armageddon, which the Bible tells us will culminate at the second coming of Jesus Christ in all His glory with the Hosts of Heaven, the Celestial Army of Starships and faithful extraterrestrials. His presence

Chapter Twelve: The World of the Wondrous

will end the battle of Armageddon, which takes place on an ancient battlefield just outside of Jerusalem, near the Valley of Jezreel. 'Har Megiddo' in Hebrew means, 'mount of blood' or 'mount of the field of blood.' At this ancient vortex, He will return from heaven and win the battle with a 'Word.' No one knows what that 'word' will be, but the Bible refers to the word of God as the sword of the spirit, cutting through to the core.

> "For the word of God is alive and powerful. It is sharper than the sharpest two-edged sword, cutting between soul and spirit, between joint and marrow. It exposes our innermost thoughts and attitudes of the heart."
> (Hebrews 4:12)

Whatever this 'Word' will be, will end the battle by causing all those aligned with Lucifer/Satan's antichrist figure to die and fill the field with blood, this may also extend to the whole planet because the bible promises that after Lucifer/Satan's kingdom is defeated, Jesus Christ sets up His Kingdom on Earth and takes over the throne of David. The New Jerusalem also called, "The Holy City" is actually a huge mothership that now exists in the upper heavens, and the bible tells us that this new city will literally come down out of the heavens and be grounded on the earth. How is this possible? Obviously, anything is possible with the Lord's technology.

> "Him that overcomes will I make a pillar in the temple of my God, and <u>he shall go no more out</u>: and I will write on him the name of my God, and the name of the city of my God, which is new Jerusalem, <u>which comes down out of heaven from my God</u>: and I will write on him my new name."
> (Revelation 3:12)

> "I saw the Holy City, the new Jerusalem, <u>coming down out of heaven from God</u>, prepared as a bride beautifully dressed for her husband."
> (Revelation 21:2)

This scripture also tells us that that any person who overcomes this world, will 'go out no more.' This relates to reincarnation, the end of it, because those whose names are written in the Lamb's book of life will be part of His Kingdom on earth. This will be the beginning of eternity. However, after the millennial reign is completed, Revelation tells us that the Lord allows Satan out of the Abyss where he has been bound for the thousand years, out to tempt the nations of the planet one more time. Eternity begins by his being expelled back to the Lake of Fire forever.

> "And he carried me away in the Spirit to a mountain great and high, and showed me the Holy City, Jerusalem, coming down out of heaven from God. It shone with the glory of God, and its brilliance was like that of a very precious jewel, like a jasper, clear as crystal. It had a great, high wall with twelve gates, and with twelve angels at the gates. On the gates were written the names of the twelve tribes of Israel. There were three gates on the east, three on the north, three on the south and three on the west. The wall of the city had twelve foundations, and on them were the names of the twelve apostles of the Lamb."
>
> (Revelation 21:10-14)

The new Jerusalem will be the shining city that will represent cosmic harmony for a thousand years. This city will not only be holy but will be blessed by the Lord's technology as a centerpiece of the universe. It will attract the faithful extraterrestrials (angels) from all over the universe. It is from the seat of this throne in Jerusalem that Christ will rule over all the kingdoms and nations of the earth, who will all be representatives of their cosmic ancestors. The reason for all the different races on earth will finally make sense, as they will be unified in harmony. However, because of the variety of nations on earth and the ease of space travel this millennium enjoys, the Lord allows Satan to deceive the nations last time, just to put them through their final test in their faithfulness to Him. He must know if they had learned the lessons from the past millennia, which is where we are right now.

Satan's Doom

Lucifer/Satan's days are numbered. At the end of this timeline, at the time of the end of the battle of Armageddon, when Christ returns with his massive fleet of starships from all the corners of the universe, He will end the battle with His breath and a Word.

[Brackets and emphasis mine]

> "But with righteousness He will judge the poor, and decide with fairness for the afflicted of the earth; And <u>He will strike the earth with the rod of His mouth</u>, [The Word of God is the Sword of the Spirit] and <u>with the breath of His Lips He will slay the wicked</u>."
>
> (Isaiah 11:4)

> "And I saw heaven opened, and behold, a white horse, and He who sat on it is called Faithful and True, and in righteousness <u>He judges and wages war</u>."
>
> (Revelation 19:11)

Chapter Twelve: The World of the Wondrous

"He is clothed with a robe dipped in blood, and <u>His name is called The Word of God</u>."

[The only one clothed with a robe dipped in blood is Jesus Christ whose blood was shed for the redemption of the sins of humankind.]

(Revelation 19:13)

Then Satan, the Beast and the Antichrist, the Trinity of Hell, defeated by Christ will be sent into the bottomless pit known as the 'Abyss' which is deep inside the Earth.

"Then I saw an angel coming down from heaven, holding the key of the abyss and a great chain in his hand. And he laid hold of the dragon, the serpent of old, who is the devil and Satan, and bound him for a thousand years; He threw him into the Abyss, and locked it and sealed it over him, to keep him from deceiving the nations anymore."

(Revelation 20:1-4)

"When the thousand years are over, Satan will be released from his prison and will go out to deceive the nations in the four corners of the earth—Gog and Magog—to gather them for battle. In number, they are like the sand on the seashore. They marched across the breadth of the earth and surrounded the camp of God's people, the city he loves. But fire came down from heaven and devoured them. And the devil, who deceived them, was thrown into the lake of burning sulfur, where the beast and the false prophet had been thrown. They will be tormented day and night forever and ever."

(Revelation 20:7-10)

"Then I heard a loud voice in heaven say, "Now have come the salvation and the power and the kingdom of our God, and the authority of his Christ. For the accuser of our brothers, who accuses them before our God day and night, has been hurled down. They overcame him by the blood of the lamb and by the word of their testimony and they did not love their lives so much as to shrink from death."

(Revelation 12:10-12)

"And the devil, who deceived them, was thrown into the lake of burning sulfur, where the beast and the false prophet had been thrown. They will be tormented day and night forever and ever...

(Revelation 21:10)

"Then death and Hades were thrown into the lake of fire. The lake of fire is the second death. If anyone's name was not found written in the book of life, he was thrown into the lake of fire."

(Revelation 21:14-15)

NOTES AND REFERENCES:

1. P.D. Ouspensky, *Tertium Organum, The Third Canon of Thought, A Key to the Enigmas of the World*, 2nd American Edition, Manas Press, St. Petersburg, Russia, 1920
2. Virginia Essene, Sheldon Niddle, *You are Becoming a Galactic Human*, Spiritual Education Endeavors; 1st edition (April 1994).

CHAPTER THIRTEEN
The Coming Kingdom

So we fix our eyes not on what is seen, but on what is unseen.
For what is seen is temporary, but what is unseen is eternal.
(2 Corinthians 4:18)

Jesus said, "My Kingdom is not of this world."
(John 18:36)

When Jesus walked the earth, He talked more about the Kingdom of God than anything else. He said, 'The Kingdom of Go' is within you,' (Luke 17:21) and 'seek ye first the Kingdom of God, and all things will be added unto you.' (Matthew 6:33) He assured us that in order to find our heart's desire, we must first find the Kingdom of God. He also instructed all of us to pray, 'Thy Kingdom Come, thy will be done on earth as it is in heaven.' (Matthew 6:10) This implies that the Kingdom of God has not yet arrived on earth.

We know from multiple promises and covenants within the scriptures that heaven will be coming to us on earth at the end of our present time. After the final battle of unfinished business is won, the Lord returns, having defeated the fallen angels and their satanic hierarchy once and for all. Scripture tells us that this final cosmic battle will be fought and won by the King of Heaven with His multitude of faithful extra-terrestrial angels, who we are told will be the final 'harvesters' of souls at the end of this age.

Where is the Kingdom of God located? Who is its King? Do others share in ruling with the King? If so, how many? Let's explore this phenomenon.

A kingdom is a government that is centered on a king. The Kingdom of God is a special government. It is set up in heaven and will rule over this earth. It will sanctify, or make holy, God's name. It will cause God's will to be done on earth as it is done in heaven (Matthew 6:9, 10).

There is a visible and invisible Kingdom of God. There are 308 scriptures on the Kingdom of God or the Kingdom of Heaven in the Bible. The Kingdom of God was the central theme in Jesus' teachings.

The visible Kingdom relates to the material or external Kingdom. The invisible Kingdom relates to the spiritual or internal Kingdom. The External Universal Kingdom which encompasses all creation is ruled by the Lord from the Heavens.

"The earth is the Lord's and everything in it, the world, and all who live in it."
(Psalm 24:1)

"The Lord has established His throne in heaven and His Kingdom rules over all."
(Psalm 103:19)

The Lord rules the Internal Personal Kingdom by revelation and through recreation or transformation, through natural revelation of creation and through spiritual revelation. This is based on the natural law of the universe that if you create something, you own it.

Our world has been in a state of rebellion towards the Creator Lord, due to Lucifer and all the fallen extraterrestrial angels that follow him. As a result, our world has been cursed, and is winding down through disintegration, heading for destruction. Planet Earth and all of its inhabitants are on this downhill slippery slope. This is why we need salvation.

The invisible Kingdom is here now, and it's growing and expanding through every person who accepts the King of the Kingdom and His gift of salvation.

What is the Kingdom of God?

The Kingdom of God (also referred to as "the Kingdom of Heaven," "the Kingdom of Christ," "the Kingdom of the Lord," and "the Kingdom,") corroborates the teachings of the entire Bible. The Scriptures reveal God being described by a number of metaphors, but the primary image which Biblical writers used for God was that of a "Divine King" (1 Samuel 8:7).

The main difference between the Kingdoms is that the Kingdom of God is a government, a benevolent dictatorship, ruled by a loving King, while the Kingdom of Heaven is the actual place governed by the Kingdom of God. The Kingdom of God governs through the Office of Christ, where Christ is the Lord of a large hierarchy of angels and extraterrestrials who are messengers and warriors, who make up the 'hosts of heaven'.

Alongside the basic conviction that God is the supreme King is the belief that He reigns over creation as His Kingdom (Psalms 47:1-9; 83:18; Daniel 4:25-26; 5:21). In this general sense, God has always been the sovereign reigning King who rules in

Chapter Thirteen: The Coming Kingdom

heaven over all things (Psalms 113:5; Matthew 5:34; Ephesians 1:20; Colossians 1:16; Hebrews 12:2; Revelations 7:15). The Kingdom of God is the rule of an eternal sovereign God over all creatures and things (Psalm 103:19; Daniel 4:3). The Kingdom of God is also the designation for the sphere of salvation entered into at the new birth (John 3:5-7), and is synonymous with the 'Kingdom of Heaven.'

When Jesus said, "the Kingdom of God is within you", He was referring to the power of Christ living and dwelling within man. There are several scriptures that reveal this:

> "Heal the sick that are there, and tell the people, <u>'The kingdom of God is near you!'</u>"
>
> (Luke 10:9)

> "But if it is by the finger of God that I cast out demons, then <u>the kingdom of God has come upon you</u>."
>
> (Luke 11:20)

> "But if I drive out demons by the Spirit of God, then <u>the kingdom of God has come upon you</u>."
>
> (Matthew 12:28)

> "Neither shall they say, see here! or, see there! for, behold, <u>the kingdom of God is within you</u>."
>
> (Luke 17:21)

> "Jesus told them, "<u>The secret of the kingdom of God has been given to you.</u> But to those on the outside everything is said in parables; so that, "'they may be ever seeing but never perceiving, and ever hearing but never understanding; otherwise they might turn and be forgiven!'"
>
> (Mark 4:11, 12)

All of these scriptures prove that the kingdom of God is already here, because when good triumphs over evil, when righteousness overcomes wrongs, when the power of the living indwelling God works through us, by forgiving sins, healing the sick, kicking out demons and setting the captives free, the kingdom of God is present here on earth.

> "Jesus answered, "I tell you the truth, <u>no one can enter the kingdom of God unless he is born of water and the Spirit</u>. Flesh gives birth to flesh, but <u>the

<u>Spirit gives birth to spirit</u>. You should not be surprised at my saying, 'You must be born again.'"

(John 3:5-7)

These are probably one of the most cryptic of all of the messages of Christ. When someone comes to Christ for salvation, they first come with faith, then with repentance. They come out of the kingdom of darkness and are translated into the Kingdom of Christ, or Light of God. This process is known as being 'born again', which is what Jesus was talking about, being born of the spirit.

Kingdom History

The Scriptures reveal that the Lord determined to accomplish the establishment of His Kingdom of Heaven on Earth through a lengthy historical process. Perhaps this process may have something to do with humans being allowed the opportunity to discover who the King is and what He is all about, in contrast to the many earthly kingdoms that have come and gone, many of which were empowered by the kingdom of darkness.

The Scriptures tell us that Satan is the god of this world (2 Corinthians 4:4), that he has the power to give men kingdoms on earth, and empower their reign. (Luke 4:5,6) We know from history that most of these kingdoms have fallen, most likely because the kings sold their souls to the god of this world, whose kingdom and power are temporary, and not eternal. We see with our own eyes that these men did not follow the Creator God. We know that these kingdoms have incorporated all kinds of abuse and cruelty, as spiritual rebellion always results in evil dictatorships. We know through American history that the United States of America was formed to break away from the restrictions of an imperialistic monarchy rule.

We are given the grace of the timeline of history to examine the contrast. As the Kingdom of God is established within us as the Internal Kingdom, we are given the grace to get to know how loving is the King of the Kingdom of God, how patient, how selfless, how inclusive, how just and how righteous He is, and that He rules through His saving grace, his power of deliverance from oppression, depression and bondages from the kingdom of darkness, through His healing love.

We know this King is a Celestial Hero, One who has overcome this world, who has conquered death and Hades Himself, and forged that path for humanity, for all those who believe on Him. This is a King that does not demand service or worship, but opens the gate of healing and deliverance to all those who choose Him and choose to repent from the kingdom of darkness. It is through His gifts of grace, salvation and deliverance that we choose to serve Him <u>willingly</u>, that it is out of our love and gratitude for

Chapter Thirteen: The Coming Kingdom

this healing King that we choose to serve His Kingdom. In return, He adopts us as His own sons and daughters, and as all adoptions go, it is permanent, without abandonment, because He chooses us as His own. With that He promises to protect His own under the shadow of His wings. He promises to all those who overcome the kingdom of darkness through His power that He will make us pillars in His Kingdom.

> "Him that overcomes will I make a pillar in the temple of my God, and he shall no more ho out: and I will write on him the name of my God, and the name of the city of my God, which is the new Jerusalem, <u>which comes down out of heaven</u> from my God: and I will write on him my new name."
> (Revelation 3:12)

The first step in establishing the Kingdom of God on earth was the choice of Abraham and his descendants as God's special people (Exodus 3:6-7; 6:2-8). The Kingdom of God was primarily limited to the people and land of Israel. The Lord asserted His kingship on earth when He delivered Israel from the Egyptian empire and brought her to the Promised Land (Exodus 15). Under Kings David and Solomon, Israel itself became a defined territory, with the sons of David sitting on the throne of God as His vice-regents (1 Chronicles 29:23; 2 Chronicles 6), and with God's royal footstool in the temple (1 Chronicles 28:2). However, the kingdom of Israel collapsed due to the idolatry practiced by its people. The Lord could no longer protect them because they had turned away from Him and turned towards other gods. The sin of disobedience to the Lord caused them to be overtaken by their enemies and sent into exile. Old Testament Israel was established as a stage from which the Kingdom of God would eventually extend to all peoples and lands of the earth (Genesis 17:17-18; 18:18; Romans 4:13-17).

The flagrant rebellion of Israel and Judah hurled the Kingdom of God into crisis. Yet, the Old Testament announced that after the exile, the Lord would remove the wicked from the earth, and establish His reign without opposition over the entire earth (Malachi 4). At that time, full obedience to God would spread to the ends of the earth, reaching both Jews and Gentiles (1 Chronicles 16:23-36; Isaiah 52:7-15; Psalms 67, 97).

The New Testament teaches that this final worldwide stage of the Kingdom of God began with the incarnation of Christ. He and John the Baptist announced the good news that the Kingdom was at hand (Matthew 3:2; 4:17; Mark 1:15). But contrary to common Jewish expectations, as Jesus and His apostles explained, the worldwide reign of God on earth would not come immediately in all of its fullness. Instead, Jesus, being a genetic descendant of King David, inaugurated this final stage of the Kingdom into His earthly ministry (Matthew 2:2; 4:23; 9:35; 27:11; Mark 15:2; Luke 16:16; 23:3; John 18:37).

"You are a king, then!" said Pilate. Jesus answered, "You are right in saying I am a king. In fact, for this reason I was born, and for this I came into the world, to testify to the truth. Everyone on the side of truth listens to me."

(John 18:37)

The inauguration of His Kingdom continues today in throughout the world:

"And this gospel of the kingdom will be preached in the whole world as a testimony to all nations, <u>and then the end will come</u>."

(Matthew 24:14)

Jesus taught that many will fall away from the faith, lawlessness will be increased and that the love of many will grow cold at the time when world evangelization is completed (Matthew 24:10-14). Further scripture supports this increasing apostasy and wickedness (2 Thessalonians 2:3; 1 Timothy 4:1; 2 Timothy 4:3; 2 Peter 3:3). Jesus needed no one to bear witness about the fallen nature of man, for He Himself knew what humans were made of, and how we have been compromised. (John 2:25). In my opinion, this is the basis for grace, and why there is a Divine Plan of Salvation in place for humans, but not necessarily for rebellious gods and fallen angels, who as Jude 1:6 says, when they rebelled, they left their first estate.

"For the kingdom of God is not a matter of eating and drinking, but of righteousness, peace and joy in the Holy Spirit,"

(Romans 14:17)

"For the kingdom of God is not a matter of talk but of power."

(1 Corinthians 4:20)

This power will reach its ultimate peak when Christ returns in glory. When that day finally comes, the will of God will be done throughout the earth just as it is done in heaven. As I point out in my chapter *Ascension or Rapture?* one of the major signs of His return will be when Matthew 24:14 and Luke 17:31-34 are fulfilled. This tells us that the Rapture will happen on a 2:1 ratio, meaning that one out of every two people on the earth will be believers in the Kingdom of God. Only the Lord knows who they really are. As I've pointed out, there are many nations around the world where belief in Christ is forbidden, where it is illegal to even own a Bible. In spite of these restrictions, are people coming to the Christ through the power of the Holy Spirit, while experiencing many miracles that are taking place through Him.

Chapter Thirteen: The Coming Kingdom

Author Jim Rutz[1] wrote in his 2005 groundbreaking book, *Megashift*, that Christianity is the fastest growing faith on planet earth today, and coined a new phrase to define the fastest growing segment of the population. He calls them "core Apostolics", or "the new saints who are at the heart of the mushrooming Kingdom of God." Rutz makes the point that Christianity is overlooked as the fastest-growing faith in the world because most surveys look at the traditional Protestant denominations and the Roman Catholic Church while ignoring Christian believers who have no part of either, such as those tucked away in China, Korea, Indonesia, Pakistan, and other places. The point is, when those numbers reach the rate that the Lord is satisfied is a 2:1 ratio, then the end will come. First the Rapture will initiate the seven-year tribulation, and then the Lord will return in all His glory with His translated saints, and two thirds of the extraterrestrial angels in the heavens to witness the final battle against the kingdom of darkness. Then His Kingdom will be established on Earth. (Revelation 3:12; Revelation 21:2)

> "I declare to you, brothers, that flesh and blood cannot inherit the kingdom of God, nor does the perishable inherit the imperishable. Listen, I tell you a mystery: We will not all sleep, but we will all be changed--in a flash, in the twinkling of an eye, at the last trumpet. For the trumpet will sound, the dead will be raised imperishable, and we will be changed. For the perishable must clothe itself with the imperishable, and the mortal with immortality. When the perishable has been clothed with the imperishable, and the mortal with immortality, then the saying that is written will come true: "Death has been swallowed up in victory."
>
> (1 Corinthians 15:50-54)

The Keys of the Kingdom

The Kingdom of God embraces all created intelligence. Both in heaven and on earth, those who willingly serve the Lord and are in fellowship with Him are included in His Kingdom. The Kingdom of God and the Kingdom of Heaven are therefore universal, in that they include created angels, extraterrestrials, ultraterrestrials, gods, alien creatures, animals and humans. It is eternal, as God is eternal, and it is spiritual, being found within all born-again believers.

God is sovereign, omnipotent, omniscient and the ruler over all of His creation. However, the designation 'the Kingdom of God' compasses that realm which is subject to God and will be for eternity. The rest of creation will be destroyed. Only that which is part of the Kingdom of God will remain. "Heaven and earth will pass away, but my words will never pass away," (Matthew 24:35).

So, when Christ promised his disciples the keys of the kingdom, what did He mean? What are those keys?
(emphasis and commentary mine)

> "When Jesus came to the region of Caesarea Philippi, he asked his disciples, "Who do people say that the Son of Man is?" "Well," they replied, "some say John the Baptist, some say Elijah, and others say Jeremiah or one of the other prophets." Then he asked them, "But who do you say I am?" Simon Peter answered, "You are the Messiah, the Son of the living God." Jesus replied, "You are blessed, Simon son of John, because my Father in heaven has revealed this to you. You did not learn this from any human being. Now I say to you that you are Peter (which means 'rock'), and upon this rock I will build my church, and all the powers of hell will not conquer it. And <u>I will give you the keys of the Kingdom of Heaven</u>. Whatever you bind (forbid) on earth will be bound (forbidden) in heaven, and whatever you loose (permit) on earth will be loosed (permitted) in heaven."
>
> (Matthew 16: 13-19)

The keys of the Kingdom of Heaven are the spiritual authority (power) given to every believer to use the power given to them from Christ's Holy Spirit to overcome the kingdom of darkness, (Satan's kingdom which rules on Earth).

> "For the Kingdom of God is not in word <u>but in power</u>."
>
> (1 Corinthians 4:20)

> "Behold, <u>I give to you power</u> to tread on serpents and scorpions, <u>and over all the power of the enemy</u>: and nothing shall by any means hurt you."
>
> (Luke 10:19)

As I've pointed out earlier in my book, serpents and scorpions represent the demonic realm of aliens and fallen angels. Serpents are the reptilians, scorpions are the insectoid aliens, both species have grays, grays can be hybrids of both.

> "You will tread upon the lion and the cobra; you will trample the great lion and the serpent."
>
> (Psalm 91:13)

Again, the lion and the cobra are metaphors for demons. Snakes are reptiles, which can come in many shapes and forms, as we have the well-known adage for

Chapter Thirteen: The Coming Kingdom

describing character. As I have mentioned in my section on Reptilians in Book One, they have the power to shape-shift. This is the realm of Satan's kingdom, and his hierarchy. The lion has also been used as a symbol for both Satan and Jesus. This counterfeit lion was brilliantly illustrated in C.S. Lewis[2], *The Final Battle*, where he introduced a counterfeit Aslan to fool the Narnians. This symbolism is repeated throughout the Bible, as Jesus was known as the Lion of Judah, yet Satan was called a roaring lion seeking someone to devour. "Be clear-minded and alert, your adversary, the devil, is prowling around like a roaring lion, looking for someone to devour." (1 Peter 5:8) The authority Christ gives to His believers is the power to crush the power of the satans and his Reptilian hierarchy, and all their demons.

"And these signs shall follow them that believe; In my name, shall they cast out devils (demons); they shall speak with new tongues; They shall take up serpents; and if they drink any deadly thing, it shall not hurt them; they shall lay hands on the sick, and they shall recover."

(Mark 16:17-18)

Jesus said, "I tell you the truth, anyone who believes in me will do the same works I have done, <u>and even greater works</u>, because I am going to be with the Father." (John 14:12)

The 'Keys of the Kingdom' are His power and authority through faith in Him, carried out through His Holy Spirit. The power to walk amongst demons and not be hurt, the power to crush demons and not be harmed, the power to bind and loose anything on earth to the extent it reaches heaven, the power to heal the sick, the power to cast out demons, even to raise the dead, are the keys of the Kingdom of God. That power can only come through faith in the Lord Jesus Christ and through receiving the anointing of His Holy Spirit. "Not by might, nor by power, but by my Spirit, says the LORD of hosts. (Zechariah 4:6)

Jesus also said, "But I tell you who hear me: Love your enemies, do good to those who hate you, bless those who curse you, pray for those who mistreat you. But love your enemies, do good to them, and lend to them without expecting to get anything back. Then your reward will be great, <u>and you will be sons (and daughters) of the Most High</u>, because He is kind to the ungrateful and wicked" (Luke 6:27, 28,35) "Forgive us our debts (trespasses), as we forgive those who trespass against us" (Matthew 6:12).

Bless those who curse you? Love your enemies? Forgive debts and trespasses? How does a human being realize this? It is almost impossible to meet this standard in our own flesh, because let's face it, humans lean towards the works of the flesh, and living for oneself. Those who do good works frequently mostly want to be recognized for it by man. We can put it down to our present two strands of DNA, but there is more than that. Besides, the Old Testament clearly stated, an eye for eye and a tooth for a tooth. As many have said, this achieves nothing but making the world blind and toothless. The New Covenant was made through Christ, who spoke head and shoulders above all the rest, raising the bar on how much to love, how often to be kind and forgiving. The only problem is that most humans are incapable of achieving these high spiritual loving standards on our own. This is why the Holy Spirit was sent, to empower every believer to have the mind of Christ, and the spirit of Christ.

> "I will give you a new heart and put a new spirit in you; I will remove from you your heart of stone and give you a tender responsive heart of flesh."
> (Ezekiel 36:26)

> "In the last days, God says, I will pour out my Spirit on all people."
> (Acts 2:17)

Those who walk with the Holy Spirit do have this incredible power. We can forgive those who have injured us, bless those who have cursed us, and love our enemies, because it is with the love of God that we can forgive our enemies, it is through the spirit of Christ that we can pray a prayer of blessing over those who have cursed us. These are clearly 'keys of the kingdom of heaven.'

Who is Called to the Kingdom?

> "And this gospel of the kingdom will be preached in all the world <u>as a witness to all the nations, and then the end will come</u>."
> (Matthew 24:14)

Jesus makes plain that the gospel of the Kingdom will be preached to the whole world in the days just preceding the end of the age. The Kingdom of God is all about God calling sinners to repentance. This was the very centerpiece of Jesus' teachings.

> "John the Baptist came preaching in the wilderness of Judea, and saying, <u>'Repent, for the Kingdom of Heaven is at hand!'</u>"
> (Matthew 3:1-2)

> "Jesus came to Galilee, <u>preaching the gospel of the Kingdom of God</u>, and saying, 'The time is fulfilled, and the Kingdom of God is at hand. <u>Repent, and believe in the gospel</u>."
> (Mark 1:14-15)

Chapter Thirteen: The Coming Kingdom

The word 'gospel' is Greek for good news or truth.

> "I say to you <u>that tax collectors and harlots enter the Kingdom of God before you</u>. For John came to you in the way of righteousness, and you did not believe him; but <u>tax collectors and harlots believed him</u>; and when you saw it, you did not afterward relent and believe him."
>
> (Matthew 21:31)

This tells us that anyone who repents is called to the Kingdom of God. You can be the worst sinner, even a Satan worshipper, and can be redeemed, through repentance and turning to Christ. The key is to repent while you're alive, while you still have breath, because, after death, everyone is judged according to what they have done based on belief. Repentant sinners are welcomed by the King.

> "He turned to the woman and said to Simon, 'Do you see this woman? I entered your house; you gave Me no water for My feet, but she has washed My feet with her tears and wiped them with the hair of her head. You gave Me no kiss, but this woman has not ceased to kiss My feet since the time I came in. You did not anoint My head with oil, but this woman has anointed My feet with fragrant oil. Therefore, I say to you, her sins, which are many, are forgiven, for she loved much. But to whom little is forgiven, the same loves little.' Then He said to her, 'Your sins are forgiven.'"
>
> (Luke 7:44-47)

<u>"Love Covers a Multitude of Sins"</u>.

(1 Peter 4:8; James 5:20)

> "...seek the Kingdom of God, and all these things shall be added to you. Do not fear, little flock, <u>for it is your Father's good pleasure to give you the kingdom</u>."
>
> (Luke 12:31-32)

The good news here is that it will be the Lord's good pleasure, His joy, to give us the Kingdom, as long as we seek the Kingdom of God. That's a good deal. That's why they call it good news.

However, the kingdom spoken of by Jesus is not the earthly kingdom that was widely inferred from the Old Testament prophesies. It is a spiritual kingdom that is now growing in the hearts of men and women, which will find its fulfillment in the eventual sovereign rule of God and the defeat of all evil. Those people who choose to belong to God's kingdom and serve Him are those who are destined to inherit eternal life in God's presence, and are invited to eat of the tree of life, which Revelation 22:2 tells us will bear twelve different fruits, which leaves will be healing medicine to all the nations of the earth. This is why the good news of the Kingdom must be preached to all the nations of the world.

Jesus often compared the kingdom of God to a seed planted in the hearts of men and women. Each of us has the seed of the kingdom within us, but it will grow only if we give it the proper "care and feeding." Jesus tells of this aspect of the kingdom in His Famous Parable of the Sower:

"Jesus left the house and went down to the shore, where an immense crowd soon gathered. He got into a boat and taught from it while the people listened on the beach. He used many illustrations such as this one in his sermon: "A farmer was sowing grain in his fields. As he scattered the seed across the ground, some fell beside a path, and the birds came and ate it. And some fell on rocky soil where there was little depth of earth; the plants sprang up quickly enough in the shallow soil, but the hot sun soon scorched them and they withered and died, for they had so little root. Other seeds fell among thorns, and the thorns choked out the tender blades. But some fell on good soil and produced a crop that was thirty, sixty, and even a hundred times as much as he had planted."

(Matthew 13:1-8)

Jesus' disciples were often just as baffled by His parables as the huge crowds of people who came to hear Him preach. Later, when He was alone with His disciples, Jesus explained the Parable of the Sower to them in plain language:

"Now here is the explanation of the story I told about the farmer planting grain: The hard path where some of the seeds fell represents the heart of a person who hears the Good News about the Kingdom and doesn't understand it; then Satan comes and snatches away the seeds from his heart. The shallow, rocky soil represents the heart of a man who hears the message and receives it with real joy, but he doesn't have much depth in his life, and the seeds don't root very deeply, and after a while when trouble comes, or persecution begins because of his beliefs, his enthusiasm fades, and he drops out. The ground covered with thistles represents a man who hears the message, but the cares of this life and his longing for money choke out God's Word, and he does less and less for God. The good ground represents the heart of a man who listens

Chapter Thirteen: The Coming Kingdom

to the message and understands it and goes out and brings thirty, sixty, or even a hundred others into the Kingdom."

(Matthew 13:18-23)

According to Jesus' explanation, three things are needed to belong to God's kingdom: understanding, commitment, and total devotion to God's Word above all else. Like the seed that falls on the hard path, a person who does not understand the Word and the commandments will fall into the temptation of evil and lose sight of God's kingdom. Like the seed that falls on the shallow, rocky soil, a person lacking a strong commitment will drift away from faith because of peer pressure, inconvenience, embarrassment or persecution. Like the seed that falls among thistles, the faith of a person who is not totally devoted will succumb to the pettiness of worldly life and the desires for wealth, power and status.

The kingdom of heaven is not some faraway place in a long-from-now time about which we can only dream; it is here and now, among and within us. Jesus put it this way:

One day the Pharisees asked Jesus, "When will the Kingdom of God begin?" Jesus replied, "The Kingdom of God isn't ushered in with visible signs. You won't be able to say, 'It has begun here in this place or there in that part of the country.' <u>For the Kingdom of God is within you</u>."

(Luke 17:20-21)

The fact that the kingdom is within implies that it is a consciousness, a way of living, thinking and believing. According to the laws of sowing and reaping, all believers are manifesting the invisible Kingdom into the visible Kingdom, because it is aligned with the Lord's will. We know it will come to earth, which is the grounding place for all manifestation of the spiritual. Nothing on earth can happen unless it is first seeded in heavenly realms.

In the Parable of the Mustard Seed (Matthew 13:31-32), Jesus again compared the kingdom of heaven to a seed, this time a mustard seed. He said the mustard seed is the tiniest of all seeds, but it can grow into the largest of plants. In other words, the kingdom of heaven is like a tiny seed within each of us. We cannot see it or touch it and we are free to ignore it. However, if we choose to nurture it, it can grow into a powerful and wonderful force within us.

We are all God's children, and if we wish to be a part of His kingdom, we must humble ourselves before the Creator like small children. We can enter *only* by the grace of God. The Lord is not "required" to admit anyone because of faith proclaimed, church services attended, good deeds done, wise words spoken, or hardships suffered. We must come on His terms, leaving our pride, arrogance, rebellion and self-centered desires behind:

> "The disciples came to Jesus, saying, "Who then is greatest in the kingdom of heaven?" "Jesus called a little child to Him, set him in the midst of them, and said, 'Assuredly, I say to you, <u>unless you are transformed</u> and become as little children, <u>you will by no means enter the kingdom of heaven</u>. Therefore, whoever humbles himself as this little child is the greatest in the kingdom of heaven. Whoever receives one little child like this <u>in My name receives Me</u>."
> (Matthew 18:1-5)

This is where the therapy of inner child work can actually pay off! Getting in touch with one's inner child, taking all the hurts and bad memories to the Lord for healing, will be the spiritual key for many to come into the Kingdom. Christ can heal and deliver a person from the unthinkable traumas that plague so many children, who grow up to be wounded adults, often confused and angry at God for allowing such injustices and crimes to happen. But with the spiritual understanding that there are essentially two main gods who battle over humans, that the God of Love does not cause these bad things to happen to children, but that the god of this world, who is satan does, in order to hold families in bondage. Once this is understood, then healing is possible.

The Gospel of John tells of the kingdom of God in terms of a spiritual birth. Just as we were born and grow in the flesh physically, we must be "born" and grow in the Spirit, spiritually. Speaking to the Pharisee Nicodemus, Jesus said we must be born again spiritually to enter the kingdom:

> "Truly, truly, I say to you, unless one is born again, he cannot see the kingdom of God." Nicodemus said to Him, "How can a man be born when he is old? He cannot enter a second time into his mother's womb and be born, can he?" Jesus answered, "Truly, truly, I say to you, unless one is born of water and the Spirit, he cannot enter into the kingdom of God. "That which is born of the flesh is flesh, and that which is born of the Spirit is spirit. "Do not marvel that I said to you, 'You must be born again.'"
> (John 3:3-7)

Saul was a Jew and a Roman citizen. His Jewish heritage meant everything to Saul, and he saw the rise of Christianity as a threat. He witnessed the stoning of Stephen, the first Christian martyr, which made him a fierce persecutor of the early Christians. He was determined to destroy the young church, and went from house to

Chapter Thirteen: The Coming Kingdom

house arresting Christians and sending them to prison. Sometime around the year 34 A.D., while on the road to Damascus, Saul was blinded by a bright light:

> "He fell to the ground and heard a voice say to him, "Saul, Saul, why do you persecute me?" "Who are you, Lord?" Saul asked. "I am Jesus, whom you are persecuting," he replied. "Now get up and go into the city, and you will be told what you must do." The men traveling with Saul stood there speechless; they heard the sound but did not see anyone."
>
> (Acts 9:4-7)

Saul was born again that day as the Apostle Paul. He became the first and most influential interpreter of Jesus' message and teachings, a passionate missionary, founder of many Christian communities, and author of several New Testament letters. Like Saul, several people experienced a sudden, intense spiritual rebirth that instantly changed their whole lives. However, for most people, spiritual rebirth is not so much an event as it is a process of becoming more and more focused on spiritual things and less and less on selfish material things. The healing process is likened to peeling an onion. Years of living on planet earth collecting wounds, disappointments, becoming disenchanted with churches and religions, we begin a process to peel and heal the many layers of wounds and disbelief accumulated in Satan's kingdom. We are translated out of the kingdom of darkness into the Kingdom of God, which takes as much time as we need. Eventually, spiritual eyesight and spiritual hearing is restored and one thinks more and more of doing God's work through serving others on earth instead of just living for ourselves.

God's kingdom will not come to total fulfillment in this present age, but at the end of the age. However, the kingdom will continue to exist and grow among the powers of evil. This is what Jesus told us in His Parable of the Weeds:

> "Jesus told them another parable: "The kingdom of heaven is like a man who sowed good seed in his field. But while everyone was sleeping, his enemy came and sowed weeds among the wheat, and went away. When the wheat sprouted and formed heads, then the weeds also appeared. "The owner's servants came to him and said, 'Sir, didn't you sow good seed in your field? Where then did the weeds come from?' "'An enemy did this,' he replied. "The servants asked him, 'Do you want us to go and pull them up?' "'No,' he answered, 'because while you are pulling the weeds, you may root up the wheat with them. Let both grow together until the harvest. At that time, I will tell the harvesters: First collect the weeds and tie them in bundles to be burned; then gather the wheat and bring it into my barn.'"

"…..Then he left the crowd and went into the house. His disciples came to him and said, "Explain to us the parable of the weeds in the field." He answered, "The one who sowed the good seed is the Son of Man. The field is the world, and the good seed stands for the sons of the kingdom. The weeds are the sons of the evil one, and the enemy who sows them is the devil. <u>The harvest is the end of the age, and the harvesters are angels</u>. (faithful extraterrestrials on assignment from the King of Heaven). As the weeds are pulled up and burned in the fire, <u>so it will be at the end of the age</u>. <u>The Son of Man will send out his angels, and they will weed out of his kingdom everything that causes sin and all who do evil. They will throw them into the fiery furnace, where there will be weeping and gnashing of teeth</u>. <u>Then the righteous will shine like the sun in the Kingdom of their Father</u>. He who has ears, let him hear."

(Matthew 13: 24-30; 36-43)

Like wheat growing among weeds, God's kingdom will exist and grow amidst the forces of evil that are so prevalent in our world.

Presently we live in a world of duality. Those who belong to the kingdom and serve God will continue to live among those who, knowingly or unknowingly, serve the powers of evil. In the end, if we are able to cling to our faith despite all the surrounding corruption, we will be freed from the evil of the world and live in perfect harmony with God. The ultimate fate of those who serve the forces of evil, whether by design or neglect, will be grim to say the least.

Being born again and entering the Kingdom of God is a process of gradually coming to follow God's commandments instead of a "sin now, pray later" attitude. It is learning and transforming spiritually to truly follow Jesus' great commandment to 'Love God with all your heart and soul and love your neighbor as yourself.' It is about entering into an intimate relationship with the Living God, just as He intended His connection to be, as was the original plan with Adam and Eve. It was their disobedience which caused them to fall away, through guilt and shame. Christ was sent to be the Healer of all guilt and shame, for He took it upon Himself for all who believe on Him will be saved. He alone restores us into right relationship with both God and with fellow humans. This is the Divine plan. God is saving and sanctifying a people who will rule on His behalf, just as He planned. All this is only possible through Jesus and our belief in Him.

"He has delivered us from the power of darkness and transferred us into the kingdom of the Son of His love, in whom we have redemption through His blood, the forgiveness of sins."

(Colossians 1:13)

Chapter Thirteen: The Coming Kingdom

Scripture tells us that it is Christ who intercedes for all His believers.

> "I have given them Your word; and the world has hated them because <u>they are not of the world, just as I am not of the world</u>. I do not pray that You should take them out of the world, but that You should keep them from the evil one. They are not of the world, just as I am not of the world. Sanctify them by Your truth. Your word is truth."
>
> (John 17:11-18)

> "But God, who is rich in mercy, because of His great love with which He loved us, even when we were dead in trespasses, made us alive together with Christ (by grace you have been saved), and <u>raised us up together</u>, and made us <u>sit together in the heavenly places in Christ Jesus</u>, that in the ages to come He might show the <u>exceeding riches of His grace</u> in His kindness toward us in Christ Jesus."
>
> (Ephesians 2:4-7)

> "For <u>our citizenship is in heaven</u>, from which we also eagerly wait for the Savior, the Lord Jesus Christ, who will <u>transform our lowly body that it may be conformed to His glorious body</u>...."
>
> (Philippians 3:20)

THE HEAVENLY KING LIVES THROUGH HIS PEOPLE ON EARTH

As I have been saying this throughout this book series, human beings were created to be vessels of a higher power, which is either God or Satan. It is up to us, each day, which supernatural power we choose. Remember, whatever God has created, Satan has counterfeited, and this goes for channeling. New Age circles are full of people channeling fallen angels and deceiving spirits and demons. This is to mimic God's Divine plan to fill human vessels with His Holy Spirit and impart all the gifts of the Spirit. So, when a person accepts Christ as his savior, His Holy Spirit comes to dwell within, allowing Him to reign on earth, through that believing and faithful human vessel. Power and authority is then given from above. As I've mentioned earlier, the manifestations are miracles, deliverance, revelation, healing, resurrection and speaking prophecies. The Holy Spirit gives words of knowledge, words of wisdom, and the discernment of spirits. This is what this book series is about!

> "I have been crucified with Christ; it is no longer I who live, but <u>Christ lives in me</u>; and the life which I now live in the flesh I live by faith in the Son of God, who loved me and gave Himself for me."
>
> (Galatians 2:20)

"For indeed, the kingdom of God is 'within you.'"

(Luke 17:20)

This is an intimate relationship with the King of Heaven: "...you will know that I am in My Father, and you in Me, and I in you. He who has My commandments and keeps them, it is he who loves Me. And he who loves Me will be loved by My Father, and I will love him and manifest Myself to him."

(John 14:20-21)

This is union, a yoga, a bonding, to yoke with the Living God, that He may then yoke to you and empower you, clean up your life, heal and deliver you, and save and sanctify you for the Kingdom.

"If anyone loves Me, he will keep My word; and My Father will love him, and We will come to him and make Our home with him. (indwelling, yoke) He who does not love Me does not keep My words."

(John 14:23-24)

"Abide in Me, and I in you. As the branch cannot bear fruit of itself, unless it abides in the vine, neither can you, unless you abide in Me. I am the vine; you are the branches. He who abides in Me, and I in him, bears much fruit; for without Me you can do nothing. If anyone does not abide in Me, he is cast out as a branch and is withered...."

(John 15:4-6)

Why People Reject His Kingdom

"Enter by the narrow gate; for wide is the gate and broad is the way that leads to destruction, and there are many who go in by it. Because narrow is the gate and difficult is the way which leads to life, and there are few who find it."

(Matthew 7:13-14)

The narrow gate is hard to find. The world is full of the broad highway, of all kinds of deceptions, propaganda, marketing, political agenda, usury, spiritual and financial bondages. The world is cursed, people are wounded, there is much anger, heartache, confusion, and disillusionment. There are many false religions, crooked spiritual paths, fallen angels masquerading as gods, ascended masters, archangels of

Chapter Thirteen: The Coming Kingdom

light. Many prefer to believe the lie, because it feels better than to see, understand and believe the Truth.

> "...woe to you, scribes and Pharisees, hypocrites! For you shut up the kingdom of heaven against men; for you neither go in yourselves, nor do you allow those who are entering to go in."
>
> (Matthew 23:13)

This woe is to all those writers of today who trust more in themselves and their arrogance then they do in the truth of scriptures. This woe is to all those who refuse to go within and see the kingdom as a little child, which requires humbling. Some are so full of pride, arrogance and bitterness, that not only are they blocked from seeing, but they block as many people as they can with false teachings, misunderstandings, and hypocrisy. These types are filled with the *religious spirit*, which I went over in great detail. This spirit does not come from God, but from Satan, who is the god of this world. The world today is still filled with Pharisees, those who breathe the spirit of unbelief, who are filled with the *religious spirit*. They mistakenly think that it is all about what they say and do to make themselves look good before others, which is often double-minded, as hypocrites say one thing, yet do another.

> "You search the Scriptures, for in them you think you have eternal life; and these are they which testify of Me. But you are not willing to come to Me that you may have life."
>
> (John 5:39)

Not being willing to come to the Lord is a huge stumbling block for many. Again, the spirit of unbelief, which produces a deaf and dumb spirit, means that a person's spiritual ears are closed to hearing the voice of the Holy Spirit. Instead they listen to the voices of demonic spirits and fallen angels masquerading as light angels, gods, spirit guides, and who knows what else. They are spiritually mute, meaning they have no understanding of the consequences of their disbelief, and do not see the fact that they are blocked with the spirit of pride. They are unable to humble themselves to the Lord, to accept the grace of Christ and allow their minds, spirits and bodies to be transformed by His Spirit.

> "The kingdom of heaven is like a certain king who arranged a marriage for his son, and sent out his servants to call those who were invited to the wedding; and they were not willing to come. Again, he sent out other servants,

saying, 'Tell those who are invited, 'See, I have prepared my dinner; my oxen and fatted cattle are killed, and all things are ready. Come to the wedding.' But <u>they made light of it and went their ways</u>..."

(Matthew 22:2-5)

Again, unwillingness and the spirit of unbelief gets in the way, which is coupled with the spirit of mockery. Making light of it and going their own way is something people do when they miss the seriousness of the destiny of their souls. They may be living a comfortable life, think that it's all about what they do to create their own reality, that it about their self-esteem, their self-will, and their self-determination that makes them who they are, but this is an illusion. Anyone's self-esteem can be hurt and broken, life force can be drained, and then who do they turn to when they feel powerless?

The scriptures say that the sun shines upon the good and the wicked at the same time. This means that God gives the breath of life to believers and non-believers. Everyone is on an even playing field. It is up to us to turn towards the Lord, yet many only do so when they are in trouble. They tend to fail to give thanks during the good times. So, they make light of it, and go their way, until trouble hits them, and there is no way out but to turn to the Creator God who alone has the power to save them.

"Jesus said to His disciples, 'Assuredly, I say to you that it is hard for a rich man to enter the kingdom of heaven. And again, I say to you, it is easier for a camel to go through the eye of a needle than for a rich man to enter the kingdom of God."

(Matthew 19:23-24)

Wealth and riches are a snare to many because they place their security in the riches on earth, when in reality, all wealth and riches on earth are temporary. "Do not store up for yourselves treasures on earth, where moth and rust destroy, and where thieves break in and steal. But store up for yourselves treasures in heaven, where moth and rust do not destroy, and where thieves do not break in and steal" (Matthew 6:19-20).

Money can buy many things, a life of comfort and financial security, but money cannot buy love, money cannot buy salvation, money cannot buy the Holy Spirit, and as Jesus said, money cannot buy you a ticket to the kingdom of heaven. This is a stumbling block for the wealthy who who put their faith in their riches, and not in God. The truth of the matter is that all money belongs to God. Remember the scripture, 'the earth is the Lord's and the fullness thereof.' Greed and hoarding are not kingdom virtues.

Chapter Thirteen: The Coming Kingdom

Giving generously to those in need gets God's attention, because He gives to all of us. Those who give, receive. It is like insurance; when we are kind and generous, there is grace for us when we need help Not all rich people are greedy, and thank God for that. The wealthy create all kinds of foundations for those in need, they pay the majority of the nations' taxes, they also create jobs through business and enterprise. Wealth in and of itself is not evil, it is all about what one does with it, that counts us worthy or not in the eyes of God.

WHO GETS REJECTED FROM THE COMING KINGDOM

These are probably some of the most frightening scriptures in the Bible. We've been talking about a Loving King, a Hero, one who laid down His life for His friends, who through His sacrifice put an end to all animal sacrifices. He became the final 'lamb of God', the only one worthy of making atonement of all the sins of humankind. But this is not automatic. It requires faith and a willingness to be healed and transformed by following God's commandments. So, for those who will not, lose their inheritance in the coming Kingdom.

> "<u>Not everyone</u> who says to Me, 'Lord, Lord,' shall enter the kingdom of heaven, but he who does the will of My Father in heaven. Many will say to Me in that day, 'Lord, Lord, have we not prophesied in Your name, cast out demons in Your name, and done many wonders in Your name?' And then I will declare to them, '<u>I never knew you; depart from Me, you who practice lawlessness</u>!'"
>
> (Matthew 7:21-23)

Heavy stuff! To be rejected by Jesus Christ, the one so full of love and mercy for humankind, has got to be the ultimate rejection of all rejections! Who are these people? Scripture reveals they are those who address Him as 'Lord', those who did the work of casting out demons, facilitated miracles in His name, and even prophesied in His name. These are Christians, and in my opinion, these are Christians in name only, those who join churches and various Christian cults just so that they can wear the badge of being a Christian. They are those who have traded in supernatural power for political gain, who are filled with the demonic *religious spirit* to do good works just to be seen and recognized as someone who is powerful. They are those whose consciences have become seared by pride, arrogance and mistakenly think that their salvation is automatic. There are those who did not humble themselves before the Lord through confession and repentance of their sins. This is why, the scripture says, 'work out your salvation with fear and trembling' (Philippians 2:12). We are not to be paralyzed with the kind of fear Satan uses, but to have the kind of fear that respects and awes God, the kind that creates wisdom (Psalm 111:10).

> "'Hear this now, O foolish people, without understanding, who <u>have eyes and see not</u>, and who <u>have ears and hear not</u>: Do you not fear Me?' says the Lord. 'Will you not tremble at My presence?'"
>
> (Jeremiah 5:21-22)

He has the power to give and take life, to save souls and to throw souls into eternal destruction. No one in the universe commands this kind of power. It is awesome. This is the kind of respect we need to have for the Lord, not to be manipulated by fear, but to humbled by it.

These are those Christians who throughout history have waged war in His name, killing thousands of innocent people, believing they were so commanded through the mistranslations and misinterpretations of His Word to carry out political agendas. These are those Christians who have initiated countless inquisitions, some who burned and hanged Jews and women and others who heard the true voice of the Holy Spirit, who were then deemed heretics by the Catholic Church. Only God knows who these people are, and only the Lord has the power to judge them justly.

> "For many are called, but few are chosen."
>
> (Matthew 20:16)

Now, for more heavy stuff. Remember, all of the sins listed, can be forgiven, and cleared through the redemption by Christ. But these scriptures are directed to the unrepentant:

> "Do you not know that <u>the unrighteous will not inherit the kingdom of God</u>? Do not be deceived. Neither fornicators, nor idolaters, nor adulterers, nor homosexuals, nor sodomites, nor thieves, nor covetous, nor drunkards, nor revilers, nor extortionists will inherit the Kingdom of God. And <u>such were some of you. But you were washed</u>, but you were <u>sanctified,</u> but you were <u>justified in the name of the Lord Jesus</u> and <u>by the Spirit of our God</u>."
>
> (1 Corinthians 6:9-11)

The key here is that many of us were those very sinners! We have repented, have been washed clean, and sanctified, made pure through the shed blood of Jesus Christ, and were thereby justified through His name and given a new spirit, the Spirit of God.

Chapter Thirteen: The Coming Kingdom

The following scriptures are directed to the unrepentant, those who by the end of the timeline have resisted the grace of God through Christ.

"...no fornicator, unclean person, nor covetous man, who is an idolater, has any inheritance in the Kingdom of Christ and God. Let no one deceive you with empty words, <u>for because of these things the wrath of God comes upon the sons of disobedience</u>. Therefore, do not be partakers with them."
(Ephesians 5:5-7)

"...the works of the flesh are evident, which are: adultery, fornication, uncleanness, lewdness, idolatry, sorcery, hatred, contentions, jealousies, outbursts of wrath, selfish ambitions, dissensions, heresies, envy, murders, drunkenness, revelries, and the like; of which I tell you beforehand, just as I also told you in time past, that <u>those who practice such things will not inherit the kingdom of God.</u>"
(Galatians 5:19-21)

"I say to you, that unless your righteousness exceeds the righteousness of the scribes and Pharisees, <u>you will by no means enter the kingdom of heaven</u>."
(Matthew 5:19-20)

"No one, having put his hand to the plow, <u>and looking back, is fit for the kingdom of God</u>."
(Luke 9:62)

This tells us that the person who moves forward, in this case using the metaphor of putting one's hand to the plow, but then looks back, or backslides, or regresses, is not fit for the Kingdom of God. Remember what happened to Lot's wife, when she was told not to look back. She disobeyed, and was turned into a pillar of salt while Sodom and Gomorrah were being nuked into glass. This is the same admonition to those who begin upward on the path, and then backslide. Don't look back into that past from which you have been redeemed. It is temporal, and will pass away. But instead, keep your eyes looking forward on the goal of inheriting the Kingdom. Keep the faith, and overcome.

Finally, the quintessential scripture at the end of the book of Revelation is one that promises reward to all those who 'wash their robes' clean. This means all those who through continual confession and repentance of every known sin, internal and external, individual and ancestral, by appropriating the cross of Christ and the blood of Jesus, will be cleansed from all sin. Many Christians think that it's just about repenting of the outward sins, but the inner ones are the ones that corrupt a person's entire spirit. Bitterness, self-bitterness, jealousy, envy, fears, and all the many avenues of the occult, hold people in bondage. Generational sins and curses must be broken, must be identified and brought before the Lord, in order to be completely broken for yourself and your descendants. Just believing in Christ does not grant automatic immunity, it is about being faithful to walk the path of cleansing, healing and deliverance with the Lord. For many this is a process, likened to peeling an onion. The older you are, the bigger the onion, the more trauma you've experienced. The deeper the onion, the more peels, but nothing is too big for the Lord's arm to save and deliver, as long as a person has faith.

> "Behold, I am coming soon! My reward is with me, and I will give to everyone according to what he has done. I am the Alpha and the Omega, the First and the Last, the Beginning and the End. "<u>Blessed are those who wash their robes</u>, that they may have the right to the tree of life and may go through the gates into the city. Outside are the dogs, those who practice magic arts, the sexually immoral, the murderers, the idolaters and everyone who loves and practices falsehood."
>
> (Revelation 22:12-14)

The tree of life was mentioned first in Genesis, along with the tree of knowledge of good and evil. Adam and Eve did not eat of the tree of life, otherwise they would still be alive today. Eden was quarantined after they disobeyed, which is why the tree of life is promised in Revelation to all citizens of the Kingdom of God.

Who Are the Citizens of the Kingdom?

Those who yoke with Christ, are kept in Him, and are one with Him. Protection is assured, because He promises adoption into His kingdom, and an inheritance that this world cannot steal from you.

> Jesus prayed: "Holy Father, keep through Your name those whom You have given Me, <u>that they may be one as We are</u>."
>
> (John 17:11)

> "...because those who are led by the Spirit of God are sons of God. For you have not received the spirit of bondage again to fear; <u>but you have received the Spirit of adoption</u>, whereby we cry, Abba, Father."
>
> (Romans 8:14,15)

Chapter Thirteen: The Coming Kingdom

"...to obtain an inheritance which is imperishable and undefiled and will not fade away, reserved in heaven for you,"

(1 Peter 1:4)

"Now, therefore, you are no longer strangers and foreigners, but fellow citizens with the saints and members of the household of God, having been built on the foundation of the apostles and prophets, Jesus Christ Himself being the chief cornerstone, in whom the whole building, being fitted together, grows into a holy temple in the Lord, in whom you also are being built together for a dwelling place of God in the Spirit."

(Ephesians 2:19-20)

The world hates the citizens of the Kingdom, because the spirit of the world, which is Lucifer/Satan's kingdom is at war with the Holy Spirit of the Kingdom:

"I have given them Your word; and the world has hated them because they are not of the world, just as I am not of the world. I do not pray that You should take them out of the world, but that You should keep them from the evil one. They are not of the world, just as I am not of the world. Sanctify them by Your truth. Your word is truth. As You sent Me into the world, I also have sent them into the world."

(John 17:12-18)

Those who are called and chosen into the coming are also called to suffer for His Kingdom in this world. Yet those who suffer are promised a greater reward.

Jesus said, "If the world hates you, you know that it hated Me before it hated you. If you were of the world, the world would love its own. Yet because you are not of the world, but I chose you out of the world, therefore the world hates you. ... If they persecuted Me, they will also persecute you... because they do not know Him who sent Me."

(John 15:18-21)

The persecution is due to the ongoing cosmic conflict and spiritual battle between the kingdom of darkness and the Kingdom of Heaven.

"Then they will deliver you up to tribulation and kill you, and you will be hated by all nations for My name's sake. And then many will be offended, will betray one another, and will hate one another. Then many false prophets will rise up and deceive many. And because lawlessness will abound, the love of many will grow cold. But he who endures to the end shall be saved. And this gospel of the kingdom will be preached in all the world as a witness to all the nations, and then the end will come."

(Matthew 24:9-14)

There is a promise to all those who are persecuted unjustly for their beliefs in Christ. The Beatitudes are probably the most famous of all Christ's teachings, which again promises rewards for those who suffer for righteousness sake and for His sake. There is a special blessing for all those who are 'poor in spirit', those who are weak, meek, pure in heart, hunger for righteousness, and those who are peacemakers.

"Blessed care the poor in spirit, for theirs is the kingdom of heaven.... Blessed are those who are persecuted for righteousness' sake, for theirs is the kingdom of heaven....Blessed are those who mourn, for they will be comforted. Blessed are the meek, for they will inherit the earth. Blessed are those who hunger and thirst for righteousness, for they will be satisfied. Blessed are the merciful, for they will be shown mercy. Blessed are the pure in heart, for they will see God. Blessed are the peacemakers, for they will be called the children of God. Blessed are you when they revile and persecute you, and say all kinds of evil against you falsely for My sake. Rejoice and be exceedingly glad, for great is your reward in heaven, for so they persecuted the prophets who were before you."

(Matthew 5:3-12)

We are also told that God has completely different standards than the world has as to who is considered worthy, and inheritors of His kingdom:

"Has God not chosen the poor of this world to be rich in faith and heirs of the kingdom which He promised to those who love Him? But you have dishonored the poor man. Do not the rich oppress you and drag you into the courts? Do they not blaspheme that noble name by which you are called?"

(James 2:5-7)

According to scripture it is through suffering trials and tribulations is the path towards being worthy of the Kingdom of God: "... 'We must through many tribulations enter the kingdom of God."

(Acts 14:22)

Chapter Thirteen: The Coming Kingdom

"We are bound to thank God always for you... for your <u>patience and faith in all your persecutions and tribulations</u> that you endure, which is manifest evidence of the righteous judgment of God, that you may be counted <u>worthy of the kingdom of God, for which you also suffer</u>."

(2 Thessalonians 1:3-5)

"Then I heard a loud voice saying in heaven, 'Now salvation, and strength, and <u>the kingdom of our God,</u> and the power of His Christ have come, for the accuser of our brethren, who accused them before our God day and night, has been cast down. (satan) And they overcame him by the blood of the Lamb and by the word of their testimony, and <u>they did not love their lives to the death.</u>"

(Revelation 12:10-11)

I believe this is why Christ said, the man who loves his life will lose it, while the man who hates his life in this world will keep it for eternal life."

(John 12:25)

War Against the Kingdom

As I have expounded upon from the beginning, this world is in a constant state of battle between the forces of darkness and the forces of light. It is an ancient cosmic drama over the ownership of human souls and the real estate of planet Earth. The battle is not limited to Earth, as I've illustrated earlier in this manuscript, but erupts all over the universe in all the star systems, on planets that have been taken over by the dark lord, which the Cosmic Christ is destined to redeem for the Kingdom of Heaven.

Our Own world, planet Earth, is under the influence of the god of this world, who is Lucifer/Satan. "...The whole world is under the sway of the evil one." (1 John 5:19) The war against the Kingdom of God is waged by his hierarchy of fallen extra-terrestrial angels, rebellious gods and their demonic intelligences and evil spirits who fight to steal the minds and souls of humankind. Their desire is to keep us from redemption, in their kingdom of darkness and deceptions. We are assured through scripture that these cosmic battles belong to God.

"Do not be discouraged because of this vast army (the satans, i.e., fallen extra-terrestrial angels). <u>For the battle is not yours, but God's</u>."

(2 Chronicles 20:15)

We are assured, that because Christ has already defeated the forces of death and Hades through His ultimate victory on the cross, that His blood is enough for all of us to overcome this world. "And they overcame him (Satan) by the blood of the Lamb and by the word of their testimony...."

(Revelation 12:11)

We are also assured and given spiritual weapons to defend ourselves in this cosmic battle, which are supernatural weapons, initiated through our faith in Christ:

"For though we walk in the flesh, we do not war according to the flesh. For the weapons of our warfare are not carnal (worldly) but mighty in God for pulling down strongholds, casting down arguments and every high thing that exalts itself against the knowledge of God, bringing every thought into captivity to the obedience of Christ, and being ready to punish all disobedience when your obedience is fulfilled."

(2 Corinthians 10:2-6)

We are also given spiritual armor through our faith which is designed to protect us from every spiritual attack. Again, this is a spiritual armor, but is it likened to the armor that medieval knights used to wear. (emphasis and commentary mine)

"Put on the full armor of God so that you can take your stand against the devil's schemes. For our struggle is not against flesh and blood, but against the rulers, against the powers, against the world forces of this darkness, against the spiritual forces of wickedness in the heavenly places. (fallen extraterrestrials, aliens, Satan's UFOs) For this reason, take up the whole armor of God so that you may be able to take a stand whenever evil comes. And when you have done everything you could, you will be able to stand firm. Stand firm, therefore, having fastened the belt of truth around your waist, and having put on the breastplate of righteousness, and as for shoes for your feet, being firm-footed in the gospel of peace, in addition to all, taking up the shield of faith with which you will be able to extinguish all the flaming arrows of the evil one, also take the helmet of salvation and the sword of the Spirit, which is the word of God."

(Ephesians 6:11-17)

Remember, this is a battle between dark and light extraterrestrial angels. The extraterrestrials that remained faithful to the Creator God are all on the side of the Cosmic Christ. As I have already said in my chapter on the Angelic Government,

Chapter Thirteen: The Coming Kingdom

everything in this world is put in charge of an angel or extraterrestrial. We are in the middle of a *Star Wars* type of battle between good and evil ET fallen angels in the universe. We also must remember that the satans, the fallen extraterrestrial angels are outnumbered 2:1, as only one third of heavens angels or ETs followed Lucifer's rebellion against the Creator God. The rest, two thirds, remained faithful.

All power and authority has been given to the King of the Kingdom by the Creator Father, who is Christ. He is the one that dispatches His angel ETs to fight our battles for us. They are the ones who defend His faithful on earth with supernatural weapons. They also uphold our supernatural, spiritual armor through our faith and our confession. I see no other way of being protected from the dangers threatened by the satans, the fallen ETs and alien demons, which attack unbelieving and ignorant humans daily. We are assured if we place our faith in the Cosmic Christ that we are given supernatural weapons, extraterrestrial angels to protect us.

> "The night is nearly over; the day is almost here. So, let us put aside the deeds of darkness and put on the armor of light."
>
> (Romans 13:12)

> "And the Lord will deliver me from every evil work and preserve me for His heavenly kingdom. To Him be glory forever and ever!"
>
> (2 Timothy 4:18)

I believe the following passage is speaking to the time in which we are living now, known as the last days, the end of this present age. This passage describes the New Age movement. There seems to be a plethora of teachers and self-proclaimed experts proclaiming all kinds of things yet turning away from the truth of what is really going on with respect to the spiritual battles over their souls, their minds and their bodies. Believing in fairy tales, turning aside to fables, believing that they will magically ascend to a higher dimension because someone channeled it to them and told them so and therefore they believe it. They follow the 'feel good' teachings, and therefore ignore the truth that we are the pawns of an ancient cosmic battle. They mistakenly believe that they are gods, that they create their own reality, ignorant of the fact that they are part of a greater reality that was created long before they were born. They mistakenly believe that they can petition ancient gods and archangels to do their bidding, answer their prayers and protect them from negativity, all the while ignoring the truth of the cause, origin and agenda of that 'negativity'. They are deceived into thinking that if they heal themselves, they can save themselves and are therefore blinded by thinking they are gods and creators, which is the agenda of Lucifer.

"Be ready in season and out of season. Convince, rebuke, exhort, with all longsuffering and teaching. For the time will come when they will not endure sound doctrine, but according to their own desires, because they have itching ears, they will heap up for themselves teachers; and they will turn their ears away from the truth, and be turned aside to fables. But you be watchful in all things..."

(2 Timothy 4:2-5)

NOTES AND REFERENCES:

1. Jim Rutz, *Megashift*, Empowerment Press (CO); 1st Edition (June 30, 2005).
2. C.S. Lewis, *The Last Battle*, published by The Bodley Head, U.K., 1956

CHAPTER FOURTEEN
The Harvest of Angels

"The harvest is at the end of the age, and the harvesters are angels."
(Matthew 13:39)

We are told through multiple scriptures that angels, who are extraterrestrials on assignment, will be called upon to complete a variety of tasks at the end of the age. The final harvest will be done through the angels, the divine extraterrestrial messengers, along with the opening up of ancient scrolls, separating the wicked from the just, and finally throwing Satan and his fallen extraterrestrial angels into the lake of fire for eternity. The Lord will order this, but it will be the task and honor of His holy faithful extraterrestrial angels to actually carry out these final tasks and complete the unfinished business between God our creator, and Lucifer with his Satanic army.

> "...<u>the kingdom of heaven</u> is like a merchant seeking beautiful pearls, who, when he had found one pearl of great price, went and sold all that he had and bought it. Again, <u>the kingdom of heaven</u> is like a dragnet that was cast into the sea and gathered some of every kind, which, when it was full, they drew to shore; and they sat down and gathered the good into vessels, but <u>threw the bad away</u>. <u>So, it will be at the end of the age. The angels will come forth, separate the wicked from among the just</u>, and cast them into the furnace of fire. There will be wailing and gnashing of teeth."
>
> (Matthew 13:45-50)

We have another clue to this end time harvest in the fulfillment of the prophecy of one of the Feasts of the Lord. The Feast of Tabernacles, known as *Sukkot* in Hebrew, or the Feast of Booths, the traditional Harvest Feast, always occurs after Rosh Hashanah and Yom Kippur. The Feast of Tabernacles comes on the full moon after the new moon of Rosh Hashanah, which always falls sometime in October as a Harvest Festival. The tradition began when the Lord redeemed the Israelites out of Egypt and gave them the promised land. At that time, He give the Israelites four main feasts of the year to commemorate His Salvation, His Promise, His Atonement and His Harvest. Jesus Christ became the final Passover Lamb, the Holy Spirit was given to all believers during Pentecost, the Day of Atonement was the day Yeshua shed His blood on the Cross of Calvary to fall on the Mercy Seat of God, for the propitiation of the sins of humankind. This leaves the Feast of Tabernacles as the final feast which has still not been fulfilled. This is the Harvest of the believers off the face of the earth at the end of this age, which the scriptures tell us in plain language will be facilitated by extraterrestrial angels.

The Feast of Tabernacles is the final harvest. The final harvest will occur in two parts, first when the rapture of the saints (believers) happens:

"For the Lord himself will come down from heaven, with a loud command, <u>with the voice of the archangel and with the trumpet call of God, and the dead in Christ will rise first</u>. After that, we who are still alive and are left <u>will be caught up together with them in the clouds to meet the Lord in the air</u>. And so, we will be with the Lord forever."

(1 Thessalonians 4:16,17)

As I've mentioned in my section on the cloud ships of the Lord, whenever scripture uses the words 'in the clouds' or 'with the clouds', it is referring to the Lord's Ships, which are cloaked in clouds of glory from His Shekinah Presence. These are the real 'light ships', which biblical witnesses described as 'clouds.' Naturally human beings are not going to be lifted up into cumulus clouds to meet the Lord in the air, but into the safety of His cloud ships, where, scripture tells us, our bodies will be translated from corporeal to non-corporeal. This includes the souls who are inside the earth according to the harvest spoken of in 1 Thessalonians 4:16,17.

Now, the final mystery is after the harvest of believing souls, when the final transformation takes place. Imagine billions of souls being taking on their ascended immortal bodies all at the same time. The Lord does this through the facilitation and cooperation of His faithful angels, holy extraterrestrials. The following is the promise to this final transformation, emphasis and comments in brackets are mine:

"If there is a natural body, there is also a spiritual body. So, it is written: "The first man Adam became a living being"; the last Adam, [which is Christ] a life-giving spirit. The spiritual did not come first, but the natural, and after that the spiritual. The first man was of the dust of the earth, the second man from heaven [Christ]. As was the earthly man, so are those who are of the earth; and as is the man from heaven, so also are those who are of heaven. And just as we have borne the likeness of the earthly man, so shall we bear the likeness of the man from heaven. I declare to you, brothers, that <u>flesh and</u>

Chapter Fourteen: The Harvest of Angels

<u>blood cannot inherit the Kingdom of God</u>, [being transformed is mandatory] nor does the perishable inherit the imperishable. Listen, I tell you a mystery: <u>We will not all sleep, but we will all be changed—in a flash, in the twinkling of an eye, at the last trumpet.</u> [the angels (extraterrestrial messengers) blow the trumpet] For the trumpet will sound, the dead will be raised imperishable, [raised from inside the earth] and we will be changed. For the perishable, must clothe itself with the imperishable, and the mortal with immortality. <u>When the perishable has been clothed with the imperishable, and the mortal with immortality, then the saying that is written will come true: "Death has been swallowed up in victory."</u> [the end of death, dying and the cycles of reincarnation]

(1 Corinthians 15:44-54)

The second harvest occurs at the end of the seven years of tribulation, at the time of the second coming of Jesus Christ, when He returns to set up His Millennial Kingdom on the Earth. This will be the final resurrection of the dead. Before the final harvest can occur, the Lord says the good news of His Kingdom is to be preached and spread throughout all the world, and then the end can come.

"And the Good News about the Kingdom will be preached throughout the whole world, so that all nations will hear it; and then the end will come."
(Matthew 24:14)

Besides the end of death, we are also told that there will be the end of heaven and earth and the beginning of a new heaven and a new earth. The end of the Bible in the book of Revelation 20 says that the believers win in the end, and our citizenship is secured in heaven. And we are assured of the end of the god of this world, Satan and his fallen angels. (Matthew 25:41; Revelation 20:10)

The following event destined to occur at the end of our timeline is that of another extraterrestrial messenger angel comes down to earth from heaven, who alone holds the key to the Abyss inside the earth. He seizes the Reptilian Beast who is Satan and binds him into the Abyss, wrapped in a great chain, for a thousand years. We are told that he is to be released, to test the nations in the coming Kingdom of God on earth, after the millennial reign, which is his very last assignment, after which he will then be sent into the lake of fire for eternity.

"<u>And I saw an angel coming down out of heaven</u>, having the key to the Abyss and holding in his hand a great chain. He seized the dragon, that ancient serpent, who is the devil, or Satan, and bound him for a thousand years. He threw him into the Abyss, and locked and sealed it over him, to keep him from deceiving the nations anymore until the thousand years were ended. After that, he must be set free for a short time."

(Revelation 20:1-3)

The Final End of Satan:

"When the thousand years are over, <u>Satan will be released from his prison and will go out to deceive the nations in the four corners of the earth—Gog and Magog—to gather them for battle</u>. (this is his final attempt at battling with Christ, as Satan is released with the Lord's permission in order to test the nations and weed out any rebellion). In number, they are like the sand on the seashore. They marched across the breadth of the earth and surrounded the camp of God's people, the city he loves. <u>But fire came down from heaven and devoured them</u>. (in other words, they get nuked). And the devil, who deceived them, was thrown into the lake of burning sulfur, (the lake of fire) where the beast and the false prophet had been thrown. They will be tormented day and night forever and ever."

(Revelation 20:7-10)

The Angels Separate The Good Earth Humans from the Evil Earth Humans:

At the end of this present timeline, all the nations and all those who proclaimed their faith in Christ will be judged by Christ, who is the King of the Kingdom. However, his holy angels (faithful extraterrestrials) are the ones who have the actual task of separating the good and the evil followers. This is when he separates his believers into 'sheep,' those who follow His commandments and listen to His voice, and those who don't, who he calls, 'goats'.

"When the Son of Man comes in his glory, <u>and all the angels with him</u>, He will sit on His throne in heavenly glory. All the nations will be gathered before him, and He will separate the people one from another as a shepherd separates the sheep from the goats. He will put the sheep on his right and the goats on his left. Then the King will say to those on his right, 'Come, you who are blessed by my Father; <u>take your inheritance, the kingdom prepared for you since the creation of the world</u>. For I was hungry and you gave me something to eat, I was thirsty and you gave me something to drink, I

Chapter Fourteen: The Harvest of Angels

was a stranger and you invited me in, I needed clothes and you clothed me, I was sick and you looked after me, I was in prison and you came to visit me.'

"Then the righteous will answer him, 'Lord, when did we see you hungry and feed you, or thirsty and give you something to drink? When did we see you, a stranger and invite you in, or needing clothes and clothe you? When did we see you sick or in prison and go to visit you?' "The King will reply, 'I tell you the truth, whatever you did for one of the least of these brothers of mine, you did for me.'

"Then he will say to those on his left, '<u>Depart from me, you who are cursed, into the eternal fire prepared for the devil and his angels</u>. For I was hungry and you gave me nothing to eat, I was thirsty and you gave me nothing to drink, I was a stranger and you did not invite me in, I needed clothes and you did not clothe me, I was sick and in prison and you did not look after me.' "They also will answer, 'Lord, when did we see you hungry or thirsty or a stranger or needing clothes or sick or in prison, and did not help you?' "He will reply, 'I tell you the truth, whatever you did not do for one of the least of these, you did not do for me.' "Then they will go away to eternal punishment, but the righteous to eternal life."

(Matthew 25:31-46)

We are told that there will be a final judgment for all those who have died, regardless of where they are in the afterlife, this is a separate judgment from the sheep and the goats. While the angels (faithful extraterrestrial messengers) will be involved in gathering these souls, it is the one on the throne, who is Christ, that will be the judge. We are also told that the lake of fire is the final death, or the second death, as the scripture calls it. This death is irreversible.

"Then I saw a great white throne and him who was seated on it. Earth and sky fled from his presence, and there was no place for them. And I saw the dead, great and small, standing before the throne, and books were opened. Another book was opened, which is the book of life. The dead were judged according to what they had done as recorded in the books. The sea gave up the dead that were in it, and death and Hades gave up the dead that were in them, and each person was judged according to what he had done. Then death and Hades were thrown into the lake of fire. The lake of fire is the second death. <u>If anyone's name was not found written in the book of life, he was thrown into the lake of fire.</u>"

(Revelation 20:11-15)

The faithful extraterrestrial angels have the task of recording the names in the book of life. These are called recording angels, extraterrestrials who literally watch everything that humans do during their lives on earth. We are told by scripture that every spoken word is judged along with every deed.

"And I say unto you, that every idle word that men shall speak, they shall give account thereof in the day of judgment."

(Matthew 12:36)

"For we must all appear before the judgment seat of Christ, that each one may receive what is due him for the things done while in the body, whether good or bad."

(2 Corinthians 5:10)

For it is the angels, extraterrestrial watchers, who record everything done by earth humans. As I've mentioned this concept before in Book Two: *Who Is God?* in my chapter on *Ancient Technology and Biblical Astronauts*[1], it is similar to the movie *Defending Your Life*[2], when Albert Brooks and Meryl Streep die and are brought to Judgment. Everything they ever did was put up before them on a movie screen. Ezekiel was taken up into a mothership and wrote about seeing visions on a wall (Ezekiel 8:1-4; 7-8,10). Today we call that television, or computer or movie screens. The ancients had no reference for such technology, so they used spiritual vernacular and called them 'visions.' Ezekiel witnessed these 'visions' on the wall of the spacecraft, while watching the Israelites in the temple of Jerusalem worshipping the idols of Ishtar, Astarte Ashtarte, which he called, 'the image of jealousy' because this idolatry made the Lord angry.

How was Ezekiel able to watch the Israelites live on the wall? Through the technology of a live feed screen. This proves that everything humans do is being recorded. Extraterrestrial angel messengers are the ones in charge of this task, to bring it before the throne of Christ on Judgment Day. Many call these beings, the Recording Angels, also known as extraterrestrial Recording Secretaries or Journalists.

"Jesus said, "But I tell you that everyone will have to give account on the day of judgment for every empty word they have spoken."

(Matthew 12:36)

These extraterrestrial messenger angels answer to the King of the Universe. He alone has the power and authority to send His extraterrestrial messenger angels on

Chapter Fourteen: The Harvest of Angels

various assignments, particularly those who are sent to guard and protect His faithful on earth. But the covenant to which you must first agree is to turn to and believe in the Lord, then get the protection of his ET angels. Here is the discernment, those who are in rebellion against the Almighty receive the *counterfeit* angels, the fallen angels which serve the Office of Satan and the lord of darkness. Here is the Lord's contract and agreement:

> "If you make the Most High your dwelling—even the Lord, who is my refuge—then no harm will befall you, no disaster will come near your tent. For he will command his angels concerning you to guard you in all your ways; they will lift you up in their hands, so that you will not strike your foot against a stone."
>
> (Psalm 91:9-12)

As I've been saying throughout this book, there are good ET angels and evil ET angels. When we turn to the Lord of Heaven and Earth, we are assured of His good angels at our side, because we choose to be on the Lord's side.

> "Then comes the end, when He delivers the kingdom to God the Father, when He puts an end to all rule and all authority and power. For He must reign till He has put all enemies under His feet. The last enemy that will be destroyed is death. ... Now when all things are made subject to Him, then the Son Himself will also be subject to Him who put all things under Him, that God may be all in all."
>
> (1 Corinthians 15:23-28)

> "Then the seventh angel sounded [the trumpet]: And there were loud voices in heaven, saying, 'The kingdoms of this world have become the Kingdoms of our Lord and of His Christ, 'and He shall reign forever and ever!'"
>
> (Revelation 11:15)

The Kingdom of God primarily refers to the era when Christ comes again to bring the final establishment of God's rule over all creation, which will include a final judgment where the righteous are rewarded and the wicked are punished. The concept of the Kingdom of God offers the goal for every believer's life: those who follow the example and teachings of Jesus will be vindicated when the Kingdom of God comes and will reign with Christ forever. For all those who follow the teachings and precepts of Christ are assured an entrance into His Eternal Kingdom.

"Therefore, brethren, be even more diligent 'to make your call and election sure, for if you do these things you will never stumble; for so <u>an entrance will be supplied</u> to you abundantly <u>into the everlasting kingdom</u> of our Lord and Savior Jesus Christ."

(2 Peter 1:10-11)

"...since <u>we are receiving a kingdom which cannot be shaken</u>, let us have grace, by which we may serve God acceptably with reverence and godly fear. For our <u>God is a consuming fire</u>."

(Hebrews 12:28)

As my readers, must know by now, I am a big fan of Enoch and his sacred scrolls which were read by all the Jewish disciples and early Christians, until they were rejected by the ecumenical councils over three centuries later. It's important to reiterate that the Books of Enoch were never taken out of the Coptic and Ethiopian Bibles and remain as the Word of God today. I am including some pertinent passages of the Word of God through Enoch:

"In those days shall the earth deliver up from her womb, and hell deliver up from hers, that which it has received; and destruction shall restore that which it owes. He shall select the righteous and holy from among them; for the day of their salvation has approached. And in those days, shall the Elect One sit upon his throne, while every secret of intellectual wisdom shall proceed from his mouth, for the Lord of spirits has gifted and glorified him. In those days, the mountains shall skip like rams, and the hills shall leap like young sheep (Psalm 114:4) satiated with milk; <u>and all *the righteous* shall become *like* angels in heaven</u>. Their countenance shall be bright with joy; for in those days shall the Elect One be exalted. <u>The earth shall rejoice; the righteous shall inhabit it, and the elect possess it</u>."

(Enoch 50:1-5)

"<u>In those days the saints and the chosen shall undergo a change</u>. The light of day shall rest upon them; and the splendor and glory of the saints shall be changed. In the day of trouble evil shall be heaped up upon sinners; but the righteous shall triumph in the name of the Lord of spirits. Others shall be made to see, that they must repent, and forsake the works of their hands; <u>and that glory awaits them not in the presence of the Lord of spirits; yet that by his name they may be saved. The Lord of spirits will have compassion on them</u>; for great is his mercy; and righteousness is in his judgment, and in

Chapter Fourteen: The Harvest of Angels

the presence of his glory; nor in his judgment shall iniquity stand. <u>He who repents not before him shall perish</u>. Henceforward I will not have mercy on them, saith the Lord of spirits."

(1 Enoch 49:1-4)

The Reapers

The extraterrestrial angels on assignment in Revelation 14 come through as grim reapers to reap those humans from the face of the earth who are in rebellion against the Lord, appointed for the wrath of God. A *reaper* reaps the mature grape clusters from the vine during the harvest. In the following passage, emphasis and commentary in brackets are mine:

> "Then I looked, and behold, a white cloud, and sitting on the cloud was one like a son of man, having a golden crown on His head and a sharp sickle in His hand.

[Again, the Biblical writers use the word 'cloud' to describe the Lord's spaceships. In this case, it specifically says, a 'white cloud', which as I've said before, indicates the Shekinah glory of the presence of the God that emanates out from the ship and appears to cloak the spaceship with a cloud. John sees a being, who he describes as one who is 'like' a son of man, indicating a human extraterrestrial, who wears a golden crown, and wields a sharp sickle. This is no ordinary 'sickle' but a powerful piece of space technology to do what John sees him do next.]

> "And another angel came out of the temple, crying out with a loud voice to Him who sat on the cloud, "Put in your sickle and reap, for the hour to reap has come, <u>because the harvest of the earth is ripe</u>." Then He who sat on the cloud swung His sickle over the earth, and the earth was reaped.

[The angel who sat on the cloud, actually sits in his space ship in space from above the earth, and takes this high tech powerful sickle and reaps the harvest on the earth in one swing.]

> "And another angel came out of the temple which is in heaven, and he also had a sharp sickle. Then another angel, the one who has power over fire, came out from the altar; and he called with a loud voice to him who had the sharp sickle, saying, "Put in your sharp sickle and gather the clusters from the vine of the earth, because her grapes are ripe." So the angel swung his sickle to the

earth and gathered the clusters from the vine of the earth, <u>and threw them into the great wine press of the wrath of God</u>. And the wine press was trodden outside the city, and blood came out from the wine press, up to the horses' bridles, for a distance of two hundred miles."

(Revelation 14:14-20)

[These people are the ones whom the Lord has promised to judge by pouring out his wrath on for their rebellion, which He spoke through the Old Testament prophet in Isaiah 66. The city he is referring to is Jerusalem, and he tells us that the blood rushes out for two hundred miles, which is greater than the size of the State of Israel today. Then the prophecy tells us, that the Lord orders the vultures and all those flesh-eating birds of the air to gather and eat of the flesh and blood of all those that the reapers had killed.]

"And I saw an angel standing in the sun, who cried in a loud voice to all the birds flying in midair, (vultures) "Come, gather together for <u>the great supper of God, so that you may eat the flesh of kings, generals, and mighty men, of horses and their riders, and the flesh of all people, free and slave, small and great</u>."

(Revelation 19:18,19)

The Great Judgment

There will be a final judgment in which the dead will be resurrected and judged according to their works. (Matthew 25:31-46, Romans 2:1-9) Everyone whose name is not found written in the Book of Life, along with Satan and his fallen angels, will be consigned to everlasting punishment in the lake of fire. (Revelation 20:11-15) Those whose names are written in the Book of Life will be resurrected and stand at the judgment seat of Christ to be rewarded for their good deeds. (1 Corinthians 4:5)

The faithful angels are working toward The Great Judgment. Each of them have been given assignments on earth to help facilitate humans getting through the Great Judgment by accepting God's Divine Plan of salvation through Christ. Ofcourse, this requires the cooperation of us humans, because of our free will, but the extraterrestrial angels on assignment exert their influence from behind the scenes in many ways, in their service to the Office of Christ. It is all about bringing glory to God at the Judgment. Those who do well will pass through the Great Judgment, those who don't, won't. Faith in Christ is key.

Yet, according to the Bible, there are a handful of scriptures that allude to those who carry the label of Christian, yet are turned away in the throne room by the

Chapter Fourteen: The Harvest of Angels

King. These are the most blood curdling scriptures in the Bible, where in Matthew 7:22,23, "Many will say to me in that day, Lord, Lord, have we not prophesied in your name and in your name, have cast out devils? and in your name done many wonderful works? And then will I profess to them, I never knew you: depart from me, you that work iniquity." That's heavy, to be rejected by Jesus Christ, when a person may think they are doing His work. What could cause a Christian to lose their way and end up with the Lord's wrath instead of His rewards? Let's consider and discern...

First, those who use the pulpit for their own gain. How many preachers and ministers end up in disgrace for abusing their powers? There are Christians who 'sell' the works of the Holy Spirit. This was not only forbidden in the New Testament, but earned a major rebuke from the disciple Peter to Simon the Magician for even thinking that the Holy Spirit can be bought. How many people today sell healing, deliverance and even exorcism? Deliverance and healing come only from the Lord. While it's perfectly understandable for churches to pass the hat around and accept offerings and donations, it not ethical to charge for prayer, healing or deliverance. This is the work of God, no man can take credit for it, whether it be for achieving fame or wealth, it is all done for the glory of God.

Angels are assigned to help expand the Kingdom by working on individuals, protecting them from various dangers, which includes they're being misled down deceptive paths. They influence earth humans with thought-forms, energy, and loving support. Angels can even cause people to avoid other people for their own good, and bring people together when the timing is right. Remember this, it is the extraterrestrial messenger angels and warrior angels who are assigned to engage in spiritual battles on behalf of humans for the Kingdom of Christ. They know which humans are owned and controlled by the Office of Satan and which ones belong to Christ. This spiritual warfare that goes on behind the scenes is the very reason for the ongoing discord on planet earth, for political divisions, arguments and outright wars. Because of the spiritual warfare, angels have the power to cause people to separate as well as come together, which would be a victory in a battle.

SPIRITUAL WEAPONS

> "For the weapons of our warfare are not carnal, but mighty through God to the pulling down of strong holds; Casting down imaginations (arguments), and every high thing that exalts itself against the knowledge of God, and bringing into captivity every thought to the obedience of Christ;"
>
> (2 Corinthians 10:4)

Strongholds are demonic intelligences, held in place through spiritual legal ground by generational curses in the ongoing presence of sin and iniquity. Who pulls down these strongholds? God's Warrior Extraterrestrial Angels! While humans would like to think, it is by their command that demons jump out of people, these prayers and affirmations only initiate the legal ground for God's Warrior Angels to intervene. This is a spiritual war, against powers, principalities, rulers of the darkness and spiritual wickedness in the heavens (Ephesians 6:12). Only mighty extraterrestrial angels can pull down these strongholds through their empowerment through Christ and His Holy Spirit.

All humans need do is to follow God's foundational commandments of faith, repentance and sanctification through Christ. Humans are empowered and encouraged to fight the good fight through the conscious practice of applying good over evil, always challenging! Yet, when initiated, they become the very 'weapons' of our warfare, which are not in our flesh, but are spiritual. Repentance is a weapon, because it is one thing Satan has always failed to do. Repentance combats pride. Forgiveness is a mighty weapon which has the victory over all kinds of evil, bitterness, murder, violence, betrayal. Worship, praise and gratitude to God are mighty spiritual weapons. Evil cannot stand the presence of God, and when humans praise and love the Lord, there He is in the midst of them, and demons are disabled.

The final spiritual weapon is knowing how the warfare with which we live daily will culminate in the ultimate battle:

> "For they are the spirits of demons, working miracles, who go forth unto the kings of the earth and of the whole world, to gather them to the battle of that great judgment day of God Almighty. Behold, I come as a thief. Blessed is he that watches, and keeps his garments, lest he walk naked, and they see his shame. And he gathered them together into a place called in the Hebrew tongue Armageddon."
>
> (Revelation 16:14)

> "And the devil (Lucifer/satan) that deceived them was cast into the lake of fire and brimstone, where the beast (Draconian/Reptilian) and the false prophet (Religious Leader/Final Pope) are, and shall be tormented day and night forever and ever."
>
> (Revelation 20:10)

Evangelical Angels?

What is even more interesting is that we have a prophecy in Revelation, revealing that at the end of time on earth, there will be an angelic extraterrestrial messenger flying

Chapter Fourteen: The Harvest of Angels

through the heavens preaching the gospel to the entire earth, for everyone to hear, in a very loud voice, or high powered translating address system, giving us humans one last chance to repent and turn back to our Creator.

> "And I saw another angel fly in mid heaven, having the everlasting gospel to preach to them that dwell on the earth, and to every nation, and kindred, and tongue, and people, saying with a loud voice, 'Fear God, and give glory to him; for the hour of his judgment is come: and worship him that made heaven, and earth, and the sea, and the fountains of waters.'"
>
> (Revelation 14:6-7)

In the last days of the end of this present age, we can expect to see the skies (heavens above the earth) to be filled with all kinds of different spacecraft and beings. Some will be working for the kingdom of darkness; others will be messenger and warriors dispatched from the Kingdom of Heaven. There is no greater evidence of this, than the fact that this prophecy will be fulfilled by extraterrestrials flying above the skies of earth shouting in a loud voice so those who live on the surface of the earth could hear, to repent, accept the good news of the gospel of heaven and be saved. This is known as the Great Commission, to preach the gospel of the Kingdom to all ends of the earth. Suffice it to say, these heavenly extraterrestrial angels have the task of the 'last call', to all those who have either rejected the invitation into the Kingdom of Heaven or for those who haven't heard it.

I wonder how they will respond? I would imagine the shock and awe of it, would be humbling. I doubt anyone would dare to say, they're being too preachy. As many evangelists on earth hear from the unbelieving crowds. Just like in bars and pubs on earth, there comes a time before closing where they shout, 'last call for alcohol', so will it be on earth during the last days, the 'last call for Grace.'

Don't wait till the very end, you can accept the invitation now by simply asking the Lord and Messiah Yeshua (Jesus Christ) to come into your heart and save you, forgive you for your sins, and wash you clean in preparation for His Heavenly Kingdom coming to earth.

Jesus spoke a lot about the Kingdom. The Kingdom of God, He said, is found within you. This is the presence of His Holy Spirit, aka the Spirit of Christ living inside you and expressing itself through you as His vessel. However, the Kingdom of Heaven is a place, which has not yet arrived.

Therefore, Jesus told us all to pray the Lord's Prayer, "Thy Kingdom Come, on earth as it is in Heaven." (Matthew 6:10) Because the Kingdom of Heaven is coming to earth! The Kingdom of Heaven is a place that is governed by the Kingdom of God, who is the Lord, King and Messiah, Yeshua/Jesus. Truth be told, it is the Body of Christ, which are all of His believers who are the redeemed from the kingdom of darkness, whose collective prayers call in the Kingdom of Heaven to actually come to earth, become reality when the prophesy is fulfilled.

NOTES AND REFERENCES:

1. Ella LeBain, *Who Is God? Book Two of Who's Who in The Cosmic Zoo? A Guide to ETs, Aliens, Gods & Angels,* Chapter Two: *Ancient Technology & Biblical Astronauts,* p.21, Skypath Books, 2015.
2. Albert Brooks, *Defending Your Life,* 1991, Geffen Pictures, Directed by Albert Brooks.

CHAPTER FIFTEEN
Ascension Or Rapture?

> "For the Lord himself will come down from heaven, with a loud command, with the voice of the archangel and with the trumpet call of God, and the dead in Christ will rise first. After that, we who are still alive and are left, will be *caught up* (raptured) together with them *in the clouds* to meet the Lord *in the air*. And so, we will be with the Lord forever."
> (1 Thessalonians 4:16-17)

> "The one who sowed the good seed is the Son of Man. The field is the world, and the good seed stands for the people of the kingdom. The weeds are the people of the evil one, and the enemy who sows them is the devil. *The harvest is the end of the age, and the harvesters are angels.*"
> "As the weeds are pulled up and burned in the fire, so it will be at the end of the age. The Son of Man will send out *his angels*, and they will weed out of his kingdom everything that causes sin and all who do evil. They will throw them into the blazing furnace, where there will be weeping and gnashing of teeth. Then the righteous will shine like the sun in the kingdom of their Father. Whoever has ears, let them hear."
> (Matthew 13:37-43)

New Agers believe in Ascension. Born Again Christians believe in the Rapture. Could they be the same? Let's discern.

New Agers think that they can ascend all by themselves by working on themselves and aligning with Higher Self. Born again believers, on the other hand, believe that they ascend into heaven's skies to meet Jesus in the air, as a group, known as the "body of Christ", not by themselves as the prophecy promises in 1 Thessalonians 4:16-17.

I learned of the Rapture when I was eighteen years old, and was told by the Assemblies of God in South Africa, 'have nothing to do with UFOs, because when the rapture happens, the devil is going to lie to the rest of the world that all the believers and saints of Jesus Christ were abducted off the planet by aliens in UFOs.'

What if that were true? That it's not aliens, but hosts of Extraterrestrial Angels on assignment from the Kingdom of Heaven? Angels who were ordered by the Lord Himself to go gather His Harvest from the earth, right before He pours out His Wrath on the Wicked. Well the whole subject matter intrigued me, which sent me on what has become a thirty-eight-year journey to find the truth. First, as bizarre as what they told me sounded at the time, I did learn there was some truth to it, however, not in the way they were trying to communicate it to me. Let's discern:

We know from Scripture that those who put their faith in the grace and salvation of the Messiah/King will be saved. These are His redeemed children, His harvest whom He saved and chose from the foundation of the world, to be redeemed for His Kingdom, delivered from the Kingdom of Darkness that prevailed on earth, during the years of the curse.

Today in New Age circles, you can't go anywhere without hearing the word 'ascension'. Many New Agers believe that they are ascending, becoming enlightened, outgrowing their human bodies and ascending into their light bodies which resides in the fifth dimension. Many believe they have been contacted by Ascended Masters who assure them that 'their ascension draweth nigh.' Well, if you've gotten to this part of my book, you will know by now that those beings masquerading as Ascended Masters are fallen angels that are intent on deceiving as many humans as possible away from the Truth. Like it or not, it's my intention to set the record straight for the good of all concerned.

New Agers believe that they can work their way towards ascension, through self-improvement techniques, like chakra balancing, and aligning with their Higher Selves. What if the individual so-called ascensions were really individual abductions done by fallen angels masquerading as Ascended Masters? The Truth Is Stranger Than Fiction!

"Don't let anyone capture you with empty philosophies and high-sounding nonsense that come from human thinking and from the spiritual powers of this world, rather than from Christ."

(Colossians 2:8)

The Ascension doctrine is one of the doctrines of demons I talked about in previous chapters. It is a counterfeit doctrine to compete with what the Bible scriptures refer to as the Rapture, when believers of Jesus Christ ascend en masse into

Chapter Fifteen: Ascension Or Rapture?

the heavens before the wrath of God is poured out on the world. "For God hath not appointed us to wrath, but to obtain salvation by our Lord Jesus Christ," (1 Thessalonians 5:9).

Christians are split into three camps regarding the Rapture, which all revolve around their beliefs and understanding of the very last days of the end times prophecies. Scriptures predict it to be the worst suffering on planet earth to date. Some believe the Rapture will happen before the Great Tribulation, others, three and half years into it, and others believe it will happen at the end of the Tribulation, just before the Wrath of God is poured out on the earth.

Many confuse the Great Tribulation, which is the seven-year reign of the Antichrist on earth, with the Wrath of God. The Tribulation period is known as the time of Jacob's Troubles, because it focuses on the persecutions of Israel, its battles during the reign of the counterfeit Messiah. This man makes a seven-year peace treaty with Israel, that he breaches after three and half years, per the book of Daniel. It is believed that many Jews and Christians will be martyred under the reign of the Antichrist. This is the wrath of Satan on the godly believers in the Lord, not the wrath of God. The seven bowls of wrath, comes from the Lord, to punish the wicked, it is not appointed to His Church. This is an important discernment.

If you've reached this point in my book, then you already understand that there is a spiritual war and cosmic battle going on over planet earth, as well as over the souls, minds and bodies of humans. You also understand by now that we're contending against a host of deceptive influences that have been cursed and cast out of the upper heavens, known as fallen angels, rebel ETs, aliens and demons. These beings have created a stronghold on earth and in the first and second heavens from which they rule (Ephesians 6:12). You also understand by now that the Bible is one of the greatest documents of extraterrestrial and alien contact left on the planet from the ancients. That what many may deem as science fiction today is really science fact, as when it comes to the technology and the technological wonders that many call miracles depicted in the Bible. When the event known as the Rapture occurs, which will remove over 3.5 billion humans from the planet at one time, it doesn't take a rocket scientist to figure out that the Lord will orchestrate that event with massive fleets of starships organized by a huge staff of extraterrestrial angel-messengers. In the true sense of the word, one could say, that yes, the rapture will be a mass abduction, but not in the sense of victimization from being abducted, but a 'lifting up' into the heavens.

The Christian Rapture is the Ascension to which New Agers aspire. The only difference is you must have Christ in you, must have repented of your sins and accepted Jesus as your only Savior, that through His blood sacrifice you are saved and *raptured* to Heaven. Most New Agers do not ascribe to that, but believe in the Ascension, nevertheless. So, which is which? Let's discern.

Being raptured means ascending to glory. The promises of God, are from glory to glory, which are within the Glory of the New Blood Covenant through Jesus Christ.

"...Now the Lord is the Spirit, and where the Spirit of the Lord is, there is freedom. But we all, with open face beholding as in a glass the glory of the Lord, are changed into the same image from glory to glory, even as by the Spirit of the Lord."

(2 Corinthians 3:17-18-KJV)

Promises of being transformed into immortal glory bodies are mentioned as the restoring of the ten strands of DNA that were genetically disabled, manipulated and downgraded by the Annunaki Alien gods. This is recorded in the Sumerian Cuneiform Tablets, established as happening approximately 4,000 BC

My research has found scriptural evidence to back up all three theories. No one therefore knows for sure when the Rapture will occur, because two-thirds of Christians maybe wrong and only a remnant may have it right. Even more reason to be ready at any time.

A remnant is now awakening, through the spiritual revival which always happens before judgment. This has always been God's pattern in the past. He sends out prophets to warn people of impending judgement, puts out a clarion call for repentance and calls souls to return to Him through Christ, the Messiah and Savior of humankind. There have been many spiritual revivals happening around the world, in countries where it's illegal to even own a bible. This is happening in places like China, where there is a growing underground church, which is thriving. In Africa, there are literally millions of Muslims leaving Islam, because they do not identify with ISIS and realize that Allah is Satan. They are turning to Jesus Christ in the millions, as I've reported in my Concluding Words in Book Two: *Who Is God?*

Many Christians who wholeheartedly believe in the rapture still cannot explain *how* the Lord will pull off such an enormous endeavor of lifting over 3-4 billion believers off the planet all at the same time, without the rest of the world noticing. Ofcourse, to believers, nothing is too hard for the Lord to accomplish. But what does the Bible say?

"For the Lord himself will come down from heaven, with a loud command, with the voice of the archangel and with the trumpet call of God,

Chapter Fifteen: Ascension Or Rapture?

and the dead in Christ will rise first. (the dead in Christ are inside heaven's dimension inside the earth, known as paradise or Abraham's Bosom in scripture). After that, we who are still alive and are left, will be <u>caught up</u> (raptured) together with them <u>in the clouds</u> (the biblical word for the Lords starships) to meet the Lord <u>in the air</u>. And so, we will be with the Lord forever."

(1 Thessalonians 4:16-17) (emphasis and brackets mine)

<u>Caught up together with them in the clouds</u>, is where Christians have attached the word 'rapture' to this verse. Many Christians have said that there is no place in the Bible that uses the word, 'rapture', yet this is simply untrue. As with many issues, much has been lost in translation. In the Latin Vulgate Bible, the Latin word *rapiemur* was used, which is where the English word 'rapture' originates. *Rapiemur* was then translated into the Greek as *harpazo* which in English is 'caught up', or 'to carry off,' 'snatch up,' or 'grasp hastily' which are the words used in 1 Thessalonians 4:16-18.

The Greek to English translations went from *harpazo* to *rapture* which involved two steps: first, *harpazo* became the Latin word *raptus*; second, *raptus* became the English word 'rapture.' In addition, there are three other places in the Bible where it relates to the mysterious disappearance of the saints, the believers in Jesus Christ, as well as ten different raptures in the Bible, which I will delineate:

THE DAY AND HOUR UNKNOWN
Emphasis and Comments in brackets are mine:

> "No one knows about that day or hour, not even the angels in heaven, nor the Son, but only the Father. As it was in the days of Noah, so it will be at the coming of the Son of Man.

[There were Nephilim on the earth in the days of Noah, the sons of God were experimenting with genetic engineering, creating giants, transhumans and all sorts of combinations of creatures, which are written in our mythologies. Today science has been tapping into genetics, through GMO food, creating transhumans, nanotechnological implants, creating Borg like humans, and as I've stated earlier in my book, the abduction phenomenon is about creating the new Nephilim; fulfilling what Jesus was talking about, that history would repeat itself in the last days that we are living in.]

"For in the days before the flood, people were eating and drinking, marrying and giving in marriage, up to the day Noah entered the ark; and they knew nothing about what would happen until the flood came and took them all away. That is how it will be at the coming of the Son of Man."

[The eating and drinking comment Jesus refers to is modern day partying, which is an escape from the world, getting inebriated. Marriage is not bad, but I believe Jesus was referring to a type of marrying that was going on in the days of Noah, which was same-sex.

[Today there are six states within the USA that allow same sex marriage unions. There is also a growing trend throughout Europe of statutes protecting gay lifestyles, making it politically incorrect to quote the Bible scriptures which outlaw it. Let's not forget history, that even though the floods came and destroyed everyone, and life had to start all over again, it wasn't long until the same pattern repeated itself in the twin cities of Sodom and Gomorrah. These had to be destroyed because of rampant homosexuality, through fire from heaven, nuclear blast from one of the Lord's spaceships.

[While it's important to note that the Almighty promised never to destroy the entire earth by flood again, He didn't say anything about fire. What Jesus is talking about here is that everyone's consciousness in the days of Noah was so focused on their pleasures and their errant lifestyles, that they didn't see it coming, and were destroyed. They were warned, but they mocked Noah.]

"Two men will be in the field; one will be taken and the other left. Two women will be grinding with a hand mill; one will be taken and the other left. "Therefore keep watch, because you do not know on what day your Lord will come. But understand this: If the owner of the house had known at what time of night the thief was coming, he would have kept watch and would not have let his house be broken into. So, you also must be ready, because the Son of Man will come at an hour when you do not expect him."
(Matthew 24:36-44; Luke 17:26,27 24:45-51; Luke 12:42-46)

Jesus said: "On that day no one who is on the roof of his house, with his goods inside, should go down to get them. Likewise, no one in the field should go back for anything. Remember Lot's wife. Whoever tries to keep his life will lose it, and whoever loses his life will preserve it. I tell you, on that night two people will be in one bed; one will be taken and the other left."
(Luke 17:31-34)

Chapter Fifteen: Ascension Or Rapture?

When we read this verse, 'Two men will be in the field; one will be taken and the other left. Two women will be grinding with a hand mill; one will be taken and the other left,' 'on that night two people will be in one bed; one will be taken and the other left' this clearly implies that fifty percent of the people will go missing. One out of every two! That would mean that by the time the rapture occurs, half the planet will have accepted Christ as their Savior.

It does say,

"And this gospel of the kingdom will be preached in the whole world
as a testimony to all nations, and then the end will come."

(Matthew 24:14)

When that goal is accomplished, the Lord will rapture His 'harvest' of believers from the face of the earth. As I've mentioned in my chapter on religion, statistically speaking, Christianity is the fastest growing religion on the planet today.

In 2005, author Jim Rutz[1] wrote a book titled, *Megashift*, and coined a new phrase to define the fastest growing segment of the population. He calls them 'core apostolics' – or 'the new saints' who are at the heart of the mushrooming kingdom of God." Rutz makes the point that Christianity is overlooked as the fastest-growing faith in the world because most surveys look at the traditional Protestant denominations and the Roman Catholic Church while ignoring Christian believers who have no part of either. He says there are over 707 million "switched-on disciples" who fit into this new category and that this 'church' is exploding in growth. "The growing core of Christianity crosses theological lines and includes 707 million born-again people who are increasing by 8 percent a year," he says. So, fast is this group growing that, under current trends, according to Rutz, the entire world will be composed of such believers by the year 2032.

At the time of the writing of this chapter (March, 2011, updated November, 2016), I researched the internet and asked how many Christians are in the world today? This is the answer I got from WikiAnswers[2]:

'Many sources mention 2.2 billion Christians in the world (about one third of the total population of the planet), but estimating numbers is fraught with difficulties. What is included among the definition of 'Christian' is not agreed upon by many of the groups involved.

The term 'Christian' in its simplest definition refers to one who believes in Jesus Christ (as God). Drawing the line between 'Christian' and those who belong to 'sects' is problematic. Add to this the fact that no-one can really tell if a person is a Christian at heart, or if they are just paying lip-service to the name. This is impossible for any but God who sees the heart to judge. The numbers can be taken, then, as a best estimate of how many identify with Christianity in some way.

However, it is now impossible to say with any certainty, as, while practicing Christians have been in decline in some Western countries, there has been a recent surge in 'membership' in parts of the West, and in the East, the numbers who are becoming new Christians daily is astronomical.

There are estimated now nearly 150 *million* Christians in China (compared with just 5,000 in the 1960s) and in South Korea, churches regularly have tens of thousands of members each. In one church, the Yoido Full Gospel Church in Seoul, there are over 1,500,000 members who meet each Sunday in several sittings in a vast hall. So, whilst it is difficult to give a definite answer to the actual number of Christians in the world (as of 2011, estimates 3.1 billion), Christianity remains the most dominant of the world, and is still growing at an astonishing rate.'

The point is that it is hard to define a Christian, because of the status of 'religion.' There are so many denominations and sects mentioned.[3] This is why there are so many people coming to Jesus Christ around the world, they are not being drawn to Him because of any religion, but because of the Holy Spirit and the miracles that are occurring daily in their lives and around the world. I have been saying this throughout this book that Jesus Christ does not belong to any religion, He is the Cosmic Christ and is there for all beings, universally. What is happening around the world is the fulfillment of this prophecy:

> "In the last days, God says, I will pour out my Spirit on all people. Your sons and daughters will prophesy, your young men will see visions, your old men will dream dreams. Even on my servants, both men and women, I will pour out my Spirit in those days, and they will prophesy."
>
> (Acts 2:17,18; Joel 2:28,29)

It is the Holy Spirit drawing men and women to Jesus Christ, in China, Korea, India and all parts of the world, and because of the Spirit, all kinds of the miracles are happening. Many people in these parts of the world are not even allowed to own a Bible, but that does not limit the Holy Spirit from doing its work. There are all kinds of reports coming out of these countries of miraculous healings, people being resurrected from the dead, and deliverance from demonic possession and oppression. Many of these people know nothing about any Christian 'religion' but they do know the Living God through Jesus Christ. Again, this is another fulfillment of prophecy:

Chapter Fifteen: Ascension Or Rapture?

"Unless you people see miraculous signs and wonders," Jesus told him, "you will never believe."

(John 4:48)

When I asked WikiAnswers, 'how many people are on planet earth today?' I got, "An exact figure is never possible." However, according to the World POP Clock Projection (U.S. Census Bureau) as of November of 2016, that number is approximately 7.5 billion people living on planet Earth, but it's changing as you read this answer, so update as needed.

So, let's do the math here, if WikiAnswers is estimating approximately 3.1 billion Christians on the planet today that is almost half of the world's population. That means that when Jesus said, 'Two men will be in the field; one will be taken and the other left. Two women will be grinding with a hand mill; one will be taken and the other left, and gave us his 1:1 ratio for our times, that's essentially 50% of the entire population! We are very close to approaching those numbers being achieved.

"Listen, I tell you a mystery: We will not all sleep (many will *ascend* and be *raptured* alive), but we will all be changed-- in a flash, in the twinkling of an eye, at the last trumpet. For the trumpet, will sound, the dead will be raised imperishable, and we will be changed. For the perishable, must clothe itself with the imperishable, and the mortal with immortality. When the perishable has been clothed with the imperishable, and the mortal with immortality, then the saying that is written will come true: "Death has been swallowed up in victory. Where, O death, is your victory? Where, O death, is your sting?" The sting of death is sin, and the power of sin is the law."

(1 Corinthians 15:51-56-emphasis mine)

We will all be changed! This means that at the time of the rapture both those who died in Christ and those who are alive on the earth, will all be transformed into their incorruptible bodies. This could be where the New Agers get the idea of ascending into the 'light body.' Only by the authority and the power of Christ will this 'ascension' happen. This is where the New Agers are misled, thinking this is something they can do themselves, with meditation or other types of metaphysical practices.

Transformation into immortality can only come through Christ. Being the Son of Man, He is the Judge of all souls, and as I've said this before in this book, if a person rejects Christ, then why would He allow him into His Kingdom? The Kingdom of Heaven is for believers, even if you have faith the size of a mustard seed, according to Jesus, that is enough. But His teachings are full of all kinds of stories where He wouldn't and couldn't perform any miracles because of disbelief.

Jesus promised to return, but in this verse, lie hidden meanings as to how and where His believers will go:

> "Do not let your hearts be troubled. Trust in God; trust also in me. In my Father's house are many <u>mansions</u>; if it were not so, I would have told you. I am going there to prepare a place for you. And if I go and prepare a place for you, <u>I will come back and take you to be with me that you also may be where I am</u>."
>
> (John 14:1-3)

As I've mentioned in previous chapters, throughout this five-book series, the word *'mansions'* has been used in the Vedic scriptures to describe *mansions* as motherships or 'cities in the air' as they describe their Vimanas. In fact, the word *'mansions'* is also used in Vedic astrology to describe the exact positions of stars known as Nakshatras, or lunar *mansions*. So, you may ask, why would Jesus choose this word to tell His disciples that there are many *mansions* in His Father's house? His Father's house is the Kingdom of Heaven, and *mansions* also refer to celestial zodiac houses, made up of millions of stars, that includes a multitude of starships as well!

That's what this book is about, not just discerning *Who's Who in the Cosmic Zoo*, but also how to discern which are the Lord's spaceships and which UFOs belong to the kingdom of darkness. Just a review for those of you who may have skipped the rest of the book and chose to begin with this chapter for some reason, the spaceships that belong to the Kingdom of God appear ethereal, they are repeatedly described in both the Old and New Testaments as 'clouds.' The Lord's ships have the capability to cloak themselves in clouds. This has alot to do with the 'glory cloud' that comes from the Lord's presence.

The UFOs most people see flying around the earth are not ethereal, or ships of light, but are metallic hardware that come from inside the planet and are controlled by Satan's Draconian-Reptilian hierarchy. Nobody ever describes them as clouds. In fact, those who have been abducted and taken onto one of their ships by gray alien demons, who have performed all kinds of sexual experiments on them, describe the interior as dark, coldly technological, and with an awful smell of sulfur. Travis Walton,[4] famous for his physical abduction experience in 1975, and author of *Fire in The Sky*, described the inside of the ship he was taken into as having what he called a green slimy jello-like substance that stuck to him, alien goo. Other abductees describe what they call angel hair, which is a sticky like spider-web-like substance that stuck to them.

Chapter Fifteen: Ascension Or Rapture?

If you go back and read my chapter on *Ancient Technology and Biblical Astronauts*, in Book Two[5], *Who Is God?* you will see that the Lord's spaceships are made of pure gold, crystals and precious gemstones which are more spectacular than the mind could imagine.

So many Christians just can't get their head around the fact that the Lord has a fleet of spaceships at His command. If He is the King of Kings and Lord of Lords, then He can have anything, right? But some may think, why does He need spaceships? If He is God, He could go anywhere with His Word and His thought. But why not travel in style? The universe is a varied place, with all kinds of different dimensional experiences, all sorts of variations in time and space, so having a space vehicle or a *mansion* in the sky can becomes one's home, one's shelter from the interstellar winds, and allow one to maintain an equilibrium instead of being tossed and changed by the fluctuations of space which could go anywhere. Plus, the Lord's starships are equipped with all the technology necessary to defeat the spaceships of the kingdom of darkness.

"When Christ, who is our life, shall appear, then shall you also appear with him in glory."

(Colossians 3:4)

As I've mentioned in greater detail in my chapter on *Ancient Technology and Biblical Astronauts*[6], you will remember that the Bible describes the Lords spaceships as being covered in jewels with crystal floors that glow like sapphires. When the Lord promises that we will appear with Him in glory, what could be a more glorious platform than one of gold and precious gemstones, which traverses the heavens safe and secure with Him?

The following scripture reveals (the brackets and emphasis are mine) that when Christ returns at the very end to claim the final victory at the battle of Armageddon, He will have with Him an armada of ships from one end of the heavens to the other.

"Jesus told his disciples: "Immediately after the distress of those days "'the sun will be darkened, and the moon will not give its light; (a solar eclipse) the stars will fall from the sky, (an alien invasion; each time the bible refers to falling stars, it is referring to fallen angels or bad/rebellious ETs) and the heavenly bodies will be shaken.' (This means their starships will be hit with mighty power causing the bad ETs (fallen angels) to shake and fall.) "At that time the sign of the Son of Man will appear in the sky, and all the nations of the earth will mourn. They will see the Son of Man coming on the clouds of the sky, (on his starships) with power and great glory. And he will send his angels (extraterrestrial messengers) with a loud trumpet call, (probably some kind of PA system into the fleet of ships) and they will gather his elect from the four winds, from <u>one end of the heavens to the other</u>. (ET Alliances and Star Nations)."

(Matthew 24:29-31; Isaiah 13:10-emphasis mine)

His elect from the four winds, from one of the heavens to the other, are the Coalition, Alliance and Federation of Star Nations that obey the command of the Cosmic Christ. Remember, Jesus Christ was given authority in all the heavens, on the earth and inside the earth. He is well known throughout the universe, and He has a lot of allies. Remember too that when Lucifer rebelled, he persuaded only 1/3 of heavens angels or stars to go with him, the other 2/3 having stayed faithful to the Lord. These combined forces will defeat the kingdom of darkness not only on earth, but in the heavens, where they have corrupted other star systems as well. This is the reason the Lord promises to create a new heaven and a new earth at the end, to cleanse the entire universe of cosmic evil. Nothing shall stay the same.

"Heaven and earth will disappear, but my Words will never disappear."
~ Jesus

(Luke 21:33)

"But the day of the Lord will come like a thief. The heavens will disappear with a roar; the elements will be destroyed by fire, and the earth and everything in it will be laid bare."

(2 Peter 3:10)

This world will be destroyed by fire. It will end with a *Star Wars* type battle between the heavenly forces of the Office of Satan and the Office of Christ. The Bible talks about the terrible Day of the Lord. Many Christians I speak to are confused about the difference between the wrath of God and the persecution of the church which is done by Satan, via the Antichrist. Satan has been persecuting God's people since they have been living on planet earth. Both Jews and Christians have been persecuted historically, and still are today. The Bible talks about the tribulation saints who are savaged by the antichrist, because they see through him and refuse to take his mark for buying and selling in his New World Order's digitalized system. However, the wrath of God is reserved for the unbelievers, not for God's own people as written in Isaiah 66 and the seven seals of Revelation 5 and 6.

Chapter Fifteen: Ascension Or Rapture?

"Do you see all these great buildings?" replied Jesus. "Not one stone here will be left on another; everyone will be thrown down."

(Mark 13:2)

"They will dash you to the ground, you and the children within your walls. <u>They will not leave one stone on another, because you did not recognize the time of God's coming to you.</u>"

(Luke 19:22)

Jesus is telling us that everything on earth will be destroyed. Jesus said, the end of the world will come instantly, unexpectedly like a 'thief in the night'. He tells everybody to be ready.

In 1881, a French Priest, Father Charles Arminjon[7], wrote *The End of the Present Word and the Mysteries of the Future Life,* which was recently translated by Susan Conroy and Peter McEnerny. In it, Father Arminjon wrote: "It will come at a time when the human race, sunk in the uttermost depths of indifference, will be far from thinking about punishment or justice."

"In those days, people will seek death but will not find it. They will long to die, but death will flee from them!"

(Revelation 9:6)

Scripture tells us that the Lord will spew, spit or vomit out of His mouth the lukewarm Christians. "So then because you are lukewarm, and neither cold nor hot, I will spew you out of my mouth." (Revelation 3:16). The world will not end by water, but by fire, and people will be caught off guard, because their consciousness is suppressed and deceived by the god of this world. People will not seek God or turn their eyes towards Heaven because of the distractions with the cares of this world. There will also be a growing belief in universalism, and the belief that everyone will be saved. There will be a denial of hell and judgment. By that time, Divine grace and mercy will have exhausted all its resources and means of action, and the antichrist will reign through the New World Order.

This is the reason why I believe that UFO disclosure may never fully happen until the reign of the antichrist, who will lie to the world. Through all kinds of mass deceptions, the antichrist will convince us that there is a threat to planet Earth from outer space. It is a threat to *him* from all those faithful extraterrestrial angels serving the Kingdom of Heaven through the Office of Christ, gearing up for the final battle with the Office of Satan.

Raptured!

Now, many in Christian circles have argued over when the rapture would occur, some believe it is supposed to happen half way through the seven-year tribulation period, others believe at the very end, others are convinced it will occur at the start of the tribulation, before the final Antichrist is revealed to the world. Since I learned about the Rapture, thirty-eight years ago, I have been through all three phases of belief of 'when', and after doing research for all three positions, which all have compelling arguments, I have become a 'Pan Tribber', meaning, all the Bible Prophecies are going to the pan out in the end, in God's way and in God's timing.

I would like to share one thing I have always believed in, that the promises of God, particularly the one that says that His Children, the redeemed of the Lord, are not appointed to God's Wrath. (1 Thessalonians 5:9) This to me has always been the key prophetic scripture that relates to the Rapture of His Redeemed from the Earth. It will happen right before the wrath of God is poured out on the earth. Another discernment that I think is important to mention, is that the wrath of God is on the wicked, the unbelievers and the rebellious towards God and His Grace. The Tribulation, upon which most Christians base their positions of when the rapture occurs, is the wrath of the Antichrist on Jews and Christians. Jesus made it very clear when He said, 'In this life, you will have tribulation, but take heart in the fact that I have overcome the world.' (John 16:33)

The promises of salvation from the wrath of God:

"And to wait for his Son from heaven, whom he raised from the dead, [even] Jesus, which delivered us from the wrath to come."

(1 Thessalonians 1:10)

"For God hath not appointed us to wrath, but to obtain salvation by our Lord Jesus Christ."

(1 Thessalonians 5:9)

"Much more then, being now justified by his blood, we shall be saved from wrath through Him."

(Romans 5:9)

"Let no man deceive you with vain words: for because of these things comes the wrath of God upon the children of disobedience."

(Ephesians 5:6)

Chapter Fifteen: Ascension Or Rapture?

Jews went through the holocaust, Christians are being beheaded, raped and tortured by Muslims on the planet today. Their only escape is through death. Make no mistake, these events are not God's wrath, but satan's wrath on God's people. Therefore, why would God take His believers off the planet during the reign of the Antichrist? He could, don't get me wrong, He's God, He can do anything, and for many years, I wholeheartedly believed this was the case, but after surviving decades of persecution and rejection from both sides of my family for my faith, and reaching my mid-fifties, I'm not so sure about that anymore. What I am sure of, is that we, His redeemed, His faithful, are saved from God's Wrath. But tribulation seems to be what goes on here, living on planet earth. And the Great Tribulation is also called the times of Jacob's troubles, which is focused on Israel. "Alas! for that day is great, so that none is like it: it is even the time of Jacob's trouble; but he shall be saved out of it." (Jeremiah 30:7) Scripture tells us of many believers that will be martyred for their faith during this great testing, so if they were raptured, then how can that be? (See, Revelation 6:9-11; Revelation 20)

I then moved from being pre-trib, to mid-trib, because, it's three and half years, the prophecy in Daniel tells us, will be when the Antichrist breaks his seven-year treaty with Israel, and declare himself to be God, demands worship and kills everyone who refuses to see him as God. I thought, surely, this would be a good time for the Lord to come and save his people, rapture them off the Earth, but then after doing even more research, I thought, how can all the people become martyred for their faith, how can Israel know the difference, that they were deceived into believing this man was their messiah, but betrays them, if the true believers who know the prophecy were taken off the planet, who would be there to help them through it and guide them to the true Messiah? So, I evolved into a post tribber, or pan tribber, as I like to call myself now. But I am going to present the research for you, so you can decide for yourself, or just be ready in any event, for rapture or death, by having your life right with God, and securing your salvation through Jesus Christ.

For those who are not familiar with this quintessential End Time Prophecy, here it is in a nutshell: The anti-Christ makes a covenant-peace treaty with Israel, called the 70th week of Daniel. (Daniel Chapter 9) It's a seven-year period (a Shemitah cycle) set aside for Israel to bring the 6000 years of Human history to a close. The 42 months of Revelation, also describes a 3-1/2-year period, and 1260 days, which is the duration of the Great Tribulation, the last half of Daniel's 70th week. It begins when the anti-Christ declares himself God in the rebuilt Temple of Jerusalem. (2 Thessalonians 2:4). This is a time known as the Abomination of Desolation, which has happened before during the reign of Antiochus (See, Book of Maccabees). Daniel says that this will happen in the middle of the 70th week (Daniel 9:27), which is

3-1/2 years also known as 'mid-trib', and Jesus said it will begin the Great Tribulation (Matthew 24:15-21)

The anti-Christ will make a 7-year covenant with Israel that will appear to bring them peace after a great world war, which culminates over Israel. The anti-Christ will bring Israel's enemies into a peace treaty, and Israel will think he's their messiah for saving them from their enemies. But in the middle of it he'll betray Israel and in Satan's power will do his best to destroy the Jews once and for all. He will fail and the Lord will emerge victorious, which will be the final *star wars* type battle of Armageddon, when Yeshua/Jesus returns as the Messiah-Warrior King, and saves Israel. However, He also says, that He will not return, until Israel can say, "Blessed is He who comes in the name of the Lord – Yeshua/Jesus." Israel has an historical lesson to learn and overcome, and that is to have their spiritual eyes open to the truth about just *who* their Messiah really is.

Remember, He purchased us for a price, which was His Divine Blood. He gave His life as a *ransom* for the multitudes. This word implies that we, the human race, have been held captive, enslaved by the god of this world, who has kept this planet in quarantine from the rest of God's creation and Cosmic neighborhood. He has oppressed the human race through demonic oppression, demonic possession and all kinds of bio-chemical manipulations, genetic downgrading and manipulations by corrupting the original DNA and image of God, along with mind control.

What I want to impress upon my readers, no matter what background or level of education you may be from, is that this undisputed historical act of what Christ did for the human race, was not about religion, but all about salvation from the captivity of the matrix that has been put in place by the god of this world, who is Lucifer/Satan. This is completely an extraterrestrial and alien war. Jesus Christ became a man, to be the ransom, the Draconian/Reptilian kingdom of darkness wanted as payment. Please read Chapter Three: *The Clash of Two Kingdoms: The Cosmic Conflict* in Book One of *Who's Who In The Cosmic Zoo?* about the transfer of spiritual power at the Resurrection of Jesus Christ, who is also known as the Second Adam. The good news is that death couldn't keep Him in the ground, He arose after not only redeeming deceased souls from hell, but emerged with the keys of Death and Hades. The power transfer took place at the Resurrection, which is the foundation of the faith of believers across all denominations and churches.

In kidnapping cases, the slave masters usually demand payment to release their prisoners. Oftentimes its money, but not always, as there are many situations where people are prisoners are traded as ransom for other prisoners. In this case, the ransom of Divine Blood, the blood of a God, who was humbled into a man, was the payment required to break the stronghold that Satan had over this planet and its inhabitants. As with everything that gets established on earth, it is first established in the spiritual

Chapter Fifteen: Ascension Or Rapture?

realms and in the heavens first. So much so, that these unseen realms become more real than the material universe, because that which is unseen, created that which is seen. (2 Corinthians 4;18)

This is exactly the case with what I am saying is an ET/Alien war over earth humans and the real estate of not only Planet Earth, but our entire solar system. But for now, let's just focus on Earth and Earth humans. There is no question about it, we were bought with a price. Question remains, do you accept His Salvation from the kingdom of darkness and all of its Archonic demonic rulers? Or do you buy into the lies of unbelief of what Christ did and *who* Jesus is?

> "Keep watch over yourselves and all the flock of which the Holy Spirit has made you overseers. Be shepherds of the church of God, which he bought with his own blood."
>
> (Acts 20:28)

> "In Him we have redemption through His blood, the forgiveness of sins, in accordance with the riches of God's grace."
>
> (Ephesians 1:7)

> "Even as the Son of man came not to be ministered unto, but to minister, and to give his life a ransom for many."
>
> (Matthew 20:28)

> "For there is one God and one mediator between God and men, the man Christ Jesus, who gave Himself as a ransom for all — the testimony that was given at just the right time."
>
> (1 Timothy 2:5-6)

> "The righteous will never be removed, But the wicked will not inhabit the earth."
>
> (Proverbs 10:30)

When doing my research on this, I came across the wonderful work of John W. Milor,[8] author of the book, *Aliens and The Antichrist: Unveiling the End Times Deception*. In it he lays out the argument for the rapture occurring before the start of the seven-year tribulation. He has graciously given me his permission to quote him in length from his chapter, *Could the Rapture of the Church be a Mass Alien Abduction?* When I read this, I felt such resonance with his words, and I knew I had stumbled upon the truth and the confirmation of what I always intuitively felt about this subject, along with what I was imprinted with in 1979 when I was a young believer. I also listened to a lecture by another prominent scholar, Dr. Chuck Missler,[9] in his DVD, titled, *The Rapture*, who also believes as Milor does, that the rapture occurs before the great tribulation, and it actually initiates the time known to the Jews, as 'Jacob's troubles.' While I'm not necessarily promoting this pre-trib belief anymore, here is what I found out, nevertheless, so you can form your own opinion or belief.

After studying Dr. Missler's work, who listed seven raptures in the Bible, I came to discover that there are actually nine listed in scripture, and possibly ten, if you take the events prophesied in 1 Thessalonians separately. But for argument sake, there are ten separate raptures or ascensions to heaven, listed in the Bible:

1. Enoch - Genesis 5:42; Hebrews 11:5 (ascended to Heaven)
2. Elijah - 2 Kings 2:1,11 (ascended to Heaven)
3. Ezekiel - Ezekiel 3:12-14; 11:1; 43:5 (lifted up in the Lord's spaceships)
4. Jesus - Mark 16:19; Acts 1:9-11; Revelation 12:5 (ascended into Heaven)
5. Philip - Acts 8:39 (ascended to Heaven)
6. Paul - 2 Corinthians 12:2-4 (ascended to the third heaven)
7. Body of Christ - 1 Thessalonians 4:17 (may be two or three separate events)
8. John - Revelation 4:1 (ascended to Heaven)
9. The Two Witnesses - Revelation 11:3-12 (ascends to Heaven)
10. The 144,000 Jews - Revelation 14:3 (ascends to Heaven)

Some Christians have argued, "There cannot be a pre-trib rapture because that would require a second resurrection at Christ's return to earth." This conclusion is drawn from Revelation 20:

> "But the rest of the dead lived not again until the thousand years were finished. This is the first resurrection. Blessed and holy is he that hath part in the first resurrection: on such the second death hath no power, but they shall be priests of God and of Christ, and shall reign with him a thousand years."
> (Revelation 20:5-6)

I have heard someone explain this passage as, "The first did not mean first in time, but rather first in kind." The first resurrection was for God's people, the second will be for the unsaved.

A quick way to shoot down the notion that the first resurrection is tied to a specific date, as opposed to a more general time frame, is to take note of the tribulation rapture of the two witnesses and the 144,000 Jewish evangelists. At the mid-point

Chapter Fifteen: Ascension Or Rapture?

of the tribulation, the two witnesses are killed by the Antichrist, resurrected by God, and then caught up into heaven (Revelation 11:3-12).

Revelation Chapter 7 describes the sealing of the 144,000 Jewish evangelists just before the Beast issues his mark. Sometime during the latter half of the tribulation, Revelation 14:3 says they will be "redeemed from the earth," standing before the throne of God.

Milor says, 'As for the rapture of the church, however, as suddenly as the *angels* arrive, they will disappear without a trace, in the twinkling of an eye (1 Corinthians 15:52), leaving the entire world to dither in complete dismay. Probably the only people who might see anything at all, if anyone, will be military personnel working at military installations like NORAD (North American Aerospace Defense Command). I doubt they'll say anything, but shortly after that time, their secrecy won't matter much anymore.' This is when the antichrist surfaces, and lies to the world that there is a real threat from outer space who has abducted nearly half of the people on planet earth. Remember the 2:1 ratio.

All those people who heard the good news of the Kingdom of God, and did not accept Christ, as well as all those who may have accepted Him but were lukewarm and are not ready, are the ones who are left behind from being Raptured. These are the ones that understand what really happened, and then become believers, who then go on to become the 'tribulation saints.'

For pre-trib critics who cite Revelation 1:17, "every eye shall see him," as proof that the rapture will not be a secret event, they are getting it confused with the <u>second coming</u>. While no one on Earth will see the Lord in the air during the Rapture, the Rapture of the Body of Christ and its after effects will certainly <u>not</u> be a secret event. I doubt that, afterwards, with all the car wrecks, plane crashes, and missing persons reports, the rapture could remain a secret occurrence. Not to mention the rise of the Antichrist, and his opportunity to create the mass delusion over the ones who are left behind, and lie to the world that billions of people were abducted by aliens from outer space and create the fear that there is a threat from an outer space invasion.

The rapture literally kicks off the Antichrist's agenda to gather the forces of the earth to wage war against the Lord and His celestial hosts. This is why us humans need to be aware of the spiritual battle which aids in discerning this cosmic war between Satan's UFOs and the Lord's celestial army. It is Satan's agenda through the manifestation of the Antichrist to get humans on his side in his war against the Almighty Creator Lord.

Let me also explain to those who have hypothesized that Satan will counterfeit the Rapture with some type of mass abduction of humans before the Lord's appointed Rapture of His Bride, the body of Christ, as to why this won't happen. First, the Office of Satan have already been abducting humans to steal genetic material, eggs, sperm, DNA, for over sixty years now, to help create a new race of humans, the new Nephilim. Today's Ufologists already know that we've been invaded against our will, so this concept is nothing new.

Secondly, if Satan's forces were to have abducted nearly half of the humans on planet on earth and all the believers in Christ were left behind, you can bet there would be mass panic at the attack by 'aliens' (fallen angel demons) from outer space, especially because Christians would know that it was not their Lord.

Thirdly, if Satan were to pull this off, he couldn't employ his final agenda. His final scheme is to deceive humans left behind in his New World Order that there is a threat from outer space, which is to convince them into siding with him in his war against the Lord of Hosts. This is why he is heavily influencing New Agers to open portals, through reenacting ancient ceremonies, that the ancient gods may come through. The experimentation at Cern's Hadron Collider in Switzerland is one of them. Humans are literally inviting them, through invocation, back to earth, which is Satan's gathering of forces to wage war against the Almighty. It truly is a Divine Appointment!

New Agers are not alone in this, as there are many types of Illuminati and Freemasonry ceremonies that invoke and worship these ancient gods as well. The ancient gods are rebels against the Almighty Creator Lord, which is the nexus of all the ancient historical cosmic dramas. The truth is Satan and all of his fallen angel ETs and aliens are the <u>real</u> threat to planet earth. He will embody the final antichrist, who will wield the power and technology of Satan's fleet of UFOs all kinds of lying wonders and miracles. (See my chapter on the Antichrist in Book Two for further elucidation on this.) This is why many believe the Rapture to be the big event that literally kicks off the time of the antichrist. The body of Christ is, literally, the 'Restrainer'.

Another interesting theory is that the Rapture of the body of Christ, as written in 1 Thessalonians 4:17 is not just one event, but two. Let's discern:

> "For the Lord himself will come down from heaven, with a loud command, with the voice of the archangel and with the trumpet call of God, <u>and the dead in Christ will rise first</u>. After that, we who are still alive and are left, will be <u>caught up</u> (raptured) together <u>with them</u> <u>in the clouds</u> (the biblical word for the Lords starships) to meet the Lord <u>in the air</u>. And so, we will be with the Lord forever." (1 Thessalonians 4:16-17) (emphasis, brackets mine)

Scripture clearly tells us that the dead in Christ are the first to be raised up. The scripture says, 'after that', meaning at a later time, the rest of the believers left will be caught up in the air to meet them (the ones who were dead in Christ and the first to be raised up) in the clouds with the Lord. When I first read this, I thought, this could be why there is such controversy about whether the Rapture is before the tribulation

Chapter Fifteen: Ascension Or Rapture?

or in the middle of the tribulation. Perhaps it is both? Perhaps this passage indicates that this will be two separate events?

First the dead are resurrected and translated, and then 'after that' meaning at a later time, the believers on Earth are Raptured up. Because of the timeline described in all the prophesies which specifically relates to the seven-year tribulation, I was not even entertaining the thought of a post-trib Rapture, because it comes from those who are confusing the Rapture with the Second Coming, which are clearly two separate events.

However, there is a possibility that all of the pre-trib, mid-trib, and post-trib arguments are all right. We see that 1 Thessalonians 4:17 is clear that there will be two separate events, one for the dead, and one for the ones left alive. But the post-trib folks hang their hat on the fact that at the second coming, those who survived the tribulation, will be caught up at that time. In fact, Christian leaders like Pat Robertson believe in a post-trib rapture. There is enough evidence in scripture to prove all three arguments. Perhaps what we need to do is piece them altogether.

Many Christians who argue against a pre-tribulation Rapture, believe that they will be persecuted at the hands of the Antichrist and his New World Order. They believe this because the Bible says there will be tribulation saints, that it must be them. Todd Strandberg[10] writes in his article arguing *The Pretribulation Rapture,* "you would think the desire to go through the tribulation would be as popular as the desire to jump into a pit filled with vipers and broken glass. As illogical as it may seem, there appears to be a large number of Christians that fully expect to get roughed up before Christ returns." They also argue the scripture that Jesus told his disciples in Matthew 24:9 they were going to be handed over to be persecuted before he returns. Jesus was talking to the Jews in Israel not the rest of the body of Christ.

The good news is that the word of God clearly states that believers will escape the wrath of God. "<u>For God hath not appointed us to wrath</u>, but to obtain salvation by our Lord Jesus Christ" (1 Thessalonians 5:9). This wrath is the Lord's anger that will be poured out during the tribulation upon the rebels. "Since you have kept my command to endure patiently, <u>I will also keep you from the hour of trial that is going to come upon the whole world to test those who live on the earth</u>." (Revelation 3:10).

Tribulation isn't the Wrath of God, but the *wrath* of the Antichrist. The Wrath of God comes last in response to the *wrath* of the Antichrist. This could be where many pre-tribbers get confused. Jesus said, "in this world, you will have tribulation, but take comfort in knowing, that I have overcome the world." The Harvest is the Rapture. The Harvest is at the *end of this age,* and the Harvester are the angels. The angels call it 'the gathering,' because it is their assignment to gather all the true believers and faithful of the Kingdom of God, and present us to the Lord, in the air. This is not only done through the agency of angels, but through spacecraft. How else can approximately 3.5 billion people disappear off the face of the earth and get to heaven?

Surprisingly, there are many Christians today who do not know the difference between the wrath of God and the persecutions from Satan. This can best be discerned by the example of Job. Satan was responsible for testing Job and taking everything away from him, including his health, in a test. If he would curse God in his sorrow and loss, without all of his abundance, would have seemed like undeserved punishment; but he did not. God allowed the test, but he was not punishing Job. God then restored Job and gave him more than he had before Satan caused his nervous breakdown.

Satan persecutes Jews and Christians because they are God's people and the apple of His eye. The Lord, however, reserves His wrath for the unbelievers, the rebels and the wicked, all those who follow Satan, the god of this world.

As I've said previously, many confuse the Rapture with the Second Coming, which clearly are two separate events. When you fuse the two events together, you end up with verses that appear to contradict each other: 1 Thessalonians 5:9, "For God hath not appointed us to wrath, but to obtain salvation by our Lord Jesus Christ," and Revelation 13:7, "And it was given unto him to make war with the saints, and to overcome them: and power was given him over all kindreds, and tongues, and nations." The Antichrist was allowed to make war with the believers (i.e., saints), all saints? Or those who are left behind?

Those who think the Church will go through the tribulation have a point, as there will be a huge number of 'carnal Christians' who may find themselves left behind. These are the ones who are Christian in name only, the ones to whom the scripture refers as 'having a form of godliness but denying its power. Have nothing to do with them' (2 Timothy 3:5). These are also the lukewarm Christians, to whom Jesus says, "because you are lukewarm, neither hot nor cold, I am about to spit you out of my mouth' (Revelation 3:10).

They will know what happened when the Rapture occurs, when the word of God will finally be quickened in them. They will cry out to the Lord for their salvation, and the Holy Spirit will save them. They will witness to others, and the Holy Spirit will save more unbelievers, and then the 144,000 Jews will be sealed, and together these people will be known as the 'tribulation saints.'

Revelation 7:3 tells us of an angel descending to earth to seal the servants of God, before the Mark of the Antichrist is stamped on the rest of humanity. This happens mid-tribulation as the mark of the Beast is demanded after the first 1260 days (3-1/2 years) are passed. The number of people who receive God's protective seal are 144,000 in number. These are the Jews from the 12 tribes of Israel, 12,000 from each tribe. If the body of Christ were there, then why aren't they being sealed as well? The angel of the Lord told Daniel that, '70 weeks are determined unto thy people' (Daniel 9:24). Scripture never mentions that the tribulation is meant to be a time of testing for

Chapter Fifteen: Ascension Or Rapture?

Christians. It does not say that the church turns against God or that God turns against the church. The reason the church is not mentioned maybe because its already gone, caught up to heaven before the tribulation punishment of the Antichrist on Israel.

Matthew 25:13 says Jesus will return at an unknown time, while Revelation 12:6 indicates that the Jews will have to wait for the Lord 1,260 days, starting when the Antichrist stands in the Temple of God and declares himself to be God (2 Thessalonians 2:4). This event will take place at the mid-point of the seven-year tribulation (Daniel 9:27). When the Jews flee into the wilderness, they know that all they have to do is wait out those 1,260 days (Matthew 24:16). There is no way to apply the phrase "neither the day nor the hour" to this situation.

The only way for these two viewpoints to be true is to separate the two distinct events transpiring here: 1) the rapture of the Church, which comes before or in the middle of the tribulation; and 2) the return of Jesus to the earth, which takes place roughly seven years later.

The Bible does not directly say the Bride of Christ will go through the tribulation. This is why Jesus spent quite a bit of time talking about the parables of the ten virgins in Matthew 25, and the need for them to be ready. Matthew 25:2-13 is a wedding story that Jesus told, which is a parable for the Rapture of the Church. Jesus clearly states that a group of people will miss out on the event, and will cry out to God to let them into the place where He resides, heaven. The ones who weren't ready did not get to partake in the wedding banquet. The wedding banquet is what will happen when Jesus, the Bridegroom, comes back to collect his Bride. The parable of the ten virgins was specifically relating to the Rapture of the Bride, the body of Christ. 'Then the angel said to me, "Write: "blessed are those who are invited to the wedding supper of the Lamb!"'" And he added, "These are the true words of God'" (Revelation 19:9).

Strandberg makes a good argument for the pretribulation Rapture, "If the Antichrist came to power with the Church still here, I do not see how he could operate. When Hitler was fighting to take over England, a number of Christians were praying for victory. Hitler made mistake after mistake, and England out-performed its enemy at every stage of the conflict. It is difficult to measure the impact of intercessory prayer in physical warfare.

Little is known of how great a role praying saints played in the defeat of Nazi Germany. If the Church were to reside on earth during the tribulation, I am sure she would give the Antichrist fits. In Revelation 11:3, the two witnesses alone give the Antichrist enough headaches. Millions of Christians who know their Bibles well would recognize the man of sin and pray fire down on his head. The post-trib view would have to plan on the Church just rolling over and playing dead the whole seven years."

Strandberg is correct. If the Church was around during the reign of the Antichrist, the church would rebuke the Antichrist. There is nothing in the scripture about this.

The New World Order and all of its tenets, plans and schemes does not involve Christians, but a pseudo Christ. The very removal of the church is literally a green light for the powers of darkness to fulfill their evil schemes and test the unbelievers. Jesus said, "Ye are the salt of the earth" (Matthew 5:13). When the believers are removed, the earth will be plunged into spiritual darkness. When this happens, the Antichrist will then be free to control the world.

Many pre-tribulation writers quote Revelation 4:1, which says, 'come up hither,' as a prophetic reference to the rapture of the Church. Revelation chapters 1 through 3 is described as the Church Age and speaks to the Church. After the shout to 'come up hither,' the Church is not mentioned in Scripture at all. The attention of Scripture switches from the Church to the Jews living in Israel.

When Jesus returns at the end of the tribulation, He will be coming for battle (Revelation 19:19-21). In Revelation 19 tells us that Jesus returns with an army. The army's members are riding on white horses, and they are clothed in fine linen that is white and clean.

Revelation 19:8 says that the fine linen represents the righteousness of the saints. If the saints of God are returning with Christ to wage war on the Antichrist, that completely rules out the belief that there will be a post-trib rapture, without believers running into each other as they are coming and going. The dead in Christ are raised first, then those left on the earth are caught up, then they are translated into their immortal bodies, given robes of white linen. They all return together to join the Lord in battle. There is an order to these events, they do not happen all at once.

The tribulation period is compared to the times of Noah and Lot by Jesus in Luke 17:28. Nobody saw the floods coming, and likewise, nobody saw fire from heaven nuking the twin cities of Sodom and Gomorra. What both situations have in common is the removal of the righteous before the wrath of God comes down on the unbelievers. This is the heart and pattern of God, that He saves and removes His own from His own wrath.

This is why Jesus said, 'Therefore, you also must be ready, because the Son of Man will come <u>at an hour when you do not expect him</u>' (Matthew 24:44). The only time frame I can think of when believers would not be expecting Jesus to return would have to be before the tribulation. The Lord was quite definite that the rapture would come as a total surprise.

Now as far as the second coming goes, the Bible couldn't be plainer. It clearly states that Jesus Christ will return 1260 days from the moment the Antichrist sits in the Temple of God and declares himself to be God, which Daniel calls the abomination of desolation. Because there exists both a known and an unknown date, many scholars have logically concluded that there must be two different events occurring;

Chapter Fifteen: Ascension Or Rapture?

the rapture and the second coming. Yet so many get these two clearly different events confused.

Scripture says the tribulation will last seven years. This is the reign of the Antichrist. Daniel tells us his rule will be split into 1260 days, (3-1/2 years), the first 1260 will begin after he makes a pseudo-peace treaty with Israel and the third temple of Solomon is rebuilt, and animal sacrifices are resumed. The second 1260 days is when he persecutes Jews and Christians, puts an end to the animal sacrifices, and sits in the temple and declares himself to be god. I believe that most believers will know if they are in the tribulation period, and that they would recognize the Antichrist. The mystery is further revealed in 2 Thessalonians, where the Apostle Paul speaks of something that will restrain the advent of the Antichrist. The restrainer's removal is required before the Antichrist can be revealed to the world.

> "And now you know what is holding him back, so that he may be revealed at the proper time. For the secret power of lawlessness is already at work; <u>but the one who now holds it back will continue to do so till he is taken out of the way</u>. And then the lawless one will be revealed, whom the Lord Jesus will overthrow with the breath of his mouth and destroy by the splendor of his coming."
>
> (2 Thessalonians 2:6-8)

WHO IS THE RESTRAINER?

Many have hypothesized that the 'restrainer' that Paul spoke about in 2 Thessalonians, as holding back the antichrist, the man of lawlessness, is the Holy Spirit. This can't be true, because the Holy Spirit is the last bastion of grace left on the planet from the mercy of the Lord, so that humankind may be saved. Today, many are being saved through the agency of the Holy Spirit alone, about which I have already written, in countries where it is illegal to even own a Bible. They are being saved through the miracles of the Holy Spirit.

There are too many scriptures referring to the tribulation period and the tribulation saints, as well as the promise of two of the Lord's witnesses to return to preach the gospel, along with three extraterrestrial angels preaching the gospel in the air to all earth humans before the end comes (Revelation 14:6-12). This is all done through the Divine grace and mercy of God through the Holy Spirit. The Holy Spirit does not leave the planet when the Rapture occurs, because many come to the Lord through the Holy Spirit during the tribulation and are saved.

The strongest argument offered against the Holy Spirit being the Restrainer is the belief that if God's Spirit was ever removed from the earth, no one could then be saved. The removal of the Holy Ghost does not have to be an all or nothing proposition. He is taken out of the way through the many 'vessels', body temples where He is housed through the body of Christ. Christian believers form a collective and are taken out of the way, which is only a degree of removal. The Holy Spirit Himself remains to bring the carnal Christians, the Jews, the 144,000 Jews from each of the twelve tribes of Israel and the unbelievers who heard the gospel but rejected it, to their final call for salvation before the wrath of the Lord is poured out on the unbelieving and the wicked.

Some have also thought that this 'restrainer' may even be a mighty angel, similar to the powerful angel who holds the key and the chain to the abyss, the one who is appointed to chain up Lucifer Satan at the end of this timeline before the millennial reign (Revelation 20:1). Even though the angels as the Lord's faithful extraterrestrial messengers have a huge role to play during the last days, it's not clear that the one to whom Paul is referring is an angel, but it could very well be a guardian extraterrestrial angel or group of angels, whose role it is to prevent another type of extraterrestrial alien being from taking over the planet, who becomes the final anti-Christ. Some have postulated that one of the Annunaki who live on Nibiru, will be the anti-Christ, as Nibiru gets closer to Earth. The Restrainer could be a fleet of spaceships that have been preventing these giant lizard aliens from taking over Earth. Or, the very quarantine around the planet, which is the electromagnetic shield, could also be seen as a restrainer.

Others believe the 'restrainer' is the body of Christ. Once the body of Christ is removed from the planet, the antichrist can be revealed. Again, we are back to the discernment between the punishment of God and that of Satan. The wrath of God is reserved for the unbelieving, rebellious and the wicked. The persecution of the Jews and Christians comes from Satan. Satan persecutes the tribulation saints, not God. Again, the fact that believers are clearly around during the tribulation rules out that it's the Holy Spirit or the body of Christ. The Restrainer must be something supernatural, as the body of Christ, despite being filled with the Spirit of Christ, are nevertheless, still in the natural world.

The Lord allows this to happen because in His Grace He saves them even after they rejected Him. Because they were left behind, their salvation is dependent on *not* taking the 'mark of the beast' which is the implant or tattoo that the antichrist decrees a necessity for his totally digitalized society. This mark must be taken in order to be able to buy and sell anything in the failing global economy that the antichrist recreates into an Orwellian New World Order.

These believers end up suffering for refusing to take his mark, as well as for not believing sooner when they were originally told about the salvation through Christ. This includes the 144,000 which have the seals of Christ. (Revelation 7:4) These are Jews and Christians from all the twelve tribes of Israel, 12,000 from each tribe. All

Chapter Fifteen: Ascension Or Rapture?

of these believers (the Bible calls 'saints') end up being persecuted by the antichrist/Satan for believing in Christ. However, the Lord pours out his wrath on the wicked, not his beloved Bride, i.e., his sheep.

This is exactly why the Rapture of His Bride, all those who believe on the Lord Jesus Christ, happens <u>before</u> the tribulation and <u>before</u> the final antichrist is revealed to the world. When the antichrist rises in power it begins the time known as 'Jacob's troubles', the seven-year tribulation period, which is designed to deceive the world and gather humans to fight a war against the Almighty Creator Lord Himself.

The Lord promises to take His beloved Bride away before this destined time period begins on the earth, 'saving' her from His appointed time of wrath which is focused on the unbelieving and rebellious. The believers of the Body were faithful to Him and prepared for His coming prior to the tribulation period. Yet, at the same time, He extends His Divine Grace to all those left behind as their very last window of opportunity to accept Him and save their souls from Satan and from hell. Promising them crowns of martyrdom, those who come to Him during the tribulation and suffer for His name's sake will be saved after all, and will see His coming millennial Kingdom.

> "Don't let anyone deceive you in any way, for that day will not come until the rebellion occurs and the man of lawlessness is revealed, the man doomed to destruction. He will oppose and will exalt himself over everything that is called God or is worshiped, so that he sets himself up in God's temple, proclaiming himself to be God. Don't you remember that when I was with you I used to tell you these things? <u>And now you know what is holding him back, so that he may be revealed at the proper time. For the secret power of lawlessness is already at work; but the one who now holds it back will continue to do so till he is taken out of the way. And then the lawless one will be revealed, whom the Lord Jesus will overthrow with the breath of his mouth and destroy by the splendor of his coming.</u> The coming of the lawless one will be in accordance with the work of Satan displayed in all kinds of counterfeit miracles, signs and wonders, and in every sort of evil that deceives those who are perishing. They perish because they refused to love the truth and so be saved. <u>For this reason, God sends them a powerful delusion so that they will believe the lie and so that all will be condemned who have not believed the truth but have delighted in wickedness.</u>"
>
> (2 Thessalonians 2:3-12)

The powerful delusion and lie that the world will believe will be that the earth is being threatened by alien invaders and that the nations must gather together to save the planet, usher in the new age, or the fifth dimension, by accepting the gods that Satan chooses. These are the ancient gods who claim that they were the creators of the human race, the original owners of planet earth. They make a further false claim to deceive earth humans that they are here to help save the planet from the threat from outer space by believing in them.

Many of these gods will be reptilian in nature, similar to the TV movie series, 'V'. They appear to be benevolent, human-looking space brothers, but was only a facade over their true reptilian bodies, shielding their vampiric natures. They are lustful for human flesh and blood, and the energy of the human soul. These beings are also known as fallen angels, the beast, the dragon, and the Nephilim, having the ability to shape shift and appear in many different forms.

This great deception that will occur will be the worst kind of delusion ever in the history of planet earth, perpetrated by the Antichrist, the fallen angels, the rebel gods and the demonic beings that serve them. While physical destruction can destroy the body temporarily, living under the influence and hypnotic spell of deception creates a condition far worse than physical death, as it destroys the human soul and spirit for all eternity. This is the danger most people today face. As time goes on, however, the deception will get even deeper.

THE TECHNOLOGY OF THE RAPTURE

Consider for a moment the possibility of a fleet of intergalactic, inter-dimensional spaceships, capable of containing in excess of three to five billion people, all the saints of the past since the crucifixion, and all the saints presently on Earth. Imagine the sky full of stealth spacecraft while hundreds of millions of people suddenly disappear. The angels will arrive and quickly circle the globe in their sky chariots, taking millions of people as they pass by. I won't even bother to go reiterating Ezekiel's wheel (Ezekiel chapters 1 and 10), (See, Book Two[11]: *Who Is God?* my chapter on *The Motherships of the Lord*) other than to say that there is every indication that advanced technology seems to be in the picture.

During the rapture of the church, this massive arrival will most likely only be visible by the people being taken up. The purpose of this mission will not to be made manifest, but simply to gather the saints prior to the "great tribulation" (a time of unparalleled suffering, both in magnitude and intensity, unlike ever before in the history of the world). Note that while the rapture of the church may not be visible, the massive arrival to occur at the second coming of Christ will not be discreet at all. Isaiah 66:15–16 speaks of *chariots like a whirlwind* raining fire down on the Earth. As I've already proved in Book Two, *chariots like a whirlwind,* in the original Hebrew meant spaceships.

Chapter Fifteen: Ascension Or Rapture?

How does He pull this off, without anyone seeing it? The Rapture is orchestrated by thousands of angels both extraterrestrials and ultraterrestrials on thousands of motherships. The scripture says, "After that, we who are still alive and are left will be <u>caught up</u> (raptured) together with them <u>in the clouds</u> (the Biblical word for spaceships) to meet the Lord <u>in the air</u> (in space). And so, we will be with the Lord forever." (1 Thessalonians 4:17). We will be 'caught up' together to be with the Lord, He does not come down to earth. The Rapture is done in stealth by angels and with the Lord's 'light' technology. Scripture also says, we will be 'translated', changed, transferred into our glory-light bodies, non-corporeal, heavenly bodies. This is the true ascension into the 'light' body that New Age fallen angels are trying to counterfeit through their various seductive and deceptive channelings.

> "Listen, I tell you a mystery: We will not all sleep, but <u>we will all be changed--in a flash, in the twinkling of an eye</u>, at the last trumpet. For the trumpet, will sound, the dead will be raised imperishable (incorruptible), and we will be changed. For the perishable (corruptible) must clothe itself with the imperishable, and the mortal with immortality."
>
> (1 Corinthians 15:51-53)

> "Now we know that if the earthly tent we live in is destroyed, <u>we have a building from God, an eternal house in heaven, not built by human hands</u>. We grow weary in our present bodies, and we long to put on our heavenly bodies like new clothing."
>
> (2 Corinthians 5:1, 2)

> "For the Lord himself will come down from heaven, with a loud command, with the voice of the archangel and with the trumpet call of God, and the dead in Christ will rise first. After that, we who are still alive and are left <u>will be caught up together with them in the clouds to meet the Lord in the air</u>. And so, we will be with the Lord forever."
>
> (1 Thessalonians 4:16, 17)

The dead shall rise first, they who are in the holding place *inside* the earth, known as Abraham's bosom. Then those on the earth will be 'caught up' and bodies are changed, a transformation takes place, nobody sees it, except maybe NORAD and by the time they register it on their radar, it will have been over and the seven-year tribulation period, known as the time of Jacob's trouble begins which becomes a green light for the Beast, the Antichrist to reveal himself to the world, and begin his plan for world domination.

Christ will *appear* visibly only to the saints in the air, in space, during the rapture of the church. The Greek word for 'appear' is *phaneros,* found in John 2:28, 3:2; 1 Peter 5:4; Colossians 3:4, means to shine, be apparent, manifest, or be seen, as Christ is to appear to the saints in the air at the rapture. Nothing is said of His appearing to the rest of Earth. [12]

During the rapture of the church, Christ will never set foot on Earth, but rather fly above it in the air. As soon as all the dead in Christ have met Him in the air, He will return to heaven with them to present them blameless before God (John 14:1–3; 1 Thessalonians 3:13, 4:16–17, and others). The rapture of the church is a New Testament doctrine which was never revealed to anyone in the Old Testament; it was first alluded to by Jesus (Luke 21:34–36), and then revealed to Paul in detail as a special revelation (1Corinthians 15:51–58; 2 Thessalonians 2:6–8). [13]

According to Milor, "the following passage reveals a mystery, and confirms that the rapture happens *prior* to the tribulation period and *prior* to the revelation of who the final Antichrist will be. To this day, nobody knows who the Antichrist is but there are many speculations. As yet, he is being restrained by <u>the very presence of the believers on the earth</u>." The believers are literally 'holding space' for Christ on earth, as they are considered to be His representatives and ambassadors on earth. Those believers who are filled with the Holy Spirit carry the vibration, frequency and mind of Christ on earth especially. Together they collectively make up the 'body of Christ' which may make up the 'restrainer' talked about in 2 Thessalonians 2:8. However, each believer has at least two angels assigned to them, one guardian, and one recording angel. So it is possible that the restrainer extends out to the Angelic realm, that when they go, so do we, as we are their harvest, that Matthew 13:39 prophesies.

I am repeating this verse, for emphasis, and have combined in brackets the translations of both the American King James version with the New International Version just for the purpose of further elucidation.

> "And you know what is restraining him now so that he may be revealed in his time. For the secret power of lawlessness (the mystery of iniquity) is already at work; but the one who now holds it back will continue to do so till he is taken out of the way. (until he [the church] be taken out of the way [raptured]). And then the lawless one (Wicked one [the Antichrist]) will be revealed, whom the Lord Jesus will overthrow (consume) with the breath (spirit) of his mouth (His Word) and destroy by the splendor (brightness) of his coming."
>
> (2 Thessalonians 2:6–8)

Another mystery revealed and prophesied in 2 Thessalonians 2:8, is that at the time of the second coming of Jesus Christ, he defeats the Antichrist with a 'Word' that comes forth from the spirit out of his mouth. Ofcourse, nobody knows what that

Chapter Fifteen: Ascension Or Rapture?

final 'Word' will be, but we do know based on scripture, that the Word of God is the 'Sword of the Spirit.' (Ephesians 6:17)

> "For the word of God is living and powerful. Sharper than any double-edged sword, it penetrates even to dividing soul and spirit, joints and marrow; it judges the thoughts and attitudes of the heart."
>
> (Hebrews 4:12)

This essentially proves that the disappearance of the body of believers will precipitate the coming seven-year tribulation, a time where all hell breaks loose on earth. This is a time when darkness reigns, the antichrist rises up, when all the prophesies in Daniel and Revelation are made manifest. The desolation of abomination, where the Antichrist sets himself up in the rebuilt third temple in Jerusalem, and demands Israel and the world to worship him as god, is one event which <u>cannot</u> happen with the presence of believers still on the planet.

Another Christian scholar who also believes that the rapture will happen before the tribulation, is John Walvoord[14], and in his book, *The Rapture Question*, he includes 50 reasons based on scripture to prove the point. I am including 10 reasons here:

1. Revelation 3:10 - The Promise of from the hour of trial; Greek, 'Ek' means exit.
2. Revelation 6:16; 1 Thessalonians 5:9 - Church is <u>not</u> the object of God's wrath.
3. Luke 21:36 - Escape (not endure) tribulation.
4. Luke 21:28 - Look up (not out); redemption.
5. 2 Corinthians 5:20 - War: calling all ambassadors home.
6. 2 Thessalonians 2 - The Restrainer (church) is removed <u>before</u> Antichrist is revealed.
7. 1 Corinthians 15:51 - In the twinkling of an eye; not an extended activity.
8. 1 Corinthians 15:52 - In the air, not the earth.
9. Revelation 12:5 - Woman is Israel not the church.
10. Revelation 19:11-14; Marriage supper: in heaven includes those raptured before.

The church, which is the group of believers in Jesus Christ, is called the 'Body of Christ' and the 'Bride of Christ' in the scriptures. [See Ephesians 5:22-23; Romans 7:14; 2 Corinthians 11:2; James 4:4.] Paul talks about the union of the Bridegroom in Ephesians 5:3. The Bride of Christ is excluded from God's wrath being poured out on the earth during the great tribulation period. [See, 1 Thessalonians 5:9; Revelation 3:10.] After the rapture of the church, those who sat on a fence for Christ, from all over the world, who have heard the truth of the gospel but did not believe until the events prophesied took place, will recognize the event(s) and many will turn to Jesus Christ to be saved. These are ones who will have to endure the persecutions of the Antichrist. It says in Daniel 7:21 that the antichrist has the power to make war on the saints, and the saints are the believers in Christ. Revelation 13:7 says that He will overcome the saints. Many will be martyred for Christ, and will be resurrected at the time of the second coming. These people are the 'Tribulation Saints.'

The Three Angels (Extraterrestrials) who preach the gospel to the world:

"And I saw another angel flying in mid heaven, having an eternal gospel to preach to those who live on the earth, and to every nation and tribe and tongue and people; and he said with a loud voice, "Fear God, and give Him glory, because the hour of His judgment has come; worship Him who made the heaven and the earth and sea and springs of waters." And another angel, a second one, followed, saying, "Fallen, fallen is Babylon the great, she who has made all the nations drink of the wine of the passion of her immorality."

Then the third angel (extraterrestrial messenger) preaches doom for all those who worship the Beast and his image, which could be a hologram.

"Then another angel, a third one, followed them, saying with a loud voice, "If anyone worships the beast and his image, and receives a mark on his forehead or on his hand, he also will drink of the wine of the wrath of God, which is mixed in full strength in the cup of His anger; and he will be tormented with fire and brimstone in the presence of the holy angels and in the presence of the Lamb. "And the smoke of their torment goes up forever and ever; they have no rest day and night, those who worship the beast and his image, and whoever receives the mark of his name." Here is the perseverance of the saints who keep the commandments of God and their faith in Jesus."
(Revelation 14:6-12)

"Do not let your hearts be troubled. Trust in God; trust also in me. In my Father's house are many mansions (dwelling places): if it were not so, I would have told you. I go to prepare a place for you. And if <u>I go and prepare a place for you, I will come again, and receive you to myself</u>; that where I am, there you may be also."
(John 14:1–3)

The Rapture differs from the second coming, that moment when the Lord returns in all His glory with this huge fleet of starships from all over the universe.

Chapter Fifteen: Ascension Or Rapture?

The rapture of the church will occur before the great tribulation (Luke 21:34–36; 2 Thessalonians 2:6–8; Revelation 1:19; 4:1).

Let's remember that the kingdom of darkness reigns on earth now, though it is restrained and limited. Our present situation on earth is not exactly living in the Kingdom of God. This is why believers pray all over the globe, "Thy Kingdom come on earth, as it is in Heaven." The return of Christ at the second coming precipitates the establishment of the Kingdom of Heaven on the earth. The prophesy states that Yeshua HaMashiach who was born out of the bloodline of King David, the root of Jesse, is to literally rule from David's throne in Jerusalem. The return of Jesus Christ to rule as King is referenced 1,845 times in the Old Testament. There are 23 out of 27 books which give prominence to this event, 17 books which feature it exclusively, with 318 references in the New Testament, in 216 chapters.[15]

> "<u>Your dead will live; Their corpses (dead bodies) will rise</u>. You who lie in the dust, awake and shout for joy, for your dew is as the dew of the dawn, And <u>the earth will give birth to the departed spirits</u>. Go, my people, enter your rooms and shut the doors behind you; hide yourselves for a little while until his wrath has passed by. See, the LORD is coming out of his dwelling to punish the people of the earth for their sins. The earth will disclose the bloodshed upon her; she will conceal her slain no longer."
>
> (Isaiah 26:19-21)

This relates to the tribulation and to the second coming of Christ. This begins when the scrolls are broken as mentioned in Revelation. It is the time of the Antichrist, when Satan's hierarchy gets the upper hand, the demonic rules and torments the unbelievers. Yet at the same time, scripture tells us that the Holy Spirit causes many to turn to Christ, after they realize what has happened. This is the time of Jacob's troubles, which is the worst time of persecution for Jews and for Christians in the entire history of the earth. Israel is brought to brink of destruction. The holocaust killed one out of every three Jews alive on the planet at that time, but during the great tribulation it is estimated that two out of every three Jews will perish (Daniel 12:1). The 'remnant' of one third will be saved.

It is interesting that this one third ratio is a constant repetitive theme throughout history. I believe it is rooted in the original rebellion when Lucifer persuaded one third of heaven's extraterrestrials angels to follow him in a rebellion against the Creator.

The purpose of the great tribulation is to get Israel to acknowledge their sin of rejecting their Messiah, who is Yeshua HaMashiach, Jesus the Christ.

"I will go and return to my place, till they acknowledge their offense, and seek my face: in their affliction they will seek me earnestly (eagerly look for me)."
(Hosea 5:15)

In his DVD, *The Rapture*, Chuck Missler[16] proves that there are distinctly two collections of scriptures that refers to the promise to come for His Bride (the body of Christ, the assembly of believers), which is the Rapture; and the other is to fulfill His commitment to Israel with His second coming to take back the throne of David and establish His Kingdom of God on Earth.

These are clearly two separate events:

The Rapture	The Second Coming of Christ
Translation; saints go to heaven	Sets up Kingdom, translated saints return to earth
Earth not judged	Earth is judged
Imminent, any moment,	Follows definite predicted signs
Not in the Old Testament	Predicted in the Old Testament
For believers only	Affects all men on earth
Before the day of wrath	Concludes the day of wrath
No reference to Satan	Satan in bound for a thousand years
He comes for his own	He comes with his own
He comes in the air	He comes to the earth
He claims the Bride	He comes with his Bride
Only His own see Him	Every eye shall see Him
Great tribulation begins	Millennial reign begins

"For the Son of Man is going to come in his Father's glory *with His Angels*, and then He will reward each person according to what they've done."
(Matthew 16:27)

Chapter Fifteen: Ascension Or Rapture?

NOTES AND REFERENCES:

1. Jim Rutz, *Megashift*, Empowerment Press (CO); 1st Edition (June 30, 2005).
2. www.answers.com/Q/How_many_people_believe_in_Christianity_worldwide?#slide=1
3. http://top101news.com/2015-2016-2017-2018/news/society/largest-religions-world/10/
4. Travis Walton, *Fire in The Sky*, 1975, Marlowe & Company; 3rd edition (August 1997)
5. Ella LeBain, *Who Is God? Book Two of Who's Who in The Cosmic Zoo? A Guide to ETs, Aliens, Gods & Angels,* Chapter Two: *Ancient Technology & Biblical Astronauts,* p.21, Skypath Books, 2015.
6. Ibid.
7. Father Charles Arminjon, France-1881, *The End of the Present Word and the Mysteries of the Future Life,* translated by Susan Conroy and Peter McEnerny, Sophia Institute Press (January 26, 2009).
8. John W. Milor, *Aliens and The Antichrist: Unveiling the End Times Deception*, Chapter Four: *Could the Rapture of the Church be a Mass Alien Abduction?* p.129, 132, iUniverse, Inc., Lincoln, NE. 2006.
9. Dr. Chuck Missler, DVD, *The Rapture: Christianity's Most Preposterous Belief*, Koinonia House, Coeur d'Alene, ID, 2010
10. Todd Strandberg, *The Pretribulation Rapture,* https://www.raptureready.com/rr-pre-trib-rapture.html
11. Ella LeBain, *Who Is God? Book Two of Who's Who in The Cosmic Zoo? A Guide to ETs, Aliens, Gods & Angels,* Chapter Four: *The Motherships of the Lord,* p.71, Skypath Books, 2015.
12. Ibid., Milor, p.147
13. Ibid., Milor, p.148
14. John Walvoord, *The Rapture Question*, p. 271. Zondervan; 1st Revised & enlarged edition (August 25, 1979)
15. Ibid., Missler, 2010
16. Ibid.

CHAPTER SIXTEEN

THE SECOND COMING AND NIBIRU

"And I will pour out on the house of David and the inhabitants of Jerusalem a spirit of grace and supplication. <u>They will look on me, the one they have pierced, and they will mourn for him as one mourns for an only child, and grieve bitterly for him as one grieves for a firstborn son</u>."
(ZECHARIAH 12:10)

"At that time the sign of the Son of Man will appear in the sky, <u>and all the nations of the earth will mourn</u>. They will see the Son of Man coming <u>on the clouds of the sky, with power and great glory</u>."
(MATTHEW 24:30)

When Yeshua Jesus Christ returns, the scripture tells us that, unlike the Rapture, every eye will see Him and all the nations will mourn for the one whom they pierced. As I've mentioned in my chapter on the Cloud ships in Book Two, each time the scripture reads, 'on the clouds' or 'with the clouds' it is referring to the Lord's spaceships, which are filled with light and the glory of God. The heavens declare the Glory of God, in Psalm 19:1, indicates His massive fleet of starships, mansions in the sky that travel amongst the stars.

Unlike the Rapture, everyone on earth will recognize Yeshua Jesus when He returns. The Rapture is done in stealth, as the Lord doesn't even put one foot upon the earth, but when He returns, everyone sees Him as He comes to end the battle of Armageddon. The celestial armies, the hosts of heaven, the faithful extraterrestrials who serve the Office of Christ and the Kingdom of Heaven, against the demonic alien armies of Satan's kingdom, under the Antichrist including the armies of the earth, will enter final combat.

Many Hollywood movies depict a fictional time where earth is invaded by alien spacecraft, warring with each other and with earthlings. Many of these movies are

Chapter Sixteen: The Second Coming and Nibiru

actually prophetic, in the sense that this scenario, which is every earth human's worse nightmare, will manifest during the reign of the Antichrist. Movies like *Independence Day, The War of the Worlds,* and even *Star Wars,* foretell of a future time where our skies are filled with the dread of alien invasions, fire from heaven, and all kinds of spaceships, alien technology and terror.

This will happen during the final days, when the gods of the past will return through the Stargates, to wage war on their Creator over the earth and its inhabitants, including us humans. Even though they all struggle amongst themselves for power, as we have seen through their many mythologies, they will somehow all team up through a type of cosmic Faustian contract with Satan's army against the Lord in the end.

Yeshua Jesus returns with His massive fleet of legions of angels, faithful extraterrestrials from all four corners of the universe, and ends the great celestial war with a 'Word' (2 Thessalonians 2:8). Then the earth and everything on it will be destroyed by fire. He will establish His Kingdom of Heaven on the purified earth, which begins His millennial reign on earth from Jerusalem (Daniel 2:44,45; 7:13,14; 7:18; Isaiah 9:6,7; Luke 1:32,33; Revelation 11:15).

Most people know that one of the main End Times prophecies that needs to be fulfilled before the end can come is the rebuilding of the third Jewish temple in Jerusalem on the Temple Mount, Mount Moriah. Yet, at this time, the Dome of the Rock, which is the second holiest Muslim temple in the world of Islam, occupies the site of the second temple. I have always felt that some kind of natural disaster will occur to destroy it, such as an earthquake, as Israelis wouldn't war with Muslims over this. There has always been tolerance of the religious diversity in Jerusalem.

The prophecy in Daniel 9 tells us that Antichrist will sit in the rebuilt temple and claim to be god and demand worship. "He will oppose and will exalt himself over everything that is called God or is worshiped, so that he sets himself up in God's temple, proclaiming himself to be God" (2 Thessalonians 2:4). But before that can happen, the ancient Ark of the Covenant must be found, which is where the spirit of God once sat upon the 'mercy seat.' The Ark of the Covenant has been missing since ancient Babylon, which is today's Iraq, invaded Israel over two thousand years ago.

In order for the Antichrist to pull off the deception that he is the messiah-king (Mashiach Nagid) of Israel, the Ark of the Covenant must be found and placed within the temple, where he will sit, while the Sanhedrin re-establishes animal sacrifices, an event described by the prophet Daniel as the 'abomination of desolation' (Daniel 9:27; 11:31; 12:7-11; Matthew 24:15; Mark 13:14). After *Raiders of the Lost Ark* went viral, I am sure, there are teams of archeologists devoted to finding the real *ark of the covenant*. With the level of technology available to us today, highly charged electrical devices such as the Ark of the Covenant could be found with advanced forms of metal detectors. I have no doubt there will be an archeological discovery in the near future.

There are literally scores of scriptures from Genesis through Revelation that point to the second coming of Yeshua Jesus, too many to reference all of them here. However, I will focus on a few choice passages.

> "See, the LORD is coming with fire, and his chariots are like a whirlwind; he will bring down his anger with fury, and his rebuke with flames of fire. For with fire and with his sword the LORD will execute judgment upon all men, and many will be those slain by the LORD."
>
> (Isaiah 66:15, 16)

Before the millennial Kingdom of God can be established on the earth, the Lord is going to destroy the earth and all of its inhabitants. Remember those who are destined to be saved during the tribulation period, will die in the Lord (Revelation 14:13) and their bodies will be raised during the resurrection. The rest of the people who joined the Antichrist's army against the Lord of Heaven, will experience the wrath of God in what has long been called, *the Day of Judgment.* This will be worse than any Hollywood movie, because no one will be left. The earth will be destroyed by fire.

THE DEATH STAR, NIBIRU, HERCOBULUS, WORMWOOD

Throughout history multiple prophesies from around the world point to the end through catastrophes. All of them agree on the appearance and passing of a giant red planet coming very close to the earth. This planet has many names, Hercobulus in Greek, Nibiru in Sumerian, the Red Kachina to Native Americans, and the Red Dragon to the Chinese. It is said to be approximately five to six times the size of Jupiter, considered a titan of our solar system, yet seems to belong to a neighboring solar system attached to a dying brown dwarf star known as Nemesis, or our sun's evil twin. Nibiru travels and orbits our solar system every 3,600 years, on its passage of Earth.

End Time Bible Prophecy points to *signs in the heavens* preceding the Second Coming of Jesus Christ. These *signs in the heavens* are extraordinary, not usual solar and lunar eclipses or blood moon eclipses as many have previously mistakenly thought. These *signs in the heavens* are the presence of other planets in our solar system showing up, which can be seen with the naked eye from Earth. Solar and Lunar Eclipses happen every six months, like clockwork. But the cyclic return of the giant planet Nibiru, happens once every 3,600 years, which is what I believe Jesus was referring to as the *sign in the heavens* preceding His return.

Chapter Sixteen: The Second Coming and Nibiru

> "I will show *wonders in the heavens above and signs on the earth below*, blood and fire and billows of smoke. The sun will be turned to darkness and the moon to blood before the coming of the great and glorious day of the Lord."
>
> (Acts 2:19, 20)

Nibiru's passage to Earth is a cyclical event causing unprecedented pole shifts and earth changes. The enormous size, the close passage, the intense radiation and its electromagnetic force this giant celestial object emits shakes the world apart. Its upcoming passage will wake up the earth, causing volcanic eruptions, high magnitude earthquakes and tidal waves. Nothing and no one will escape this cataclysm.

> "And then shall appear *the sign of the Son of man in heaven*: and then shall all the tribes of the earth mourn, and they shall see the Son of man coming in the clouds of heaven with power and great glory."
>
> (Matthew 24:30)

> "Immediately after the tribulation of those days the sun will be darkened, and the moon will not give its light, and *the stars will fall from heaven*, and the powers of the heavens will be shaken."
>
> (Matthew 24:29)

The stars falling from heaven are all those rebel extraterrestrials who joined Lucifer's rebellion against the Lord. This points to their end, as 'the powers of the heavens will be shaken' means that the Lord will destroy their planets, their space portals and even their star systems. This will be a truly ominous time.

I am of the belief that the events described in Matthew 24:29, 30 Joel 2:31, Acts 2:19, 20; Revelation 6:12 relate to an astronomical event that is not an ordinary cycle. Many false prophets and teachers in the past seven years have used these scriptures and attached them to Blood Moon Lunar Eclipses, but the Triad of Blood Moon Eclipses of 2014-2015 have come and gone, and the end of the world, nor the rapture has occurred yet. This is because the events described in these end time scenarios are not normal eclipses, but the presence of a giant planet that cyclically orbits our solar system every 3,600 years, which wreaks havoc, causes earth changes, and has also been blamed on rearranging our solar system.

The ancients had many names for this titan Hercobulus, Nibiru, aka Planet X today. Wormwood in the book of Revelation 8; Marduk in the Babylonian religion; Phateon in the Greek literature; Nemesis in the Greek mythology; Apollyon in Babylonian mythology; Revelation 9:11; Apollo in Greek mythology; "G1.9" as a working title by NASA; along with "The Death Star" by NASA, and Planet GJ1214B.[1]

> "Then the third angel sounded his trumpet, and a great star burning like a torch fell from heaven and landed on a third of the rivers and on the springs of water. The name of the star is Wormwood [Nibiru and the comets that travel with it]. A third of the waters turned bitter like wormwood oil, and many people died from the bitter waters. Then the fourth angel sounded his trumpet, and a third of the sun and moon and stars were struck [this comet like object that travels in the orbit of Nibiru will graze our solar system, it is believed that it is heading for a collision to graze the bottom third of Jupiter, which will remove a piece of Jupiter to plunge into earth and other planets in our solar system]. A third of the stars were darkened, [from its trail of comets] a third of the day was without light, and a third of the night as well [from the passing of this giant planet blocking out the sun, causing the poles to shift, upsetting the natural cycle of day and night as we know it]."
>
> (Revelation 8:10-12- BSB – Emphasis Mine)

There have been many names of 'The Destroyer' aka "Death Star" during its course through the history of mankind. These are the recorded ones: Lucifer, Satan, The Dragon, The Great Snake, The Destroyer, The Serpent, The Devil, Marduk, Nibiru, Shiva, Hercolubus, Wormwood, The Dark Star, The Death Star, The Red Star, The Red Planet, The Planet of the Crossing, The Winged Disk, The Tenth Planet, The Dark Twin, Black Star, The Freightener, Comet Elenin (NASA), P-7X by Astronomer John Anderson, Science Digest, November 1982; Planet X by NASA Astronomer Robert S. Harrington– Planet X as the Tenth Planet–1993; Tyche, Nemesis, Wormwood, The Second Sun. The Blue Star, Blue Kachina, Fiery Red Dragon of Old, Chinese Guest Star 1054 AD[2], Death Angel that passed-over Egypt, the Terrible Comet. Eris, the name given by NASA to the newly discovered 10th planet could also be Planet X according to various astronomers and authors; Kepler 22 System; aka Planet Christ; Raja Sun; Great Star.

"The Destroyer" is mentioned in the Old Testament Jewish Bible as well as mentioned in the ancient writings of the Egyptians. See, Exodus 12:23; Jeremiah 6:22-30; Jeremiah 48:7-10; Isaiah 16:4-5; Jeremiah 4:1-10; Jeremiah 51:18; 51:54-58; Revelation 12:3-4, 9, 12-15; Isaiah 54:16-17.

Matthew 24:29 tells us of a double eclipse of both the sun and the moon, which is physically impossible as eclipses happen like clockwork, every six months, there is at least a pair of solar and lunar eclipses, which take place two weeks apart. Solar Eclipses can only occur on New Moons, and Lunar Eclipses can only occur on Full Moons. However, this scripture is telling us, along with Joel 2:31 that the sun and

Chapter Sixteen: The Second Coming and Nibiru

the moon are darkened and the heavens are shaken. This is the presence of this giant planet Nibiru.

Nibiru orbits around a brown dwarf star called Nemesis, known as our sun's evil twin. It is called the *Death Star,* because it always brings destruction in its path. It will bring with it comets, asteroids, fireballs (fire from heaven) and meteors. Because of its status as a dying star, it absorbs into its energy field all kinds of space junk, and while it passes the earth at a tremendous speed, it will not only cause earthquakes and tsunamis on earth, it will literally cause fire to rain down from heaven, due to the comets that orbit with it.

Nibiru is the *sign in the heavens* that Jesus warned us about in Matthew 24. It is being viewed by amateur astronomers all over the world today. It is a like a mini solar system, which appears to be overlapping our solar system. As Nibiru orbits around our Sun, it will pick up energy and speed, and even though it will travel 225 million miles from earth, it's energy field will nevertheless be felt on earth, which is the cyclical cause of pole shift on earth. As it passes, it will literally cause Earth to turn upside down. The Prophet Isaiah predicted this, as well as the terrible Day of Lord, who returns on the final quake.

THE POLE SHIFT AND BIBLE PROPHESY

The following are scriptures from the Jewish Bible that clearly makes reference to pole shifts:

> "Behold, the Lord lays the earth waste, devastates it, distorts its surface and scatters its inhabitants."
>
> (Isaiah 24:1)

> "It is God who removes the mountains, they know not how, when He overturns them in His anger; Who shakes the earth out of its place, And its pillars tremble."
>
> (Job 9:5-6)

> "Though the earth should change and though the mountains slip into the heart of the sea."
>
> (Psalms 46:2)

> "Yet once more I will shake not only the earth, but also the heaven."
>
> (Hebrews 12:26-27)

This expression, "Yet once more," denotes the removing of those things which can be shaken." Proves that this has happened before, and will happen again! The Book of Genesis describes past pole shifts; Revelations describes the next one.

"I will drive him like a peg in a firm place, and he will become a throne of glory to his father's house."

(Isaiah 22:23)

These scriptures tell us the Lord is saying that a pole shift was coming again, bringing with it a new North Pole. It will seem firmly established. Like a throne, it will be a central location for the new "house." The word house here is referring to the house of stars, the new pole star and its constellation. Each North Pole Star guides its own unique era, which we can go back into history and study to confirm its associations. When the North Pole Star was Thuban in Draco, during the Prehistoric Jurassic Era, the dinosaurs walked the earth. When the sun stood still in the Long Day of Joshua (Joshua 10:12-13), the pole was migrating to a new location in 1448BC.

Immanuel Velikovsky postulated back in the 1950s, that the dinosaurs disappeared during a passing of the planet Nibiru which came too close to the earth, and literally destroyed all life.[3] The Dinosaur Dynasty was destroyed. As I mentioned in Book One of *Who's Who in The Cosmic Zoo?* that many Ufologists believe that not all were destroyed, but hid inside the earth, and were transformed into humanoid *sauroids*, which are draconian-reptilian-humanoid-lizard men. That would certainly explain how these reptilian beings established themselves inside the earth.[4]

Isaiah 22:25 tells us though that the pole shift is not a permanent fix: "In that day," declares the Lord of hosts, "the peg driven in a firm place will give way; it will even break off and fall, and the load hanging on it will be cut off, for the Lord has spoken." This peg, which seems to hold the position of the North Pole, (with the load hanging on it being the earth) is not as permanent as it first seems.

In 1279 BC when there was three days of darkness, the sun went down at dawn 6 AM which is now 6 PM, this refers to pole shifts. The sun appeared to stand still on the opposite side of earth in Egypt for three days of darkness which were three days that were 12 hours long.[5]

Revelation 16:18-20 "there was a great earthquake, such as there had not been since man came to be upon the earth, so great an earthquake was it, and so mighty... And the cities of the nations fell... and every island fled away, and the mountains were not found." This is referring to the end times pole shift, which I believe is presently in progress as the evidence is mounting that the north and south poles are currently shifting.

NOAA & NASA have been recording the magnetic declination of the earth's slowly accelerating electro-magnetic shift that's affecting weather and making it slightly difficult for air traffic controllers and pilots to navigate landings at the exact coordinates. Scientists hypothesize that the final shift of magnetic poles will happen when we hit zero point and no one knows when that will happen or what to expect during the very,

Chapter Sixteen: The Second Coming and Nibiru

very brief time lapse at zero point. NOAA & NASA just want to inform the public so they don't panic during zero point. Just breath, relax, and meditate through it.

RAS scientists further warn that this rapid shifting of the North Pole will increase the destabilization of our Earth's weather systems which has caused historic droughts to occur world-wide, most importantly in the United States, Mexico-Central America and Brazil's Amazon forest regions.

Unknown to most people, and as reported by London's Independent newspaper, the magnetic north pole is moving faster than at any time in human history, threatening everything from the safety of modern transport systems to the traditional navigation routes of migrating animals.

Scientists now say that magnetic north, which for two centuries has been in the icy wilderness of Canada, is currently relocating towards Russia at a rate of about 40 miles a year. The speed of its movement has increased by a third in the past decade, prompting speculation that the field could be about to "flip", causing compasses to invert and point south rather than north scientific proof they say sudden shift soon.[6]

> "Immediately after the distress of those days "'the sun will be darkened, and the moon will not give its light; the stars will fall from the sky, and the heavenly bodies will be shaken.'
>
> (Matthew 24:29)

> "I will show wonders in the heaven above and signs on the earth below, blood and fire and billows of smoke."
>
> (Acts 2:19)

The Book of Noah, found in the Dead Sea Scrolls, records the pole shifts with Noah's flood. "Noah saw the Earth had tilted and that its destruction was near." (Noah 65:1) Sounds like a pole shift to me.

The so-called apocrypha were Jewish texts of record and of prophecy, which were rejected by the Roman Bible Editors. Just like the Book of Maccabees which tells us all about the story Hanukah, a Feast of the Lord that is ingrained in Jewish tradition and celebrated by Yeshua, so were other books included in some Catholic bibles but not in Protestant ones. The Book of Noah is not included either, even though it is referenced in the Book of Jubilees, as well as the Book of Enoch, despite all of them being found in the Dead Sea Scrolls. The Book of Enoch, was always included in the Coptic Bible. The Church of Rome deleted it, then about a thousand years later, included the Books of Enoch again.

Another apocryphal book that didn't end up in the final cut of the Bible we know is Esdras. 2 Esdras 2:4-8 tells us "The sun will suddenly start shining at night, and the moon in the daytime. Blood will drip from trees; stones will speak; nations will be in confusion; the movement of the stars will be changed. A king unwanted by anyone will begin to rule, and the birds will fly away. Fish will be washed up on the shores of the Dead Sea. The voice of one whom many do not know will be heard at night; everyone will hear it. The earth will break open in many places."

2 Esdras 5:5 adds "And the course of the stars will be changed."

Bruce Killian wrote in *Joshua's Longest Day*, that pole shifts are recorded in the Bible, from the very beginning. Several important events in the Scriptures involved pole shifts – where the North and South Poles moved thousands of miles to a new location in less than a day. Spring of 1448 BC is when the Israelites entered into the promised land, marking the beginning of a new era. What I find interesting about this date, which was the last time Nibiru passed the earth, is that the rebirth of the State of Israel occurred in the Spring of 1948 and one hundred years from that time, will be 2048.

Jesus said, this generation shall not pass away until all these things have come to pass (Matthew 24:34). As I stated in Book One of *Who's Who in The Cosmic Zoo?* scholars disagree on how long a biblical generation is, some say seventy years, others eighty years and others one hundred years. This is quintessential in determining the year Nibiru will pass earth again, and the year the Son of Man will return. If a biblical generation is seventy years, then that puts us in 2018, which at the time of the publication of this manuscript is only a little more than a year away. However, if a biblical generation is eighty years, then that puts us at 2028, whereas if Jesus was referring to a hundred-year generation, then we're looking at 2048. The fact that the same set of celestial circumstances of a pole shift caused by the passing of Nibiru to earth, is recorded in both Biblical and exo-biblical texts is confirmation to the fact that this cycle will re-occur the year Jesus returns. Yes, His Words are, 'no man knows the day or the hour, of the return of the Son of Man' (Matthew 24:36), but He says nothing about the year.

> "So the sun stood still, and the moon stopped, till the nation avenged itself on its enemies, as it is written in the Book of Jasher. The sun stopped in the middle of the sky and delayed going down about a full day."
>
> (Joshua 10:13)

> "And the Lord hearkened to the voice of Joshua, and the sun stood still in the midst of the heavens, and it stood still six and thirty moments, and the moon also stood still and hastened not to go down a whole day. And there was no day like that, before it or after it, that the Lord hearkened to the voice of a man, for the Lord fought for Israel."
>
> (Book of Jasher, Chapter 88:64-65)

Chapter Sixteen: The Second Coming and Nibiru

"The sun and moon stood still in their habitation: at the light thine arrows they went, and at the shining of thy glittering spear."

(Habakkuk 3:11)

"Who shakes the earth out of its place, and its pillars tremble; Who commands the sun not to shine, and sets a seal upon the stars;"

(Job 9:6, 7)

"In that day there will be an altar to the Lord in the midst of the land of Egypt, and a pillar to the Lord near its border. It will become a sign and a witness to the Lord of hosts in the land of Egypt; for they will cry to the Lord because of oppressors, and He will send them a Savior and a Champion, and He will deliver them."

(Isaiah 19:19-20)

The pyramids at Giza are not in the center of modern Egypt near Cairo, but at the start of the Nile Delta, the old border between Upper and Lower Egypt many thousands of years ago.

Will the pyramid's measurements, warnings, and prophecies finally be understood? If the pyramid's missing top were added on, (representing completion of the world) the pyramid would be 5780 inches high. It is believed the inch is an ancient unit, and that this may correspond to Hebrew calendar year 5780 - or possibly December 2019, for completion of the world at the next pole shift.[7]

The missing piece is called the cornerstone. The Bible tells us that Yeshua HaMashiach (Jesus Christ) is the cornerstone.

"The stone the builders rejected has become the cornerstone; This is the LORD's doing, and it is wonderful to see."

(Psalm 118:23)

Blue Kachina vs. Red Kachina

The solar system Nemesis is comprised of Nibiru and other planets as well. The Native Americans called the two large planets, the Blue Kachina and the Red Kachina. The Red Kachina refers to Nibiru, because of the amount of iron in its energy field. The Blue Kachina is a large blue planet with stripes, seen during sunset and sunrise since 2015. Please Google it, and you will see pictures and videos, along with another smaller white planet, which many astronomers believe to be its moon.

The white planet has an odd depression, which looks very similar to the Death Star in the movie, Star Wars.

The Blue Kachina is close to the sun, whereas the Red Kachina, Nibiru is projected to be outside of Neptune, heading towards the Sun. It will pass earth twice, once on its way towards the Sun, and then on its way back out into its 3,600-year orbit around our solar system. I think some authors get these two planets confused, as they do not behave similarly, but are part of the same Nemesis system.

We know that Nibiru is on a 3,600-year orbit around the sun, but the Blue Kachina appears every 2,000 years. It is my belief that it was the Blue Kachina that eclipsed the Sun during the crucifixion of Christ over 2,000 years ago. "From the sixth hour until the ninth hour darkness came over all the land." (Matthew 27:45; Mark 15:33; Luke 23:44) At the same time of the three hours of darkness, there was a great earthquake, which caused the rocks to split and people who were dead were miraculously resurrected back to life, while Jesus hung dead on the cross. The eclipse of the Blue Kachina is what cause the earthquake.

> "At that moment the curtain of the temple was torn in two from top to bottom. *The earth shook, the rocks split and the tombs broke open.* The bodies of many holy people who had died were raised to life. They came out of the tombs after Jesus' resurrection and went into the holy city and appeared to many people. When the centurion and those with him who were guarding Jesus saw the earthquake and all that had happened, they were terrified, and exclaimed, "Surely he was the Son of God!" (Matthew 27:51-53)

We know that Jesus was crucified when He was thirty-three years of age. It is quite possible that it was the Blue Kachina shining brightly in the sky during the time of His Birth which is also known as the Star of Bethlehem, because it can take thirty-three years for it to eclipse the sun and cause an earthquake. We know from the Bible record that not only were there three hours of darkness, which is not a usual duration of a solar eclipse of the moon, but the eclipse of a much bigger and slower planet. It is my belief that it was the Blue Kachina planet of the Nemesis system which came close to the sun. This planet is close to the sun at the time of the publication of this manuscript, and it is being seen by the naked eye, photographed and videographed all over the world.

The events described as happening after the Crucifixion do not match in severity those caused by the Red Kachina (Nibiru) when it passes the earth. The severity of these events mark the difference between the Blue Kachina and Nibiru eclipses. Both create eclipses of the sun that are much longer than our usual thirty minutes or so. At the time of the Crucifixion the darkness is recorded as lasting for three hours. This was the eclipse of a planet, not the moon. Neither was it Nibiru, it was the Blue Kachina. Both cause

Chapter Sixteen: The Second Coming and Nibiru

earthquakes, but Nibiru's passing and eclipse of the sun can last a whole day, as the previous Bible records have indicated, as well as the future terrible Day of the Lord to come.

The Neumayer Station in Antarctica has a twenty-four-hour live cam which reveals this blue planet rising before the sun, and it is most definitely a blue planet, not red. Nibiru is much larger and much more of a maverick. Because of the iron oxide, it shows up as a red-brown, and absorbs all kinds of space junk in its atmosphere, making it look like it has wings. Nibiru is the destroyer, it wreaks havoc in our solar system. Some passes of the Earth are closer than others, which is why it is blamed for the destruction of the dinosaurs. It has sent hundreds of comets to pummel the Earth.

> "And to YOU who are in fear of my name the sun of righteousness will certainly shine forth, with healing in its wings; and YOU will actually go forth and paw the ground like fattened calves."
>
> (Malachi 4:2)

The Sun with healing in its wings, is obviously the coming of the Lord, which will cause those on the earth to literally paw the ground, because they have been saved. The scriptures also reveal that the pole shift will be over very quickly. The bypassing of the earth by Nibiru will be literally catapulted out from the sun, with tremendous energy and thrust as it soars away into its elongated orbit around the solar system. The astronomers have said it could all be over in 60-90 minutes, and the Bible promises, the entire shift will all be over in an hour. So perhaps the astronomers are 30 minutes off in their calculations?

> "On this account you too prove yourselves ready, because *at an hour* that you do not think to be it, the Son of man is coming." (Matthew 24:44)

> "the master of that slave will come on a day that he does not expect and *in an hour* that he does not know," (Matthew 24:50)

> "...while they stand at a distance because of their fear of her torment and say, 'Too bad, too bad, you great city, Babylon you strong city, because *in one hour your judgment has arrived*!' (Revelation 18:10)

The passing of Nibiru will cause a great earthquake which may register as a ten or above on the seismogram. This one will literally flip the poles and finalize the new earth changes, creating massive tidal waves which will take over land masses, and land masses that will appear that are now under water.

"And I saw when he opened the sixth seal, and *a great earthquake occurred*; and the sun became black as sackcloth of hair," (Revelation 6:12)

"and *there will be great earthquakes*, and in one place after another pestilences and food shortages; and there will be fearful sights and from heaven great signs." (Luke 21: 11)

We know that this is not the first time the poles have shifted, causing earth changes and total darkness for three days, as history records that during the ninth plague of Exodus, the three days of darkness, which took place in 1279BC.8

It is the day when the Sun will set hours later than expected that should be the trumpet in the skies, the flashing red light, the announcement you have been waiting for that now is the moment to drop all and rush to your safe location.

"And it must occur in that day,' is the utterance of the Sovereign Lord Yahuah, 'that *I will make the sun go down at high noon, and I will cause darkness for the land on a bright day*."

(Amos 8:9)

"And it must occur that anyone fleeing from the sound of the dreaded thing will fall into the hollow, and anyone coming up from inside the hollow will be caught in the trap. For the very floodgates on high will actually be opened, and the foundations of the land will rock. The land has absolutely burst apart, the land has absolutely been shaken up, the land has absolutely been sent staggering. The land absolutely moves unsteadily like a drunken man, and it has swayed to and fro like a lookout hut. And its transgression has become heavy upon it, and it must fall, so that it will not rise up again. "In that day the Lord will punish the powers in the heavens above and the kings on the earth below. They will be herded together like prisoners bound in a dungeon; they will be shut up in prison and be punished after many days. The moon will be dismayed, the sun ashamed; for the Lord Almighty will reign on Mount Zion and in Jerusalem, and before its elders—with great glory."

(Isaiah 24:18-23)

The wealthy families of the world, the bankers, the elite have been building underground communities in group bunkers for decades now. I believe that this is how this end time prophesy refers to them, who are also known as the kings of the earth, because as the old saying goes, the men with the gold rule the world. These people are known as the elite because they rule the banks of the world, they have had

Chapter Sixteen: The Second Coming and Nibiru

information and have known about the coming of Nibiru for decades now, but suppressed that information from the public.

The prophecy states that the Lord will use their own bunkers and 'safe place' as a prison and a trap for them where they will receive their punishment from him. He literally locks them away by moving the earth, so they cannot escape. This appointed punishment for these despotic earthly kings receive vengeance that turns the earth on them, for what they have done to billions of others, by not warning people of what they knew was coming. See, Revelation 6, the sixth seal.

The sun and moon are drastically obstructed during this cosmic event. The moon being dismayed, comes from the Hebrew word *chafer*, which means to confuse, as the moon is dependent on its light from the sun as it is set in orbit around the earth. The earth will be moved in its wobble and it will flip upside down, so the moon will need to adjust accordingly, meanwhile the sun is ashamed, because the sun will not shine, due to the passing of Nibiru and all of its comets, meteors and space junk in its path, which fulfills the end time prophecy of Joel 2:31, "The sun will be turned to darkness and the moon to blood before the coming of the great and dreadful day of the LORD."

In the following passage from Isaiah 2:10-22, which is the prophecy of the Terrible Day of the Lord, it seems clear that it will be the LORD Himself who will be appearing in the skies, not just a planet, which is why others have called the passage of Nibiru, the planet of Crossing, and the Sign of the Son of Man at the End of the Age.[9]

> "Go into the rocks, hide in the ground from the fearful presence of the Lord and the splendor of his majesty! **The eyes of the arrogant will be humbled and human pride brought low; the Lord alone will be exalted in that day.** The Lord Almighty has **a day in store for all the proud and lofty, for all that is exalted (and they will be humbled)**, for all the cedars of Lebanon, tall and lofty, and all the oaks of Bashan, for all the towering mountains and all the high hills, for every lofty tower and every fortified wall, for every trading ship and every stately vessel. *The arrogance of man will be brought low and human pride humbled; the Lord alone will be exalted in that day, and the idols will totally disappear.* People will flee to caves in the rocks and to holes in the ground from the fearful presence of the Lord and the splendor of his majesty, when he rises to shake the earth. In that day people, will throw away to the moles and bats their idols of silver and idols of gold, which they made to worship. They will flee to caverns in the rocks and to the overhanging crags from the fearful presence of the Lord and the splendor of his majesty, *when he rises to shake the earth*. Stop trusting in mere humans, who have but a breath in their nostrils. Why hold them in esteem?"
>
> (Isaiah 2:10-22, NIV)

Warning of Coming Destruction

"<u>I will sweep away everything from the face of the earth</u>," declares the LORD. "I will sweep away both men and animals; I will sweep away the birds of the air and the fish of the sea. The wicked will have only heaps of rubble when I cut off man from the face of the earth," declares the LORD."

Against Judah

"I will stretch out my hand against Judah and against all who live in Jerusalem. <u>I will cut off from this place every remnant of Baal, the names of the pagan and the idolatrous priests--those who bow down on the roofs to worship the starry host, those who bow down and swear by the LORD and who also swear by Molech, those who turn back from following the LORD and neither seek the LORD nor inquire of him</u>. Be silent before the Sovereign LORD, for the day of the LORD is near. The LORD has prepared a sacrifice; he has consecrated those he has invited. On the day of the LORD's sacrifice I will punish the princes and the king's sons and all those clad in foreign clothes. On that day, I will punish all who avoid stepping on the threshold, who fill the temple of their gods with violence and deceit. "On that day," declares the LORD, "a cry will go up from the Fish Gate, wailing from the New Quarter, and a loud crash from the hills. Wail, you who live in the market district; all your merchants will be wiped out, all who trade with silver will be ruined. At that time, I will search Jerusalem with lamps <u>and punish those who are complacent</u>, who are like wine left on its dregs, who think, 'The LORD will do nothing, either good or bad.' Their wealth will be plundered, their houses demolished. They will build houses but not live in them; they will plant vineyards but not drink the wine.

The Great Day of the LORD

"The great day of the LORD is near-- near and coming quickly. Listen! The cry on the day of the LORD will be bitter, the shouting of the warrior there. <u>That day will be a day of wrath, a day of distress and anguish, a day of trouble and ruin, a day of darkness and gloom, a day of clouds and blackness, a day of trumpet and battle cry against the fortified cities and against the corner towers. I will bring distress on the people and they will walk like blind men, because they have sinned against the LORD. Their blood will be poured out like dust and their entrails like filth</u>. Neither their silver nor their gold will be able to save them on

Chapter Sixteen: The Second Coming and Nibiru

the day of the LORD's wrath. <u>In the fire of his jealousy the whole world will be consumed, for he will make a sudden end of all who live in the earth."</u>

(Zephaniah 1:2-18)

It is quite clear from Bible Prophecy, that the Lord will use these celestial wrecking balls to bring about His Wrath on the wicked and the earth. Remember, the earth was cursed in Genesis 3, and these Judgements that are coming on the Earth will affect all the beings, both on the surface, in the air, and inside the planet. As a student of astronomy and astrology for over twenty-five years, I have studied planetary patterns and their effects on earth changes and on human behavior. I observed that earthquakes and severe weather patterns happened during solar and lunar wobbles, and solar and lunar eclipses. How much more would the eclipse of another celestial object like the planets in the Nemesis system, i.e., the Blue and Red Kachina, have on the movements of the earth?

I also observed that the Lord used these astronomical and astrological cycles to propagate his judgements and rewards. Some people would be blessed by certain cycles, while others were cursed by them. This leads me to my conclusion that the Lord uses the cycles and movements of the planets to officiate his judgments on the earth and its inhabitants. However, before He does so, He always sends messengers to warn us of impending judgments and there is always a call to repentance to Him, so that those who do heed His calling may be saved. Salvation is not just to save your physical life, but more importantly, your soul life in the Age to Come. Repentance brings God's grace and forgiveness. That's the promise and covenant of the Lord. The next book in this book series, will be Book Four: *Covenants*, where I will detail all the covenants of God, and all the spiritual contracts and agreements. A covenant is a two-way agreement. If you do this, God will respond. It is not single sided. You must make a choice and God will pour out His grace, forgiveness and salvation on all who repent to Him, no exceptions!

"Repent, for the kingdom of heaven has come near."

(Matthew 4:17)

"For it is by grace you have been saved through faith, and this not from yourselves; it is the gift of God, not by works, so that no one can boast."

(Ephesians 2:8-9)

Earth Changes From A Binary Brown Dwarf?

Various official astrophysics and solar research labs around the world all agree that something very, very unusual is taking place in our solar system. A partial list includes the following:

- Recent solar sunspot activity highest in 8000 years | • Space.com
- Sun's magnetic field has decreased in size by 25%
- The long-term increase in solar irradiance is heating both Earth and Mars. | • National Geographic
- 300% increase in galactic dust entering our solar system | • New Scientist
- Mercury's magnetosphere experiencing significant increases
- Venus exhibiting a 2500% increase in its "green glow"
- Mars showing a rapid appearance of clouds and ozone
- Mars observations reveal up to 50% erosion of its ice features within a 12-month period
- Jupiter plasma torus increasing; its moon Io exhibiting the same changes
- A 200% increase in the density of Io's plasma torus
- Jupiter's Disappearance of White Ovals since 1997 - recent increase in storms
- Io's ionosphere is 1000% higher
- Jupiter's moon Europa much brighter than scientists expected
- Jupiter's moon Ganymede is 200% brighter
- Saturn's plasma torus is 1000% more dense
- Aurorae first seen in Saturn's polar regions in recent years
- Uranus was featureless in 1996 - exhibiting huge storms since 1999
- Uranus in 2004 was also markedly brighter than in 1999
- Neptune is 40% brighter in the near-infrared range based on observations from 1996 - 2002 |• SSEC
- Neptune's largest moon, Triton, seems to have heated up significantly since the Voyager space probe visited it in 1989 | • MIT
- Pluto observations reveal a 300% increase in atmospheric pressure
- The average surface temperature of the nitrogen ice on Pluto has increased 2 degrees Celsius over the past 14 years. | • MIT[10]

As a result of the magnetic poles shifting, along with the presence of Nemesis/Nibiru in our solar system, there has been and will continue to be an increase in all natural earth phenomena, until the changes are complete, and the Lord returns to recreate the earth and the heavens.

Please keep the science and the bible prophecy in mind when the liberal world tries to guilt trip you into the false belief that global warming is caused by you, and what type of light bulbs you may or may not use. This is complete and utter nonsense! The only thing earth humans are responsible for is pollution and abuse of earth's resources, animals and stewardship of them, for which we will be held accountable. The earth changes are caused by outside forces beyond our control. So, when you see monster storms, freak weather patterns in unusual areas, intensified

Chapter Sixteen: The Second Coming and Nibiru

earth quakes, volcanic activity and tornadic eruptions, please remember the facts. Our earth is being affected by our sun's activity along with Nemesis, our sun's evil twin, the brown dwarf star and its orbit of planets, in which the big one is Nibiru.

Mental illnesses will increase as well, as the human brain is wired to receive impulses from the sun and neighboring stars. We are all made up of star stuff, so we respond and react to what is going on in our cosmic neighborhood, whether we are consciously aware of it or not. All mental illnesses are caused by the absence of love. Jesus prophesied that this would be a major sign before His Second Coming.

> "Because of the increase of wickedness, the love of most will grow cold. But the one who perseveres to the end will be saved."
>
> (Matthew 24:12, 13)

This is what we can expect an increase in the following activities:

Super storms, earthquakes, volcanic activity;
Expect the unexpected, increasingly, as the pole shift approaches.
poles moving or earth wobble (has to do with declination line);
solar flares, sunspot activity;
Sudden large rogue waves in new places;
Sudden Hurricanes in unusual places;
Sudden tornadoes out of season;
Extremes in drought, heavy rains, out of season snows, flooding, severe storms;
Mysterious Booms, methane flashes, odd underground trumpet sounds;
Disrupted cell phone, television and radio signals;
Unusual animal behavior, disrupted species migration patterns;
Unusual increases in violent behavior in human beings;
Increasingly severe earthquakes;
Rising Sea Levels;
Mass animal death;
Insect invasion;
Red colored milk colored rain;
Red/blood colored water, rivers, lakes, streams;
Storm surge on coastlines with no storm apparent;
Freak Storms;
Out of Season Weather;
noticeable polar air masses in new areas of earth;
Some parts of the world getting colder;
Some parts of the world getting warmer.[11]

Climate change needs to be the language used to describe our situation, not the term global warming. Some temperatures have increased, other parts have decreased, over the globe as a whole due to the pole shift, which does not average out to a complete warming. These are due to earth changes and the end of this present processional age due to the disturbance of Earth's magnetic axis.

Jesus told us all these things would happen preceding His Second Coming:

> "Jesus left the temple and was walking away when his disciples came up to him to call his attention to its buildings. "Do you see all these things?" he asked. "Truly I tell you, *not one stone here will be left on another; everyone will be thrown down."*
>
> As Jesus was sitting on the Mount of Olives, the disciples came to him privately. "Tell us," they said, "when will this happen, and *what will be the sign of your coming and of the end of the age?"*
>
> Jesus answered: "Watch out that no one deceives you. For many will come in my name, claiming, 'I am the Messiah,' and will deceive many. You will hear of *wars and rumors of wars, but see to it that you are not alarmed. Such things must happen, but the end is still to come. Nation will rise against nation, and kingdom against kingdom. There will be famines and earthquakes in various places. All these are the beginning of birth pains."*
>
> (Matthew 24: 1-8, NIV)

New Heavens And New Earth

After all the cataclysmic death and destruction of the passing of Nibiru, we have the promises that God will create a New Heavens and a new earth. Jesus promised that not a single stone would be left. "Do you see all these things?" he asked. "Truly I tell you, not one stone here will be left on another; everyone will be thrown down." (Matthew 24:2) This flattening of the earth, the future rebuilt third temple of Jerusalem is very much in the plans and intentions of religious Jews to erect a third temple in Jerusalem. This will be the future place from which the antichrist will rule, another chapter in Bible Prophecy that must be fulfilled before the end of this age, according to the very Words of Jesus Himself.

After all these events have come to pass and been fulfilled according to the Divine Plan of God, we are given hope for a New Age to come, a New Earth which will be changed into Heaven on Earth. We are told that a heavenly city will be coming, called the New Jerusalem, that will lay over the old flattened Jerusalem, and that the Lord Himself will rule over the whole earth, from it. Both the Old Testament prophecy

Chapter Sixteen: The Second Coming and Nibiru

through the Prophet Isaiah and the Book of Revelation given by Jesus Christ to St. John, completely matches this glorious future event.

> "Behold I will create new heavens and a new earth.
> The former things will not be remembered,
> nor will they come to mind."
>
> (Isaiah 65:17)

> "Then I saw a new heaven and new earth, for the first heaven and the first earth had passed away, and there was no longer any sea. I saw the Holy city, the new Jerusalem, *coming down out of heaven from God*, prepared as a bride beautifully dressed for her husband and showed me *the Holy City, Jerusalem coming down out of heaven from God*, and its brilliance was like that of a very precious jewel, like a jasper, clear as crystal."
>
> (Revelation 21:1)

In this verse, it is quite clear that this Holy Heavenly City is the Bride of Christ. So many people confuse the Body of Christ, which is made up of all the redeemed believers who have accepted the salvation through the Blood of Christ, with the Bride of Christ. The Bride of Christ is this Heavenly City, which is where the Throne of Christ is. This is where He will rule and reign from, inside His Bride.

In Book Two, *Who Is God?* I detailed that this heavenly city coming out of the heavens and landing on the earth is in fact a huge Mothership of the Lord. (See, Chapter Four of *Who Is God?*[12]) Motherships are huge cities. The detailed description in St. John's vision, describes a mother ship so phantasmagorical, a shining light dressed in precious jewels, gold and crystals, with twelve gates. Only ships have gates. Let's face it, cities don't just fly out of the heavens and land on earth with twelve gates, just like that. This is the description of a Mothership that is probably close to the size of the earth. Its signifies the beginning of the Millennial Reign of Christ on earth, which scripture says will be the beginning of the New Age.

Signs of the End of the Age

The big cosmic events at the end of the age will be the passing of the giant planet Nibiru. This is what will cause the sun to go dark, and the moon to not give its light. Jesus said, "'the sun will be darkened and the moon will not give its light (an eclipse of the sun by Nibiru). The stars will fall from the sky, (each time the bible refers to falling stars, it is referring to fallen angels or bad/rebellious ETs), and the heavenly bodies will be shaken." (Matthew 24:29; Isaiah 13:10). This means their starships will be hit with mighty power causing the bad ETs (fallen angels) to shake and fall.

> "At that time the sign of the Son of Man will appear in the sky, and all the nations of the earth will mourn. They will see the Son of Man coming <u>on the clouds</u> of the sky, with power and great glory. (in a fleet of starships). And he will send his angels (ET messengers and alliances) with a loud trumpet call, and they will gather his elect from the <u>four winds</u> from one end of the heavens to the other (ET Alliances of Star Nations)."
>
> (Matthew 24:30-31)

We know that we are in the end of days of the age of Pisces, based on the processional ages. We know, based on bible prophecy, that we are getting close to the second coming of Christ, and closer to the rapture/ascension of all believers by witnessing all the events that are happening on our planet right now. But how close are we?

When Jesus walked the Earth, He spoke extensively about His Coming Kingdom and the end of our present age. He gave signs to look for, advice to follow, and prophesies about the end of this present time line. He told us the worst of times will culminate in His glorious second coming and the establishment of the Kingdom of Heaven on Earth.

The following comes from Luke 21:5-36; with my emphasis and commentary:

> "Some of his disciples were remarking about how the temple was adorned with beautiful stones and with gifts dedicated to God. But Jesus said, "As for what you see here, the time will come when not one stone will be left on another; every one of them will be thrown down."
>
> "Teacher," they asked, "when will these things happen? And what will be the sign that they are about to take place?" He replied: "<u>Watch out that you are not deceived</u>. For many will come in my name, claiming, 'I am he,' and, 'The time is near.' Do not follow them. When you hear of wars and revolutions, do not be frightened. These things must happen first, but the end will not come right away."
>
> Then he said to them: "Nation will rise against nation, and kingdom against kingdom. There will be great earthquakes, famines and pestilences in various places, and fearful events and <u>great signs from heaven</u>. "But before all this, they will lay hands on you and persecute you. They will deliver you to synagogues and prisons, and you will be brought before kings and governors, and all on account of my name. This will result in your being witnesses to them. But make up your mind not to worry beforehand how you will defend yourselves. For I will give you words and wisdom that none of

Chapter Sixteen: The Second Coming and Nibiru

your adversaries will be able to resist or contradict. You will be betrayed even by parents, brothers, relatives and friends, and they will put some of you to death. All men will hate you because of me. But not a hair of your head will perish. By standing firm you will gain life.

"When you see Jerusalem being surrounded by armies, you will know that its desolation is near. Then let those who are in Judea flee to the mountains, let those in the city get out, and let those in the country not enter the city. For this is the time of punishment in fulfillment of all that has been written. How dreadful it will be in those days for pregnant women and nursing mothers! There will be great distress in the land and wrath against this people. They will fall by the sword and will be taken as prisoners to all the nations. Jerusalem will be trampled on by the Gentiles until the times of the Gentiles are fulfilled.

"There will be signs in the sun, moon and stars. On the earth, nations will be in anguish and perplexity at the roaring and tossing of the sea. Men will faint from terror, apprehensive of what is coming on the world, for the heavenly bodies will be shaken. At that time, they will see the Son of Man coming in a cloud with power and great glory. When these things begin to take place, stand up and lift up your heads, because your redemption is drawing near."

He told them this parable: "Look at the fig tree and all the trees. [this represents Israel] When they sprout leaves, you can see for yourselves and know that summer is near. Even so, when you see these things happening, you know that the kingdom of God is near. I tell you the truth, this generation [a biblical generation is seventy - one hundred years; depending on scripture interpretation] will certainly not pass away until all these things have happened. [I believe Jesus is talking about Israel. Israel was reborn in 1948. 1948 + 70 brings us to 2018. If a biblical generation is 80 years as some have said, then that brings us to 2018. If it is one hundred years as some have hypothesized, then that would mean the end of this generation would be 2048] Heaven and earth will pass away, but my words will never pass away.

"Be careful, or your hearts will be weighed down with dissipation, drunkenness and the anxieties of life, and that day will close on you unexpectedly like a trap. For it will come upon all those who live on the face of the whole earth. Be always on the watch, and pray that you may be able to escape all that is about to happen, and that you may be able to stand before the Son of Man." (Luke 21:5-36; emphasis and commentary are mine)

"This is how it will be at the end of the age. The **angels** will come [faithful extraterrestrials that serve the Kingdom of Heaven

under the authority of the Lord Jesus Christ]
and separate the wicked from the righteous"

(Matthew 13:29)

"<u>As the new heavens and the new earth that I make will endure before me,</u>" declares the Lord, "so will your name and descendants endure. From one New Moon to another and from one Sabbath to another, all mankind will come and bow down before me," says the Lord. "<u>And they will go out and look upon the dead bodies of those who rebelled against me; their worm will not die, nor will their fire be quenched, and they will be loathsome to all</u> mankind."

(Isaiah 66:22-24)

"Notice how God is both kind and severe. He is severe toward those who disobeyed, but kind to you if you continue to trust in his kindness. But if you stop trusting, you also will be cut off."

(Romans 11:22)

"And everyone who calls on the name of the Lord will be saved."

(Acts 2:21)

What is The Day of The Lord?

"Howl ye; for <u>the day of the LORD</u> is at hand; it shall come as a destruction from the Almighty. Therefore, shall all hands be faint, and every man's heart shall melt: And they shall be afraid: pangs and sorrows shall take hold of them; they shall be in pain as a woman that travails: they shall be amazed one at another; their faces shall be as flames. <u>Behold, the day of the LORD cometh</u>, cruel both with wrath and fierce anger, to lay the land desolate: and he shall destroy the sinners thereof out of it. *For the stars of heaven and the constellations thereof shall not give their light: the sun shall be darkened in his going forth, and the moon shall not cause her light to shine.* [this is caused by the passing of Nibiru and its trail of comets into our solar system, blocking the sun's light which would cause the moon to have nothing to reflect from.] And I will punish the world for their evil, and the wicked for their iniquity; and I will cause the arrogance of the proud to cease, and will lay low the haughtiness of the terrible. I will make a man more precious than fine gold; even a man than the golden wedge of Ophir. <u>Therefore, I will shake the heavens,</u> [collision of

Chapter Sixteen: The Second Coming and Nibiru

<u>planets with Nibiru</u>] and <u>the earth shall remove out of her place,</u> [pole shift] <u>in the wrath of the LORD of hosts, and in the day of his fierce anger.</u>"

"Before them *the earth shakes, the heavens tremble, the sun and moon are darkened, and the stars no longer shine.* [all caused by the passing of Nibiru and its trail of comets in our solar system]. "That <u>terrible day of the LORD</u> is near. Swiftly it comes— <u>a day</u> of bitter tears, a day when even strong men will cry out. It will be <u>a day</u> when the LORD 's anger is poured out— <u>a day</u> of terrible distress and anguish, <u>a day</u> of ruin and desolation, <u>a day</u> of darkness and gloom, <u>a day</u> of clouds and blackness, <u>a day</u> of trumpet calls and battle cries. Down go the walled cities and the strongest battlements! "Because you have sinned against the LORD, I will make you grope around like the blind. Your blood will be poured into the dust, and your bodies will lie rotting on the ground." Your silver and gold will not save you on that day of the LORD 's anger. For the whole land, will be devoured by the fire of his jealousy. He will make a terrifying end of all the people on earth. The sun will be turned to darkness and the moon to blood before the coming of the great and dreadful <u>day of the LORD</u>."

(Isaiah 13:6-18-Emphasis Mine)

Clearly all this will happen in a day. The prophecy repeats itself eleven times. Eleven is the number of disaster. Scripture also tells us; it will come swiftly. This celestial body is not only five times the size of Jupiter, but it is moving through its orbit around our sun at an astronomical rate of many million miles per minute. It will pick up speed after it makes its orbit around the sun and passes the earth for its final destruction, which multiple astronomers predict will take place in 24-36 hours. It will happen just that fast.

The *Day of the Lord* is the Biblical, Old Testament term used to describe the judgments which God will pour out on the world as outlined in the book of Revelation. This is a time when God will actively intervene in the affairs of humanity with devastating impact. These judgments will be experienced by the entire world population at a time when society has been lulled into a false sense of security. The world will think it has achieved "peace and safety" and then sudden destruction from God will come. This is known as *The Terrible Day of The Lord,* because it is a time of judgment on the earth and the wickedness of humanity. It does not simply come out of nowhere. This is a cosmic event, that is scheduled and planned by the Lord, by using the rogue orbit of the planet Nibiru's passing through our solar system, to wreak havoc throughout our solar neighborhood. He uses this as an opportunity to punish the wicked and eventually recreate the heaven and earth. I am including this prophetic judgment here in its entirety for those who never read it in the Bible.

Before then the earth shakes, the heavens tremble, the sun and moon are darkened, and the stars no longer shine. The Prophet Zephaniah predicted the end of this world, which will be a Judgment on the Whole Earth in the *Day of the Lord*. That on the *Day of the Lord*, He will destroy everything by fire. This is what inspires people to evangelize the world, to lead people into repentance towards the Creator, Lord and Savior. The Lord desires to save humans, but will only do so if humans choose His Salvation and repent and turn toward Him. Sadly, many don't even believe in Him anymore. They judge the Lord based on His many imperfect followers. But humans are not saved by humans, but by the Grace of God, so no man can boast (Ephesians 2:8). In any event, here is the quintessential End Time Prophecy from the Prophet Zephaniah (625BC), which corroborates with the Prophet Isaiah (740-681BC):

"I will sweep away everything from the face of the earth," "When I destroy all mankind on the face of the earth," declares the Lord. "I will sweep away both man and beast; I will sweep away the birds in the sky and the fish in the sea—and the idols that cause the wicked to tumble." "When I destroy all mankind on the face of the earth," declares the Lord, "I will stretch out my hand against Judah and against all who live in Jerusalem. I will destroy every remnant of Baal worship in this place [Islam], the very names of the idolatrous priests—those who bow down on the roofs to worship the starry host, those who bow down and swear by the Lord and who also swear by Molech, those who turn back from following the Lord and neither seek the Lord nor inquire of him." Be silent before the Sovereign Lord, <u>for the day of the Lord</u> is near. The Lord has prepared a sacrifice; he has consecrated those he has invited. "<u>On the day</u> of the Lord's sacrifice I will punish the officials and the king's sons and all those clad in foreign clothes. <u>On that day</u>, I will punish all who avoid stepping on the threshold, who fill the temple of their gods with violence and deceit. "<u>On that day</u>," declares the Lord, "a cry will go up from the Fish Gate, wailing from the New Quarter, and a loud crash from the hills. Wail, you who live in the market district; all your merchants will be wiped out, all who trade with silver will be destroyed. At that time, I will search Jerusalem with lamps and punish those who are complacent, who are like wine left on its dregs, who think, 'The Lord will do nothing, either good or bad.' Their wealth will be plundered, their houses demolished. Though they build houses, they will not live in them; though they plant vineyards, they will not drink the wine." The great <u>day of the Lord</u> is near—near and coming quickly. The cry on <u>the day of the Lord</u> is bitter; the Mighty Warrior shouts his battle cry. <u>That day will be a day of wrath</u>— <u>a day</u> of distress and anguish, <u>a day</u> of trouble and ruin, <u>a day</u> of darkness and gloom, <u>a day</u> of clouds and blackness—<u>a day</u> of trumpet and battle cry against

Chapter Sixteen: The Second Coming and Nibiru

the fortified cities and against the corner towers. "I will bring such distress on all people that they will grope about like those who are blind, because they have sinned against the Lord. Their blood will be poured out like dust and their entrails like dung. Neither their silver nor their gold will be able to save them on the day of the Lord's wrath." In the fire of his jealousy the whole earth will be consumed, for he will make a sudden end of all who live on the earth."

(Zephaniah 1:1-18)

The *day of the Lord,* will coincide with the arrival and passing of the Destroyer, the planet Nibiru aka Hercobulus. This is scheduled, on route, and on its way. It cannot be stopped, it is the *sign in the heavens* prophesied in the scriptures, that will end this world's system, and bring about the judgments of God upon the earth.

NOTES AND REFERENCES:

1. http://jardalkalataol.blogspot.com/2015/09/nibiru-and-isaiah-24.html
2. https://grahamhancock.com/bournewp1/
3. Immanuel Velikovsky, *Earth in Upheaval,* Paradigma Ltd (December 1, 2012)
4. Ella LeBain, *Who's Who in The Cosmic Zoo? Book One, A Spiritual Guide to ETs, Aliens, Gods & Angels, Third Edition,* Chapter Five: Draconian/Reptilians, p.154-177.
5. http://biblepoleshifts.webs.com/
6. Pole Shifts - Growing Evidence for Catastrophic Shifts Past and Present https://www.youtube.com/watch?v=6Ka1Yf0_zjM
7. Bruce Killian, *Joshua's Long Day,* scripturescholar.com
8. Lance Lee Osbourn, *Poles Are Moving: What to Expect,* June 2, 2013, https://www.facebook.com/notes/lance-lee-osbourn/poles-are-moving-so-what-to-expect-/652217308124970
9. Doug Elwell, *Planet X, The Sign of the Son of Man, and the End of the Age,* Defender Publishing LLC (January 1, 2011)
10. *Watchman Bible Study* 2005–2016 www.watchmanbiblestudy.com/Articles/Watchman/6thSeal_PlanetX.html
11. Ibid., Lance Lee Osbourn, *Poles Are Moving: What to Expect,* June 2, 2013
12. Ella LeBain, *Who Is God? Book Two of Who's Who in The Cosmic Zoo? A Guide to ETs, Aliens, Gods & Angels,* Chapter Four: *The Motherships of the Lord,* p.71, Skypath Books, 2015.

CHAPTER SEVENTEEN
THE COSMIC CHRIST

"I AM not of this world."
~ JESUS CHRIST (JOHN 17:14)

"Jesus said, "I have other sheep <u>that are not of this sheep pen</u>.
I must bring them also. They too will listen to my voice,
and there shall be one flock and one shepherd."
(JOHN 10:16)

This statement from Jesus Christ Himself tells us that while He walked amongst us as a flesh and blood human being, He was not of this world, He came from another. This qualifies Him as an Extra-Terrestrial Savior God. He is not an 'alien' in the true sense of the word, because He is human just like the rest of us. He is extra-terrestrial, and His deity is confirmed by His life, death and miraculous resurrection, and what transpired afterwards. He also said that He has other sheep, whose flock is not of 'this' sheep pen, and that He intends to bring them in as well, to become one flock with one shepherd. While Jesus often spoke in cosmic riddles which we call parables, only those who believed on Him were given revelation from His Holy Spirit to understand His words. The others thought He was a madman who had no idea what He was talking about. Let's investigate, and discern...

The very term *Cosmic Christ* offends some Christians, because like those who adhere to the replacement theology heresy, they think that Jesus belongs to them alone, that the Jews lost their chance. The New Agers preach an alien gospel, so to even suggest that there is something 'cosmic' about Christ is enough to create cognitive dissonance in funda-mental Christians. Perhaps their implants are sputtering simply because of a lack of understanding of the 'Words' reflected in how the Scriptures actually reveal this as truth. Let's unpack the Word, in order to illuminate the truth here.

John 10 is Jesus' dissertation as Himself being the Good Shepherd and those who follow Him as His sheep. When talking about those who hear His voice versus those who don't He also mentioned He had sheep that were not of this pen, meaning not

Chapter Seventeen: The Cosmic Christ

of this earth. The more we peel back these scriptures, the more clearly they indicate that He was given authority over all things in the heavens, on the earth and inside the earth, the more we realize that His salvation extends beyond earth humans, which is written in the heavenly scrolls, to the names of the very stars themselves. (See, Book Five: *The Heavens*, my chapter: *The Word of God in the Stars* for further elucidation).

Jesus also told us that "The harvest is at the end of the age, and the harvesters are angels." (Matthew 13:39) We know that the angels are the faithful extraterrestrials that serve the Kingdom of Heaven, and Christ rules from the Throne of Heaven at the right hand of the Creator Lord of all the Heavens and Earth. So, if the harvesters are extraterrestrial angels, they won't stop at planet earth, but will be harvesting other believers around the cosmos, bringing them into one flock under one shepherd.

We are also told that the New Jerusalem is a city made of gold and precious jewels that will literally be downloaded out of the heavens, grounded onto the new earth, after all the wicked are destroyed, and Satan and his fallen angels are bound and thrown into the lake of fire. This holy heavenly city is the seat of the King of the kingdom of heaven, a place that unites all nations both in the heavens and on earth. It will be a place where those in the heavens will come through, perhaps inter-dimensionally, perhaps even through interstellar travel. The New Jerusalem is the City of Peace, which will establish peace in the heavens and on earth, ruled by the Prince of Peace, the Prince of Princes, the Mighty Counselor.

> "I saw the Holy City, the new Jerusalem, coming down out of heaven from God, prepared as a bride beautifully dressed for her husband. And I heard a loud voice from the throne saying, "Now the dwelling of God is with men, and he will live with them. They will be his people, and God himself will be with them and be their God. He will wipe every tear from their eyes. There will be no more death or mourning or crying or pain, for the old order of things has passed away." He who was seated on the throne said, "I am making everything new!"
> (Revelation 21:2-4)

This prophesy points to the next age, when Heaven literally comes to earth. But the Holy City that is known in the heavens will be downloaded to earth. It will be a cosmic hub for all the universe to visit, just as I would imagine it is now, only situated in the heavens. the promise of the King on the throne is that He is making everything new. The old order, which is the system of things we live in, including the New World Order, or World out of Order, will have all passed away. This will be a time when humankind will unite through one 'Cosmic Shepherd' and both earth humans and extraterrestrials will live in peace and harmony, and Earth will be delivered from cosmic evil and its subsequent quarantine.

The Power And Authority Of Jesus Christ

"The Lord says to my Lord, "Sit at my right hand until I make your enemies a footstool for your feet."" (Psalm 110:1) That scripture reveals that the two Lords are Yahuah and Yeshua/Jesus. In Hebrew, the first word 'Lord' is the word, YHVH, which is Yahuah, the second word Lord uses the word, Adonai, which means Lord.

"After the Lord Jesus had spoken to them, he was taken up into heaven and he sat at the right hand of God."
(Mark 16:19)

"But from now on, the Son of Man will be seated at the right hand of the mighty God."
(Luke 22:69)

"But when this priest had offered for all time one sacrifice for sins, he sat down at the right hand of God."
(Hebrews 10:12)

"To which of the angels did God ever say, "Sit at my right hand until I make your enemies a footstool for your feet"?
(Hebrews 1:13)

"Therefore God exalted him to the highest place and gave him the name that is above every name, that at the name of Jesus every knee should bow, in heaven and on earth and under the earth"
(Philippians 2:9-10).

"God raised Jesus from the dead and "seated him at his right hand in the heavenly realms, far above all rule and authority, power and dominion, and every title that can be given, not only in the present age but also in the one to come. And God placed all things under his feet"
(Ephesians 1:20-2).

"The Son is the radiance of God's glory and the exact representation of his being, sustaining all things by his powerful word. After he had provided purification for sins, he sat down at the right hand of the Majesty in heaven. So, he became as much superior to the angels as the name He has inherited is superior to theirs."
(Hebrews 1:3-4)

Chapter Seventeen: The Cosmic Christ

"All things were made by Him; and without Him was not anything made that was made."

(John 1:3)

This reveals to us, that Yeshua was around from the beginning of creation and created life. There are created beings and there are creators, Jesus is a creator with the Almighty El Shaddai, also known as the Heavenly Father, Yahuah (YHVH). Yahushua (Yeshua) was the manifestations of the Heavenly Father in the flesh. Therefore, He was called the Son of God and the Son of Man. He was God who walked among His people.

"For by Him all things were created: things in heaven and on earth, visible and invisible, whether thrones or powers or rulers or authorities; all things were created by Him and for Him."

(Colossians 1:16)

This remains one of the greatest mysteries to humankind: how a mere man could be God, and how God could come as a man with the fate of taking on the sins of the world, die nailed to a tree, and then walk among His people shortly thereafter, as if no suffering ever happened to Him?

The Word Became Flesh

"In the beginning was the Word, and the Word was with God, and the Word was God. He was with God in the beginning. Through him all things were made; without him nothing was made that has been made. In him was life, and that life was the light of men. The light shines in the darkness, but the darkness has not understood it."

(John 1:1-5)

The mystery continues, in that the world was in spiritual darkness and many could not recognize Him. Many knew He was coming, as there were multiple prophets who preceded Him, telling He was to come. But when He arrived, they missed Him.

"He was in the world, and though the world was made through him, the world did not recognize him. He came to that which was his own, but his own did not receive him. Yet to all who received him, to those who believed in his name, he gave the right to become children of God—children born not of natural descent, nor of human decision or a husband's will, but born of God. <u>The Word became flesh and made his dwelling among us</u>. We have seen his glory, the glory of the One and Only, who came from the Father, full of grace and truth."

(John 1:10-14)

To understand this, we must accept the truth that God's ways are not our ways. It was God's Will that He should come as a Savior to His people, this is the meaning of His name, Yahushua, which means Yahuah (YHVH) saves. God became a man, and walked among His people to save them first spiritually from the spiritual darkness of the world that came through the curse of sin from Adam. He promised He would come in this way, in Genesis 3:15. While the Jews at the time, were expecting the Messiah to save them from the Romans, the second coming, will be such a triumph over much darker forces of tyranny and bondage, than the Romans.

"For the law was given through Moses; grace and truth came through Jesus Christ. No one has ever seen God, but God the One and Only, who is at the Father's side, has made him known."

(John 1:17-18)

Does Christianity own Jesus Christ? Absolutely not! Firstly, let's remember that Yeshua was Jewish. Yes, he came for the whole world, but His purpose as Savior and Redeemer is not limited to one group of people over another, or even limited to our planet, this is why He is the Cosmic Christ.

Anyone who believes in His atoning sacrifice on the cross to save humans from the bondage of the god of this world, Lucifer Satan and his hierarchy of fallen angels, demons and evil spirits, can be saved. You do not need to belong to any religious sect, cult, or church group, but only to have the belief and understanding that Christ is the savior of this world and of the Cosmos. Anyone can be saved from the curse of the kingdom of darkness.

Before the Word was written as words of the scriptures, the story of salvation, of the coming King and the coming Kingdom, had been set and written into the stars for all the universe to see. This is about the Cosmic Drama between the Creator and his rebellious sons who became fallen angels.

Therefore, the Creator Almighty God planned the Cosmic Christ who was sent as God in the flesh to redeem humankind from the bondage of the fallen angels and their lead fallen son Heylel/Lucifer who then became Satan, the adversary. Because they were created immortal beings they were allowed dominion over certain star systems and planets. This is what set up the mock up for cosmic battles, not limited

Chapter Seventeen: The Cosmic Christ

to their rebellion against the Creator but mostly between themselves over power and control over who has dominion over which galaxy and star system.

They became gods with a small 'g' in the experiment of creating life on other worlds. Many have had a great deal of experience in control issues over their human subjects. Our history is rich with stories of such brutal human suffering under the direct and indirect influences of these gods (fallen angels). They demanded worship and created slavery. They instituted bondage of all kinds. To ensure this plan for humanity would work for them, they used genetic engineering to manipulate human DNA, so humans would have a real hard time finding their own power.

Therefore, earth humans today have only two strands of DNA. Our top geneticists have discovered there are ten strands of missing DNA in humans. This explains why humans only use 10% of our brains, and that amount is even debatable for some.

These fallen angel 'gods' have created karma with us humans. The path of evolution is the Creator's constant in the universe, with all creation eventually evolving or transforming into something else, whether it lives or is destroyed.

Everything is energy. Energy can never be destroyed, only transformed. Even the force of a black hole can recreate that which it compressed, it's molecular structure may be rearranged, but spirit will find a way to bump it into matter eventually. So, it is with the fallen angel gods, as they are not immune to the Creator's force of evolution. Some may evolve out of the karma they created for us humans and continue to create, while others will be cast even deeper into darker denser worlds to work out their karma or receive their punishment, which is promised in Revelation.

The Cosmic Christ Defeats The God Of This World

Lucifer or Satan is known as the god of this world, the prince of the powers of the air of Ephesians 2:2. He has the power to set up kingdoms on earth, and give power and authority to his chosen kings, lords and presidents. This is why Lucifer or Satan tested Jesus during His fast in the desert, tempting Him by offering Him power over all the kingdoms of the world. Jesus didn't argue with Satan's right to offer this to him, because He knew that Satan had spiritual legal authority over the earth after the curse. But Jesus did rebuke and correct Satan during His test.

> "The devil led him up to a high place and showed him <u>in an instant all the kingdoms of the world</u>. And he said to him, "<u>I will give you all their authority and splendor, for it has been given to me, and I can give it to anyone I want to</u>. So, if you worship me, it will all be yours." Jesus answered, "It is written: 'Worship the Lord your God and serve him only.'"
>
> (Luke 4:5-8)

This was how Lucifer lured extraterrestrial fallen angels to align with him, by giving them a kingdom on earth. They built huge structures to venerate and honor themselves. They created religions so others could worship them as they all had god complexes, as does Lucifer. This is why they made agreements with him, for power. It was when Israel began to honor this Faustian Contract and worship gods other than that of Abraham, Isaac and Jacob, God took His protection off them, and gave them up to their enemies. This was a violation of the first commandment. They fell into Satan's temptations, through his many fallen angels, the pseudo gods.

When Jesus Christ was offered a kingdom on earth, He declined and resisted the temptation to align with Lucifer's power trip, knowing full well from whence His true power springs. Jesus knew where His throne belonged and with whom, which is next to the Creator Father in Heaven. He said He was not of this world. He will however make a show of Lucifer Satan and spoil his stronghold. "And having disarmed the powers and authorities, he made a public spectacle of them, triumphing over them by the cross." (Colossians 2:15)

One of the earliest prophesies written down of the coming of the Christ as Savior was in the Pseudepigrapha book, *The First Book of Adam and Eve*[1]:

"Then Adam said to God: "O Lord, take You my soul, and let me not see this gloom anymore; or remove me to some place where there is no darkness." But God the Lord said to Adam, "Indeed I say to you, this darkness will pass from you, every day I have determined for you, until the fulfillment of My covenant; when I will save you, and bring you back again into the garden, into the house of light you long for, in which there is no darkness. (See John 12:46 for cross reference)

"I will bring you to it, in the kingdom of heaven." Again, said God to Adam, "All this misery that you have been made to take on yourself because of your transgression, will not free you from the hand of Satan, and will not save you. But I will. When I shall come down from heaven, and shall become flesh of your descendants, and take on Myself the infirmity from which you suffer, then the darkness that covered you in this cave shall cover Me in the grave, when I am in the flesh of your descendants. And I, who am without years, shall be subject to the reckoning of years, of times, of months, and of days, and I shall be reckoned as one of the sons of men, in order to save you." (Chapter XIV: 1-5)

The *First Book of Adam and Eve* was not included in the Bible because the Roman church fathers questioned its validity. Others have postulated that it was rejected out of

Chapter Seventeen: The Cosmic Christ

the Old Testament and Talmud first by the Jews because it predicted the life of Jesus Christ, just as did the *Books of Enoch*. Ironically, all of Christ's disciples, who were Jewish, quoted from *Enoch's Scrolls*. The book, *First Book of Adam and Eve*, was a version of the story of Adam and Eve handed down by word of mouth from generation to generation, until someone finally decided to write it down. This was an Egyptian in Arabic with later versions found in Ethiopic, dated approximately 300 years before Christ. Parts of it have been found in the Jewish Talmud and the Islamic Quran, confirming what a vital role it played in the genesis of human wisdom. It was translated into English in the 1800s by Drs. Malan and Trump and later by Rutherford Hayes.

The Divine Plan of Salvation was planned from the beginning of world, as it is written in ancient texts, including the Bible. Just in case one was illiterate, as most ancient people were, it was first written in the stars. (See, Book Five: *The Divine Plan of Salvation Written in the Stars*, and *The Word of God in the Stars* in Book Three of *Who's Who in The Cosmic Zoo*) The earliest scripture in the book of Genesis 3:15, "And I will put enmity between you and the woman, and between your offspring and hers; he will crush your head, and you will strike his heel." Christ was struck on His heels on the cross, yet He crushed the head (authority) of Satan through His victory on the cross. He will finish His work at the second coming in the culminating battle of Armageddon. Later in the New Testament, "The God of Peace will soon crush Satan under your feet" (Romans 16:20).

Old Testament Prophecies Fulfilled in Jesus Christ

When I first became saved after meeting Yeshua in the Negev desert of Israel in July of 1979, I was shown that the Old and New Testament were like right and left legs, they need each other to walk. The Old Testament was the prophetic book, and the New Testament was the fulfillment of those prophesies. All sixty-six books in today's canon were penned by Jews. The Old Testament prophets were pointing the way to the birth of the Messiah. The New Testament prophets were used to communicate the New Blood Covenant which was offered to ALL humankind, including Jews and Gentiles.

All of the disciples were Jewish. The early church was all Jewish, until Paul was sent to spread the Gospel of the Good News of Salvation to the Gentile World. That was when the scriptures were changed, manipulated and edited. In 325 A.D., Roman Emperor Constantine could not compete with the growing Christian movement, so as the old saying goes, if you can't beat them, join them. That wasn't *exactly* what Constantine did. Instead, being a devout pagan who worshipped the Sun God Mithras, he knew that he couldn't control the Empire if there were two different belief systems, so he found a way to *incorporate* Christianity into his already established Babylonian religion of Mithraism.

He set up a council of scribes to sort through all the Jewish scrolls that the early Christians used to support their beliefs, and altered many of the texts to fit into his Roman agenda. There are approximately eighteen Jewish scrolls (books) that were rejected from the Bible Canon. These later became known as the Pseudepigrapha or Apocrypha. They were heavily discredited by the Church of Rome, casting doubt on their origin or efficacy of being the Word of the Lord.

It's important to note that nearly all of these Great Rejected Texts are mentioned within the Bible canon. The mainstream Christian fundamentalist who believes that the Bible is the unadulterated Word of God from Genesis to Revelation must then look into the missing books, which are mentioned in the Bible.

Another thing I was taught as a young Bible scholar, was that in order to prove scripture, there had to be *corroborating* texts in both Old and New Testament. Rogue scriptures were considered to be additions or edits done by the Church of Rome to support their agenda to oppress Jews and delete all things Jewish, including the *Jewish Jesus* by deleting the Book of Maccabees. This book tells the story of the miracle of lights that is celebrated annually by Jews called Hanukah. Even Jesus celebrated Hanukah. But the agenda of the Emperor Constantine, which is revealed in Constantine's Creed, was that any Judaization was considered to be anathema. That meant you couldn't worship on the Sabbath, but only on Sunday, which is the day Rome worshipped the Sun god; you couldn't celebrate any of the Feasts of the Lord, because they were considered to be Jewish, in spite of the fact that these were called Feasts of the Lord, not Feasts of the Jews. You were not allowed to refuse unclean meat, as by all of these actions you were anathema to Rome, persecuted and killed.

Then approximately twenty years later, the Nicaean Creed was established from the Seven Ecumenical Councils and the Constantine Creed was reiterated as well as expanded upon to include any Judaization by belief in reincarnation was now anathema to Rome. Reincarnation was deleted by the Romans, not by the true Christians and certainly not by the Jewish scribes, because Rome wanted everyone on the same page as Rome. You either submit to the Church of Rome or you go to hell. There were no second chances. It was simply a fear tactic to control the masses. But rejection of God's Word as given to the Jews, does not negate God's Word or cause it to cease to exist. We know today that Jesus specifically said, "Heaven and Earth will pass away, but my Words shall never pass away." So even though His Word was suppressed and shortened, it still holds true. I assert it becomes even more relevant today.

I really want my readers, who consider themselves to be Christians, to ask yourself this question: do you follow the Word of the Lord? Or are you still under the auspices of Rome? Because if you adhere to Constantine's Creed, you have this opportunity to repent, and as the book of Revelation says, "Come away from her, the Whore of Babylon." What many modern-day Christians fail to understand is that these Creeds

Chapter Seventeen: The Cosmic Christ

were not just against Jews, and anything Jewish, they were a direct rebellion against the God of Israel, who is the true Christ and Father of humanity. As I included in Book Two: *Who is God?*[2] Constantine's Creed in my Conclusion, so you know exactly of what you are repenting, if you don't know already.

One of the reasons the Roman Empire fell was that many Roman soldiers, and even some emperors, repented from the Roman religion of paganism and became Christians. After the destruction of the Second Temple in 70 A.D., it wasn't long before the Roman Empire crumbled and the Jews dispersed throughout the Diaspora. Call it a curse, or call it a blessing, it depends on your perspective. Rome was invaded by barbarians who essentially kicked out the emperors and took over.

The other reason the books of Paul and Thecla were rejected hinged on Roman morality, or immorality. A very significant portion of Paul and Thecla works preached celibacy, which went against the Roman free-for-all code. They did not want their women refusing sex to their Roman husbands because of their faith in Christ.

The Book of Paul and Thecla was rejected and deleted from Paul's writings, in spite of the fact that it records one of the most remarkable miracles of God. This one is equal if not bigger and better than what the Lord performed for Daniel in the Lion's Den, when he closed the mouths of the hungry lions and protected His Prophet Daniel from harm. In the Book of Paul and Thecla, after Paul betrayed his apprentice Thecla, whom He led to the Lord, she was given over to the Roman authorities to be thrown to the Lions in the Coliseum before thousands of people. The Lord entered into the very lionesses who were there to eat her, who instead protected Thecla from the male hungry lions. Then as if that's enough, Thecla threw herself into a pool filled with hungry seals, in order to prove that she could baptize herself, and the Lord kept their mouths shut so no harm would come to His anointed. But I suppose this story was too extravagant for the Church of Rome, even though it was true. I go into more detail about Thecla's role as the first female evangelist in Book Two: *Who Is God?* in my chapter on *Who Created Sexism?*[3]

Be that as it may, we are living in the last days of the end of this age, and nearly all of these Great Rejected Texts are relevant to End Times Prophesies. The *Books of Enoch*, even though omitted from the Church of Rome's version of the Bible Canon, remained through the Coptic Christians, the Egyptian believers in Jesus who did not submit to Roman rule. They kept the *Books of Enoch* in their Bibles, while the Roman Canon deleted it. Enoch was the first man to ascend into the heavens without dying. Enoch was used as a scribe and a prophet for the Lord. His Words do in fact contain the Word of the Lord, and I will prove this to you, because He accurately predicted the life, death and resurrection of Jesus Christ, as does the Old Testament scriptures. There are approximately 355 Old Testament scriptures which prophesy the life, death, resurrection and the return of Jesus Christ.

I have to include these scriptures to prove to Jews and the rest of the world that Jesus (Yeshua) was prophesied from the beginning of scriptures. Then I will prove to you that Enoch's books corroborate the Word of God in both the Old and New Testament. You will see the bigger picture of End Time Bible Prophecies, in order to apply it to current events, as much of it was written for a time such as this.

There were many prophecies in the Old Testament pertaining to the coming Christ. "There shall come a Star out of Jacob, and a Scepter shall rise out of Israel. Out of Jacob shall come One that shall have dominion" (Numbers 24:17, 19) and, "But thou, Bethlehem Ephrata, though thou be little among the thousands of Judah, yet out of thee shall he come forth unto me that is to be ruler in Israel; whose goings forth have been from of old, from everlasting." (Micah 5:2) Most Jews recognize these scriptures as pertaining to the Messiah, but somehow they don't accept that it has anything to do with Jesus. I shall prove to you otherwise. As you know, I am one of thousands of Jews who believe and accept Jesus as Messiah, Savior, Healer and Deliverer of this World. And, yes, seeing is believing, but vision only comes when the spiritual veils are removed by God, to illuminate truth, whether that be to see the hand of God working in your life, or to *see* the revelation behind the Word of God. Both go hand in hand.

Micah 5:2 led the wise men of the east to come to Jerusalem saying, "Where is he that is born King of the Jews? for we have seen his star in the east, and have come to worship him." From this they knew that out of Bethlehem, from the tribe of Judah, "shall come a Governor, that shall rule my people Israel." (Matthew 2:2; 6)

During the times of the Temple, genealogical records were stored and available there. However, after the Messiah died, it wasn't long afterward, approximately thirty-seven years later, in 70 A.D., the second temple was destroyed along with all of its genealogical records. Jews scattered to all the nations of the world in the Diaspora. Many Bible Scholars believe that was a fulfillment of the prophesy that the Scepter departed from Judah (Israel), because now there is no longer any certainty that any Jew can prove he or she descended from the tribe of Judah.

"Lo, I come: in the volume of the book it is written of me."

(Psalm 40:7)

"The testimony of Jesus is the spirit of prophecy."

(Revelation 19:10)

Chapter Seventeen: The Cosmic Christ

"...all things must be fulfilled, which were written in the law of Moses, and in the prophets, and in the psalms, concerning me."

(Jesus Christ, Luke 24:44)

"And beginning at Moses and all the prophets, he expounded unto them in all the scriptures the things concerning himself."

(Jesus Christ, Luke 24:27)

"For had ye believed Moses, ye would have believed me: for he wrote of me."

(Jesus Christ, John 5:46).

"To Him give all the prophets witness"

(Acts 10:43).

The Seed was first mentioned in Genesis 3:15, then confirmed to Abraham, to Isaac, and to Jacob. Now it is confirmed to Judah. The leadership, according to Jacob, was to go to Judah, but this did not happen for over six hundred years. Moses came from Levi, Joshua from Ephraim, Gideon from Manasseh, Samson from Dan, Samuel from Ephraim and Saul from Benjamin. But when David finally became king, Judah became the dominant tribe. Judah held the scepter and did not relinquish it until after the coming of Shiloh. Shiloh is the Messiah, the Lion of the Tribe of Judah, who is none other than Yeshua HaMashiach, the Lord Jesus Christ. Shiloh (šīlō Hebrew: שִׁלֹ or šīlōh Hebrew: שִׁילֹה) is a person mentioned in Genesis 49:10 as part of the benediction given by Jacob to his son Judah. Jacob states that "the scepter will not depart from Judah... until Shiloh comes." When the temple was destroyed in 70 A.D. and the Jews were forced to disperse of out Judah, this prophesy was then fulfilled.[4]

Old Testament Scripture	Messianic Prophecy	New Testament Fulfillment
1. Genesis 3:15	Seed of a woman (virgin birth)	Galatians 4:4-5, Matthew 1:18
2. Genesis 3:15	He will bruise Satan's head	Hebrews 2:14, 1John 3:8
3. Genesis 3:15	Christ's heel would be bruised with nails on the cross	Matthew 27:35, Luke 24:39-40
4. Genesis 5:24	The bodily ascension to heaven illustrated	Mark 16:19, Revelation 12:5
5. Genesis 9:26, 27	The God of Shem will be the Son of Shem	Luke 3:23-36
6. Genesis 12:3	Seed of Abraham will bless all nations	Galatians 3:8, Acts 3:25, 26
7. Genesis 12:7	The Promise made to Abraham's Seed	Galatians 3:16
8. Genesis 14:18	A priest after the order of Melchizedek	Hebrews 6:20
9. Genesis 14:18	King of Peace and Righteousness	Hebrews 7:2
10. Genesis 14:18	The Last Supper foreshadowed	Matthew 26:26-29
11. Genesis 17:19	Seed of Isaac (Genesis 21:12)	Romans 9:7
12. Genesis 22:8	The Lamb of God promised	John 1:29
13. Genesis 22:18	As Isaac's seed, will bless all nations	Galatians 3:16
14. Genesis 26:2-5	The Seed of Isaac promised as the Redeemer	Hebrews 11:18
15. Genesis 28:12	The Bridge to heaven	John 1:51
16. Genesis 28:14	The Seed of Jacob	Luke 3:34
17. Genesis 49:10	The time of His coming	Luke 2:1-7; Galatians 4:4
18. Genesis 49:10	The Seed of Judah	Luke 3:33
19. Genesis 49:10	Called Shiloh or One Sent	John 17:3
20. Genesis 49:10	Messiah to come before Judah lost identity	John 11:47-52

Chapter Seventeen: The Cosmic Christ

21. Genesis 49:10	Unto Him shall the obedience of the people be	John 10:16
22. Exodus 3:13-15	The Great "I AM"	John 4:26, 8:58
23. Exodus 12:3-6	The Lamb presented to Israel 4 days before Passover	Mark 11:7-11
24. Exodus 12:5	A Lamb without blemish	Hebrews 9:14; 1Peter 1:19
25. Exodus 12:13	The blood of the Lamb saves from wrath	Romans 5:8
26. Exodus 12:21-27	Christ is our Passover	1Corinthians 5:7
27. Exodus 12:46	Not a bone of the Lamb to be broken	John 19:31-36
28. Exodus 15:2	His exaltation predicted as Yeshua	Acts 7:55, 56
29. Exodus 15:11	His Character-Holiness	Luke 1:35; Acts 4:27
30. Exodus 17:6	The Spiritual Rock of Israel	1Corinthians 10:4
31. Exodus 33:19	His Character-Merciful	Luke 1:72
32. Leviticus 1:2-9	His sacrifice a sweet smelling savor unto God	Ephesians 5:2
33. Leviticus 14:11	The leper cleansed; a sign to the priesthood	Luke 5:12-14; Acts 6:7
34. Leviticus 16:15-17	Prefigures Christ's once-for-all death	Hebrews 9:7-14
35. Leviticus 16:27	Suffering outside the Camp	Matthew 27:33; Hebrews 13:11, 12
36. Leviticus 17:11	The Blood-the life of the flesh	Matthew 26:28; Mark 10:45
37. Leviticus 17:11	It is the blood that makes atonement	Romans 3:23-24; 1John 1:7
38. Leviticus 23:36-37	The Drink-offering: "If any man thirst"	John 7:37
39. Numbers 9:12	Not a bone of Him broken	John 19:31-36
40. Numbers 21:9	The serpent on a pole-Christ lifted up	John 3:14-18, 12:32

41. Numbers 24:17	Time: "I shall see him, but not now."	John 1:14; Galatians 4:4
42. Deuteronomy 18:15	"This is of a truth that prophet."	John 6:14
43. Deuteronomy 18:15-16	"Had ye believed Moses, ye would believe me."	John 5:45-47
44. Deuteronomy 18:18	Sent by the Father to speak His word	John 8:28, 29
45. Deuteronomy 18:19	Whoever will not hear must bear his sin	Acts 3:22-23
46. Deuteronomy 21:23	Cursed is he that hangs on a tree	Galatians 3:10-13
47. Joshua 5:14-15	The Captain of our salvation	Hebrews 2:10
48. Ruth 4:4-10	Christ, our kinsman, has redeemed us	Ephesians 1:3-7
49. 1 Samuel 2:35	A Faithful Priest	Hebrews 2:17, 3:1-3, 6, 7:24-25
50. 1 Samuel 2:10	Shall be an anointed King to the Lord	Matthew 28:18, John 12:15
51. 2 Samuel 7:12	David's Seed	Matthew 1:1
52. 2 Samuel 7:13	His Kingdom is everlasting	2Peter 1:11
53. 2 Samuel 7:14a	The Son of God	Luke 1:32, Romans 1:3-4
54. 2 Samuel 7:16	David's house established forever	Luke 3:31; Revelation 22:16
55. 2 Kings 2:11	The bodily ascension to heaven illustrated	Luke 24:51
56. 1 Chronicles 17:11	David's Seed	Matthew 1:1, 9:27
57. 1 Chronicles 17:12-13	To reign on David's throne forever	Luke 1:32, 33
58. 1 Chronicles 17:13	"I will be His Father, He...my Son."	Hebrews 1:5
59. Job 9:32-33	Mediator between man and God	1 Timothy 2:5
60. Job 19:23-27	The Resurrection predicted	John 5:24-29
61. Psalms 2:1-3	The enmity of kings foreordained	Acts 4:25-28
62. Psalms 2:2	To own the title, Anointed (Christ)	John 1:41, Acts 2:36
63. Psalms 2:6	His Character-Holiness	John 8:46; Revelation 3:7

Chapter Seventeen: The Cosmic Christ

64. Psalms 2:6	To own the title King	Matthew 2:2
65. Psalms 2:7	Declared the Beloved Son	Matthew 3:17, Romans 1:4
66. Psalms 2:7, 8	The Crucifixion and Resurrection intimated	Acts 13:29-33
67. Psalms 2:8, 9	Rule the nations with a rod of iron	Revelation 2:27, 12:5, 19:15
68. Psalms 2:12	Life comes through faith in Him	John 20:31
69. Psalms 8:2	The mouths of babes perfect His praise	Matthew 21:16
70. Psalms 8:5, 6	His humiliation and exaltation	Hebrews 2:5-9
71. Psalms 9:7-10	Judge the world in righteousness	Acts 17:31
72. Psalms 16:10	Was not to see corruption	Acts 2:31, 13:35
73. Psalms 16:9-11	Was to arise from the dead	John 20:9
74. Psalms 17:15	The resurrection predicted	Luke 24:6
75. Psalms 18:2-3	The horn of salvation	Luke 1:69-71
76. Psalms 22:1	Forsaken because of sins of others	2 Corinthians 5:21
77. Psalms 22:1	"My God, my God, why hast thou forsaken me?"	Matthew 27:46
78. Psalms 22:2	Darkness upon Calvary for three hours	Matthew 27:45
79. Psalms 22:7	They shoot out the lip and shake the head	Matthew 27:39-44
80. Psalms 22:8	"He trusted in God, let Him deliver Him"	Matthew 27:43
81. Psalms 22:9-10	Born the Savior	Luke 2:7
82. Psalms 22:12-13	They seek His death	John 19:6
83. Psalms 22:14	His blood poured out when they pierced His side	John 19:34
84. Psalms 22:14, 15	Suffered agony on Calvary	Mark 15:34-37
85. Psalms 22:15	He thirsted	John 19:28
86. Psalms 22:16	They pierced His hands and His feet	John 19:34, 37; 20:27

87. Psalms 22:17, 18	Stripped Him before the stares of men	Luke 23:34, 35
88. Psalms 22:18	They parted His garments	John 19:23, 24
89. Psalms 22:20, 21	He committed Himself to God	Luke 23:46
90. Psalms 22:20, 21	Satanic power bruising the Redeemer's heel	Hebrews 2:14
91. Psalms 22:22	His Resurrection declared	John 20:17
92. Psalms 22:27-28	He shall be the governor of the nations	Colossians 1:16
93. Psalms 22:31	"It is finished"	John 19:30, Hebrews 10:10, 12, 14, 18
94. Psalms 23:1	"I am the Good Shepherd"	John 10:11, 1Peter 2:25
95. Psalms 24:3	His exaltation predicted	Acts 1:11; Philippians 2:9
96. Psalms 30:3	His resurrection predicted	Acts 2:32
97. Psalms 31:5	"Into thy hands I commit my spirit"	Luke 23:46
98. Psalms 31:11	His acquaintances fled from Him	Mark 14:50
99. Psalms 31:13	They took counsel to put Him to death	Matthew 27:1, John 11:53
100. Psalms 31:14, 15	"He trusted in God, let Him deliver him"	Matthew 27:43
101. Psalms 34:20	Not a bone of Him broken	John 19:31-36
102. Psalms 35:11	False witnesses rose up against Him	Matthew 26:59
103. Psalms 35:19	He was hated without a cause	John 15:25
104. Psalms 38:11	His friends stood afar off	Luke 23:49
105. Psalms 38:12	Enemies try to entangle Him by craft	Mark 14:1, Matthew 22:15
106. Psalms 38:12-13	Silent before His accusers	Matthew 27:12-14
107. Psalms 38:20	He went about doing good	Acts 10:38
108. Psalms 40:2-5	The joy of His resurrection predicted	John 20:20

Chapter Seventeen: The Cosmic Christ

109. Psalms 40:6-8	His delight-the will of the Father	John 4:34, Hebrews 10:5-10
110. Psalms 40:9	He was to preach the Righteousness in Israel	Matthew 4:17
111. Psalms 40:14	Confronted by adversaries in the Garden	John 18:4-6
112. Psalms 41:9	Betrayed by a familiar friend	John 13:18
113. Psalms 45:2	Words of Grace come from His lips	John 1:17, Luke 4:22
114. Psalms 45:6	To own the title, God or Elohim	Hebrews 1:8
115. Psalms 45:7	A special anointing by the Holy Spirit	Matthew 3:16; Hebrews 1:9
116. Psalms 45:7, 8	Called the Christ (Messiah or Anointed)	Luke 2:11
117. Psalms 45:17	His name remembered forever	Ephesians 1:20-21, Hebrews 1:8
118. Psalms 55:12-14	Betrayed by a friend, not an enemy	John 13:18
119. Psalms 55:15	Unrepentant death of the Betrayer	Matthew 27:3-5; Acts 1:16-19
120. Psalms 68:18	To give gifts to men	Ephesians 4:7-16
121. Psalms 68:18	Ascended into Heaven	Luke 24:51
122. Psalms 69:4	Hated without a cause	John 15:25
123. Psalms 69:8	A stranger to own brethren	John 1:11, 7:5
124. Psalms 69:9	Zealous for the Lord's House	John 2:17
125. Psalms 69:14-20	Messiah's anguish of soul before crucifixion	Matthew 26:36-45
126. Psalms 69:20	"My soul is exceeding sorrowful."	Matthew 26:38
127. Psalms 69:21	Given vinegar in thirst	Matthew 27:34
128. Psalms 69:26	The Savior given and smitten by God	John 17:4; 18:11
129. Psalms 72:10, 11	Great persons were to visit Him	Matthew 2:1-11
130. Psalms 72:16	The corn of wheat to fall into the Ground	John 12:24-25

131. Psalms 72:17	Belief on His name will produce offspring	John 1:12, 13
132. Psalms 72:17	All nations shall be blessed by Him	Galatians 3:8
133. Psalms 72:17	All nations shall call Him blessed	John 12:13, Revelation 5:8-12
134. Psalms 78:1-2	He would teach in parables	Matthew 13:34-35
135. Psalms 78:2b	To speak the Wisdom of God with authority	Matthew 7:29
136. Psalms 80:17	The Man of God's right hand	Mark 14:61-62
137. Psalms 88	The Suffering and Reproach of Calvary	Matthew 27:26-50
138. Psalms 88:8	They stood afar off and watched	Luke 23:49
139. Psalms 89:27	Firstborn	Colossians 1:15, 18
140. Psalms 89:27	Emmanuel to be higher than earthly kings	Luke 1:32, 33
141. Psalms 89:35-37	David's Seed, throne, kingdom endure forever	Luke 1:32, 33
142. Psalms 89:36-37	His Character-Faithfulness	Revelation 1:5, 19:11
143. Psalms 90:2	He is from everlasting (Micah 5:2)	John 1:1
144. Psalms 91:11, 12	Identified as Messianic; used to tempt Christ	Luke 4:10, 11
145. Psalms 97:9	His exaltation predicted	Acts 1:11; Ephesians 1:20
146. Psalms 100:5	His Character-Goodness	Matthew 19:16, 17
147. Psalms 102:1-11	The Suffering and Reproach of Calvary	John 19:16-30
148. Psalms 102:25-27	Messiah is the Preexistent Son	Hebrews 1:10-12
149. Psalms 109:25	Ridiculed	Matthew 27:39
150. Psalms 110:1	Son of David	Matthew 22:42-43
151. Psalms 110:1	To ascend to the right-hand of the Father	Mark 16:19
152. Psalms 110:1	David's son called Lord	Matthew 22:44, 45
153. Psalms 110:4	A priest after Melchizedek's order	Hebrews 6:20

Chapter Seventeen: The Cosmic Christ

154. Psalms 112:4	His Character-Compassionate, Gracious, et al	Matthew 9:36
155. Psalms 118:17, 18	Messiah's Resurrection assured	Luke 24:5-7; 1Cor. 15:20
156. Psalms 118:22, 23	The rejected stone is Head of the corner	Matthew 21:42, 43
157. Psalms 118:26a	The Blessed One presented to Israel	Matthew 21:9
158. Psalms 118:26b	To come while Temple standing	Matthew 21:12-15
159. Psalms 132:11	The Seed of David (the fruit of His Body)	Luke 1:32, Act 2:30
160. Psalms 129:3	He was scourged	Matthew 27:26
161. Psalms 138:1-6	The supremacy of David's Seed amazes kings	Matthew 2:2-6
162. Psalms 147:3, 6	The earthly ministry of Christ described	Luke 4:18
163. Proverbs 1:23	He will send the Spirit of God	John 16:7
164. Proverbs 8:23	Foreordained from everlasting	Revelation 13:8, 1Peter 1:19-20
165. Song. 5:16	The altogether lovely One	John 1:17
166. Isaiah 2:3	He shall teach all nations	John 4:25
167. Isaiah 2:4	He shall judge among the nations	John 5:22
168. Isaiah 6:1	When Isaiah saw His glory	John 12:40-41
169. Isaiah 6:8	The One Sent by God	John 12:38-45
170. Isaiah 6:9-10	Parables fall on deaf ears	Matthew 13:13-15
171. Isaiah 6:9-12	Blinded to Christ and deaf to His words	Acts 28:23-29
172. Isaiah 7:14	To be born of a virgin	Luke 1:35
173. Isaiah 7:14	To be Emmanuel-God with us	Matthew 1:18-23, 1Tim. 3:16
174. Isaiah 8:8	Called Emmanuel	Matthew 28:20
175. Isaiah 8:14	A stone of stumbling, a Rock of offense	1Peter 2:8
176. Isaiah 9:1, 2	His ministry to begin in Galilee	Matthew 4:12-17

177. Isaiah 9:6	A child born to Humanity	Luke 1:31
178. Isaiah 9:6	A Son given by and through Deity	Luke 1:32, John 1:14, 1Tim. 3:16
179. Isaiah 9:6	Declared to be the Son of God with power	Romans 1:3, 4
180. Isaiah 9:6	The Wonderful One, Peleh	Luke 4:22
181. Isaiah 9:6	The Counsellor, Yaatz	Matthew 13:54
182. Isaiah 9:6	The Mighty God, El Gibor	1Cor. 1:24, Titus 2:13
183. Isaiah 9:6	The Everlasting Father, Avi'Ad	John 8:58, 10:30
184. Isaiah 9:6	The Prince of Peace, Sar Shalom	John 16:33
185. Isaiah 9:7	Inherits the throne of David	Luke 1:32
186. Isaiah 9:7	His Character-Just	John 5:30
187. Isaiah 9:7	No end to his Government, Throne, and kingdom	Luke 1:33
188. Isaiah 11:1	Called a Nazarene-the Branch, Netzer	Matthew 2:23
189. Isaiah 11:1	A rod out of Jesse-Son of Jesse	Luke 3:23, 32
190. Isaiah 11:2	Anointed One by the Spirit	Matthew 3:16, 17, Acts 10:38
191. Isaiah 11:2	His Character-Wisdom, Knowledge, et al	Colossians 2:3
192. Isaiah 11:3	He would know their thoughts	Luke 6:8, John 2:25
193. Isaiah 11:4	Judge in righteousness	Acts 17:31
194. Isaiah 11:4	Judges with the sword of His mouth	Revelation 2:16, 19:11, 15
195. Isaiah 11:5	Character: Righteous & Faithful	Revelation 19:11
196. Isaiah 11:10	The Gentiles seek Him	John 12:18-21
197. Isaiah 12:2	Called Jesus-Yeshua	Matthew 1:21
198. Isaiah 22:22	The One given all authority to govern	Revelation 3:7
199. Isaiah 25:8	The Resurrection predicted	1Corinthians 15:54
200. Isaiah 26:19	His power of Resurrection predicted	Matthew 27:50-54

Chapter Seventeen: The Cosmic Christ

201. Isaiah 28:16	The Messiah is the precious corner stone	Acts 4:11, 12
202. Isaiah 28:16	The Sure Foundation	1Corinthians 3:11, Matthew 16:18
203. Isaiah 29:13	He indicated hypocritical obedience to His Word	Matthew 15:7-9
204. Isaiah 29:14	The wise are confounded by the Word	1Corinthians 1:18-31
205. Isaiah 32:2	A Refuge-A man shall be a hiding place	Matthew 23:37
206. Isaiah 35:4	He will come and save you	Matthew 1:21
207. Isaiah 35:5-6	To have a ministry of miracles	Matthew 11:2-6
208. Isaiah 40:3, 4	Preceded by forerunner	John 1:23
209. Isaiah 40:9	Behold your God	John 1:36; 19:14
210. Isaiah 40:10.	He will come to reward	Revelation 22:12
211. Isaiah 40:11	A shepherd-compassionate life-giver	John 10:10-18
212. Isaiah 42:1-4	The Servant-as a faithful, patient redeemer	Matthew 12:18-21
213. Isaiah 42:2	Meek and lowly	Matthew 11:28-30
214. Isaiah 42:3	He brings hope for the hopeless	John 4
215. Isaiah 42:4	The nations shall wait on His teachings	John 12:20-26
216. Isaiah 42:6	The Light (salvation) of the Gentiles	Luke 2:32
217. Isaiah 42:1, 6	His is a worldwide compassion	Matthew 28:19, 20
218. Isaiah 42:7	Blind eyes opened.	John 9:25-38
219. Isaiah 43:11	He is the only Savior.	Acts 4:12
220. Isaiah 44:3	He will send the Spirit of God	John 16:7, 13
221. Isaiah 45:21-25	He is Lord and Savior	Philippians 3:20, Titus 2:13
222. Isaiah 45:23	He will be the Judge	John 5:22; Romans 14:11
223. Isaiah 46:9, 10	Declares things not yet done	John 13:19

224. Isaiah 48:12	The First and the Last	John 1:30, Revelation 1:8, 17
225. Isaiah 48:16, 17	He came as a Teacher	John 3:2
226. Isaiah 49:1	Called from the womb-His humanity	Matthew 1:18
227. Isaiah 49:5	A Servant from the womb.	Luke 1:31, Philippians 2:7
228. Isaiah 49:6	He will restore Israel	Acts 3:19-21, 15:16-17
229. Isaiah 49:6	He is Salvation for Israel	Luke 2:29-32
230. Isaiah 49:6	He is the Light of the Gentiles	John 8:12, Acts 13:47
231. Isaiah 49:6	He is Salvation unto the ends of the earth	Acts 15:7-18
232. Isaiah 49:7	He is despised of the Nation	John 1:11, 8:48-49, 19:14-15
233. Isaiah 50:3	Heaven is clothed in black at His humiliation	Luke 23:44, 45
234. Isaiah 50:4	He is a learned counselor for the weary	Matthew 7:29, 11:28, 29
235. Isaiah 50:5	The Servant bound willingly to obedience	Matthew 26:39
236. Isaiah 50:6a	I gave my back to the smiters.	Matthew 27:26
237. Isaiah 50:6b	He was smitten on the cheeks	Matthew 26:67
238. Isaiah 50:6c	He was spat upon	Matthew 27:30
239. Isaiah 52:7	Published good tidings upon mountains	Matthew 5:12,15:29,28:16
240. Isaiah 52:13	The Servant exalted	Acts 1:8-11; Eph. 1:19-22, Philippians 2:5-9
241. Isaiah 52:14	The Servant shockingly abused	Luke 18:31-34; Matthew 26:67, 68
242. Isaiah 52:15	Nations startled by message of the Servant	Luke 18:31-34; Matthew 26:67, 68

Chapter Seventeen: The Cosmic Christ

243. Isaiah 52:15	His blood shed sprinkles nations	Hebrews 9:13-14, Revelation 1:5
244. Isaiah 53:1	His people would not believe Him	John 12:37-38
245. Isaiah 53:2	Appearance of an ordinary man	Philippians 2:6-8
246. Isaiah 53:3a	Despised	Luke 4:28-29
247. Isaiah 53:3b	Rejected	Matthew 27:21-23
248. Isaiah 53:3c	Great sorrow and grief	Matthew 26:37-38, Luke 19:41, Hebrews 4:15
249. Isaiah 53:3d	Men hide from being associated with Him	Mark 14:50-52
250. Isaiah 53:4a	He would have a healing ministry	Matthew 8:16-17
251. Isaiah 53:4b	Thought to be cursed by God	Matthew 26:66, 27:41-43
252. Isaiah 53:5a	Bears penalty for mankind's iniquities	2Corinthians 5:21, Hebrews 2:9
253. Isaiah 53:5b	His sacrifice provides peace between man and God	Colossians 1:20
254. Isaiah 53:5c	His sacrifice would heal man of sin	1Peter 2:24
255. Isaiah 53:6a	He would be the sin-bearer for all mankind	1John 2:2, 4:10
256. Isaiah 53:6b	God's will that He bear sin for all mankind	Galatians 1:4
257. Isaiah 53:7a	Oppressed and afflicted	Matthew 27:27-31
258. Isaiah 53:7b	Silent before his accusers	Matthew 27:12-14
259. Isaiah 53:7c	Sacrificial lamb	John 1:29, 1Peter 1:18-19
260. Isaiah 53:8a	Confined and persecuted	Matthew 26:47-27:31
261. Isaiah 53:8b	He would be judged	John 18:13-22
262. Isaiah 53:8c	Killed	Matthew 27:35
263. Isaiah 53:8d	Dies for the sins of the world	1John 2:2
264. Isaiah 53:9a	Buried in a rich man's grave	Matthew 27:57

265. Isaiah 53:9b	Innocent and had done no violence	Luke 23:41, John 18:38
266. Isaiah 53:9c	No deceit in his mouth	1Peter 2:22
267. Isaiah 53:10a	God's will that He die for mankind	John 18:11
268. Isaiah 53:10b	An offering for sin	Matthew 20:28, Galatians 3:13
269. Isaiah 53:10c	Resurrected and live forever	Romans 6:9
270. Isaiah 53:10d	He would prosper	John 17:1-5
271. Isaiah 53:11a	God fully satisfied with His suffering	John 12:27
272. Isaiah 53:11b	God's servant would justify man	Romans 5:8-9, 18-19
273. Isaiah 53:11c	The sin-bearer for all mankind	Hebrews 9:28
274. Isaiah 53:12a	Exalted by God because of his sacrifice	Matthew 28:18
275. Isaiah 53:12b	He would give up his life to save mankind	Luke 23:46
276. Isaiah 53:12c	Numbered with the transgressors	Mark 15:27-28
277. Isaiah 53:12d	Sin-bearer for all mankind	1Peter 2:24
278. Isaiah 53:12e	Intercede to God in behalf of mankind	Luke 23:34, Romans 8:34
279. Isaiah 55:3	Resurrected by God	Acts 13:34
280. Isaiah 55:4a	A witness	John 18:37
281. Isaiah 55:4b	He is a leader and commander	Hebrews 2:10
282. Isaiah 55:5	God would glorify Him	Acts 3:13
283. Isaiah 59:16a	Intercessor between man and God	Matthew 10:32
284. Isaiah 59:16b	He would come to provide salvation	John 6:40
285. Isaiah 59:20	He would come to Zion as their Redeemer	Luke 2:38
286. Isaiah 60:1-3	He would shew light to the Gentiles	Acts 26:23
287. Isaiah 61:1a	The Spirit of God upon him	Matthew 3:16-17
288. Isaiah 61:1b	The Messiah would preach the good news	Luke 4:16-21

Chapter Seventeen: The Cosmic Christ

289. Isaiah 61:1c	Provide freedom from the bondage of sin	John 8:31-36
290. Isaiah 61:1-2a	Proclaim a period of grace	Galatians 4:4-5
291. Jeremiah 11:21	Conspiracy to kill Jesus	John 7:1, Matthew 21:38
292. Jeremiah 23:5-6	Descendant of David	Luke 3:23-31
293. Jeremiah 23:5-6	The Messiah would be both God and Man	John 13:13, 1Ti 3:16
294. Jeremiah 31:22	Born of a virgin	Matthew 1:18-20
295. Jeremiah 31:31	The Messiah would be the new covenant	Matthew 26:28
296. Jeremiah 33:14-15	Descendant of David	Luke 3:23-31
297. Ezekiel 34:23-24	Descendant of David	Matthew 1:1
298. Ezekiel 37:24-25	Descendant of David	Luke 1:31-33
299. Daniel 2:44-45	The Stone that shall break the kingdoms	Matthew 21:44
300. Daniel 7:13-14a	He would ascend into heaven	Acts 1:9-11
301. Daniel 7:13-14b	Highly exalted	Ephesians 1:20-22
302. Daniel 7:13-14c	His dominion would be everlasting	Luke 1:31-33
303. Daniel 9:24a	To make an end to sins	Galatians 1:3-5
304. Daniel 9:24a	To make reconciliation for iniquity	Romans 5:10, 2Cor. 5:18-21
305. Daniel 9:24b	He would be holy	Luke 1:35
306. Daniel 9:25	His announcement	John 12:12-13
307. Daniel 9:26a	Cut off	Matthew 16:21, 21:38-39
308. Daniel 9:26b	Die for the sins of the world	Hebrews 2:9
309. Daniel 9:26c	Killed before the destruction of the temple	Matthew 27:50-51
310. Daniel 10:5-6	Messiah in a glorified state	Revelation 1:13-16
311. Hosea 11:1	He would be called out of Egypt	Matthew 2:15
312. Hosea 13:14	He would defeat death	1Corinthians 15:55-57

313. Joel 2:32	Offer salvation to all mankind	Romans 10:9-13
314. Jonah 1:17	Death and resurrection of Christ	Matthew 12:40, 16:4
315. Micah 5:2a	Born in Bethlehem	Matthew 2:1-6
316. Micah 5:2b	Ruler in Israel	Luke 1:33
317. Micah 5:2c	From everlasting	John 8:58
318. Haggai 2:6-9	He would visit the second Temple	Luke 2:27-32
319. Haggai 2:23	Descendant of Zerubbabel	Luke 2:27-32
320. Zechariah 3:8	God's servant	John 17:4
321. Zechariah 6:12-13	Priest and King	Hebrews 8:1
322. Zechariah 9:9a	Greeted with rejoicing in Jerusalem	Matthew 21:8-10
323. Zechariah 9:9b	Beheld as King	John 12:12-13
324. Zechariah 9:9c	The Messiah would be just	John 5:30
325. Zechariah 9:9d	The Messiah would bring salvation	Luke 19:10
326. Zechariah 9:9e	The Messiah would be humble	Matthew 11:29
327. Zechariah 9:9f	Presented to Jerusalem riding on a donkey	Matthew 21:6-9
328. Zechariah 10:4	The cornerstone	Ephesians 2:20
329. Zechariah 11:4-6a	At His coming, Israel to have unfit leaders	Matthew 23:1-4
330. Zechariah 11:4-6b	Rejection causes God to remove His protection	Luke 19:41-44
331. Zechariah 11:4-6c	Rejected in favor of another king	John 19:13-15
332. Zechariah 11:7	Ministry to "poor," the believing remnant	Matthew 9:35-36
333. Zechariah 11:8a	Unbelief forces Messiah to reject them	Matthew 23:33
334. Zechariah 11:8b	Despised	Matthew 27:20
335. Zechariah 11:9	Stops ministering to those who rejected Him	Matthew 13:10-11
336. Zechariah 11:10-11a	Rejection causes God to remove protection	Luke 19:41-44
337. Zechariah 11:10-11b	The Messiah would be God	John 14:7

Chapter Seventeen: The Cosmic Christ

338. Zechariah 11:12-13a	Betrayed for thirty pieces of silver	Matthew 26:14-15
339. Zechariah 11:12-13b	Rejected	Matthew 26:14-15
340. Zechariah 11:12-13c	Thirty pieces of silver cast in the house of the Lord	Matthew 27:3-5
341. Zechariah 11:12-13d	The Messiah would be God	John 12:45
342. Zechariah 12:10a	The Messiah's body would be pierced	John 19:34-37
343. Zechariah 12:10b	The Messiah would be both God and man	John 10:30
344. Zechariah 12:10c	The Messiah would be rejected	John 1:11
345. Zechariah 13:7a	God's will He die for mankind	John 18:11
346. Zechariah 13:7b	A violent death	Mark 14:27
347. Zechariah 13:7c	Both God and man	John 14:9
348. Zechariah 13:7d	Israel scattered as a result of rejecting Him	Matthew 26:31-56
349. Zechariah 14:4	He would return to the Matthew of Olives	Acts 1:11-12
350. Malachi 3:1a	Messenger to prepare the way for Messiah	Mark 1:1-8
351. Malachi 3:1b	Sudden appearance at the temple	Mark 11:15-16
352. Malachi 3:1c	Messenger of the new covenant	Luke 4:43
353. Malachi 3:6	The God who changes not	Hebrews 13:8
354. Malachi 4:5	Forerunner in spirit of Elijah	Matthew 3:1-3, 11:10-14, 17:11-13
355. Malachi 4:6	Forerunner would turn many to righteousness	Luke 1:16-17

THE BOOK OF ENOCH PROPHESIES JESUS CHRIST

The *Book of Enoch* is considered scripture in the *Epistle of Barnabas* (16:4) and by many of the early Church Fathers, such as Athenagoras, Clement of Alexandria, Irenaeus and Tertullian, who wrote in 200 A.D. that the *Book of Enoch* had been rejected by the Jews because it contained prophecies pertaining to Christ.[5]

Although widely known at the time of the development of the Jewish Bible canon, 1 Enoch was excluded from both the formal canon of the Tenakh and the typical canon of the Septuagint. One possible reason for Jewish rejection of the book might be the textual nature of several early sections of the book that make use of material from the Torah; for example, 1 Enoch is a *Midrash* of Deuteronomy 33. Another reason may be the fact that Enoch accurately predicted that the Son of Man would come, suffer for His people, and then live forever as the Lord of Spirits. The Jewish scholars, the Pharisees, rejected Yeshua as being their Messiah, in spite of the fact that He fulfilled every prophecy, except of course His Second Coming, which is yet to come.

The content in 1 Enoch detailed descriptions of fallen angels, which could also be a reason for rejection from the Hebrew canon at this period - as illustrated by the comments of 'Trypho the Jew' when debating with 'Justin Martyr' on this subject. Trypho said: "The utterances of God are holy, but your expositions are mere contrivances, as is plain from what has been explained by you; nay, even blasphemies, for you assert that angels sinned and revolted from God."

However, later on the Church Fathers denied the canonicity of the book, and some even considered the letter of Jude uncanonical because it refers to an "apocryphal" work. By the 4th century, it was mostly excluded from Christian lists of the Biblical canon, and was omitted from the canon by most of the Christian church (the Ethiopian Orthodox Church and Coptic Church being the exception).

What many Jews today forget, in spite of their tradition of memorializing historical events, was that ancient Jews believed in a Lesser Yahuah, or Lesser God, which is evidenced in Jewish literature before the time of Christ. This being was believed to be a Great Being who was *Second in Command* in the Universe. The Bible reveals this being to be Yeshua HaMashiach, Yahushua, Yeshua, Jesus the Christ.

The Books of Enoch reflect this truth, which was deliberately covered up by both the Catholic Church Fathers and the Jewish Pharisees, because they refused to accept Yeshua as Messiah.

The New Testament reveals this Being to have been the Christ. The mystery of this super powerful Being is revealed in the Book of Enoch, quoted by the apostle Jude. Notice what Enoch wrote about this ancient Being![6]

The Book of Enoch contains captivating discernment into the existence of a super-powerful Being, who was also called the "Son of Man," long before there was a human being called the "Son of Man". The only other person in history crowned with the title, "Son of Man" was Jesus Christ, who can be discovered within the pages of Enoch's scrolls. This ancient man of God "walked with God" (Genesis 5:24), before the time of Noah and the Flood.

The Old Testament Pseudepigrapha, as edited by James H. Charlesworth, in which are three books translated from ancient Middle Eastern languages, the Ethiopian or Coptic texts which is called Enoch, the seventh generation from Adam. The Ethiopic book of Enoch, which is also known as I Enoch and 2 Enoch, is considered the oldest

Chapter Seventeen: The Cosmic Christ

of the three. According to Genesis Chapter 5, Enoch walked with God, then simply vanished, because God "took Him," is affirmed in many of the Haggadic Stories among Jews in ancient times.

The book of Enoch, or I Enoch, states God took Enoch to heaven, where he was taught the secrets of the Universe. He was taught the language of the angels which was ancient Hebrew, also known as Aramaic, and he was given glimpses into the future of humanity, the End of Times and the Final Divine Judgment.

It is important to note that Enoch's Scrolls were known to most Jews, especially the Essenes, the early Christians and Jesus Himself. Jude, the brother of Christ, quoted from Enoch in his epistle, indicating his reliance on its credibility, importance and authority. He quoted from Enoch as if it was the very Word of God Himself: "And Enoch also, the seventh from Adam, prophesied of these, saying, 'Behold, the Lord cometh with ten thousands of his saints, to execute judgment upon all, and to convict all that are ungodly among them of all their ungodly deeds which they have ungodly committed, and of all their hard speeches which ungodly sinners have spoken against him.'" (Jude 14-15)

The Ethiopic Book of Enoch says, "Behold he comes with ten thousands of his saints, to execute judgment upon them, and destroy the wicked, and reprove all of flesh for everything which the sinful and ungodly have done, and committed against him."

Enoch was also quoted by the authors of the book of Jubilees, the Twelve Patriarchs, the Assumption of Moses, 2 Baruch and 4 Ezra, all texts rejected by the Church of Rome because of their Jewish origins, beliefs, and the fact that they contained the inspired Word of God. It is important to remember that the Jews were chosen by the Lord Yahuah to be the preservers of knowledge, discernment and to be a 'set apart' people in the world, wholly (holy) unto Himself. The rebellion of the Roman emperors was against the God of gods, with their long history steeped in idolatry and rebellion. Instead Rome was influenced by fallen angels to create many religions, to confuse people. It completely avoids the Creator and His Divine Plan. Remember that the fallen angels were and continue to be in rebellion against the Lord of the Universe.

When the Roman Catholic Church began to dominate in the first millennia, it proved to be a continuation of the original Babylonian religion. This religion was rooted in a belief in a Trinity, originally Semiramis, Nimrod and Tiamat, or in the Egyptian mythos as Isis, Horus, Osiris. They incorporated the belief in the Trinity into Roman Catholicism, keeping in line with the Mother Church of Rome, and switched out the gods for Mary, Jesus and the Father God, which was contrary to the teachings of the book of Enoch. E. Isaac wrote, "The relegation of I Enoch to virtual oblivion by medieval minds should not diminish its significance for Christian origins; few other apocryphal books so indelibly marked the religious history and thought of the time of Jesus." Enoch reveals God as righteous and just, the Creator of the world, the holy lawgiver, the dispenser of history and ultimate judge of all.

I Enoch discusses the existence of the one and only Heavenly Messiah also known as the Cosmic Christ (chapters 45-57). "The Messiah in is called the Righteous One, and the Son of Man, is depicted as a PRE-EXISTENT HEAVENLY BEING who is resplendent and majestic, possesses all dominion, and sits on his throne of glory passing judgment upon all Mortal and spiritual beings." (1 Enoch)

The Book of 1 Enoch focuses on the theme of the Final Judgment, the Wrath of God on the future destruction of the wicked, and the triumph of the righteous and redeemed. It communicates the coming resurrection of the righteous who have died, the coming of the Messiah to judge the world, the fate of sinners, including the fallen angels, and apostate Jews. Central themes emphasized in Enoch's book are that sinners are financial manipulators and abusers, political oppressors, and are the socially unjust people of the world who will be judged harshly if they fail to repent.

The Book of Enoch reveals statements dating back centuries before the times of Christ, of a Being with Great Power and Authority over creation, who was the First Creation of God. He was also foretold to become the Messiah from the foundation of the World.

Enoch declares:

"At that place, I saw the One to whom belongs the time before time. And his head was white like wool, and there was with him another individual, whose face was like that of a human being. His countenance was full of grace like that of one among the holy angels. And I asked the one -- from among the angels – who was going with me, and who had revealed to me all the secrets regarding the One who was born of human beings, 'Who is this, and from whence is he who is going as the PROTOTYPE OF THE BEFORE-TIME?' And he answered me and said to me, 'This is the *Son of Man*, to whom belongs righteousness, and with whom righteousness dwells. And he will open all the hidden storerooms; for the Lord of the Spirits has chosen him, and he is destined to be victorious before the Lord of the Spirits in eternal uprightness. This *Son of Man* whom you have seen is the One who would remove the kings and the mighty ones from their comfortable seats and the strong ones from their thrones. He shall loosen the reins of the strong and crush the teeth of the sinners. He shall depose the kings from their thrones and kingdoms"

(I Enoch 46:1-5)[8]

In Richard Laurence's translation of 1 Enoch, who was the Archbishop of Cashel, and Professor of Hebrew in the University of Oxford, 1821, he wrote (emphasis mine):

Chapter Seventeen: The Cosmic Christ

"There I beheld the *Ancient of Days*, whose head was like white wool, and with him another, whose countenance resembled that of a man. His countenance was full of grace, like that of one of the holy angels. Then I enquired of one of the angels who went with me, and who shewed me every secret thing, concerning this *Son of Man*; who He was; whence He was; and why He accompanied the *Ancient of Days*."

"He answered and said to me: This is the *Son of Man*, to whom righteousness belongs; with whom righteousness has dwelt; and who will reveal all the treasures of that which is concealed; for the *Lord of Spirits* has CHOSEN him; and his portion has surpassed all before the *Lord of Spirits* in everlasting uprightness." (Enoch 46:1, 2)[9]

These scriptures prove that the *Son of Man* – who sits with the *Ancient of Days* and accompanied Him – will execute judgment, hurling kings from their thrones, and punished all who lift up their hands against the Most High God, who I have already identified as YAHUAH.

Enoch's Words clearly parallel the New Testament description of Jesus Christ, who is identified as the "Logos" or "Word" of God, who was with God "in the beginning" (John 1:1-4). Enoch calls this Person the "Prototype of the Before-Time." Paul says Christ was the "firstborn of every creature" (Colossians 1:15). Christ Himself was referred to often as the "Son of Man," just as Enoch foretold. He also says He was "the beginning of the creation of God" (Revelation 3:14).

The fact that Enoch speaks of this primordial Being as "the Prototype of the Before-Time," specifies that He was the first One made in the very image and likeness of God, the only begotten Son, (John 3:16) which also indicates that there will be more like Him in the future, who were the Elohim, who also were the Sons of God, but not the first born of creation, but sons nonetheless.

The Book of Enoch translation of Charles E. Isaac described this Person as follows:

"At that place, I saw the One to whom belongs the time before time. And his head was white like wool, and there was WITH HIM another individual, whose face was like that of a human being. His countenance was full of grace like that of one among the holy angels. And I asked the one – from among the angels -- who was going with me, and who had revealed to me all the secrets of the One who was born of human beings, 'Who is this, and from whence is he who is going as the PROTOTYPE of the Before-Time?' And he answered me and said to me, 'This is the Son of Man, to whom belongs righteousness, and with whom righteousness dwells. And he will open all the hidden storerooms; for the Lord of the Spirits has chosen him, and he is destined to be victorious before the Lord of the Spirits in eternal uprightness.'" (I Enoch 46:4)[10]

You can see that Enoch clearly referred to an Individual chosen by God – the "Before-Time" – who was a "Prototype" of Himself and who was also called "The Son of Man," because He would later be transformed into a human being, and who would be victorious over all enemies. Clearly this is evidence of the Pre-Existent Messiah?

Enoch continues:

"At that hour, that Son of Man was given a name, in the presence of the Lord of the Spirits, the Before-Time; even before the creation of the sun and the moon, before the creation of the stars, he was given a name in the presence of the Lord of the Spirits. He will become a staff for the righteous ones in order that they may lean on him and not fall. He is the light of the Gentiles and he will become the hope of those who are sick in their hearts. All who dwell upon the earth shall fall and worship before him; they shall glorify, bless, and sing the name of the Lord of the Spirits. For this purpose, he became the CHOSEN ONE; he was concealed in the presence of the Lord of the Spirits prior to the creation of the world, and for eternity. And he has revealed the wisdom of the Lord of the Spirits to the righteous and the holy ones, for he has preserved the portion of the righteous because they hated and despised this world of oppression (together with) all its ways of life and its habits in the name of the Lord of the Spirits; and because they will be SAVED IN HIS NAME and it is his good pleasure that they have life." (I Enoch 48:2-7)[11]

I think it's incredibly revealing that this Person was even given a name before the creation of the sun, moon, and stars and the material Universe. He was to be a "light to the Gentiles." He was the "Chosen One," who was concealed by God prior to the creation of the world. He was to be the "Savior," and all those who would be saved would obtain salvation "in His name." This being is none other than Yeshua HaMashiach, aka The Lord Jesus Christ.

Peter declared of Christ, "Nor is there salvation in any other, for there is no other name under heaven given among men by which we must be saved" (Acts 4:12). Enoch accurately predicted and prophesied that this being was the Logos, or Word of God who is Jesus Christ!

Matthew said of Yeshua Jesus Christ, that He dwelt in Capernaum, in the regions of Zebulun and Naphtali, fulfilling the prophecy of Isaiah, who wrote:

Chapter Seventeen: The Cosmic Christ

"The land of Zebulun and the land of Naphtali, by the way of the sea, beyond the Jordan, Galilee of the Gentiles: The people who sat in darkness have seen a great light, and upon those who sat in the region and shadow of death, Light has dawned."

(Matthew 4:13-16)

In the Laurence translation[12], this passage in 1 Enoch reads:

"In that hour was this Son of man invoked before the Lord of spirits, and his name in the presence of the Ancient of days. Before the sun and the signs were created, before the stars of heaven were formed, his name was invoked in the presence of the Lord of spirits. A support shall He be for the righteous and the holy to lean upon, without falling; and He shall be the light of nations.

"He shall be the hope of those whose hearts are troubled. All, who dwell on earth, shall fall down and worship before him; shall bless and glorify Him, and sing praises to the name of the Lord of spirits.

"Therefore the ELECT and the CONCEALED ONE EXISTED in His presence, BEFORE THE WORLD WAS CREATED, AND FOR EVER."

(1 Enoch 48:2-5)

These words clearly show the belief and teaching that existed in ancient times among the Jewish people, even in a book regarded as authoritative by the apostle Jude, of the existence of a great *Son of Man* – the *Elect* – the *Concealed One* who existed before the heavens and the earth were formed – One who dwelt in the *presence* of the *Ancient of Days*! Jesus said,

"For nothing is concealed that won't be revealed, and nothing hidden that won't be made known and come to light."

(Luke 8:17)

And that includes Him being revealed! The Book of Revelation and the Prophet Isaiah said:

"Look, he is coming with the clouds," and "*every eye will see him*, even those who pierced him"; and all peoples on earth "will mourn because of him." So shall it be! Amen."

(Revelation 1:7)

> "Listen! Your watchmen lift up their voices; together they shout for joy. When the LORD returns to Zion, *they will see it with their own eyes.*"
>
> (Isaiah 52:8)

In 1 Enoch Chapter 49, we read:

> "The *Elect One* stands before the *Lord of the Spirits*; his glory is forever and ever and his power is unto all generations. In him dwells the spirit of wisdom, the spirit which gives thoughtfulness, the spirit of knowledge and strength, and the spirit of those who have fallen asleep in righteousness. He shall judge the secret things."
>
> (I Enoch 49:2-4)

Compare this passage to the Laurence translation:[13]

> "But iniquity passes away like a shadow, and possesses not a fixed station; for the *Elect One* stands before the *Lord of Spirits*; and his glory is for ever and ever; and His power from generation to generation. With Him dwells the spirit of intellectual wisdom, the spirit of instruction and of power, and the spirit of those who sleep in righteousness; He shall judge secret things. Nor shall any be able to utter a single word before Him; for the *Elect One* IS IN THE PRESENCE of the Lord of Spirits, according to his own pleasure."
>
> (Enoch, Part II, 2-4)

Paul wrote in Hebrews 1:1-3, that Christ, in His pre-incarnate form, was appointed by God the Father as "heir of all things, by whom also He made the worlds: who being the brightness of his glory, and the express image of His person, and upholdeth all things by the word of His power" (Hebrews1:1-3). Christ was "the image, the prototype" of the invisible God, "the firstborn of every creature" or "all creation" (Colossians1:15-16). He is the Elect One, and the Chosen One, of God. Remember that the Lord chose and transformed Saul who later became known as Paul, because he was as scribe and an educated man. He already knew the Scriptures, which is why I believe the Book of Enoch's Scriptures match Paul's writing in the New Testament, almost verbatim. No coincidence, but Inspired Word of God.

Yeshua Jesus is the One prophesied by the Old Testament Prophet Isaiah, written in the 8th Century BCE, when he wrote of the coming Messiah eight hundred years before His birth on earth:

Chapter Seventeen: The Cosmic Christ

"There shall come forth a Rod from the stem of Jesse, and a Branch shall grow out of his roots [this implies that Jesse would both be his ancestor, as well as his descendent, since this "Branch" was to grow out of his own roots, as well as come forth as a branch from his stem!]. The Spirit of the LORD shall rest upon Him, the Spirit of wisdom and understanding, the Spirit of counsel and might, the Spirit of knowledge and of the fear of the LORD."
(Isaiah 11:1-2)

I think any scholar with reasonable knowledge of these ancient scriptures can conclude that Yeshua Jesus Christ is the only human being in history to fulfill these ancient prophecies! The fact that Enoch described Christ as having existed ages before His human birth and conception, and that he wrote that He was present AT CREATION makes the Book of Enoch a match to the Bible and should be added to the Bible Canon. It ought to be studied in Churches today, especially for its prophetic value. Its relevance to End Times Prophecies, is priceless.

Did Jesus quote the Book of Enoch?

Jesus did quote from the Book of Enoch, and extensively and at least referenced, the Book of Enoch in the New Testament.

In spite of the fact that the Book of Enoch was not included in the Biblical canon except in the Ethiopic Orthodox Churches, its influence on the New Testament writers simply cannot be denied, particularly the references from Jude and 2 Peter. Unquestionably the most comprehensive account of the Nephilim is found in 1 Enoch. This is arguably one of the most captivating pieces of literature to have ever been written to explain not only the past, but also the End Times scenarios on earth. In spite of the controversy amongst scholars, theologians, and Bible students, I continue to hold the view that it should be studied today by all Bible scholars, pastors, evangelists and End Times prophets.

After much research, I found some incredibly close comparisons from the Book of Enoch, which was written centuries before Christ, with the words of Yeshua Jesus Christ in the New Testament. If Jesus preached from the Book of Enoch, it is only logical to deduce that Enoch's Words had to predate the life of Christ. The dating of the books of Enoch varies from scholar to scholar. However, it seems that most agree the earliest parts of the book were written during the pre-Maccabean period. As I mentioned earlier, that the Book of Maccabees is also considered one of the Great Rejected Texts by the Church of Rome, because of its *Jewishness* and celebration of the God of Israel. Jesus celebrated Hanukah, so we know that the Book of Maccabees was available to Him when He was a Rabbi. This would place Enoch's scrolls way before 164 BCE, however, dates for the earliest portions have ranged from sometime in the 300's BCE to 200 BCE.

R. H. Charles was the leading expert on the subject in the early part of the 20th century. While I have looked at other translations, I tend to favor Charles, because it seems to be the most concise and coherent. He argued that the Book of Enoch was written over a period of years, that the latest portions were written in 64 BCE. The earliest portions were written during the above mentioned pre-Maccabean period. However, even Charles stopped short of claiming his dates as exact.[15]

If Jude 14 quotes from the Book of Enoch, then that makes Enoch's words scripture. "And about these also Enoch, in the seventh generation from Adam, prophesied, saying, "Behold, the Lord came with many thousands of His holy ones." (Jude 14)

Now I invite you to compare the words of Christ to the words written down centuries before in the *Book of Enoch*:

Chapter Seventeen: The Cosmic Christ

Words of Jesus Christ	Word of God in Book of Enoch
"Blessed are the meek, for they shall inherit the earth." (Matthew 5:5)	"The elect shall possess light, joy and peace, and they shall inherit the earth." (Enoch 5:7 {6:9})
"The Father judges no man, but hath committed all judgment unto the son." (John 5:22)	"The principal part of the judgment was assigned to him, the Son of man." (Enoch 69:27 {68:39})
"shall inherit everlasting life." (Matthew 19:29)	"those who will inherit eternal life." (Enoch 40:9 {40:9})
"Woe unto you that are rich! For ye have received your consolation." (Luke 6:24)	"Woe to you who are rich, for in your riches have you trusted; but from your riches you shall be removed." (Enoch 94:8 {93:7}).
"Ye also shall sit upon twelve thrones, judging the twelve tribes of Israel." (Matthew 19:28)	"I will place each of them on a throne of glory." (Enoch 108:12 {105:26})
"Woe unto that man through whom the Son of man is betrayed! It had been good for that man if he had not been born." (Matthew 26:24)	"Where will the habitation of sinners be . . . who have rejected the Lord of Spirits. It would have been better for them, had they never been born." (Enoch 38:2 {38:2})
"between us and you there is a great gulf fixed." (Luke 16:26)	"by a chasm their souls are separated." (Enoch 22: 9, 11 {22:10, 12})
"In my Father's house are many mansions." (John 14:2)	"In that day shall the Elect One sit upon a throne of glory, and shall choose their conditions and countless habitations." (Enoch 45:3 {45:3})
"that ye may be called the children of light." (John 12:36)	"the good from the generation of light." (Enoch 108:11 {105: 25})
"the water that I shall give him shall be in him a well of water springing up into everlasting life." (John 4:14)	"all the thirsty drank, and were filled with wisdom, having their habitation with the righteous, the elect, and the holy." (Enoch 48:1 {48:1})

"For the Father judges no man, but has committed all judgment unto the Son." (John 5:22)	"And there was great joy amongst them, and they blessed and glorified and extolled, because the name of that Son of Man had been revealed unto them. And he sat on the throne of his glory, and the sum of judgment was given unto the Son of Man, and he caused the sinners to pass away and be destroyed from off the face of the earth, and those who have led the world astray. With chains shall they be bound, and in their assemblage-place of destruction shall they be imprisoned, And all their works vanish from the face of the earth. And from henceforth there shall be nothing corruptible; For that Son of Man has appeared, and has seated himself on the throne of his glory, and all evil shall pass away before his face, And the word of that Son of Man shall go forth, and be strong before the Lord of Spirits." (Parable III: 26-29, 1 Enoch)
"Notwithstanding in this rejoice not, that the spirits are subject unto you; but rather rejoice, because your names are written in heaven." (Luke 10:20)	"And this is the second Parable concerning those who deny the name of the dwelling of the holy ones and the Lord of Spirits. And into the heaven they shall not ascend, and on the earth they shall not come: Such shall be the lot of the sinners who have denied the name of the Lord of Spirits, who are thus preserved for the day of suffering and tribulation. On that day Mine Elect One shall sit on the throne of glory and shall try their

Chapter Seventeen: The Cosmic Christ

	works, and their places of rest shall be innumerable." (Parable II; 1 Enoch 45:2-3)
	"I swear unto you, that in heaven the angels remember you for good before the glory of the Great One: and your names are written before the glory of the Great One. Be hopeful; for aforetime ye were put to shame through ill and affliction; but now ye shall shine as the lights of heaven, ye shall shine and ye shall be seen, and the portals of heaven shall be opened to you." (1 Enoch 104:1-2)
"And Jesus said unto them, Verily I say unto you, that ye which have followed me, in the regeneration when the Son of man shall sit in the throne of his glory, ye also shall sit upon twelve thrones, judging the twelve tribes of Israel." (Matthew 19:28) "When the Son of man shall come in his glory, and all the holy angels with him, then shall he sit upon the throne of his glory." (Matthew 25:31)	"And now I will summon the spirits of the good who belong to the generation of light, and I will transform those who were born in darkness, who in the flesh were not recompensed with such honor as their faithfulness deserved. And I will bring forth in shining light those who have loved my holy name, and I will seat each on the throne of his honor. And they shall be resplendent for times without number; for righteousness is the judgment of God; for to the faithful He will give faithfulness in the habitation of upright paths." (1 Enoch 108:12-13) "And he said unto me: "Enoch, why dost thou ask me regarding the fragrance of the tree, and why dost thou wish to learn the truth?"

Then I answered him saying: "I wish to know about everything, but especially about this tree." And he answered saying: "This high mountain which thou hast seen, whose summit is like the throne of God, is His throne, where the Holy Great One, the Lord of Glory, the Eternal King, will sit, when He shall come down to visit the earth with goodness. And as for this fragrant tree no mortal is permitted to touch it till the great judgment, when He shall take vengeance on all and bring everything to its consummation forever. It shall then be given to the righteous and holy. Its fruit shall be for food to the elect: it shall be transplanted to the holy place, to the temple of the Lord, the Eternal King."

"Then shall they rejoice with joy and be glad, and into the holy place shall they enter; and its fragrance shall be in their bones, and they shall live a long life on earth, such as thy fathers lived: And in their days shall no sorrow or plague or torment or calamity touch them." Then blessed me the God of Glory, the Eternal King, who hath prepared such things for the righteous, and hath created them and promised to give to them." (1 Enoch 25:1-7)

Chapter Seventeen: The Cosmic Christ

JESUS CALLS ENOCH SCRIPTURE:
In the book of Enoch, Enoch was told to tell the fallen Watchers this:

> "And He answered and said to me, and I heard His voice:
> "Fear not, Enoch, thou righteous man and scribe of righteousness: approach hither and hear my voice. And go, say to the Watchers of heaven, who have sent thee to intercede for them:
> 'You should intercede for men, and not men for you: Wherefore have ye left the high, holy, and eternal heaven, and lain with women, and defiled yourselves with the daughters of men and taken to yourselves wives, and done like the children of earth, and begotten giants as your sons?
> And though ye were holy, spiritual, living the eternal life, you have defiled yourselves with the blood of women, and have begotten children with the blood of flesh, and, as the children of men, have lusted after flesh and blood as those also do who die and perish.
> Therefore, have I given them wives also that they might impregnate them, and beget children by them, that thus nothing might be wanting to them on earth. But you were formerly spiritual, living the eternal life, and immortal for all generations of the world. And therefore, I have not appointed wives for you; for as for the spiritual ones of the heaven, in heaven is their dwelling".
> (Enoch Chapter 15:1-7)

> "Ye shall shine as the lights of heaven, ye shall shine and ye shall be seen, and the portals of heaven shall be opened to you. And now fear not, ye righteous, when ye see the sinners growing strong and prospering in their ways: be not companions with them, but keep afar from their violence; for ye shall become companions of the hosts of heaven."
> (Enoch 104:5-6)

> "And I will bring forth in shining light those who have loved My holy name, and I will seat each on the throne of his honor. And they shall be resplendent for times without number; for righteousness is the judgment of God; for to the faithful He will give faithfulness in the habitation of upright paths."
> (Enoch 108:12-13)

> "Yeshua said to them, "Do you not therefore err, because you do not know the scriptures, nor the power of God?"
> (Mark 12:24)

Some scholars believe that Yeshua was referring to Enoch's writings as well as Moses (i.e., the Torah).

> "For when they shall rise from the dead, they neither marry, nor are given in marriage; but are like/even as the angels which are in heaven."
>
> (Mark 12:25)

Enoch teaches the resurrection and translation of the elect-righteous-redeemed, and that they will be companions of and as, the host of heaven, who do not marry nor give in marriage.[16] After studying the scriptures of both Enoch and the Bible Canon, I believe Enoch's scriptures were Divinely Inspired by the Father in Heaven. The scriptures speak of Enoch ascending into the heavens accompanied by angels (extraterrestrials) and showing Enoch the ten heavens, and teaching Enoch the language of God, and making him a 'scribe'. See, Book Five: *The Heavens* on the ten heavens revealed through Enoch. I believe Enoch wrote many more scrolls than what we have salvaged today. Knowing how controversial are the three Books of Enoch we do have, one can only imagine how provocative and threatening the rest of Enoch's other scrolls were! No wonder why the dark forces sought to destroy them and suppress their power, just as they've done with a lot of other valuable pieces of Scripture, historical records of deep antiquity, causing the human race to be a species with amnesia.

The Destruction of Satan

> "The great dragon was hurled down--that ancient serpent called the devil, or Satan, who leads the whole world astray. He was hurled to the earth, and his angels with him."
>
> (Revelation 12:9)

> "And I saw an angel coming down out of heaven, having the key to the Abyss and holding in his hand a great chain. And he seized the dragon, that ancient serpent, who is the devil and Satan, and bound him in chains for a thousand years. The angel threw him into the bottomless pit, which he then shut and locked so Satan could not deceive the nations anymore until the thousand years were finished. Afterward he must be released for a little while."
>
> (Revelation 20:1-3)

Chapter Seventeen: The Cosmic Christ

"And the devil, who deceived them, was thrown into the lake of burning sulfur, where the beast and the false prophet had been thrown. They will be tormented day and night forever and ever."

(Revelation 20:10)

In reference to the fallen angels:

"And the angels who did not keep their positions of authority but abandoned their own home--these he has kept in darkness, bound with everlasting chains for judgment on the great Day."

(Jude 1:6)

"For God did not spare angels when they sinned, but sent them to hell, putting them into gloomy dungeons to be held for judgment."

(2 Peter 2:4)

"In that day, <u>the LORD will punish the gods in the heavens and the proud rulers of the nations on earth.</u> They will be herded together like prisoners bound in a dungeon; they will be shut up in prison and be punished after many days."

(Isaiah 24:22)

Gods, herded together like prisoners? Gods sent to a dungeon and punished? Which God has the power and authority to pull something like this off? Perhaps this is why He is called, God 'Almighty', which distinguishes Him from the god and gods of this world, whose fate is prison and eventually the lake of fire.

Is Jesus The Cosmic Christ?

Is Jesus Christ limited to the Saviour of just Planet Earth? Is Christ Jesus the Cosmic Christ, Saviour of the Universe? The word says, 'all power under the Heavens, High Heavens, and authority over the lower Heavens, the stars, dimensions, parallel universes, planetary spheres. When the fallen sons of God (Bene HaElohim) and angels fell from heaven they were limited to dominion over one third of the stars of the lower heavens.

"For we war not against flesh and blood, but against powers, principalities and cosmic rulers of the darkness and spiritual wickedness in heavenly places."

(Ephesians 6:11)

The fallen sons and angels, the rebellious ETs, joined Lucifer who is now known as Satan the adversary, rebel, counterfeiter and god of this world. They still have the powers of angels. Since they have fallen, their powers are perverted, distorted and darkened. They were cast down to the lower heavens, infiltrating other stars and planets, infecting them with their disease of cosmic evil.

In the Zohar, the heavens are viewed as dual, and there are Milky Way stations that are dominated by what they call the Dark Lord with his Death Star Fleet. They refer to him as the Empire of Darkness, and state that the Dark Lord's agenda is to create a universe where chaos reigns supreme. But thankfully, that is not what the Creator Lord had in mind, which is why the discernment of worlds, stars, and star fleets is imperative now. The Zohar's Kabbalah comes across as a script right out of *Star Wars* or *Star Trek*. They make reference to portions of the cosmos as cosmic evil, the Empire of Darkness, and to some of the Hebrew Fire letters as representatives of Death Stars, and negative battle stations.[17]

J.J. Hurtak writes in *The Book of Knowledge: The Keys of Enoch*®:

"For the Pleiades will come the cross of Redemption through the image of the Lamb of God. And the Lamb will be seated upon the Throne of God, and he will carry the sword of Light which will behead the energies of the fallen suns and all those who shout blasphemies against the Father, the Paradise Sons (Elohim) and the Holy Spirit-Shekinah.

Thus, the Pleiades and Orion give the mathematics for every chemical sacrifice required in life from Genesis to Revelation. And at the end of our program, those who carry the image of the Lamb will be separated from those who carry the image of the Bear (Ursa Major) and the Dragon (Alpha Draconis), the fallen spiritual powers controlling the old linear astronomy of the Babylonian sciences, forcing man to do homage to the lower heavens." (Key106:32-33)[18]

The heavens have been cursed by the dominions of the fallen angels and the Dark Lord, Lucifer Satan's forces. This is the promise from the Creator in the book of Revelation to create a new heaven and a new earth, Revelation 21:1: "Then I saw a new heaven and a new earth, for the first heaven and the first earth had passed away, and there was no longer any sea." The old heavens have been corrupted, and when the Creator recreates the heavens, all cosmic evil will be obliterated, and we will remember it no more.

As it says in Psalm 103:19, "The Kingdom of the Lord has dominion over all."

Chapter Seventeen: The Cosmic Christ

"We see the Pleiades in terms of the organic seed of the *Pneumatikoi,* the spiritual people of the Christ Race. And we see the Pleiades in terms of the greater sacrifices of Light and Cosmology.

Pneumatikoi Gk. - The spiritual adepts of the Christ Body in this world. Those possessing not only the outpouring of the gifts of the Holy Spirit, but possessing the higher 'Gnosis' or 'Wisdom' of the Father's Cosmic Law and redemptive vehicle of "light" which cannot be separated from the Living Light. *Pneumatikoi Priesthood* are the "mystics" who seek to elevate humanity to participate in the higher worlds of Light through work on both the 'inner' and 'outer' planes.[19]

The sixth key, then, shows how the higher lights can modulate the physical universe which is controlled by the force fields of '666' so that the pure thoughts of the Masters working with the '777' principle stars in the cluster of the Pleiades have the power to materialize a new heavens and new Earth, so that the former things will not be called to mind." (Key 106:37-38)[20]

When the fallen sons and angels were ousted from the high heavens, God did not destroy them, he instead allowed them dominion over other worlds and dimensions so he could work out His Divine Plan for Evolution and Salvation through them.

> "For by him all things were created: things in heaven and on earth, visible and invisible, whether thrones or powers or rulers or authorities; all things were created by him and for him."
>
> (Colossians 1:16)

> "And through him to reconcile to himself all things, whether things on earth or things in heaven, by making peace through his blood, shed on the cross."
>
> (Colossians 1:20)

The fallen sons and Satan answer to God and both operate under "agreements" and "legal contracts" which are binding in Heaven. Satan reports back to God, he is the accuser/celestial prosecutor of the brethren,

> "Then I heard a loud voice in heaven say: "Now have come the salvation and the power and the kingdom of our God, and the authority of his Christ. For the accuser of our brothers, who accuses them before our God day and night, has been hurled down."
>
> (Revelation 12:10)

The Most High God uses Satan to test and try souls as part of the Divine Plan of Salvation and Evolution in this Grand Experiment called 'Life on Planet Earth.' Suffering brings us closer to God, purifies the soul through burning mega units of negative karma and teaches us compassion.

> "For such *are* false apostles, deceitful workers, transforming themselves into the apostles of Christ."
>
> (2 Corinthians 11:13)

> "And no marvel; for satan himself is transformed into an angel of light."
>
> (2 Corinthians 11:14)

Lord Of The Cosmos

As the One who will judge the nations, He is both Judge and Jury:

> "He will judge between the nations and will settle disputes for many peoples. They will beat their swords into plowshares and their spears into pruning hooks. Nation will not take up sword against nation, nor will they train for war anymore."
>
> (Isaiah 2:4)

> "In the presence of God and of Christ Jesus, who will judge the living and the dead, and in view of his appearing and his kingdom,"
>
> (2 Timothy 4:1)

When Christ returns, He comes to judge and make war, he *wears the crowns of total universal sovereignty* (Revelation 19:12). He is not only the Judge and the Captain, but also the sovereign King. Remember, He won these crowns by His obedience to His Father's Will as our Substitute. (John 17:2) When David conquered the Ammonites he took the crown of the defeated king and placed it upon his own head, in addition to the crown he already had as King of Israel. (2 Samuel 12:30) In the same sense, Christ has, by virtue of His conquests, taken all the crowns of the universe and placed them upon His own head, in addition to the crown He possesses as God and Creator of all things. And He is coming to make war with and execute judgment upon those who dispute His right to total sovereignty. (Isaiah 45:9)

From those scriptures, we see that Jesus is: The Son of God; Superior to the angels; Heir to all things; The One who made the universe; The radiance of God's Glory;

Chapter Seventeen: The Cosmic Christ

The exact representation of God's Glory; The One who sustains all things by His powerful word; The sacrifice that bought our purification from sin; Now sitting at the right hand of God in Heaven; Jesus is superior to everything. This includes Satan and the forces of darkness that wage war against us daily (Ephesians 6:12; 1 Peter 3:22). Jesus defeated Satan at the cross and will eventually bring every enemy under His feet. These enemies will then be cast into the Lake of Fire (Revelation 20:14-15).

Jesus demonstrated God's authority in his ministry on earth. He delegated that authority to His disciples and to anyone else who would believe in Him. Here are the details:

Jesus has authority over all things: Jesus claimed that all authority had been given to him in heaven and on earth in Matthew 28:18. He then proved that authority by driving demons out of people, healing the sick and forgiving sins.

Jesus gave his authority to his disciples: Jesus said, "I have given you authority to trample on snakes and scorpions and to overcome all the power of the enemy; nothing will harm you (snakes and scorpions are aliens and demons). However, do not rejoice that the spirits submit to you, but rejoice that your names are written in heaven." (Luke 10:19-20)

Jesus gave his authority to those who believe in him: This is an amazing benefit of believing in Jesus that was foreshadowed in Psalm 91:13: "You shall tread upon the lion and the cobra, the young lion and the serpent you shall trample underfoot." Jesus has given his believers the authority to trample Satan and his forces.

COSMIC CHRIST = FREEDOM

Freedom - when you're free you can operate in a different manner. Freedom from curses is being free to be blessed, free to receive love and mercies. Freedom is more important than love, because one cannot receive and give love unless one is liberated. So many are wounded, brokenhearted. Christ heals the broken hearted and came to bind up their wounds, giving freedom to love again. Jesus Christ delivers. Jesus said, "I give you authority and power to cast out demons, (Luke 10:19) heal the sick, cure diseases and restore the broken hearted." I came to set you free. (Isaiah 6:20) to release them from the hold of the enemy, so that the kingdom of darkness is destroyed.

Religious Spirits

> "They will act religious, having a form of godliness but denying its power, they will reject the power that could make them godly. Stay away from people like that!"
>
> (2 Timothy 3:5)

Religion is a form of godliness without power. (Matthew 23) It is a system without the spiritual power to bring forth transformation. It is void and empty. Religion doesn't save anybody. Religion is controlled by *'Religious Spirits.'* *Religious spirits* are not sent by God, as these demon spirits hold a person in bondage. There is always a power struggle between light and darkness. The core issue is being able to tell the difference between God's voice from that of the fallen angels, the Satans, the *religious spirits*.

Religious spirits are designed to mentor others in an attempt to mould them into their own image with an aura of respectability. The image of a *religious spirit* deceitfully appears righteous. *Religious spirits* are camouflaged by image. They are really full of hypocrisy, pride, false humility, self-righteousness, criticism, legalism and rebellion. The aim of the game is control.

In the *Book of Enoch*, Enoch refers to Satan as 'the satans'. Satan is a Hebrew word which means adversary. Lucifer became the adversary, the Satan. However, he also has a group of fallen angels that are in rebellion against the Creator God and His Creation, us humans. So, when Enoch repeatedly refers to them as 'the satans', he is clearly referring to the hierarchy of evil that is programmed to attack humans, in every which way and form.

Remember these were once beings of great light. Lucifer was the Chief Cherub, whose name literally means 'angel of light', so he and his minions use light to deceive humans. Humans are hooked in by their fascination with light, their false promises of ascension, and their seemingly endless powers of control and magic. This is why humans need to develop the muscle of discernment. Discernment of spirits is so important to see *Who is* <u>Really</u> *Who in the Cosmic Zoo.* There is a whole spirit world hell-bent on destroying earth and its human family. They will use any form of manipulation or control tactics to keep humans in the bondages of ignorance.

Religious spirits are employed to keep the power of the spiritual relationship that the Creator intends with humans blocked, by putting earth humans under a hypnotic spell through religion and through the appearance of being pious, and super spiritual. These *religious spirits* are employed in every religion on this planet including the New Agers. Yet the Creator and His Holy Spirit see right through this. There is nothing new under the sun as Jesus rebuked the Pharisees for their stubborn, stiff necked ways of religious legalism and denying the Spirit. Christ said in Matthew 5:20-44, that obeying the "letter of the Law" is a matter of *physical action*, whereas obeying the "spirit of the Law" requires more than just outward actions—it also involves an *attitude of the mind*—referred to by Paul as a "circumcision of the heart" (Romans 2:28-29).

The fruits of the Spirit are love, joy, peace, patience, kindness, goodness, faithfulness, gentleness, and self-control (Galatians 5:22). The fruit of a *religious spirit*, by contrast, is self-righteousness, legalism, hypocrisy, a carnal view of Christ and the

Chapter Seventeen: The Cosmic Christ

spiritual path, false humility, dead works, traditions, and instability. The purpose of the *religious spirit* is to stand in the way of God's work and corrupt our perception of Messiah, the Holy Spirit and the Creator's Will. When we begin to notice in ourselves or in others a self-righteousness, a false humility, the doing of vain works or keeping empty traditions, stubbornness and carnal focus, we know we are on the sheepfold, and may wisely take heed. Carnal means everything that is done in the flesh. The focus then becomes on 'doing' and to avoid 'being' and flowing and being prompted by the Holy Spirit.

The Holy Spirit doesn't inhabit anything that is bound in dead religious form. The True Church of Christ is built on living stones, "the living Stone rejected by humans but chosen by God and precious to Him you also, like living stones, are being built into a spiritual house to be a holy priesthood, offering spiritual sacrifices acceptable to God through Jesus Christ. But you are a chosen people, a royal priesthood, a holy nation, God's special possession, that you may declare the praises of him who called you out of darkness into his wonderful light." (1 Peter 2:5, 9)

We need to keep this in mind at all times, and to examine ourselves honestly regularly. There is a continuous clash between the kingdom of darkness and the kingdom of light, and most of us realize at one time or another that we are the rope in the spiritual tug-of-war. The Kingdoms of this world are not those to which we belong, nor are we inheritors of darkness.

Humans were created to be the chosen vessels of the Spirit of God. We were given free will, so we can discover this love relationship on our own, and not as robots to blindly worship and be used by God. That is the relationship imposed by the fallen upon us. The spiritual battle exists in our minds, whereas the Satanic--the adversaries work to counterfeit everything God intended for us. They are the corruption in a pure, simple, good relationship. In New Age circles channeling is very popular, this act of being used as a vessel, yet most New Agers have no way or intention of discerning by whom they are being used as a channel. (See, Book Four: *Covenants,* my chapter, *Who's Channeling Who?*)

The entities that attend come as angels of light, speaking words we want to hear, hooking us in and lulling our minds. We can allow their false spirits to embody and use us without realizing it has even happened. Some of us have been given power, wealth and fame as a result of channeling. The spirits sandwich just enough truth to obfuscate the deceptions and lies included. So many channelers have been used to mislead people, exactly the *modus operandi* of the fallen angels. *Religious spirits* and fallen angels are used constantly both in churches, synagogues and mosques as well as in New Age circles to titillate the fragile egos of humans, giving them the appearance of power which is actually void of real power.

Eternal rewards are given based on our faithfulness to God, how we have used what we have to accomplish what we have been called to be, and to do. We wisely do what He has told us to do. Faith without works is dead.

The Church is known for its willingness to serve, but not without an agenda. Serving just to get people saved can be the uses of a religious agenda. It's manipulative as it serves the appearance in the world. *Religious spirits* exude a manipulative atmosphere, designed to keep others away, and so continues the false belief that the church is bondage. Many churches, synagogues and mosques are indeed in bondage to these *religious spirits*. These fallen may hook in millions, but also turns off thousands. The world hates the system with an agenda. In order to shift out of the agenda, we must really care for people, and love them as Christ commanded us. His love is the reason, after all. Agendas produce religion, religions are void of real power and love.

Religious spirits wreak of death. Being alive in the Holy Spirit of God attracts people! Those who serve the Holy Spirit genuinely want to see others blessed and for them to succeed, through the unconditional love they share with Jesus Christ. All other agendas, hidden or proclaimed, are manipulative and of darkness, even the religious ones. Power can and does leave the church, which can no longer heal, bless, or empower, but instead exerts bondage to *religious spirits*. The appearance of piety through dogma replaces the liberating freedom of God's Holy Spirit.

When true power flows through us, it brings us into a closer relationship with Creator. Jesus said, "I and the Father are One'.

True servants do not have personal agendas. Their only aim is to further the well-being of others by manifesting the love of God in a world that is dying.

The truth does not give us the right to control or manipulate each other. This is where the stronghold of the *religious spirit* shows its face. We are not elite in a hierarchy.

"Whoever exalts himself will be humbled, whoever humbles himself will be exalted."

(Matthew 23:12)

Destiny For Believers Of Christ

Believers and those who are counted as worthy of the Kingdom of God are promised not only immortality, but equality with the angels in heaven. As we've already established, the angels of the Bible are faithful extraterrestrial messengers who serve the Creator of Heaven and earth. They have all kinds of powers, talents, and skills to fulfill the roles they have to play all around the cosmos. This promise comes from Jesus Christ Himself.

Chapter Seventeen: The Cosmic Christ

"And Jesus answering said unto them, the children of this world marry, and are given in marriage: But they which shall be accounted worthy to obtain that world, and the resurrection from the dead, neither marry, nor are given in marriage: Neither can they die any more: for they are equal unto the angels; and are the children of God, being the children of the resurrection.
(Luke 20:34-36)

"For when they (the faithful) shall rise from the dead, they neither marry, nor are given in marriage; but are as the angels which are in heaven."
(Mark 12:25; Matthew 22:30)

"After that, we who are still alive and are left will be caught up together with them in the clouds to meet the Lord in the air. And so, we will be with the Lord forever."
(1 Thessalonians 4:17)

"For the perishable must clothe itself with the imperishable, and the mortal with immortality. When the perishable has been clothed with the imperishable, and the mortal with immortality, then the saying that is written will come true: "Death has been swallowed up in victory."
(1 Corinthians 15:53, 54)

Immortality in brand new glorious bodies, equal to those of the ET angels in heaven, is the reward and destiny of those whose faith is in Christ, and in what He has done for humankind. This glorious renewal, by the way, is not exclusive to just us humans. This means that all humans who will be redeemed from the kingdom of darkness and translated into the Kingdom of God will be transformed into immortal extraterrestrial angels, and be given similar gifts, abilities and roles to serve the Kingdom of Heaven, just as the angelic faithful extraterrestrial messengers do now.

Notes and References:

1. Joseph B. Lumpkin, *The Lost Books of the Bible: Section One: Lost Scriptures of the Old Testament: The First Book of Adam and Eve*, p.10-62, Fifth Estate Publishers, Blountsville, AL. 2009.
2. Ella LeBain, *Who Is God? Book Two of Who's Who in The Cosmic Zoo? A Guide to ETs, Aliens, Gods & Angels,* Concluding Words, p.501-559, Skypath Books, 2015.

3. Ibid. pp. 485-499
4. http://www.accordingtothescriptures.org/prophecy/353prophecies.html
5. http://www.realdiscoveries.info/BOOK-OF-ENOCH.php
6. William F. Dankenbring, *The Book of Enoch and the "Prototype" or "Chosen One" of God,* http://www.triumphpro.com/enoch-and-the-prototype.htm
7. The Old Testament Pseudepigrapha, edited by James H. Charlesworth
8. Charles E. Isaac, translation, edited by James H. Charlesworth, from the volume, *The Old Testament Pseudepigrapha,* Hendrickson Publishers; Volume Set ed. edition (February 1, 2010)
9. Richard Laurence, Archbishop of Cashel, and Professor of Hebrew in the University of Oxford: Parker, 1821, translation 1 Enoch, http://www.sacred-texts.com/bib/bep/bep01.htm
10. Charles E. Isaac, translation, edited by James H. Charlesworth, from the volume, *The Old Testament Pseudepigrapha,* Hendrickson Publishers; Volume Set ed. edition (February 1, 2010)
11. Charles, R. H., *The Apocrypha and Pseudepigrapha of the Old Testament, Volume Two: Pseudepigrapha.* Apocryphile Press., p. 185. ISBN 978-0-9747623-7-1 (2004)
12. Ibid., Richard Laurence. *The Book of Enoch* (Oxford: Parker, 1821)
13. Ibid.
14. APOCRYPHA 1st Maccabees of the King James Bible 1611, 1 Maccabees www.Scriptural-Truth.com
15. *The Book of Enoch,* http://www.israel-a-history-of.com/the-book-of-enoch.html
16. *Jesus Christ Accepted Book of Enoch,* http://www.city-data.com/forum/religion-spirituality/966511-jesus-christ-accepted-1-enoch-scripture.html#ixzz2j01rZmcI
17. Dr. Philip S. Berg, *The Zohar, Volume II: Parashat Pinhas,* p 88-89, Kabbalah Publishing, 1987
18. J.J. Hurtak, *The Book of Knowledge: The Keys of Enoch®*: p.57., The Academy for Future Science, Los Gatos, CA. 1977.
19. Ibid., p. 598
20. Ibid., p.57

CONCLUDING WORDS

"The time is coming when everything that is covered
up will be revealed, and all that is secret will be
made known to all."
(Luke 12:2)

"Behold, I will create a New Heavens and a New Earth. The former
things will not be remembered, nor will they come to mind."
(Isaiah 65:17)

"Then I saw a new heaven and a new earth, for the first heaven and
the first earth had passed away, and there was no longer any sea."
(Revelation 21:1)

Spiritually speaking, people are being tested collectively with the religious spirit demon and the demon of fear. Fear wreaks havoc on your brain and nervous system, it causes anxiety, anxious behavior, impatience and irrational thinking. We are called to be fearless in the saving Grace of the Lord Jesus, His Spirit gives us courage, to face fears and conquer them. Courage is feeling the fear but moving forward despite it. Fear paralyzes, this is the technique Gray aliens use during abduction experiences, sleep paralysis, which keeps the spirit/mind/soul bodies in bondage, eventually manifesting in the physical body. We must repent to the Lord for our fears. Everything that is not of faith is fear. There are essentially two forces in the universe, fear and love, and in our relationship, walk with the Lord, faith is the opposite spirit of fear, because faith comes from love.

> "All of creation *groans* as in the pains of childbirth, there are *groanings* in the spirit, that only God understands, to be redeemed of the bondage to death and the curse of this world."
>
> (Romans 8:22)

Salvation is extended to ALL of creation, not just earth humans. All of creation groans in their bondage to the curse, that includes animals, and yes alien life. Many of our animal species on this planet are alien lifeforms, all kinds of *out of this world* creatures live in the oceans and at the bottom of the ocean are found luminous creatures that are alien life forms. On the surface, insects are alien to this world, spiders, reptiles, all representatives or ambassadors of alien life forms planted on this planet long ago. Clearly, not all alien life forms are demonic, but certainly misunderstood.

"Jesus said to them, "Go into all the world and preach the gospel *to every creature - all creation*."

(Mark 16:15)

Therefore, I have Concluded that Yeshua/Jesus is the Cosmic Christ. He is not just the Savior of humankind but the Savior of all creatures, great and small, who have their place in the foundation of the world. The miscreants or Nephilim will be judged when He returns and most will end up in the Lake of Fire which was prepared for satan who is the Dragon, aka Reptilian Beast, and his fallen angels and their demons. Those aliens which were created by God, who did not rebel against the Creator, or those who repent to their Creator, will be saved. This is the Good News of the Gospel of the Kingdom of Heaven. The Great Commission is to communicate this Grace to ALL CREATION! Think about that, that means all beings that were Created by the Creator per the Laws of Creation, are included in this call for Salvation through Grace. It doesn't, however, include miscreants, Nephilim, rejects that were experiments and were created outside of God's laws, these the Lord considers perversions. However, if these fallen beings repented, then they would be given new bodies, just like the rest of us are promised at Christ's Return.

There is so much political correctness in our world today over race, culture, religion and gender! Humanity is imploding with intolerance and political (in)correctness, so how on earth can humans accept others unlike themselves, when we're still working at trying to accept each other? This is precisely why we need a Savior to straighten things out here, and there is an awful lot of sorting out to do when He returns.

Angels, UFOs and Mars

In Book One of *Who's Who in The Cosmic Zoo?*[1] I included a rather lengthy chapter on *Life on Mars* and the *Mars Jump Room*, edited by one of the most outspoken whistleblowers of the Truth Movement, Andrew Basiago, who participated in the 1980's CIA secret time travel project, "Project Pegasus". I also mentioned the beginning of the marketing campaign to recruit civilians to join privately funded corporations to set up Mars colonies, which is happening now through the ambitious private enterprise space projects of Elon Musk.

Concluding Words

> "The United States has had a secret presence on Mars since 1964. Keeping the secret space program secret is a major emphasis of mainstream science reporting about Mars."
>
> -- Andrew D. Basiago

David Flynn[2] was the first researcher who exposed the "alien-rebel angel agenda" and he was attacked for exposing them with a rare form of brain cancer, simply because he knew too much. I was internet friends with David Flynn, who gave me permission to quote him the year before he passed. He was the first of the Mars researchers to connect the dots between earth's Sidon-Cydonia region and coincidentally Cydonia on Mars. Ancient Sidon aka Cydonia is today's Lebanon. Cydonia was connected to Rome, and the sons of the covenant were dependent on knowledge from heaven. Note that Jezebel, the evil Queen of Israel, married King Ahab, was from Sidon-Cydonia.

St. Albertus Magnus in 1280 AD said, "...the powers of all things below originate in the stars and constellations of the heaven, and all these powers are poured down into all things below by the first circle of the constellations." He references the constellations that surround our earth as a spherical zodiac path, just as the neo Pythagorean zodiac is mirrored on the earth. Atlas the Magi said, "he knows the depth of all the seas; and he, no other, guards the tall pillars that keep the sky and earth apart." (Odyssey 1.52)

David Flynn was the first to connect the dots to the Mars-Earth Connection. Flynn made the connection that the Prime Meridian which goes through Cydonia Earth and the Prime Meridian is the same as that which goes through Cydonia Mars. No coincidence there. This was deliberate Divine Design.

Flynn revealed through his extensive research that the structures on earth connect with structures on Mars. He demonstrated that ancient earth religions and the early mythologies of Egypt, Greece, and Rome were rooted in the Mars-Earth Connection.[3] This explains why all mythologies venerate Mars as their god of war. No coincidence that in astrology, Mars rules war and aggression. The Roman god of war, Ares, became the astrological sign Aries, which is a sign of war and aggression.

Mars Exopolitics

Exopolitics is a growing field of study that defines human policies in dealing with extraterrestrials and aliens. I devoted a chapter in Book One to the relevance and importance of exopolitics now on earth.[4] As of today, exopolitics focuses primarily on how terrestrial governments should deal with the alien presence on earth. But what about the foreign policy of exopolitics? How do we conduct ourselves when we inhabit other planets? Who gets to own the real estate of Mars?

There is so much evidence of a US based space station on Mars being released lately through NASA photos from the Rovers, along with whistleblowers, that it would make one's head spin. For those who want to study and research in depth and see these photos of objects being photographed on Mars, there are several Facebook groups devoted to the expose' of Mars. The Mars Anomaly Society led by whistleblower Andrew Basiago is one dedicated to the discernment of these photos.

In the nascent age of space technology, to travel in our solar system, and land on a planet fit for habitation, what happens when there's competition? Who's to say that the Americans can stake claim to Mars real estate, when faced off against Chinese or Russian prior claims? Or do we stop at just the Big Three? How will they negotiate space for their individual space stations? How will the planet be claimed? If a group of earth humans detonates a nuclear bomb on Mars, what are the implications to earth and the rest of our solar system? What kind of accountability do earth humans have in space?

Who gets to make the rules on Mars? The Aliens? In fact, when earth humans land on Mars, then they are the aliens or extraterrestrials. Something to think about. Therefore, in light of these questions and more, the field of exopolitics is growing in the governments of earth's exopolitics, and needs to become part of the US Presidential foreign policies, and the US Space Program.

The Chief Cornerstone and the New Jerusalem

There are many people who believe that the New Jerusalem is a giant cube. They also believe that the rebuilt temple of Solomon is where the Antichrist will sit and proclaims himself God. This temple is shaped like a rectangle. But what if the New Jerusalem is a pyramid? This fits all the dimensions given in scripture and makes perfect sense. The pyramid shape fits into the grand scheme of things, and lines up with Bible prophecy in several ways that a giant cube doesn't seem to fit.

The New Testament description of the New Jerusalem, "the city lies foursquare, and the length is as large as the breadth: and he measured the city with the reed, twelve thousand furlongs. The length and the breadth and the height of it are equal." (Revelation 21:16)

While this scripture was thought of as a giant cube before, it's important to keep in mind the prophecy that Christ is the chief cornerstone that the builders rejected.

> "The stone which the builders refused is become the head stone of the corner."
> (Psalm 118:22)

Concluding Words

"And have ye not read this scripture; *The stone which the builders rejected is become the head of the corner*:"

(Mark 12:10)

"Jesus saith, unto them, did ye never read in the scriptures, *the stone which the builders rejected, the same is become the head of the corner*: this is the Lord's doing, and it is marvelous in our eyes?"

(Matthew 21:42)

In Masonry, the cornerstone is also known as the foundation stone. It is the first stone set in the construction of a masonry foundation, upon which all other stones will be referenced, thus determining the position of the entire structure. It seems that the chief cornerstone would be where all corners met. In a cube this doesn't fit, but if the top four corners were to all to meet at the same place, the shape would change from a cube to a pyramid, while keeping all the dimensions given in scripture.

Relating back to Christ being the chief cornerstone, notice in a pyramid shape that the capstone consists of four corners all meeting in one place, at the top. That would make Him the capstone of the pyramid shape. Relate that to the body of Christ. He is the head [capstone] and we are all the body [base] of the pyramid. No coincidence that pyramids are found all over the Earth. The three pyramids of Giza are 19.47 degrees apart from one another, the exact same set of three pyramids were found on the Moon and on Mars. Coincidence? Or Divine Design?

Richard Hoagland [5] described the D&M Pyramid as the "Mathematical Rosetta Stone of Cydonia." In his groundbreaking book, *The Monuments of Mars*, Richard Hoagland dismisses the possibility that the numerical relationships and alignments that he refers to as the "Geometry of Cydonia" couldn't be coincidental. He postulates there is a definite formation in the Cydonia region of Mars which he named the D & M Pyramid. Hoagland named the D & M Pyramid after Vincent DiPietro and Gregory Molenaar, who were two computer scientists who worked at the Goddard Space Flight Center, and unexpectedly found the "Face" on Mars while working on the Viking imagery. They proposed the hypothesis that this formation may have been a bilaterally-symmetric, five-sided pyramid at one time in the past.

Cydonia and the pyramids all rest at 19.47 degrees from the equator. On Earth, pyramids are exactly at 19.47 degrees north of the equator on the Yucatan peninsula in Mexico. The Hawaiian pyramids are at 19.47 degrees north of the equator as well. The earth is 21,600 nautical miles around. This measurement is based on the ratio of 360 x 60 first used by the Phoenicians and still in use by modern ocean and flight navigators.

The number 6,480 is exactly 1/4th of the total 25,920 years it takes earth to complete one circuit through the signs of the zodiac, this is known as the Processional. 6,480 years is unique because it marks the duration between a series of global cataclysms left in earth's historic and geologic record.[6] 3,600 years is the approximate orbit of the return of the Red Planet or Nibiru/Hercolubus passing earth and its orbit around the Sun.

A three-dimensional sphere with a three dimensional pyramid inside it with its tip aligned to the North or South either way would create the three-dimensional shape of *The Star of David*, where the base of the pyramid touches the sphere, at latitude 19.47.

The Star of David used to be called the Seal of Solomon. This is the sacred geometry of the Merkavah, which is a three-dimensional living starship. I wrote about the Merkavah in Book Two: *Who Is God?*[7]

When the fallen angels were kicked out of the heavenly city, the New Jerusalem, they instructed their children, the Nephilim/Annunaki Giants, on how to construct a mirror image of it here on earth, the Great Pyramid of Giza. The Great Pyramid of Giza is missing its capstone. It faces due North more accurately than we can position buildings today so that each side faces the four cardinal points of the compass. Its shadow has predicted equinoxes and solstices. Originally it was to have a solid gold capstone that was a scale model of the pyramid itself. It was never put in place because the builders rejected it. Only on a pyramid can a capstone also be the head of the corner. (Psalm 118:22 and Matthew 21:42)

Just as Christ is the capstone of the New Jerusalem, the Antichrist will announce that the capstone of the Great Pyramid represents himself, in order to deceive us into believing that he has completed prophecy and that he is god. "And the second beast performed great signs to cause even fire from heaven to come down to earth in the presence of the people." (Revelation 13:13) This is alien technology, advanced weaponry coming down from UFOs. This means he will be controlling a fleet of UFOs. This is the army of the beast, aka antichrist in the final last days on earth.

The Illuminati know this image and have it depicted as the Eye of Horus on the U.S. one dollar bill. If you remember the movie, *Stargate*, this event took place, where the ancient being, Ra, travelled in his spaceship shaped like a pyramid that landed atop the pyramid on the second earth through the Stargate. The concept as illustrated in a Hollywood movie as truth is often hidden within science fiction films, which is why I say, *the Truth is Stranger than Fiction*.

The Bible refers to the New Jerusalem as the Temple of God, it is 1500 miles wide by 1500 miles high, which as I analyzed in Book Two,[8] was none other than a *Mothership of the Lord*, the Holy Heavenly City. It's smaller grounded version of this Temple is the Great Pyramid. The Bible says the Antichrist will show himself to be God while sitting in the temple of God. To give this some perspective, if one corner of the New Jerusalem were placed on Los Angeles, a second corner would sit on Mexico

City and a third corner would land on St. Louis, Missouri, and the final corner on Edmonton, Alberta. This is the size of the heavenly city that comes down out of the heavens and lands on the scorched earth.

> "The one who is victorious I will make a pillar in the temple of My God, and he will never again leave it. Upon him I will write the name of My God, and the name of the city of My God (the new Jerusalem that comes down out of heaven from My God), and My new name."
>
> (Revelation 3:12)

> "Who opposes and exalts himself above all that is called God, or that is worshiped; so, that he as God sits in the temple of God, shewing himself that he is God."
>
> (2 Thessalonians 2:4)

People have always assumed this is the temple in Jerusalem, but what if the pyramid is a replica of God's heavenly temple and Jesus/God is the capstone? Wouldn't it make more sense, to be in the proper position when you claim to be God, sitting inside the rebuilt capstone of the earthly replica of the heavenly temple?

Also in the same verse, it calls the faithful believers who are the redeemed "Pillars" in the temple of the Lord in the New Jerusalem. There is a reference to this mentioned in Isaiah 19:19, which many Bible scholars believe refers to the Great Pyramid because the great Pyramid is in the middle of Egypt and yet sits on the border of where Egypt used to be separated into two halves.

> "In that day shall there be an altar to the LORD *in the midst of the land of Egypt*, and a pillar at the border thereof to the LORD." And it shall be for a sign and for a witness unto the LORD of hosts in the land of Egypt: for they shall cry unto the LORD because of the oppressors, and he shall send them a savior, and a great one, and he shall deliver them.
>
> (Isaiah 19:19-20)

> "And the City Lieth (is laid out as a square) four-square, and the length is as large as the breadth: and he measured the city with the reed, twelve thousand furlongs. The length and the breadth and the height of it are equal."
>
> (Revelation 21:16)

I believe that the New Jerusalem City will be a Pyramid Shape with a Square Foundation. It's the square foundation of the pyramid that I believe gets people confused into the thinking that it's a cube.

The ancient Egyptians word for ascension, or *to ascend* is the word for pyramids. While many have been led to believe that the pyramids of Giza were built by Israelite slaves, in 2,200 BC, I believe they were built by extraterrestrials, more specifically fallen sons of heaven. These fallen ones were counterfeiting the shape of the motherships of the Lord, built on our earth at the time of Atlantis, approximately 10,000 years ago, simultaneously with those built on the Moon and Mars. These giant structures were not intended as burial tombs, but as energy capacitors, to harness the free energy, and were used to generate their spaceships.

Remember everything that satan has done, is an imitation, a counterfeit of what the Creator has already designed, only Satan's version is cursed, distorted and perverted. It does not have the light and love energy which are God's creative forces. Satan not only counterfeits God's creations, but also other heavenly creations, as His Living starships, His creatures and His beings. Satan is attempting to genetically modify humanity by corrupting its image on earth and replacing it with Nephilim miscreants, alien-human hybrids and Cyber-genetic Borg-like human hybrids. Such genetic experiments are already taking place on earth now. This is what Jesus meant when He warned that the last days would be like the days of Noah. Genetic modification is exactly what was going on then, which led the Lord to destroy the miscreants, the Nephilim that invaded the earth, with the Great Deluge.

Another coincidence or Divine Design, is that the Speed of Light is 299,792,458 meters per second, and the Great Pyramid of Giza lays exactly on 29.9792459 North Latitude. Personally, I find these numbers to be too coincidental to be easily debunked. There's patterns in numbers no matter which level of science, mathematics or physics you operate from. This was no doubt Divine Design. There are no coincidences! The fact that the Prophet Isaiah predicted that the Pyramid in Egypt would be an altar to the Lord, and that the Lord would send the Egyptians a Savior to deliver them, is End Time Prophesy, that the Lord is the golden cornerstone that was rejected.

The Bible describes the New Heaven and the New Earth as the New Jerusalem in Revelation 21 that hovers over the old earth as a beautiful phantasmagorical Crystal City adorned with precious gemstones, that literally comes out of the heavens and lands over the renewed earth. The dimensions of this Crystal City are that of a pyramid.

> "I, John, saw the holy city, New Jerusalem, coming down, from God out of heaven, prepared as a BRIDE adorned for her husband having the glory of God, and her light was like unto a stone most precious, even like unto jasper stone clear as CRYSTAL."
>
> (Revelation 21:2)

Concluding Words

New Jerusalem is crystalline and because it's made of precious gems and therefore has no need for artificial light, nor does it depend on the light of the sun to shine through it, for the glory of God lightens it, who is Yeshua/Jesus, the Messiah of God, the Light of the World, just as John 8:12 states. He literally enlightens the crystal city with His presence, because He is the light of life. The light of His presence emanates from within the city where He rules and reigns, and comes through the crystalline city walls which in turn lights up the entire outside world.

> "Having the glory of God, and her shining was like unto a stone most precious, as a jasper stone clear as crystal, and had a great wall and high, and had [k]twelve gates, and at the gates twelve Angels, and the names written which are the twelve tribes of the children of Israel. On the East part, there were three gates, and on the North side three gates, on the South side three gates, and on the West side three gates."
>
> (Revelation 21:11-13-GNV)

"The foundation of the city walls are garnished with twelve different types of crystalline gems, starting with jasper, to sapphire, chalcedony, emerald, sardonyx, sardius, chrysolite, beryl, topaz, chrysopragus, jacinth and finally amethyst. Each layer diffusing its beautiful color both within and without the city of pure gold like unto crystal." (Revelation 21:18). Everything in the New Jerusalem is see through, transparent and beautiful, capturing and radiating the Lord's light simultaneously.

Even the streets are made of pure gold like transparent glass "and the street of the city is pure gold, as shining glass." (Revelation 21:21)

The descriptions of this Grand Mothership of the City of God, match the language of the Prophet Ezekiel's description of the starship of the Lord, that He was taken up into. What is glass but crystalline in nature out of the Throne of God itself was described by Ezekiel which had the appearance of a sapphire stone.

> "And above the firmament that was over their heads, was the fashion of a throne like unto a Sapphire stone, and upon the similitude of the throne was by appearance, as the similitude of a man above upon it. [the Lord] And I saw as the appearance of amber, and as the similitude of fire around about within it to look too, [fire that fuels the ship] even from his loins upward: and to look too, even from his loins downward, I saw as a likeness of fire, and brightness round about it. As the likeness of the bow, that is in the cloud in the day of rain, so was the appearance of <u>the light round about</u>."
>
> (Ezekiel 1:26-28 -GNV-1599-emphasis mine)

As far as the true shape of New Jerusalem, it is easy to see how many misinterpret it as a cube, because they are focusing only on the measurements. However, the key word in the description which are repeated multiple times, is the word "crystal", an important linguistic that reveals understanding of its true shape. Quartz crystals are formed naturally into pyramid shapes. The pyramid shape corroborates with multiple scriptures that describe the Lord's House as a Mountain, which is why it's called, the 'mountain of the Lord's house.'

> "And the city lay [p]foursquare, and the length is as large as the breadth of it, and he measured the city with the reed, twelve thousand furlongs: and the length, and the breadth, and the height of it are equal. And he measured the wall thereof a hundred forty and four cubits, by the measure of man, that is, of the Angel."
> (Revelation 21:16-17-GNV-1599)

John described this city to be higher than Mt Everest, which is only about six miles above sea level. Perhaps John saw the base measurements of the cube, which is the bottom of the pyramid, without necessarily understanding that the area it occupies is a three-dimensional space extending as high as it is wide. Then you have the language that refers to the measure of man, that is of the Angel. This is extraterrestrial language for space technology. This city is 1500 miles wide and high, and it is most certainly out of this world, like nothing anyone in our human history has ever witnessed before, and it's coming to Earth!

A pyramid is much more beautiful than a Cube sitting on the *sphere* of the Earth. Its Beauty comes from the Golden Section also known as 'the divine proportion' or 'phi,' which is 1.618 proportion. This proportion is incorporated into the side slope of a perfect pyramid as seen in the Giza model, even though it's a scaled down counterfeit version of the Crystal City. Giza, is just a 1/10,000 counterfeit version of the New Jerusalem that uses these sacred geometric measurements and proportions. It isn't any coincidence that Giza has base lengths of 792 feet in correspondence to 7920-mile diameter of the Earth. And it is no coincidence that its height 504 feet, the square root of 'phi' which is 1.272, that correlates to Plato's sacred number of 1x2x3x4x5x6x7 or 5040. Suffice it to say, magnificence of the divine proportion would make the New Jerusalem a Crystal Pyramid.

A pyramid is the shape that brings together static and living geometry, straight lines and curves, two dimensional flat surfaces and three dimensional volumes in outer space. Pyramids are a link between the physical realm and the spiritual realm. The Merkavah is a living three-dimensional star of David, which are made up of equal three dimensional pyramids interlocking, that represent the meeting of the physical and spiritual realms. The fact that the New Jerusalem is a Crystal Pyramid is consistent with

Concluding Words

the sacred geometry and symbolism that has manifested in ancient Jewish texts and traditions, whose histories are intertwined with Ancient Egypt as well.[9]

END TIME APOSTASY

Apostasy is a falling away from the original truth. There is so much confusion due to a watered-down version of the truth, that many fail to recognize what is truth anymore. The *Religious Spirit* is responsible for creating division amongst believers. Messianic Jews for Jesus view the Scriptures differently than Gentile believers, who are taught heresies trickled down from the Church of Rome and the Catholic Churches. Even though most born again Christians do not belong to Catholic churches, their denominations have never repented from its heresies, blatant outright anti-Semitic lies and their anti-Jewish agenda that were the "agenda of the Church of Rome" and still are today. Most Christians haven't a clue that they are vessels of this heresy which does NOT please the Lord. They accept and believe the ancient lies as Truth. Most Christians listen to others, instead of allowing the Lord to illuminate and reveal the truth of scriptures to them. This is why the Lord moved me to put these books together, to teach and remind today's Church of ancient forgotten truths.

My books expose the heresies dictated by the Church of Rome, the Replacement Theology that essentially rejects Christianity's Jewish Roots, Jewish texts, and Jewish beliefs, the very roots of the Christian Faith, distinguishing it from the Church of Rome. The Constantine and Nicaean Creeds are alien implants that are in direct rebellion towards Yahuah, the God of Israel. This is what led Martin Luther to promulgate Replacement Theology, the very falsehood that inspired the Jewish Holocaust. Many Christian Churches have never repented of these false beliefs and continue to teach them to this day, which are anti-Semitic, anti-Israel and Antichrist heresies. These are spiritual implants, which essentially work in the Christian life as spiritual limitation devices, implanted into minds and spirits and eventually wreaks havoc in bodies, unbeknownst to them.

I have come across so many Christians who are of this funda-*mental* mind control, who can't identify truth when they see it, because they've been programmed to believe in lies. They reject truth because it means they must repent of the lies, and spiritual pride stands in the way, blocking them from even having a teachable spirit. This is the *Religious Spirit* at work. They call the truth false and mistakenly think the false teachers carry truth. This is nothing but the presence of the twisted serpent at work.[10] (See, Leviathan, Book One of *Who's Who in The Cosmic Zoo?*) As I've discerned and shared throughout this book series, the *Religious Spirit* does NOT come from the Creator God. It comes from the fallen angels and their alien stranglehold, the demonic stronghold, as they seek to maintain power over humankind. Biblically speaking, the *Religious Spirit* comes from the Church of Thyatira, which was Jezebel's church of false prophets.

The Jezebel demon comes from the ancient goddess Ashtoreth who chose to remain in rebellion to the Lord. They became ancient enemies. Lilith, in the original Adam and Eve story, later became Ashtoreth. Lilith was given to Adam first, but she rebelled against him and the Lord, so the Lord gave Eve to Adam, using Adam's own DNA. However, the Lord allowed Lilith to live, just as He did to all the other fallen angels, although some were imprisoned. The Books of Enoch tells us that there are angels bound in a prison in the 5th heaven, and angels bound in a prison inside the earth, that will be released during the End Times. These angels will be used to punish the wicked during the End Times Great Tribulation period. That's the prophecy, we can't forget that piece.

Phoenician, Ishtar, Astarte can also be found in other pantheons including that of the Greek, who identified her with Aphrodite, also known as Astarte. Satan is afraid of women and men in Christ who pray, and especially those who know "who" they are in Christ. Women are persecuted and subjugated by satan in Islam. In fundamental Christianity, women are subjugated and forbidden positions of teaching and ministry because satan envies women their creative powers. Satan cursed women by using them to create Nephilim. This kind of alien rape continues to this day, as there are many reports of women being raped by lizard like beings, while ensuring the physical and moral nightmare which follow a resultant pregnancy. This is today's hybridization program, which I detailed in Book One.

It's a vicious cycle, because women were overpowered by the 200 *BeneHaElohim* who became the fallen angels that were filled with lust by mating with the earth women who gave birth to the Nephilim, which most likely happened through rape, spells and seductions. This was not the woman's fault, nor was the event in the Garden of Eden, if you read the entire story in the Apocryphal Rejected Jewish texts, *The First and Second Books of Adam & Eve*,[11] which, unlike Christianity who tends to blame the woman for the fall, the Jewish Apocrypha reveals it was the manipulations of Lucifer/satan who hated the fact that humankind (the Evadamic Race) were elevated over Lucifer/satan to have authority on the earth, so he tried all kinds of stunts and schemes to murder them, but each time, the Lord sent His Angels to protect them and save them. These are the good ETs, the celestial angels who serve the Lord and His Kingdom of Heaven, and His Will on earth.

What transpired in the Garden epitomizes the quintessential warfare that all of humanity is subjected to because Lucifer/satan doesn't want humans to inherit the earth. This is what the Lord promised would happen, whether satan agrees with it or not. Women are subjugated by the religious spirit in most religious circles NOT by the will of God, but by the will of satan, as I proved through Old Testament scripture in Book Two, *Who Is God?*[12]

The hierarchies which are at work, which I discern in greater detail throughout my entire book series, are markedly different evil spirits, demons, Archdemons, fallen

Concluding Words

angels, Archons, despotic kings and their kingdoms. As individual spiritual warriors, we're never alone, when the Lord Yahuah assigns His Angels to watch over us, who stand with us against these demonic strongholds. (Psalm 91:11) And just as heaven's angels are not all equal in their authority, powers and abilities, so it is with the counterfeit kingdom of darkness.

While we as spiritual warriors are empowered with the authority in Christ in the spirit realm to bind evil spirits and demons, some demonic strongholds require joining our faith with others by standing in agreement with another on the God's Word. "Where two or more agree on anything on earth, so shall it be in heaven, we are given powers to bind and loose," (Matthew 18:19-20). These are the spiritual keys of heaven empowered to every true believer in Christ. The more the faithful pray in agreement with one another, the more these prayers will resonate with God and with Heaven's Angels, who are dispatched on assignment by the Lord to fulfill His faithful. There is strength in unity and satan knows this. He counters by sending spirits of strife, discord and religious spirits to keep the Church divided.

Eric Barger[13] of *Take a Stand Ministries*, writes, *Is Hyper Critical Name Calling Contending for the Faith*:

> "Under the guise of "discernment," some individuals have been using their platform in the apologetics community as a means to promulgate a brand of sad, critical Christianity...these so-called "super discerners" operate with a grating, holier-than-thou brashness... Besides the actual issues themselves, the environment created is frankly a twisted form of religious bigotry that has created enemies amongst their parties who have been and should still be allies... True Christians can have a difference of opinion on many issues without trying to decimate or play "gotcha" with those we disagree with."

We are part of a greater body, the Body of Christ, and when we join in faith and synchronize together, all that we represent individually coalesces, connecting with other like-minded souls, forming a bigger picture which has the power to call down the very powers of Heaven to take out the Archonic strongholds, the big satans, the Despotic Kings and Dark Princes. This can only be done as a group. "The weapons we fight with are not the weapons of the world. On the contrary, they have divine power to demolish strongholds." (2 Corinthians 10:4) There are some princes (Archdemons) and despotic kings that can only be brought down by the Lord Himself. As His Word says, "The battle is mine, says Yahuah." (1 Samuel 17:47; 2 Chronicles 20:15) As believers we need to do our part, then surrender and trust Him to do the rest. That requires faith, patience and often long suffering.

My books are put together to save souls for the Kingdom of Heaven. Most of my readers make up their own mind by reading these books themselves and allowing the Holy Spirit to guide them into all truth, through the Scriptures presented and the original Hebrew explained.

I have been called into the study of Prophesy since the Lord appeared to me in the Negev, in 1979. I graduated with a degree in Biblical Hebrew from Sde Boker, Israel. I spent two years as a Missionary in South Africa and witnessed on the front lines the Spiritual Revival that took place right before the proverbial discharge hit the fan, bringing down apartheid.

I have endured being rejected from my Jewish and Catholic families for 38 years for my faith, and my knowledge of Scripture. Interesting coincidence that most Jews don't know their own Scriptures, they rely on their Rabbis to interpret it to them, just as most Catholics don't read their own Bibles either, they rely on their Priests to teach and interpret it for them. Neither are receiving revelation of the Word directly from the Lord's Holy Spirit, both rely on man's interpretation or misinterpretation, as the case may be. So, here I was in a family of both Jews and Italian Catholics, both sides threatened that I knew more of God's Word than they did. How dare I speak the Word to them? I was neither a Rabbi nor a Priest? Their level of ignorance was stunning, when my step sister suggested I join a convent and become a Nun, which was the antithesis of being a born again Messianic Completed Jew not to mention a recovering Catholic.

Here in America, I don't know too many American Christians who have endured decades of persecution and rejection for my faith as I have. Jesus said, you know them by their fruits, and I often feel I have giant watermelon-sized fruits of long suffering in this area, unlike the modern-day Pharisees who divides churches with their funda-MENTALISM and judgments of others, which quite frankly is the cause of most apostasy and falling away, and the cause of the formation of the New Age, which are made up of 95% Christians who have left the churches for those very reasons. Ironically now, I am attacked and persecuted more by so-called Christians, than non-believers and Jews who don't accept Jesus, because I expose heresy and the demonic *religious spirit* on both sides. Well, somebody's got to do it!

For the life of me, I couldn't understand this, it caused me to leave the churches back in the 1980s, where I felt totally disenchanted with the 'church scene' and so-called Christians. Where was Christ in the Christian? I would constantly ask. I found solace in Metaphysical and Spiritual New Age circles, where I met many like-minded souls who had similar experiences, all who have come out of Christian churches, some Jews as well. Then after losing spiritual ground to the enemy during some of the worst life and death battles of my life, I was brought to my knees back in repentance to the Savior, after exhausting every New Age god under the sun to deliver me from the grips of overpowering Archonic, reptilian demonic alien forces. Jesus showed up for me, again, and took my hand and told

Concluding Words

me after I almost died from a heart attack caused by vampirism, when I had my life force literally drained out of my body to the point of death by reptilians, and He told me, He loved me, He was going to restore me, and that He wanted me to complete my books and He would guide me through the editing process and that He wanted me to share all that I learned along with my testimony of His Saving Grace with the world. Well here I am, and here is the end of Book Three: *Who Are the Angels?* God is faithful.

However, since I returned wholeheartedly back to the Lord, I have come full circle and experienced the same kind of persecution, rejection and maligning that caused me to leave the church in the first place over thirty years ago. Only now, I have identified it as an Archonic Stronghold, which is the spirit of religion and its crackerjack box full of spiritual limitation devices and implants. This is what the Lord showed me, this is the discernment teaching and the measurement stick He uses when it comes to the churches. Remember, the scripture in Matthew 25, which refers to the return of Jesus Christ coming to Judge the Church and separate His Sheep from the goats, who end up in the Lake of Fire. I don't know about you, but I'd rather be rejected by men then get rejected by the Lord Jesus Christ, who is the King of kings and Lord of lords. So, take heed to the discernment herein which is His plan for His Final Judgment on the Church when He separates His Sheep from the Goats:

> "When the Son of Man comes in his glory, and all the angels with him, then he will sit on his glorious throne. Before him will be gathered all the nations, and he will separate people one from another as a shepherd separates the *sheep from the goats*. And he will place the sheep on his right, but the goats on the left. Then the King will say to those on his right, 'Come, you who are blessed by my Father, inherit the kingdom prepared for you from the foundation of the world. For I was hungry and you gave me food, I was thirsty and you gave me drink, I was a stranger and you welcomed me, I was naked and you clothed me, I was sick and you visited me, I was in prison and you came to me.' Then the righteous will answer him, saying, 'Lord, when did we see you hungry and feed you, or thirsty and give you drink? And when did we see you a stranger and welcome you, or naked and clothe you? And when did we see you sick or in prison and visit you?' And the King will answer them, 'Truly, I say to you, as you did it to one of the least of these my brothers, you did it to me.'
>
> "Then he will say to those on his left, 'Depart from me, you cursed, into the eternal fire prepared for the devil and his angels. For I was hungry and you gave me no food, I was thirsty and you gave me no drink, I was a stranger and you did not welcome me, naked and you did not clothe me, sick and in prison

and you did not visit me.' Then they also will answer, saying, 'Lord, when did we see you hungry or thirsty or a stranger or naked or sick or in prison, and did not minister to you?' Then he will answer them, saying, 'Truly, I say to you, as you did not do it to one of the least of these, you did not do it to me.' And these will go away into eternal punishment, but the righteous into eternal life."

(Matthew 25:31-46 – ESV)

"He who saves souls is wise", and that is what my books are designed to do for the Kingdom of Heaven. The Creator King Jesus is calling souls back into right relationship with Himself, not to join some cult or religion. Relationship is the way of Love. Religion creates bondage. The Lord gives freedom from bondage. Right relationship with God fosters freedom. Freedom is everything in Life and Love. The *Religious Spirit* originates from the Church of Thyatira, which was Jezebel's church. Christian churches are split and fragmented because of this counterfeit spirit. This is exactly where discernment of spirits must be taught, but sadly some churches are blind. The following chart is an easy comparison to the seven churches of the Book of Revelation, which are both ancient and end times churches.

THE SEVEN CHURCHES OF REVELATION

EPHESUS	SMYRNA	PERGAMOS	THYATIRA	SARDIS	PHILADELPHIA	LAODICEA
Rev. 2:1-7 Once on fire for Christ but now becoming indifferent.	Rev 2:8-11 Persecuted, Poor, but ever faithful and resolute!	Rev. 2:12-17 Permissive, sheltering false teachers, following false doctrines.	Rev. 2:18-29 Idolatrous, seduced into corrupt beliefs and pagan rituals.	Rev. 3:1-6 A church in name only, without results and spiritless.	Rev.3:7-13 Exemplary! Faithful to God's Word and filled with his Love!	Rev. 3:14-22 Self-Indulgent, Rich, and Ostentatious, full of worldly pride.
BACKSLIDING CHURCH	**STEADFAST CHURCH**	**LICENTIOUS CHURCH**	**LAX, PAGAN CHURCH**	**DEAD CHURCH**	**FAVOURED CHURCH**	**LUKEWARM CHURCH**
Criticism: "Thou has left thy first love...."	No Criticism!	Criticism: "Thou has them that hold the doctrines of Baalam and the Nicolaitans."	Criticism: "Thou sufferest that Jezebel to teach and seduce my servants to commit fornication..."	Criticism: "Thou has a name that thou livest and art dead. I have not found thy works perfect."	No Criticism!	"I will spew thee out of my mouth...Thou art wretched, miserable, poor, blind and naked..."
Counsel: "Remember from whence thou art fallen and repent."	Counsel: "Fear not! Be faithful unto death and I will give thee a Crown of Life!"	Counsel: "Repent, or I will come unto thee quickly!"	Counsel: "Hold fast to what (little) ye have till I come."	Counsel: "Strengthen what (little) remains. Hold fast and repent."	Counsel: "Hold that fast which thou hast, that no man take thy Crown."	Counsel: "Buy my gold and white raiment to clothe thee...and anoint thine eyes."

Concluding Words

If the enemy can infiltrate the body of Christ like a virus does, then the entire body becomes diseased, and can't function in its empowered warrior capacity, it becomes weakened through the Religious Spirit, which creates more strife, apostasy, and disgrace to the body of Christ than the lusts of the flesh could do.

No spirit received more Woes (curses) from Jesus than the *Religious Spirit*, eight woes altogether. I listed them all in Book Two: *Who Is God?*[14] and contrast them to the opposite spirit in each of the eight corresponding beatitudes. True believers focus on winning the spiritual battle over evil through strengthening the "good" in ourselves. We do this through acceptance, kindness and a will to forgive those who are unloving, bitter and jealous to us. The *Religious Spirit* is a jealous spirit which essentially states that we can't be blessed by God through His Spirit without being a legalist or a believing the way the church does. That church can't accept something supernatural, or outside of its limited understanding of scripture, or not in keeping with its own perception of God.

Jesus was crucified by this evil spirit, which came through the Pharisees and the Sanhedrin, who were intensely threatened and jealous of Him, because He performed miracles they could only dream of. Instead of praising and thanking God for these miracles, they attacked and falsely accused Him for doing the works of Beezelbub. Jesus wisely responded, "Satan cannot cast out Satan." And so it is, with those with the evil demonic *religious spirit*, they cannot cast out satan either from themselves or from others because they have no power in the spirit realm.

Many Christians do not know or understand the mysteries of Heaven nor the intricacies with which the beings of Heaven work. The children of Israel accused Jesus of being of the devil because they did not understand Him nor know by which power He performed His miracles. Christians today hold the same fears those ancient Jews did, making them Modern Day Pharisees. It is this fear that closes the door to Divine Truth.

It is the quintessential false spirit that masquerades as religion which has caused so many to turn their backs on God and His Divine Plan of Salvation. The disgraceful behavior of so many so-called Christians, and religious people, rankles the best of us!

The *religious spirit* is expressed through rejecting others who simply do not think like us, or those who come from a different background and perceive scripture from a different perspective. I, myself, understand the original meaning in Hebrew of the Scriptures, and have a totally different view than that of a Catholic priest or Fundamental Pastor. The religious spirit is pervasive in the Modern-Day Church, on the internet and on Social Media.

The *Religious Spirit* manifests as an intolerant attitude. For example, the Rapture divides the Church into three groups: 1. Pre-Trib; 2. Mid-Trib; 3. Post Trib, relating to beliefs about the timing of the Rapture with respect to the Seven-Year Tribulation. Allowing myself to get suckered into this division, which clearly can get us maligned by certain church circles, I stated my viewpoints on Facebook to the so-called born again Christians that I was "Pan-Trib," meaning that all the Bible prophecies are going to "pan" out eventually in God's Perfect Timing. For this and this alone, I was blocked and unfriended by them. How Christ-like and loving of them? Not! Do Christians think the Lord Jesus Christ is pleased with their strife and division over such matters, that are beyond their understanding? I believe I presented all viewpoints in this manuscript, to let my readers decide. Be that as it may, believers should live every day as if it was their last day on earth. Whether they leave this world through death or through Rapture, the point is, to be spiritually ready no matter what happens.

I was also unfriended for my viewpoints and "knowledge" of ETs and Aliens. How dare I assert that there are good ETs in the Bible? But I don't make this up, it's in God's Word, which I believe I have proven sufficiently through scripture in my five-book series. After all, I'm just a messenger and an experiencer of ETs, aliens, gods and Angels. I have been maligned for my viewpoints on the alien presence and Extraterrestrials in Biblical Prophecy. But these so-called Christians refuse to examine their own beliefs, which frequently go against Scripture and the very heart of God, making their tenets in fact heresies. They defend their own views to the point of telling lies, refusing to be teachable, to yield ground, to admit that perhaps they don't know everything about the Bible or God's End Times Prophesies. It is wicked to call others false, or to judge another's faith based on their own ignorance and misunderstandings of Scripture.

It blows my mind that for centuries, Jews were persecuted for rejecting Jesus. This was the major excuse for the Jewish Holocaust in World War II. When Jews become Messianic, and accept Jesus as our Messiah, the Lord brings us home and opens our eyes by removing the veil. He reinstates our original purpose He called us Jews for, which is to be holders of ancient knowledge and teachers to the Gentiles (the Nations). Gentile Christians need to be reminded of this historical fact. Romans 1 is very clear, that the Gospel goes first to the Jew and then the Gentile. Just because Gentile Christians are blinded by the *religious spirit*, doesn't make Messianics false for seeing what they don't see, or are too prideful to admit.

The problem that the *religious spirit* has created in the Modern-Day Pharisees in the churches will destroy the spiritual side of Christianity, if we remain unaware of it. This demonic spirit dressed up as religious pride causes Christians to believe they are defined as a Christian by being antigay or anti-abortion or anti-sin of any kind, that somehow that makes them a good Christian. Where are the Christians who are Anti-the Religious Spirit? Am I the only one? Shouldn't a Christian be defined by belief in Christ the Savior, by being on the side of the Lord, and not necessarily what we rail against? The very word Christian means we are for all the qualities that Christ exhibited, as He commanded us, the qualities of love, mercy, forgiveness, understanding, compassion, tolerance, patience, humility, goodness and wisdom. As

Concluding Words

His vessels, we express these qualities through His Spirit. Herein lies the rub and the spiritual discernment between the failing Christians and the trying Christians, the sheep and the goats, as Jesus Himself taught us, "by their Fruits, you will know them." (Matthew 7:20)

The *religious spirit* influences to judge those who are not like you, or judge the part of us that we hate in ourselves but which we see in others. This is known as classic psychological projection. Like the famous example of Muslims and Christians who kill gays but are themselves closet gays, this is the shadow-self making itself known. It can only be healed by bringing it into the light of Christ, who has more acceptance and understanding of it then the best of us do.

We need to heal this practice if we want to survive as a body. We're not called to give up. We are called to overcome. So, if one way clearly hasn't worked in the past, which is rejecting someone because of religion, then perhaps it's time to try it God's way? There is nothing more insidious than so called religious people masquerading as light when they're full of bitterness, jealousy, rejection, fear and spiritual witchcraft (controlling energies). That's Satan's personality. Not Jesus.

"And no wonder, for Satan himself masquerades as an angel of light."
(2 Corinthians 11:14)

Jesus said by their fruits, you will know who are my disciples. (Matthew 7:20) False accusations, finger pointing, is nothing but narcissist psychological projection to cover up our own lies and hatred of Truth of the One true God. Ofcourse there is a difference between accusations motivated by righteous indignation, as when a prosecutor is making accusations not for the sake of covering up their own sins, but for the sake of exposing corruption for the good of the community.

"And I heard a loud voice saying in heaven, now is come salvation, and strength, and the kingdom of our God, and the power of his Christ: for the accuser of our brethren is cast down, which accused them before our God day and night."
(Revelation 12:10)

The spiritual lesson that we can discern from this is that the Lord is not happy with us "putting up with" false teachings and doctrines within our churches. We must stand up for the truth and expose any error, which is the purpose of this five-book series. We are certainly not to "commit fornication" with apostate churches like the Roman Catholic Church or any other fallen church that maligns Jews, Messianics, true Christian believers, or one which bears the fruits of the *Religious Spirit* who is Jezebel.

The End Time Prophesy scriptures point to a great error and apostasy found within Christianity all around the world. Those who are taught to hate Israel, hate Jews, hate those who are filled with the Holy Spirit, are part of that apostasy. The Roman Catholic Church has the largest church membership with over 1 billion around the world. The Bible reveals this church, which sits on seven hills, is Rome, to be apostate. Many of the Protestant churches are now heading back to Rome, back to the "mother" (Mother of harlots). The apostate world is preaching ecumenism, the principle or aim of promoting unity among the world's Christian churches. Ecumenism is presently being driven by the Catholic Church to unite all churches as a One World Religion, which the Vatican desires to head, as a nave from which the antichrist can rule. We, however, must remain steadfast to the truth by uniting around the Savior and upon the Rock who is the Lord Jesus Christ, and be obedient to Him. He told us to come out of Babylon and to stay separate from her many heresies, because God is going to pour out His wrath upon her and anyone who continues to commit fornication with her. Follow Jesus, not Jezebel! To those who overcome, God will grant them to rule over the nations with Jesus. (See, Revelation 2:26; 3:21)

I am focusing on exposing the demonic spirit of religion in this one of kind series of books, five in all, to illuminate the spiritual truth that behind a facade of piety may lie the god of this world, not that of Heaven. Just because someone or some church appears to be religious, doesn't mean they are being led by the light of God, but by the god of this world, whose modus operandi is to use religion to wield power over the masses and enslave humanity with falsehoods, half-truths and religious implants.

Jesus, on the other hand, is the Living God, which He has proven billions of times in the lives of His true followers, that He is here to save souls from the clutches of the god of this world and his fallen angels, who have been deceiving humans through religion for millennia. "I have come to set the captives free" are the Words of the Messiah, and when you have been set free, as I have from both the clutches of religions and the alien abductions connected with them, you will understand 'Who' the Lord Jesus Christ is in reality. He is inviting us into right relationship with Him, not to follow some legalistic religion that is void of His Grace and Power.

Disclosure of ETs, Aliens and Angels

This standing tenet that all aliens and extraterrestrials are fallen angels, Nephilim demons, is a half-truth. And when it comes to half-truths, we had better be careful that we don't get hold of the wrong half! The persecutory spirit that is inspired by fear, cognitive dissonance, ignorance and the *Religious Spirit* is hamstringing Christians with respect to this subject. I say to you that the Jezebel spirit is enmeshed in alien abductions, reptilian rape and ritual satanic abuses. Many Christians are still

Concluding Words

getting abducted, and are experiencing all kinds of symptoms of alien interference but haven't a clue how to stop it in their lives. Even if you take alien abductions out of the equation, many Christians don't even know how to obtain true deliverance from the Lord, who came to set the captives free. (Isaiah 61:1; Luke 4:18)

I used to have all kinds of physical problems, until the Lord delivered me from alien abductions and through His Grace guided me into repentance of all things that belonged to that realm. But it didn't happen overnight, it took years for me to get over all the traumas and pain they caused me. My life is a testimony to the Grace of God. The fruits of the Spirit are deliverance and healing from the bondages of the god of this world. All illness comes from satan, demons and curses. Repentance is the *key* to God's outpouring of forgiveness and Grace, which brings healing.

In Book Four: *Covenants*, I go into much more detail on spiritual limitation devices, which are alien implants put into us humans and how to get free of them. First you must be able to identify them as such, just like any problem. The Truth Shall Set You Free, but first it may frustrate and anger you. This is called cognitive dissonance, which we discussed in depth in Book Two: *Who Is God?*[16]

Spiritual legal ground is the number one reason many Christians are not healed. I am a retired paralegal/legal assistant of twenty-five years. The Lord showed me how the legal world and the spiritual realm of spiritual legal ground are connected through His Word which details the rules of engagement of the spirit world. The Lord says in Hosea 4:6, "My people perish for lack of knowledge." Implants belong to the Kingdom of darkness. The spiritual implants which come from Heaven are packed into the Living Word. When you speak the Word, who is the Living Logos, over yourself, and others speak the Word over you, you are essentially implanting the Word into your spirit, your mind and body. You can alter the conditions of a problem by simply speaking the Word over it, in faith. This is an example of a positive implant. When I use the word implant, I am referring to etheric implants, not physical technological devices.

However, the Kingdom of Darkness counterfeits the Kingdom of Heaven. Everything God created has been stolen, counterfeited, distorted and perverted. God allows this to happen as it is part of the proof of His Grand Experiment. Well, people can and are awakening within the Grand Petri Dish of life on earth. We can identify the duality, discern the spirits of both kingdoms, and choose rightly. It is possible because we have the choice, and we must choose wisely. I am living proof that someone who has been delivered of alien implants can live to tell. Not all implants are physical, in fact most are etheric in substance, which program the mind/body/spirit towards illness. The dis-ease in spirit, in auric, then becomes physical.

There are so many Christians who struggle with all kinds of illnesses and conditions! They are not free, as I've been observing this for years, and it all comes down to implants and spiritual legal ground. I'm going to share with you in Book Four: *Covenants* how to be free from alien implants, through scripture.

Antisemitism runs rampant throughout Christian churches and 'Woe to those who' will get judged by the Lord for it. (Genesis 12:3) It is based on ignorance and misunderstanding of 'who' the Lord is and what His Word means. His Truth is right there, both in today's canon and in the exobiblical texts, which Jews have never rejected nor forgotten.

I believe that there are four main reasons why people won't accept the existence of extraterrestrial life.

1. People have invested so much emotionally, spiritually and financially into their religious institutions and dogma, based their entire lives on their beliefs. By accepting the fact of alien life would cause serious cognitive dissonance, would go against everything they were taught to believe. The Christian fringe, however, accepts the reality of aliens in the Bible, but are blinded by the false belief that they're all demons. Not all are evil, as this book proves and we must learn to discern the differences.
2. People resist the idea of extraterrestrial intelligences because our higher education systems deny it totally. Few of us have good exposure to the sciences. There are many scientists who won't even entertain the idea of alien life. They too fear the unknown. Therefore, the best thing to do is to deny it and remain skeptical, despite the plethora evidence in the multiple cases of alien abductions, UFO sightings, whistleblowers, contactees, and experiencers' reports. Our younger generation is different in that like all youngsters, they are curious, and many are awakening and starting to question everything around us.
3. Most people haven't experienced the phenomenon themselves, so they cast doubt and aspersions on those who have. Once people experience it, as they say, seeing is believing, and it's a game changer. What usually follows is questioning everything around us. #2 gets reinforced by #3 and #2 will cancel or adapt #1
4. The UFO Cover-Up, Truth Embargo and Official Denial of the alien presence by the governments of the world is very much in effect. This trickles down to the masses to also be in denial.

Truly there is nothing new under the sun. The Alien presence goes way back into the ancient past. The Alien presence is chronicled in the ancient past, in the Bible and exobiblical scriptures in detail. Religious systems have covered it up through a combination of mistranslations, erroneous transliterations and misinterpretations. My book

Concluding Words

series exposes these ancient truths from the world's major religions and scriptures. The Truth is Stranger Than Fiction!

The Truth Embargo is an aspect of deception which is multi-layered, cultivated over sixty years of government cover ups, as referred to by the Disclosure Project.[17] There are multiple reasons for government cover ups of UFOs, namely National Security. The US government is involved with the alien presence on earth, in the form of legal agreements with them. Secondly, other governments of the world have also been involved with the alien presence, and are well-aware of the exopolitical situation that the world faces.

Thirdly, there is competition between these governments for advanced technology and weaponry. If full disclosure were to happen, it may come back to the compromise of National Security. It would betray the aliens with whom the authorities have legal contracts. This brings me to the fourth reason for the Truth Embargo, and that is the preparation in partnership with the alien presence for an upcoming Space War. The governments of the world, who have been experimenting and developing space technology for over sixty years, are not going to reveal their plans nor preparations for what they discern to be a threat to their nation or the world regarding the aliens. They are depending on one or more groups of aliens to protect them in this war, and they are also preparing to defend themselves with advanced space technology, in case they are betrayed.

In addition, parts of these treaties involve keeping the aliens, and their sharing and mentoring of advanced space technology and weaponry, Top Secret. The aliens themselves are in conflict with other alien groups over the control of the real estate and space over earth and this solar system. They are using the superpowers of this world to help fight their own enemies. I told you, the *truth is stranger than fiction*.

The Biblical War of Armageddon is a real-life *Star Wars*, fought in the space above the earth, over the earth, and through the inner earth. The governments of this world are out for their own self-preservation and they do not want to betray the aliens, who have helped them to develop a fleet of spacecraft in preparation for this final battle. The Bible says that the Kings of the Earth will fight with the Antichrist against not only Jerusalem, an ancient space portal, but against the Creator Lord.

> "Why are the nations in an uproar and the peoples devising a vain thing? *The kings of the earth* take their stand and the rulers take counsel together <u>against the LORD</u> and against His Anointed, saying, 'Let us tear their fetters apart and cast away their cords from us!'"
>
> (Psalm 2:1-3)

> "And it shall come to pass in that day, that the LORD shall punish the host of the high ones that are on high, and *the kings of the earth upon the earth.*"
>
> (Isaiah 24:21)

The host of the high ones means the commander of the archons, the rulers of darkness, the spiritual wickedness in the heavens, the alien races, who manifest the antichrist on earth. This host will lead these alien armies along with the kings of the earth to wage their final battle against the Lord and His Angels, the Celestial Warriors of Heaven. This will culminate in a Star Wars battle.

> "And the heaven departed as a scroll when it is rolled together; and every mountain and island were moved out of their places. And the *kings of the earth*, and the great men, and the rich men, and the chief captains, and the mighty men, and every bondman, and every free man, hid themselves in the dens and in the rocks of the mountains; and said to the mountains and rocks, fall on us, and hide us from the face of him that sits on the throne, and from the wrath of the Lamb:"
> (Revelation 6:15-17)

> "For God has put it into their hearts to carry out His purpose by uniting to give their kingdom to the beast, until the words of God are fulfilled. And the woman you saw is the great city that rules over the *kings of the earth*."
> (Revelation 17:18)

The final battle between the Antichrists armies and the Celestial Armies of Heaven, commanded by the Lord of Hosts, will be a *Star Wars* battle. The Battle of Armageddon, also known as the Battle of the Great Day of the Lord Almighty in detailed in Revelation 19:7-21, points to Christ as the righteous Warrior-King. We see Him coming to do battle with the host (fallen angels) of Satan's armies which in truth is a war or campaign against the hosts of heaven and their King. This war is necessitated by the evil ambitions of humanity's kings of the earth and their evil source of power, who is Satan, the god of this world (2 Corinthians 4:4).

Jesus Himself tells us when this final battle will take place: "Immediately after the distress of those days the sun will be darkened, and the moon will not give its light; the stars will fall from the sky, and the heavenly bodies will be shaken. At that time the *sign of the Son of Man will appear in the sky*, and all the nations of the earth will mourn. They will see *the Son of Man coming on the clouds of the sky*, with power and great glory. <u>And he will send his angels with a loud trumpet call, and they will gather his elect from the four winds, from one end of the heavens to the other.</u>" (Matthew 24:27-31) These are the extraterrestrial warriors who will be gathered, and who will heed the call of war to assist their Creator Lord and King of Heaven.

This final *Star Wars* battle and the Glorious Appearing of the Lord Jesus and His gathering of His fleet of extraterrestrial angels will take place "immediately after the distress of those days," that is, at the end of the Tribulation and before the Millennium. The Lord Jesus Christ will time His coming at the most dramatic point in all history. The Antichrist who will be satan incarnate and the False Prophet (the Vatican Priests, or the Pope), will inspire the armies of the world to invade Israel in a gigantic effort to rid the world of the Jews and true Christians, to fight against Jesus Christ.

> "Then I saw another *angel flying in midair*, and he had the eternal gospel to proclaim to those who live on the earth – to every nation, tribe, language and people."
> (Revelation 14:6)

Tweaking the time-space continuum is like plucking a string in the string theory. The extraterrestrial messengers *who are the Angels* will be judged for their effect on us through their interventions. In the end, we will be asked to judge whether they were beneficial to the human race. Their comings and goings have become imprinted in our psyches. How they have made us feel was indelibly etched into our collective soul memories. As a result of their intervention, many of us have abandonment issues. We remember in our souls when we lived with them for a time, and we felt they were parents to us, but then they left the planet, physically. These are the Elohim Angels, the Good ETs. They're mentioned throughout the Bible scriptures, and their imprint was permanently left on the Earth.

Who Are The Human Angels?

> *"To love for the sake of being loved is human,*
> *but to love for the sake of loving is angelic."*
> ~ Alphonse de Lamartine (1790-1869)

What are the signs of a human angel? Can heaven's angels be born into a flesh and blood into human body? Do angels reincarnate? These are the types of questions most people either think about or ask when discussing the existence of angels. How often do we praise someone who has helped us in kind, performed a good deed for us in our time of need, and say, 'oh, you are such an angel!' Or, how often do we call our children angels? Or what about that old saying to describe a child who behaves perfectly in front of strangers, but at home gets up to all kinds of mischief, a street angel and a house devil. Are these just metaphors? What about appealing to the angel side of our better natures?

These sayings have become part of our lingo and culture, yet, do we mean what we are saying? Or is it just poetry?

There is a book called, *We Are Human Angels,* penned by authors who choose to remain anonymous, but only call themselves, *human angels,* which is summed up and defined as such:

"☆ If since childhood you have wanted to change the world and have not stopped believing... ☆ If you have always dreamed of relieving the sorrows of all living beings... ☆ If you feel that you have a special talent to help others... ☆ If you have an out of the ordinary sensitivity... ☆ If you have overcome difficult trials in your life... ☆ If you think that despite everything, life should be lived with joy... ☆ If, while always trying to give meaning to your suffering, you believe that there must be a way to stop yours and others suffering...☆ If in your heart there is no room for hatred and resentment... ☆ If you always try to change evil into good and darkness into light... ☆If you always follow your heart even when it seems to be the hardest thing to do... ☆ If you have always had a vision of heaven on earth and would like to spread it throughout the world... ☆ If you have the ability to read people and know what is hidden within their hearts...☆ If you silently bless everyone you encounter in your life... ☆ If you, from the very beginning, have always felt a sense of not belonging to this world... ☆ If you have never been able to relate yourself with any group of people, but you have always had a deep desire to connect yourself with your Souls' family here on earth... ☆ If the search for truth is your greatest passion... ☆ If you live with honesty even when it hurts...☆ If you believe in the healing power of Love... ☆ If you still have the same dreams you had when you were a pure-hearted child... ☆ If you feel you were born for a greater purpose and would like to express it...you are a Human Angel and you are just trying to remember." [18]

It's a calling, a heart and soul thing. The whole Gospel of salvation pivots on inviting Christ into our heart and becoming *born again* to His Higher Calling of our soul, which is the angel of our better nature. It is that space where God lives inside us through His Holy Spirit, so we can do the works of Christ on earth. Then we not only become citizens of Heaven's Kingdom and servants of the Most High God, but a human messenger, aka, angel. It's possible, it's happening, and thank God there are many people on earth who are following their inner calling who are being obedient to God's Grace and Will.

Love covers a multitude of sins. This is the way of the Kingdom; this is the way of the Angels. Heaven's Angels get excited when humans act like angels on earth. Simple things go a long way like, showing a kindness to strangers, letting someone in front

Concluding Words

of you on line, or in traffic, holding doors open for others, helping strangers, feeding the poor, praying for the sick, clothing the naked; after all these were the commands of the Lord to all those who follow Him. Remember He is the Lord of the Angels, regardless of whether that angel lives in heaven or on earth.

But can one of heaven's angels incarnate on earth? To say no would be a complete denial of our history. We've had both fallen and faithful angels make their mark on our planet, and with God all things are possible. To sum things up, every Angel that appears in the Bible stories was a man, without wings, but certainly with the ability to fly, and move through the dimensions at will. This made them extraterrestrial messengers and extraterrestrial warriors. These men took on the appearance and feel of a fleshly man at times, to fulfill an assignment, and then transformed back into their non-corporeal bodies. Some were seen in visions in their true form, which is why so many Renaissance artists depicted them with halos and wings, because of the light that emanated from them. Most however appeared as ordinary men, to carry out specific assignments on order from Heaven.

If you are called to assist the community by doing the work of the angels, anonymously, not necessary taking any credit for yourself, then perhaps you are a human angel, as the Lord says, "Your Heavenly Father sees what you do in secret. If you pray and fast, do it unto God in secret, do not broadcast it to the world, that's what the Pharisees do, to get attention, that's the *Religious Spirit* at work. When you give, do it unto God, keep it secret and your Heavenly Father will reward you." (Matthew 6:2-16)

Many of us have experienced the fruit of the Spirit of the Angels when we've been helped by what was appeared an invisible hand, healed, saved, or protected.

The Bible says that the redeemed of the Lord for the Kingdom will end up at the Final Judgment, judging Angels. This mystery runs deep, because in the Kingdom, everything is flipped opposite from the way it is on earth. The last shall be first, the first shall be last, the greatest among you is your servant. The weak are made strong and the strong are made weak: "But God chose the foolish things of the world to shame the wise; God chose the weak things of the world to shame the strong." (1 Corinthians 1:27) And, "My grace is sufficient for thee: for my strength is made perfect in weakness." (2 Corinthians 12:9)

Today, Heavens' Angels' work on earth is to do the Will of God, respond to the Logos, the Living Word, who is the Lord of Hosts. When you speak the Living Word out of your mouth, Angels respond. When you align yourself with being bathed in the goodness of God, living in gratitude for all of God's gifts, and praise and worship your Creator, you are living as a Human Angel, because that's exactly what Heavens Angels do. As we discussed, there are angels in heaven whose role is to praise the Lord all the live long day. So, think about it, when you do the same, what does that make you?

> "Be not forgetful to entertain strangers: for thereby some have entertained *angels* unawares."
>
> (Hebrews 13:2)

When you extend your hand of mercy to others, what does that make you? I can tell you that no good deed goes unpunished as the saying goes, and your reward is great in heaven, even though you may suffer for it on earth. Angels put themselves in danger for others. Angels are heroic, brave and fight evil with the weapons that are not of this world. When you align with the supernatural realm of Heaven's Kingdom, through being obedient to the Lord, through His Word, and living through His Spirit, then you too are doing the Kingdom's work, and you are an earth angel, or human angel expressing heaven's way on earth.

> "But those who are considered worthy of taking part in the age to come and in the resurrection from the dead will neither marry nor be given in marriage, and they can no longer die, for **they are like the angels**. They are God's children of the resurrection."
>
> (Luke 20:35-36)

> "Be Kind, For Everyone You Meet Is Fighting a Hard Battle."
> ~ Philo, 10BC

- FINIS -

Notes and References:

1. Ella LeBain, Book One of *Who's Who in The Cosmic Zoo?* Chapter Five: Martians, Life on Mars, p. 308-323, Tate Publishing. 2013.
2. David Flynn, *Cydonia: The Secret Chronicles of Mars*, End Time Thunder Publishers (2002).
3. Ibid.
4. Ella LeBain, Book One of *Who's Who in The Cosmic Zoo?* Chapter Two: Exopolitics and Divine Jurisprudence, p. 43-62. Tate Publishing. 2013.
5. Richard Hoagland, *The Monuments of Mars: A City on the Edge of Forever*, Frog Books; 5th Edition (2001).
6. Art Green Field, *The Alien Agenda Revealed*, 2009. http://www.scribd.com/doc/17117471/W...rt-Green-Field

Concluding Words

7. Ella LeBain, *Who Is God? Book Two, A Guide to ETs, Aliens, Gods & Angels,* Chapter Two: *Ancient Technology & Biblical Astronauts,* p.27-41 Skypath Books, 2015.
8. Ibid., Chapter Four: *Motherships of the Lord,* p.71-88
9. David Jay Jordan, *New Jerusalem Is a Crystal Pyramid,* http://www.davidjayjordan.com/NewJerusalemisaCrustalPyramid.html
10. Ella LeBain, Book One of *Who's Who in The Cosmic Zoo?* Leviathan, p. 304. Tate Publishing. 2013.
11. Joseph B. Lumpkin, *The Lost Books of the Bible: The Great Rejected Texts -Section One: The First and Second Books of Adam Eve,* p.10-85, Fifth Estate Publishers, 2009.
12. Ella LeBain, *Who Is God? Book Two, A Guide to ETs, Aliens, Gods & Angels,* Chapter Twenty-Nine: *Who Created Sexism?* p.485-500 Skypath Books, 2015.
13. Eric Barger, *Is Hyper Critical Name Calling Really Contending for the Faith?* http://www.ericbarger.com/ Take A Stand Ministries
14. Ibid., Ella LeBain, *Who Is God? Book Two, A Guide to ETs, Aliens, Gods & Angels,* Concluding Words, p. 525-528
15. Ibid., *Who Is Allah? Baal Worship,* p. 359-386
16. Ibid., p. 7
17. Steven Basset, *The Paradigm Research Group,* http://www.paradigmresearchgroup.org/
18. Excerpt from the Introduction of *We are Human Angels: A Crash Course for Human Angels,* Human Angels; 2nd Edition (April 16, 2012).

NOTES AND BIBLIOGRAPHY

All Bible quotes from www.biblehub.com

Chapter One: The Clash of Two Kingdoms

1. Robert Sepehr, *Species with Amnesia,* Createspace, 2015
2. Dr. R.H.C. Charles, *The Book of Jubilees* (London: A & C Black, 1902).
3. W.F. Albright, *Our Future is in Our Past,* W.F. Albright of Archeological Research, http://www.aiar.org/
4. Ella LeBain, *Who's Who in The Cosmic Zoo? Book One, A Spiritual Guide to ETs, Aliens, Gods & Angels, Third Edition,* Tate Publishing & Enterprises, 2013.
5. *What is Generation in the Bible?* http://www.bible-codes.org/old-prophecy_5c-Yeshua-codes.htm
6. http://www.teachingfaith.com/spiritual-warfare-ebook

Chapter Two: The Angelic Government

1. Ella LeBain, *Who's Who in The Cosmic Zoo? Book One, A Spiritual Guide to ETs, Aliens, Gods & Angels, Third Edition,* Chapter One. Tate Publishing & Enterprises, 2013.
2. Geoffrey Hodson, *The Kingdom of the Gods,* The Theosophical Publishing House, London, U.K., Adyar, India, 1952
3. http://www.sacred-texts.com/chr/tbr/tbr023.htm
4. *The Sons of God and the 24 Elders,* http://www.jesus-resurrection.info/sons-of-god.html
5. Ella LeBain, *Who's Who in The Cosmic Zoo? A Spiritual Guide to ETs, Aliens, Gods and Angels, First Edition,* 2012, Trafford, Indiana.

6. Ella LeBain, *Who's Who in The Cosmic Zoo? Book One, A Spiritual Guide to ETs, Aliens, Gods & Angels, Third Edition,* Chapter One. Tate Publishing & Enterprises, 2013.
7. Ella LeBain, *Who Is God? Book Two, Who's Who in The Cosmic Zoo? A Guide to ETs, Aliens, Gods & Angels,* Chapter Three: Ancient Astronaut Theory, p.49, Skypath Books, 2015.
8. Ella LeBain, *Who's Who in The Cosmic Zoo? Book One, A Spiritual Guide to ETs, Aliens, Gods & Angels, Third Edition,* Chapter One. Tate Publishing & Enterprises, 2013.
9. Ibid.

CHAPTER THREE: THE CELESTIAL HIERARCHY OF ANGELS

1. Ella LeBain, *Who's Who in The Cosmic Zoo? Book One, A Spiritual Guide to ETs, Aliens, Gods & Angels, Third Edition,* Tate Publishing & Enterprises, 2013.
2. Ann Madden Jones, *The Yahweh Encounters: Bible Astronauts, Ark Radiations and Temple Electronics, A Controversial Interpretation of the Holy Bible,* The Sandbird Publishing Group, Chapel Hill, North Carolina, 1995.
3. Ibid.
4. Ibid.
5. Gustav Davidson, *A Dictionary of Angels: Including the Fallen Angels,* The Free Press, A Division of MacMillan, Inc., New York, 1967. p.193
6. Ibid.
7. Ibid., p. 194
8. Louis Ginzberg, *The Legends of the Jews,* 1909. Volume II. 303. http://www.pseudepigrapha.com/LegendsOfTheJews/index.htm
9. Ibid., Gustav Davidson, *A Dictionary of Angels: Including the Fallen Angels,* p.194
10. Ibid.
11. Ibid.
12. Ella LeBain, *Who's Who in The Cosmic Zoo? Book One, A Spiritual Guide to ETs, Aliens, Gods & Angels, Third Edition,* Tate Publishing & Enterprises, 2013, p.248-293

CHAPTER FOUR: ANGEL PROTOCOL

1. Joseph B. Lumpkin, *The Lost Books of the Bible: The Great Rejected Texts,* Fifth Estate Publishers, Blountsville, AL. 2009.

Notes And Bibliography

2. *Jewish Encyclopedia,* http://www.jewishencyclopedia.com, West Conshohocken, PA, originally published in 1906.
3. Ibid.
4. Ibid.
5. Philo Judaeus of Alexandria, *idem,* "On Dreams," i. 22
6. Ella LeBain, *Who Is God? Book Two of Who's Who in The Cosmic Zoo? A Guide to ETs, Aliens, Gods & Angels,* Skypath Books, 2015.
7. Philo, Ibid.
8. Philo, Ibid.
9. Ibid.
10. Joe Kovacs, *Shocked by the Bible, The Most Astonishing Facts You've Never Been Told,* Thomas Nelson, Nashville, Tennessee. 2009.
11. Ella LeBain, *Who's Who in The Cosmic Zoo? Book One, A Spiritual Guide to ETs, Aliens, Gods & Angels, Third Edition,* Tate Publishing & Enterprises, 2013.
12. Ella LeBain, *Who Is God? Book Two of Who's Who in The Cosmic Zoo? A Guide to ETs, Aliens, Gods & Angels,* Skypath Books, 2015.
13. John J. Parsons, *Parashat Vayera-The Angel of the LORD, Further Thoughts on Parashat Vayera,* www.hebrew4christians.com
14. Henry M. Morris, *The Genesis Record: A Scientific and Devotional Commentary on the Book of Beginnings.* Grand Rapids, Michigan: Baker Book House. (1976). pp. 337, 499–502.
15. Wikipedia. < http://en.wikipedia.org/wiki/Jacob>
16. Josephus. *The Antiquities of the Jews,* Book II, 2.4.18
17. Strong's Concordance 3478, 8280, 6439.
18. Josephus. *The Antiquities of the Jews,* Book II, 2.4.18
19. Judah David Eisenstein, "Porging". *Jewish Encyclopedia.* New York City. (1901–1906). LCCN:16014703. Retrieved 2008-11-19.
20. Joshua Trachtenberg, *Jewish Magic and Superstition: A Study in Folk Religion,* New York: Behrman's Jewish Book House. 1939.
21. Ibid. Trachtenberg 1939, p. 80
22. Joseph B. Lumpkin, *The Lost Books of the Bible: The Great Rejected Texts,* Fifth Estate Publishers, Blountsville, AL. 2009.
23. Ella LeBain, *Who Is God? Book Two of Who's Who in The Cosmic Zoo? A Guide to ETs, Aliens, Gods & Angels,* Skypath Books, 2015. Chapter: *Gods or ETs? Who Are The Biblical God(s)?,* sub-section: *Yahweh or Jehovah? Yahweh, the Counterfeit God*
24. Ella LeBain, *Who's Who in The Cosmic Zoo? Book One, A Spiritual Guide to ETs, Aliens, Gods & Angels, Third Edition,* Chapter: *Ashtar Command,* p.127 Tate Publishing & Enterprises, 2013.

Chapter Five: Celestial Warriors: Extraterrestrials With Extraordinary Powers

1. John Milton, *Paradise Lost*, 1667. http://www.paradiselost.org/
2. Guy Malone, *Hosts of Heaven*, 2007. http://www.alienresistance.org/hostsofheaven.htm
3. Rav. Simon B. Laḳish, *The Jewish Encyclopedia* http://www.jewishencyclopedia.com, West Conshohocken, PA, originally published in 1906
4. Ibid.
5. Ella LeBain, *Who Is God? Book Two of Who's Who in The Cosmic Zoo? A Guide to ETs, Aliens, Gods & Angels*, Skypath Books, 2015. Chapter Four: *Mother Ships of The Lord*, subsections, *The Cloud Ships, The Clouds of Heaven*. pp. 71,75,77
6. R. Johanan, *The Jewish Encyclopedia* http://www.jewishencyclopedia.com, West Conshohocken, PA, originally published in 1906

Chapter Six: Fallen Angels

1. R. H. Charles, (trans.). *The Book of Enoch*, 1917. http://www.sacred-texts.com/bib/boe

Chapter Seven: The Watchers, The Nephilim and Satan's Ministers

1. R. H. Charles, (trans.). *The Book of Enoch*, 1917. http://www.sacred-texts.com/bib/boe
2. *The Jewish Encyclopedia* http://www.jewishencyclopedia.com, West Conshohocken, PA, originally published in 1906
3. Philo, *Concerning the Giants* II: 6-9

Chapter Eight: Stars Who Fell From Heaven

1. R. H. Charles, (trans.). *The Book of Enoch*, 1917. http://www.sacred-texts.com/bib/boe
2. *The Jewish Encyclopedia* http://www.jewishencyclopedia.com, West Conshohocken, PA, originally published in 1906

Notes And Bibliography

3. Albert Barnes, *Barnes Notes on the Bible*, Baker Books; 19th edition (February 1, 1983).

CHAPTER NINE: FALLEN ANGELS OR EVIL SPIRITS?

1. C.S. Lewis, *The Screwtape Letters*, published by Geoffrey Bles, U.K., 1942
2. C.S. Lewis, *The Last Battle*, published by The Bodley Head, U.K., 1956
3. John Keel *Operation Trojan Horse*, ISBN 978-0962653469 G.P. Putnam and Sons, NY, NY, 1970. p. 192
4. Ibid., (Keel 266).
5. Dr. John Mack, *Abduction, Human Encounters with Aliens*, Scribner, (August 1, 2007), p.402
6. Michelangelo di Lodovico Buonarroti Simoni, *Moses*, Wikipedia-Moses/Michelangelo c. 1513 – 1515, San Pietro in Vincoli, Rome.
7. Stephen Spielberg, *War of the Worlds*, 2005.
8. Ella LeBain, *Who's Who in the Cosmic Zoo?* Book One, Third Edition, Chapter on *Giants*, p.208, Tate Publishing, 2013.
9. Ibid. p.280-289.
10. Jennifer LeClaire, *Satan's Trio: Defeating the Deception of Jezebel, Religion and Witchcraft*, Revelation Media Networks, Chosen Books, Minnesota. 2014.
11. Ella LeBain, Book Two: *Who Is God?* Chapter Twenty-Two: *Who Is Allah?* p.359, Skypath Books, 2015.
12. Ibid.

CHAPTER TEN: PURGATORY

1. Ella LeBain, *Who Is God? Book Two of Who's Who in The Cosmic Zoo? A Guide to ETs, Aliens, Gods & Angels*, Skypath Books, 2015. Chapter Twenty-Eight: *What Happens When You Die?* p. 455-485
2. St. Catherine of Genoa, *Fire of Love! Understanding Purgatory*, Sophia Institute Press, Manchester, New Hampshire. 1996. (Originally published in France, 1493)
3. Venerable Bede, *Historia Ecclesiastica, Ecclesiastical History of the English People*, 731 AD. Bede's Ecclesiastical History of England, A.M. Sellar's 1907 Translation. From the Christian Classics Ethereal Library.
4. Karma Lingpa, *Tibetan Book of the Dead*, aka *The Bardo Thodol, Liberation Through Hearing During the Intermediate State, the Profound Dharma of*

Self-Liberation through the Intention of the Peaceful and Wrathful Ones. (1326–1386)
5. George Anderson, *Extra-Terrestrials: Friend of Foe?* Illuminet Press; 1st Edition, (August 1993).
6. Ella LeBain, *Who's Who in The Cosmic Zoo? Book One, A Spiritual Guide to ETs, Aliens, Gods & Angels, Third Edition,* Chapter: Grays, p. 248-289. Tate Publishing & Enterprises, 2013.
7. Ibid, Karma Lingpa, *Tibetan Book of the Dead,* (1326-1386)
8. Ibid.
9. C.S. Lewis' *Chronicles of Narnia, The Voyage of the Dawn Treader,* Geoffrey Bles, U.K. 1952.
10. The Constantine and Nicean Creed, 365AD, Council of Laodicea, Stefano Assemani, Acta Sanctorium Martyrum Orientalium at Occidentalium, Vol. 1, Rome 1748, page 105 https://tjcoop3.wordpress.com/the-constantine-creed/
11. Todd Burpo, Lynn Vincent, *Heaven Is for Real: A Little Boy's Astounding Story of His Trip to Heaven,* Thomas Nelson, October 31, 2010.
12. Kevin and Alex Malarkey, *The Boy Who Came Back from Heaven: A Remarkable Account of Miracles, Angels, and Life beyond This World,* Tyndale House (June 30, 2010).

CHAPTER ELEVEN: IS HELL FOR REAL?

1. Taylor Marshall, *Why Did Christ Descend Into Hell?,* 2012. http://taylormarshall.com/2012/01/why-did-christ-descend-into-hell.html
2. Ella LeBain, *Who's Who in The Cosmic Zoo? Book One, A Spiritual Guide to ETs, Aliens, Gods & Angels, Third Edition,* Chapter Three: *The Clash of Two Kingdoms: The Cosmic Conflict,* subsection: *From Adam's Failure to the Second Adam's Victory,* p. 71-73.
3. Dante Aligheri. *Dante's Inferno,* Parts 1-3 epic 14th Century Poem *Divine Comedy, Purgatorio* and *Paradiso.* 1320.
4. Ella LeBain, *Who's Who in The Cosmic Zoo? Book One, A Spiritual Guide to ETs, Aliens, Gods & Angels, Third Edition,* Chapter Five: *Aghartians,* p. 98-104.
5. Ella LeBain, *Who Is God? Book Two of Who's Who in The Cosmic Zoo? A Guide to ETs, Aliens, Gods & Angels,* Skypath Books, 2015. Chapter Two: *Ancient Technology and Biblical Astronauts,* p. 21-46
6. Ibid.
7. Ibid.
8. Ibid.

9. Howard Storm, *My Descent into Death: A Second Chance At Life*, Harmony; First U.S. Edition (February 15, 2005).
10. Bill Wiese, *23 Minutes in Hell One Man's Story About What He Saw, Heard, and Felt in that Place of Torment*, Charisma House; 1st edition, January 30, 2006
11. Ella LeBain, *Who's Who in The Cosmic Zoo? Book One, A Spiritual Guide to ETs, Aliens, Gods & Angels, Third Edition*, Chapter Five: Draconian/Reptilians, p.154-177.

CHAPTER TWELVE: THE WORLD OF THE WONDROUS: THE KINGDOM OF GOD

1. P.D. Ouspensky, *Tertium Organum, The Third Canon of Thought, A Key to the Enigmas of the World*, 2nd American Edition, Manas Press, St. Petersburg, Russia, 1920
2. Virginia Essene, Sheldon Niddle, *You are Becoming a Galactic Human*, Spiritual Education Endeavors; 1st edition (April 1994).

CHAPTER THIRTEEN: THE COMING KINGDOM

1. Jim Rutz, *Megashift*, Empowerment Press (CO); 1st Edition (June 30, 2005).
2. C.S. Lewis, *The Last Battle*, published by The Bodley Head, U.K., 1956

CHAPTER FOURTEEN: THE HARVEST OF ANGELS

1. Ella LeBain, *Who Is God? Book Two of Who's Who in The Cosmic Zoo? A Guide to ETs, Aliens, Gods & Angels*, Chapter Two: *Ancient Technology & Biblical Astronauts*, p.21, Skypath Books, 2015.
2. Albert Brooks, *Defending Your Life*, 1991, Geffen Pictures, Directed by Albert Brooks.

CHAPTER FIFTEEN: ASCENSION OR RAPTURE?

1. Jim Rutz, *Megashift*, Empowerment Press (CO); 1st Edition (June 30, 2005).
2. www.answers.com/Q/How_many_people_believe_in_Christianity_worldwide?#slide=1

3. http://top101news.com/2015-2016-2017-2018/news/society/largest-religions-world/10/
4. Travis Walton, *Fire in The Sky*, 1975, Marlowe & Company; 3rd edition (August 1997)
5. Ella LeBain, *Who Is God? Book Two of Who's Who in The Cosmic Zoo? A Guide to ETs, Aliens, Gods & Angels*, Chapter Two: *Ancient Technology & Biblical Astronauts*, p.21, Skypath Books, 2015.
6. Ibid.
7. Father Charles Arminjon, France-1881, *The End of the Present Word and the Mysteries of the Future Life*, translated by Susan Conroy and Peter McEnerny, Sophia Institute Press (January 26, 2009).
8. John W. Milor, *Aliens and The Antichrist: Unveiling the End Times Deception*, Chapter Four: *Could the Rapture of the Church be a Mass Alien Abduction?* p.129, 132, iUniverse, Inc., Lincoln, NE. 2006.
9. , Dr. Chuck Missler, DVD, *The Rapture: Christianity's Most Preposterous Belief*, Koinonia House, Coeur d'Alene, ID, 2010
10. Todd Strandberg, *The Pretribulation Rapture,* https://www.raptureready.com/rr-pre-trib-rapture.html
11. Ella LeBain, *Who Is God? Book Two of Who's Who in The Cosmic Zoo? A Guide to ETs, Aliens, Gods & Angels*, Chapter Four: *The Motherships of the Lord*, p.71, Skypath Books, 2015.
12. Ibid., Milor, p.147
13. Ibid., Milor, p.148
14. John Walvoord, *The Rapture Question*, p. 271. Zondervan; 1st Revised & enlarged edition (August 25, 1979)
15. Ibid., Missler, 2010
16. Ibid.

Chapter Sixteen: The Second Coming and Nibiru

1. http://jardalkalataol.blogspot.com/2015/09/nibiru-and-isaiah-24.html
2. https://grahamhancock.com/bournewp1/
3. Immanuel Velikovsky, *Earth in Upheaval,* Paradigma Ltd (December 1, 2012)
4. Ella LeBain, *Who's Who in The Cosmic Zoo? Book One, A Spiritual Guide to ETs, Aliens, Gods & Angels, Third Edition,* Chapter Five: Draconian/Reptilians, p.154-177.

5. http://biblepoleshifts.webs.com/
6. Pole Shifts - Growing Evidence for Catastrophic Shifts Past and Present https://www.youtube.com/watch?v=6Ka1Yf0_zjM
7. Bruce Killian, *Joshua's Long Day*, scripturescholar.com
8. Lance Lee Osbourn, *Poles Are Moving: What to Expect*, June 2, 2013, https://www.facebook.com/notes/lance-lee-osbourn/poles-are-moving-so-what-to-expect-/652217308124970
9. Doug Elwell, *Planet X, The Sign of the Son of Man, and the End of the Age*, Defender Publishing LLC (January 1, 2011)
10. *Watchman Bible Study* 2005–2016 www.watchmanbiblestudy.com/Articles/Watchman/6thSeal_PlanetX.html
11. Ibid., Lance Lee Osbourn, *Poles Are Moving: What to Expect*, June 2, 2013
12. Ella LeBain, *Who Is God? Book Two of Who's Who in The Cosmic Zoo? A Guide to ETs, Aliens, Gods & Angels*, Chapter Four: *The Motherships of the Lord*, p.71, Skypath Books, 2015.

Chapter Seventeen: The Cosmic Christ

1. Joseph B. Lumpkin, *The Lost Books of the Bible: Section One: Lost Scriptures of the Old Testament: The First Book of Adam and Eve*, p.10-62, Fifth Estate Publishers, Blountsville, AL. 2009.
2. Ella LeBain, *Who Is God? Book Two of Who's Who in The Cosmic Zoo? A Guide to ETs, Aliens, Gods & Angels*, Concluding Words, p.501-559, Skypath Books, 2015.
3. Ibid. pp. 485-499
4. http://www.accordingtothescriptures.org/prophecy/353prophecies.html
5. http://www.realdiscoveries.info/BOOK-OF-ENOCH.php
6. William F. Dankenbring, *The Book of Enoch and the "Prototype" or "Chosen One" of God*, http://www.triumphpro.com/enoch-and-the-prototype.htm
7. The Old Testament Pseudepigrapha, edited by James H. Charlesworth
8. Charles E. Isaac, translation, edited by James H. Charlesworth, from the volume, *The Old Testament Pseudepigrapha*, Hendrickson Publishers; Volume Set ed. edition (February 1, 2010)
9. Richard Laurence, Archbishop of Cashel, and Professor of Hebrew in the University of Oxford: Parker, 1821, translation 1 Enoch, http://www.sacred-texts.com/bib/bep/bep01.htm

10. Charles E. Isaac, translation, edited by James H. Charlesworth, from the volume, *The Old Testament Pseudepigrapha*, Hendrickson Publishers; Volume Set ed. edition (February 1, 2010)
11. Charles, R. H., *The Apocrypha and Pseudepigrapha of the Old Testament, Volume Two: Pseudepigrapha*. Apocryphile Press., p. 185. ISBN 978-0-9747623-7-1 (2004)
12. Ibid., Richard Laurence. *The Book of Enoch* (Oxford: Parker, 1821)
13. Ibid.
14. APOCRYPHA 1st Maccabees of the King James Bible 1611, 1 Maccabees www.Scriptural-Truth.com
15. *The Book of Enoch,* http://www.israel-a-history-of.com/the-book-of-enoch.html
16. *Jesus Christ Accepted Book of Enoch,* http://www.city-data.com/forum/religion-spirituality/966511-jesus-christ-accepted-1-enoch-scripture.html#ixzz2j01rZmcI
17. Dr. Philip S. Berg, *The Zohar, Volume II: Parashat Pinhas*, p 88-89, Kabbalah Publishing, 1987
18. J.J. Hurtak, *The Book of Knowledge: The Keys of Enoch*®: p.57., The Academy for Future Science, Los Gatos, CA. 1977.
19. Ibid., p. 598
20. Ibid., p.57

Concluding Words

1. Ella LeBain, Book One of *Who's Who in The Cosmic Zoo?* Chapter Five: Martians, Life on Mars, p. 308-323, Tate Publishing. 2013.
2. David Flynn, *Cydonia: The Secret Chronicles of Mars*, End Time Thunder Publishers (2002).
3. Ibid.
4. Ella LeBain, Book One of *Who's Who in The Cosmic Zoo?* Chapter Two: Exopolitics and Divine Jurisprudence, p. 43-62. Tate Publishing. 2013.
5. Richard Hoagland, *The Monuments of Mars: A City on the Edge of Forever*, Frog Books; 5th Edition (2001).
6. Art Green Field, *The Alien Agenda Revealed*, 2009. http://www.scribd.com/doc/17117471/W...rt-Green-Field
7. Ella LeBain, *Who Is God? Book Two, A Guide to ETs, Aliens, Gods & Angels*, Chapter Two: Ancient Technology & Biblical Astronauts, p.27-41 Skypath Books, 2015.

Notes And Bibliography

8. Ibid., Chapter Four: *Motherships of the Lord*, p.71-88
9. David Jay Jordan, *New Jerusalem Is a Crystal Pyramid*, http://www.davidjayjordan.com/NewJerusalemisaCrustalPyramid.html
10. Ella LeBain, Book One of *Who's Who in The Cosmic Zoo?* Leviathan, p. 304. Tate Publishing. 2013.
11. Joseph B. Lumpkin, *The Lost Books of the Bible: The Great Rejected Texts -Section One: The First and Second Books of Adam Eve*, p.10-85, Fifth Estate Publishers, 2009.
12. Ella LeBain, *Who Is God? Book Two, A Guide to ETs, Aliens, Gods & Angels*, Chapter Twenty-Nine: *Who Created Sexism?* p.485-500 Skypath Books, 2015.
13. Eric Barger, *Is Hyper Critical Name Calling Really Contending for the Faith?* http://www.ericbarger.com/ Take A Stand Ministries
14. Ibid., Ella LeBain, *Who Is God? Book Two, A Guide to ETs, Aliens, Gods & Angels*, Concluding Words, p. 525-528
15. Ibid., *Who Is Allah? Baal Worship*, p. 359-386
16. Ibid., p. 7
17. Steven Basset, *The Paradigm Research Group*, http://www.paradigmresearchgroup.org/
18. Excerpt from the Introduction of *We are Human Angels: A Crash Course for Human Angels*, Human Angels; 2nd Edition (April 16, 2012).

About the Author

1. Hal Lindsey, *The Late Great Planet Earth*, Bantam, NY; 27th Printing edition (1977).
2. Eric Von Daniken, *Chariots of the Gods*, Bantam Books, NY. 1968, translation by Michael Heron (1970)
3. Zecharia Sitchin, *The Earth Chronicles, Nine-Book Series Set: Twelfth Planet, Stairway to Heaven, War of Gods and Men, Lost Realms, When Time Began, Cosmic Code, End of Days, Genesis Revisited, and Divine Encounters* Mass Market Paperback —Avon Harper (1995)
4. G. Cope Schellhorn, *Extraterrestrials in Biblical Prophecy*, Horus House Press. Wisconsin. (1989)

ABOUT THE AUTHOR

Ella LeBain is the author of a book series entitled *Who's Who in The Cosmic Zoo? A Spiritual Guide to ETs, Aliens, Gods & Angels: An End Time Guide to the Mass Deception.*

Ella LeBain, who is originally from New York City, was educated in Israel. She received a Social Sciences Degree from the Biological Research Center of the Negev in 1979 where she was schooled in Biblical Hebrew. She then went on to receive an Astronomy Degree from the Hayden Planetarium in New York City in 1982. She spent two years working as a missionary in apartheid South Africa in the early 1980s, where she embarked on what has become a thirty-seven-year journey to get to the truth about UFOs, Aliens, ETs, gods, and angels and how they all fit into the end of our age scenario.

Ella has spent twenty-five years in the field of UFO research, investigating alien abductions, and she has had many supernatural experiences of her own along the way, many of which have shaped the writing of these books.

Ella has collected vast amounts of information from a variety of sources, in addition to her own experiences which have been incorporated into the Book set. Book One is a type of encyclopedia, covering *Who's Who in the Cosmic Zoo of ETs and Aliens* in an A-Z compendium.

Book Two - *Who Is God?* Focuses on the Cosmic Drama and identifies and discerns "who" are the so-called ET gods of ancient history based on both biblical and exobiblical scriptures.

Book Three – *Who Are the Angels?* Focuses on the hierarchy of angels (extraterrestrial messengers) both the fallen ET angels and those who have remained faithful to the Creator, how they have been interacting with humankind for millennia and the important roles they play at the end of this age.

Book Four – *Covenants* focuses on spiritual legal ground, and the spiritual contracts that are represented in the ancient scriptures.

Book Five – *The Heavens* discerns the heavenly scroll and God's Word written first into the Stars before the downloading of the written scrolls on Earth, the afterlife, the millennial reign, and Heaven on Earth in the age to come.

Ella LeBain is also an International Deliverance Minister and a member of ISDM (International Society for Deliverance Ministers). While serving as a missionary in apartheid South Africa from 1979 – 1981, Ella witnessed front and center the spiritual revival that was taking place before the end of apartheid. Ella has witnessed the raising of the dead, demonic deliverances, supernatural healings, and miracles through the Living God.

Ella is a retired legal assistant of twenty-five years, where she made her living as a professional freelance paralegal, working on projects in New York City, Florida, and Colorado. Ella retired sixteen years ago to complete her books and become a stay-at-home Mom. Ella is the mother to a teenage daughter. She is happily married to her soul mate and shares a house with three cats. In her spare time, Ella likes to horse around with her equine partners every chance she gets. Horseback riding is her favorite past time and therapy, in Colorado.

Ella LeBain is available for interviews, lectures, and book signings.
Contact: ellalebain@whoswhointhecosmiczoo.com
http://www.whoswhointhecosmiczoo.com

Who Is Ella LeBain?

"Condemnation without investigation is the highest form of ignorance."
~Albert Einstein

Why this book series is important to me, is because I have lived much of it, as an experiencer and a witness to the Saving Grace of God. Here are some highlights of my testimony and background and what led me to compile *Who's Who in the Cosmic Zoo?* My full testimony will be released in my 6th book, *CinderElla's Shadow,* which will be published after this five-book series is completely released. It's more important to me to publish what I have learned, before I share the details of my story as to how I obtained this knowledge through my experiences, for I am just a mere witness and messenger.

I am an Italian Messianic Jew, who has seen Yeshua/Jesus Christ a half a dozen times in the five and half decades I've been alive on earth. They say seeing is believing. I think the reason He reveals Himself to people, is so we can be witnesses to the fact that He is alive, as real and close as our breath, and holds the power over *all* evil. How do I know, because I have been saved from horrible evil done to me by aliens and demons who tried to destroy me several times, I have no fear of death, because I know 'who' watches over me, and more importantly, 'who' lives inside my heart and soul.

At age 15, I was sent to Israel to complete my education. I graduated in 1979 with a Matriculation Degree in Social Sciences, and then went on to obtain a Basic Astronomy degree in New York City in 1984. I became a Jew for Jesus in 1979, spent two years as a missionary in South Africa from 1979-1981, where I was told, 'have nothing to do with the UFO phenomenon, because it's a plot from the devil to deceive the world after the Rapture, that the believers were abducted by aliens in UFOs'. That statement caused me to start digging and researching to understand, why they would say such a thing to me, at the young age of 18, and where was the truth in it? I can honestly say, I have found the answers, which I am presenting to you in this book, and throughout my five-book series, *Who's Who in The Cosmic Zoo?*

I believe knowledge empowers and ignorance endangers per Hosea 4:6, and sharing this knowledge is my burning passion before I share the gory details of my personal stories. However, I have been known to pepper my books with relevant pieces of my stories, so those of you who have been following this book series, will be able

Who Are The Angels? *Ella LeBain*

to put my life puzzle together in the end and understand why these books became my life work. However, this material is not about me, but suffice it to say I am an experiencer of ETs, Aliens, gods and Angels. I am a real-life person, and yet by the Grace of God, go I.

I was orphaned at age six, as an only child, and then again at age fifteen when I was estranged and abandoned from my father for most of my life who died in 2007, without ever meeting his own flesh and blood granddaughter, my millennium baby, born in 2000. I met Jesus in 1979 when I was eighteen years old, after matriculating at Sde Boker, Negev, Israel. I was waiting on a visa to travel to South Africa with a friend, which took about a month. In the meantime, I was helping my Principal clean out her office, as ours was the last class of the Nativ Angli (Native English Speakers) at Sde Boker. She had a book on her shelf titled, *The Late Great Planet Earth*, by Hal Lindsay,[1] which she gave to me, said she had no use for it.

I later found out it belonged to David Ben Gurion and sat on his coffee table in his office in 1972 not long before he died. He was buried at Sde Boker. After completing Hebrew studies, which included Tenakh in Hebrew, (Old Testament Bible), and before I could even complete reading *The Late Great Planet Earth*, I saw Jesus in the Negev desert appear to me and heard Him say, "I am the Messiah, follow me." So, I did. Sde Boker was above the Wadi Nahal Zin, which is where historians believed to be the spot where Jesus fasted for forty days and nights and was tested by satan in the desert. We would take hikes down the Wadi often throughout my time at Sde Boker.

My visa came through, I travelled to Capetown where I then spent two years working as a Missionary in apartheid South Africa. I served the Capetown and Johannesburg Assemblies of God as a missionary around South Africa. I witnessed front line and center the outpouring of God's Grace in a spiritual revival all over Southern Africa right before the end of Apartheid. I witnessed a woman who was raised from the dead, miraculous healings and demonic deliverances and exorcisms take place right before my very eyes.

I lived for six months in Zululand at Kwa Sizabuntu, where I witnessed a twenty-three-year-old woman die of kidney disease. Everyone in the entire village called on Jesus to come heal her. Instead she died. The village mourned and prepared for her burial. An hour later, she woke up, completely healed and told everyone that she met Jesus. She said she was climbing up a mountain, and Jesus was at the top. She said she felt like there were chains around her ankles holding her down, making it difficult for her to climb the mountain, and that Jesus met her where she was at. She said He told her that those chains around her ankles represented her resentments, and that He had forgiven her and was going to give her, her life back. She wanted to stay with him, but He told her she had to go back and tell everyone what God has done for her, and that He wanted her to forgive her family and teach them about His forgiveness and that He would be with her always, and she would see Him again.

There was a lot of witchcraft going on in her ancestry, and now that she and her family were saved by the Lord, He wanted them to know His forgiveness. Forgiveness healed her. I will never forget her story. God is real. And He often sends people back to life because He wants them to be a 'witness' to His Love, Grace and Power. It's that simple and to teach a lesson, which is to learn forgiveness. After all, it was His forgiveness of her, that was imprinted into her, to pass it on to her family. That was His instruction, she was obedient, and they lived on doing their work on earth for the Lord.

When I began my work as a Missionary, they gave me a room to live in, in their church in Johannesburg, that was my home base, and I served in the Teen Challenge Center, and did street work, mainly counseling alcoholics and leading them to God's Deliverance. My elders who took very good care of me, saw all my stuff in my trunk that followed me from NY to Israel to Capetown, to Johannesburg. And in it were my books, albums, and personal items. They saw what I was reading, and told me in no uncertain terms, that I should have nothing to do with the UFO phenomenon, that it's a plot from the devil, that when the Rapture happens, he was going to lie to the rest of the world, that all the true believers in Jesus were abducted by aliens. Well, at the age of eighteen, I was passionate to serve the Lord, and didn't want to do anything to displease him, so I gave up my books to them in repentance. They burned them.

They renewed my visa three times in the two years I lived there to continue to serve as their missionary. Then when the 3rd visa expired, the authorities told them I had to go back to the United States to renew my visa. I believe that was God's hand saving me for what was coming down, that I was hearing them prophesy in the churches, blood in the streets and dark times ahead for South Africa. Sure enough, six months later, began the riots and curfews and Apartheid was overturned. I was thrilled to have witnessed its prophecy and its fulfillment. I saw the amazing outpouring of God's spirit all around their land, right before this major shift happened. I was glad I wasn't there during its transition phase, I felt saved out of a dangerous situation. Praise the Lord for His lovingkindness to me.

While I lived in Zululand, in a compound farm called Kwa Sizabuntu that was built around sugar fields. There was so much open space, and then there were rows and rows of sugar cane growing. I remember eating it raw and squeezing and sucking the sugar juice out of the cane. I would hang out in the grass field adjacent to the sugar cane fields, sometimes with my friends, and other times alone. One afternoon I took my blanket out to the field to sunbathe and pray. I fell asleep on my blanket in the sun, the sun was always tranquilizing to me. Then I was woken up by an audible voice, calling my name and saying 'Get Up!' I opened my eyes and about a hundred yards ahead of me, was a huge swarm of bees flying in my direction. I got up off my blanket just in time, and ran to the side to get out of their path. I watched the swarm, which looked like a dark moving cloud, pass right over my blanket.

I was saved by my Guardian Angel. I will never forget that day. So, you see, when you are witness to the reality of the supernatural, God's Love, God's Grace, God's Salvation, God's Deliverance, there is nothing else to do but tell everyone about it and serve God's Kingdom.

I go into more stories of miracles I witnessed and when I came close to death twice in my life, one from an illness and one from the treachery of neighbors, in full detail in *CinderElla's Shadow*. God is real, and so are His Angels, the good ETs. I had multiple encounters during the most challenging and difficult times of my life. God has been faithful to me, an orphan, abandoned by both my biological and step families. I felt cursed, but God blessed me and saved me multiple times.

I was interfered with by Grays and Lizard men, and the Lord brought me through so much drama, and battles, when they nearly drained the life force right out of me, leaving me spiritually and emotionally raped. I learned I was abducted since I was two years old. I remember my parents keeping the story of my nose bleeds alive, until they died, that they used to come in and find me upside down in my crib with nose bleeds and how they always had to change the sheets.

It wasn't until I reached my thirty-something years, that I could connect the dots to these earliest of my childhood memories. I remember it, and I remember not being able to talk, and trying to tell my mother what was going on, and felt like she couldn't do anything about it, it was a feeling of intense powerlessness. Then when I was six, my mother became sick with Bone Marrow Cancer, she ended up in the hospital, and when I used to visit her, her body was covered in bruises, then she died a few months after my sixth birthday. I remember one visit to her in the hospital I got a splinter in my finger, so they took me to her nurse, and put me in this chair with a table attached to it so she could work on removing the splinter from my finger. I fainted, because she stuck a needle into me.

I was typically in every sense of the word, 'needle phobic'. Every time my step mother took me to the doctor's office to get vaccinations, I would pass out and faint. I had sleep paralysis for decades, and a handful of times I would wake up and see them putting me back in my bed, or coming to take me. I had an implant put into my nose, I think it was the entry point in right nostril, it felt like a tiny bead that would never go away.

In 1995, I woke up to what was happening to me, when my period was late, and then I thought I got my period, but miscarried a baby, that my body seemed to release the entire placenta and sac which I put into a zip lock bag because I never saw anything like that come out of my body and I was taken to the emergency room, which was determined that I was eight weeks pregnant and lost a baby. They said everything was intact, but the fetus was missing.

In my grief and depression, crying on the couch to God about what happened, I had a being show up before me on the couch, who was this white wispy-haired blond being with white silver skin and big teal eyes, telepathing to me loudly, in my head, that she was the reason this had to happen and thanked me and beamed all this white light energy to me, then disappeared. I realized that they have been taking fetuses from me for a long time, because I used to miss sometimes two or three periods and then go through these freaky heavy bleeds, then things would calm down, but I got to admit, my cycles were not always regular, I thought it had to do with the fact that I had culture shock, because I lived in foreign countries. I suffered such intense migraines and used to get terribly painful ear infections as a child.

When I was in my twenties and thirties it was migraines. It was then that I got into Deliverance work, and found that breaking generational curses, delivered me of alien interference once and for all. For years, I was using the name of Jesus, or pleading the blood, they would leave, but would still return. It was then I learned about cancelling spiritual legal ground, which is the focus of Book Four: *Covenants,* and ended all contracts and agreements with alien abductions once and for all.

> *"The weak can never forgive.*
> *Forgiveness is an attribute of the strong."*
> ~ GANDHI

Since I was thirteen years old, I began reading books on Astrology and UFOs. I was drawn to Eric Von Daniken's classic and prophetic work, *Chariots of the Gods,*[2] in the early 1970s. Years later I met and interviewed Zecharia Sitchin after his epic work, *The Earth Chronicles,*[3] was completed. Then in 1992 I was handed a copy of G. Cope Schellhorn's book, *Extraterrestrials in Biblical Prophecy,*[4] which completely changed my life and answered many of the questions I was researching for years.

As a child, I was the subject of very intense spiritual battles and religious warfare over me, which felt like a curse to me. Therefore, I do not identify with religion, or being 'religious' per se, but I do identify as a *citizen* of the Kingdom of Heaven, and more importantly, I belong to the Lord of Hosts, who saved my life and soul more than once. Suffice it to say, my entire testimony is summed up in this Word:

"When my father and my mother forsake me, then the Lord will hold me close."

(Psalm 27:10-NLT)

All in all, I grew up to realize, that it's way more important and eternally valuable to be in right *relationship* with the Creator, than to follow any specific earth religion. While I do come from a Judeo-Christian background, I learned to eat the meat, and throw out the bones. Or for those who are vegetarian, drink the juice and spit out the pits. Discernment is both a spiritual and an intellectual muscle, that must be developed in order for human beings to live freely in the Saving Grace that Messiah Jesus so freely offers us.

The supernatural realm is real. It is full of both good and evil, I am a witness to that. But without *discernment*, the average Joe and Jane, can't always tell *Who is Who in the Cosmic Zoo*, because evil often masquerades as good and can hide behind so called *religious* people.

> "Woe to those who call evil good and good evil, who put darkness for light and light for darkness, who put bitter for sweet and sweet for bitter."
>
> (Isaiah 5:20)

*Life is a Chance. * Love is Infinity. * Grace is Reality.*

www.ingramcontent.com/pod-product-compliance
Lightning Source LLC
Chambersburg PA
CBHW080527170426
43195CB00016B/2488